Women, Housing and Human Settlements

Women, Housing and Human Settlements

SEHGAL. N

Ess Ess Publications

4837/24, Ansari Road, Darya Ganj,
New Delhi,110 002
Phone : 3260807

First Published : 1995

ISBN : 81-7000-177-3

Rs. 575/-

Published by :

Ess Ess Publications

4837/24, Ansari Road, Darya Ganj,
New Delhi,110 002
Phone : 3260807

Composed by :

Classic Computer Services
RZ-128/6K, Lane No. 9, East Sagar Pur,
New Delhi-46

To the memory of
My noble and loving friend
S. K. Sethi

Quem di diligunt
Adolescens moritur dum valet, sentit sapit
'Whom the gods love die young, while still
they can enjoy Health, tastes and senses'

PLAUTUS

PREFACE

Women are, in every way, disadvantaged in their participation in the human settlements sector. They are excluded from decision-making on programmes and projects which fundamentally affect their lives, they are handicapped in obtaining property and in gaining access to credit for both housing and business purposes, and they are systematically excluded from employment in all but the most elementary roles in the construction, finance and real estate industries. Women face legal, cultural and educational difficulties in overcoming the obstacles they face in all these areas. Despite the discrimination from which they suffer, women have made and continued to make substantial contribution to the development, operation and maintenance of human settlements. Without their unpaid and unrecognized labours, human settlements in the developing countries would cease to function. Women are a resource which the governments of developing countries can no longer ignore, if they wish to realize the potential of human settlements development for supporting economic growth and for establishing the infrastructure for social advancement and productivity improvements.

In the developing countries, cities are growing rapidly, and governments must meet increasing human settlements demands from very limited resources. Removing the barriers which prevent women from making a full contribution to the human settlements sector should be a high-priority issue, not only because women have the same fundamental rights as men to share in the development process but also because governments can obtain enormous benefits from enabling women to expand their roles in the management of housing, infrastructure and community services. It is clear that development strategies followed over the past two decades, designed to increase economic growth and industrial output, have been in fundamental conflict with the interests of the poor majorities of populations, paradigms, giving special attention to the human settlements sector, through which they can bring about sustainable and equitable growth, and in which women can have the role they deserve.

This publication is intended to make a modest contribution to the development by providing a brief overview to women's concerns in the areas of human settlements decision-making, employment in the human settlements sector and property rights. These are important issues in the context to the Global Strategy for Shelter to the Year 2000 which aims at facilitating access for all to adequate shelter, but with particular emphasis on the participation of the poor and disadvantaged, amongst whom women represent a substantial majority.

SEHGAL. N

CONTENTS

1. Introduction 1
2. Doing What comes Naturally ? Women and Environment in Development 45
3. Room for One's Life : Women, Houses and Social Change 81
4. Gender and Housing : Broadening the Debate 93
5. Food for thought : making women visible 121
6. Social Action Theory and the Women's Movement : An Analysis of Assumptions 128
7. Gender Matters in Third World Development Projects: The Dangers of Gender Blindness 138
8. HIC Women and Shelter Network 176
9. Women, Environment and Urbanization : Guide to the Literature 186
10. Women and Solid wastes in Poor Communities 209
11. The Problems of Living with In-Laws 216
12. Women's Participation Strengthens NGO Projects : Sri Lanka 235
13. Women and Environmental Aspect of Human Settlement in the Third World 243
14. Women, Shelter and UNCHS 258
15. Women in Human Settlement Development and Management 322
16. Women and Human Habitat 339
17. Indian Women and the House 358
18. Women and Water in Rural Maharashtra 372
19. Women's Roles in Creating the Urban Habitat of 384
20. Women and Urban Housing Crisis: Impact of Public Policies and Practices in Uganda 403
21. Gender in Two Slum Cultures : Sri Laka and Thailand 437
22. Gender and Housing 454
23. Rehousing the Urban Poor : Looking at Women First : Argentina 482
24. Gender and State Bias in Jamaican Housing Programs 501
25. Equality for Women-What We Need Doing 528
26. Shelter, Women and Development : Beating a Path Towards Women's Participation 541

CHAPTER-1

Introduction

Why Focus on Women ?

The question is not whether women are involved in the human settlements development process, but rather how they are. All over the world, women play a large part in building and maintaining settlements. The level and extent of women's participation in house construction vary in different cultures, ranging from assisting the men to having total responsibility. Providing a Safe and Clean environment, especially in poor urban neighbourhoods, is hard and difficult work, done mostly by women. Yet when it comes to formulating settlements policies, planning settlements and designing housing programmes, women are seriously under-represented, and hardly consulted. As a result, women's work in providing and maintaining shelter remains invisible, unrecognized and unrewarded, and their needs unplanned for.

An estimated 20 to 35 per cent of all households world-wide are headed by women. This number is growing. In certain African and Latin American countries the percentage is as high as 45. Such households may be headed by unmarried women and widows, or married women, often with children, who are de facto heads of household because the husbands have left home for economic or political reasons, often not communicating with their families for long periods.

There are several things that women-headed households have in common: they are generally much poorer than those headed by men; they predominate in informal and poor urban settlements, where they are also among the poorest; they face many problems in their attempts to secure a place to live, as well as in their daily fight for survival.

In 1992 a group of women doing research in Ecuador to collect information that would help determine indicators to measure lack of services (among other things) made an interesting observation: The number of school-age girls not attending school was a good indication of lack of services, especially water. Why? Women are responsible for cleaning, fetching water and fuel, and looking after children. Where services are lacking and women find it difficult to cope, girls are withdrawn from school to help their mothers. This will naturally affect their school performance, their chances in life, and their possibilities for eventually leading a better life than their mothers.

Women spend a large amount of time and energy fetching water over long distances. In certain rural areas in Africa, it is estimated that during the dry season, women may expend as much as 85 per cent of their total daily energy intake on fetching water, and may carry loads as heavy as 30 kilograms over rough terrain. Moreover, the incidence of anaemia in women increases dramatically during the dry season, due to the combination of a reduced supply of food and an increase in the distances covered in search of water.

In rural as well as in poor urban settlements women and children are more exposed to water-borne diseases than men, since they are the ones primarily responsible for fetching water.

Women build homes and neighbourhoods despite the serious constraints facing them--such as low incomes, lack of access to credit, lack of land rights and security of tenure, lack of recognition and often outright harassment by authorities. Women's organizations are doing a lot to provide services. It is not difficult to see why water and daycare are favourite projects of women's organizations in poor neighbourhoods. But in the process, the burden on women is often increased.

National governments, non-government organizations NGOs, donor agencies and international organizations need to give greater recognition to the situation and needs of women. More gender-sensitive planning and housing policies are required to ensure that housing projects are more people-friendly and take into account the requirements of men, women, girls and boys.

Legal and traditional barriers to women's access to shelter need to be removed. Women need to be educated on their rights: what is possible; what needs to be lobbied for. Credit programmes for the poor, especially women, should be increased. More women in decision-making positions at local, national and international levels can help push through the required change in attitudes, policies and programmes. This can only happen if women have the relevant training. People's organizations can also fight for change, especially if they have the right information and support.

UNCHS (Habitat) recognizes that the participation of all sectors--public, private and community--is necessary for the success of the Global Strategy for Shelter to the Year 2000 (GSS) with the goal of facilitating shelter for all. It realizes that the full mobilization and participation of women is vital to this process: Removing the constraints that women face can help to make their participation more visible, and effective.

Improving the status of women, enabling them to take a more active part in the human settlements process as a whole and incorporating gender issues into the entire work programme of UNCHS (Habitat) and human settlements development in general -- these are priority issues connected to the following problems: the lack of gender-awareness among both at the grassroots and among human settlements professionals, the exclusion of women in the human settlements development process, the exploitation of women's labour in that development process, and the absence of women at decision-making levels.

In order to respond to these issues, UNCHS (Habitat) has a specific "Women in Human Settlements Development Programme". One basic objective of this Programme is: to facilitate UNCHS (Habitat) fulfilment of its mandate to (a) promote women's equal participation GSS and all human settlements development and (b) mainstream gender issues in its various new and on-going programmes, projects and activities. The Programme also supports Governments, NGOs and Community-based organizations (CBOs) in their commitment to a process of training and organizational development which foster gender awareness, gender sensitivity and gender competence among-their staff.

1995 will be the year assessing the achievements of two women's decades. In 1996 Habitat II will be looking back at two decades since the Vancouver Conference on Human Settlements, paying attention to the special needs and contributions of women. These dates and related events provide a good opportunity to put a human settlements agenda into women in development programmes.

B. SOME QUESTIONS FOR DISCUSSION

Women are disadvantaged with regard to access to good, secure housing, as well as safe and clean neighbourhoods. At the same time they bear an inordinately heavy burden in providing their families with food, personal care and clean homes. They are also active in organizations that are engaged in improving communities and neighbourhoods. This often means hard work for women for almost no tangible rewards.

Can you imagine what life would be like without our mothers, sisters, wives, our neighbourhood women's group that runs the water kiosk ?

Here are some questions that we can think about in our homes, schools and universities, with our religious groups and neighbourhood organizations, in our local municipalities, villages and national parliaments. If we give them serious consideration, we may begin to be more appreciative and supportive of what women are doing to sustain our village, towns, cities and countries. They might also help us to change any stereotyped views we may have of women as "just" mothers, home-makers, seamstresses . . . What about some women architects, city planners, engineers . . . ?

(B.1) HOUSING : POLICY, PLANNING, MANAGEMENT AND DESIGN.

What do you understand "gender-sensitive" or "gender-aware" programmes?

- Programmes for women?
- Programmes with special components for women?
- Programmes that take account of everybody's needs and contributions, including men and women, boys and girls?

  The last answer is the correct one. Can you think of any projects or programmes in your municipality or country which are gender- sensitive?

Why should we emphasize better shelter for women?

Because:

- it is one of their basic rights,
- currently they are disadvantaged in this area,
- women form a large proportion of the population of poor communities, where housing and services are inadequate,
- at present, women's housing concerns are largely ignored at the national policy-making level, and are therefore unrecognized and unplanned for,
- nearly one third of the world's households are headed by women,

- they spend more time in the house than any other family member,
- many women conduct economic activities in the house,
- governments need to ensure that women and men--especially the poor-- have basic rights in housing, which include services like water, sanitation, waste disposal, transport, schools, clinics, markets, shopping centres and recreation facilities,
- all human resources--including those of women--need to be tapped for shelter development.

Why should urban housing be given greater priority ?

Because:

- the urban population is rising rapidly; it is estimated that nearly half of the world's' population will live in urban centres by the year 2000.
- poor urban households often live in worse housing conditions than poor rural households. Women form the majority in this group.
- many women are forced into urban or peri-urban concentrations due to traditional lack of access to rural land, war, disasters, and the inability to make a living in the rural areas.

What are the consequences of planning cities, towns and settlements without involving women ?

- House designs are inappropriate. For example, kitchens and working areas are too small.
- Community facilities such as schools, parks, health and shopping centres are inappropriately located.
- Low-income neighbourhoods are designed in a way that does not allow women to work in or around the home. This is reinforced by zoning regulations that prohibit commercial activity in residential areas.
- Food growing is either prohibited or unplanned for.

What are the consequences when there are no women in local authorities ?

- Women's informal-sector employment is outlawed.

- Waiting lists for council rental housing give priority to "families", which are often assumed to be male-headed.
- Public home-ownership projects also define families in the same way.
- Women's personal safety is not taken into account when locating recreational areas distributing public lighting, bus stops and other amenities.

(B.2) LAND

Why is land so critical in shelter development especially for women?

Because:

- land may be used collateral to get a loan to buy or improve shelter,
- it can provide security for women and their children,
- it may serve as a saving which appreciates over time,
- women are currently denied land for various reasons.

How can women be assisted to surmount the existing traditional legal barriers that prevent them from owning land and other property like housing?

Through:

- forming pressure groups to advocate women's property rights,
- educating women on these rights,
- providing girls with formal education and improving women's literacy levels in order to raise awareness on their rights,
- legislating on issues hampering women's property rights.

What can governments do to make land available to poor women other low-income members of society?

- Earmark state land for them,
- Set up site-and -service schemes, and make sure women's needs are specifically addressed,
- Set up community and trusts.

(B.3) FINANCE FOR HOUSING

How do most women in poor communities finance their shelter?

- Through personal savings and informal loans from relatives and friends.
- Many women form savings and credit cooperatives.

What are some of the main problems that women face in obtaining credit from conventional financial institutions?

- Financial institutions do not like to give small loans, which is often what women want.
- Many women have low, irregular incomes and therefore do not qualify for loans because they cannot assure repayment.
- In some countries, women can only borrow on the strength of a male relative's signature.

What are some of the ways in which women can be assisted to acquire the credit in a form most convenient to them?

- Women are already forming savings and credit cooperatives.
- More support can be given to these groups, especially in their income-generating activities.
- Revolving funds can be set up from which such groups can borrow.
- NGOs can intervene with banking institutions on behalf of women.

(B.4) ENVIRONMENT

How best can communities in general--and women in particular--be supported in their efforts to improve their dwellings, services and immediate surroundings?

Through:

- helping them form self-help groups such as cooperatives, women's groups, associations and savings clubs,
- strengthening their self-help efforts on matters concerning land acquisition, credit, building construction and maintenance,
- encouraging networking among community groups, NGOs, public and private shelter agencies, polytechnics, universities and government bodies.

How can one ensure that shelter is environment-friendly ?

Through:

- constructing dwellings using materials that have no toxic effects.
- cutting down on the use of energy by taking full advantage of prevailing climatic conditions such as solar heating.
- using water carefully.
- recycling waste.

How can housing be designed to reduce indoor pollution caused by smoky cooking fires. Which affect the eyes and respiratory tracts of millions of women and children worldwide each year?

Through:

- using fuel-efficient kitchen appliances.
- assisting women to make appropriate technologies for cooking on a do-it-yourself basis.
- funding projects where local artisans can produce such technologies cheaply.
- improving ventilation by increasing size of openings to kitchens.
- designing kitchens in consultation with women. (Several NGOs working in poor neighbourhoods are already doing this.)

(B.5) INFORMATION AND NETWORKING

What measures can be taken to improve research, documentation and dissemination of information on women and shelter development?

Actively involve women in gathering data on women's shelter concerns. Using grassroots professional as well as women. This has already been tried with very interesting results. It needs to be more widely applied. The date thus collected should be used in policy-making and planning as well as in designing courses and learning materials for, say, urban planners.

Disaggregate data so that the true situations of women and men is easily discernible.

What can be done to improve women's access to information on housing and credit opportunities, and human-settlements issues in

general, especially since women form the majority of the illiterate?

Media--both folk and modern--are already being used to communicate the local concerns of women. However, it has not been used enough for housing and shelter issues. Some community shelter networks use "talking newsletters" (audio cassettes) to get over the literacy barrier.

Study tours and exchange visits have proved to be useful means of gaining first-hand information. Even visiting a group in a neighbouring district can be quite inspiring.

(C) HOUSING, THE LIVING ENVIRONMENT AND WOMEN'S HEALTH

Some 2.4 billion people, representing 48 per cent of the world's population, live in urban areas. In 1990 it was estimated that 37 per of the developing world's population lived in urban areas. About one third of this group lived in informal settlements with poor housing and inadequate or no services. Their number continues to grow.

It is estimated that at least 600 million people living in urban areas of developing countries live in what might be termed life- and health-threatening homes and neighbourhoods. Women and children are the most severely affected by this situation, since they spend the most time at home. For example, an estimated 70 million women and children world wide suffer from severe indoor pollution from cooking fires, giving rise to respiratory and other health problems.

After food, housing is the largest item of poor families expenditure. Many such families (33 per cent globally, 45 to 50 percent in some African and Latin American countries) are headed by women. When incomes decline, their food and health budgets suffer, leading to malnutrition, early childhood deaths and reduced productivity.

Every day some 50,000 people, mostly women and children, die as a result of poor shelter, polluted water and inadequate sanitation. It is estimated that one in four of the world's population does not have access to clean drinking water and that in many developing countries, about 50 per cent of the urban population has no water within 200 meters of their dwelling.

Water and Services: the Women's Burden

32 per cent of the population of developing countries lacks easy

access to safe drinking water. In the least developed countries, this figure goes up to 53 per cent and in sub-Saharan Africa, it is as high as 59 per cent. In some countries as much as 80 per cent of the population lacks ready access to safe water.

The poor very often pay more for water than the rich, through informal and often unsafe supplies. For example in Nairobi, Kenya, residents of informal settlements pay water vendors 5 to 10 times more per unit than other residents pay to the city authorities. This is a common pattern in many cities in developing countries.

In situations where there is no water, it is women and older girls who have to provide it. Medical research has documented cases of permanent damage to women's health directly attributed to carrying water-among them spinal and pelvic deformities, and degenerative rheumatism. More immediate problems include exposure to water-borne diseases, chronic fatigue and the risk of miscarriage for pregnant women.

In some parts of rural Africa, where women may use as much as 85 per cent of their daily energy intake fetching water, 40 per cent of non-pregnant and 63 per cent of pregnant women are anaemic. The incidence and severity of anaemia increase during the dry season.

Access to health facilities is equally limited. 37 per cent of pregnant women in developing countries have no access to pre-natal care.

The Socio-economic Status of the Invisible Majority

It is estimated that world-wide 33 per cent of all households are headed by women. Death of a husband, divorce, war, large-scale displacement, labour migration as well as single motherhood result in women-headed households. For example, it is estimated that 70 to 80 per cent of refugees world-wide are women and children. In some southern African countries, as many as 50 per cent of rural households are headed by women as a result of men moving to towns in search of jobs, often not sending enough money home.

Women, a majority of the world's population receive only a small share of developmental opportunities. Even though women comprise more than 50 per cent of the world's population, they own only 1 per cent of the world's wealth. They are often excluded from education, from the better jobs, and from political systems.

In education, women still lag far behind men, especially in developing countries. Female literacy rates are low: 20 to 50 per cent of male levels.

In higher education, the disparities are even more stark. Female enrolment ratios in higher education in developing countries are typically only half the male ratios. In sub-Saharan Africa, women's enrolment rates for tertiary education are only a third of those of men. Even in industrialized countries, women are poorly represented in scientific and technical study: in Austria, the ratio of female to male third-level students in these fields is 25 per cent, in Austria 25 per cent, in Canada 29 per cent and in Spain 28 per cent.

Lack of education is partly responsible for women's disadvantage in the world of work and in political life. Women's are much less likely to be employed than their male counterparts, and working women are lower paid than men. In all industrialized countries. Women's wages are significantly lower. In Belgium and France, they earn about three quarters of the average male wage, and in Japan only about half. Female unemployment levels are typically about 1.5 times male levels. As for decision-making, men continue to dominate centres of business and government. Even in countries where women's representation is relatively high-such as Finland, Norway and Sweden-women account for only one third of the legislators. In developing countries, the figures range from 0 to 14 per cent.

However, in many countries and areas of life, even these kinds of comparisons are not easy to make because the data on women do not exist. Thus both the contributions that women make to development, and the discrimination against them, are hidden. This is gender blindness.

Finally, it is necessary to think of these and other statistics individually, and in combination, for example: think of a woman who is poor, under-nourished and probably anaemic; who has to carry water over a long distance; who gets water from a polluted source; who has to walk a long distance for pre-natal care and immunization for her children; who lives in a house with no proper sanitary facilities; who has to earn an income but has no access to childcare facilities. . . Then one begins to get an idea why it is necessary to focus specifically on women.

(D) PLANNING AND MANAGEMENT: BY AND FOR WHOM?

What is planning and management?

Human settlements planning follows a number of stages: the identification of needs, the formulation of goals and objectives, and the mobilization of resources needed (such as land, finance and personnel), implementation, monitoring and evaluation. Human settlements management is the operation, or running, and maintenance of the existing shelter, infrastructure, social services, as well as the overall organization and sustaining of our villages, towns and cities. Planning and management in shelter development, therefore, involve the provision, operation and maintenance of housing and related infrastructure and services, such as water, sanitation, refuse collection, transport, household energy, health centres, schools and shopping facilities; and, even more importantly, building and consolidating communities.

Planning for whom ?

A very basic assumption in human settlement planning is that it is for people. In other words, housing, water, health facilities and similar services are provided for the use of a given population. Therefore people should participate in the planning and management of such services, to ensure that they are suitable for their needs and to help communities feel responsible for managing and maintaining these services.

In the last decade, much has been said and written about people's participation in development. However, for a long time the people often participated only in project execution, and rarely at the planning or design stages. Indeed people became more and more involved as governments became less capable of providing for all their needs. They would be involved in providing labour and in making some other contribution in cash or kind.

In the last few years, the failure of many urban local authorities to provide services has resulted in communities, especially women, organizing to manage services, in particular water, health and daycare. One line of graffiti from a Latin American city expresses the burden of communities in managing services. It reads: "Participation? Don't tell me about my people's participation, I want to know what the government's participation is."

What then can be done to involve people in planning and in

higher-level management? Who does the planning and for whom? Gender-aware planning and management means taking into account the needs and situations of all members of any given society: men, women, boys and girls, It also means the effective participation of all, or at least the fair representation of all in the process.

Women have for a long time been involved in the management of communities. Indeed this often constitutes a burden for them. However, they have been largely excluded from higher levels of planning, decision-making and management. This is due to many factors, particularly cultural attitudes, and lack of appropriate education, the two often being related. Neglect of women's needs can also be attributed to a general lack of awareness and concern as well as an absence of meaningful data and statistics, and essential basis for good planning.

What are the results of planning without women?

The most obvious ill effects of planning without consideration for, and the participation of, women are most easily seen in towns and cities. Examples are: the absence of daycare facilities, the inappropriate location of public water points and of children's play parks, inadequate lighting of streets and public areas, and "modern" house designs that do not take into consideration women's traditional use of space. These are all areas that affect everybody, and women in particular. They are often inadequately addressed, leading to inconvenience and even risk, especially for women and children.

Planning laws that prohibit economic activities and food growing in residential areas render women's survival strategies illegal, and are one more example of planning that excludes women.

How can the situation be improved ?

Women's needs, along with those of men, can only be adequately met if women and men participate equally in human settlements planning and management at community; local and national levels. For this to happen, several issues need to addressed.

Women's education

World figures for literacy, higher education and enrolment in scientific and technical courses reveal that women are lagging far behind men. As a result, there are few women engineers, architects, planners and bank managers. These are all areas related to human settlements planning, development and management. One reason why women do not enrol in education in these fields is the traditional perception of what jobs are suited to women and men respectively.

One Tanzanian woman tells the story of how several years ago she turned up at the university as a student of engineering. She was shocked to find that no separate toilet facilities were provided for women student. Obviously nobody expected a woman to enrol! Similarly, in Uganda, most government technical training institutes, which are residential, have no boarding facilities for women.

More democratic participation of women

Women's participation in settlements development needs to move forward from community management to higher levels. Although community-based activities help give women the experience to move to "bigger and better things", very often even people's organizations are not democratic enough and do not give women the opportunity to participate as leaders.

In many urban popular movements, it is common for women to be heavily involved in the day-to day work of providing basic needs. However, it is the men who take the decisions, negotiate with local authorities and manage the finances. Fortunately some non-governmental organizations (NGOs) are trying to reverse this trend and to ensure that community-based organizations (CBOs) can become a starting point for building women's capacities and confidence, to enable them to participate in planning and management.

SPARC, an NGO that works with pavement dwellers in Bombay, India, has been developing a methodology for ensuring that community intervention provides a clearly defined space for the democratic participation of women in the organizations of slum dwellers, at various levels. This has helped to bring about some change in the attitudes of men in these organizations, and in the women's perception of themselves-thereby increasing the women's capacity to take some responsibility for planning and managing their settlements.

Participation of women in political life is also crucial. More women are needed in local and national governments. This can only come about with more education of women, as well as building awareness among both men and women that women can and must have a role to play.

Decentralized planning is more likely to involve the people and , therefore, more women. But even with decentralization a conscious effort has to be made to ensure that women are involved at levels that can help to bring about change.

Towards more gender-sensitive data

The 1993 *Human Development Report* by UNDP describes women as the "non-participating" majority. Indeed women's contribution in many areas of development has often been described as "invisible". Even countries with a high Human Development Index, high literacy or employment figures do not look so good when their vital statistics are disaggregated by gender. In other words, the position of women in most societies, even in the more developed countries, is one of relative disadvantage. Therefore data are needed not just on levels of education, but male and female levels of education; male and female human settlements professionals; male and female community leaders and politicians; and so on.

Participatory research is one way of ensuring that meaningful data are collected. This approach involves the people who are likely to be affected by development programmes. The Women in Human Settlements Development Programme of UNCHS (Habitat) is in the process of developing a set of indicators to measure the participation of women in human settlements development. The methodology includes conducting the research using professional, NGO and grassroots women in each of the communities surveyed. The results so far have been very interesting. A next step could be to promote the use of the research findings in local and national planning in the respective countries.

Education for policy-makers and planners

Gender-sensitization seminars for policy-makers and development workers, both men and women, are now on the curriculum of some university departments. Workshops are also being conducted or sponsored by some international development agencies. The Women and Human Settlements Development Programme of UNCHS (Habitat) is organizing gender-awareness workshop at national and regional levels. There should be more of them at the national level also. Perhaps one day, a qualification in this area will become a requirement for jobs in local and national planning!

(E) HOUSING POLICY: STARTING RIGHT

Housing policies are meant to provide the guiding framework for satisfying the housing needs of all groups in society. They also lay the ground rules by which plans of action and strategies are formulated. The Global Strategy for Shelter to the Year 2000 (GSS), launched by the United Nations in 1988, lays emphasis on country-level action and defines the principal role of governments as that of "enabling". This means that for the most part, the role of national governments will be to establish the right legislative, institutional and financial framework that will enable the formal and informal private business sector, non-governmental organizations (NGOs), communities and individual households to contribute most effectively to shelter development. The GSS also points out the need to address the special problem faced by women, in order to improve their participation, both as contributors and beneficiaries in the shelter process.

However, policy-makers often fail to recognize or acknowledge the need to given specific attention to women's concerns. Some of these include legal and customary discrimination, severe poverty, limited access to credit, low levels of education and training, and the triple burden of earning an income, managing the home and family and (very often) managing the community. A national housing policy, should address all these issues if, is to be effective in mobilizing, and benefitting all sections of society.

Policies should seek to remedy conflicts, exploitation, and omissions that limit women's participation in the housing development and management process, and also bar them from their rightful access to adequate housing.

Examination of many countries' housing policies reveals that gender inequalities are either ignored or, worse, reinforced. For example, the proposal on a housing policy and strategy for a future South Africa presents specific strategies to eliminate class and race inequalities but does not map out a plan of action to eliminate the inequality between genders. This is in spite of the fact that the proposals are based on information that shows that 50 per cent of the households in the rural areas are female-headed and that many urban women, married and single, are severely disadvantaged. What chances are there that the gender issue will be addressed in the implementation of the policy?

Housing policies must cut across several sectors, and address the gender issue in each sector. Otherwise they will inevitably fail, due to the deeply ingrained inequalities in many societies.

There are numerous examples of this which can be cited with reference to issues central to housing planning, development and management. The following examples illustrate policy contradictions among various national socio-economic policies that can adversely affect the shelter situation of number of people:

In Jamaica, during the International Year of Shelter for the Homeless, 1987, the Ministry of Housing was supporting the efforts of low-income households (many of them female-headed) in house improvements within the informal sector. At the very same time, the Ministry of Agriculture was involved in a campaign against squatters.

Another case of contradiction refers to Uganda, where the housing policy states "equal opportunities" for training and yet the practice in education is still based on traditional gender classification of jobs. Thus there are no boarding facilities for girls in government technical institutes. How then can women compete for skilled jobs within the construction sector (for example) without access to the necessary training?

Land and property ownership for women is yet another area where many countries have either no laws, or no clear guidelines for dealing with traditional discrimination against women, even while declaring equality for all.

Women have fewer options than men in terms of paid employment because of the commitment to other tasks around the home, notably child-rearing. Planning laws that prohibit income-generating activities in designated residential areas do not take into account the women (and men) who earn their livelihood in the informal sector in many cities. These are policies which fail to recognize the social and economic dimensions of shelter.

It is not just women who suffer because of gender-discriminatory policies, but their families and ultimately the whole society. A survey carried out in the United Kingdom of Great Britain and Northern

Ireland revealed that building societies were reluctant to grant mortgages to single women. Public housing allocation procedures favoured two-parent families, thus pushing single women with children, elderly women, and disabled women into substandard housing.

Housing information and statistics, the basis on which policies are formulated, often do not provide a true picture of the role and position of women. For instance, in calculating the value of houses, they take into account only the monetary contributions of the male as head of household, disregarding contributions by the woman, which may include cash and labour. This may have adverse implications for the woman in case of separation. The role of women in poor communities in providing shelter for themselves, often with little or no external assistance, and the needs and resources of women-headed households are often regarded.

It must be reiterated that gender discrimination is often subtle and sometimes happens during policy implementation. Even where good policies exist on paper, the practice may be very different. Similarly, good policies may be adopted at the national level, yet somehow become ineffective during implementation at sub-national and local levels.

Women remain under-represented at the global, national, regional and community levels of decision-making and therefore make minimal contributions to the formulation of policies. This has to be corrected through better education and information for women, as well as general awareness-building for all.

Sufficient detailed facts about the state of the housing sector should be obtained, in relation to overall economic, social and environmental development. The availability of statistics and indicators which quantify the specific disadvantages women face in relation to men, as well as their contribution and progress towards equality, can influence changes in public perception and hence policies. Such indicators are now being developed by UNCHS (Habitat) in collaboration with communities, NGOs and local governments in nine different countries: Bolivia, Colombia, Costa Rica, Ecuador, Ghana, Sri Lanka, Uganda, the United Republic of Tanzania, and Zambia. This is only the pilot stage. It is hoped that eventually more national governments and international agencies will make efforts to disaggregate data to allow analysis on the basis of gender. This will form a sound basis for the formulation and implementation of gender aware housing policies.

(F) TOWARDS A SAFER ENVIRONMENT

Over the past decade, and especially in the years leading to the Earth Summit in Rio de Janeiro, Brazil, in 1992, the deteriorating environment has been a major cause for concern among governments, the United Nations system, citizens groups, intergovernmental organizations and communities all over the world, In the industrialized West the issues have mainly revolved around environmental problems brought about by rapid technological and industrial advancements, such as toxic wastes, environmental pollution and climate changes. In the developing countries, the issues have tended to revolve around environmental problems brought about by people's abuse of the very environment on which they depend for survival such as resource depletion, deforestation, lowered water table and environmental degradation.

The destruction of the environment is not only an ecological issue but a critical housing issue as well. In rural areas around the world, a large majority of people depend directly on nature for building materials. Commercialization and/or destruction of important indigenous building materials such as wood and straw means that poor people who cannot afford to buy building materials are systematically being unplugged from their traditional life-support systems.

In unplanned informal urban settlements, environmental degradation is both a cause and a result of poor-quality housing. Lack of basic services and infrastructure (such as water treatment) poses environmental hazards which, in turn, affect the quality of life of those communities. For instance, if there are no sanitation facilities in a settlement (resulting in environmental and health problems), the community living there has no choice but to build their own facilities, without proper engineering techniques, financial aid, and government assistance. Such services may be sub-standard, and therefore potentially hazardous to the community.

These problems have particular implications for women. As primary users and also providers of services in urban and rural (especially informal) settlements, women are constantly exposing themselves to health hazards brought about by unsanitary and toxic environments. In both rural and urban areas, women are the primary users of house space and are responsible for running the house on a day-to day basis. They are the main providers of life-support systems-food, fuel, water, building materials-for their families and are, therefore, the first to feel the adverse effects of environmental degradation.

It is, therefore, not surprising that long before the environment became a popular theme for seminars and conferences, women were spearheading campaigns to protect the environment on issues ranging from toxic waste dumping to deforestation. This is because women, often being the poorest, and definitely being the least literate and the most powerless, are major victims of environment abuse.

In India, forests are considered valuable not only because they are life-sustaining, but also because trees are believed to have unique spiritual and healing powers. But forests that once provided food, fuel, fodder, medicine and spiritual comfort to rural women are being destroyed at an alarming rate. Commercialization of forests has turned vast tracts of land into privately-owned, single-species tree farms owned and controlled by men.

However, in the 1970s, an inspiring grassroots movement gained momentum in the hill district of Uttar Pradesh in Northern India when rural women began physically embracing trees so that loggers could not cut them. The Chipko Movement, as it is called, ("chipko" means "to hug") succeeded in articulating women's need to have access and control in the management of the forests on which they depend for day-to day survival. This kind of environmental activism is not new in India. As early as the three centuries ago, a woman called Amitra Devi led 300 villagers into a forest where they lost their lives while trying to save sacred trees by clinging to them.

Elsewhere in India, a woman called Medha Patkar has been protesting the building of a staggering complex of 3600 large and small dams over the Narmada River by organizing hunger strikes, demonstrations, sit-ins, road blocks and rallies. If the dams are built, they will submerge 245 village and thousands of hectares of vibrant forests and fields. They will also lead to the displacement and possible destitution of at least 100,000 people and destruction of their livelihood, culture and economies.

Environmental activism is not just the preserve of women in developing countries. In the United States of America, for example, women's membership in grassroots environmental and human settlements organizations and other "green" movements often surpasses that of men. One of the more well-known cases is that of Lois Gibbs, a former home-maker who currently heads the anti-toxic movement in the United States. In 1978, as a result of Gibbs' work, 900 families were evacuated from a toxic landfill in her working class neighbourhood in the town of Love Canal. She has since formed the Citizens' Clearing House on Hazardous Wastes that advises over 6000 citizen groups (the majority organized by women) on how to fight toxic-waste dumping in their neighbourhoods.

Women have thus been at the forefront of voluntary movements aimed at preserving life on this planet. Why then, one may ask, is the national international leadership of powerful environmental and human settlements organizations and lobbies dominated by men? Why are male-dominated governments setting the agenda and developing strategies? Why does activism continue to be a mere extension of the unpaid work do at home, that is cleaning up after others?

If it is true that those who face a problem are the most effective creators of solutions to the problem, then doesn't it make sense to involve women not merely as implementors of the solution but as planners and decision-makers-that is, the creators of the solution?

Women's lack of participation in mainstream, well-financed "development"organizations has already resulted in disastrous consequences. For example, many leading environmental and human settlements groups today blame overpopulation for the human-settlements crisis threatening the planet. Says the united States-based Sierra Club: "The continuing rapid rate of population growth is a core problem contributing in a major way to nearly all other environmental problems."

This is a view shared by many governments and aid agencies. The issue increasing population and decreasing agricultural yields is a critical topic on the global environmental agenda. Rapid urban expansion has no doubt led to a host of environmental and health problems, such as poor sanitation and lack of other basic social services, especially in the growing unplanned settlements in developing countries' cities and towns. Increasing populations have also put enormous pressure on agricultural land and small subsistence farms.

But according to research conducted by the Urban Management

Programme, a joint programme of the United Nation Development Programme, UNCHS (Habitat) and the World Bank, the underlying causes of environmental degradation and the resulting costs to public health and productivity are "inappropriate economic policies, inadequate investment in pollution control, deficient regulatory and institutional frameworks weak management capacities, inadequate cost recovery and insufficient political will and public awareness." In other words, blaming environmental destruction on overpopulation or urban growth as causes raises the real root of the crisis: skewed development priorities.

And so it is with environmental and human settlements problems. The question is not how women can be prevented from becoming victims of exploiters of the environment; the question is how women can gain control over their own environment so that can make decisions about its management.

Change can be brought about only if women are included not only in the management of the environment but in its very definition. There is a widespread tendency among environmentalists to divorce the human form the natural. But saving the enviroment does not mean getting rid of the people who live in it. Just as saving the rain forest means preserving the lives and livelihood of the people who inhabit it, saving our human settlements must necessarily include incorporating the decisions, views and participation of those who depend on the environment to create safe, secure shelter and life-support systems for their families and communities. That is why women must be involved at every stage in the process of managing and preserving the environment.

(G) A PLACE OF HER OWN: WOMEN AND LAND

Throughout the world, women face various constraints related to access to land and property. Laws, customs and economics prevent women from owning, inheriting and using land. This in turn adversely affects their access to shelter, and their contribution to shelter development.

In Kenya, where thousands of women get together in hundreds of groups to deal with many issues confronting women, land buying is one significant objective of many of these of these groups. Women get together specifically to pool their savings to buy land, or to start some economic activity that will eventually enable them to do so. This is true of both rural and urban women. It also applies to the very-low-income and the relatively better off middle-income groups. Membership includes single women with no children, women heads of household and married women.

The names of such groups are interesting. Some popular names (in various Kenyan languages) are:

Hodari, courageous, hard-working

Kugeria, to try, or to be determined

Kujitokeza, to stand up for oneself, to stand up to be seen, to dedicate oneself

Mugorogoro, a small tin used to measure grain in the market. The idea behind this name is that of slow accumulation of resources.

It is difficult to give exact translations of these names, but all contain the ideas of courage, trying hard, standing up for oneself, emerging from oblivion, and doing it bit-by-bit. They reflect the situation of women regarding land and property ownership: it is a hard struggle all the way.

In many customary law situations, women may have no right to own land except through fathers, husbands, sons or other male relatives. This can make the situation of widows with no sons, or unmarried women, very difficult. Even for married women with sons, their access is dependent on their being on good terms with the concerned males. There are legal systems in which women are treated as minors, unable to make transactions without a male relatives's consents. In Zimbabwe such a law was repealed recently.

Even in traditional and modern societies where women have the right to own and inherit land, the introduction of cash economies coupled with the growing importance of land as a commodity result in women having little chance of owning land. This is due to the high cost of land, as well as women being unaware of any existing rights. All this is taking place at a time when land is becoming increasingly important as means of getting credit for economic activities and for building houses, among other things.

Lack of access to land has other serious implications. For women in the subsistence economy, land means a place to live, to work, to grow food and to get building materials. In rural areas where population pressure, widespread cultivation of cash crops or commercial exploitation such as logging are eroding traditional lands, the burden of women to maintain shelters and feed families is increasing.

It is no surprise therefore that women have been organizing around the protection of traditional lands and ecosystems in many countries both developed and developing. In Papua New Guinea, where many men work away from the villages, leaving the women to defend the land, women are fighting not only against the logging companies, but also against a system that only allows land transfers among men. They are fighting to be recognized as rightful owners of land as part of the community, and to be fully involved in decisions concerning its exploitation.

In poor urban areas, women also face problems related to land ownership and use. Studies have shown that women-headed households predominate among low-income and informal settlements. Low-income settlements tend to be located on marginal, often hazardous land. precisely because this is the least attractive to land developers, and therefore, less likely to be targeted for evictions. However, settlements on such land tend to be crowded, dangerous and either lack space on which to grow food, or are too polluted for food growing.

Town planners and housing project designers often fail to plan or legislate for land for informal economic activities as well as subsistence food and livestock raising. Yet is well known that in many urban households, people (especially women) are growing food and keeping small livestock for subsistence, because they do not earn enough to pay for all their food requirements.

Eviction of residents of informal settlements is perhaps the most dramatic (and often violent) manifestation of the fight for land the position of the poor in this fight. Women suffer the most when such events occur. It is they who have to look after the family without a shelter, lose their food-growing areas, and often crops. Being the majority of informal-sector workers, they also lose their work support networks.

Women have therefore been prominent in struggles against eviction, and for regularization of tenure in informal settlements. There are several instances where residents have been able to come to some agreement with the authorities, and have gained recognition of their right to stay on and use the land. While such agreement may not be formal or official to the extent of providing titles to the land, they nevertheless recognize residents' rights.

Villa El Salvador, in Lima, Peru is one such example. Similar cases can be cited in Mexico City and in Sao Paolo, Brazil. In bangkok, Thailand, "land-sharing" has emerged as one way of accommodating the needs of both the occupants and the legal landowners, In Lusaka. Zambia, a group of grassroots women managed in 1992 to convince the local authority not to destroy an informal settlement without providing an alternative for the residents. They convinced authorities that eviction was against the human and housing rights of those people concerned.

The community land trust is a form of ownership where the land belongs to a community, And individuals have ownership rights over their house (structure) and user rights over the land. This model helps to remove land from the speculative market, thus making it more accessible to marginalized groups, which include poor women.

It must be pointed out that many factors can influence whether or not residents manage to get their occupation rights recognized. One significant factor is the level of community organization and consciousness. The more successful cases are those in which the whole community, men and women, has been mobilized. Access to legal aid, information, training on organizing and negotiating and the presence of truly representative community leaders all increase the chances of the community succeeding in gaining the right to stay.

Apart from the legal, economic and policy constrainsts to women's access to land, the systems for land delivery in many countries pose problems to any citizen trying to acquire land. The situation is more difficult for the poor, and even more so for women, who may not have the necessary money and information.

In one East African country it is estimated that obtaining a land title requires 33 separate transactions involving government bureaucracy, in a protracted process that may take up to three years. No doubt there are those who are able to go through the necessary process in a short time. It all depends on the amount of money, knowledge and personal clout one may have,

What would a rural widow do to obtain a title deed under such circumstances? She would probably be forced to spend several hours travelling from her village to the nearest land office, located in town.

Once there she would then join the queue, which would be mostly made up of men. While discreetly feeding her baby she would worry whether her other children at home had eaten. Being illiterate, she would be forced to make friends quickly with the man ahead of her in the queue. How else would she fill out the relevant forms? If she is patient enough, she may undergo this kind of procedure several more times, in the hope that in the end the piece of paper might provide her with some form of security. Without it there are possibilities that her in-laws can chase her off the property.

This is not the only country where land- delivery systems are centralized, tedious, inefficient and expensive and where women continue to be the ones that suffer most form it.

In Kenya the government has recently taken the positive step of publishing a guide on land transactions. This book describes all the stages of land purchase and transfer, including the required documentation and charges.

The status quo rooted in sex discrimination and gender insensitivity will change only when women start lobbying for better living conditions, which include land rights. Such action will draw women's plight to the attention of policy-makers, legislators, politicians and women leaders, who can influence change.

The issue of linking finance and credit to land ownership also needs to be explored further one women's behalf. The women themselves are finding practical ways of overcoming the land ownership barrier. Through self-help groups they are forming savings clubs variously known as "tontines", "merry-go-rounds" and "sou-sou". One could, borrow a leaf from Trinidad and Tobago where the "sou-sou" (penny-by-penny) venture originated from the need to enable squatters to buy land. The system does not assume members' households are male-headed, nor does it require a strong collateral base such as a regular income or a credit record, which women often lack.

Such groups have recognized that they are disadvantaged under both traditional and modern land ownership practices, and have taken steps to overcome this disadvantage, albeit within an unfair system.

More fundamental change is needed to help women overcome barriers to land ownership. Land reform cannot be ignored in this process. To date, little research has been carried out on the question of women's access to land, and how the constraints they face could be addressed. Research could help identify the constraints, and the data gathered used to legislate for women's equal access to property.

Another approach is lobbying for land reform. During the last decade in Zambia, women parliamentarians lobbied, with the help of a lawyers' association, to pass an inheritance law so that when a man dies, his wife is guaranteed 25 per cent of his land, while 50 per cent goes to his children, and the rest to other dependents.

Pressure groups, however, do not have to be confined to parliamentarians. Women from different walks of life are getting together to lobby for their rights. Women legislators, lawyers, policy-makers, planners and community organizers all have roles in providing the relevant information, and pressing for the right legislation and action.

The Global Strategy for shelter to the Year 2000 defines the major role of governments as that of enablers. Land is one area where government's enabling role is critical. Enabling means removing constraints for all sections of the community, facilitating people's initiatives, and paying special attention to those who are currently disadvantage. Women form a large proportion of this group.

(H) HOUSING THAT MEETS THE NEEDS OF ALL

Housing can be simply described as a place to live in peace, safety and dignity; as such it is recognized as a human right. This definition implies security, privacy, access to a means of making a livelihood and a base from which to develop. Safety also implies a clean and healthy environment. To many, housing represent an investment, a source of income and a symbol of permanence and security.

However, many do not have access to this right and even among those who do, many have no say in how their housing is developed. This is especially true of the poor in developing countries, and more so for women who are the majority of the poor.

Very often adequate care is not taken in designing, planning and implementing housing programmes and projects to make sure that the needs of all users are addressed.

An interesting phenomenon has been observed in low-income public housing projects in Africa, Asia and Latin America: as soon as residents assume ownership of the houses, they start making changes. People knock down walls to make bigger rooms, put in partitions to enclose certain areas, make extensions and generally change the interior to suit themselves. As one woman in a new neighbourhood in Nairobi, Kenya, was heard to say, "Instead of putting in two bathrooms in the house, they should have provided a place to store charcoal. .."

How should women participate ?

In many traditional societies women participate in the construction and maintenance of their homes. In urban areas in developing countries, up to 70 per cent of the housing is built by "informal" or unpaid labour, a great proportion of which is women's labour. Women may plaster walls, lay bricks pack down new mud floors or help repair a roof. In some instances, women are solely responsible for constructing homes. Yet, because this occurs in the "informal" sector where little or no money is exchanged, women's contribution and experience go unrecognized. On the other hand, women are left out of the modern, formal construction sector.

There are many good reasons why women should participate in housing development. One of them is that they have as much right to participate in projects which profoundly affect their lives as men. Women are the primary users of housing. They are therefore the most affected by housing and settlement projects. This is especially true given the amount of time they spend in the house: women often have to combine employment with household and child-rearing roles, and therefore have to work in and around the home.

In rural areas, and in unplanned urban settlements, women are also the main providers of services. For example, a large proportion of women's self-help projects are concerned with water and daycare. Official housing projects with self-help components have tended to depend a lot on women's labour.

This kind of participation, which in many cases has been a big burden, has been imposed on women by circumstances, and by official insensitivity to women's needs and circumstances.

What is needed is the participation of women and men in the planning and design of settlements -houses, neighbourhoods and cities.

Some specific difficulties faced by women in shelter projects

When women are not consulted at the planning and design stage of human settlements development, their needs and priorities may not be taken into account. These may be related to particular cultural requirements, or to the need to combine income-earning and household tasks. This can cause severe problems. Women's lives can be adversely affected by introducing services that are inappropriate to their needs. For example, in a neighbourhood in El Salvador, women would not use the public toilets provided because a gap was left at the bottom of the door that exposed their feet, offending their notion of privacy. In Bangladesh, because of similar reasons of privacy, women could only use toilets before sunrise and after sunset, causing inconvenience and severe physical discomfort.

Women often have to work in or near the home. The failure of architects and planners to recognize this has resulted in house designs that do not take into consideration the needs of women. In addition, zoning regulations separate residential and business activities, thus prohibiting the development of income-earning activities in the home or locally in residential areas. This has at times led to harassment of women who have no choice but to locate businesses in areas not accepted by local authorities.

Failure to acknowledge the many roles that women play also leads to undue demands being made on women's time. This happens in public-sector interventions that do not consider women's special needs and situations. It is especially true in site-and-service projects and squatter-upgrading programmes where households are expected to participate in housing construction. Absence of day-care facilities, coupled with the fact that women may not be able to afford the loss of income resulting from time taken off from economic activities, make participation difficult for women. Incorrect assumptions about women's ability to devote their time to self-help projects and to participate in the community process have thus often resulted in women being left out. In such projects some women end up contracting labour because they do not have enough time to do the work themselves. This is too expensive and may place them in heavy debt, often forcing them to sell their plots.

Negative effects of relocation, and non-participatory upgrading

Non-participatory relocation and upgrading schemes have also tended to disrupt women's lives and economic activities. As a result, women often lose their mutual support networks through which they arrange employment, credit and childcare, among other things.

Similarly, when upgrading changes single-storey housing to high-rise apartments, women forced to move to upper storeys lose considerably in the value of the house as a place from which to make a living, a street-level dwelling being more convenient as a place for business, especially if it involves vending.

Under-employment in the construction sector

Another obstacle faced by poor women is lack of suitable employment in the modern construction sector so that they can both escape poverty and gain valuable skills to be used to build and improve their homes. Although in many traditional societies women were partly or wholly responsible for house building, jobs offered to them in the modern formal sector are often limited to menial tasks like carrying water and sand. Moreover, the participation of women in the formal construction sector is amazingly low, especially in developing countries.

Lack of training

Lack of training is the most significant cause of under-representation and the low status of women in the construction industry. Lack of understanding of this sector also makes it easy for women to be exploited when they have to hire artisans to build for them. Maintenance of the house poses the same problem to the woman who has no understanding of building.

Training of women can mobilize unemployed or underemployed labour resources, resulting in a more balanced distribution of jobs in the construction industry, and help women to acquire shelter through self-help construction. Skills acquired can also be used in house maintenance. One women's building cooperative in Cincinnati in the United States of America started with women heads of households learning simple house maintenance skills.

Jamaica also offers a positive example of training women for the construction industry. In this case, training was designed to meet identified needs and specific job openings in the construction industry. It must be noted, however, that measures to change the attitude of building-site supervisors are required if more women are to be able to use their new skills.

Some specific problems of the poorest Women-headed households

A group that is not given due attention is the increasing number of women heads of household who have exceptionally low incomes and can hardly participate in many conventional housing projects. For example, in a site-and-service project in Quito, Ecuador, female heads of households formed 30 percent of the total applicants, but 46 per cent of them did not qualify for access to the scheme because their incomes were too low. In Dandora, Kenya, some women households heads could not afford to construct their houses according to specified standards and were forced to resell their plots. In Dodoma, United Republic of Tanzania, a programme of the Low Cost Housing Unit for supporting employment-based housing cooperatives left out a large percentage of women who did not have the minimum financial resources required.

Many women cannot afford to make the downpayments in such projects. Nor can they afford to repay fixed sums because of irregular incomes, and they lack collateral to get loans in the first place.

In spite of these problems, a number of successful credit programmes for women have been established, oriented towards employment, as a first step to housing. Examples include the Self-Employed Women's Association in India, with 13,000 members, and the Women in Development Loan Fund in Barbados.

Overcoming the obstacles

For women to benefit from shelter development equally with men, both their special needs and their autonomous demand for shelter should be taken into account in policies, plans and programmes. This will also help to ensure that women's needs and concerns are incorporated in the design and implementation of housing projects. The issue of women and shelter has to be addressed in comprehensive programmes for increasing women's participation in settlement planning and management, at local and national levels. Such programmes will have to include better access to appropriate training as a prerequisite.

An essential starting point is gender sensitization of policy-makers, planners and human settlements professionals. This is one area in which women are under-represented even in developed countries. For example, in Toronto, Canada, out of an estimated 2000 architects, only about 10 per cent are women. Moreover only 10 per cent of the

200 are actively applying gender concerns to their work. Obviously gender awareness needs to be raised in both men and women!

Fundamental changes in understanding, policy and planning are required if women's housing issues are to be adequately addressed. What is needed is a policy approach that acknowledges that women have different housing needs from those of men; that in many societies there are specific constraints that limit women's access to housing on the basis of gender, regardless of income; and that women in poor communities are doubly constrained.

(I) DEMYSTIFYING MONEY TALK

Nubia lives in an informal settlement in a Latin American city. She has several children and no husband. Nubia wants a house. It is the best investment she, her mother and her sisters know of. It is also security for her and her children. No bank would lend Nubia money. She has no bank account, no savings, and no proper job. Her "savings" are in a television set and a pair of gold earrings, paid for in instalments. "Is it not ridiculous that they have TV's and gold jewellery when they don't even have flush toilets in their houses?" This is the comment of more well-to-do observers. But then there is no instalment-purchase plan for a flush toilet. On the other hand, it is possible for Nubia to give her TV or gold jewellery as downpayment for a plot in the informal land market. Some of her friends have done so.

The poor face many problems in obtaining finance for shelter from conventional finance markets. Financial institutions prefer to give big loans. Small loans are not good business. However, the poor cannot afford to take big loans because their monthly incomes are too small for the repayments required. High interest rates make repayment doubly difficult.

Eligibility criteria usually require relatively high and regular incomes. Many of the poor have low and irregular incomes in informal employment.

Lack of substantial savings-which banks like to see before lending-is another stumbling block. The requirement for collateral or other security, often in the form of land or other legal property. Automatically excludes most poor people.

Women form the majority of the poor and, as such, suffer all the above constraints. In addition, there are specific factors that bar women from the credit market. For example:

Women's legal status, where women are classified as minors and cannot acquire credit or only on husbands's or male relative's guarantee, is one problem.

Definitions of households where the man is assumed to be the head of the family, and "normal" families have a male head and bread-winner lead to discrimination against female heads of households. They disregard the woman's income when assessing the income eligibility of "normal" households.

Take Nubia as an example. If she had money in the bank, she would not be needing a loan, not for the kind of housing purchase or development she is likely to be interested in. With her laundry job, she sees no way of saving enough to buy a house, even in her squatter settlement.

Most house purchases or improvements by the poor in developing countries are through cash payments from family savings or from informal loans. However, family house purchases are often not the best solutions for a woman like Nubia. Since she is single, she is expected to contribute towards her parents house. Indeed, she has contributed 25 per cent of the purchase price. Her parents in turn have helped their sons to buy their own houses. And Nubia? She is expected to live with her parents; but she is thirty-two and does not wish to live with them anymore. Her married friends are not much better off. They have little hold on property to whose acquisition they have directly or indirectly contributed.

What Nubia would really like is a convenient savings plan, where her small savings would enable her to have small loans for whatever she needs a loan for-not necessarily for buying a house, not right now anyway. But being able to satisfy some of these other immediate needs brings her closer to acquiring a house some day.

Nubia is like many women among the poor in developing countries: cut off from the conventional housing market that requires large downpayments and expensive credit, in order to buy ready-made housing that is often not suitable for the buyer. Many are not eligible for, do not want, cannot afford, and are even afraid of credit as it is currently available.

A credit scheme for house improvement in a poor rural district in Kenya had to change its approach when project staff realized that even repaying the very small loans offered would have been a heavy burden on the women involved. Besides, the women's first priority was raising money for school fees for their children. The new approach involved giving small loans to women's income-generating groups, for shelter-related activities. With some technical assistance, the women learned to make stabilized soil blocks and fibre-concrete roofing tiles for sale. Much later they also learned construction skills. Several years after the start of the project, the women's groups are taking loans for shelter-related income activities; some groups are now thinking of home improvements. A side benefit for the women has been that the materials-production and construction skills gained means they can do their own construction, or supervise the artisans they hire to do the construction for them. Money was lost before through artisans' incompetence or dishonesty.

The Working Women's Forum (WWF) which was started in 1978 in madras, India, has a credit programme that lends to individual women in poor communities, through community-based groups. Loans are small, but a beneficiary takes a new loan on completion of payment of the previous one. The WWF's experience has been that the priorities of the women change as their economic situation improves with each successive loan. Priorities change from paying debts to making trade investment to buying households goods to improving the house. By the fifth or sixth loan, almost all borrowers were improving roof, walls or floors.

The WWF started off acting as an intermediary for official lending institutions, helping women through bank bureaucracy, and guaranteeing their loans. Eventually it started its own credit cooperative society for women because the banks were not flexible enough for the women clients of the WWF. Even with the credit cooperative, the WWF had to fight against conventional procedures and requirements. For example, making groups rather then individuals responsible for loans was against existing government rules governing savings cooperatives.

Beneficiaries recounted what a difference it made securing loans through the WWF; "We were all women . . .they were patient and explained everything and helped us to fill the forms . . .Before, if we went to the big banks in our dirty *sarees*, they treated us badly. . .so next time one borrowed a *saree* form a friend, then they said "your *saree* is worth a lot of money, why do you want a loan?". . . So either way you could not win. Here (WWF) they do not ask us if we own property or land, they just ask about our business enterprise, what we will do with the loan and how we can repay . . ." The repayment rates have been very good, and the programme has expanded into several other states of India.

There are other innovative credit programmes that help women improve their incomes and their shelter. The Grameen Bank in Bangladesh is one of the best known. Women's World Banking and national women's finance trusts are also making their contribution.

There are many successful credit schemes whose experience can be drawn upon. What is needed is the recognition of the special problems of women in acquiring finance for shelter, and the political will to do something about the problem. Women's organizations, non-governmental organizations (NGOs), national governments and international agencies can assist in financing and promoting housing finance and credit programmes that benefit both men and women.

The involvement of women in policy-making is also essential. Already some progress for women's access to credit has been made through the work of associations of women bank managers, and women development workers. More needs to be done, for example, to make the necessary education and training available to women, so that they can be in decision-making positions. Steps should also be taken, at the national level, to improve women's land and property rights. Last but by no means least, is the need to make information on credit opportunities and procedures available to women. Both governments and NGOs have a responsibility in this task.

(J) NETWORKING: SHARING SUCCESS, PROBLEMS AND EXPERIENCES

"Sharing, exchanging, learning, solidarity . . ." These are some of the words we use when we talk about networking. Sharing experiences, problems, strategies, successes, failures and lessons learned can play an important role in furthering common interests, and in developing the political will and strength to push for change.

Networking is very simply talking *to* each other, taking *about* each other and talking *for* each other for a common cause. It is a learning process that involves sharing information and knowledge and building solidarity. Networking around critical issues can cut across geographic, cultural, ideological and class divisions. Recognition of, and support for, women's role in the development, management and maintenance of human settlements is one such issue.

At the end of 1987, the International Year of Shelter for the Homeless (IYSH), a group of 90 women from East and Southern Africa met in Harare, Zimbabwe, to talk about the shelter situation of women in sub-Saharan Africa. This group identified lack of information as a serious constraint to women's ability to control and improve their living environment. Similarly, the National Campaign for Housing Rights in India recognizes the right to information as one of a cluster of rights making up the right to housing. Networking is part of information sharing.

If can be carried out at different levels, between different types of groups and organizations and using various types of media. At local and national levels, groups of women from different parts of one country can and do visit each other to exchange information and skills, and to formulate joint action programmes on a wide range of issues. These include acquisition of skills related to house construction and infrastructure, environmental health, how to make neighbourhoods safe and how to provide community facilities such as day-care centres.

Recently a group of Tanzanian women community leaders representing women's housing groups visited women's housing cooperatives in neighbouing Kenya. The tour was coordinated by the Housing and Building Research Institute of the University of Nairobi. The Tanzanian women saw, among other things, what the Kenyan women were doing in building-materials production and construction. One Tanzanian woman remarked during the visit, "We had thought of doing construction, but we always wondered what would happen when we got to the roof. It was quite an experience seeing a woman in an overall, on top of a house, doing the roof. Now we can learn to do roofing too. "They in turn taught some of the Kenyan women a simple and cheap way of making water tanks and pots from sand and cement. The Tanzanians videotaped the visits as well as the discussions, to share them with the women in their housing groups. They say the video has been provoking lively discussion.

Regional and inter-regional level exchange between grassroots as well as professional women has been taking place through seminars or direct country-to-country exchanges, enabling women to discuss and to learn from each others' experiences. Exchanges between community-based women's organizations have been facilitated by non-governmental organizations (NGOs) as well as donor and international organizations. This is well illustrated by an exchange visit involving the women from the *barrios* of Bogota exchange took place in 1990, with the help of SPARC, and NGO working with pavement dwellers in Bombay, FEDEVIVIENDA, a Colombian NGO, and Homeless International, a British NGO that funds shelter programmes in developing countries. A group if Indian women first visited Bogota; then their Colombian counterparts returned the visit soon after.

What was the purpose of this exchange? What can women from informal settlements in Bogota and Bombay learn from each other, coming as they do from different cultures, living miles from each other, not even having a common language? "For me, this experience has been very good", one Colombian woman said. "I can see that all of us from different neighbourhoods are fighting for a better future. We are struggling but we are gaining this future . . ." And a woman from Bombay said of the exchange, "we thought they were much better off than us. . . but then we came to understand that they face the same problems: How to make yourself visible so that the authorities will negotiate with you over your right to land on which to build your house, how to arrange meetings when you have children to look after, and how to deal with men who feel threatened. . . "

For the two NGOs, SPARC and FEDEVIVIENDA, it was a good opportunity to look at each other's methods of making interventions in poor communities, supporting women's initiatives, and organizing on women and human settlements issue. One observer has remarked that the experience has been a real confidence builder for the Colombian women. This experience has been widely disseminated through the newsletter of the Women and Shelter Network of the Habitat International Coalition, (HIC), an international alliance of NGOs working on shelter issues. It has aroused a lot of interest and it is quite possible that other such exchanges may happen in the future. The HIC Woman and Shelter Network, founded in 1988, believes that women's initiatives in the struggle for better living conditions can be strengthened by networking.

Effective networking must respect the diversity of experience, understanding, ideologies and strategies that exist. It must assist people to learn from both the successes and failures of others. Through networking, professional women can learn not only form each other but also from grassroots women, creating a dialogue between popular knowledge and more formal knowledge. In turn, the policy-makers, the planners, the designers of housing projects and training programmes can use this knowledge in their work, for better human settlements.

The UNCHS (Habitat) Women in Human Settlements Development Programme organized a meeting at the end of 1992, to discuss indicators for measuring the participation of women in human settlements development. This was an interesting networking experience in which women form Africa, Asia and Latin America, representing grassroots, NGO and professional women who had participated in a survey, exchanged their experience of the survey process. During the discussions, the grassroots women underscored their need to work with professional women on this kind of activity. On the other hand, they were also quite emphatic in their views on the survey method, the questionnaires, what changes they would like made, and what they thought to be the most critical indicators of women's participation in human settlements. Several groups indicated that they had started or were going to start discussing environmental health awareness in their communities. They would begin in the neighbourhoods where they had carried out the surveys, using some of the research findings. The professional women involved in the exchange will incorporate some of the lessons in their work in the future.

Networking also helps to build solidarity. Just knowing that there are others engaged in the same struggles, advocating and promoting the same goals, makes a difference. Associations of women bankers are already making an impact in some countries on women's access to credit. Associations of women lawyers are fighting for property rights for women; planners and project designers have been networking for more gender-sensitive zoning laws and housing designs, as well as better consideration for female heads of households. A network of professional women that brings together lawyers, bankers, planners and policy-makers in government as well as NGOs could be very interesting. The HIC Women and Shelter Network is already linking such women from NGOs, and lobbying governments.

From their experience, many women from developing countries know that it makes a lot of difference to their work when they network, at however informal a level, with other women in decision-making positions in the official national machinery. Kenya, in the process of identifying indicators for measuring access to housing, is already benefiting from the experience of a woman senior policy-maker who has been networking with the NGO community. She is ensuring that indicators on women's housing situation and their contribution are included in the set of national indicators under preparation. In Uganda, now in the process of formulating a national shelter strategy, the woman responsible for the project has been involved in regional networking on women and shelter issues for several years. This experience is being reflected in her country's shelter planning at the national level.

Networking needs resources-people and money. A lot of activity is already taking place, but it needs support and encouragement. Newsletters, exchange visits and meetings need planning and money. The women and Human Settlements Programmes of UNCHS (Habitat) is committed to encouraging and facilitating the exchange process through support for existing networks.

Governments should also be encouraged to support networking on women and shelter issues, as well as the participation of the NGO and community sectors in the shelter process. These are the sectors in which many of the women and shelter issues are being addressed. Interventions are being made and innovative ideas are being tried out. They are also the sectors that are doing a lot of work with very few resources. Networking helps to share these few resources, and a wide body of knowledge among a large group of people.

Networking is the kind of activity that reaps slow, long-terms, qualitative benefits. It is not the kind of activity that has immediate and spectacular results-except in occasional cases. It is therefore often difficult to justify resource allocation in terms of cost-effectiveness. Networking, however, is an important part of people-oriented development. It is also a vital tool for empowering women, for the promotion of women as agents of change in the shelter development process. Thus it is worth allocating the necessary resources to networking.

(K) HUMAN SETTLEMENTS INFORMATION: EQUAL ACCESS, EQUAL CONTROL

Is there adequate information on women in shelter development?

The answer, unfortunately, is “No” There exists little useful information on the roles, needs and contributions of women in shelter development. This is partly because not enough appropriate research has been done in this area, and women remain invisible in many research findings. Equally important is the fact that policy-makers and project managers do not make use of the scanty information that exists. Women's views needs and contributions are often neglected in policy formulation implementation, not just because of lack of information, but also because of lack of concern about the situation of women.

For their part, women lack essential information on shelter development such as policies, projects, credit facilities and opportunities. As a result they miss out on the few possibilities available to them. This is partly due to the fact that information about some of these policies, projects and credit facilities has not been widely distributed and publicized. Another reason why women lack information is that many of them live in isolation and poverty, many are illiterate and cannot obtain information from the print media and they are often too poor to own a radio or television set.

Fortunately, steps are being taken to improve information gathering and sharing, and the interaction between policy-makers, women and men. These involve international organizations, non-governmental and community-based organizations (NGOs and CBOs). However, national public-sector institutions are generally lagging behind in this area.

Why is more awareness on women in shelter development needed?

Women, more than other members of the family, spend a lot of time in the home and it is only fair that their views and needs be taken into account, particularly in designing houses and other services. It is now acknowledged that official policies and programmes on shelter development cannot succeed without women's full participation. Women cannot participate fully unless they have access to information on policies, projects and other entitlements. In a study in Paraguay, 50 per cent of the women interviewed mentioned lack of information as the main reason for not improving their housing conditions, whereas only 16 per cent of the men mentioned that factor.

Women's roles, needs views and contributions are crucial for the effective formulation implementation of appropriate gender-sensitive policies, programmes and projects. Otherwise policy-makers will continue to make plans based on inaccurate, gender-blind information. A documented example is that of Ibn Khalkdoun, a squatter-settlement upgrading project in Tunisia. Because of a lack of awareness and concern, policy-makers decided to build modern-style houses-resulting in the reduction of internal space which is very important in that particular culture where women have to spend most of their time indoors. The house design gave rise to mental depression, and in some cases, suicide among the women. If the women had been consulted about their needs this situation would not have arisen. Another example is that of policy-makers in Boa Vista, Brazil, who, lacking awareness on different family structures of the target population, made a ruling that applicants for housing loans could only be fathers of at least two children. This immediately excluded 43 per cent of the target population made up women-headed households. Unfortunately these kinds of mistake may be repeated elsewhere, if this kind of information is not publicized and if policy-makers are not sensitive to women's concerns.

What has been done to facilitate information sharing and gender awareness in shelter development ?

Some progress is being made. In 1988, UNCHS (Habitat) started a series of five separate regional seminars aimed at improving communication and the participation of women in human settlements. Support communication materials for use in training were developed and disseminated. These training programmes were aimed at highlighting the role of information and communication in enhancing the role of women in shelter development. The participants were policy-makers in government, and NGOs working with women. The seminars are slowly contributing to the development of gender awareness among policy-makers in shelter development.

The Women in Human Settlements Programme of UNCHS (Habitat) has run a number of gender-awareness workshops for men and women in shelter development so that they become sensitive to gender issues in their implementation.

Women are creating their own media in which they determine the information and issues to be disseminated. Information and news networks such as Her Say in the United States, Agence Femme Information in France, and the Caribbean Women's features Syndicate, have been created to disseminate information on women. Much relevant information on women in shelter development comes from newsletters that are specifically concerned with gathering and disseminating information on women and shelter. The Habitat International Coalition's Women and Shelter newsletter is one example.

At the grassroots levels, women are using dance and drama, puppet shows, music slides, video film and sound tapes to enhance gender awareness and inform other women about development projects and facilities. For example, Sistren, the Jamaican all-women theatre, is using theatre to examine and comment on the role of women in development and their experiences in the ghetto. The Amauta Association of Cusco, Peru, was formed by women who participated in shelter building but were denied access to the decision-making body by men. They developed their own audio-visual materials to formulate solutions to their problems.

The southern Africa People's Dialogue on Land and Homelessness uses "talking newsletters", audio-cassettes that contain information and discussions on poor communities shelter issues.

In order to improve women's access to information, adult literacy programmes have been started in most developing countries by NGOs, government agencies and CBOs. In Egypt, for example, women make up 70 per cent of the audience for radio literacy courses.

What are some of the obstacles to information sharing and gender awareness in shelter development ?

Lack of gender awareness of some of the policy-makers in the media and in institutions making policies on shelter development is a big disadvantage. The policy-makers, mostly men, decide on the information to be collected and disseminated. A lot of the information is gender-blind. Even in developed countries, few programmes are devoted to homelessness and other issues related to shelter development. Serious issues like shelter are not usually scheduled on prime time on television or radio, nor are they given front page coverage in the print media.

About 40 per cent of women in the world are illiterate and cannot read about policies and projects on shelter development. Even those who can read have problems understanding the technical language used in documents on shelter development. In Asia, less than 5 per cent of the female population has access to television, while in Africa the proportion is less than 1 per cent. The "talking newsletters" mentioned earlier could be interesting to use in such a situation, as could more radio programmes.

What needs to be done ?

Women researchers and professionals should carry out surveys to provide information and statistics on women's roles, needs views and contributions in shelter development-to be made available for use by policy-makers and project managers working in government. International organizations and NGOs.

Training workshops to promote the gender awareness of both female and male decision-makers in shelter development, like those run by the Women in Human Settlements Development Programme of UNCHS (Habitat), should be extended to include some men and women from the popular media.

Adult literacy programmes for both women and men should be promoted to enable women to read newspapers, official documents, advertisements of new projects and available facilities on shelter development. CBOs could be encouraged to buy radios to be shared by the members.

Women-controlled media should collect and disseminate information on women in shelter development. Information on shelter projects and programmes should be announced on radio, at churches, markets, community meetings and schools-as well as at mother-and-baby, clinics in residential areas. Drama and songs can also be used to inform both women and men about issues in shelter development. Social workers and extension officers can visit the potential beneficiaries in their homes. More female projects workers should be used to enhance women's participation.

they can relate more easily to the messages.

Television is probably the most powerful media of communication in the world today. Its influence, in shaping attitudes and concepts is unquestionable. However, at present the impact created by this is predominantly negative.

For community based programme "group media" is more powerful. This refers to all media that facilitate communication within a group and between that group and other group of individuals. Music, theatres, slides, video films, flip charts and sound tapes are among the more frequently used group media. Women has found this effective especially in areas where the literacy rate is high and the mass media including radio is under Govt. monoply. Alongwith these, women have experimented with puppet shows, street theatre, comics and dance and have found each useful depending upon the context and purpose.

They have also observed that traditional forms of communication could be used effectively to bring women into the core of development process especially in rural areas.

CONCLUSION

Thus, it is becoming apparent that National Development targets can only be achieved if women are approached as the main agents of change. In the interest of National Development as a whole, the total sum of their available knowledge and talent, their contributions to Human Settlement Development is indispensable to progress and the development of Humanity.

CHAPTER-2

Doing What Comes Naturally ? Women and Environment in Development

Cecile Jackson

1. ECOFEMINISM, WOMEN, ENVIRONMENT AND DEVELOPMENT

The dominant discourses on women and environment-i.e. ecofeminist and Women,Development and Environment[1] (WDE) literatures — emphasize the affinity of women with their environments, yet gender analysis offers a preferable alternative conceptual framework as the basis for understanding, and intervening in, the local specificities of men's and women's environmental relations. I will first give a brief account of ecofeminist and WDE ideas before discussing the themes of closeness of women to their environments and altruism. Finally I examine the view common to both these discourses that women are the appropriate target group to mobilize for conservation and consider how a gender analysis of environmental relations might lead to rather different perspectives.

Ecofeminism takes different forms characterized broadly as cultural ecofeminism and social ecofeminism (Plumwood, 1992, p. 10)—the criticisms made here relate mainly to the former, but there is considerable common ground between the two. "A basic assumption common to all ecofeminist positions is the rejection of the assumed inferiority of women and nature and of the superiority of reason, humanity and culture" (Plumwood, 1992, p. 13). Both are ecocentric, in that nonhuman life is seen as morally considerable (Eckersley, 1992) and both bracket women with nature. Our concentration on cultural ecofeminism here is justified by the apparent ascendancy of this element, especially among activist environmental groups in the West, as well as by the influence (acknowledge by Rodda, 1991, p. 4) of cultural ecofeminism upon WDE literature, primarily through Vandana Shiva. Critiques of ecofeminism from a development perspective (Agarwal, 1991; Rao 1991, Jackson, 1993) have drawn attention to its biological determinism and essentialism, and the absence of social, material or historical context.

Recent years have seen a proliferation of books, reports, conferences and activity related to women and environment both in the West and the Third World[2] and both international organizations and NGOs have adopted the linkage. Key ecofeminist theorists have not seen any problems with extending their analysis to the Third World.

> Ecological feminism . . . has grown up especially in the women's, peace and ecology movements . . . In the Third World...the connection between women's interests and the health of nature is especially apparent (Plumwood, 1992, p.10).

How are ecofeminist ideas reflected in development literature and practice? The exploitation of women and the environment are now commonly portrayed as having gone hand in hand, and both are seen as victims of "development" (Shiva, 1989b). It is taken as self-evident that harm to nature equals harm to women, because of the pervasive perception that women are closer to nature.[3] One might, however, question whether the general awareness that the burden of degradation falls disproportionately upon women does not rather derive from growing awareness of the reproductive labor of women (for example, wood and water collecting) in development discourse? This does not seem to be the case — much of the WDE literature does not use the concept of reproduction in its analysis.[4] Nor does it use gender analysis either, preferring to deal with "women." Instead, the linkage of women and environment is either assumed or asserted and taken as prescribing a course of action in which women are mobilized for conservation.

The nature of the WDE literature is noticeably different from earlier work of WID — it is not led by academics, it is very anecdotal (e.g., Dankelman and Davidson, 1989)[5] and not concerned to establish clear evidence or strong argument but takes it position as self-evident and it is characterized by a strong presumption that women have an affinity with the environment. For example, a report which found that people working on anti-desertification projects were usually only rewarded with food and that most such workers were women concludes that women are very committed to the environment, not that women were the poorest and, unlike men, work for only food. In most cases women *volunteer* for the work, driven by their strong desire to restore the land" (Monimart, 1991, p. 41) and the report further claims that "the women have got to their feet and are trying to halt this [environmental] destruction" (1991, p.39). Another example is in an article which remarks on the fact that women only collect dry wood for fuel . . .

> Women have rules about fuel collection that expressly prohibit the cutting down of living trees. Dead and downed wood is preferred. In addition, certain species may be protected by custom or religious sanction. In parts of India women water the peepul tree as an act of piety (Fortmann, 1986,p. 40).

What is not said here is that dead wood is lighter and easier to carry. Environment-friendly management practices by women can be explained in terms of rational short-term interest but are too often understood with an implicit assumption that women are caring, nurturing and selfless beings committed to both future generations and the environment for its own sake. The theme of women mobilizing in defence of the environment involves repeated reference to the same instances — Chipko, the silkworm development by women on wastelands in West Bengal, the Guarari Community Development Project, the Kenyan Green Belt Movement — and Sontheimer reads these as showing women "working together and. . .uniting their voices to demand that both their rights and nature be treated justly" (Sontheimer, 1991, p. iii). She goes on to claim that

> The motivation for their actions is based on the full recognition that without a healthy environment, their is no life. [Women] express their concern for local ecological problems and a philosophy of living with nature rather than against it (Sontheimer, 1991, p. iii).

Another feature of WDE discourse is that it is propagated by NGOs in particular. One of the key documents is the NGO Forum of the 1985 UN Decade for Women Conference in Nairobi. The papers given there demonstrate many of the features of WDE thinking. Women are urged to "rally to protect the soils and water systems of their lands, so that hunger is not invited to stalk the generations" (Martin-Brown, 1985), they "have a special role to play to stop the death of our continents and even the planet" (Maathai, 1985) and it is "up to women to save the environment" (Barrow quoted by Dankelman, 1985). Women are said to have "healing hands" and it is alleged that "Forest operations like picking out seedlings from nurseries are best suited to women. . . .The job needs women's patience and nursing instinct" (Aloo, 1985). A number of papers assert that "as women are the most affected by the energy crises" they should also be considered as the most effective in tackling the crises (Dankelman, 1985; Landazuri, 1985). Vandana Shiva claims that "women want development that ensures water and food. Men want development that generates cash and "Contracts" (Shiva, 1985, P. 61). Finally, "the invisible bond existing between women, the environment and development" (Dankelman, 1985, p. 17) is affirmed throughout. We will next examine the validity of two major themes in WDE discourses — the special relationship between women and their environments and the altruistic behavior of women in the protection and defense of nature.

2. WOMEN AND ENVIRONMENT: THE ESSENTIALIST LINKAGE

The ecofeminist conception of the inherent closeness of women and nature is expressed by Vandana Shiva — "(The) organic process of growth in which women and nature work in partnership with each other has created a special relationship of women with nature. . ." (1989b, p. 43) — and widely endorsed in WDE literature (Davidson, 1989). Essentialism is also expressed in WDE literature by the very general level at which information is presented—women are given as a homogenous category, not only within countries but across nations too. (Dankelman and Davidson, 1989). The absence of gender terminology is significant — for gender affirms the socially grounded nature of identities as women and men, and eschews essentialism. But because women have not been at the forefront of tree logging or mining or rainforest burning does not mean that they are naturally more caring about the environment.

Much of this paper is focused at the micro level in order to reveal the variability of incentive structures experienced by individual men and women, but an equally strong critique of WDE could be made which points out the necessity to locate environmental attitudes within particular economies. For example, two recent studies of Kenya and Tanzania reach opposite conclusions on how gender affects environmental behavior — for Kenya, Gould (1992, p. 15) describes an area of high male outmigration and suggests that "women, as environmental managers, are able to assert their *de facto* responsibilities and knowledge to sustain the on-farm resources of the household economy" while Eele, Duncan and Lawson for Tanzania (1992, p. 18) found that, even after accounting for other variations such as holding size, male farmers were more likely than female to make a conservation investment. Clearly, it is not possible to characterize women as inherently environment friendly.

Women as a group do not experience environmental degradation in a uniform manner — these effects are mediated by the *livelihood system.* Some women may have remittances from migrant males, or more diverse livelihoods, or assets that may be liquidated, or kin-based entitlements which ameliorate the effects of environmental degradation. For example, the effects of logging in Malaysia upon rainforest inhabitants is varied. Hunter-gatherer Penan men have resisted assimilation into wage work with the logging companies and the negative effects on their livelihood system are felt equally by men and women since "property" rights and divisions of labor are barely differentiated. Both men and women have been involved in the protests and road blockades against logging. The shifting cultivating Iban on the other hand, through the practice of "*bejalai*" (journeys undertaken by young men for material gain and prestige) have embraced wage work, especially in Brunei, and remit to their wives and mothers who are increasingly responsible for farming. The absence of males makes it difficult to fell new lands, in order to follow old ones, and women therefore are driven to continue repeatedly cultivating the same plots, with negative effects on soil fertility and crop yields. Neither Iban men or women have become involved in the protests against logging — the addition of wages to livelihood portfolios compensates for the absence of male labor and buffers the potentially negative experience by women of environmental degradation (Heyzer, 1992).

Environmental relations of particular women also depend upon a class-gender system. As Agarwal documents for South Asia (1991, pp. 38-44) the adverse effects of environmental degradation fall particularly upon poor women, and Hobley (1991) shows how gender and class intersect in the use of forest resources in nepal. The latter omstamce demonstrates that dependence on forest resources and participation in decision making by women regarding forest use is variable — low caste men and in particular low caste women were dominated in meetings.

In addition to the class-gender effects there are other distinctions between women which are significant. Inequalities among women exist even at the household level where seniority frequently patterns divisions of labor, access to and control of resources and decision-making powers. For example, in Zimbabwe older women within households can, and do, send junior wives, son's or daughters to collect fuel wood (McGregor, 1991, p. 206). In 65 households randomly sampled in the Chivi Communal Area of Zimbabwe[6] 42% were households with only one adult woman. Of the whole sample 31% collected water alone and 36% collected wood alone, 27% did not collect water at all themselves and 14% did not collect wood themselves. Thus a considerable number of women are seen to share and delegate these tasks. Since there are power relations between woman within the same household, a younger woman in Chivi is frequently dominated by more senior household women, and carries a disproportionate burden of wood and water collection. Thus the division of labor may allocate wood collection to wives but if a wife can delegate the means by which she meets that responsibility then the incentive toward replanting (increased time in collection) may not be felt equally by all women of a household. Life-cycle processes intervene in various ways to pattern the incentives to positive environmental management. But age is not only significant in that women of different seniority have differently structured constraints and opportunities with regard to environmental relations. Societies are not socially reproduced without change and younger women have experienced a different history from older women and their attitudes and expectations differ as a result. The aspirations of young women in rural Zimababwe today are different from those of their mothers as young women. To posit a special relationship between women and their environments which ignores such multiple sources of difference is problematic, because women bear socially formed gender, as well as other, identities.

A further problem with the "special relationship" between women and environments is that it ignores the context within which environmental relations are nested — women relate to natural resources as part of their livelihood strategies, which reflect multiple objectives, powerful wider political forces and, crucially, gender relations, i.e. social relations which systematically differentiate men and women in processes of production and reproduction. Microstudies of resource use reveal that the relations of women to environments "cannot be understood outside the context of gender relations in resource management and use" (Leach, 1991, p. 14). When WDE writers limit their analysis to women, an essentialism is expressed in not only the failure to disaggregate the category "women" but also the failure to realize that women are gendered in relation to men — this is discussed further below.

Finally, essentialist viewpoints are unsatisfactory in that they are static and give no account of historical change and the shifting meanings of environmental relations. The significance of the historical moment can be seen in the changing meaning of environmental degradation in Zimbabwe — during the settler regime deliberate flouting of conservationist laws and regulations, such as the sabotage of contour ridges and the encroachment of arable cultivation into grazing areas, was an expression of profound alienation and the politics of racial domination; the same laws and regulations in postindependent Zimbabwe remain unpopular amongst some sections of the rural population but they do not have the same significance and meaning.

To summarize — there cannot be a special relationship between women and environments because women are not a unitary category, and their environmental relations reflect not only divisions among women but also gender relations and the dynamics of political economies and agroecosystems.

3. WOMEN AS CARERS OF COMMON PROPERTY AND COMMUNITY

The idea that women "naturally" care for the environment as an extension of their caring roles is expressed by Bernadette Vallely of the Women's Environment Network —"Women's priorities are usually oriented towards the good of the community thus placing more emphasis on the protection of the environment and the resources within it" (WEN, 1989). This is perhaps as untenable a generalization as that which assumes altruism within the household (Folbre, 1986). The suggestion that "women are involved in *community managing* work undertaken at a local community settlement level in both urban and rural contexts" (Moser, 1989, p. 1801) is not unique to WDE discourse and is generally problematic and inadequately theorized.[7] Collective action with regard to the environment has been "naturalized" for women, but not for men, on the basis of implied altruism and with a failure to scrutinize the private interests of women adequately. In the WDE context, the view of Vandana Shiva that women are responsible for community and forest management is questionable — for most forests in India are managed not by women but by *panchayats* which notably lack women members (DN, 1990, p. 795). Here, WDE writers fail to distinguish clearly between working and managing, and employ a crude and simplistic understanding of gender divisions of labor.

Women's reproductive work does bring them into frequent contact with common property resources but the nature of this contact is generally misunderstood by WDE writers who assume that those who work with the resource manage that resource. "Manage" is a polysemic word — but in development discourses it predominantly implies control over decision making and planning in accordance with objectives. Common property users act in the context of rules and conventions devised by a range of institutions — unlike farm laborers, wood collectors are not working under the farm managers' directon and supervision but their actions (e.g. to cut live or dead wood), have to be situated within these institutional frameworks. In Kenya, the provision of fire-wood is a woman's task, but tree growing is not and women were found to have minimal involvement in tree regenerative activities (Bradley, 1991, p. 149). In this instance tree planting by women is a subversive activity since adjudication in land disputes is done on the basis of tree ownership (Bradley, 1991, p. 283).[8] Without a gendered analysis of common property institutions women as users cannot be directly equated with common property rights managers. Even the gendered planning frameworks devised for project planners the distinction between access to resources and control of resources is routine (Overholt *et al*, 1985). This distinction reflects not only the difference between use and management but also the differentials in property rights which make the access by women to resources more deeply conditional upon social relations than those of men. More of this is pursued below, but the point being made with regard to community welfare is that the high visibility of women in the use of communally held resources cannot be taken as either indicating a greater commitment to "community" than that of men or as imparting a community management role to women. We return below to the problem of the reductionist understandings of gender devisions of labor which cannot be represented as descriptions of work allocation — they involve differential social relations of production, including power relations and differential resource access, culturally specific understandings of gender identities and capabilities. Gender divisions of labor also necessitate exchange and cooperation between men and women.

In India, as elsewhere in the Third World, many women do indeed cut wood for sale. Refusal to accept that women are agents of environmental degradation and the determined attempt to construct a positive image of women as custodians of, and carers for, the environment is to obscure and prevent a more useful analysis. In addition, the policy implications of accepting the "community management" role of women often means extending unpaid work done by women. For example, Thomas-Slayter's study of class, gender and resource management in rural Kenya shows that

> When there are community-based, labor-intensive tasks to be done, it is the women, not the men in the community, who are mobilised to undertake them. If a road needs repair, if gulley erosion must be stabilised, if a school needs maintenance, it is the women who are asked to provide these services (1992, p. 818).

The reasons for this are found in the male domination of public office, the presence of women's groups facilitating the mobilization of women, and the realization by women that if they fail to do such work it will remain undone. Women are said by Thomas-Slayter to be more responsive to calls for voluntary public works because improved roads and schools are perceived to bring better health and education for individual families — areas of women's responsibility within the particular gender divisions of labor in Katheka. This example shows the need for a class-gender analysis (women's groups are predominantly composed of poorer women); that community action by women may be rooted in individual family welfare, reflective of the subordination of women (public work demands are made by chiefs and branch chairmen of KANU), and legitimated by gender divisions of household responsibility; and that there is a danger of community mobilization (in environmental as well as infrastructural projects) deepening exploitation of women's labor. we can begin to see the consequences of the ecofeminist project of simply inverting the valuation given to divisions of labor — to applaud the unpaid community work done by women without an accompanying analysis of whether such work is consistent with women's gender interests is to open the way for entrenching exploitation.

The instance often cited to support both the view of women as both community spirited and of their willingness to mobilize collectively in defense of the environment is the Chipko movement which developed in mid-late 1970s in Garhwal division of Uttar Pradesh out of a Gandhian social development movement. This movement emerged in a context where there was anger over government forest policy which denied local use of trees while giving logging rights to large companies.

Floods during the 1970s and land slips were perceived by these social workers as caused by deforestation (Jain, 1984, p. 1788). The initial involvement of women was accidental, but they then became the mainstay of a movement which spread widely and focused on demonstrations, in which trees were hugged, to prevent logging.

Chipko is usually represented as demonstrating women's concern for conservation, and taken as an example of spontaneous environmental and community commitment by women.[9] Recently, questions have been raised as to how we are to understand Chipko:

> Locating Chipko culturally and historically provides a long overdue corrective to the popular conception of Chipko, which is that of a romantic reunion of humans, especially women, with nature (Guha, 1989, p. 173).

Guha sees Chipko as essientially conservative and anti-change and locates Chipko within a local history of peasant protest based on charismatic, populist leadership, asceticism and religious imagery, and the charismatic Chipko leader Sunderlal Bahuguna's followers "look to him to restore a pristine state of harmony" [Guha, 1989, p. 171]. Further both Guha and Jain (1984, p. 1789) deny that Chipko is a feminist movement. Women of the region supported the campaign for prohibition,[10] organized by the Ghandian social development organization that spawned Chipko, during the 1960s. Later women became involved in large numbers in tree hugging, but the leadership has been predominantly male. It has been claimed that as the Chipko movement developed it took on more of a feminist quality as women came to oppose, for the first time, not only men from beyond their community but also local men, including their husbands. Guha points out, however, that this is not new, for the anti-alcohol demonstrations were also such. The shortcomings of essentialist interpretations of Chipko which ignore history become apparent, for the image of a woman hugging a tree in front of a bulldozer has a context which contributes to its meaning.

For Guha Chipko is

> only one in a series of protest movements against commercial forestry dating from the earliest days of state intervention. . . .the peasantry was protesting against the denial of subsistence rights which state policy has wrought. Essentially the movement was a response to a perceived breach of the informal code between the ruler and the ruled known as the "moral economy" of the peasant (1989, p. 174).

In this light the Chipko movement appears more as a conservative affirmation of the moral economy, a contract which sustains power structures, including that of the subordination of women.[11] Women may be more susceptible to mobilization on the basis of breaches in the moral economy since the weight of subsistence work has fallen on them following male outmigration in the region. Hill women are also culturally and historically less subordinated than plains women and the Chipko women should not be taken out of this context and projected as submissive and obedient wives who, through their veneration of nature and instinctive understanding of ecological principles, rose up spontaneously and risked life and limb for their forests. Community action by women in the Chipko case does not seem to support a view of rural woman as profoundly altruistic but rather shows them as responding to wider political and economic change (principally commercialization) within the context of specific gender relations.

The focus of attention on Chipko tends to obscure that fact that in many villages where environmental degradation has occurred this has not led to women's protest movements. A legitimate counterargument may be made that the documentation of women's protest is lacking both because of gender blindness in historical records and because the "everyday forms of resistance," in struggles by women are by nature invisible. It seems inappropriate, at this stage, to make any generalizations about the likelihood of political action by women in defense of the environment.

4. GENDER PERSPECTIVES ON CONSERVATION

Women act a agents in both environmentally positive and negative ways but until we begin to approach such agency free of essentialist presuppositions about women's predisposition to conservation and of reductionist understanding of gender divisions of labor, and with improved gender analytical frameworks, we have little prospect of identifying either points where gender equity and environmental conservation can be simultaneously addressed by development interventions or where they cannot.

It is frequently asserted that women are more severely affected by environmental degradation and that they will be the "natural" constituency for conservation activities. The combination of this with the women/nature linkage sustained by ecofeminist influenced discourse leads to the assumption that they can be mobilized in defense of the environment. In examining the question of how far women may be mobilized for environmental conservation we will consider, with

African examples, the centrality of gender relations (rather than women) to environmental degradation. It will be argued, against the essentialist ecofeminist position, that women have no inherent closeness to nature, but a socially constructed relationship with natural resources which varies for different group of women and for individual women during the course of a lifetime. There is a need to recognized that many women are frequently agents of environmental degradation because of gender and class relations and that the alleviation of poverty will not necessarily change this. It is suggested that a gender analysis leads to a very different perspective from that of synergism or the "win-win" policies which the World Bank defines as "action which promote income growth, poverty alleviation, and environmental improvement" (1992, p. 2). This section examines a range of incentives and disincentives toward environment friendly behavior by women (e.g. the adoption of conservation technologies or the practice of regenerative resource use), illustrates the potential for conflicting gender and environmental interests and draws out some of the development policy conclusion.

The severity of environmental degradation has been seen to have a greater impact on women because of the overrepresentation of female headed households among the poor (who depend more critically upon common pool resources) and because of the gender divisions of labor within households which allocates work such as firewood and water collection to women — precisely the tasks which have become much more difficult with environmental change such as deforestation and falling water tables. From a gender analysis standpoint, however, the costs of degradation cannot be seen as accruing predominantly to women without an enquiry into how gender divisions of labor are contested and change under environmental stress, without an account of men's environmental relations and without an investigation of the context within which degradation occurs.

(a) *Environmental knowledges*

Before looking at property relations we could consider the distribution of environmental knowledges. It is often held that women know more than men about the environmental because of gender divisions of labor which assign women to many of the reproductive tasks which bring them into daily contact with fields, forests and rivers. "[women] have a profound knowledge of the plants, animals and ecological processes around them" (Dankelman and Davidson, 1989,

p. xi). This view leads to the assertion that women's knowledge equips them for effective conservation and justifies rthe identification of women as the relevant target group for conservation projects. Women's knowledges, however, cannot be considered in isolation from men's for there are variations in who acquires what knowledge. In Chivi Communal Area of Zimbabwe women knew more than men about some crop varieties, men know more about local soil classification and there was variation in knowledges between research sites. The lived experience of women's land relations, characterized by relative mobility and insecurity, means that women are more usefully seen as having differently constituted environmental knowledges (possibly greater understanding of spatial and lesser of temporal variation) rather than as knowing more, or less, than men.

More significantly, the problem of accessing women's knowledge is unrecognized. Knowledges are manufactured and expressed through social proceses and there fore reflect gender relations. For examples, in Hobley's study of decision making in forest use in Nepal she shows how "relations of dominance between men and women gained their full expression at . . . forest meetings" and quotes one woman thus

> The foreigners told the villagers that because women are the forest users they must also be members of the forest committee. . . . The men agreed to this. . . . However women were informed of a meeting only when a male committee member chanced to meet them. Even if women attend meetings they cannot voice their opinions: they cannot speak against the opinions of their seniors. When the men have finished speaking that is the end of the meeting. . . . Men do not tell women they cannot speak at the meetings but the men do not want to be opposed by women (1991, p. 148).

Particular women (low caste and younger women) were particularly inhibited, as were poor men — one low caste man said "If they [the poor] stand and speak the wind blows their sound away. If they sit and speak no-one can hear them" (Hobley, 1991, p. 149). The politics of articulating knowledge and of "mutedness" (Ardener, 1975) are not seen as problematic by WDE writers and activists who seem to have no model of ideological domination. What Kandiyoti terms "patriarchal bargains" (1988)[12] may include suppressing environmental knowledge because displayed knowledge can be construed as a property claim or simply as inappropriate to women's behavior. As one woman in the Nepali case above remarked — if women speak out at meetings "men will say that the hen has started crowing" (Hobley, 1991, p. 148).

The implications of the problem of mutedness (the social and ideological domination which leaves groups, such as women, inhibited in vocabulary and voice) for development practice are wide ranging. In particular, it leads one to question the expectations of "participation" in development — consultation with women may not unproblematically reveal gender interests. For example, how would a participatory development approach respond to women's wide spread support for dowry in Maharashtra (Vlassoff, 1991) or for sex determination tests both of which can ben seen as contrary to the gender interests of women? We cannot assume that women have a monopoly upon environmental knowledge, that their knowledges can necessarily be expressed in order to be accessed and validated by development agencies or that views articulated by women are free from the imprint of gender relations. Participatory resource conservation has much to commend it, but articulated views of participators should not mistaken for the truth — scepticism, "triangulation" (Khon Kaen University, 1987), secondary sources and objective indicators remain important in project appraisal and design.

(b) *Property relations*

Much WDE activity is NGO based and the curious and unsatisfactory lack of attention to property relations in WDE literatures may reflect the pressures upon many NGOs toward politically safe agendas — the issue of land rights for women in contentious. This section indicates the central importance of property relations to understanding how incentives toward conservation are differentiated for women and men.

(i) *Individual property relations*

Property relations mediate the ways in which women and men relate to their environments. Individual property,[13] such as is found on arable land in Zimbabwe, is not private in the sense of being bought, sold and rented, but are allocated to individual males and inherited by their eldest sons. Patrilineal inheritance of land allocation, means that in such societies women do not usually have primary rights to land. Land which women farm on their own account is obtained through allocation by a husband or relative and these secondary rights are conditional, most commonly, upon marriage. Clearly, for women in these circumstances commitment to land improvement practices, such as building contour ridges will be filtered through perceptions of security to tenure radically different from those of men with primary land rights. They are likely to have much shorter time preferences than men, and given the nature of many conservation pracitces such as tree planting in which the returns are slow, we should rather expect that women to be less, rather than more, inclined than men to adopt conservation practices.

In circumstances where women do not generally have individual private property rights in land, such as Zimbabwe's communal areas, any land which may be acquired by a woman often has a very temporary nature — both allocations from husbands and borrowings from friends or neighbours are usually subject to periodic changes in location since land givers become nervous about claims being made after long periods of continued use. This is also the case in parts of West Africa — for example, the Maguzawa of Nigeria (Jackson, 1981) and in Sengal (David, 1992, p. 10). Women who borrow land in this way are both aware of the insecurity of tenure from this source and reluctant to invest in land improvements which benefit the landowner rather than themselves. David found that women in Senegal carry out fewer conservation techniques on their personal plots than they did on the plots for household use (1992,p. 9), partly because their personal plots are reallocated each year. In circumstances such as these conservation interventions which yield returns within a year, such as mulching, are more likely to be adopted by women for use on personal plots than those with longer term pay-offs. Without an appreciation of how men and women's land use, within households, varies it is difficult to avoid repeating, in the context of conservation, the mistakes made in gender-blind rural development (e.g., Carney, 1988; Jackson, 1985).

Gender analysis in development has shown how land tenure in Africa embodies labor rights — especially the rights of men to the labor of women. One implication of this for development policy and research is that the tasks done by women cannot be taken as representing women's choices alone. The Senegal case shows the needs to distinguish between land farmed by a woman on her own account and that farmed as part of household responsibilities. In the latter case, where decision-making structures override women's wishes, the preferences of male household heads may be expressed (e.g., adoption of recommended conservation practices may be evident) but this cannot be taken as evidence of enthusiasm by women for environmental coservation. Gender divisions of labor may mean that women do a particular task, such as maintaining ridges, but this does not mean that they have chosen to do this — for women, even less than for others, one cannot assume that action reflects choice. We return below to the question of choices and decisions. As we discussed above, there are limits to what can be understood from a mechanistic understanding of gender divisions fo labor or jural concepts of land "ownership" which neglect the social relations of land tenure.

The significance of patriliny[14] for resource management, however, goes beyond its operation as a system of inheritance of land. Patrilineal descent ideology excludes women: they do not obtain land and they are not expected to have the same concern for the long-term state of the land. Women will also experience differently those aspects of belief systems relating to land for shona of Zimbabwe the ancestral spirits of chiefs govern particular territories of land, and

> . . . a strong emotional bond exists between individual and the territory of their ancestors. The desire to live there is equalled only by the desire to be buried there. An important notion in the organising of political and moral experience is the idea of living "at home". Home is essentially the home of the dead. Life is good if you live where your ancestors lived before you (Lan, 1985, p. 20).

Yet women are seldom "at home" and even when they are they are excluded from real membership of the patrilineage — people consider that in human reproduction the woman is simply a vessel and contributes only the blood, very, very few women become *mhondoro* mediums and in general women play "a very insignificant part . . . in everything to do with the ancestors, the past or the authority of the lineage" (Lan, 1985, pp. 94-95). Women would seem to be both materially and ideologically alienated from the land.

Where women do inherit and hold land in their own right patrilocality often combines with religious and gender ideology in mediating the relations between women and land. For example, in Islamic, patrilineal northern Nigeria, Muslim women have gained the right to inherit a half share of land upon the death of their fathers, but given patrilocality of marriage and wife seclusion norms it is extremely difficult for married women to make use of such land directly. This is not to deny the importance of latent land rights in intrafamily bargaining. The limitations of conceiving of the problem as one of jurally defined land rights, as do most women and environment writers (e.g., Dankelman and Davidson, 1991) become clear. Land rights have significance for environmental relations as part of a wider set of social relations of production and reproduction, yet the gendered analysis of this by scholars such as Whitehead (1984) is absent from the women and environment discourse. Rather than assuming that women can be expected to have greater commitment than men to land improvement it may be more realistic for development agents to endeavor to build in stronger incentives to land conservation for women land users.

(ii) *Common property rights*

Although, as has frequently been pointed out, gender divisions of labor often assign women responsibility for collecting fuelwood and water there are other uses made of CPRs which are conversely gendered. For example, in Zimbabwe, the rights to grazing resources are predominantly exercised by prosperous men with large cattle herds and the smallstock, which is of mixed gender and class ownership, are a small proportion of the total livestock population supported by the vegetation.[15] Similarly, men use CPRs for construction timber, for house, granary and cattle *kraal* building, to a much greater extent than women, and children of both genders are probably the major food collectors from CPRs in no famine times. In times of famine women certainly depend for famine foods on CPRs (Iliffe, 1990, p. 15) but the significance of this has to be seen in the context of other shifts in the conjugal contract at such times. For Zimbabwe it would be difficult to contend on the basis of the gender division of labor that women had a greater interest in CPR reproduction.

One of the shortcomings of the WDE approach is that it does not allow the analysis of change in the relationship between women and their environments in either the short or long term. Adaptations to fuelwood shortages may indeed be damaging to women where it involves additional labor time, but we cannot assume this from statements about the distances to fuelwood sources in the past and currently (Agarwal, 1991, p. 83) without examining whether substitution in tasks has not occurred. The IFPRI study in Nepal (Kumar and Hotchkiss, 1989) concluded that deforestation necessitated and additional 1.1 hours per day in wood, fodder and grass collection by women and observed that deforestation leads to a reduction in women's field labor of 1.5 hours per pay.[16] Studies of *changing* fuelwood use show complex processes of adaptation. When common property fuelwood becomes scarce, there may be an increase in on-farm woody biomass (Bradley, 1991, p. 274),[17] there may be an increase in purchasing of firewood or there may be technical change, e.g., the use of carts for wood collection. Property relations, gender relations and divisions of labor are all mutable. A meticulous study of the "fuelwood crisis" in southern Zimbabwe concludes that men have become increasingly involved in fuelwood collection in the past 30 years, in particular in cutting larger trees and using carts or axes for transport (McGregor, 1991, p. 295).

Commoditization is a strong theme in WDE literature and women are portrayed as relating to the environment for the purpose of "sustenance" while men exploit it for cash (Shiva, 1989b, 96-97) — a view common to much WID literature too (Whitehead, 1990, pp 54-68). This is questionable for CPRs in Zimbabwe where women collect fuelwood not only for food cooking but also for income earning activities such as brewing beer[18] and firing pots. Other market oriented use of CPRs by women include collecting insects and fruits as well as clay for pottery. Moreover, since women's goat rearing is often more market oriented than men's cattle keeping it could be argued that men use CPRs in a more subsistence-oriented way as cattle are seldom sold and are primarily inputs to arable farming, from which only small surplusses are generated for sale by the majority of farmers, and furthermore men's use of timber is predominantly subsistence oriented. Development projects and programs concerned to target their activities effectively need an understanding of men's as well as women's use of CPRs and a localized livelihood specification rather than crude assumptions that women rely upon common pool resources more than men and are subsistence oriented in their uses of CPRs.

(c) *Space: Diversity and distance*

This section considers the linkages between women's mobility, autonomy and environmental relations in the context of patrilineal and patrilocal societies. When men are migrating in large numbers from rural areas of the Sahel suffering from climatic change, encouraging women in "insistence on staying on their home ground and holding back the disappearing earth, men and water" (Monimart, 1989, p. 33) as one NGO report on the Sahel does, needs to be questioned by development practitioners — what price, in the welfare of women, should be paid in the interests of the environment?

The way in which women relate to their environments reflects gender differentials in degree and type of mobility and experiences of place and space. While men may have a continuing relationship with the same area of CPRs during their lifetimes, women frequently do not. If the making of marriage relocates the great majority of women in patrilocal societies, divorce will also frequently lead to further mobility. Rural-rural male migration also changes the long-term relationships of men with particular CPRs, but much rural-urban male migration does not have this effect, given that migrants return to their areas of origin. For women, however, who in some parts of Africa, such as Nigeria, constitute the majority of rural-rural migrants (Mortimore and Wilson, 1965, p. 35) the movements consequent on marriage, divorce and widowhood mean that they may well have a shorter term knowledge of, and commitment to, any particular set of CPRs. Clearly, the degree to which this is true depends on the extent of patrilocality, the degree of exogamy, the divorce rate, the age gap between spouses, as well as the perceptions by women of the security of their long-term usage of particular CPRs, i.e. of the subjective probabilities of events which would lead to their movement elsewhere.

Environmental dislocation seems to affect women more than men because of patrilocal marriage, the dominant form in Zimbabwe (although in some areas brideservice practices lead to at least temporary uxorilocal marriages which means that women are outsiders in the place they come to live. As Wilson (1990, p.265) points out, for southern Zimbabwe, land pressure in patrilineal societies leads to low male mobility but in Chivi Communal Area 69% of a sample of 65 women were born in a place beyond regular walking distance from their martial homes. The importance of patrilocality in influencing environmental relationships depends on the distance between the natal homes of spouses which is not only related to the degree of exogamy but also to settlement patterns and population densities — high population densities, evenly distributed and stable settlements may mitigate the impact of patrilocality while aspects of environmental adaptation such as risk avoidance may exacerbate it. It has been suggested, for India, that households make marriage alliances across wide distances as a strategy for risk management in precarious environments. Given the great local variation in rainfall in semiarid zones the probability of drought striking neighbors at the same time in greater than that of it occurring simultaneously in two widely separated areas, and therefore affines may be more useful in times of drought if they are not close neighbors (Rosenzweig, 1988, p. 249). If this were the case then women in more risky agro-ecosystems may tend to marry over wider distances, be more alienated from natal environments and experience variable relations with their conjugal environments depending on some of the factors we disucss in (d) below. In addition, Dyson and Moore (1983) point out that marriage distance is negatively related to women's autonomy in India, and this has been confirmed by Vlassoff (1991) — risk aversion for the household is at least partly purchased at the cost of individual women's security and power. A high degree of distance involved in patrilocality seems to negatively influence environmental attitudes and the autonomy of women, although it may be an effective element in household level coping with environmental vulnerability. A some what different process has a comparable outcome in southern Zimbabwe where Wilson (1990, pp. 263-266) shows that in clayveld ecosystems with unstable interannual agro-pastoral productivity, numbers of marriages are also unstable whereas in the more stable sandveld ecosystems numbers of marriages are not linked to rainfall, given the more stable crop and animal productivity, and therefore ability of men to acquire bridewealth. Thus in dry years clayveld women are more likely to contract marriages in sandveld areas (very different ecosystems in terms of vegetation species, soil types, rainfall variability, plant productivity, nutrient regimes), and one might predict that drought deepens the environmental dislocation of women.

Finally, class-related variations in marriage residence are likely to pattern the significance of patrilocality. Where social differentials are maintained through marriage alliances the restricted range of potential marriage partners may lead to a greater physical distance between the natal homes of spouses, and thus environmental dislocation for women, particularly of higher classes. For example, in the dry Indian state of Rajasthan where atatus hypergamy requires women to marry men of higher status the high status Rajputs have the longest average distance of marriage migration (Billig, 1991, pp. 344-346).[19] Mechanistic models of marriage alliances which fail to allow for the agency of women,i.e. their choices, preferences and decisions as individuals and the impact of these on outcomes, are unsatisfactory of course, but the points being made here are simply that a woman's environmental relations are influenced by the livelihood strategies of others, as well as themselves, to varying degrees depending on a constellation of power relations at the household level; that environmental stress does not only have a direct impact upon the daily reproductive labor of women but, perhaps more significantly, it changes social reproduction; that male-dominated household adaptations to environmental stress can be premised upon the exchange of women; that tradeoffs emerge between the interests of individuals, particularly women, and those of households as well as, in certain contexts, environmental conservation.

Although long distances of movement on marriage are seen as negative for women and for the environment in the examples given above, the implications of different types of female mobility needs to be seen in cultural and historical context. Divorce rates in many rural African communities are high and rising. The marital careers of Hausa women in northern Nigeria show an average of 2.3 marriages during a lifetime — interleaved with periods at natal homes (*iddah*) and punctuated by periods of courtesanship for some women (Jackson, 1981, p. 227). Divorce (which is almost exclusively initiated by women[20]) of Hausa women in Nigeria, and consequent mobility, is an indicator of their relatively strong in trahousehold bargaining position and here conservationist development, based on stable households and long-term returns to investments, should consider the implications of constraining the opportunism of women which has been significant in resisting subordination. Similarly, in southern Africa there has been a continuing struggle by women for freedom of movement. Early colonial laws which introduced western notions of marriage were utilized by women to challenge control by male elders of women which had operated through the bridewealth system (Lovett, 1989, pp. 47-169). In Zimbabwe there was also an opening up of opportunities for women to support themselves outside the kinshipbased production systems, e.g., by beer brewing for mining compounds. Gender conflicts centered on the struggles for autonomy

> Those women who were attempting to evade lineage control grew ever more imaginative in the 1920s, as the infrastructure brought in by the Occupiers provided new openings. The trains were used by groups of "roving prostitutes" to move from one location to the next following the rail workers' pay days. Other women used the trains to run away (Jeater, 1989, p. 3).

The increasing mobility of women induced an alliance of colonial officials and male elders in preventing the movement of women to towns and in buttressing the bridewealth system to control women. Changes in the practice and meaning of bridewealth continued, however, and currently in Chivi Communal Area there is a tendency toward alternative forms of marriage (still patrilocal with little or no bridewealth payment and distinct instability. The improved position of women, indicated by greater personal freedom and autonomy, may not coincide with environmental reproduction — on the contrary, because the payoff to conservation work depends on long-term residence the increased mobility of women is likely to lead to shorter time preferences and hence both more short-term management and less interest in conservation. Women's mobility here may be antithetical to conservation. The assumption that there are "synergistic interventions" which improve the position of women at the same time as protecting and conserving the environment requires reexamination.

(d) *Intrahousehold dynamics and relations*

The crude and universalized conception of a singular gender division of labor leads to an overemphasis of the "closeness" between women and their environments, and obscures the lifecycle differences in the way the genders relate to environments. Household development cycles mediate gendered resource relations in locally specific ways, but they are an important part of understanding the processes of environmental degradation and regeneration. For example, the impact of male outmigration upon rural women can bring about changing domestic development cycles which alters resource use. Domestic devlopment cycles interact with differentiation in complex ways and rural households do not all progress upon a single trajectory of household formation, growth and decline (Murray, 1989). Household size and resource access, however, is related to the age of the household head in Zimbabwe (GFA, 1986), with older households being larger and better resourced in terms of access to livestock and land. Superimposed upon this, as in other parts of Africa, are powerful tendencies toward nucleation of households which are at least partly related to gender conflict — younger women prefer to set up their own domestic units at an earlier age in order to capture migrant remittances more effectively without competition from husband's kin. This exposes such women), however, to more acute crises in reproductive labor, such as wood and water collection, and a greater tendency to environmentally negative behavior. Remittances allow farm labor to be hired but there is virtually no commoditized fuelwood or water provision available in Chivi Communal Area. In another manner, domestic development cycles can be seen to pattern the impact of male outmigration upon resource use by women. In West Africa complex domestic groups frequently have households nested within compounds — a compound head (usually senior male) has overall control over constituent households (the consumption units) (see Hill, 1972, for an account of this for the Hausa). Male migrant remittances have been found in Senegal to be controlled by the compound head (David, 1992) rather than the spouse of the migrant, as in Zimbabwe, and therefore the wives of migrant junior males are not able to use remittances to substitute for absent male farm labor as in Zimbabwe or for commoditized reproductive services.

How far do relations within households influence environmental behavior? Intergenerational relations may be argued to influence women, as mothers, toward concern to conserve environments in order to secure future benefits for children. As Shiva puts it "Women naturally think of the next generation" (Shiva, 1989a, p. 5). This argument would only apply to sons as daughters would, like their mothers, find that patriliny and patrilocality intervene between them and their environmental relations. But for a number of reasons this may not be a significant factor for mothers — partly because the implicit contract of trusteeship and inheritance excludes them, and partly because of wider economic and political changes. In Chivi, the majority of rural women desire a future in which their sons obtain formal sector jobs, and thus the rational investment for mothers is in the education of sons rather than the fertility of the farm. Rights in children are, of course, gender differentiated in a number of ways — on divorce women may be allowed to keep a child whilst very young (but relinquish it at a certain age) but usually divorced women are alienated from their children and the probability of this too colors the responsibility felt by individual women for the futures of their children.

Intrahousehold relations between genders are critical to the decision-making processes which pattern resource management. Adoption of a conservation technology will depend on intrahousehold negotiations yet the WDE literature shows no awareness of the debates over the nature of the household, the characterizations of altruism and self-interest of household members or of attempts to model intrahousehold relations and decision making. While the flaws of models of households as unitary bodies with joint utility are well known, the problems with methodological individualism, on the other hand, seem to have been forgotten. It is problematic to assume male household heads to be altruistic as in New Household Economics, but it is also unsatisfactory to assume individual women are altruistic within the community or household.[21] At least a focus upon the household allows scrutiny of intrahousehold relations, which an individualized treatment of women obscures. The gross generalizations inWDE literature are innocent of the strictures in this earlier gender scholarship against ethnocentrism and the problem of generalizing domestic group functions across widely differing societies.

There is a need to unpack the idea that women's "responsibilities" make them environment friendly — the responsibility to provide firewood for cooking a meal may lead a woman, when faced with a firewood shortage, to plant a tree but it may also lead her to pull up a wooden fence and burn it, to argue for the purchase of a fuel efficient stove, to insist on the purchase of charcoal, to delegate fuelwood collection to a younger woman in the household or any number of alternative responses. As well as the issues of time preferences and livelihood strategies, these responses depend on the bargaining position, within the household, of individual women. Sen (1987) models intrahousehold relations in terms of cooperative conflict, i.e. both "the coexistence of extensive conflicts and pervasive cooperation in household arrangements" (Sen, 1987, p. 5). He suggests that individuals within households have variable perceptions of self-interest and variable perceptions of the value of the contributions to household welfare by themselves and others and that the bargaining strength of individuals within a household depends not so much on the objective quantity of labor or incomes contributed but on the value that is attributed to those contributions to household welfare. Outcomes of intrahousehold negotiations over resource management, where men and women have differing preferences, will be affected by the bargaining strength of parties which in turn reflects their breakdown positions (i.e. their situations in the event of the breakdown of cooperation — such as divorce). Where divorce for women is difficult and remarriage rare, as in northern India, then a woman may be less able to bargain strongly and outcomes are more likely to reflect male preferences. Where an individual has a low sense of their self-worth (perceived interest response), and where they perceive the claims of others as having greater legitimacy (perceived contribution response), they are also liekly to concede to the priorities of other parties. With such a model decision making is understood with a primary focus upon power within households which refract wider societal gender relations. The quality of "altruism" attributed to women, which is "revalued" by WDE discourse, can be seen as symptomatic of powerlessness, the inability to exercise self-interest (despite objective evidence for discrimination against women) and idological domination. We could also question whether environmental altruism is not therefore profoundly at odds with the project of gender equality.

Divisions of rights and responsibilities within households are therefore not static but mutable, contested and responsive to changes in societal level gender relations. They also change under stress. While in Chivi it is broadly seen as women's responsibility to provide household staples in normal years, there are stages in food-shortage coping strategies where food provisioning in early stages of crisis falls on men. In 65 households of chivi Communal Area 41% of men thought that women alone should provide grain for household consumption in normal years, whereas 97% felt that in drought years men should provide grain for household consumption. Women of the same households were asked the same question independently and 60% of them felt that in normal years women should provide grain whereas 84% said that in drought years men should provide household grain. When rains and crops fail, responsibility for food provision shifts from women to men — where a household male has a job, wages are expected to be used for food purchases, or failing this livestock owned by men are expected to be sold. Thus women may be less concerned than men about food security and be less risk averse in crop choice preferences, where they perceive a partner's capacity to provide such insurance. Where such preferences are combined with increasing decision-making powers of women in agriculture, in this example because of the absence of male migrants, the unpalatable truth may be that what is progressive for women has negative impacts upon food security and sustainability.

Differential income control by men and women has also been crudely simplified in WDE discourse to a characterization of women as largely engaged in subsistence production. This is a misleading generalization — for southern Africa, women have, e.g., in Malawi (Vaughan, 1985) and Mozambique (Young 1977), been early adopters of cash cropping as well as contributing a major proportion of labor to cash crop production and the involvement of women in commoditized crops reveals the error in assuming women to be confined to subsistence production. But more significant is the failure to recognize that technological change in agriculture is responded to, and patterned by, intrahousehold negotiations and exchanges. In the Cameroons such processes, following the introduction of irrigation into the farming system, led to a situation in which women were partially rewarded by their spouses for the additional labor on irrigated fields (Jones, 1986) and in Hausaland of northern Nigeria secluded women on an irrigation scheme successfully negotiated payment from spouses for crop processing. The existence of intrahousehold transfer (as well as collective consumption) shows how misleading it is to view the successful adoption of a technology, e.g., field terracing, as a matter of individual decision making for women, or men, in isolation, and how incorrect to assume that commoditized and noncommoditized production exist as bounded elements in household production.

Kinship, marriage and conjugal contracts can be major elements in both the continuing subordination of women and explanations for why women are inhibited from taking more positive attitudes to environmental conservation. We would not wish to imply that the social institutions of kinship and marriage determine an inevitable exploitation of the environment by women - clearly there is wide variation in the extent to which norms are adhered to, women make choices within a range possibilities, change occurs in many directions and we cannot generalize the negative elements in women's environmental relations.

5. CONCLUSION

We have attempted to identify weaknesses in the WDE approach and to expand discussion in the direction of a broader gender analysis which is better theorized, free of essentialism, empirically detailed and capable of revealing policy tradeoffs, between the objectives of progressive change for women and environmental conservation, where they exist. Key points are that women's environmental relations cannot be understood in isolation from men's; women have no inherent closeness to their environments; community work and defense of natural resources by women has politically ideological, social and economic explanations; women's environmental knowledges are social products; gendered analysis of property relations is a precondition for understanding differential incentives of men and women toward conservation; gender divisions of labor cannot be reduced to task allocation; environmental relations have historical, spatial and temporal dimensions of significance; and gendered environmental decision making needs to seen through the lens of intrahousehold relations of both cooperation and conflict. Policy perspectives require an emphasis upon local-level research, planning and specification to identify target groups and design incentives which are not based upon gender stereotypes. While points of synergistic leverage on gender equity and environmental conservation may be identified in this way we need to confront tradeoffs, expose alternatives and make choices free from unrealistic notions of a generalized synergy.

NOTES

1. There is an inevitable arbitrariness about labeling literatures—some views carry a mixture of approaches, some edited collections bear papers reflecting several perspectives — but I would consider the following to represent ecofeminist discourse; Cox (1992); Merchant, (1982, 1992); Plumwood, (1986, 1988, 1992); Ruether, (1979); Shiva, (1989a and 1989b); Warren (1987, 1990), WEN (1989) Gray, (1981), Eastlea, (1981), King, (1989), Griffin, (1978). What I call the women and environment literature is influenced by ecofeminist ideas which emphasize the "natural" affinity of women with their environments, even if these are not explicitly recognised, for example, Sontheimerr (1991), Dankelman and Davidson (1989), Rodda (1991), Monimart, (1989), Munyakho, (1985) Special Issue of The Society for International Development Journal Development (1992, No.2); IUCN, (1987). Much of the large 'grey literature in this field is not formally published. Finally, one can perhaps discern an alternative approach which could be called, after Agarwal, "feminist environmentalism" e.g., Agarwal (1991); Leach, (1991); DAWN, (1988); Cecelski. (1987); Kelkar and Nathan (1992).

2. For example, in Britain there is the Women's Environmental network (WEN) which began in 1988 and which campaigns environmental issues, both national and international. "WEN's ecofeminist philosophy elevates the feminine aspect of intuition as a leading mechanism for the preservation of life." (Cox, 1992 p.290). In the international political arena, women environmentalists, dominated by ecofeminists such as Vandana Shiva have been meeting as the International Policy Action Committee since 1990 to influence the 1992 UNCED. The Women for Life on Earth emerged out of the peace movement. "In making the connection between women and the fate of the Earth, they explored issues of chemical and radioactive pollution, alternative technology, alternative healing and women's spirituality" (Cox, 1992, p.289).

3. See de Beauvior (1988), Brown and Jordanova (1982), MacCormack (1980), Ortner (1974).

4. In gender analysis, reproduction is taken to have several levels — biological reproduction, daily and generational reproduction as well as social reproduction. The women and environment literature (Dankelman and Davidson, 1989; Sontheimer, 1991; Rodda, 1991) does not use this framework and simply describes the gender division of labor — and that narrowly in terms of tasks.

5. One example of the poor scholarship is seen in the following extract

In Zimbabwe, a woman too poor to purchase new millet seeds used traditional ones, Later droughts caused others' harvests to fail, but her crop survived. A women's organisation purchased 25 bags of her traditional seeds and distributed them to other women throughout many villages" (van Brakel, 1986 quoted in Dankelman and Davidson, 1989, p.18), 'New' presumably means hybrid seed, yet this is extremely uncommon in Zimbabwe. Hybrid maize is widely used but hybrid millet is not and doubts are raised about whether the correct crop is named. When one seeks to check the source one finds it is not given in the bibliography. Hence the making of a myth.

6. This draws on field work experience in Chivi Communal Area of Zimbabwe in 1988-89 during which time data were collected for a study of environmental degradation, gender and rural livelihoods. Chivi is a large dry Communal Area in southern Zimbabwe. The support of ODA for this research is gratefully acknowledge.

7. Moser refers to a "spatial division between the public world of men, and the private world of women" (1989, p.1801) including the neighborhood, without reference to the debates over the inadequacy of the public:private dichotomy, without considering the degree to which collective action reflects not community commitment but private interest, without any discussion of what is meant by "community" and without adequate empirical support for such a generalization. Although she criticizes the expectation for women to be "selfless and pure" (1989, p.1819) in their community work, and recognizes that community work by women is seen as nonproductive and not valued, there is no discussion of the implications of this for gender planning and policy.

8. The 1958 land Code in Malaysia a recognised fruit tree planting as establishing indirect land rights (Heyzer, 1992. p.31).

9. The essentialist currents in the representations of Chipko are clear. It is suggested, with reference to the Chipko slogan "what do the forests bear? Soil, water and pure air" that the Chipko women have "a holistic under standing of the environment in general and forests in particular" (Agarwal, 1991, pp.35-34). It is not clear, however, that an understanding of hydrological cycles can be read off from such a slogan. The long-term influence in the area of the Gandhian social development activists who were responsible for the mobilization around their perception of deforestation as causing landslides and floods would seem to be significant. The verities of women's environmental knowledge has to be seen in the light of current thinking which suggests that geological forces rather than deforestation is the likely cause of landslides and flooding downstream (Thompson and Warburton, 1985). The manner in which Chipko has been represented is revealing. It has been portrayed as a case of spontaneous, "natural" environmental conservation by women, with little attempt to look for other explanations; it has been categorized as a women's movement — simply because of the presence of women, despite male leadership; the style of the accounts given of Chipko activities is emotional and dwells on the images of defenceless women hugging trees and singing songs. The Chipko movement has had three identifiable groups within it and it is interesting, and predictable, that women and environment writers have identified not with the reconstructionists/technocentrics of Bhatt, nor the marxists but the romantic/ecocentric Sunderlal Bahuguna. During the 1980s two strands developed within the Chipko movement — that led by Chandi Prasad Bhatt who believes in conserving and developing resources to benefit the local community while preserving ecological balance, and that led by Sunderlal Bahuguna, politician, journalist and ecologist who does not support agroforestry or local industries using the forest in any way.

10. Shiva even interprets the anti-alcohol protests by women as ecological, by claiming that they realize that "the generation of cash for liquor involves over-exploitation of eco-systems, which disrupts the hydrological cycle and creates water scarcity" (1985; p.62).

11. The populist character of Chipko is apparent in Guha's analysis — in addition to the moralism it is antistate and the leadership influenced by peasant martyrs (Guha. 1989a, p.70-177).

12. Kandiyoti uses the term patriarchal bargains to cover the manner in which, women, within the particular set of gender relations,

and from a position of relative but variable weakness, negotiate the best terms possible for themselves. This involves both compromise and struggle.

13. Space does not permit an adequate treatment of land tenure, or indeed many of the social relations which are used here to raise questions — they are invoked in a stylized manner for the purpose of argument.

14. I would not wish to suggest that patriliny orders all land access — it is emphasized and simplified here to demonstrate a major influence on women's environmental attitudes — nor would I wish to suggest that matrilineal societies do not alienate women from land. The environmental relations of women in matrilineal societies is an interesting area for research.

15. Five goats are reckoned to be the equivalent of one cow in terms of Livestock Units.

16. The study shows the negative effects of deforestation upon agricultural productivity, real incomes and nutrition as a consequence of the withdrawal of women's labor from agriculture.

17. Which may or may not be available to women to use for firewood.

18. Beer brewing has been shown to demand substantial amounts of wood which is live and of large dimensions since this gives the required slow burn. This distinguishes such usage from fuel for domestic cooking (McGregor, 1991, p.208). 19. Billig's analysis shows that the potentially positive effect of high sex ratios on the position of women in the marriage market is countered by status hypergamy, of several types, as well as factors such as population growth which leads to larger availability of women in the younger age cohorts (Billig, 1991, p.356).

20. A study of the court records of two districts in Hausaland revealed the degree to which divorce cases are brought by women and the grounds given for divorce (Jackson, 1981).

21. In Hausa households women lend grain to husbands (and charge interest) for their own household consumption, they sell the manure from their goats to husbands for use on household fields, they buy relish ingredients, such as groundnut oil, from themselves with the money given by husbands for daily meal preparation (Jackson, 1981).

REFERENCES

Agarwal, B., "Engendering the environment debate: Lessons from the Indian subcontinent," CASID Distinguished Speaker Series. No. 8, Center for Advanced Study of International Development (East Lansing, MI: Michigan State University, 1991).

Aloo, T., "Forestry and the untrained Kenyan woman" in D. Munyakho (ED), *Women and The Environmental Crisis: A Report of the Proceedings of the Workshops on Women, Environment and Development, July 10-20, Nairobi kenya NGO Forum* (Nairobi: Environment Liaison Centre, 1985).

Ardener, E. Belief and the problem of women." in S. Ardener (Ed), *Perceiving Women* (London: Malaby, 1975), pp. 1-18.

Biehl, J., "Ecofeminism and deep ecology: Unresolvable conflict?", *Our Generation*, Vol. 19, No. 2 (1988), pp. 19-32.

Beinart, W., "Soil erosion, conservationism and ideas about development: A southern African exploration 1900-1960," *Journal of Southern African Studies*, Vol. 11, No. 1 (1984).

Billig, M., "The marriage squeeze on high-caste Rajasthani women." The Journal of Asian Studies, Vol. 50, No. 2 (1991), pp. 341-360.

Bradley, P.N., *Woodfuel, Women and Woodlots, Vol. 1, Foundations of a Woodfuel Strategy for East Africa* (london: MacMillan, 1991).

Brown, P., and L. Jordanova, "Oppressive dichotomies," in Open University, *The Changing Experience of Women* (Oxford: Martin Robertson, 1982(, pp. 189-399.

Bruce, J., "Homes divided," *World Development*, Vol. 17 No. 7 (1989), pp. 979-1136.

Carney, J., "Struggles over crop rights and labor within contract farming households in a Gambian irrigated rice project," *Journal of Peasant Studies*, Vol. 15, No. 3 (1988), pp. 334-349.

Cecelski, E., "The rural energy crisis, women's work and family welfare: Perspectives and approaches to action," World Employment Programme Research Working Paper No. WEP10/WP35 (Geneva: International Labour Office, 1984).

Cox, C., "Ecofeminism" in G. Kirkup and L. Keller (Eds.), *Inventing women: Science, Technology and Gender* (London: Open University and Polity Press, 1992).

Dankelman, I., and J. Davidson, "Land: Women at the centre of the food crisis" in S. Sontheimer (Ed.), *Women and The Environment: A Reader* (London: Earthscan Publications, 1991).

Dankelman, I., and J. Davidson, Women and Environment in the Third World: Alliance for the Future (London: Earthscan Publications, 1989).

Dankelman, I., "In a word . . . Rapporteur's summary" in D. K. Munyakho (Ed), *Women and the Environmental Crisis: A Report of the Proceedings of the Workshops on Women, Environment and Development. July 10-20; Nairobi Kenya NGO Forum* (Nairobi: Environment Liason Centre, 1985).

David, R., "The effects of male out-migration on women's management of the natural resource base in the Sahel," Mimeo (London: SoS International, 1992).

Davidson, J., "Restoring women's link with nature," *Earthwatch*, No. 37 (1989), pp. 2-3.

DAWN, *Development Crises and Alternative Visions: Third World Women's Perspectives* (New York: Monthly Review Press, 1987).

De Beauvoir, S., *The Second Sex* (London: Picador, 1988).

DN, "Women and forests," *Economic and Political Weekly* (April 14, 1990), pp. 795-797.

Dyson, T., and M. Moore, "Kinship structure, female autonomy and demographic behaviour", *Population and Development Review*, Vol. 9, No. 1 (1983), pp. 35-60.

Eastlea, B., *Science and Sexual Oppression: Patriarchy's Confrontation with Women and nature* (London: Widenfield and Nicholson, 1981).

Eckersley, R., *Environmentalism and Political Theory: Toward an Ecocentric Approach* (London: University College London Press, 1992).

Eele, G., A. Duncan, and A. Lawson, "Environmental change and the response by small-holder farmers: some evidence from Tanzania," Paper given at the Annual Conference of the British society for Population Studies, Exeter College (Oxfor: September 9-11, 1992).

Folbre, N., "Hearts and Spades: Paradigm of household economics," *World Development*, Vol. 14, No. 2 (1986). Pp. 245-255.

Fortmann, L., "Women in subsistence forestry," *Journal Forestry*, Vol. 84, No. 7 (1986), pp. 39-42.

GFA — Gesellschaft fur Agraprojekte in Ubersee, "Study on the economic and social determinants of livestock production in the Communal Areas — Zimbabwe," Report to Dept. of Veterinary Services of Ministry of lands, Agriculture and Rural Resettlement, Zimbabwe (Harare: GFA, 1986).

Gould, B., "Population growth, environmental stability and migration in Western Province, Kenya," Paper given at the Annual Conference of the British Society for Population Studies, Exeter College (Oxford: September 9-11, 1992).

Gray, E. Dodson, *Green Paradise Lost* (Wellesley, MA: Roundtable, 1981).

Griffin, S., *Woman and Nature: The Roaring Inside Her* (New York: Harper and Row, 1978).

Guha, R., *The Unquiet Woods: Ecological Change and Peasant Resistance in the Himalays* (New Delhi: Oxford University Press, 1989).

Heyzer, N., "Rainforest management and indigenous livelihoods: a Malaysian case study," Paper prepared for the UNRISD Meeting on the Social dimensions of Environment and Sustainable Development (Malta: April 1992).

Hill, p., *Rural Hausa: A Village and A Setting* (Cambridge: Cambridge University Press, 1972).

Hobley, M., "Gender, class and use of forest resources: Nepal" in A. Rodda (Ed.), *Women and The Environment* (London: Zed Boods, 1991).

Iliffe, J., *Famine in Zimbabwe 1890-1960* (Gweru Zimbabwe: Mambo Press, 1990).

International Union for Conservation of nature (1987) *Women and the World Conservation Strategy*, Report on the first Strategy Workshop held at IUCN, Switzerland (Zurich: IUCN, 1987).

Jackson, C., "Environmentalisms and gender interests in the Third World," *Development and Change*, Vol. 24, No. 4 (1993).

Jackson, C., "Change and rural Hausa women: A study in Kura and Rano Districts, Northern Nigeria," Ph.D. thesis (London: Wye College, University of London, 1981).

Jain, S., Women and people's ecological movement: A case study of women's role in the Chipko movement in Uttar Pradesh." *Economic and Political Weekly* (October 13, 1984), pp. 1789-1794).

Jeater, J., "The closing gap: African women and European morality in Southern Rhodesia 1915-30," Paper for the African History Dept Seminar, School of Oriental and African Studies (London: University of London, Janurary, 1989).

Jones, C., "Intrahousehold bargaining in response to the introduction of new crops: A case study from North Cameroon" in J. Moock (Ed.), *Understanding Africa's Rural Households* (Boulder and London: Westview Press, 1986).

Kandiyoti, D., "Bargaining with patriarchy," *Gender and Society*, Vol. 2, No 3 (1988), pp.274-290.

Kelkar, G., and D. Nathan, *Gender and Tribe: Women, Land and Forests* (New Dehli: Kali for Women, 1991).

Khon Kaen University, *Proceedings of the 1985 International Conference on Rapid Rural Appraisal* (Khon Kaen: Khon Kaen university, , 1987).

King, Y., "The ecology of feminism and the feminism of ecology," in J. Plant (Ed,) *Healing the Wounds: The promise of Ecofeminism* (Philadelphia: New Society Publishers, 1989).

Kumar, S., and D. Hotchkiss, "Consequences of deforestation for women's time allocation, agricultural production, and nutrition in hill areas of Nepal," Research Report 69 (Washington, DC: International Food Policy Research Institute, 1988).

Lan, D., Guns and Rain: *Guerillas and Spirit Mediums in Zimbabwe* (London: Currey, 1985).

Lanzaduri, H., "The missing link: Decision-making and the Latin American woman" in D. Munyakho (Ed.), *Women and The Environmental Crisis: A Report of the Proceedings of the Workshops on Women, Environment and Development, July 10-20, Nairobi Kenya* NGO Forum (Nairobi: Environment Liasion Centre, 1985).

Leach, M., "Gender and environment: Traps and opportunities," Paper prepared for the Development Studies Association conference (Swansea: September 11-13, 1991).

Lovett, M., "Gender relations, class formation and the colonial state in Africa," in J. Parpart and K. Staudt (Eds.), *Women and the State in Africa* (Boulder, CO: Lynne Rienner Publishers, 1989), pp. 47-69.

MacCormack, C., "Nature, culture and gender: A critique," in C. MacCormack and M. Strathern (Eds.), *Nature, Culture and Gender* (Cambridge: Cambridge University Press, 1980).

Martin-Brown, M., "Healing hands," in D. Munyakho (Ed.), *Women and the*

Environmental Crisis: A Report of the Proceedings of the Workshops on Women Environment and Development, July 10-20, Nariobi Kenya NGO Forum (Nairobi: Environment Liasion Centre, 1985).

McGregor. J., *Woodland Resources: Ecology, Policy and Ideology, An Historical Case Study of Woodland Use in Shurugwi Communal Area, Zimbabwe*, Ph.D. thesis (Loughborough: Loughborough University, 1991),

Merchant, C., *Radical Ecology: The Search for a Livable World* (New York: Routledge, 1992).

Merchant, C., *The Death of Nature: Women, Ecology and the Scientific Revolution* (London: Wildwood, 1982).

Mies, M., *Patriarchy and Accumulation on a World Scale: Women in the International division of labour* (London: Zed Books, 1986).

Monimart, M., "Women in the fight against desertification," in Sontheimer (Ed.), Women and the Environment: A Reader (London: Earthscan Publications, 1991).

Monimart, M., "Women in the fight against desertification," International Institute for Environment and Development, Drylands Programme, Issues paper No. 2 (London: IIED, 1989).

Mortimore, M., and J. Wilson, "Land and Population in the Kano closed-settled zone," Department of Geography Occasional Paper No. 1 (Lagos: Ahmadu Bello University, Nigeria, 1965).

Moser, C., "Gender planning in the Thire World: Meeting practical and strategic needs," *World Development*, Vol. 17, No. 11 (1989), pp. 1799-1825.

Munyakho, D. K. (Ed.), *Women and The Environmental Crisis: A Report of the Proceedings of the Workshops on Women, Environment and Development, July 10-20, Nairobi Kenya NGO Forum* (Nairobi: Environment Liason Centre, 1985).

Murry, R., "Class, gender and the household: The developmental cycle in Southern Africa," *Development and Change*, Vol. 18, No. 2 (1987), pp. 236-249.

Omvedt, G., "Peasants and the ecological future," *Economic and Political Weekly* (February 10, 1990), pp. 321-323.

Ortner, S., "Is female to male as nature is to culture?" in M. Rosaldo and L. Lamphere (Eds.) *Woman, Culture and Society* (Stanfard, CA: Stanford University Press, 1974).

Overholt, C., M. Anderson, K. Cloud, and J. Austin, *Gender Roles in Development Projects: A Case Book* (West Hartford: Kumarian Press, 1985).

Overseas Development Administration, "Population, environment and development: An issues paper for the Third UNCED Preparatory Committee," Mimeo (London: ODA, 1991).

Plumwood, V., "Beyond the dualistic assumptions of women, men and nature," *Ecologist*, Vol. 22, No. 1 (1992), pp. 8-13.

Plumwood, V., "Woman, humanity and nature," *Radial Philosophy*, Vol. 48 (1988), 16-24.

Plumwood, V., "Ecofeminism: An overview and discussion of positions," *Australian Journal of Philosophy*, Vol. 64 (1986), pp. 120-138.

Rao, B., "Dominant constructions of women and nature in social science literature," Pamphlet 2, *Capitalism, Nature, Socialism* (New York: Guilford Publications, 1991).

Rodda, A. (Ed.), *Women and the Environment* (London: Zed Books), 1991

Rosenzweig, M., "Risk, private information and the family," *American Economic Review* (1988), pp. 245-250.

Ruether, R., New Woman, New Earth (New York: Seabury Press, 1979).

Salleh, A., "Ecofeminism/ecosocialism," *Capital, nature, Socialism*, Vol. 2, No. 1 (1989), pp. 129-134.

Sayers, J., *Biological Politics: Feminist and Anti-Feminist perspectives* (London: Tavistock Publications, 1982).

Sen, A., "Gender and cooperative conflicts" (Helsinki: WIDER, 1987).

Shiva, V., *Staying Alive: Women, Ecology and development* (London: Zed Books, 1989a).

Shiva, V., "Escaping from masculine time," *Earthwatch* No. 37 (1989b), pp. 4-5.

Shiva, V., "Where has all the water gone? The case of water and feminism in India," in D. Munyakho (Ed.), *Women and The Environmental crisis: A Report of the Proceedings of the Workshops on Women, Environment and Development, July 10-20, Nairobi Kenya NGO Forum* (Nairobi: Environment Liasion Centre, 1985).

Sontheimer, S. (Ed.), *Women and the Environment: A Reader* (London: Earthscan Publications, 1991).

Thomas-Slayter, M., "Politics, class and gender in African resource management: The case of rural kenya." *Economic Development and Cultural Change*, Vol. 40, No. 4 (1992), pp. 809-827.

Thompson, M., and M. Warburton, "Uncertainty on a Himalayan scale," *Mountain Research and Development*, Vol. 5, No. 2 (1985).

Vaughan, M., "Household units in southern Malawi," *Review of African Political Economy*, Vol. 34 (1985), pp. 35-45.

Vlassoff, C., "Progress and stagnation: changes in fertility and women's position in an Indian village," *Population Studies*, Vol. 46 (1991), pp. 195-212.

Warren, K., "The power and promise of ecological feminism," *Environmental Ethics*, Vol. 12 (1990), pp. 125-146.

Warren, K., Feminism and ecology: Making the connections," *Environmental Ethics*, Vol. 9, No. 1 (1987), pp. 3-20.

Whitehead, A., "Food crisis and African conflict in the African countryside," in H. Bernstein et al. (Eds.), *The Food Question: Profits Versus People?* (London: Earthscan, 1990).

Whitehead, A., "Men and women, kinship and property: Some general issues" in R. Hirschon (Ed.), Women and Property, Women as Property (London: Croom Helm, 1984).

Whitehead, A., "Some preliminary notes on the subordination of women," *Bulletin of the Institute of Development Studies*, Vol. 10, No. 3 (1979), pp. 10-13.

Wilson, K., "Ecological dynamics and human welfare: A case study of population, health and nutrition in Southern Zimbabwe," Ph.D. thesis (London: Department of Anthropology, University, College 1990).

Women's Environmental Network, "Women, environment, development seminar report" (London: WEN, 1989).

World Bank, *World Development Report* (New York: Oxford University Press. 1992).

Young, M., "Fertility and famine: Women's agricultural history in Mozambique," in R. Palmer and N. Parsons (Eds.), *The Roots of Rural Poverty in Central and Southern Africa* (Berkeley: University of California Press, 1977).

Zimmerman, M., "Feminism, deep ecology and environmental ethics," *Environmental Ethics*, Vol. 9, No. 1 (1987), pp. 21-44.

CHAPTER-3

Room for One's Life: Women, Houses and Social Change

Maria Muller

Introduction

The word "room", used in the title, has a double meaning. It refers to physical space which is or might be occupied by something, and in particular to the space which is part of a house, enclosed by walls and a ceiling. The word "room" also stands for opportunity, or scope for doing something. Both meanings of room are implied in this paper. Together they express the relationship that exists between the qualities of the physical space a person occupies and the opportunity he or she has for exercising his or her personal qualities in the life of the family and the community. This connection is obvious in the case of houses, which are supposed to be the domain of women. The physical dimensions and location, structural quality and symbolic value of houses have great impact on the scope for women for living their lives.

The argument of this paper is based on the recognition that the culture of a society, and particularly its value system, contains internal conflicts. Values, as expressions of collective interests, are in conflict with each other, as social groups in a society have conflicting interests. we consider men and women as constituting separate social groups who often have opposing interests in scarce resources. Specifically they have conflicting interests in access to, control over and the use of houses.

Conflicts within the value system of a society are exasperated in periods of socio-economic change in which a redistribution of interests takes place. Value patterns must be redefined in order to rationalise the new distribution of interests. Change in the value system does not occur smoothly. If the dominant social group, in this case men, feels threatened, it will oppose any changes that facilitate the access to resources which the other group needs in the changed situation. Men will oppose changes, for example, which would allow women greater access to the legal system, to capital, knowledge and to land and houses. In particular, the aim of women to obtain an `ideal' house becomes a focal point for cultural and economic conflict, as a house is a capital asset as well as the symbolic expression of the social order.

THE PERSPECTIVE OF WOMEN

My point of departure is the social position of women, in particular of those women who have little education, live in poor urban neighbourhoods in Third World cities and who are in general disadvantaged in the struggle for economic advancement in a modern urban society. The line of argument of this paper is that women have strong interests in living in an `ideal' house, as the house is the basic condition for them to achieve their goals in life. For men the house has not that fundamental value. Although women have this strong interest, often it is almost impossible for them to obtain and to keep their ideal house, because of socio-economic and cultural obstacles put in their way. Women face obstacles because they belong to the urban poor, and because they are women. First I will show in which sense housing is important to women, and also indicate the difficulties women experience in obtaining a house. Finally, I will give an explanation for these difficulties. conflicts of interests and conflicts within the value system play a role here.

To do this I follow Nas and Prins (1988, pp. 114—131) in their conception of housing as a dynamic process, consisting of creating housing and of being housed. But I want to broaden this conception by saying that the creation of housing is also an element in a comprehensive strategy to obtain certain ends in life, both short-term and long-term, ranging from sheer survival to establishing a permanent base for one's family, and to safeguarding capital investment. The dynamic element of housing refers, therefore, not only to activities resulting in the `ideal house' (housing as an aim), but also to activities in which housing is used for further goals (housing as a means). More concretely, one can say that an ideal house enables both men and women to arrange their life in the way they prefer. This holds particularly true for women.

WOMEN'S ROLES

A woman's life is structured by a combination of roles. Worldwide, women are assigned the reproductive roles of mother and housewife. In many low-income communities women have in addition the productive role of income earner. The reproductive role, supported by norms and sanctions, tie women to the house and the immediate neighbourhood. The best income-earning opportunities for women, therefore, are those that can be performed in the house or neighbourhood. The size of the house and its location in relation to work opportunities determine to a large extent the potential of women to earn an income, since their physical mobility is restricted. They can only escape this restriction through relying on mutual assistance among neighbours or by getting more women in the house who can help with the housework. Being tied to the neighbourhood causes women to be more dependent than men on neighbourhood social network and on infrastructural services in the immediate environment. This is the central issue in the difference in gender interests regarding housing. Men are not tied to the house through social roles and obligations. They are free to choose whether to use the house as a workshop or whether to spend long hours travelling to their work. Women (especially poor women) do not have that choice if they want to look after the daily needs of their family as well as earn an income. Of course, not all women have to perform productive duties. Yet also women who are predominantly occupied with reproductive duties regard the house and neighbourhood as their main area of work.

Although the social expectations determine to a large extent women's lives, other considerations too influence women's strategies. Ann Schlyter concludes from her converstions with women in Lusaka, Zambia that even the poorest woman "wants her family to survive and to live a life of human dignity according to her own aspirations and culture" (Schlyter, 1988, p. 29). I want to add that this `human dignity' includes creating some freedom of action and independence for oneself, earning respect, and obtaining a degree of autonomy in one's own life. Women tend to grasp any opportunity to carry out their own business, however small scale, and be involved in activities which yield social recognition (e.g. in religious groups). `Freedom of action' and `respect' have of course a cultural content, but they help to explain why women attach that importance to living in a particular house and even to obtaining a house of their own.

In addition there are the women heads of households who are, forced by circumstance or by choice, solely responsible for their children. The economic condition of these households varies considerably.

It is, however, important to recognise that women who head households are the primary income-earners and that therefore the combination of roles proves to be particularly burdensome to them (Moser and Peake, 1987, p. 14).

The neighbourhood-based social network is an important source of support for women. In periods of sudden crisis— financial or otherwise—the neighbouring women lend each other goods and exchange services for which they normally would have to pay (see also Maher, 1974). In addition, the neighbouring women also keep each other informed about the world around them through their informal visiting. This social exchange serves to develop collective ideas about how to view events and how to judge the behaviour of the actors (Plantenga, 1987). So-called gossiping, therefore, thought so typical of women, is in fact an attempt to give meaning to events seen in their proper context (from the point of view of the women) and to confirm or to modify prevalent values and norms.

The `ideal' house then for women is the house that, through its location and lay-out, enable women to carry out this combination of roles in an ideal manner. This means, in particular, that the house should enable women to engage in economic activities. Secondly, the house should facilitate social contact with neighbours and relatives who make up the support network of women. And finally, considering the increasing number of women who head a household, it must be possible for women to obtain independent access to the `ideal' house by renting, buying or building, so that they may establish or maintain their own household with their children.

THE HOUSE AS A SOURCE OF INCOME

A house can enable women to earn income in several ways. If the house is situated within easy reach of centres of employment, women can find paid work—often informal and often part-time—while keeping travel time and travel costs to a minimum. A change in house location can have a disastrous effect on the ability of women to look after their children. In Paramaribo, Surinam, for example, the increase in land values in the city centre caused house rents to rise steeply, thus forcing low-income women to move to the city's periphery. As the women still kept their jobs in the city centre, they spent move time away from their families than before. They partly solved the ensuing problem by breast-feeding their babies for only five instead of 10 months. The result was a strong increase in child mortality (Lamur, 1986).

If women cannot leave the house because of child care and domestic duties, or because it is considered `improper' for them to move in public, women use the house itself as a place of business. Small scale trading from their house—if the zoning by-laws allow it—is a common sight in many low-income neighbourhoods. Moreover, the whole cottage industry in the textile and electronics sectors is based on this fact: that women use their own premises to produce cheaply for the middlemen and entrepreneurs.

Significant in this respect is the title of a paper, "My Work Grows with my House," about Bandung, West Java (Van Velzen, 1987, pp. 105-115). The title refers to the local cottage industry which provides work for a large number of women. The women produce snacks which are sold by a chain of middlemen and eventually reach the markets and shops. The two women described arc of different socio-economic status, yet each makes a substantial contribution to household income. One woman, living in a small one-roomed house, works alone, assisted only by her husband and children at the end of their working day. The other women occupies with her husband, children and relatives a relatively spacious house. the largest room and the kitchen are used as a production centre where about 15 women work daily. Whether the house consists of one room or of several rooms, the economic enterprise dominates its use. Only in the evening, after the day's production, can normal family activities take place. The women lament the fact that their house is too small to allow the enterprise to expand and they are continuoulsy thinking of ways to increase the space by adding a verandah or an outside kitchen or by building a second storey onto the house. The size of the house is one of the important factors that determine the production capacity of these women.

THE HOUSE AS A SCENE OF SOCIAL CONTACT

An essential element of social networks of neighbouring women is that they are developed over a period of time, and that they require investment in time and attention. Women must see each other frequently and assist each other over a number of years. Thus these social relationships are 'tested' and strengthened. It was noted in

Lusaka, for example, that women did not want to move from their own section in a settlement because of the good relationships with their neighbours. The reason is that unless neighbourship is supported by kinship, former neighbours lose contact very quickly.

We can learn from an example from Morocco how house lay-out and neighbourhood planning affect the potential for contact between neighbouring women (Buitelaar, 1987, pp. 61-62). In Sidi Slimane, a small town, middle class houses are built in a closed Arabic style, adjoining each other. The outside walls have no windows. The rooms are built around an inner court yard, which is their only source of daylight. The roof is the women's favourite place. From there they have a good view of the whole neighbourhood without being seen themselves. Neighbouring women talk to each other from the roof top, as they do not easily walk into each other's houses just for a chat. Sitting there, they exchange information, help each other with various chores, watch their children, and follow events in the neighbourhood (see also Warnock Fernea, 1976).

Many shops are located in the narrow streets, enabling women to do quick shopping and to contact the shopkeepers who sell the clothes which they sew at home. Although the women stay inside the house most of the time—as is expected of them—they do keep in touch with the world around. Yet many men and women strive to move one day to the former French neighbourhood built in European style. There the houses stand far apart, each on its own plot and surrounded by a garden and fence. Casual contact is obstructed, while the sloping roofs prevent social gatherings. The streets are wide and there are few shops in the residential area. These architectural and planning features increase women's isolation and prevent the exchange of services so vital for women. They hinder women in their economic transactions with shop-keepers.

HOUSE OWNERSHIP

The ideal house thus enables women to fulfill their culturally determined roles in a situation of economic scarcity and uncertainty; a situation, moreover, where women depend for emotional support and information sharing on women, rather than on men.

If this can be said for married women, It holds even more true for women household heads, who are both economically and socially in a weaker position. The latter, however, have also to face the issue of how to obtain their own house, so that they can live with a greater degree of independence.

A house of one's own is one of the great aims of women households heads. They expect from house ownership the basic security which a rented dwelling connot provide. Ownership would free them from the constraint of regular monthly payments, so much in conflict with their irregular work and income situation. Moreover, as indicated above, women view house ownership as a form of investment which will support Them now as well as in their old age. In fact, it is said of Low income illiterate women tenants in Lusaka that they "were desperate for a place of their own" (Schylter, 1988, p. 97). If, in the case of the husband's death or of divorce, a woman has any funds available, her first priority of investment is a house of her own (Schlyter, 1988, p. 103). Sometimes relatives help with the purchase of a house.

In George, a legalised low-income settlement in Lusaka, there are two types of houses, i.e. those made of mud bricks and those made of concrete blocks. In each type there is a range from the well constructed and maintained to the poorly built and badly maintained ones. It was found that in 1985 half of the houses sold to women were sold at a very low price. These were the mud brick houses which were in an old and dilapidated condition (Schlyter, 1988, p. 104). Not all the women household heads were very poor, however, as a few women could afford to pay a high price for modern, well-constructed concrete houses. These women had formal employment or were successful marketeers (Schlyter, 1988, p. 105).

The assumption stated above that women have a strong interest in living in an ideal house and in obtaining a house of their own, is supported by several observations. In the George area in Lusaka, for example, it was noted that in the years 1982-1985, after the completion of the upgrading process, only a small proportion of houses changed ownership (Schlyter, 1988, p. 109) Only 4% of the sellers were women, while 14% of the buyers were women. Women will do everything possible to defend their house ownership, as this is one of the few means available to them to maintain independence and security. They are very reliable in their payment of service charges. For them these payments constitute a higher priority than for men.

Further still, women will literally defend their houses against the brute force of the police who try to remove people from settled residential areas. Reports from cities as far apart as Bucaramanga (Colombia) and Manila (Philippines) mention that women are in the forefront of the battle, risking their life for the right to keep their house (Meertens, 1987, pp. 33-51; Medel-Anonuevo and Hilhorst, 1987, pp. 137-151). They fight against political decisions taken in the name of development or modernisation.

VALUES AS CONSTRAINTS

The previous paragraph has indicated two main problems women experience with respect to housing. First, as women it is often impossible for them to acquire house ownership. And secondly, as members of the working classes they must confront the market forces which increase the price of land and housing and may result in their being forced to move from their homes. At the centre of both problems is a conflict of interest and of values.

The fundamental value conflict regarding the role of women in relation to the house is expressed in the hostory of unplanned settlements. During the first phase of a squatter settlement in Bucaramanga, when workers were needed to organise and build temporary houses and to defend the place against physical attack, women were respected workers. Men accepted that women played a public role in order to establish a homestead. In the consolidation phase, however, when negotiations took place between community leaders and city authorities, the men did not allow woemn to play a public role. Women kept their `proper' place, at home with the children (Meertens, 1987). A similar conflict of values and norms was observed in Guayaquil, Ecuador (Moser, 1987, pp. 166-194).

Another conflict refers to women's productive role, largely associated with their home. Women are expected to do productive work for the benefit of the household. At the same time they are restricted by the limitations placed on the work they may carry out. Certain jobs are considered `unsuitable for women'. When, some years ago, the first women street sweepers were employed by Nairobi City Council, there was a hue and cry against women's so-called trespassing on the job rights of men. Job stereotype restrictions on women's public mobility, underpinned by normative statements about women's proper place being at home, serve to exclude women from training for the most remunerative jobs. Together these cultural conceptions, reinforced by real competition on the labour market, increase women's dependence on the house for productive work.

Another major area of conflict pertains to women's independent access to house ownership. In many countries women are extremely restricted as to their legal rights to own property. In Zambia, for example, women may acquire a title deed or an occupancy license to a house only with the consent of her husband. At divorce the woman must always leave the house. At the husband's death the widow does not inherit any property according to customary laws (Schlyter, 1988, pp. 55-61). These legal concept serve to restrict access to a scarce commodity, which is one of the reasons why any constitutional changes meet strong opposition.

However, these customary concepts fly in the face of present day reality where more women stand on their own and are in need of independent rights to house ownership than before. If in the past brothers or brothers-in-law cared for widows and separated women without difficulty, today it is different. Relatives are no longer able or willing to care for additional family members in the same way as they used to. Instead they may assist a woman with purchasing or rebuilding her own house. Their support, however, cannot automatically be counted upon. One must conclude that the two parts of the normative system of rights and obligations are changing at unequal pace. "While the right of women to be cared for by their husband's brother or their own brother is taken away from the urban women, they are still not given the rights to the property which they as spouses have obtained together with their husbands" (Schlyter, p. 60). The traditional inheritance rights, by which property acquired by the husband with the help of the wife is passed on to the husband's relatives, are still claimed by these relatives.

A final source of value conflict concerns the appreciation of modernisation. One source of conflict is the political decision to boost the presumed international image of a modern country by removing `unsightly' low-income residential area. Obviously, the national goal of being `modern' is in conflict with the interests of the poor and of women. As explained above, the removal of a house, which is the source of income and the scene of social ineraction, hits deeply at women's lives.

More subtle is the appeal to modern values made by women themselves. Their aim to earn respect by living in a `modern' house may appear to conflict with their other aims, such as managing their roles in an efficient manner, and gaining a certain amount of freedom of manoeuvre. The case study from Morocco has already shown that women foster the ideal of living in the French residential area, which is regarded as the expression of social mobility. At the same time, the `modern' style of housing restricts their physical mobility and increases their economic and social dependence. A final example comes from Lusaka, where some women prefer to build a modern concrete block house, even if their meagre means only allow them a very small, badly constructed one-roomed dwelling (Schlyter, 1988, pp. 119-120). In the western observer's view a well-built mud brick house would have provided a healthier, less cramped space more conducive to family life and productive work. The women's main aim was, however, to be considered modern, urban women. A concrete house served as a symbol of that status.

CONCLUSION

The starting point for this paper has been that the value of a house for different social groups is deeply influenced by culture and gender interests.

I have looked at housing from the perspective of the user—low-income urban women in the Third World—and taken account of the values and norms guiding their behaviour, their aims in life, and their strategies for achieving these aims. From this point of view a house is a crucial element in women's strategies. Generalising about women's aims, we can say that they are closely associated with their roles as mother, housewife and income earner (granting all their cultural and class determined variations). To carry out these roles with a certain amount of freedom of manoeuvre, and while earning social recognition, women require their own source of income and their own network of social relationships. The ideal house enables women to achieve all this.

It is obvious that women, complled to stay near home, have an intense interest in living in an `ideal' house, and that this interest touches the centre of their existence as a responsible social being, as mother, domestic worker and income earner. For men, interest in a house is different, as they have a wider array of economic opportunities and social contacts, less circumscribed by the lay-out and the location of the house. Women's definition of an `ideal' house, and the value they attach to living in such a house is for this reason likely to be different from those applied by men.

One might expect that—if all were equal—the significance of the ideal house for women would be reflected in normative patterns and distribution systems in society. But all are not equal, and fundamental changes in the system of production are taking place, creating even greater social inequality between men and women. And so interests, backed by values, succeed in impeding the access to good housing to women. These values are, for example in the spheres of training and availability of jobs, the exercies of public roles, and the legal status of women. But the situation is not static. Case studies should be collected which document that values and norms are not strictly adhered to, and that women find in practice ways and means to circumvent the norms. Thus they contribute to the wider recognition and acceptance of social change in the value systems of their societies.

REFERENCES

Buitelaar, M., "Ontmoetingen met vrouwen in Sidi Slimane, Marokko," in Muller, M.S. and Plantenga, D. (Editors). *De Volkswijk,* pp. 59-70, 1987.

Kleinpenning. I.M.G. (Editor), "Competition for Rural and Urban Space in Latin America and its Consequences for Low Income Groups." *Nederlandse Geografische Studies,* No. 25. Nijmegen, Amsterdam, 1986.

Lamur. H.E., in Kleinpenning, I.M.G. (Editor), *Urban Survival Strategies and Infant Mortality in Paramaribo, Surinam,* pp. 164-173, 1986.

Maher, V., *Women and Property in Morocco; their Changing Relation to the Process of Social Stratification in the Middle Atlas.* Cambridge University Press, London, 1974.

Medel-Anonuevo, C. and Hilhorst, T., "Overleven in Armoede; Vrouwenorganisatie in een Volksbuurt by Manila, Filippijnen" in Muller, M.S. and Plantenga, D. (Editors), *De Volkswijk,* pp. 137-151, 1987.

Meertens, D., "Vrouwen in invasiewijken: een case study in Bucaramanga, Colombia," in Muller, M.S. and Plantenga, D. (Editors), *De Volkswijk,* pp. 33-51 1987.

Moser, C.O.N. and Peake, L. (Editors), *Women Human Settlements and Housing.* Tavistock Publications, London, 1987.

Muller, M.S. and Plantenga, D. (Editors), *De Volkswijk, Woning en Werkplaats; Overlevingsstrategieen van Vrouwen in Derde-Wereldsteden.* Koninklijk Instituut voor de Tropen/NOVIB, Amsterdam, 1987.

Nas, P.J.M. and Prins, W.J.M., "House, Culture and Development," in *Bijdragen tot de Taall-, Land-en Volkenkunde,* Vol. 144, pp. 114-131, 1988.

Plantenga, D., "De stad en haar Volksbuurten: Informele netwerken van sociale relaties tussen Vrouwen in een Volksbuurt Van Rao de Janeiro, Brazilie," in Muller, S. and Plantenga, D. (Editors), *De Volkswijk,* pp. 81-103, 1987.

Schlyter, A., *Women Householders and Housing Strategies; the Case of George, Zambia.* The National Swedish Institute for Building research, Lund, 1988.

Van Velzen, A., "Mijn werk groeit met mijn Huis mee; Vrouwen in de Huisindustrie in Bandung, West Java," in Muller, M.S. and Plantenga, D. (Editors), *De Volkswijk*, pp. 105-113, 1987.

Warnock Fernea, E., *A street in Marrakech.* Anchor Press/doubleday, New York, 1976.

CHAPTER-4

Gender and Housing : Broadening the Debate

Moira Munro and Susan J.Smith

Introdution

One of the most conspicuous themes of housing research explores the significance of structured inequalities in access to residential space, Theoretically and empirically the majority of effort has focused on household incomes, modes of consumption and forms of class relations as the key determinants of differentiation in the housing system. 'Race' (more properly, racism) has also received attention, as analysts increasingly regard the housing system as a set of mechanisms and practices that mediate (ie both reflect and reproduce) axes of social differentiation other than those directly contingent on the accumulation or display of material wealth. But if social theory (and the housing research it informed) was late in affording racism (embedded in a legacy of nationalism and imperialism) analytical significance on a par with class inequality (embedded in capitalism), it was long overdue in recognising the related salience of gender relations (particularly in their patriarchal form) to an understanding of the operation of markets and institutions.

Even now, there are only a handful of housing studies incorporating theories of gender relations into explanatory frameworks accounting for the operation of the housing system, despite the fact that the importance of considering gender relations in general and the structure of patriarchy in particular, is now well-established in a range of fields related to housing most notably in social policy studies (eg Baldsock and Cass, 1983; Dale and Foster, 1986, Williams, forthcoming, Wilson, 1977; Ungerson, 1985) and in studies of work and labour markets, including research on domestic labour and on paid employment opportunities (see, for instance, some of the papers edited by Crompton and Mann, 1986).

As Watson (1986a) shows one reason why neither housing nor urban studies have been quick to incorporate gender alongside class and 'race' into analyses of social and spatial differentiation and segmentation within the housing stock, is that much of the relevant research is concerned primarily with the roles and requirements of specific groups of *women.* There are some inportant reasons for this emphasis, not least the fact that 'mainstream' urban studies were predominantly either gender-neutral in tenor, or actively subsumed women beneath the structures of a 'male' world. Thus, it is hardly surprising that a large proportion of the 'women and housing' literature is concerned with descriptive and prescriptive analyses of the problems faced by women in particular segments of the housing market,and it is worth mentioning some of these.

The difficulties posed by different locations, particularly poorly serviced suburbs, are a common theme (see Allport, 1983; Morrow-Jones, 1986), as are the problems women face in gaining access to owner occupation (Schafer and Ladd, 1981; Shear and Yezer, 1985; Watson and Helliwell, 1985) or negotiating complex public housing access rules and obstructive bureaucracies (Brailey, 1986) Brion and Tinker's (1980) pioneering text focuses even more spcifically on the problems peculiar to women. They draw attention to problems encountered either because of discrimination arising out of legal or technical anomalies (eg the traditional - but now less common - tendency for tenancies to be registered and mortgages granted in men's names) or because of demographic and physiological characteristics (notably the longevity of women relative to men, and women's greater susceptibility, irrespective of age, to rheumatism and arthritis). An extension of this kind of approach is found in the awakening of public and academic interest in the problems of domestic violence against women (discussed by Wilson, 1983) and the far-reaching behavioural and psychological consequences of the threat of rape (assessed by Warr, 1984) Drawing on both these themes (women in relation to the spatial and tenure-based differentiation of the housing market and women's special needs) a variety of studies have been initiated which focus systematically on the plight of women in different kinds of households one-parent mothers (Leavitt, 1985; Vincent, nd); single women (Austerberry and Watson, 1983); homeless women (Cyrenians, 1985; Gilbert 1986; Watson and Austerberry, 1986); black women (Omarshah, nd; GLC, 1984; Immigration Widows Campaign, 1984); and so on.

Research exploring women's disadvantage has undoubtedly been of importance in identifying large areas of unmet social need and in exposing a range of discriminatory policies and practices. It is moreover unlikely that the achievements of the 'women and housing' focus have exhausted themselves in this respect. However there is a point beyond which this essentially descriptive and exploratory kind of study cannot go. It has become apparent that such an approach though vital as a first step, gives too narrow and partial a base for reformulating urban theory. In housing studies particularly, it encourages the tendency to present women's issues as some form of 'special need' rather than as an integral part of the 'normal' concerns of housing policy. It is important, therefore, to adopt a conceptual and theoretical perspective broad enought to show how and why the housing system is drawn into the production and reproduction of gender-based inequalities (a point developed more generally by Hayden, 1980; McDowell, 1983; Saegart, 1980)

This paper is written as a contribution to that wider project. We begin by sketching our preferred analytical framework, arguing that gender differences in housing attainment express not only the reproduction of patriarchy but also the reproduction of labour relations and of social inequality more generally. This outline prefaces and contextualises and analysis of the different predictors of housing attainment amongst yound (23 year-old) men and women. Our discussion focuses particularly on the housing consequences of women's and men's labour market position drawing attention to the neglected role of working mothers in sustaining owner-occupation in some household types. We also focus more specifically on how the effects of income and occupation are mediated by the presences of children to affect the attainment of housing and residential location.

Explaining gender differences in housing

Payne and Payne (1977) suggest that housing is not simply an index of the achievement of life chances but also (p 134) the means by which the inequalities of the occupational structure are transferred into the wider social structure. We would argue that housing embodies in this way not just a set of economic relations, but also a form of gender relations. These two concerns obviously overlap (there are marked gender inequalities in the labour market) but neither is reducible to the other, Indeed, housing studies are one pathway to a broader understanding of just how class and gender relations are articulated. To this end we suggest it is necessary to explore three analytical frameworks. None is in itself sufficient to explain observed gender differences in housing outcomes. Together, however, they provide some foundation for a more comprehensive theoretical account of the housing system. These frameworks, which are discussed in turn below, relate to the role of family status, labour market conditions and housing history (or generational factors) as predictors of gender differences in housing circumstances. These frameworks enable us to embrace the role of housing in the reproduction of patriarchal relations, in the reproduction of labour power, and in the reproduction of social inequality respectively. We discuss these breefly in turn.

Austerberry and Watson (1983) and Watson (1986a, 1986b) have established the importance of family structure as a key focus for gender and housing research by exposing the orientation of the housing system to the need of 'conventional' families. They show that non-family households (particularly one-parent families) are marginalised by housing allocation systems, and that the net effect of this is a bias against women (who, for instance, comprise 90 per cent of Britain's single parents). Watson (1986b) explains this by tying housing markets and institution into the predominantly patriarchal form of gender relations that characterises advanced market economies. 'Family' households (consisting of husband, wife and children) are, she argues, an important arena in which patriarchal relations are sustained. Because such gender inequalities are also embedded in the structure and organisation of the major institutions, the selective operation of the housing system is bound to favour those (conventional) households which sustain patriarchy rather than those (unusual) family types which might challenge this pattern of inequality. Extending this kind of reasoning we might expect 'conventional' couples to attain owner occupation more readily than other household types, though we might also expect that 'conventional' couples with children will more easily gain access to council housing should they require it (for instance, early in the housing career).

While recognising the importance of Watson's thesis, we would argue that a more complex interpretation is required to account for the fact that while some non-family households obviously are marginalised within the housing market, others (eg single men) often are not. Moreover, those households best placed in the housing market (dual income, no children) are not always those most obviously patriarchal in their organisation. These anomalies arise, we suggest, because while housing systems undoubtedly do operate to reproduce gender relations, they also (and through essentially the same mechanisms of production, allocation and exchange) reproduce other sets of social relations. In view of this, the effect of family status cannot be considered apart from the effect of a second explanatory framework, relating to labour market conditions. Indeed given the strong links between labour and housing markets (see Munro, 1987) it is imposible to understand gender differences in housing outcomes without making explict reference to labour market variables. This is true in two senses.

First and most obviously there is a link between access to economic power (represented by paid employment) and ability to pay for houing (Murphy and Sullivan, 1986). Ability to pay has a profound influence on housing choice; it determines the range of tenure options available in the private market it limits the quality and location of properties available; and even in the public sector, economic security enhances tenants' ability to wait for an 'acceptable' offer, so securing them access to better quality properties in that tenure also (Clapham and Kintrea, 1986). It is well established that women and men are highly segmented at work, and that women tend to occupy jobs which have low pay and low status. In 1985 full-time women workers earned about two-thirds of the men's average (Department of Employment, 1986), but this understates the difference between men's and women's earning as women constitute the vast majority of the part-time labour force. About 28 per cent of women are part-time workers (Martin and Roberts, 1984) and in 1985 part time workers earned just 22 per cent of the male full-time wage. Thus, women are immediately disadvantaged in their ability independently to gain access to housing because of their low earnings capacity relative to that of men. Watson and Helliwell (1985) thus argue that the direct discrimination women encounter at the hands of housing exchange professional is compounded by labour market factors which undermine women's purchasing power.

A second important link between housing and labour market occurs because the location of housing affects job opportunities. This occurs either when areas are stigmatised by potential employers (McGregor, 1979) or when houseprice differentials or difficulties of access to local authority housing are sufficient to inhibit access to the locations where work is available. These geographical links between housing and labour markets, although usually described in gender neutral terms, are particularly disadvantageous to women, whose access to private transport is still relatively limited and whose greater average domestic and child-care responsibilities frequently make long journeys to work impossible. Thus, women are likely to experience the housing constrainst imposed by labour market conditions differently from men, and this is a further reason why labour market variables are an essential component of any explanation of gender differences in housing outcomes.

In addition to conceptualising these differences in terms of the reproduction of patriarchal and labour relations, it is important to recognise that the way in which family status and labour market position are mapped onto housing outcomes varies over time. The housing system is not a static reflection of enduring social relations. It may provide some illuminating snapshots of contemporary norms, but it also expresses-indeed, in some circumstances promotes-changes in the form of social inequality that accompany macroeconomic, political and demographic trends, Because of changes both at the level of political economy and in the sphere of housing policy, gender differences in housing circumstances can only accurately be interpreted in terms of the relative achievements of men and women in a given birth cohort. This provides a certain amount of analytical 'control' over inter-temporal and inter-generational changes, while facilitating study of the impact within a particular cohort of for instance the differential inheritance of material wealth.

In order to combine these three conceptual frameworks, the analysis which follows explores the independent and combined effects of family status, labour market position and the inter-generational transmission of wealth on housing attainment in Britain, using the National Child Development Survey (NCDS).[1]

Our discussion is based on the experiences and achievements of a subset of the 12,000 individuals interviewed in 1982, focusing on the 5,000 respondents who had formed independent households and moved into owner occupation or council renting. The analysis was restricted to these two tenures, because they currently form the only realistic options for long term housing for most households. Payne and Payne (1977), moreover, have argued that the initial achievement of either of these tenures is a fundamental divide that sets the pattern of the housing career, In this report, therefore, we focus primarily on the predictors of tenure attainment amongst very youthful independent households, for the moment excluding those who will eventually attain one of the main two tenures but whose entry has been delayed, for instance, by a long training or extended education, or because they have not yet formed independent households that would be eligible for local authority housing. This means that, initially at least, we must regard owner occupation as an index of housing achievement. Our rationale for doing so is not so much that owner occupation is an unequivocally better option than public renting for all households, as a recognition that an ability to achieve ownership early in the housing 'career' may be good indicator of future housing prospects. It is nevertheless true that as ideological and financial pressures have increased the 'attractiveness' of owner occupation this tenure is increasingly seen as a 'good' in itself.

The aim of our analysis is to find those factors that tend to predispose young households towards owner occupation or local authority renting. Our discussion above, as well as the weight of past research that has examined tenure choice and housing market outcomes (albeit in a genderneutral framework) has given us some a *priori* hypotheses about the factors which we expect to be significant. Here, we extend earlier analyses to study not only the relative importance of these factors but also to assess their differential effect on men and women in a single age cohort.

The analysis

Our aims as specified above are best fulfilled by the application of a logit model.[2] A set of seven independent variables was chosen in order to construct a relatively parsimonious model while still including all three main influences on tenure attainment. These variables are listed in Table 1, Which also indicates the expected sign associated with each coefficient. The dependent variable, TENURE, is dichotomous distinguishing local authority renters from those who achieve owner occupation.[3] Below, we discuss first a model applied to the entire subsample and then models constructed separately for the male and female subpopulations. In all three cases we used a forward stepping procedure as advocated by Goodman (1972).[4] Initaially we allowed only one way terms to enter the model, but then allowed significant interaction terms to enter as well.[5]

Table 2 presents the final model as fitted to the entire subsample (of men and women together). This model fits well ($p^2 = 0.293$)[6] without being too complex, and all the one-way terms have the signs we expect. Eight interaction terms improved the fit of the model significantly enough to merit inclusion.[7]

This model affirms the importance of family status for the achievement of owner occupation, as the strongest single effect in increasing the probability of being an owner results from having a partner. A useful summary of the magnitude of effects that results from a particular factor is given by the relative odds ratio.[8] The relative odds ratio of having a partner compared to not having one is 15.7, which implies that those with partners (91.8 per cent of the sample) are nearly 16 times more likely to be owners than those without, holding other things constant. The other family status variable (NOKIDS) also has a very strong effect, confirming that those who do not have children are nearly 13 times more likely to be owner occupiers than those who do. (Family status variable also appear in the two-way interaction terms. The three largest (and significant) terms are between SEX, and PARTNER, PARTNER and FAMNETD and NOKIDS and ECSTATD. The interaction terms between NOKIDS and FAMNETD is also significant. These interaction terms are discussed in more detail below.

Parental tenure (which might tbe interpreted either as an index of the transmission of cultural

Table 1: Independent variables used in the analysis

Variable group	Variable name	Categories	Expected sign[5] of coefficient
Gender	SEX	1. Female	
		2. Male	+
Labour market	ECSTATD	1. In paid employment	
		2. Not a wage worker	-
	FAMNETD1	1. Low	
	(family net income)	2. Medium	+
		3. High	+
Family status	PARTNER[2]	1. No partner	
		2. Living with partner	+
	NCKIDS	1. At least I dependent child	
		2. No children at home	+

Inter-generat-ional *Variables*	GIFT[3]	1. Received gift/inheritance
		2. Not received gift/inheritance -
	PARTEND[4] (paremaltenure)	1. Owner
		2. Public renter -
		3. Other -

Notes (1) The sample is divided equally into these three categories.

(2) Refers to spouse or cohabitee

(3) Value at least £ 500

(4) As identified when the respondent was aged 16

(5) Each coefficient estimates the effect of being in category 2 (or 3) of a variable, rather than in category 1, on the probability of owning rather than renting

Table 2 : Final fitted model for the whole sample

Variable	Coefficient	Coeff/SE
SEX	0.25580 E-01	0.2782*
GIFT	- 0.46190	- 6.118
PARTNER	0.68768	4.484
NOKIDS	0.59745	9.423
ECSTATD	- 0.58004	- 4.967
PARTEND (1)	-0.64087	- 10.05
(2)	- 0.86715 E-01	- 0.9055*
FAMNETD (1)	0.16607	0.9137*
(2)	0.17786	0.6777*
SEX*PARTNER	- 0.39317	- 4.669
SEX*ECSTATD	- 0.17155	- 2.751
GIFT*FAMNETD (1)	0.10772	1.107*
(2)	0.19243	1.637*
PARTNER*ECSTATD	0.15949	1.476*
PARTNER*FAMNETD (1)	- 0.38636	- 2.398
(2)	0.27231	1.156*
NOKIDS*ECSTATD	- 0.18170	- 2.875
NOKIDS*FAMNETD (1)	- 0.14699	- 2.123
(2)	- 0.68499 E-01	- 0.7981*
ECSTATD*FAMNETD (1)	0.15724	2.103
(2)	- 0.92163 E-01	- 0.8699*
CONSTANT	0.37609	2.176

$* \frac{\text{Coeff}}{\text{SE}} < 2$ (ie not significant)

LL(0) = - 2491.232

Log likelihood = 1760.84

Likelihood ratio p^2 = 0.293

Note : LL(O) is the log likelihood with only the constant fitted.

norms and aspirations or as a proxy for the potential for intergenerational transfer of housing wealth), has the second largest independent effect on tenure attainment. It appears only as a oneway term, implying that its effects are independent of other factors. It has a greater bearing on the probability of owning rather than renting than does the receipt of gifts or inheritances (even though this latter variable might be expected to provide a more direct index of help with the costs of housing and entry into the owner occupied sector). The odds ratios indicate that those whose parents were owners are 13 times more likely to be owners than those whose parents rented from the local authority, and that those who received a gift or inheritance are six times more likely to be owners than those who did not.

The overall model also exposes the salience of labour market position. At this aggregate level, it suggests that the security of having regular paid employment has a greater independent effect on tenure attainment for all respondents than does household income (the coefficent on ECSTATD exceeds those on FAMNETD, and the latter is surprisingly weak). Both these variables are also prominent in the model's interaction terms, but their full significance does not become apparent until the model is disaggregated to consider male and female respondents separately (which we move on to later).

Gender does not exert a significant independent effect on tenure attainment. This might be expected, given the structure of the sample (which is dominated by couples), though it is perhaps surprising that the age difference of respondents partners (as an index of earning power and job security) does not act through gender to make a greater difference to the overall model (the men's partners had an average age of 22.6 years and the women's of 26.3 years, and 71 percent of women with partners as compared with 65 percent of men with partners are owner occupiers). The model does, however, confirm the importance of examining the interaction of gender with other factors, as two out of the six significant interaction terms involve SEX.

The largest of the interaction terms in this aggregate model is between SEXand PARTNER which implies that the influence of having a partner on tenure attainment is different for men and women. The direction of this relationship can be interpreted either as an indication that men with out partners are less disadvantaged in tenure terms (ie more likely to be owners) than are women without partners, or conversely, that having a partner confers a bigger advantage on women than men in terms of access to owner occupation. Either way, the prominence of this interaction term is probably a reflection of men's and women's different average earning capacity women's lower average incomes (and the general expectation that they will leave the labour force for a period of child care) typically make them dependent on the existence of a second wage to secure a mortgage. This issue is taken up in more detail later in the discussion.

The second largest interaction terms in this model is between PARTNER and FAMNETD. This implies that the effect on tenure of having a partner varies with family income. The effect of having a partner is particularly important in raising the probability of owning amongst those with low incomes relative to those with medium incomes. The overall positive effect on owning of having a partner remains dominant, but it is considerably more important to those on low incomes to have a partner if they are to achieve owner occupation. This interaction term also implies that the lack of a partner is much less disadvantageous in tenure terms to those with medium incomes than it is to those with low incomes.

The third largest significant interaction term in this model is between NOKIDS and ECSTATD. This term applies mainly to women and it will be explored more fully in the gender-specific models introduced below.

The fourth largest significant interaction term that between SEX and ECSTATD which points to the different importance of having paid work for men and women in the attainment of owner occupation. It suggests that, while gender alone is not a good predictor of tenure attainment, it is important, though in different ways, in some categories of work status. Most notably, to be male and out of work decreases the chance of being an owner occupier more than to be female and out of work (45 per cent of unwaged women but only 26 percent of unwaged men have achieved owner occupation). Put another way, this means that amongst male owners, 94 per cent have had to secure full time employment, whereas amongst female owners, the proportion drops to 60 per cent. This again reflects women's relatively high dependency on a partner's income to achieve owner occupation, as well as the different responsibilities for child care that typically fall to young men and women.[9]

The model discussed above in not gender differentiated, in that it cannot adequately allow for the possibility that men and women, even in ostensibly similar household types (and the majority of respondents in our subsample are couples, with or without children) do not arrive at their housing outcomes through essentially the same processes. Yet, our aim in using this data set was always to investigate the different housing experiences of men and women, and to specify the extent to which apparently similar factors have different absolute or relative effects on their respective housing outcomes.

The fitted models for women and men separately are given in Tables 3 and 4. Using the men's data set, no interaction terms were large enough to be selected,and an acceptable fit (p^2 = 0.266) was achieved simply by fitting the independent

Table 3 : The final fitted model for men

Variable	Coefficient	Coeff/SE
GIFT	-0.50699	-4.5251
NOKIDS	0.64445	9.497
ECSTATD	-0.59618	-5.122
PARTEND (1)	-0.60216	-5.982
(2)	-0.54729 E-01	-0.3592*
FAMNETD (1)	-0.17306	-1.869*
(2)	0.77285	6.848
CONSTANT	0.66562	4.436

$* \frac{\text{Coeff}}{\text{SE}} < 2$ (ie not significant)

LL (0) = -958.044

Log likelihood = -703.094

Likelihood ratio (p^2) = 0.266

Table 4 : The Final fitted model for women

Variable	Coefficient	Coeff/SE
GIFT	-0.50699	-4.5251
PARTNER	1.1619	7.996
NOKIDS	0.64657	8.214
ECSTATD	-0.47875	-3.247
PARTEND (1)	-0.65986	-8.068
(2)	-0.10503	-0.8578*
FAMNETD (1)	-229659	-2.227
(2)	0.57469	3.541
GIFT*FAMNETD (1)	0.22611	1.736*
(2)	0.65447E-01	0.4137*
PARTNER*ECSTATD	0.27643	1.952*
NOKIDS*ECSTATD	-0.22032	-2.837
NOKIDS*FAMNETD (1)	-0.20675	-2.456
(2)	-0.15526 E-01	-0.1528*
CONSTANT	0.24151	1.387

$* \frac{\text{Coeff}}{\text{SE}}$ <2 (ie not signigicant)

LL(O) = -1532.404

Log likelihood = -1063.671

Likelihood ratio $\rho 2$ = 0.306

effects of the six remaining independent variables (five of which are in the final model). When applied to women's tenure attainment however, the same model proved unsatisfactory (in particular the goodless of fit chi-squared statistic was significant, implying the esistence of nonrandom difference between the model and the observed outcomes). Significant improvement was achieved by allowing two-way interaction terms to enter the model and the final fitted form included four such terms (two with significant coefficients), with a good overall fit (ρ^2 = 0.306). The differences bwtween the two fitted models indicate that there are differences not only in the range of factors that affect the housing outcomes of men and women, but also in the relative importance of the influences that *are* shared.

Amongst men, the largest independent effect on tenure attainment in family income, where the odds ratio indicates that having a high rather than a low income increases the chances of owning 22 times. Amongst women, while income is not insignificant (it is fourth largest coefficient, and the analysis shows that women in high income households are nearly 10 times as likely to be owners as are those in low income households), by far the largest effect comes from having a partner. The relative odds ratio shows that women with a partiner were over 100 times as likely to be owners as woemn who were single, holiding other factors constant. For men, having a partner has no direct effect on tenure attainment as the term PARTNER does not enter the men's model.

The importance of a partner's income to women seeking owner occupation is apparent from the marked differences in housing outcomes for single men and women is our sample. Ninetyseven per cent of female owners, but only 82 per cent of renters live with a partner and only 29 per cent of single women compared to 76 per cent of single men had achieved ownership by the age of 23. Young men, therefore, are much more able than young women significantly to increase their likelihood of gaining access to owner occupation through raising household incomes (largely by exploiting their own earnings potential in a way that is often denied to working women by the structure of the labour market). Indeed, this seems the only feasible route for men to take, and in accord with this, in terms of housing outcomes the fact of working or not is (in the present economic climate) relatively more important to men that to women in housing terms.

The effects of inheritance and gifts are broadly the same for men and women and we shall leave discussion of this for another essay.[10] In the remainder of the paper we discuss, firstly the importance of economic and labour market variables, and, secondly the importance of family variables, for men's and women's tenure attainment as revealed in the gender-spceific models.

Housing, employment and income

As described briefly above, the gender-specific models imply a different relative role for income and emplyment in the attainment of owner occupation between young men and women. (This is reflected in the fact that income effects are revealed more clearly in these models than for the sample as a whole.) The odds ratios imply that men's chances of becoming owners are 22 times higher if they have high family income rather than low. For women the effect is halved, as having 'high' income increases the probability of owning only 10 times. Similarly, being in work increases men's chances of owning by nearly 11 times, but for women the probability is increased by under seven times. Thus income and employment have different effects on tenure outcome for men and women, and this is ilustrated in Table 5.

This table suggests that it may be as well that women's family income is not mapped onto tenure as markedly as men's since by the age of 23, women are more likely to live in low income households than men, irrespective of whether they own or rent

Table 5 : Income distribution by tenure

Income	Low		Medium		High		Total	
Women	n	%[1]	n	%	n	%	n	%[2]
Owners	595	27.1	642	29.2	961	43.7	2,198	67.2
Tenants	634	59.1	337	31.4	101	9.4	1,072	32.8
ALL	1,229	37.6	979	29.9	1,062	32.5	3,270	100.00
Men								
Owners	220	16.9	487	37.3	597	45.8	1,304	65.6
Tenants	322	47.1	269	39.3	93	13.6	684	34.4
ALL	542	27.3	756	38.0	690	34.7	1,988	100.0
All								
Owners	815	23.3	1,129	32.2	1,558	44.5	3,502	66.6
Tenants	956	54.4	606	34.5	194	11.0	1,756	33.4
ALL	1,771	33.7	1,735	33.0	1,752	33.3	5,258	100.0

Notes : (1) Percentages total across

(2) Percentage total down

their homes (though, overall, more than twice the proportion of tenants as owners have low incomes), while almost two-fifths of the women (nearly 60 per cent of female renters), but little more than a quarter of the men fall into the low income group.

Whereas, in the men's model, economic status, household income and family status have independent effects on the probability of owning, for women, economic status or family income appears in both significant (and both non-significant) interaction terms (see below). It is important to note, then, that the effects of women's economic activity are mediated through their family position. Traditionally, such effects have been hidden in analyses of housing focusing primarily on the household unit. However, when tenure outcomes are considered in relation to the economic activity of both partners in a couple, the relevance of women's earning capacity becomes clear (see Table 6)

Table 6 shows that, in our subsample, there are just two common owner occupier household types amongst couples households where both partners are in work (66 per cent) and households where the man is in work and the woman is economically inactive (25 per cent). In only 1.5 per cent of owner occupier couples is the women the only earner. For couples who are local authority tenants, however, the typical pattern of economic activity is quite different. Just 26 per cent of such couples are both in work in 42 per cent of cases the man is in work and the women has no paid employment, and in 18 per cent of such couples the man is unemployed and the women economically inactive. It is somewhat less rare for only the woman to be in work-a pattern adopted by 3 per cent couples who rent from the local authority. Socio-economic group is also strognly associated with tenure outcome. Nineteen per cent of women and 22 per cent of menowner occupiers are professional/intermediate workers and a further 60 per cent of women and 19 per cent of men owner occupiers have other non-manual employment. This contrasts sharply with local authority tenants, amongst whom just 9 per cent of men and 8 per cent of women work in professional occupations.

We have already demonstrated that in order to achieve owner occupation, 23 year-old women are more reliant than their male counterparts on having a partner. It is clear from Table 6 however that once in a partnership, women's income can be of considerable importance to owner occupying couples. Nevertheless in 87 per cent of such.

Table 6 : Joint economic activity by tenure

	Owners		Council tenants		Total	
	n	%[1]	n	%	n	%
Both employed	2,195	66.4	386	25.8	258	53.7
Man employed Woman inactive	809	24.5	627	41.9	1,436	29.9
Man unemployed						

Woman inactive	59	1.8	274	18.3	333	6.9
Man unemployed						
Woman employed	53	1.6	63	4.2	116	2.4
Both unemployed	9	0.3	26	1.7	35	0
Other	181	5.5	122	8.1	303	6.3
	3,306	68.8	1,498	31.2	4,804	100.0

Note : (1) percentages total down

households (owner occupiers where both partners work) the man earns over half the joint income and on the crucial issue of job security, 58 per cent of men but only 45 per cent of women describe their employment as very secure (the comparable figures for renters are 46 per cent and 38 per cent). Since both income and job security are crucial in obtaining a mortgage, this more detailed examination of the evidence confirms that women must typically rely on their partners' income and employment to attain owner occupation. There is, though, one socio-economic stratum in which women's work is particularly important for households seeking to attain or sustain owner occupation and we consider this in some detail.

Table 5 and 6 and the evidence from comparing the socio-economic profiles of owners and tenants, indicate a striking polarisation between the two tenures in terms of incumbents' earning capacity, employment status and skills. This evidence bears testimony to the pervasiveness of what Forrest (1982) terms the 'residualisation' of the local authority sector. This process involves the increasing concentration of poor and benefitdependent households (ie those with few options in the market) in the council sector, as owner occupation is extended 'downmarket' to accommodate a greater proportion of middle and low income households. during the 1980s, this extension of owner occupation bas been achieved mainly by tenure switches (throught the right-to-buy council hosues at a discount), though the process has been encouraged throughout the post war period by a range of direct and indirect subsidies to lower income house buyers

Women's wages may play an important but relatively neglected role in these twin processes of 'commodification' and residualisation by virtue of their importance to one particular category of male partners-those in skilled manual employment. Unlike most other categories of employee, skilled manual workers are prominent in both main tenures (accounting for 47 per cent of male owners and 51 per cent of male local authority tenants). This group has been identified as most pertinent to government's policies for increasing home ownership. Consequently, their shift into owner occupation is expected to make an important contribution to the extension of a 'property owning democracy' (and as a corollary, to the continued residualisation of the local authority stock). To assess the scope for this contribution, we attempted to distinguish more closely the factors that divide local authority tenants from owner occupiers among male skilled manual workers and it was here that the role of women's paid employment became apparent.

Amongst males, skilled manual workers depend crucially on their own employment status and on their household income to attain owner occupation. This is reflected in the fact that Just 3 per cent of male skilled mannual wokers are unemployed in owner occupation in contrast to 20% of those in local authority housing. However women clearly play an important role in determining whether owner occupation is sustained, as 79 per cent of owning couples where males are in skilled manual occupations include a female partner who works (compared to 66 per cent in the sample as a whole). Differences in family net income between tenure groups are also very marked where the respondent is a male skilled manual worker amongst this group, only 39 per cent of those with low incomes as compared with 83 per cent with high incomes as compared with 83 per cent with high incomes are owner occupiers. Amongst owner occupiers, moreover, male manual workers are more likely to have children than are male non-manual workers : 14 per cent of professional workers but fully 29 per cent of skilled manual workers had children by the age of 23. Given the importance to manual workers of having two workers in the household to raise family incomes sufficiently to support owner occupation, their prospects for attaining and sustaining this tenure must rely to a greater than average extent on the efforts of working mothers.

Evidence from the NCDS provides striking confirmation of the polarisation between tenure sectors of households with different earnings capacities, employment profiles and unemployment rates (or it confirms the pervasiveness-even by 1982, and even amongst relatively 'new' households-of the process usually referred to as residualisation). What perhaps has not fully been appreciated in previous work is the role of women's labour within the present drive to extend owner occupation. It is now clear that amongst households containing male, skilled, manual workers (the key group in the expansion of owner occupation) it is necessary to have two people working in order to sustain the 'ideal' of home owner occupation. While this is increasingly recognised as part of the 'common sense' associated with house purchase in the dynamic markets of the south, it is perhaps less commonly acknowledged as a more general constraint on home-ownership amongst young families in Britain as a whole.

The role of the family

A second striking aspect of the models given in Tables 2 and 3 is the importance to both men's and women's housing outcomes of having children. Strong independent effects occur in both models (having children is second in importance to income for men, and third (after partner and parental tenure) for women). The relative odd ratios indicate that both men and women without children are about 13 times more likely to be owners than those with. Thus, whereas 45 per cent of the sample have at least one child, this includes less than one-third (30 per cent) of owners and fully three-quarters (75 per cent) of renters.

Whether because of eligibility rules (which favour young 'conventional' families with low incomes), patterns of demand or lack of alternative opportunities, the relationship between parenthood and renting for men is direct and independent: it holds for all levels of income and employment and persists irrespective of inheritance or parental tenure. For 23-year-old males (and their partners who on average, are even younger), being in a household with children has a direct (inhibiting) effect on their early access to owner occuption (see also Murphy and Sullivan, 1986). Amongst women, on the other hand, the efficacy of parenthood as a predictor of tenure attainment interacts significantly with two other varibles: economic status and family net income.

The consequences of parenthood for housing outcome are different for working mothers than for the unwaged (as indicated by the interaction between NOKIDS and ECSTATD). The for findings are, at first glance, counter-intuitive, for amongst women without paid employment, Parenthood appears to *increase* the probability of home-ownership. What this probably implies is that those households with children who can afford to buy their home can also afford to allow mothers not to work, whereas, amongst renters with children, the necessity for mothers to work is greater. Consistent with this, the consequences of parenthood for tenure attainment also vary with income (as reflected in the second significant interaction term in the women's model, between NOKIDS and ECSTATD). This interaction term is most relevant for medium and low income groups. Whereas having a medium rather than low income would ordinarily increase the probability of wonership, amongst parents, the effect of this income increment is dampened. Not surprisingly, when low income groups have children, their probability of renting (which is already high) is greatly in creased.

Early parenthood, directly, or in interaction with income and employment variables, is a very powerful predictor of the likelihood of renting amongst young adults. Whether or not this matters ie; whether or not renting is a disadvantage or an asset, overall-depends on its implications both for future housing opportunities and for current housing experiences (as indexed by housing conditions, residential satisfaction and so on).

As regards the future, this cohort's housing career will become apparent from subsequent sweeps of the NCDS. It is not necessary to speculate much further here except to note that although there is evidence from earlier research that the first attainment of owning or public renting is a good indicator of future trend patterns, this may be a legacy of the time when a buoyant private rented sector provided a 'gateway' to the other major tenures, and when public renting was seen as a generally available alternative to owning. Currently, the public sector is declining in size and scope and new provision is almost exclusively orientated towards a narrow range of special' needs. The 'average' renter is therefore likely increasingly to aspire to owner occupation to avoid remaining in a residual public sector. Thus 87 per cent and 82 per cent of male and female renters respectively, hope to buy a place of their own at some time in the future.[12] Many of these will have the opportunity to buy their council home, and whether or not this is an asset or a liability depends very much on where they live and on the kind and quality of accommodation they have been allocated.

There remains, then, the question of what consequences the greater likelihood of renting amongst parents has for current housing experiences. Given the overall improvement of housing conditions in the last 40 years (by this we mean improvement in amenities rather than in the structure of the buildings), it is not surprising that the majority of owners and renters were not experiencing housing deprivation as measured by the traditional indicators of shared or inferior basis amenitites. Amongst couples, moveover, the presence or absence of children had no discernible consequences for the type of dwelling occupied: over 80 per cent of these households live in a house or bungalow rather than a flat, irrespective of whether they have children. parent hood does, however, make a difference in the dwellings available to single mothers, who are much more likely to live in a house than are their childless counterparts (the proportions are 65 per cent and 39 per cent, respectively, whereas over all, the proportion of single women living in a house is 53 per cent).

Parenthood also, and predictably, increases the density of room occupancy for both couples and singles. Nineteen per cent of couples with children but only half a per cent of those without live at densities on one or more persons per room. Amongst single people however, it is striking that, irrespective of whether they are parents, women have, on average, less residential space than men. Seventy-three per cent of single men but only 65 per cent of single, childless women and 23 per cent of single mothers live at densities of less than half a person per room.

Residential location is at least as important as living conditions for the quality of life, and, because both intra-urban and regional location is so important in relation to differential house price inflation, this factor is also important for families' housing futures: this is true for both renters and owners, since it gives an indication of whether the purchase of a council home is a good investment. In any sector, then, location is a good indication of the ability or potential of dwellings to store and accumulate wealth. Fortunately, the individual records of the NCDS have been tagged with ACORN codings (derived from the 1971 census) which alows us to make a broad classification of respondents according to whether they live in poor, intermediate or good neighbourhoods of predominantly public or private sector dwellings[13]. The findings are given in Table 7, which shows the relationship between parenthood and quality of residential environments. It is clear from this table that, irrespective of whether respondents live in areas which are predominantly owner-occupied or in areas where renting is more common-this is irrespective of whether they live in neighbourhoods whose residents were supposedly housed according to need or where they gained access according to ability to pay-families with children are more likely to live in poorer environments than those without.

Within ownership zones the effect of children is to decrease the probability of living in the best environments and increase the probability of living in poorer neighbourhoods. This can be interpreted as a straightforward consequences of the economics of housebuying *vis a vis* the costs of raising children. In renter zones, by contrast, those eligible for the `better' estates achieve such locations irrespective of the presence of children, and the main effect of parenthood is to increase the probability of renting in poor rather than in

Table 7 : The consequences of family structure for residential location

	Area type[1] Poorest[2]		Interm-ediate[3]		Best[4]		Total
Public renting[6]	n	%[5]	n	%	n	%	
Children	373	34.6	205	19.0	500	46.4	1,078
No children	193	25.8	206	27.5	350	46.7	749
Total	566	31.0	411	22.5	850	46.5	1,827
Owner occupation[7]							
Children	341	28.2	535	44.3	331	27.4	1,207
No children	435	21.8	843	44.2	719	36.0	1,997
Total	776	24.2	1,378	43.0	1,050	32.0	3,204
Whole sample							
Children	714	31.2	740	32.4	831	36.4	2,285
No children	628	22.9	1,049	38.2	1,069	38.9	2,746
Total	1,342	26.6	1,789	35.6	1,900	37.8	5,031

Notes: (1) Based on the ACORN classification described in footnote 13.

(2) In predominantly public sector neighbourhoods this includes ACORN categories 16, 21 and 23 (peripheral, high rise and `stressed' estates); in owner-occupied neighbourhoods it includes ACORN 11, 12, 25, 26, 27 (Low quality inner and declining areas and low status terraces with immigrants).

(3) In rented districts this includes categories 19, 20 and 22 (middle income, demographically ageing estates); in owner dominated zones it includes mixed and older terraces with low unemployment, rural areas, student and 'affuent' inner areas (notably, categories 2, 4, 8, 9, 10, 13, 14, 15 and 24).

(4) ACORN categories 1, 13, 17, 18 (recent and family estates, council sector) and categories 5, 6, and 30-34 (modern private housing, suburbs and commuter villages in owner-occupied zones).

(5) Percentages total across.

(6) Areas dominated by renting.

(7) Areas dominated by owning.

intermediate areas. This must be interpreted as a reflection of the housing allocation system which, though it is supposed to house according to need, has many informal rules and procedures and which, because of the pressures to ration a limited resource fo uneven quality *quickly*, often works according to criteria other than need. This is well documented by Clapham and Kitrea (1986) and by Henderson and Karn (1987), and it includes a combination of stereotyping (in which, for instance, a single mother may be deemed less deserving of a `nice' home than a conventional family) and the (income-related) ability of prospective tenants to reject offers and wait for a better opportutniy.

Conclusion

The key implications of our preliminary work on men's and women's housing attainment in modern Britain, based on the cohort tracked by the NCDS, are as follows. Firstly, labour market position, the intergenerational transfer of wealth and family status are all, singly or in interaction, important influences on young people's tenure attainment. We have shown in this paper that the precise combinations and relative effects of these variables vary between men and women, even within a single birth cohort.

Secondly, the variables that reflect labour market position, economics status and income clearly operate in different ways to produce distinctive housing outcomes for men and women. The process by which these outcomes are produced from given labour market variables needs further investigation. However, we have shown that male, skilled manual workers (whose flight from local authority renting is now critical for the continual extension of owner occupation) rely more on women's earnings that do other men in the cohort, in their attempt to attain owner occupation.

Furthermore, since the greater propensity of manual workers than of non-manual workers to have children persists even in owner occupation, it seems likely that the continued extension of owner occupation may be sustained partly by working mothers. The so-called `commodification' of housing, and its corollary in the 'residualisation` of the public sector, apparently relies more on women's work than has hitherto been recognised. Thirdly, while having a partner may have more far-reaching consequences for women than for men early in their housing `career', parenthood-a second element of family status-is an important factor affecting tenure and residential location for both men and women. The most obvious housing consequence of early child-bearing is its influence on families eligibility for, or restriction to, the public rented sector. Our analysis suggests that the public sector, even by 1982, was not able to meet the demand for subsidised housing that exists amongst young families. One consequence is that such households (whose disposable in come is reduced by expenditure on children) are over-represented in the poorer segments of the housing market. However, even those 23-year-old parents who have secured a council tenancy seem more likely to live in poorer areas than do their childless counterparts. Existing feminist theory suggests that `conventional' families are favoured by the housing bureaucracy. Our analysis indicates that, because housing systems simultaneously reproduce more than one aixis of inequality (ie; because they mediate labour as well as gender relations), this direct link cannot always be made.

Our analysis so far has been essentially exploratory, and the points we have reised require further elaboration. We have, however, drawn attention to a surprisingly neglected area of mainstream housing studies and illustrated the salience of 'gender' for studies of tenure attainment, for research on the process of residential differentiation, and as a centrepiece of conceptual and theoretical discussion of key shifts in the structure of the housing system. In so far as housing is one of a range of markets and institutions responsible for the reproduction of social inequality, it is clear that an appreciation of the role of gender relations is as central to the explanatory task as are the more commonly specified (and, of course, intimately related) axes of inequality relationg to `race', class and the social relations of consumption.

NOTES

1. This is based on a cohort of all children born in one week in 1958. We are using the fourth sweep, completed in 1981. when the respondents were 23 years old.
2. Longit models have many advantages for the analysis of social surveys, but perhaps the major one is that they are specifically designed for the estimation of models where there is a dichotomous dependent variable (in our case either owning or renting). In such a case multiple regression analysis is inappropriate because ordinary least squares estimation leads to biased and inconsistent estimators (Payne, C., 1977).

3. Logit modelling here provides an estimation of the probability that a person (or household) with a particular characteristic or combination of characteristics is an owner-occupier rather than a renter. Having assessed the combined effect of a set of independent variables , an estimation of the relative effects of each one can also be made. For each independent variable, the coefficient estimated gives the log-odds that an individual falling into each category of that variable owns rather than rents. That is if Y_i is the 0/1 outcome of an event following the form Y_i = BXi + e_i (where B is a matrix). A logistic transformation gives the probability that Y_i = 1 as;

$$P_i = \frac{1}{1+e^{-X_iB}} \quad \text{and} \quad 1 - P_i = \frac{1}{1+e^{X_iB}}$$

where the estimation maxismises the likelihood function L = Prob (Y_i). This gives coefficient estimates which represent the log of the odds of the occurrence of Y_i/ ((P_i) / (1 - P_i)). The translation antilog (conefficient* 2) converts the additive, regression like coefficients into multiplicative parameters, which can be interpreted as `odds' rather than `logodds' (Haberman, 1974). It can be seen that variables which have a positive effect on the probability of owning (ie odds > 1) will be associated with a positive estimated coefficient. The model was fitted using the statistical package BMDP.

4. This allows the progressive inclusion in the model of any term (from the set previously specified) which passes a given lower limit of the maximum likelihood ratio. An alternative approach would be to choose a priori a model whose terms could be justified on the grounds of past empirical work and substantive theoretical agruement. In our case, whilst we have been able to inform our choice of variables from previous empirical and theoretical work we have little guidance either concerning which of the many possible models is most probable, or concerning the interaction terms that are likely to prove to be most important.

5. This allowed us, first, to test the hypothesis that each of the independent variables acts on the dependent variable additively and independently, and secondly to identify interactions between each pair of independent variables (to see, for instance, whether the effect of family status on housing outcomes varies according to income). The hierarchical rule in operation allowed the introduction of second (or higher) order terms only when each of the lower order terms had been entered, since the interpretation of the higher order terms would be difficult in the absence of this restriction.

6. Two different goodness of fit measures are used in previous work. The first is based on the reduction in the chi-squared statistic between the model in which only the constant is fitted and the final model (Payne, 1977); and the second compares the in-crease in log likelihood between these same two models (Hensher and Johnson, 1981). Neither is exactly analogous to the R^2 statistic usually reported in regression analysis and here we will favour the rho^2 (p^2) statistic based on log likelihood because it is more suitable where some cell counts are small. Hensher and Johnson (1981) point out `that values of p^2 between 0.2 and 0.4 are considered extremely good fits so that the analyst should not be looking for values in excess of 0.9 as is often the case when using R^2 in ordinary regression' (p51).

7. The goodness of fit chi-squared (C^2 = 2s [Obs. Ln (Obs/Exp]) can be used to test whether additional terms improve the fit of the model significantly. To test whether second order terms should be added to the overall model, for instance, we compare

C^2 (F) (the C^2 (F) the C^2 of the model including only first order terms, with C^2 (S) (the C2 of the model including second order terms), where C^2 (F) - C^2 (S) has a chi-squared distribution, with degrees of freedom equal to the difference between the degrees of freedom in the two models. For the whole model, C^2 (F) = 253.153, DF = 164; C^2 (S) = 155.323, DF = 152 so the test statistic has a value of 97.83, DF = 12, which is significant at the 0.995 level.

8. We follow Francis and Payne (1977) who note that 'a convenient way to interpret the relative effect of different factors and the levels within them is to look at the relative odds ratio for pairs of levels within each factor'. We are interested, they observe, in odds ratios which depart from 1. . . . . . the greater the departure the higher the difference between the two levels' (p255). For example, within the factor SEX, the logit model provides an estimate of the odds of men owning rather than renting. The relative odds ratio (of women/men) simply calculates the ratio of these two odds, giving an estimate of the relative odds of women owning compared to men. The more this ratio departs from one, the greater the discrepancy between men's and women's probability of ownership.

9. The two remaining significant interactions terms both identify the relatively small effects on tenure attainment that result from having a low rather than a medium household income. The interaction between ECSTATD and FAMNETD show, predictably, that for those respondents who are out of work it is less disadvantageous in tenure terms to have a medium household income than a low income. Similarly, the interaction between NOKIDS and FAMNETD implies that if there are some children in the household it is more disadvantageous to have a low than a medium income.

10. In both models the effect of having had owner-occupying parents is strongly positive and additive (for women the odds ratio is 14, and for men 11). Similarly the effect of having received a gift is positive and additive in both models (with odds ratios of six for women and eight for men).

11. The generally higher demand for public housing from younger families can be inferred from the difference between male and female respondents in the survey. Just over a third of men (34 per cent) but only 29 per cent of women (whose partners are on average older than 23) have had to resort to an application for public housing during their short 'career'.

12. Amongst parents however, women are more likely than men to perceive this option as unavailable (the proportions are 16 per cent and 10.5 per cent), and this probably reflects women's greater likelihood of being single parents.

13. ACORN (a classification of residential neighbourhoods) defines enumeration districts according to their mix of characteristics, based on a multivariate analysis of census data. It is essentially a marketing device, produced by CACI. The NCDS used the 1971 classification which distinguished 35 area types (whose components and labels are different from those used in the later, 1981, classification, which is now more widely adopted in social research).

REFERENCES

Allport, C. (1983). Women and suburban housing. P. Williams (ed) *Social process and the city,* 64-87 Sydney: Allen and Unwin.

Austerberry, H. and Watson, S. (1983). *Women on the margins.* London: City University Housing Research Group.

Baldsock, C. and Cass, B. (eds) (1983). *Women, social welfare and the state.* London: Allen and Unwin.

Brailey, M. (1986) Women's access to council housing. *Occasional Paper* 25 Glasgow: The Planning Exchange.

Brion, M. and Tinker, A. (1980) *Women in housing: access and influence.* London: Housing Centre Trust.

Clapham,D. and Kintrea, K. (1986). Rationing choice and constraint: the allocation of public housing in Glasgow. *Journal of Social Policy,* 15: 51-67.

Crompton, R. and Mann, M. (1986). *Gender and Stratification.* Cambridge" Polity Press.

Cyrenians (1985). *Women and Homelessness* London: National Cyrenians Women and Homelessness Group.

Dale, J. and Foster P. (1986) *Feminists and state welfare.* London: Routledge and Kegan Paul.

Department of Employment (1986). *New Earnings Survey* London: HMSO.

Forrest, R. (1982). The social implications of council house sales. J. English (ed) *The Future of Council Housing,* 97-114. London: Croom Helm.

Francis, J. G. and Payne, C. (1977). The use of the logistic model in political science; British Elections, 1964-1970. *Political Methodology,* 4: 233-270.

Gilbert, J. (1986). *Not just a roof.* Birmingham: Birmingham Standing Conference for the Single Homeless.

Goodman, L. A. (1972). A model for the analysis of surveys. *American Journal of Sociology,* 77: 1035-1086.

Greater London Council (1984). Black women and housing. Unpublished report by the Director General.

Haberman, S. J. (1974). *The analysis of frequency* data Chicago: University of Chicago Press.

Hayden, D. (1980). What would a non-sexist city be like? Speculations on housing, urban design and human work. *Sings,* 5: 5171-5187.

Henderson, J. and Karn, V. (1987). Race, class and state housing. Aldershot Gower.

Hensher, D.A and Johnson, L. W. (1981). *Applied Discrete Modelling.* London: Croom Helm.

Immigration Widows Campaign (1984). *Trial by separation.* London: IWC.

Leavitt, J. (1985). The shelter-service crisis and single Pauents. Birch, E. L. (ed) *The Unsheltered Women* 153-176. New Jersey: Centre for Urban Policy Research.

McDowell, L. (1983). Towards an understanding of gender division of urban space. *Environment and Planning D: Society and Space,* 1: 59-72.

Mc Gregor, A. (1979). Area externalities and unemploment. Jones, C. (ed) *Urban Deprivation and the Inner City,* 92-112 London: Croom Helm.

Martin, J. and Roberts, C. (1984). *Women and unemployment: a lifetime perspective.* Department of Employment, OPCS London: HMSO

Morrow-Jones, H. A. (1986). The geography of housing elderly and female households. *Urban Geography* 7: 263-269.

Munro, M. (1987). *Housing and labour market interactions, a review.* Discussion Paper 12, Centre for Housing Research Glasgow University: Glasgow.

Murphy, M. and Sullivan, O (1986). Unemployment housing and household structure among young adults. *Journal of Social Policy* 15: 205-222.

Omarshah, S. n. d. *Asian women and housing*. London ASHA Asian Women's Aid Research Project.

Payne, C. (1977). The log linear model for contingency tables. O'Muircheartaigh, C. A. and Payne, C. (eds.) *The Analysis of Survey Data, Vol 2,* 105-144. London: Wiley and Sons.

Payne. J. and Payne, G. (1977). Housing pathways and stratification: a study of life chances in the housing market. *Jorunal of Social Policy,* 6: 129-156.

Saegart, S. (1980). Masculine cities and feminine sub-urbs: polarised ideas, contradictory realities. *Signs* 5: 596-611.

Schafer, R. and Ladd, H. (1981). *Discrimination in Mortgage Lending*. Cambridge, Mass: MIT Press.

Shear, W. B. and Yezer, A. M. J. (1985). Discrimination in urban housing finance: an empirical study across cities. *Land Economics,* 61: 292-302.

Ungerson, C. (1985). (ed) *Women in social policy, a reader*. London: Macmillan.

Vincent, J. n.d. *The housing needs of young signgle mothers.* Social Policy Research Ltd.

Warr, M. (1984). Fear of victimisation: Why are women and the elderly more afraid? *Social Science Quarterly,* 65: 691-702.

Watson, S. (1986a). Women and Housing or Feminist Housing Analysis: Housing Studies 1: 1-10.

Watson, S. (1986b). Housing and the family - the marginalization of non-family households in Britain, *In ternational Journal of Urban and Regional Research,* 10: 8-28.

Watson, S. and Austerberry, H. (1986). *Housing and homelessness.* London: Routledge and Kegan Paul.

Watson, S. and Helliwell, C. (1985). Home ownership- are women excluded? *Australian Quarterly,* 57: 21-31.

Willaims, F. (forthcoming). *Social policy, a critical introduction: issues of class, race and gender.* Cambridge: Polity Press.

Wilson, E. (1977). *Women and the Welfare State. London:* Tavistock.

Wilson, E. (1983). *What is to be done about violence against women?* Harmondsworth: Penguin.

Moria Munro and Susan J. Smith: Glasgow University Centre for Housing Research.

The authors are grateful to the ESRC data archive for supplying a copy of the NCDS data and to the NCDS User Support Group, City University for advice on its use. We would also like to thank Hal Kendig and two referees for helpful comments on an earlier draft of the paper.

CHAPTER-5

Food for Thought : Making Women Visible

Pamela L. Sayne

---

1. Introduction [(1)]

This Paper outlines the major contribution made by women (particularly poor women) to sustaining life and how this contribution is misunderstood or ignored. It suggests that the lack of investment in women's knowledge, skills and technologies contributes to the erosion of the resource base and makes impossible the achievement of sustainable development. Thus a consideration of sustainable development demands a gendered analysis.

Women globally are more often expected to provide the daily food for communities and families than to provide food for thought on sustenance itself. This reflects a situation that must be addressed in order to achieve the continued existence of our species and all other on this finite earth. The message is quite straightforward: we must all (and I do mean all of us) understand and use a gendered analysis in addressing human settlements and global environments. Why am I insistent on this point? Leaving aside for the moment the essential demographic and political fact that although women are majority of the world's population we hold title to only 1 per cent of the world's property; it is essential to realize that women and men have differing relationships to the environment. I will argue that women (and particularly women involved in the subsistence sector) have a great deal to teach us about human settlements and the possibility of "sustainable development".

First, I must address the term "sustainable development". This expression is now commonly used in contexts that render its two parts contradictory, with the contradictions built into organizations, households and countries. There is a simple way to express this contradiction: men develop it, women clean and sustain it.

Vandana Shiva, in her book *Staying Alive* illustrates the contradiction in the phrase "sustainable development" and what can happen when academic work fails to acknowledge a gendered bias.[2] She writes:

"In December 1987, two prizes were awarded in Stockholm: the Nobel Prize for economics was given to Robert Solow of Massachusetts Institute of Technology for his theory of growth based on the dispensability of nature. In Solow's words, The world can, in effect, get along without natural resources, so exhaustion is just an event, not a catastrophe. At the same time, the Alternative Nobel Prize (the popular name for the Right Livelihood Award), instituted for vision and work contributing to making life more whole, healing our planet and uplifting humanity honoured the women of the Chipko movement who, as leaders and activists, had put the life of the forests above their own and, with their actions, had stated that nature is indispensable to survival.".

Shiva brings to our attention and eminent economist making the life-threatening suggestion that our world can get along without natural resources about as easily, and with as little consequence, as we can get along without food. We do not need to look very far to find the tragedies due to lack of natural resources or to go very long ourselves without food or water to know the impending results. Solow's approach does not sustain life. The acknowledgment of the contradiction at the heart of the phrase "sustainable development" is the beginning of a gendered analysis.

Many researchers, Vandana Shiva among them, have reported on the Chipko movement in northern India. In the forested Himalayan foothills that are their home, the Chipko women have taken a political initiative against the reductionist economistic approach which views forests as tree producing facilities whose purpose is to generate capital and jobs for the development of a market economy. These women know that the forests directly provide a renewable source of fuel, shelter, fodder, food and medicines for the local human inhabitants and for the diversity of other life in the area. These women know that the earth's resources are indispensable to our health and survival, and that women are indispensable to our understanding of our earth. And we only need to be conscious of our own experience as living beings to understand this basic principle.

Women's knowledge and the specificity of women's role in sustaining life has all too often been peripheral to discourse on what has come to be called "sustainable development". Yet women are not, and cannot be, separable from a sustainable life, despite the dominance of Solow's world view. Nor are women's ways of knowing separable.

The Chipko women teach us that diversity must be strengthened, not isolated and questioned. They teach us that, by themselves, test tube solutions to environmental concerns are not appropriate. The wholeness and complexity of our environment must be acknowledged. The essential arrogance of the western scientific approach, exemplified in Solow's words, will only lead to more ignorance of the past and tyranny in the future, in the name of development.

Women, particularly poor women, continue to play the primary role in taking care of the planet and its inhabitants. This has been demonstrated throughout history as women have provided the sustainable subsistence living for their communities. Indigenous women in many parts of the globe still have knowledge about forest management, the medicinal use of plants, and an understanding of crop management that has been passed down through the centuries. Indigenous women have not only sustained their communities but have also done so with little environmntal degradation to our planet. Ironically, this has been accomplished through what has now become, in the development industry, a problem to overcome: women have accomplished sustainable human settlements though the subsistence economy. A number of accounts demonstrate how an ecological balance between human settlements and natural resources was achieved, only to become unbalanced through insensitive, and ultimately unsustainable, "development".

This hindsight is only useful if one continues to be intent on (to use a metaphor) driving in reverse. Without the enhanced perception of a gendered analysis to guide us into the future, a crash is inevitable. In spite of women's central role for thousands of years in contributing to sound, ecologically sustainable development, men have dominated the public discussion, data collection, and political agenda, rendering women silent, invisible, and valueless within the dominant global political economy. Women have been so invisible that some people, in the core of their hearts, may secretly believe that I am making this up. the lack of awareness of women's role in subsistence economies and the lack of documentation with which to locate women in demographic and urbanization patterns has left the role of women in sustaining communities invisible. Therfore, women's struggles for survival and quality of life are little understood or supported within dominant development strategies. Two examples can illustrate this.

Urban poor women in industrially overdeveloped countries struggle to produce subsistence, shelter and other basic services for themsleves and their families. Their efforts, if they are recognized at all, often become merely a subsidiary concern of municipal planning policy. For instance, a number of homeless women in Toronto, forced to use emergency shelters because of domestic violence, have been struggling for over five years to get one small, permanent, non-profit housing project built. Meanwhile, they have witnessed massive corporate and governmental resources being allocated to the "development" of a domed stadium. Giving priority to such development projects is a very common scenario.

There are numerous examples from the Third World which show how women's traditional role in constructing housing is ignored, while young men are trained to build with costly, non-indigenous materials. Housing thus becomes inaccessible to women because of building codes which promote costly imported materials and western-style building technologies. The lack of investement in women's knowledge, skills and "technologies" contributes to the erosion of the resource base and defeats the goal of achieving sustainable communities. Women thereby begin to lose access to basic resources for survival, as have the women in industrialized countries. There are not isolated situations. Instead, there is a global trend toward viewing women, like natural resources, as ultimately dispensable to development.

Despite women's continuing invisibility, their are some things we do know about women. We know, for instance, that 30 to 50 per cent of the world's households are led by women, and that the number of women-led, single parent families is increasing both in the over-industrialized and the under-industrialized worlds, as is poverty for women and their dependent children. We know that female migration has increased due to poverty caused by drought, floods, environmental degradation, lack of access to land, wars, and other preventable disasters.

We know that there are few reliable statistics on women's economic activities because they are often subsistence activities and therefore not included in government statistics such as Gross Domestic Product. We know that poor health and starvation follow when women's subsistence crop production, which feeds their families, is changed to cash crop production for export. Hence, as the GDP of a country increases with cash crop production, increased ill health and malnourishment among women and children often result. Even though this is common knowledge, our political and economic will has not been strong enough to change a practice which is supported by the World Bank and other institutions of "development".

We also know that the lack of recognition and support of the subsistence sector is a major cause of both environmental degradation and increasing proverty. We know that women, as the main producers in the subsistence sector, are directly and immediately faced with the consequences of the increasing pollution of the air, land and water, global warming, and the destruction of the earth's ability to supports us. As once arable land became unusable, women and the families they support face worsening health and nutrition, increasing birth defects, and hunger.

Women also know that, as our non-renewable use of natural resources for energy increases each year, we must begin to ask fundamental questions such as by whom and in whose interests are these resources being depleted and destroyed.

II PROSPECTS FOR THE FUTURE

WHAT CAN WE do to ensure that we have some prospects for the future, and that our children's children will inherit a world that can sustain them? Development must be measured in real terms of satisfied human need, not in false terms of the scale of a market economy (eg. GDP) which ignores the actual value of natural resources, women and life itself. As Marilyn Waring, a feminist economist, clearly illustrates, health must be measured by clean air and water, not by the amount of money spent to clean up polluted waters or to build air pollution control.(3) Housing must be measured by those having secure and safe homes, not by the cost of construction or the number of dwellings built. Simply counting new dwellings built does not guarantee people secure and affordable homes in such dwellings. Construction costs do not reflect jobs or income generation for women, children, the elderly, the disabled, the sick and others who contribute to the community and are required to pay for homes.

The subsistence economy needs to be recognized, protected, planned for, and enabled. This requires changing legislation, women's access to land, women's mangagement of resources and technological improvement of traditional, local building materials and other domestic technologies. And most important, as Gita Sen and Caren Grown clearly state, The perspective of poor and oppressed women provides a unique and powerful vantage point from which we can examine the effects of develpment programmes and strategies."[4]

As Vandana Shiva documents, reductionist thinking underlies the basis of the market economy, and contributes to killing the diversity of life, our planet, and women.[5] Yet very often it is women, the poorest of the poor, who have the knowledge to sustain our planet and human life. Political will must support women, and prevent the destruction of generations of knowledge, the evolution of planetary life and, eventually, humanity itself. A political will that insists on a system using a market economy that does not work in the best interest of sustaining life, will surely lead us to further destruction as a planet and as a life form. The indigenous knowledge of local communities in managing their ecosystems needs to be recognized and respected before it is lost. Gender based, community centred planning, and a celebration of diversity must be the way of the future and must be central to all discourse on human settlements.

This approach should be reflected in statistics through the disaggregation of data based on gender. Individual not household income, hours of work, production, and consumption (market and subsistence) must be understood as a means to measure the human condition. This would make visible how women's position has been weakened by rural to urban migration; women's role has been changed from producer to consumer, while she has lost access to resources and political strength, thereby becoming "dispensable" to "development". Women's and their communities means of survival are clearly threatened by "development" as their relation to the land, shelter and community is changed.

Means must be provided for women to meet and exchange information about their specific role in society and how it is hindered or assisted by "development" programmes. Women engaged in subsistence production must be asked how we can protect what remains of the earth's resources for the benefit of all.

We must break down the barriers between academics, activists and practitioners and implement processes that clearly represent social, cultural and economic diversity, including gender. This is absolutely essential for the survival of our species and the living planet.

In conclusion. I hope this paper provides adequate food for thought. Some may consider this offering of food for thought to be more in the nature of bad tasting medicine! I'm trying to resist the urge to simply say that it's good for you, so urge instead that if you find the notion of gendered analysis to be indigestible, you should perhaps continue to ruminate. And for those of you, sisters and brothers, who already have seen the absolute necessity of incorporating a gendered analysis in your activities, then I say simply, "Keep up the Struggle".

REFERENCES

1. This paper was adapted from a presentation made on behalf of the Women and Shelter Group of the Habitat International Coalition to the international colloquium on Urbanization and the Environment. Human Settlement and Sustainable Development, University of Toronto, June 22 1990.
2. Shiva, Vandana (1989) *Staying Alive,* Zed Books Ltd. London.
3. Waring, Marilyn (1988). *If Women* counted, Harper and Row, New York.
4. Sen, Gita and C. Grown (1987), *Development, Crisis, and Alternative Visions,* Monthly Review Press, New York.
5. See not 2.

Addional reading

World commission of Environment and Development (1987), *Our Common future,* Oxford University Press, New York.

Lewenhak, Sheila (1988), *The Revaluation of Women's Work,* Croom Helm, London.

Redclift, Michael (1987), *Sustainable Development,* Methuen and Co, Ltd., London.

Mies, Maria (1986), *Patriarchy and Accumulation on a World Scale,* Zed books Ltd., London,

Sticher, Sharon (1982), *Migrant Labour in Kenya: Capitalism and African Response, 1985-1975,* Longman Group Ltd., Essex, UK.

CHAPTER-6

Social Action Theory and the Women's Movement : An Analysis of Assumptions

Bill Lee and Wenedy Weeks

Introduction

Assumptions and theoretical assertions underpinning social change interventions demand constant re-examination and reflection in light of the realities of the populations at which they are aimed. Brandwein (1984: 169-70) suggests that most social movements become caught up and eventually reproduce the thought and structure and thus, the conditions they seek to overthrow. It is crucial to examine the underlying assumptions of theory to create genuine social change strategies. This paper suggests that when some key assumptions underlying social action-oriented community organization theories are placed against the experience of Women's Movement organizing, they must be questioned. this has implications for future theory development in community organization in general and social action organizing in particular.

Community Organizing Assumptions

Many writers point out the difficulties and complexities of defining community organization. (Aldred, 1977: 421)

Theories and practice are based on a wide range of assumptions about the nature of society, the origin of social problems and the efficacy of various strategies for organizing. The ideological spectrum is broad indeed, covering as it does consensus views like those of Ross (1967), centralized planning conceptions like those of Perlman and Gurin (1972) and Moynihan (1969), and so-called conflict analyses like those of Alinsky (1969), Freire (1972), and Piven and Cloward (1977). Clearly then these last four authors are not representative of community organization theory in general. They have come to occupy a critical position within the discipline relative to social action. Indeed, if we accept Brager and Specht's view of Rothman's well-known topology as the creation of "analytical extremes", these four authors fall within the social action category. In other words they occupy a position within community organization theory which views the interests of disadvantaged groups as differing radically from those who have power. They perceive community organization or social action as an attempt to alter formal institutional policies or to make changes in the distribution of power. (Brager and Specht 1973: 127.) Their influences on theory and practice can be seen variously in the work of a number of writers, (Staples, 1984; Rubin and Rubing 1981 Kahn, 1982; Lee, 1985; Speeter, 1979; Booth, 1976). The authors of this paper have chosen the social action orientation as most appropriate for consideration of community organization theory in relation to the women's movement, which has identified women as an oppressed group. According to Hole and Levine, both 19th century and 20th century feminists have "engaged in a fundamental re-examination of the role of women in all social, political, economic and cultural institutions" (Hole and Levine, 1973; 1). The women's movement is concerned with changes in the personal and socio-political consciousness and behaviour of women, and with the redistribution of power (Adams et al, 1985; Booth, 1976; Mitchell, 1971).

Wilson (1977; 9) asserted that community workers have two major lessons to learn from the Women's Movement. First "that daily life is political" and, second, that women must speak for themselves, She wrote "community workers must learn to listen to women instead of telling them what they want, what they are `really' like, and how they should be".

This paper examines assumptions concerned with analysis with analysis of society; target population; the basis for unity in action; the nature of "community", and arenas for organizing. The assumptions implicit in the theories of the selected authors are examined in relation to the important realities and experiences identified as underlying women's movement organizing.

Class Conflict or Sexism ?

The selected theorists generally assume a conflict analysis of society. Whether they are referring to "elites" and "poor people" as do Piven and Cloward, Alinsky's "haves" and "have-nots," or the oppressors and oppressed characterized by Freire, they essentially accept Piven and Cloward's dictum that, "those who control the means of physical coercion, and those who control the means of producing wealth have power over those who do not" (1977: 1). They characterize society as an arena for class struggle, or at least a place where certain groups have less access to power and resources than others. In a sense these authors are concerned with the problem of alienation, with the effect of powerlessness and a lack of understanding of the events in which they are caught (Brager and Specht, 1973: 125).

While the class or conflict analysis is a perspective accepted by some parts of the women's movement (Adams et al, 1985), women's movement organizing rests on an analysis of sexism. Sexism has been defined by Mitchell as "the inferiorization (Attitudinal and actual) of one sex by the other" (1971: 64). Safilios-Rothschild calls it the "entire range of attitudes, beliefs, practices, policies, laws and behaviours discriminating against women or against men on the basis of their gender".

The absence in the selected community organizing theories of any appreciation of the complex interplay between gender and other variables, for example, class, limits the direct usefulness of their social analysis for amny aspects of women's movement organizing. In a manner similar to other social science practitioners and action theorists, the four authors do not differentiate on the grounds of sex either of the group to be organized or of the organizer.

Only the Poor ?

The second common assumption of the four theorists is the orientation of their organizing frameworks around "poor people". None of the authors suggest that their theoretical frameworks might be differentially applied to groups of people possessing attributes additional to that of poverty—race or sex, for example—which might specify the disadvantaged experience further. This is not necessarily to suggest that the authors are unaware of cultural variation. Alinsky (1972: 84-5) for example, refers to the importance of the organizer "getting into the experience and culture of the group to be organized". Freire (1972: 89) focuses considerable attention on action coming out of "awareness of the shared objective situation of the people". Piven and Cloward (1977: 20, 21, 36) suggest that organizers have little effect on protest movements and that the extent and nature of a people's protest is shaped by their daily experience, and the social/institutional context in which they find themselves. However, what appears to be missing is a sense that organizing theory can profit by the consideration of the unique experiences of particular groups of people—in this case, women and the women's movement. The authors in contrast appear to assume that the theoretical frame-works can be generally applied to a wide range of particular situations.

There is a further limitation with theories which assume a general disadvantage or common poverty when considering women's movement organizing. First is the obvious point that women are not all poor in economic terms. The women's movement, like the more recent environmental, anti-nuclear, or consumer movements, has the potential for cutting across class lines. There has in fact been considerable debate on women's class position (McKee, 1989). Traditional sociological analyses have relied on variables such as the income and occupational status of the male adult, as head of household and have attributed social class to families. Wives and daughters have automatically been attributed the social class of father or husband, More recently the presence of single women, female heads of households, women's over-representation in poverty and low-income groups have challenged this traditional view. It has, for example, been suggested that housewives are working class in view of their domestic labour and relation to the means of production, although it is unlikely that they will share a working class consciousness: Daniels and Murnane (1980: xii) conceptualise the class difference within the context of a broad women's movement in a way which is useful. They describe two groups of women—separate by class and politics rebels against exclusion from privilege on the one hand, and against exploitation on the other". They suggest that the two groups cannot be regarded separately because of the broad women's movement but nevertheless must be understood "as part of the wider relationship between classes".

Basis for Unity

A second problem with the general theory of disadvantage, is that the women's movement does not unite in consiousness or action on the basis of socio economic class or poverty, but on the basis of gender—"sisterhood". "Sisterhood" is the consciousness of being a woman, socially and politically—it is solidarity with women.

Smith describes sisterhood as the discovery of the "Objectivity of our oppression". She says :

That discovery is made in relation to other women, in our discussions with other women, in exploring with other women the dimensions of the oppression. For we discover oppression . . . .not as something which is peculiar to yourself . . . .but as something which is indeed imposed upon by society and which is experienced in common with others . . .Once sisterhood was our basis, once we took the standpoint of women, once we were feminists, we had to deal with that . . . .we had to take up aspects of the women's experience which hadn't counted for us before . . . .(1977: 10-16).

Women as Community ?

Another shared assumption of the selected theorists is that there is a community to organize, Women's movement community organizing has had to build a community of women, because the structure of women's lives, more often than not, has militated against community.

Sociologists have described the socialization of women as including fewer experiences of group-bonding and team or group experience defined by gender, that that of their make counterparts. As adults, women's domestic labour and the personal commitments this involves means that they are concerned with the personal sphere of everyday life. Fox (1980: 209) comments that : ''organizing housewives remains very difficult... because of the privatized nature of their work.'' Piven and Cloward (1977: 21) in noting that protest varies with people's context, comments that:

Institutional life aggregates people or disperses them, moulds group identities, and draws people in the settings within whcih collective action can erupt.

A final barrier to women's sense of community is their fragmentation in the paid labour force. In spite of the occupational sex-segregation, women are frequently spread throughout different establishments or in different departments. Clerical and sales workers (two of the largest occupations for women) are clear examples of this. Twenty-five per cent of women in the paid labour force are part-time workers and women comprise the majority of employees through many establishments. Women in senior management positions, political and academic life, the traditional professions, or in blue-collar work are all isolated by their limited presence in an otherwise male-dominated work place. Indeed, their ability to function in the workplace is impinged upon by the intransience of the traditional expectations of women as homemakers. As married women have entered the paid labour force in greater numbers they have moved into a ''double workday'', with their privatized domestic labour now in addition to their labour in the paid workforce.

Public and Private Spheres ?

The existence of family and personal life has almost ignored by community organization theorists. It has been assumed that community organizing takes place only in the public sphere- the state, community life and the paid work place. The emphasis by the Women's movement on "the personal is political" has meant that the family and personal life have become targets for social action. Division of household labour, and wife battering have, for example, been identified as social issues demanding organizing and social action. For Alinsky, the targets of community organizing include both powerful institutions and mass organizations (Alinsky, 1972: 3; Reitzes and Reitzes, 1980; 40 71). This is therefore applicable to women's movement organizing in the public sphere and the paid work place. Freire however recognizes personal consiousness as a key focus for organizing. He sees the oppressed as the objects of their own actions- the social order is the focus for reform, but only as, and after, the oppresed liberate themselves from the ''contradictions of the concrete, existential situation by which they are shaped'' (Freire, 1972: 30). Piven and Cloward point out that action targets must be accessible to the protestors. They note that:

> Institutional roles determine the strategic opportunities for definance, for it is typically by rebelling against the rules and authorities associated with their everyday activities that people protest (1977: 21).

While these insights are very applicable to women's movement organizing, the authors have not developed the link nor considered the implicatons for organizing women.

The women's movement has been concerned with demanding changes in women's social role (Adams *et al,* 1985: 30). Signs of discontent with women's social role are not new - Chesler (1970) has argued that this was a component of women's mental illness. Bernard has documented the lesser happiness of women with the institution of marriage (1971: 145-162). The extent of mood-changing drugs prescribed for women in response to unhappiness, anger and depression offers another example. The women's movement has, however, attempted to promote less self-destructive approaches to discontent. Greer wrote of women's tendency to rebellion, when what was needed was a revolution-of consciousness and action (Greer 1972: 292ff).

There are a growing number of significant examples of personal action among middle class and educated women: sharing with spouses, housework and child care; separate names and bank accounts; an increasing rate of women initiating separations and divorces; delayed marriage; a greater number of single women taking action in regard to their role in the family. This has not been organized social action, and most women would probably continue to describe this as "Personal" not "political" action.

Similarly the women's movement has supported action directed to changes in individuals' everyday life. As with the family, this may be seen as the personal level of political change or described as "changes in life-style". In the tradition of social change which appears to follow Marcuse or Greer, making individual changes in consciousness and life-style appears to have absorbed much of women's energy.

Many women who have been active in the women's movement for a number of years have in fact made major and enduring changes in the structure of their personal and social lives in conjunction with their changing consciousness. Some have moved into education and pursued chosen careers; some have "come out" as gay; some have separated from a spouse, and whether separated or within a marriage, some have developed new patterns of shared child care and domestic work and/or co-operative living arrangements. In addition to the major changes in lifestyle, many have made a host of smaller changes often explicitly as political acts, from returning to their own (their "maiden") name; to changing their language to include the feminine; and withdrawing support from the cosmetic and fashion industries, etc.

What have all these changes to do with social or political action? Reich (1974) wrote that we had learned that an economic democracy was at least possible, but asserted that the struggle ahead was to develop "self-regulating" character structure, i. e., people who were capable of living democratically. He interpreted Lenin's prediction of the "withering away of the State" to refer to this new, democratic, self-regulating character structure and consciousness. The individual changes in everyday life within the women's movement are precisely about this struggle for democracy and equality between people. This is consistent with what Freire refers to as the peoples "incessant struggle to regain their humanity" (1972: 33).

CONCLUSION

The assumptions of the selected theorists appear to be too narrow in light of the experience of women's movement organizing. Our analysis has implications for future theory development as well as for women's community organizing.

First, to be directly useful to women's organizing, social action theory must learn from the Women's Movement that gender is a key variable in social analysis, and that the structure of women's lives must be understood in developing action theories for women organizing.

Second, the selected theorists tend to assume a geographic community. Attention needs to be paid to the understanding of women comprising functional as well as or rather than ones' geographic communities (Plant, 1974; Lee, 1980). The task of organizing women demands new tools and strategies in view of the barriers to community which arise from the structure women's lives, (i.e. their socialization, the privatization of domestic labour, their double workday and fragmentation in the paid labour force).

Third, there appears to be natural linkage between Freirean-oriented theoriests and practitioners and the Women's Movement in relation to the identification of "the personal is political". Unfortunately, there appears to have been relatively little interchange between the two groups on the theoretical level, although there is recent evidence that some practitioners (McGuire, 1987; ICAE, 1986) are testing Freirean concepts. It would be intersting to see more discussion, research and theory develop in this area.

Finally, it is important to see the family and individual's everyday life as chosen arenas for action within the Women's Movement. These previously invisible spheres should be brought into consideration for organizing theory. Issues such as sexual harassment, violence against women, and equal pay for work of equal value pose important challenges for organizers to develop imaginative strategies.

This paper has attempted to highlight the necessity and the potential for interchange between the Women's Movement and social action theorists within community work. Clearly there are rich and interesting issues that are crucial to both. Thus, the strength of the two will be enhanced significantly by further dialogue and reflection between them.

Bill Lee is Associate Professor of Social Work to McMaster University, Hamilton, Ontario, Canada and *Wendy Lee,* Director, Department of Social Work, Philip Institute, Melbourne, Australia.

BIBLIOGRAPHY

Adamson, Nancy, Briskin, Linda, McPhail, Margaret, (1985), *Feminist Organizing for Change,* Toronto, Oxford University Press.

Alfred, Neil, (1977), "community Development: Problems and Perpectives", *International Review of Community Development,* No. 37-38, Summer, pp. 241-257.

Alinsky, Saul, (1972), *Rules for Radicals,* New York, Vintage Books.

Bernard, Jessie, (1976), "The Paradox of a Happy Marriage" in Vivian Gornick and barbara Moran, *Women in Sexist Society,* Basic Books.

Both, Heather, (1976), *Direct Action Organizing: A Handbook for Women,* Chicago, Midwest Academy.

Brager, George and Specht, Harry, (1973), *Community Organizing, New York,* Columbia University Press.

Brandwein, Ruth A., (1984), "Feminist Thought Structure: An Alternative Paradigm of Social Change for Social Justice" in *Toward Social and Economic Justice,* David G. Gil and Eva A. Gil (eds), Cambridge, Massachusetts, Shankman Publishers Co. Inc.

Chesler, Phyllis, (1970), *Women and Madness,* New York, Doubleday.

Daniels, Kay, and Murnane, Mary, (1980), *Up the Hill All the Way:* A Documentary History of Women in Austrialia, University of Queensland Press.

Fox, Bonnie, (ed.), (1980), *Hidden in the Household,* Toronto, The Women's Press.

Freire, Paulo, (1972), *Pedagogy of the Oppressed,* New york, Herder and Herder.

Gallagher, Anne, (1976), "Women and Community" in *Women in the Community, (ed.)* M. Mayo. London: Routledge and Kegan Paul.

Greer, Germaine, (1971), *The Female Eunuch.* London, Paladin.

Guettel, Charnie, (1974), *Marxism and Feminism.* Toronto, Canadian Women's Press.

Hole, Judith and Levine, Ellen, (1973), *Rebirth of Feminism,* New York, Quadrangle Books Edition.

Kahn, S., (1982), *Organizing, New York,* McGraw Hill Company.

Lee, Bill, (1986), *Pragmatics of Community Organization,* Mississauga, Commonact Press.

McGuire, Pat, (1987), *Doing Participatory Research: A Feminist Approach,* International Council for Adult Education, Toronto.

Mckee, Janet, (1989), "The Effect of Domestic Labour and Gender on the Relationship Between Class and Political Attitudes", *Atlantis,* Volume 14, Number 2, pp. 63-71.

Mitchell, Juliet, (1971), *Women's Estate,* Penguin, Chapter 1.

Moynahan, Daniel, (1969), *Maximum feasible Misunderstanding: Community Action in the war on Poverty,* New York, The Free Press.

Perlman, Robert and Gurin, Arnold, (1972), *Community Organization and Social Planning,* New York, John Wiley and Sons, Inc. and The Council for Social Work Education.

Piven, Frances Fox, and Cloward, Richard A., (1977), *Poor People's Movements,* Why They Succeed and How They Fail, New York, Vintage Books.

Plant, Raymond, (1974), *Community and Ideology,* London, Routledge and Kegan Paul.

Reich, Wilhelm, (1974), *The Sexual Revolution,* New York, Farrar, Straus & Giroux.

Reitzes, Donald C. and Reitzes, Deitrich C., (1980), "Saul D. Allinsky's Contribution to Community Development" in *Journal of the Community Develpment of Society,* Vol. 11, No. 2, Fall.

Roberts, Wayne, (1976), *Honest Womenhood,* Feminism, Femininity and Class Consciousness Among Toronto Working Women 1893 to 1914, Toronto New Hogtown Press, Chapter 1.

Ross, Murray, (1967), *Community Organization: Theory, Principles and Practice,* Harper and Row, New York.

Rubin, Herbert J. and Rubin, Irene, (1986), *Community Organization and Development,* Columbus, Ohio, Merill Publishing Company.

Safilios-Rothschikd, Constantina, (1974), *Women and Social Policy,* New Jersey, Prentice-Hall.

Smith, Dorothy E., (1977), *Feminism and Marxism,* Vancouver, New Star Books.

Speeter, Greg, (1978), *Power: A Repossession Manual,* Massachusetts, Citizen Involvement Training Project.

Staples, Lee, (1984), *Roots to Power,* New York, Praeger, Special Studies.

Wilson, Elizabeth, (1977), "Women in the Community", In *Women in the Community,* Marjorie Mayo (ed.), London, Routledge & Kegan Paul, Chapter 1.

Women's Council International Council for Adult Education, (1986) Voices Rising: *A Bulletin About Women and Popular Education.*

CHAPTER-7

Gender Matters in Third World Development Projects: The Dangers of Gender Blindness.

Dr. M. M. Batra

In recent years there has been an increasing awareness that as development has proceeded, or not proceeded, in Third World countries, the impact on men and women has been different. In fact, there is substantial evidence that women have consistently lost out in the process.

Some of the inequalities between men and women had their basis in colonial rule. Although social relations between men and women, as between other groups, were by no means egalitarian in many pre-colonial settings, there is no doubt that colonial capture and the introduction of exploitative labour regimes led to a marked deterioration in the social and economic status of women relative to that of men. The development of a world economy, and the spread of wage labour in both agricultural and industrial production, assumed very different roles for women and men in the economy, sometimes excluding women from wage employment while relying on their unpaid work on family farms or on low-paid work within the informal sector. Even since the Second World War, when national governments and multilateral and bilateral aid agencies have initiated development programmes and projects, there is overwhelming evidence that such assistance has generally bypassed women or sometimes made women worse off. Such was the concern of development professionals that 1975 was declared International Women's Year, followed by the Decade for the Advancement of Women 1976-85. But even after these initiatives there is considerable concern about the lack of understanding of gender relations and the fact that development policies and projects are still in the main gender blind if not actually biased against women.

Why has development affected women and men differently ? Are women too weak and powerless to take advantage of the challenges and opportunities that development offers ? Is it tradition or backwardness that keeps women in a secondary position in Third World societies ?

Do planners and policy makers discriminate against women because they make mistaken assumptions about women's roles and involvement in production and reproduction ? Or, more fundamentally, is the whole process of development, both as historical social change, and in terms of development policies and projects, deeply rooted in the unequal relations between men and women so that it is necessary totally to rethink the objectives and strategies of development ?

This chapter will help address these questions by presenting a framework for thinking about gender relations. First, some basic analytical concepts are introduced to help in understanding the social processes that give rise to the disadvantaged position of women. Then some ways in which women are subordinated. These concepts are then used to look at some development initiatives and examine how they have affected men and women differently. Finally, some attempts to make women's issues and interests more central in the development field, and argue that the effects of more recent economic policies indicate that there is still a long way to go.

But-be warned-the conclusion of this chapter is that we can't think in terms of analysing development and then looking at its effect on women. On the contrary, whether it is recognized or not, development process or policy inevitably affects and is affected by the relations between the genders in any society. All policies, however technical or neutral they may appear to be, will have gendered implications. One task is to understand how different aspects of social and economic organization are already based on a system of gender relations and thus to clarify how assumptions about the roles of men and women form the backdrop against which policies are formulated, even if these assumptions remain unspoken and unacknowledged.

Conceptualizing gender and understanding gender relations

'Gender' rather than 'sex' is the key concept here because we are concerned with the social roles and interactions of men and women rather than their biological characteristics. Gender relations are social relations, referring to the ways in which the social categories of men and women, male and female, relate over the whole range of social organization, not just to interactions between individual men and women in the sphere of personal relationships, or in terms of biological reproduction. In all aspects of social activity, including access to resources for production, rewards or remuneration for work, distribution of consumption, income or goods, exercise of authority and power, and participation in cultural and religious activity, gender is important in establishing people's behaviour and the outcome of any social interatction.

As well as interactions between individual men and women, gender relations describe the social meaning or male and female, and thus what is considered appropriate behaviour of activity for men and women. What is considered as male or female work, or male or female attributes, behaviour or characteristics, varies considerably between different societies and different historical periods. But it is also important to realize that notions of gender identity, and thus what is fitting for men and women to do or be, have a strong ideological content. For example, in Britain, with nearly 50% of women of working age in the labour force. If the Good Lord had intended us to have equal rights to go out to work he wouldn't have created men and women. *These are biological facts.* In rural sectors of the Third World both men and women often report that women don't do any agricultural work, or that they are just involved as family helpers, or carry out only demestic work, In fact, many of their waking hours are spent in activities such as weeding and harvesting, or collecting animal fodder or fuel wooe, which have a direct effect on the productivity of agriculture whether the output is used for self- provisioning or processed and sold on the market.

Because notions of gender roles and activities have such a strong ideological content, policy often reflects normative or prescriptive versions of female and male roles rather than activities actually practised by women and men. But, as will become clear later, it is essential to understand the precise nature of what women and men actually do, and their real contribution to production and reproduction, if development policy is to crease being biased against women.

Using women as an analytical category

Although most people accept that women and men have different social positions, it is of course true that other social divisions such as class, race, ethnicity and age will also affect people's life chances. However, in common with much feminist literature, this chapter 'starts from the premise that all women share a common experience of oppression and subordination'.

It is possible to gain some notion of women's common interests, even though the forms of women's oppression and subordination vary widely, both historically and across or within specific societies.

For example, all women are potentially vulnerable to violence from men. Many women in third world avoid travelling or walking alone at night. However, if a woman is rich enough she can avoid some of the constraints this places on her life by driving her own car, or using expensive forms of transport such as taxis. But her vulnerability to male violence stems from the fact that she is a woman, not from her economic circumstances. Her economic power may be deployed to mitigate the constraints and threats that male violence imposes on her as a woman, but it cannot abolish them.

Other situations can look different. In January1991 rich women in Riyadh sought to challenge the very strict code of conduct that gender relations in contemporary Saudi Arabia imposed on them. They organized a drive-in to the centre of the city, dismissed their chauffeurs and drove their expensive cars themselves. The authorities retaliated by dismissing many of them from their employment in the University. Again, in this situation the constraints on their action stemmed directly from their gender, which was the basis of the social and political control on their autonomy. Being rich gave them big cars and chauffeurs, but it could not allow them the freedom to drive. Many examples given in this chapter detail the work burden of poor women in the Third World which systematically exceeds that of men in the same households (and therefore, the same class position). Without focusing on the social relations which produce and perpetuate this situation, it is impossible to go beyond a mere description of the conditions of women in different situations. But if we are concerned to devise policy initiatives and promote social changes which will improve the material and social condition of women, we need to understand how profound and pervasive the structures of women's subordination really are.

How gender makes a difference

One way of measuring how people's gender makes a difference to their share of the benefits of society is to examine macro-level indicators which are differentiated by sex. Tables 1 and 2 show some further differences (wage rates and political participation) for selected countries and regions. On all the indicators shown, it is clear that women have an unequal share in some of the benefits of development'.

Although national average figures hide an enormous amount of variation'by class, occupation and so on, they cannot hide the importance of gender in determining people's access to resources or opportunities.

Competing concepts; subordination or patriarchy

We can go further than talking about *inequality* whith respect to gender relations: we can say that men are dominant and women are **subordinated.**

Subordination of women: A phrase used to describe the generalized situation whereby men as a group have more social and economic power than women, including power over women. As a result, women come off worse in most measurable indices of the outcome of social and economic processes. In short, the way the two genders related to each other is that the male gender is dominant and the female gender is subrodinate.

Another term which is often used to describe the unequal relations between men and women is *patriachy*. This was originally an anthropological terms which described the kind of social systems in which authority is vested in the male head of the household (the patriarch) and other male elders within the kinship group. Older men were entitled to exercise socially sanctioned authority over other members of the household or kinship group, both women and younger men.

Some writers prefer to use the term patriarchy to describe the general situation of male dominance over women, in order to develop an analysis of the structures of patriarchy within specific societies. However, the form this relationship of domination/subordination takes differs strikingly between different societies and is constantly undergoing change and negotiation, we therefore prefer to use the term *subordination* as it has no connection with any specific system of social organization and does not rest on the basis of a specific structure of male authority over women.

Subordination of women

Although the subordination of women is universal, this does not mean that gender relations are the same in every society. In every case, the social meaning of being female or male will be the result of the history of that society, influenced by the nature of the local economy that evolved over time, religious beliefs and political systems. It is necessary to analyse each situation separately in order to understand the precise nature of gender relations, the different factors which influence them, and how gender relations themselves have an impact on social and economic development. It would be a mistake, for example, to pick out one independent variable such as religion and assume that the gender ideologies and ralated gender roles implied by that religion have a uniform, or even a determining, impact on the specific relationship between men and women.

2 Structures of subordination

How and where are women subordinated? The mechanisms of distribution of resources and exercise of power between women and men vary widely, but one can expect to find structures of subordination in areas of life such as property relations, divisions of labour, in law and the state, and in how households are organized. Although we look at these areas separately, there are links between them which will become apparent (for example, between state policy and property relations, or sexual divisions of labour and household organization).

Table 1 Wages of females as a percentage of wages of males

	1977	1986
Developing countries		
Cyprus	49.6	56.1
El Salador	80.8	81.5[a]
Hong Kong	—	77.9
Kenya	55.6	75.6[a]
South Korea	44.7	48.5
Singapore	—	63.4a
Sri Lanka	—	75.5
Developed countries		
Czechoslovakia	67.4	67.9
France	75.8	79.5
West Germany	72.3	72.9
Greece	68.8	76.9
Japan	46.0	42.5
New Zealand	73.3	71. 8
Sweden	87.4	90.4
United Kingdom	70.8	67.9

Source: UN (1989) Report on the World Social Situation, United Nations, Geneva, p. 13.

[a]Based on 1985.

Table 2 Percentage of women in parliament

	Lower chamber of bicameral assembly		Upper chamber of bicameral assembly	
Region	1975	Latest year	1975	Latest year
Africa	4.1	6.3	—	4.9
Asia	13.2	12.8	6.9	6.9
Latin America and Caribbean	3.4	10.6	4.2	6.5
North America	3.6	7.0	2.9	7.4
Oceania	1.9	4.9	9.4	22.4
Europe	13.2	17.6	6.4	8.2
Soviet Union	32.1	34.5	30.5	31.1

Source ; UN (1989) Report on the World Social Situation, United Nations, Geneva, p. 13.

Property relations: ownership and access to land

Systems of land tenure and inheritance vary widely. In most cases women have use rights rather than outright ownership rights to land. Where full rights to ownership exist in traditional legal codes, a women's share is not usually equal to a man's. And even where traditionally women are entitled to inherit land, new laws often reduce women's rights to succession. For example, the Colombian land reform law confined land redistribution to married males over 18, and deprived women of rights they had in the pre-reform system (Whitehead, 1985, p.53).

Even where women have customary use rights to land, these are rarely exercised in their own right, but only through kin relationships with individual men-brothers, fathers, other male relatives or, most commonly, husbands. In many African systems which prescribe the payment of bridewealth to the husband's family, women very often can only farm residual land after the rest of the kin group have had their allocation, even though, as wives, they are required to work on their husband's land. Without direct ownership or right to farm land, a woman has little say in the allocation of the income or crops. Since, as we detail below, men and women have different responsibilities within a household, lack of access to land can mean not just dependence on the haed of the household, but real difficulties in meeting her own and her children's needs for food and clothing.

Even in quite different systems where property is combined in marriage, which is common in many Asian societies, a woman rarely receives direct proceeds from the land, but depends on her husband to support her and her children. Although property relations are determined at the level of social and legal institutions, women's subordination in this realm has important consequences reaching into the allocation of resources, income and product within the household (Whitehead, 1985, pp. 55-6).

The sexual division of labour

Another important aspect of women's subordination is the allocation of different tasks and responsibilities to men and women. Strictly this should be called the `gender division of labour'; however, although it refers to social, not biological, categories, the term, *sexual division of labour* is generally used. One division often made is that between productive work and domestic labour. Women are generally regarded as responsible for the latter, although men may also play a role (Table 3). However, it does remain true that women carry out the bulk of what has been called reproductive work-including biological, generational and daily reproduction. In Britain in 1988, 72% of women claimed total responsibility for domestic work; and in Cuba, where by law, men are supposed to share domestic tasks, 82% of women is Havana and 96% of the women in the countryside have sole responsibility for domestic chores (Momsen, 1991).

Table 3 Gender divisions of time use in Nepal

	Time input into village and domestic work (%)	
	Men	Women
Cooking and serving	10	90
Cleaning	5	95
Maintenance	7	93
Laundry	10	90
Shopping	54	46
Other domestic	22	78
Childcare	16	84
Animal husbandry	55	45
Family farm enterprise	45	55
Gathering and hunting	60	40
Fuel gathering	34	66

House construction	72	28
Food processing	13	87
Water collection	8	92
Outside earning activity	69	31
Local market economy	43	57

Source : adapted from Joss, S. (1990) `Your husband is your god', GADU Pack no. 12, OXFAM, Oxford.

In many Third World societies, in the urban informal sector and in the rural economy, it is extremely difficult in practice to distinguish between domestic labour and productive work. Many apparently domestic tasks are part of maintaining production. But allocation of time to different activities including so-called domestic labour in rural production systems does vary to a certain extent according to the seasonal and other demands of production. Table 4 gives a seasonal breakdown of time spent on different tasks by men and women. The sexual division of labour within both agricultural and household tasks is fairly rigid. During peak times, women's time allocated to domestic work is reduced-though only by 13%. Men's domestic tasks are usually of a different nature (house maintenance, fencing, preparation of land for gardens etc.). In this example, women have much longer work time overall and consequently less time for leisure or sleep in both peak and slack seasons.

Table 4 Gender divisions of time use (hours per month) in the dry zone of Sri Lanka

	Peak season		Slack season	
	Male	Female	Male	Female
Agricultural production	298	299	245	235
Household tasks	90	199	60	220
Fetching water and firewood	30	50	30	60
Social and religious duties	8	12	15	15
Total work hours	426	560	350	530
Leisure/sleep	294	160	370	190

Source : Momsen, (1991) Women and Development in the Third World, Routledge, London, table 4.3

The sexual division of labour therefore operates not just between domestic and productive work but within each category of work as well. Also, what is considered to be a male or female occupation varies considerably between different societies, and in some cases between different groups and classes within the same society. A number of activities which are `male' in one place (petty trade in North India, for example) are predominantly female tasks in others, such as Jamaica or Nigeria. On the other hand, the vast majority of domestic servants are women is South American cities, whereas in Lagos they are men; most typists in Jammaica are women, but not so in Madras (Figure 2).

The sexual division of labour may be modified to respond to changes in economic circumstances which alter the supply of men or women to carry out 'male' or 'female' tasks. For example, when the plough was introduced earlier this century in Zimbabwe, women were displaced from tasks associated with the preparation of ground for farming. However, in recent years, with large scale male out-migration from rural areas, women have largely taken over ploughing and land preparation. In the northern province of neighbouring Zambia, the response to male out-migration has been different. Women have responded by hiring in casual labour to carry out traditional male tasks such as tree cutting and ploughing.

Gender roles have their own dynamic, evolving and adapting over many generations, exhibiting considerable resistance to changes in economic circumstances, or even to market forces. Often strategies which avoid changing the sexual division of labour are pursued, as in the Zambian case. Another example occurred when many women, often mothers of young children, migrated from Sri Lanka and other South Asian countries to the high-income Gulf states during the 1980 to work as domestic servants. Most often their childcare and domestic work at home devolved on other female family members, rather than on the fathers or male kin. This persistence of a strict sexual division of labour in domestic work is common all over the world (possibly more so than in household production) and should warn us not to assume to readily that gender relations can be modified or changed in response to change in the demand for or availability of male or female labour.

Sexual divisions of labour are neither constant in any particular society nor parallcled between different societies. But in every society there are clear demarcations which define what is approapriate, or possible, for women and men in that society-demarcations which may be transgressed by individuals without necessarily challenging the principle of allocation of tasks according to gender. Box 2 gives an example of how sexual divisions of labour are established in childhood and are carried through into adult life.

The state, law and gender relations

The state influences how women are viewed in society in various ways: through legislation, in how public institutions are staffed and run, and through social policies. These mechanisms can affect whether women are seen as autonomous individuals or as dependents of men. In some countries, women's civil rights (in divorce, custody of children, ownership of property, autonomy in matters of employment, financial contracts) are discriminatory. Entitlement to benefits such as health insurance, pensions and welfare payments are often linked to women's relationship with men, rather than granted in their own right. In many countries the police and law courts treat physical and sexual assaults of women within the family quite differently from other forms of assault.

The state also appoints public officials in the judiciary, the civil services, Industrial planning and regulatory boards, etc. Where such appointments are not adequately shared between men and women it reinforces the notion that primarily it is men who have the authority and competence to represent the whole population in serious matters. While many discriminatory laws have been repealed, particularly in the socialist Third World countries, in many places the extensive powers and practices of the state continue to legitimate unequal rights and unequal treatment of men and women.

Gender relations within households

In developing countries, most households are the site of many different kinds of activity: residence and consumption, subsistence and market production, distribution of resources and output, socialization of children, care of the elderly, and so on. these activities may take place in a single unit or in several connected ones. Different members of households may have different rights (over property, labour and income) and obligations (particular productive tasks, food provision, domestic work, etc.), often depending on age and marital status, as well as sexual divisions of labour.

Development policies are often directed to an idealized model of households where production, income and consumption are shared: they are seen to have convergent interests in which all members contribute according to their ability and share the benefits according to their needs. However, empirical studies have shown that far from being a unit in which all resources and benefits are pooled equitably,, the use of resources and labour, and the distribution of income and output, have constantly to be negotiated, and intra-household relations are often conflictive (Dwyer & Bruce, 1988). In different household systems men and women have different responsibilities in terms of work in domestic or other activities, obligations to provide food and other resources (water and cooking fuel), and cash income to meet family needs such as school fees, clothing, agricultural inputs, etc. In some households, far from a pooling situation, women trade grain they have grown themselves for cash to buy clothing and other necessities. In others, women's labour in family farms and enterprises give them no direct rights to cash, no 'owned resources' to exchange for cash, and little influence in deciding how household income is to be allocated between competing demands. In each of these cases, intra-household relations can be seen as a form of co-operative conflict (Sen, 1987): although household members may depend on each other in terms of labour and output, there is considerable negotiation and conflict about how such inputs and benefits should be distributed.

As well as these intra-household divisions, the distribution of inputs and benefits can also systematically disadvantage women. For many households, especially those on the margins of subsistance, women contribute a major proportion of their labour time, and their total income, to the needs of the household, particularly to their children. In contrast, men tend to have considerable autonomy over how they spend their income:

''A general finding is that women's income is almost exclusively used to meet collective household needs, whereas men tend to retain a considerable portion of their income for personal spending. A key source of male bargaining power within the household is determining what proportion of their income to pass on to other household members. Rather than personal spending money for male adults being residual after other household needs have been met, it is often a priority and the amount allocated to household expenditure is residually determined by the difference between male income and personal spending. The good husband is the one who strictly limits his personal spending, but his prerogative to enjoy such spending remains.''

3 Using gender to analyse development

In the previous sections we have mapped out some basic concepts necessary to analyse the changing social relations of gender. We have stressed that the precise nature of gender relations differs according to specific historical contexts. We will now see how these concepts can be applied by analysing briefly two examples of change in developing countries.

Women and Green Revolution

The 'Green Revolution' is regarded as an important example of successful development. A technological package based on new seeds, but with biochemical, mechanical and institutional aspects (i.e. new forms of credit and training) has been responsible for substantial increases in production of wheat and rice, particularly in Asia.

The Green Revolution started in the mid-1960s and continues today. It is probably the first systematic attempts to increase worldwide food production. Agricultural production is increased in three ways: average yields are increased, the area devoted to agriculture is extended, and the number of crops grown in a year is increased.

The major technical elements are:

1 Mechanization - the introduction of tractors, and other machinery for harvesting and irrigation etc. These may be used to extend the cropped area; often machines are used to replace labour.

2 Biochemical innovations - such as new seed varieties and new inputs such as fertilizers, pesticides and weed killers. These can all increase crop yields.

Most assessments of the impact of the Green Revolution in India recognize that as well as increasing overall productivity, it has also increased socio-economic stratification. This has resulted in worsening of income distribution between rich farmers on the one hand and poor farmers on the other, many of whom have joined the ranks of landless labourers.

The economist, Bina Agarwal (1985a), has used gender to analyse this particular devlopment process within the three major rural groups or classes in India, identified as:

1 agricultural labour households (which have no land or insufficient land for household subsistance);

2 small cultivator households (which have sufficient land to provide for household needs using family labour);

3 large cultivator households (which have sufficient land and other resources to farm using hired, i.e. paid, labour, and which do not use the women of the household for field work).

For women in the landless or land-short households the impact of Green revolution technology was complex. The numbers of households in this group incresed (including a large number of female headed households) and there was a rise in the number of women who had to hire themselves out as casual wage workers because many families were living on lower material resources than before the changes. Women had to increase their time and energy devoted to agricultural work for wages as well as maintain their subsistence production and domestic labour to ensure their household's survival. Women were squeezed between conflicting demands - the need to earn income, and the need to increase time devoted to domestic activities.

While there was a rise in the total amount of hired labour required by larger farm households, the increase in employment has not been gender neutral. The new technology package requires additional labour for tasks such as transplanting and weeding (normally women's work) but it is not clear that this has kept pace with the increase in the numbers of women seeking such work. Other activities, particularly harvesting, threshing and grain-processing, have been subject to substantial mechanization, reducing the employment opportunities for poor women. The widespread adoption of grain processing mills has vastly reduced women's employment in dehusking of rice, for example (Agarwal, 1985a).

The Green revolution has at best had a mixed impact on the employment opportunities and incomes of poor women. Statistics show increases in days worked and in wage rates, but the latter have been offset by price increases (Agarwal, 1985a, p. 97). Even where women's incomes have improved, it is not clear that they experience the benefits: women in landless and land-short households continue to suffer chronic deficits in food intake, both in absolute terms and in relation to men.

Women working as casual wage labour also face health hazards from standing in water containing fertilizers and pesticides to do weeding and transplanting (Figure 3). There are reports of women field workers suffering intestinal and parasitical infections, leech bites, skin complaints, rheumatic joints, arthritis and gynaecological infections (Agarwal, 1985b. p. 329).

Women from small cultivator households are in a different position. Although in general they are not required to work outside family farms for wages, their work within the family holdings has intensified. New seed varieties shorten the gestation period and make possible two harvests a year. Since most of women's agricultural tasks are not mechanized, their work burden has increased. In addition, they still carry the burden of domestic work. They are of course subject to the same health hazards described above.

Total household incomes of this group have in general increased, but decisions on the spending of this income remain biased against women. For instance, substantial shares of the extra income have been spent on tractors which save male labour time - but few households in this group have invested in home-grinding mills which would reduce women's domestic work burden in food processing.

The impact on women from large cultivator households is more closely linked to the considerable rise in household incomes. Although male bias in intra-household distribution remains, women have generally shared in the new prosperity. But even prosperity has implications for women. With increasing wealth, women are withdrawn from field production (a common way of demonstrating prosperity), but this does not necessarily signal an increase in women's autonomy. First, there may be an increase in domestic labour as women are responsible for preparing food for the increased numbers of hired labourers, and for other farm management tasks. Secondly, women's ability to bargain over allocation of household income may be further constrained. Withdrawal from field work can often lead to total seclusion and an increase in women's dependence on men.

The effect of the Green Revolution therefore cannot be measured just in terms of increased production or rises in aggregate household incomes.Consideration should also be given to the increases in women's workloads and to the fact that women often fail to receive an equitable share in the extra income earned, even though their labour is often central to achieving higher levels of productivity. Increased demand for casual waged work for women from the poorest households has not necessarily increased household income where, as has often been the case, real wage levels have declined. Since women are in danger of losing out (of working harder, for less reward, with added health risks), this policy for improvement in agricultural productivity cannot be considered an unqualified success.

Development projects: the dangers of gender blindness :

Many development initiatives have been introduced in areas of the Third World in the form of large-scale projects financed by external aid and organized by technical experts. One well-known example was the attempt in the 1970s to introduce irrigated rice production in an area in The Gambia where, traditionally, men had farmed groundnuts as a cash crop (with the aid of family labour) and women had cultivated rice for household consumption on unirrigated wetlands (Figure 4). The irrigation project was unsuccessful largely because the planners failed to understand the specific dynamics of gender relations within the local household-based farming system (Dey, 1982; Carney, 1988).

"The lack of success stemmed in part from [a] 'male dominant', 'domestic sharing' model of the household which shaped the project. An initial assumption was that the men were the rice growers with full control over the necessary resources. Incentive packages included cheap credits, inputs and assured markets offered to male farmers. But it was women who traditionally grew rice for household consumption and exchange, within [a] kind of complex set of rights and obligations...The scheme proposed to develop irrigated rice production of common lands to which women had secured use rights. Backed by project officials, men established exclusive rights to these common lands, pushing the women out to inferior scattered plots to continue cultivating traditional rice varieties. All access to inputs, labour, and finance was mediated through husbands, and women became notably reluctant to participate in their planned role as family labour. For what work the women did do on the irrigated rice fields husbands had to pay their wives... the disappointingly low levels of improved rice production arose substantially from these misunderstandings."

As well as assumptions about the structure and operation of households, the planners took other things for granted. first, they assumed that women were 'free' labour - that their labour would not have to be recompensed in any way, and thus involved no resource cost. Secondly, they assumed that women's labour had no existing productive use and therefore was available for intensive application to irrigated rice production. In fact, women were busy with their own rice lands in the rainy season, during which men did not have access to their labour and therefore did not grow a further rice crop as planners had expected. Men only grew rice in the dry season when their women were free to work for them (for wages) and when they themselves earned higher wages elsewhere. In addition, ignoring that women were farmers in their own right, planners neither took advantage of women's expertise in swamp land rice nor helped women to improve their own output.

The Gambian example illustrates two further points. Women are not necessarily the passive victims of circumstances with no possibility of resisting. By refusing to make their labour available at no cost and to the convenience of the male farmers involved in irrigated rice production, the Gambian women demonstrated their determination to defend their existing gender position as separate producers, albeit with various obligations as well as rights within the household. The example demonstrates that in households where men and women hold separate purses with no pooling of cash income, and have responsibility for different items of household expenditure and food production, as well as different access to resources for production, it cannot be assumed that increasing household production and incomes will of necessity improve the living standards of all members.

4 Putting gender on the development agenda

The concern with the effects of development on women goes back some 10-20 years. The UN's Decade for the Advancement of Women (1976-85), which was preceded by the International Women's Year in 1975, was the culmination of successful pressure by women activists and academics (Pielta & Vickers, 1991). The argument was that development policies, co-ordinated by the leading multinational agencies, such as the World Bank, UNIDO and FAO, as well as many bilateral development agencies and NGOs, had ignored the needs of poor women in Third World countries.

It was not just in economic terms that the marginalization of women needed to be addressed. There was concern that women were being 'left out' in four critical areas: political rights; legal rights; access to education and training; and their working lives (Boyd, 1988).

'Women in Development' policies

The new emphasis led many agencies and experts to commit themselves to women in Development policies in order to enable women both to enjoy the fruits of development, and to make and appropriate and necessary contribution to the development process. Many development agencies financed projects aimed at helping poor women, particularly setting up income-generating projects ranging from poultry and fishing co-operatives to handicrafts and school uniform sewing, with various inputs of credit, technical expertise and training provided. Of course, women's labour was unpaid, since the income depended on the sale of the project's output.

A parallel development was the establishment of Ministries for Women's Affairs or Women's Bureaux, particularly in Commonwealth countries. These were charged with negotiating and co-ordinating the activities of the various international agencies keen to finance projects for women. These agencies also helped to raise the profile of women's issues, and divert some aid resources to targeted women's groups. Unsurprisingly, they were chronically understaffed and under-resourced and most have found it extremely difficult to meet their broad range of objectives (Gorden, 1985).

A major criticism of the Women in development approach is that its basic assumptions are flawed: it starts from the premise that women have been excluded from development. But as our previous discussion has clearly illustrated, women's time, energy, work and skills are involved in every aspect of the development process; it is the inequality of gender relations and the continuing subordination of women that ensure that women's contribution is not matched by recognition and remuneration in social, political and economic terms.

The shortcomings of the Women in development approach, which focuses on women rather than on gender relations, is illustrated by research which has assessed various projects aimed at inproving the situation of poor women (Buvinic, 1986). Most projects focused on one aspect of women's problems (often lack of access to cash income) without considering the implications of such initiatives. For example, income-generating projects do not take into consideration how women's time budgets are already overstretched. Furthermore, many projects were staffed by unpaid leaders, with little commercial or technical expertise available, rather than professional salaried workers.

Many projects are based on what are assumed to be women's traditional skills (embroidery, handicrafts etc.), though in many cases the women have no direct experience of these activities. Few have identified any attainable market and as a result are continually dependent on further aid for survival.

Increasing visibility of women ?

One clear advance from the UN Decade has been an enhanced understanding of the nature and variety of women's work in the Third World. This has been accompanied by an increasing recognition that conventional methods of collecting statistics consistently underestimate the extent of women's work (waring, 1989; But even a more comprehensive recording of women's paid work would not represent the real extent to which all economies rely on women, both in productive activities and in the range of reproductive activities discussed above.

"Women often contribute to family earnings in a number of ways, making it important that all income-earning activities be reported. For example, a woman may help on the family farm or in a family enterprise. During the off-season she may take in laundry, produce handicrafts, brew beer for sale, or work on someone else's farm. Especially if she is poor, she may scrape together a living by engaging in several such activities. Unless there is an inquiry into time use or a sequence of questions on multiple jobs, secondary occupations may well be omitted...Unpaid family work on farms and in small non-farm enterprises is an important part of women's work in developing countries...A special effort is often necessary to make certain that it will not be overlooked."

In spite of the increase in research and awareness of the specific circumstances of women, there was still no evidence at the beginning of the 1990s that the implications of taking gender seriously are understood or acted upon at the level of macroeconomic planning.

5. Structural adjustment policies: lesson from the past

the 1980s saw widespread implementation of structural adjustment policies, which were intended to transform Third World economies into efficient and competitive producers for international markets.

What have we learned about the nature of gender relations that might be relevant to the analysis of those market-oriented policies? It should be clear that economies do not only work through market relations. Given the complexity of gender relations within smallholder households, the invisibility of women's work both in the rural and urban sectors, and the multiple and complex roles women actually perform, market-only policies such as structural adjustment are likely to have specific, and probably negative, effects on women.

For example, women agricultural producers may grow marketable crops, but their energies are often directed to producing food for household consumption. If prices are allowed to rise as an incentive to increasing marketed production, women will often be in a situation where they are under pressure from husbands and other male kin to work harder in order to produce more cash crops at the expense of household food. Women also often find that their workload is increased because new crops and technology intensify the need for weeding and other female agricultural tasks. Even so, they will not necessarily be compensated by payment for their labour or increased cash income from the sale of the new crops. Further more, there is no certainty that cash earned will be used to purchase food to compensate for the reduction in their own provisioning, or that the moeny earned will be sufficient to purchase equivalent food products on the open market.

These problems are borne out by a nutritional study carried out in Zambia in 1988, after an adjustment programme had been in place. It was found that `in the predominantly maize growing areas it is the children of the farmers growing maize for sale who are most likely to suffer from nutritional stress' (feldman, 1989, p.17). In this case, it was also suspected that the extra burden of work imposed on women by producing for the market gave them less time for childcare, infant feeding and food preparation. Thus, as well as underestmating the centrality of women's work in agricultural production, policies based on market models also ignore women's domestic or reproductive roles. Not only is time taken away from non-market production, it can also squeeze the time required to carry out essential domestic tasks. Women will always attempt to stretch themselves in order to meet their multiple obligations, with the result that their total work burden is increased, but their ability to ensure the well being of their families is jeopardized, to say nothing of their own health and welfare.

Raising prices as an incentive to increase agricultural production for sale, plus the reduction of state control of food markets has meant shrply rising prices for consumers. Together with increased costs of housing, water, school fees and medicines, households can only survive by acquiring several incomes. Women especially have been forced to find alternative income sources, mainly in the informal sector of the economy (Figure 5). A recent survey in Dar Es Salaam showed that women of all classes were doing extra work for cash (Feldman, 1989, p. 25). Young girls contrubuted by selling cooked food before and after school. In addition, 58% of households reported that they had reduced the number of meals taken from three to two.

The other plank of structural adjustment policies -that of reducing government spending-has had specific and direct effects on women, who, as teachers health workers and public sector office workers, have often taken the brunt of cuts in public sector employment. Many women have had to turn to the informal sector for work. Cuts in public services such as health and education have also taken their toll on the poor. In some places, healthbudgets have been reduced by 50% or more, and a lack of foreign exchange has led to shortage of medical supplies within state-run hostpitals and health centres. In Tanzania, mortality of children under 5 has inccreased since 1980 from 193 per thousand to 309 in 1987. In Zambia there has been a sharp increase in childhood malnutrition, and a decline in the child immunization programmes. The uptake of antenatal care has also fallen off. In countries such as Jamaica, where the government has introduced charges for previously free public health care, many women, who face declining incomes and increased prices for basic needs, have simply been unable to afford medical attention for themselves or their children (Antrobus, 1988).

Reduction in other areas of state expenditure also affects women in ways which are less obvious. Housing, sanitation, clean water, programmes, rural road projects-all these have been the victims as governments seek to reduce 'unnecessary' or 'unproductive' expenditure. But all these services affect the ability of women to manage their conflicting roles. Without rural roads, women are unable to travel to urban centres for health care, for education, or to market their own crops. Without sanitation and clean water, women use much time and energy fetching water from insanitary and distant points; intestinal and other diseases afflict children and adults alike, adding care of the sick to women's already overburdened tasks.

In some countries, governments have also introduced or increased school fees as a means of raising revenues. This has contributed to the marked fall-off of enrolment of girls in schools, for several reasons. Additional expenditure cannot be justified where household incomes are falling. The possibility of women obtaining a job where literacy is necessary is slight. Girls have been with drawn from school in order to care for younger children as women have increasingly had to take up income-generating work. The girls themselves are also required to contribute to household income either by assisting relatives, or working as domestic servants (Pittin, 1990).

Adjustment policies which favour deregulation of the market are premised on ideas about 'getting the prices right'- that is, eliminating what are seen to be distortions in the market. But within a conceptualization of the economy which ignores any analysis of gender, women's time and energy have no price: they become further stretched. As carnings of other members of the household declin, women extend the range of income-generating activities, seeking new sources of cash and investing their time and resources in new activities- hence the increase within the urban economy of activities such as vegetable growing, petty trading, beer brewing, poultry keeping and tailoring (Figure 6). Common strategies to reduce household expenditure initially focus on purchasing cheaper commodities, either by seeking cheaper sources of supply or by purchasing more basic goods which require home processing-both of which involve time and work undertaken by women. As the crisis deepens, items of expenditure are eliminated. As the total amount of goods and services the household can afford to buy falls, the share of women and girls of these shrinking resources also tends to decline. For example, it is common for male family members' food consumption to be protected as food intake of women and young girls is sacrificed.

A more market-oriented economy will not have negative consequences for all women in Third World economies. Increased market-based economic relations tend to cause increased stratification in the economy, with some groups doing better and being in a position to accumulate, as was the case in the Green Revolution. Inevitably, groups who have weaker claims on resources lose out. For many women in both rural and urban Third World communities, adjustment has meant increasing workloads and falling living standards as they have struggled, often unsuccessfully, to maintain their standard of living and to ensure the basic survival of their households.

6. A challenge for the 2000s

The 2000s will present enormous challenges to all those who are concerned with development. However, all development issues require analysis from the perspective of gender realtions if they are to be successful and serve the needs of women as well as men. There is some evidence that the World Bank is drawing back from its 1980s policy agenda and prioritizing areas of social investment which are crucial to women's survival. But other key issues such as environmental conservation, political stabilization and democracy all need to be subjected to a similar scrutiny. Efforts to halt soil degradation will not succeed if they rely on (unlimited and unrewarded) applications of women's scarce time and energy resources; democracy will be meaningless unless women are represented and have full acess to political office and power. The whole of the development agenda will need to be reformulated if the message that gender matters is to be taken seriously.

REFERENCES

Agarwal, B. (1985a) 'Women and technological change in agriculture: the Asian and African experience', in Ahmed, I. (ed) *Technoligy and rural Women*, Allen and Unwin, London.

Agarwal, B. (1985b) 'Rural women and high yielding variety rice technology', in International Rice Research institute (eds) *Women in Rice Farming*, Gower press, Aldershot.

Algar, H. (1972) 'The oppositional role of theUlama in twentieth-century Iran', in Keddie, N. (ed.), *Scholars, Saints and Sufis*, University of California Press, Berkeley.

Amin, S. (1976; 1978) *The Arab Nation*, Zed Press, london.

Amin, S. (1990a) *Maldevelopment*, Zed Press, London.

Amin, S. (1990b) *Delinking*, Zed Press, London.

Anderson, M.B. (1985) 'Technoligy transfer: implication for women', in Overholt, C., Anderson, M.B., cloud, K. & Austin, J.E. (eds) *Gender Roles in Development Projects:* a casebook, pp. 60-8, Kumarian Press, Connecticut.

Anon (1982) *Independent Kenya*, Zed Press, London.

Antrobus, P. (1988) 'Consequences and responses to social and economic deterioration: the experience of the English-speaking Caribbean', Workshop on Economic Crisis, Household Strategies and Women's Work, Cornell University Ithaca, NY.

Arnold, B. (1986) *Police Power and Colocial Rule: Madras*, 1989-1947, Oxford University Press, Delhi.

Arrighi, G. (1990) 'Marxist century, American century: the making and remaking of the world labour movement', New Left Review, 179,pp.29-63.

Asia labour Monitor (1988) *Min-Ju No-Jo: South Korea's new trade unions,* Asia Monitor Resource Centre, Hong Kong.

Atkinson, L. (1989) "Two decades of contraceptive research: prospects for the 21st century', in UN (eds) *World Population Prospects* 1988, United Nations, New York.

Azarya, V. (1988)'Recordering State-Society Relations: incorporation and disengagement', in Rothchild, D. & Chazan, N. (eds) *The Precarious Balance: state and society in Africa*, pp. 3-21, Westview Press, Boulder.

Bagchi, A.K. (1972) *Private Investment in India,* 1900-1939, Cambridge University Press, Cambridge.

Baker,J. (1990) Speech, Washington DC, October 22 1990, US Information Agency, Washington DC.

Barbier,E. (1989) *Economics, Natural Resource Sacricity and Development: conventional and alternative views,* Earthscan, London.

Bardhan, P. (1974) 'On life and death questions', *Economic and Political Weekly,* 9 August, pp.1293-1304.

Barratt brown, M. (1963) *After Imperialism,* Heinemann, London.

Bates, R. H. (1981) *Markets and States in Tropical Africa*, university of California Press, Berkeley.

Batra, Madan Mohan.. A Socio Economic Study of Licenced Porters at Delhi Railway Station.. Mobile, KADRAS 1966.

Batra, M.M. * Planning In India: Development Pospective

*Towards 21st century, 1987 Leading issues in Economic Development V.K. Publishing Home, 1994.

Bayly, C. A. (1983) *Rulers, Townsmen and Bazaars,* Cambridge University Press, Cambridge. Bayly, C. A. (1989) *Imperial Meridian: the British Empire and the World,* 1780-1830, Longman, London.

Beecham, D. & Eidenham, A. (1987) "Beyond the mass strike: class, party and trade union struggle in Brazil', *International Socialism,* Series 2, 36, pp.3-48.

Beneria, L. 91982) *Women and development: the sexual division of labor in rural societies,* Praeger, New York

Berliner, P. (1978) *The Soul of Mbire,* University of california Press, Berkeley.

Bernier, F., trans. Constable, A. & Smith, V. (1916) *Travels in the Mogul Empire* 1656-1668, Oxford University Press, Oxford.

Bernstein, H. (1983) 'Development', in Thomas, A. & Bernstein, H. (eds) The *'Third World' and 'Development'*, Block 1 of the Open University course U204 *Third World Studies,* The Open University, Milton Kenyas.

Bernstein, H. (1988) 'Production and producers', in crow, B. & Thorpe, M. (eds) *Survival and Change in the Third World,* Polity Press, oxfor.

Blacking, J. (1976) *How Musical is Man?*, Faber, London.

Blacking, J. (1980) 'Political and musical freedom in the music of some black South African churches', in holy, L. & Stuchlik, M. (eds) *The Structure of Folk Models*, pp.35-62, Academic Press, London.

Boyd, R. (1988) *A Global View of Women after the UN Decade*, Centre for Developing Area Studies, McGill University, Motreal, Working Paper No.56, October 1988.

Brandt, W. *et al.* (1980) *North-South: a programme for survival, Report of the Independent Commission of International Development Issues*, (The Brandt report), Pan Books, London

Brown, S. (1974) *New Forces in World Politics*, Little brown, Boston.

Buchanan, A. (1982) *Food, Poverty and Power*, Spokesman, Nottingham.

Bundy, C. (1977) 'The Transkei Peasantry, c.1890-1914: Passing through a time of stress', in Palmer, R. & Parsons, N. (eds) *The Roots of Rural Poverty*, heinemann, London.

Bundy, C. (1979) *The Rise and Fall of the South African peasantry*, Heinemann, London.

Burridge, K. (1969) *New Heaven, Hew Earth*, Blackwell, Oxford.

Burton, J. (1972) *World Society*, Cambridge University Press, Cambridge.

Buvinic, M. (1986) 'projects for women in the Third World: explaining their misbehaviour', *World Development*, 14(5).

Callinicos, A. (1987) 'Imperialism, capitalism and the state today - a review of Nigel Harris's *The End of the Third World'*, *International Socialism*, Series 2, 35, pp. 71-115.

Cardoso, F. H. & Faletto, E. 91979) *Dependency and Underdevelopment in Latin America*, University of California Press, Berkely (first published 1971).

Carney, J. (1988) 'Struggles over crop rights and labour within contract farming households in a Gamiban irrigated rice project', *Journal of Peasant Studies*, 15(3) (April).

Carson, R. (1962) *Silent Spring*, Houghton Mifflin, Boston Mass., and Penguin, Harmondsworth.

Cernea, M. (1985) *Putting People First; sociological variables in rural development*, Oxford University Press, New York.

Chambers, R. (1983) *Rural Development: Putting the last first*, Longman, London.

Chambers, R. (1988) 'Sustainable rural livelihoods', in *The Greeting of Aid; sustainable livelihoods in practice*, Earthscan, London.

Chambers, R. (1989) *The State and Rural Development: ideologies and an agenda for the 1990s*, IDS Discussion Paper No. 269, Institute of Development Studies, Brighton.

Chandra, Bipan *et al.* (1989) *India's Struggle for Independence*, Penguin, Harmondsworth.

Chen, L. C., Huq, E. & D'Souza, S. 91980) *A Study of Sex-Biased Behaviour in the Intra-Family Allocation of Food and the Utlization of Health Care Services in Rural Bangladesh*, International Centre for Diarrhoeal Disease Research, Bangladesh, and Department of Population Sciences Harvard School of Public Health.

Chen, R. S. (ed.) (1990) *The Hunger Report,* The Alan Shawn Feinstein World Hunger Program, Brown University, Providence, Rhode Island.

Choi Hyung Sup (1988) 'Guidelines for Future Development of Steel Technology', *Journal of Materials Education*, 10(3), pp. 286-99.

Cliff, L. & Cunningham, G. L. (1973) 'Ideology, organization and the settlement experience in Tanzania', in Cliffe, L. & Saul, J. S. (eds) *Socialism in Tanzania*, vol.2, East African Publishing House, Nairobi.

Colclough, C. & Manor, J. (1991) *States and Markets? New-liberalism and the Development Policy Debate*, Oxford University Press, Oxford.

Connolly, B. & Anderson, R. (1988) *First Contact: New Guinea's highlanders encounter the outside world*, Penguin Books, Harmondsworth.

Coplan, D. (1979) 'The African musician and the Johannesburg entertainment industry, 1900-1960', *Journal of Southern African Studies*, 6(2) (April), pp.135-64.

Coplan, D. (1982) 'The urbanization of African music: some theoretical observations', *Popular Music*, 2, pp.113-29.

Coplan, D. (1985) *In Township Tonight! South Africa's black City Music and Theatre*, Longman, London.

Cornia, G. A. (1987) 'Adjustment policies 1980-85: effects on child welfare', in Cornia, G. A., Jolly, R. & Stewart, F. (eds), *Adjustment with a Human Face: protecting the vulnerable and promoting growth, a study by UNICEF*, Clarendon Press, Oxford.

Coulson, A. (1982) *Tanzania: a political economy,* Clarendon Press, Oxford.

Crowder, M. (1968) *West Africa under Colonial Rule*, Hutchinson, London.

Crowder, M. (1987) 'Whose dream was it anyway? Twenty-five years of African independence', *African Affairs*, 86(342) (January), pp.7-24.

CSCE Joint Declaration (1990) Joint Declaration on CSCE, 19 november 1990, US Information Service, Washington DC.

Cummings, B. (1989) 'The abortive aberture: South Korea in the light of Latin American experience, *New Left Review*, 173 (January-February), pp.5-34.

Curtin, P.D.(1969) The Atlantic Slave Trade, University of Wisconsin Press, Wisconsin.

Curtin, P. D. (1984) *Cross-Cultural Trade in World History,* University Press, London.

Das Gupta, J. (1989) 'India: democratic becoming and combined development', in Diamond, L., Linz, J. & Lipset,S.(eds)*,Democracy in Developing Countries: Asia*, pp.53-104, Adamantine Press, London.

Davey, B. (1975) *The Economic Development of India*, Spokesman University Paperback 20, Nottingham.

Davidson, B.(1978) *Africa in Modren History*, Penguin, Harmondswarth.

Day, R. (1977) 'Trotsky and Preobrazhensky: the trouled unity of the Left opposition', *Studies in comparative Communism,* 10, pp. 77-91.

De Lancey, M., Elliot, S., Green, D., Menkhaus, K, Moqtar, M. & Schraeder, P. (1988) *World bibliographical Series:Somalia*, Clio Press, Oxford.

Denitch, B. (1990) *The End of the cold War,* Verso, London.

Dessalegn Rahmato (1987) *Famine and Survival Strategies: a case study from Northeast Ethiopia,* Addis Ababa University, Institute of development Studies, Addis Ababa. Food and Famine Monograph Series No 1.

Dey, J. (1982) 'Development planning in The Gambia: the gap between planners' and farmers' perceptions, expectations and objectives', *World Development,* 10(5).

Dhaouadi, M. (1988) 'An operational analysis of the phenomenon of th other underdevelopment in the Arab world and in the third world', *International Sociology,* 3(3) (September), pp.219-34.

Diamond, L., Linz,J.& Lipset, S.(eds)(1988)*Democracy in Development Countries: Africa,* Adamantine Press, London.

Diamond, L., Linz,J.&Lipset,S.(eds)(1989)*Democracy in Developing countries: Asia,* Adamantine Press, London.

Diaz, B. (1963) The *Conquest of New Spain,* penguin, Harmondswarth.

Dicken, P. (1986) *Global Shift,* Harper and Row, New York.

Dirks, N. B. (1988) *The Hollow Crown: ethnohistory of and Indian Kingdom,* Cambridge University Press, Cambridge.

Breze, J. & Sen, A, (1989) *Hunger and Public Action,* Clarendon Press, Oxford.

Dubb, A. (1974) 'The impact of the city', in Hammond-Tooke, W. D. (ed.) *The Bantu Speaking Peoples of Southern Africa,* 2nd edn, pp.441-72, Routledge & Kegan Paul, London.

Dwyer, D. & Bruce, J. (eds) (1988) *A home Divided: women and income in the Third World,* Stanford University press, Stanford, Cal.

Dyson, T. & Moore, M. P. (1983) 'On kinship structure, female autonomy and demographic behaviour in India', *Population and Development Review,* 9 pp.35-60.

Ebrahim, G. J. & Ranken,J. P. (1988) *Primary Health care:reorienting organisational support,* Macmillan London.

Eckstein, A. (1977) *China's Economic revolution,* Cambridge University Press, Cambridge.

Edwards, M. (1989) 'The irrelevance of development studies', *Third World Quarterly,* 11(1) (January), pp.116-35.

Eisenstadt, S.(1966) *Modernization: protest and change* Prentic-hall, Englewood Cliffs, N.N.

Eisenstadt, S. N. (1973) *Tradition, Change and Modernity,* Wiley-Interscience, London.

Ellman, M. 'Did the agricultural surplus provide the resources for the increase in investment in the USSR during the first Five Year Plan?', *Economic Journal,* 85,pp.844-63.

Elson, D. (ed). (1991) *Male Bias in the Development Process,* Manchester University Press, Manchester.

Wnloe, C. (1989) *Bananas, Beaches and Bases,* Pandora, London.

Erlich, A. (1960) *The Societ Industrialization Debate 1924-8,* Harvard University Press, Cambridge, Mass.

Erlich, P. (1968) *The Population Bomb,* Ballantine books, New York.

Erlmann, V. (1985) 'Black political song in South Africa - some research perspectives', in Horn, D. (ed.) *Popular Music Perspectives,* vol.2, pp.187-209, International Association for the Study of Popular Music, Exeter.

Erlmann, V. (1990) 'Migration and performance: Zula migrant workers' Isicathamiya performance in South Africa, 1890-1950', *Ethnomusicology,* (Spring/Summer), pp.199-220.

Fallers, L. (ed.) (1964) *The King's men,* Oxford University Press, Oxford.

Fanon, F. (1961; 1963; 1967; 1969) *TheWretched of the Earth, trans.* C. Farrington, Penguin, Harmondsworth.

Farooq, G. M. & DeGraff, D. S. (1990) 'Fertility and development: an introduction to theory, empirical research and policy issues', *Training in Population, Humman resources and Development planning,* 7, International Labour Office, Geneva.

Feldman, r. (1989) 'Women for a change: the impact of structural adjustment on women in Zambia, Tanzania and Mozambique', War on Want, London.

Frank, R. & Chasin, B. (1981) 'Peasants, peanuts, profits and pastoralists', *Ecologist,* 11, pp. 156-68.

Freire, P. & Shor, I. (19876) *A Pedagogy for Liberation* Macmillan, London.

Friedman, S. (1987) *Building Tomorrow Today: African workers in trade unions* 1970-84, Ravan Press, Johannesburg.

Fukuyama, F. (1989) 'The End of History?' *The Public Interest,* Summer, p.63.

Fukuyama, F. (1990) 'Forget Iraq - history IS dead', *The guardian,* 7 September.

Galbraith, J. K. (1972) *The New Industrial State,* Andre Deutsch, London (2nd edn) (Penguin, harmondsworth 1974).

Galbraith, J.K. (1990) 'The price of world peace', paper prepared for 1990 Oslo conference sponsored by the Norwegian Nobel Peace Committee and the Elie Wiesel foundation for Humanity on the Continuing issues of hate and conflict as the Cold War ends, reprinted in *The Guardian,* 8 September 1990.

Gandhi, M. K. (1928) *Young India,* Viking Press Ganesan, London.

Gann, L. H. & Duignon, P. (1967), *Burden of Empire an appraisal of Western Colonialism in Africa South of the Sahara,* Hoover Institution Press, Stanford.

Gastil, R. D. (1988) *Freedom in the World: political rights and civil liverties, 1987-88,* University Press of America, lanham, MD.

Geertz, C. (1984) 'Culture and social change: the indonesian case', *Man,* 19, p.511-32.

George, S. (1976) *How the Other Half Dies,* Penguin, harmondsworth.

Ghai, D. (ed.) (1965) *Portrait of a Minority: Asians in east Africa,* Oxford University press, Oxford.

Gheerbrant, A. (ed.) (1961) *The Incas,* Orion Press, New York (Avon Books, 1966).

Ginwala, F., Mackintosh, M. & Massey, D. (1991) *Gender and Economic Policy in a Democratic South Africa,* DPP Working Paper No. 21, the Open University, Milton Keynes.

Goldsworthy, D. 91988) 'Thinking politically about development', *Development and Change,* 19(3)(July), pp.505-30.

Gordon, D. 91988) 'The global economy: new edifice or crumbling foundations? *New Left Review,* 168 (March), pp.24-65.

Gordon, S. (1985) 'Ladies in limbo', Commonwealth Secretariat.

Goulet, D. (1971) *The Cruel choice: a new concept in the theory of development*, Atheneum, New York.

Gramsci, A. (1988) 'Some Theoretical and practical Aspects of 'Economism', in Forgacs, D. (ed.), *A Gramsci Reader*, Lawrence and Wishart, london.

Gronow, P. (1983) 'The record industry: the growth of a mass medium', *Popular Music*, 3, pp.53-75.

Guha, R. (1989) *The Unquiet Woods: ecological change and peasant resistance in the Himalaya*, Oxford University Press, Delhi.

Guia del Tercer Mundo (1981) Periodistas del Tercer Mundo, Mexico.

Gwynne, R. B. N. (1990) *New Horizons? Third World Industrialisation in an International Framework*, Longman Scientific and Technical, London.

Habib, I. (1969) 'Potentialities of Capitalistic development in the economy of Mughal India', *Journal of Economic History*, 29, pp.32-78.

Halliday, F. & Molyneux, M. (1981) *The Ethiopian Revolution*, Verso, London.

Halliday, F. (1978) 'Revolution in Afghanistan', *New Left Review*, 112, pp.3-44.

Halliday, F. (1979) *Iran: dictatorship and development*, Penguin, Harmondsworth.

Halliday, F. (1980) 'Warand revolution in Afghanistan', *New Left Review*, 119, pp. 20-41.

Halliday, F. (1981) 'The North Korean enigma', *New Left Review*, 127, pp.18-52.

Halliday, F. (1987) *The Making of the Second Cold War*, Verso, London.

Halliday, F. (1989) *Cold War, Third World*, Abacus, London.

Halliday, F. (1990a) 'The End of Cold War', *New Left review*, 180, pp.5-23.

Halliday, F. (1990b) *Cold War, Third World*, Hutchinson, London.

Hamm, C. (1989) '*Graceland* revisited', *Popular Music* 8(3), pp.299-304.

Han Sung-joo (1989) 'South Korea: politics in transition', in Diamond, L., J. & Lipset, S.(eds), *Democracy in Developing Countries: Asia*, pp.267-303, Adamintine Press, London.

Harris, M. (1969) *The Rise of Anthropolicical Theory*, Routledge and Kegan Paul, London.

Harris, n. (1986) *The End of the Third World*, I. B. Tauris, London.

Harris, N. (1987) *The End of the Third World*, Penguin, london.

Harris, B. (1989) 'Differential female mortality and health behaviour in India', *Ld'A-QEH Development Studies Working Papers*, Oxford.

Hartmann, B. & Standing, H. (1989) *The Poverty of population Control: family planning and health policy in Bangladesh*, Bangladesh International Action Group (BIAG), London.

Hartmann, B. 91987) *Reproductive Rights and Wrongs: the global politics of population contro and contraceptive choice*, Harper & row, New York.

Hartmann, J. (1990) 'The rise and rise of private capital', in O'Neill, N. & Mustafa, K. (eds) *Capitalism, Socialism and the Development Crisis in Tanzania*, Avebury, Aldershot, pp.233-54.

Hayter, T. (1989) *Exploited Earth*, Earthscan, London.

Headrick, D. P. (1988) *The Tentacles of Progress: technology transfer in the Age of Imperialism, 1850-1940,* Oxford University Press, New York.

Heering, L. (1990) *Health Inputs and Impacts: a case study on the mediating role of mother's characteristics and practices on health of children in Indonesia,* Institute of Social Studies Working Paper No. 81, PO Box 90733, 2509 LS, The Hague, Netherlands.

Held, D. (1987) *Models of Democracy,* Polity Press, Cambridge.

Henderson, J. 91989) *The Globalisation of High Technology Production,* Routledge, London.

Hewitt, T., Johnson, H. & Wield, D. (eds) (1992) *Industrialization and Development,* Oxford University Press The Open University, Oxford (Book 2 of this series).

Hinton, W. (1972) *Fanshen,* Penguin, Harmondsworth.

Hobsbawm, E. & Ranger, T. (1983) *The Invention of Tradition,* Cambridge University Press, Cambridge.

Hobsbawm, E. (1968) *Industry and Empire,* Penguin, Harmondsworth.

Hubi K. 91986) 'The nomadic livestock production system of Somalia', in Conze, P. & Labahn, T. (eds) *Somalia: agriculture in the winds of change,* Epi Verlag, Hamburg.

IFPI (1981) 1981 World Sales, International Federation of Phonogram and Videogram Producers, London.

IFPI (1989) *The I.F.P.I. Review 1988/89,* International Federation of Phonogram and Videogram Producers, London.

Iliffe, J. (1979) *A Modern History of Tanganyika,* Cambridge University Press, Cambridge.

ILO (1976) *International Recommendations on labour Statistics,* International Labour Organization, Geneva.

ILO (1989-90) *Labour Statistics,* International Labour Organization, Geneva.

ILR (1988) 'Interview with Crispin Beltran', *International Labour Reports,* 27/28, Summer, pp.18-19.

IWHC 91986) *The Contraceptive Development Process and Quality of Care in Reproductive Health Services,* International Women and Health Coalition (with The Population Council), Meeting, 8-9 October, New York.

Jackson, K. 91989) 'The Philippines: the search for a suitable democratic solution, (1946-1986)', in Diamond, L., Linz, J. & Lipset, S. (eds), *Democracy in Developing Countries: Asia,* pp.231-265, Adamantine Press, London.

Johnson, R. W. (1972) 'French imperialism in Guinea', in Owen, E. R. J. & Sutcliffe, R. B. (eds) *Studies in the Theory of Imperialism,* Longman, London.

Hohnson, H. & Bernstein, H. (eds) (1982) *Third World Lives of Struggle,* Heinemann, London.

Johnson, Samuel (1810) *Dictionary of the English Language,* F. & C. Rivington, London.

Jordan, b. (1985) *The State: authority and autonomy,* Blackwell, Oxford.

Joss, S. (1990) *The economies of small: appropriate technology in a changing world,* Intermediate Technology Publications, London.

Karl, T. (1990) 'Dilemmas of democratization in Latin America', *Comparative Politics,* 23(1) (October), pp.1-21.

Kauffman, R. (1979-80) 'Tradition and innovation in the urban music Zimbabwe', *African Urban Studies,* 6, pp. 41-8.

Kegley, C. W. & Wittkopf, E. R. (1989) *World Politics,* Macmillan, London.

Khan, A (1990) 'The impact of international labour migration on the rural 'Barani' areas of modern Pakistan', PhD thesis, University of Sussex, Brighton.

King, M. (1990) 'Health is a sustainable state', *The Lancet,* 336, 15 September.

Kitching, G. (1980) *Class and Economic Change in Kenya,* Yale University Press, new Haven.

Kitching, G. 91982) *Development and Underdevelopment in Historical Perspective: populism, nationalism and industrialization,* Methuen, London.

Kitching, G. (1989) *Development and Underdevelopment in Historical Perspective,* Routledge, London (2nd revised edition).

Kloosterboer, W. (1960) *Involuntary Labour Since the Abolition of Slavery,* E. J. Brill, Leiden.

Kluckhohn, C. & Kroeber, A. (1952) *Culture,* Peabody Museum Papers, Harvard University, Cambridge, Mass., 67(1).

Krasner, S. (1985) *Structural Conflict,* University of California Press, Berkeley.

Krikler, J. (1987) 'Reflections on the transition to socialism in South African agriculture', Africa Perspective, New Series, 5&6, pp.95-120.

Laing, D. (1986) 'The music industry and the 'cultural imperialism' thesis', *Media, Culture and Society,* 8(3), pp.331-41.

Lappe, F.M. & Schurman, R. (1988) *Taking Population Seriously,* Earthscan Publications, London.

Lawand, T. A., Hvelplund, F., Alward, R., & Voss, j. (1976) 'Brace Research Institute's *Handbook of Appropriate Technology* (1975)', in Jequier, N. (ed.) *Appropriate Technologuy: problems and promises,* pp.124-36. OECD, Paris.

Leach, E. (1954) *The Political Systems of Highland Burma,* Cambridge University Press, Cambridge.

Lenin, V. I. (1939) *Imperialism: the highest stage of capitalism. A popular outline,* English version, International Publishers, New York (first published in Moscow 1916).

Lewis, I. (1965) 'The northern pastoral Somali of the Horn', in Gibbs, J. (ed.) *Peoples of Africa,* Holt, Rinehart and Winston, New York.

Lewis, I (1975) 'The dynamics of nomadism: prospect for sedentarization and social change', in Monod, T. (ed.) *Pastoralism in Tropical Africa,* Oxford University Press, London.

Lewis, I. (1985) *Social Anthropology in Perspective,* Cambridge University Press, London.

Leys, C. (1975) *Underdevelopment in Kenya,* Heinemann, London.

Lipset, D. (1989) 'Papua New Guinea: the Melanesian ethic and the spirit of capatalism,

1975-1986', in Diamond, L., Linz, J. & Lipset, S (eds) *Democracy in Developing Countries: Asia,* pp. 383-421, Amamantine Press, London.

Low, D. A. (1973) *Lion Rampant: essays on the study of British Imperalism,* Cass, London.

Mackintosh, M. (1981) 'Gender and economics: the sexual division of labour and the subordination of women', in Young, K.etal. (eds) *Of Marriage and the Market: women's subordination in international perspective,* CSE Books, London.

Maitan, L. (1976) *Party, Army and Masses in China,* New Left Books, London.

Maliyamkono, T. & Bagachwa, m. (1990) *The Second Economy in Tanzaniz,* James Curry, London.

Mamdani, M. (1973) *From Citizen to refugee: Ugandan Asians Come to Britain,* Frances Pinter, London.

Mamdani, M. (1976) *Politics and Class Formation in Uganda,* Heinemann, London.

Mamdani, M. (1983) *Imperialism and Fascism in Uganda,* Heinemann, London.

Mangat, J. S. (1969) *A History of the Asians in East Africa,* Clarendon Press, Oxford.

Mann, M. (1984) 'Capitalism and militarism', in Shaw, M. (ed.)*War, State and Society,* Macmillan, London.

Mannoni, D. (trans. Powesland, P.) (1956) *Prospero and caliban: the psychology of colonization,* Methuen, London.

Manuel, P. (1988) *Popular Musics of the Non-Western World: an introductory survey,* Oxford University Press, New York.

Markowitz, I. L. (1977) *Power and Class in Africa,* New Jesey, Prentice-Hall.

Martorell, R. (1988) 'Nutrition, infection and growth', *Clinical Nutrition,* 7(4), pp.156-67.

Martorell, R. (1989) 'Body size, adaptation and function', *Human Organisation,* 48(1), pp.15-20.

Mass, B. (1976) *Population Target: the political economy of population control in Latin America,* Charters Publishing, Ontario.

Mayall, J. (1990) *Nationalism and International Society,* Cambridge University Press, Cambridge.

McFarlane, B. (1984) 'Political economy of class struggle and economic growth in China 1950-1982', in Maxwell, N. & McFarlane, B.(eds) *China's Changed Road to Development,* Pergamon, Oxford.

McKeown, T. (1979) *The Role of Medicine,* Basil Blackwell, Oxford.

McLelland, D. (1963) 'The achievement motive in economic growth', in Hoselitz, B. F. & Moore, W. E. (eds) *Industrialization and Society,* UENSCO and Mouton, The Hague.

McNeill, W. H. & Waldman, M. R. (1973) *The islamic World,* Oxford University Press, New York.

Medows, D. H., Meadows, D. L., Randers, J;, & Behrens, W. III (1972)*The Limits to Growth,* Earth Island Ltd, London.

Meintjes, L. (1990) 'Paul Simon's *Graceland,* South Africa, and the mediation of musical meaning', *Ethnomusicology,* 34(1) (Winter), pp.37-73

Michaelson, K. L. (1981) *And the Poor Get Children: radical perspective on population dynamics,* Monthly Review Press, New York.

Michalak, S. J. (1983) *UNCTAD, Heritage* Foundation, Washington DC.

Misra, B. B. (1976) *The Indian Political Parties: an historical analysis of political behaviour up to 1947,* Oxford University Press, Delhi.

Mister, R. (1988) 'Refugees and Nomads: successes and failures in Somalia', in Poulton, R. & Harris, M. (eds) *Putting People First,* Macmillan, London.

Moghadam, V. (1991) 'Women's employment in the Middle East and North Africa: gender, class and state policies', Mimeo, UNU/World Institute of Development Economics Research, Helsinki.

Momsen, J. (1991) *Women and Development in the Third World,* Routledge, London.

Moore, B. (1966), *Social origins of Dictatorship and Democracy: lord and peasant in the making of the modern world,* Beacon Press, Boston.

Moore, B. (1967) *Social origins of Dictatorship and Democracy,* Allen Lane, london (Penguin, 1973).

Moore, B. (1969) 'Tolerance and scientific outlook', in Wolff, R., Moore, B. & Marcuse, H. (eds), *A Critique of Pure Tolerance,* pp.65-91, Cape, London.

Morrison, D. (1982) 'A critical examination of A. A. Barsov's empirical work on the balance of value exchanges between the town and the country', *Soviet Studies,* 34, pp. 570-84.

Mueller, R. (1983) 'Measuring women's poverty in developing countries', in Buvinic, M. *et al,* (eds) *Women and Poverty in the Third World,* Johns Hopkins University, Baltimore, MD.

Murphy, Y. & Murphy, R. F. (1974) *Women of the Forest,* Columbia University Press, New York.

Mutloatse, M. (ed.) (1987) *Umhlaba Wethu: a historical indictment,* Skotaville Publishers, Johannesburg.

Nair, S. (1989) *Imperialism and the Control of Women's Fertility,* Campaign Against Long Acting Contraceptives, Amsterdam.

Nandy, Ashis (1983) *The Intimate Enemy: loss and recovery of self under colonialism,* Oxford University Press, Delhi.

Nathan, A. (1986) *Chinese Democracy,* Tauris, London.

Nolan, P. (1976) 'Collectivization in China: some comparisons with the USSR', *Journal of Peasant Studies,* 3, pp. 192-220.

Nolan, P. (1989) *The Political Economy of Collective Farms,* Blackwell/Polity Press, Oxford.

Nzula, A. T., Potekhin, I. I. & Zusmanovich, A. Z. (1979) *Forced Labour in Colonial Africa,* Zed Press, London (first published in Moscow, 1933).

Oliver, R. & Fage, J. D. (1962) *A Short History of Africa,* Penguin, Harmondsworth.

Open University (1989) *Living with Technology: a foundation course, T102; Block 6 Health,* The Open University, Milton Kenynes.

Pacey, A. (1990) *Technology in World Civilization,* Basil Blackwell, Oxford.

Payne, P. R., Whitehead, A. & Young, K. (1984) 'The continuing subordination of women in the development process', in Young, K. *et al.* (eds), *OF Marriage and the Market: women's subordination in international perspective,* 2nd edn, Routledge, London.

Perham, M. & Simmons, J. (1948) *African Discovery,* Penguin, Harmondsworth.

Pielta, H. & Vickers, J. (1991) *Making Women matter: the role of the United Nations,* Zed Press, London

Pittin R. (1990) 'Women, work and ideology in the context of economic crisis : a Nigerian case study', *ISS Working Paper,* Sub Series on Women, History and Development, no. 11.

Population Reports (1987) 'Norplant implants', *Population Reports, Series K,* 3, March-April, Population Information program, Johns Hopkins University, Baltimore, MD.

Potter, D. C. (1986) *India's political Administrators; 1919-1983,* Calrendon Press, Oxford.

Poulton, R. & Harris, M. (eds) (1988) *Putting People First,* Macmillan, London.

Prince, r. (1989) 'South Africa-music in the shadows', in *Rhythms of the World,* pp.98-107, BBC Books, London.

Pye, L. (1985) *Asian Power and Politics: the cultural dimensions of authority,* Harvard University Press, Cambridge, Mass.

Rakovsky, C. (1981) 'The Five Year Plan in crisis', *Critique,* 13, pp. 5-54.

Randall, V. (ed) (1988) *Political Parties in the Third World,* Sage, London.

Ranger, T. (1985) *Peasant Consciousness and Guerilla War in Zimbabwe,* James Currey, London.

Ravenhill, J. (1990) 'The North-South balance of power', *International Affairs,* 66(4), pp.731-48.

Raza, S.H. (undated) Unpublished Papers, India Office Library, MSS, Eur. F. 180/29.

Redclift, M. 91987) *Sustainable Development: exploring the contradictions,* Routledge, London.

Reddy, A. K. N. (1979) *Mazingira: the world forum for environment and development,* no. 8.

Riskin, C. (1988) *China's Political Economy,* Oxford University Press, Oxford.

Robbins, A. & Freeman, P. (1988) 'Obstacles to developing vaccines for the Third World', *Scientific American,* November, 259(5), pp.90-5.

Robinson, F. C. R. (1971) 'Consultation and control: the United Provinces' government and its allies, 1860-1909', *Modern Asian Studies,*5(11), pp.313-36.

Robinson, R. (1988) 'Authoritarian states, capital-owning classes, and the politics of newly industrializing countries: the case of indonesia', *World Politics,* 41(1) October), pp.52-74.

Rogow, D. (1986) 'Quality care in international family planning: a feminist contribution', in IWHC (eds) *The Contraceptive Development Process and Quality of Care in Reproductive Health Services,* International Women and Health Coalition (with The Population Council), Meeting, 8-9 October, New, York.

Roseberg, C. G. & Nottingham, J. (1966) *The Myth of 'Mau Mau': nationalism in Kenya,* East African Publishing House, Nairobi.

Ritberg, R. I. (1983) 'Nutrition and history', in Rotberg & Rabb (eds) *Hunger and History: the impact of changing food production and consumption patterns on society,* Cambridge University Press, Cambridge,

Rungta, R. S. (1970) *The Rise of Business Corporations in India, 1851-1900,* Cambridge University Press, Cambridge.

Rustow, D, (1970) 'How does a democracy come into existence?', *Comparative Politics,* 2, pp.37-63.

Ruthven, M. (1984) *Islam in the World,* Penguin, Harmondworth.

Rycroft, D. (1957) 'Zulu male traditional singing', *African Music* 1(4), pp.33-5.

Rycroft, D. (1977) 'Evidence of stylistic continuity in Zulu 'town' music', In KPW Festschrift Committee (eds) *Essays for a Humanist: an offering to klaus Wachsmann,* Town House Press, New York.

Sahlins, M. (1976) *Culture and Practical reason,* Aldine, Chicage.

Salvadori, C. (1983) *Through Open Doors: a view of Asian cultures in Kenya,* Kenway Publications, Nairobi.

Sanders, D. (with Richard Carver) (1985) *The Struggle for Health: medicine and the politics of underdevelopment,* Macmillan, London.

Sandhy, R. & Sandler, J. (1986) *The Tech and Tools Book: a guide to technologies women are using world-wide,* International Women's Tribune Centre, New York, and Intermediate Technology Publications, London.

Schiff, L.M. (1939) *The Present Condition of India: A Study in Social relationships,* Quality Press, London.

Seers, D. (1963) 'The Limitations of the special case', *Bulletin of the Oxford Institute of Economics and Statistics,* 25(2) May.

Seers, D. (1969; 1979) 'The meaning of development', in Lehmann, D. (eds) *Development Theory: four critical studies,* Frank Cass, London.

Selden, M. (1971) *The Yenan Way in Revolutionary China,* Harvard University Press, Cambridge, Mass.

Selden, M. (1984) 'The logic - and limits - of Chinese socialist development', in Maxwell, N. & McFarlane, B. (eds) *China's Changed Road to Development,* Pergamon, Oxford.

Sen, A. (1975) *Employment, Technology and Development,* Clarenden Press, Oxford.

Sen, A. (1981) *Poverty and famines: an essay on sntitlement and deprivation,* Oxford University Press, Oxford.

Sen, A. (1984) *Resources, Values and Development,* Basil Blackwell, Oxford.

Sen, A. K. (1987) 'Gender and cooperative conflicts', Mimeo, World Institute of Development Economics Research, Helsinki.

Sen, G. (1989) 'Fertility decline and women's autonomy: another look', paper presented at the International Economics Association, Athens, 28 August-1 Septmber.

Shaban, M. A. (1971) *Islamic History: a new Interpretation*, Cambridge University Press, Cambridge.

Shiviji, I. (1976) *Class Struggles in Tanzania*, Heinemann, London.

Silverblatt, I. (1988) 'The Universe has turned inside out. There is no justice for us here'. Andean Women under Spanish Rule', in Etienne, M. & Leacock, E. (eds) *Women and Colonization: anthropological perspectives*, Praeger, New York.

Singer, H. W. (1989) *Lessons of Post-War Development Experience: 1945-1988*, Discussion Paper no. 260, April, Institute of Development Studies, Brighton.

Sivan, E. (1985) *Radical Islam*, Yale University Press, London.

Smelser, J. J. (1968) 'Toward a theory of modernization', in Smelser, N. J. (ed.) *Essays in Sociological Explanation*, Prentice-Hall, Englewood Cliffs, N.J.

Snow, R. (1972) *Red Star over China*, Penguin, Harmondsworth.

Soto, H. de (1989) *The Other Path: the invisible revolution in the Third World*, Harper & Row, New York.

South Commission (1990) *The Challenge to the South*, Oxford University Press, Oxford.

Standing, G. (1981) *Labour Force Participation and Development*, International Labour Organization, Geneva.

Stapleton, C. & May, C. (1989) *African All-Stars: the pop music of a continent*, Paladin, London.

Strake, L. (1990) *Signs of Hope*, Oxford University Press, Oxford.

Stein, B. (1977) 'Privileged land-holding', in Frykenberg, R. E. (ed) *Land Tenure and Peasant in South Asia*, Orient Longman, New Delhi.

Stein, B. (1990) *Vijayanagara*, Cambridge University Press,Cambridge.

Stein, S. J. (1972) 'Bramilian Slavery re-examined', in Winks, R. W. (ed.) *Slavery: a comparative perspective*, New York University Press, New York.

Thaiss, G. (1972) 'Religious Symbolism and Social Change: the drama of Husain', in Keddie, N. (ed.) *Scholars, Saints and Sufis*, University of California Press, Berkeley.

Thelwell, M. (1982) 'Looking for work in Kingston', in Johnson, H. & Bernstein, H. (eds) *Third World Lives of Struggle*, Heinemann, London.

Therborn, G. (1978) 'The rule of capital and the rise of democracy', *New Left Review*, 103 (May-June), pp.3-41.

Thuku, H. (1970) *An Autobiography*, Oxford University Press, Nairobi.

Tinker, H. (1974) *A New System of Slavery*, Oxford University Press, Oxford.

Tinker, I. (1979) *New Technologies for Food Chain Activities: the imperative of equity for women*, Office of Women in Development, Agency for International Development, Washington DC.

Toye, J. (1987) *Dilemmas of Development: reflections on the counter-revolution in development theory and policy*, Basil Blackwell. Oxford.

Tracey, A. (1987) 'A word from the editor', *African Music*, 6(4), p.3.

Treece, D. (1988) 'Your enemy is our enemy', *International Labour Reports,* 26, March/ April, p.13.

Turton, D. (1988) 'Anthropology and Development', in Leeson, P. & Minogue, M. (eds) *Perspectives on Development,* Manchester University Press, Manchester.

UNDP (1990) *Human Development Report 1990,* United Nations Development Programme, Oxford University Press, Oxford.

UNFPA (1989a) *The State of World Population, 1989,* United nations Population Fund, New York.

UNFPA (1989b) *1988 Report,* United Nations Population Fund, New York.

UNFPA (1990a) *Investing in Women: the focus of the '90s,* United Nations Population Fund, New York.

UNFPA (1990b) *Population Issues: a briefing kit,* United Nations Population Fund, New York.

UNICEF (1988) *Asian and Pacific Atlas of Children in National Development, UNICEF* East Asia and Pakistan Regional Office with the co-operation of the United Nations Economic and Social Commission for Asia and the Pacific (ESCAP).

UNICEF (1990) *State of the world's Children,* Oxford University Press, Oxford.

Visaria, P. (1990) *Concepts and Measurement of Unemployment and Underemployment in ESCAP Countries: a comparative study,* Working Paper No.31, The Gujarat Institute of Area Planning, Ahmedabad.

Walby, S. (1990) *Theorizing Patriarchy,* Blackwell, Oxford.

Wallerstein, I. (1989) 'The Myrdal Legacy: racism and underdevelopment as dilemmas', *Cooperation and Conflict,* 24, pp.1-18.

Wallis, R. & Malm, K. (1984) *Big Sounds from Small Peoples: the music industry in small countries,* Constable, London.

Wallraff, G. (1985) *The Lowest of Low,* Methuen, London.

Waring, M. (1989) *If Women Counted: a new feminist economics,* Macmillan, London.

Warnock, J.W. (1988) The politics of hunger, Methuen, Toronto.

Warren, B. (1980) *Imperialism: pioneer of capitalism,* Verso, London.

Washbrook, D. A. (1981) 'Law state and agrarian society in colonial India', *Modern Asian Studies,* 15(3), pp.649-721.

WCED (1987) *Our Common Future* (The Brundtland Report), Oxford University Press, Oxford.

Weiner, M. (1965) 'India: two political cultures', in Pye, L. & Verba, S. (eds) *Political Culture and Political Development,* Princeton University Press, Princeton.

Whitcombe, E. (1972) *Agrarican Conditions in Northern India; col.1: The United Provinces under British Rule, 1860-1900,* University of California Press, Berkeley.

Whitehead, A. (1985) 'Effects of technological change on rural women: a review on analysis and concepts', in Ahmed, I. (ed.) *Technology and Rural Women,* Allen and Unwin, London.

Whitehead, A. (1990) 'Food crisis and gender conflict in the African countryside', in Bernstein, H., Crow, B., Mackintosh, M. & Martin, C. (eds) *The Food Question: profits versus people,* Earthscan, London.

WHO (1989) *World Health Statistics Annual,* World Health Organization, Geneva.

Willetts, P. (1978) *The NonOaligned Movement: the origins of a Third World alliance,* Francis Pinter, London.

Wink, A. (1986) *Land and Sovereignty in India: agrarian society and politics under the eighteenth century Maratha Svarajya,* Cambridge University Press, Cambridge.

Winner, L. (1977) *Autonomous Technology: technics-out-of-control as a theme in political thought,* Massachusetts Institute of Technology Press, Cambridge, Mass., and London.

Wolf, E. (1982) *Europe and the People without History,* University of California Press, Berkeley.

World Bank (1980) *World Development Report 1980,* Oxford University Press, Oxford.

World Bank (1983) *The Effect of Piped Water on Early Childhood Mortality in Urban Brazil, 1970-76,* Thomas Merrick, World Bank, Washington DC.

World Bank (1984) *World Development Report 1984,* Oxford University Press, Oxford.

World Bank (1985) *Quantitative Studies of Mortality Devline in the Developing World,* by Julie Da Vanzo, Jean-Pierre Habicht, Ken Hill & Samuel Preston, World Bank, Washington DC.

World Bank (1987) *Sri Lanka and the World Bank: a review of a relationship,* World Bank, Washington DC.

World Bank (1990) *World Development Report 1990,* Oxford University Press, Oxford.

Worsley, P. (1964; 1967) *The Third World,* Weidenfeld and Nicholson, London.

Worsley, P. (1979) 'How many worlds?', *Third World Quarterly,* 1(2), pp. 100-8.

Worsley, P. (1984) *The Three Worlds,* Weidenfeld and Nicholson, London.

Wuyts, M., Mackintosh, M. & Hewitt, T. (eds) (1992) *Development Policy and Public Action,* Oxford University Press/The Open University, Oxford (Book 4 of this series).

Young, K. (1989) *Women and Economic Development: local, regional and national planning strategies,* Berg/UNESCO.

CHAPTER-8

HIC Women and Shelter Network

I. WHY WOMEN AND SHELTER ?

WOMEN ALL OVER the world are concerned with the basic sustenance of their families. In urban slums and squatter settlements, it is the women who have to provide water and other services. In Africa, women spend much of their time transporting fuelwood and water. In Latin America, women sustain urban settlements in other ways. For example, in Lima, Peru there are about 3,500 communal kitchens run by women and 7,000 groups providing milk to children.[(1)] When shelters are threatened with demolition it is the women who lead the struggle to protect families homes. box I provides an example from South Africa, in Regina Ntongana's description of how women worked and organized in Crossroads. Yet women's central role in the production of subsistence is unrecognized and unplanned for. Women all over the world are responsible for work in the home. In the Third World this means providing basic services like water, fuel and even growing and processing as well as cooking the food. As pointed out by an African regional network meeting in 1991.

"Both economic and land use planners neglect the subsistence resource base because women have no vioce. It is a historical fact and not a biological necessity that women handle subsistence. Neglect of this sector is damaging not only to women but to whole societies and planetary ecosystems. If women's central role is not recognized sustainable development can never be achieved. Women must have the opportunity to fully participate in the planning implementation and mangement of their habitat.

Women worldwide do not have the same access as men to land and shelter. Because of their traditional role, they are more responsible for household and neighbourhood services: they are more active neighbourhood organizations than men, although they are seldom the formal representatives.

II. WOMEN'S ROLE IN HABITAT INTERNATIONAL COALITION

IN 1988, HABITAT Inernational Coalition (HIC) launched its Women and Shelter Network to address the information gap on these issues and to develop a support network for community based organization dealing with women and shelter worldwide.

Habitat International Coalition is formed by over 200 non-governmental organizations from over 50 nations working in housing or related subjects.[2] It acts as an international pressure group in defence of the rights of the homeless, the poor and the inadequately housed. Orginally formed in 1976 after the United nations Conference on Human settlements (Habital) in vancouver. Habitat International Coalition has been in the process of transforming itself into a more grassroots and Third World oriented coalition since 1987-the year designated by the United Nations as the International Year of Shelter for the Homeless (IYSH).

There were a number of women and organizations active on women's issues involved in the 1987 initiative to change and broaden the coalition's focus so integrating women and their shelter concerns became an important part of this. A group of women from concerned NGOs met in New Delhi in early 1988 to advise the Coalition on how to integrate women and shelter issues into its organizational process. Although most of these women met each other for the first time. They rapidly developed a common understanding of the urgency of the issue and what needed to be done. SPARC and the Federation of building and Woodworkers from India, Klongtoey Community Development Credit Union from Thailand, Mazingira Institute of Kenya, RADI from Senegal, the Construction Resource and Development Centre of Jamaica. Rooftops Canada, and the IYSH Trust form the UK shared their understanding of what it is that motivates women to take action on issues affecting their daily lives.

It was not difficult to develop a plan of action for Habitat Inernational coalition based on this clear common understanding. but the difficulties arose when that common understanding was not so quickly achieved in other members of the coalition and there was considerable debate as to the right of the Women and Shelter Group to advise the Coalition The actions that this group had recommended at their 1988 New Delhi meeting did not seem so obvious to them.

Nevertheless, the Plan of Action of the HIC Women and Shelter Group was adopted by the Coalition's General Assembly in New Delhi.

Debate within Habitat International Coalition centred on the recommendation of the Women and Shelter Group's Plan of Action to have three members of this group (which by now was constituted as a subcommittee of the Board) sitting on the Board. The Women and Shelter Group had proposed that a Women and Shelter Network be established, and that its representatives would eventually be the ones sitting on the Board. The idea was that at least three of the 20 or so Board members should represent women's issues and be active at policy level within the organization. A constitutional amendment allowing for this was passed at the Coalition's General Assembly in Cartagena in 1989.

The changeover from the original Board members to a representative group is now taking place. Meanwhile, women are beginning to have more impact within Habitat International Coalition's Board, and there is a better integration of women' issues in all aspects of the Coalition's work. One example of this is the close collaboration of the HIC Women and Shelter Network and the Asian Coalition of Housing Rights on grassroots networking and evictions in Asian countries. Another example is the inclusion of women's concerns in all working groups at the International Forum organized by the Coalition on Sustainable Development in Mexico in early 1991. This happened because the working group on Women and Shelter split up so different members could work in each of the other groups. Several of the working group were in fact men, making it clear that it is the issues that are important, and not the gender of the participant.

III. BUILDING A NETWORK

MEANWHILE, THE HIC Women and Shelter Network has been growing, in a decentralized and organic way. The original Women and shelter Group was set up during the discussions and debates among members of Habitat International Coalition about how the Coalition should be transformed. But the Group is also still in its own process of transformation. Its major goal defined in the plan of Action in New Delhi in 1988 is to establish the Women and Shelter Network. Its structure is intended to be participatory, representative and accountable. "The establishement of the Women and Shelter Group on a permanent basis and the launching of the Women and Shelter Network are not ends in themselves but a means of ensuring that all activities of HIC recognize and incorporate women's concerns and issues relative to shelter."

The Women and Shelter Network aims at a decentralized decision-making process that truly reflects shelter priorities at the grassroots level. As a structure, it should simply provide a channel that permits links between women in different poor communities. In 1991 the network is producing the third issue of its newsletter (in Engligh. French, Spanish and Portuguese) through its secretariat now based at Mazingira Institute in Nairobi. But this international linking is only a superficial manifestation of the nework. Its major priority is support and encouragement of women's activities on shelter improvement at the community level in the countries and regions. The network mainly exists to strengthen and support their efforts to organize themselves through various means. The newsletter serves as one forum for amplifying the voice of women from poor communities.

"Initiative centres" are organizations that work with or represent community based organizations dealing with women and shelter. As and when they join the network, information on what they are doing can be shared with others, and in turn the network can encourage and sustain their work. The system of initiative centres is still in its early stages and each region is developing its own strategy on how to network. Groups of initiative centres communicate through the network, and one from each region is nominated to sit on the HIC Women and Shelter Group. This policy making group is the link with the HIC Board, so initiative centres have to think about joining the Coalition as well.

MUCH OF THE networking in Asia evolved around the work of SPARC, Mahila Milan and the National Federation of Slum Dewllers in India making links at the regional level through the Asian Coalition for Housing Rights (whose Secretariat is based in Bangkok). The work of SPARC in linking groups of women pavement and slum dwellers between neighbourhoods and cities was described in some detail in an NGO profile in *Environment and Urbanization* Vol. 2. No. 1 in April 1990. Mahila Milan is a community based organization of women which started originally in Bombay. Through meeting women in other communities, women are able to learn from each other about how to lobby for their rights to secure shelter. Women from poor communities are able to get exposure as to how other organizations of women deal with issues. They learn how women's participation is different in different communities and how this works. Women from grassroots organizations in eight followed by the Asian People's Dailogue held in Seoul, Korea in June 1989. [(3)]

Other groups in Asia have accessed the network through its newsletter. One of these, the "Design and Research Group on House Kitchens" promotes better conditions for urban women. As a result of joining the network, the group is organizing meetings with community social workers in Nanjing and Beijing (china) based on issues translated from the newsletter, and is distributing the newsletter in other parts of the country through the Chinese Women's Federation.

Networking in Latin America has focused around efforts to link the work of the numerous NGOs, networks and coalitions already operating in the region, and to strengthen their activities. A regional meeting in Bogota in February 1991 identified the initial structure of initiative centres as well as regional priorities. A series of meetings of local grassroots and support groups in Bogota is already underway, focusing on women's concerns at neighbourhood level. In addition, as a result, women's issues are becoming a major concern across the board in the entire programme of at least one NGO.

Box 1: Regina Ntongana of Crossroads in Cape Town, South Africa.

"I was born in Cape Town in 1939, but I stayed with may granny untill she died in 1959 and I moved to Cape Town to join my mother. We lived in a shack on open land in what is now called Nyanaga Secton four. In 1965, I married a man from Transkei. Under apartheid law, he was not allowed to live in Cape Town because Transkei was his "homeland". Because of that law in 1974 I was sent to live in Transkei. I had four children when I went there and two of them died there. I was living with my husband's family. It was a desert. We lived in huts with no means of survival, so I decided I must come back.

That same year I was back in Cape Town at Brown's Farm, a township near Nyanga with a squatter camp shared by black and "coloured" people. I shared a house in a backyard for one year untill the Administration Board came and told us we had to move away because it was designated for "coloureds" only, We were told to move to a place called Crossroads.

The women decided to get together and think how to live here. We chose women from each area and walked to the churches to ask for help. First we built a school, then a clinic with church help. At first we were 16, then 20 elected women. We organized funds for rent and services and the churches helped.

In March 1975 there was a big raid on crossroads and many people were arrested and charged with trespass. But we brought a case in court and won, because some among us qualified to stay in Cape Town. In July 1976 Crossroads was declared an "emergency camp" which meant it could stay. In spite of that ruling, in 1976 they started moving many people, especially women, to Transkei. But we organized so that if anyone was being arrested they started to scream and others came to help. They arrested a few and destroyed their houses, but again our organizing succeeded, because they would come back and find the same people and the shacks rebuilt after a few days!

In 1977 we organized a play called "Exodus" about what was happening to us. Nobody taught us, it came out of our own experience. It took us three or four months to work it out. Women played all the parts. We went all over with that play thanks to donations. When we came back we continued organizing activities like the creche and adult schools. Three of us ran the advice office, supported by an NGO. We helped people on their rights, pensions,

when they lost their jobs and so on. But trouble was coming. there were more demolitions for rent arrears, and our chairman was replaced by Johnson Ngxobongwana who caused a lot of problems.

The community agreed to a plan for redevelopment. Some agreed to go to a new area and they set up the New Crossroads Committee. But not everybody was included in the plan so the community was divided. I stayed behind in Old Crossroads and we continued organizing through our women's organization Nomzamo. But we got caught up in the power struggles that went on between Ngxobongwana and other men over who controlled Crossroads. Ngxobongwana didn't want advice but

only put forward his own ideas. When we complained about him he burned our houses. Many of us were attacked and some killed. In 1983 all my belongings were stolen and I had to escape and move over to New Crossroads.

As for me, I have got may own house now in New Crossroads, but the struggle against evictions goes on. I work as a field worker for the Surplus People's Project (SPP), a support NGO. We advise and support people in urban and rural areas who are threatened with eviction. We also have lawyers in SPP who check the case and advise. The communities can call us by phone and we make visits once a week, but basically we get them to organize themselves. They elect a committee and take action with the authorities themselves. Through adult schooling the committees have also learned to translate so we are not needed when they have to deal with the whites.

I have learned many tactics during this time. We learned how to confront the white police by doing it. For example, we used to tip buckets from the latrines on the roads when we wanted action on services. That affects the motorists. One Sunday, they came arresting all the men. We women surrounded the police can and beat on it and screamed untill they got so fed up they let the men out. We followed even ministers into their offices as delegations of women. And we learned that the press is powerful.

If you are really fighting for people then you must forget who you are and just do it. I never gave in. As a leader you must be like that, but it is hard to find leaders like that. It's like being a washing line. When there is a lot of wet washing on it hangs down really low. If you're a leader its like the washing is hanging on you. Then you go up when it dries and you can take it off. Then you get another load. I shall go on as long as I have my health."

Networking in Africa began before the formation of the Women and Shelter Network through a regional meeting on women and shelter in 1987 which defined priorities and actions. Nevertheless, while there are many African grassroots women's groups, the infrastructure to support them is very weak. This was identified by a francophone Africa regioanl group meeting in Dakar in June 1990. An anglophone Africa meeting in April 1991 identified concrete actions needed to build the network. Participatnts from 11 countries including Portuguese-speaking Mozambique shared experiences, including those of network members form other regions. The need for exchange visits, especially between grassroots groups, was recognized as a high priority. A number of African NGOs are now considering taking of an initiative centre and holding local meetings to develop strategies.

In South Africa, women have been taking an active role in the struggle against apartheld, which is also a struggle for the right to land and housing for black people. Box 1 illustrated this, in the words of a participant at the SouthAfrican Peoples Dialogue on Land and Homelessness in Johannesburg in March 1991. As a result of that meeting, a women's Forum was established to give a platform and refuge to homeless women.

Networking in the North, in Europe and North America, has been slow to develop. This is partly the result of the history of Habitat International coalition which has largely consisted of NGO members who support settlements work in Third World countries. A strong commitment emerged in the Women and Shelter Group to build a network based on organizations dealing with local women and shelter issues in the North as well as in the South. The process of contacting such organizations and involving them in the network is underway, The lead is being taken through Canada's National Action Committee on the status of women (NAC) and through the contacts of Rooftops Canada. Homesles International in the UK and Shelter Sweden, all of whom support Third World work but are governed by boards made up of NGOs dealing with housing in their home countries.

V. ACTION FOR CHANGE

WOMEN'S CENTRAL ROLE in human settlements has not yet been properly recognized, let alone supported. The HIC Women and Shelter Network can contribute towards removing women's mantle of invisibility. Women's central role in maintaning the home through providing food and services, defending and maintaining the home and neighbourhood, earning and saving income, must be seen and rewarded. The Network can help strengthen and provide support for women's struggles and organizations and give them the legitimacy they deserve.

The HIC Women and Shelter Plan of Action developed in 1988 aims at change through a number of strategies at different levels. The primary strategy of energizing and supporting action at the grassroots level is being pursued in a decentralized way through networking in the regions. However, action across the regions is also occurring in a number of ways. For example, grassroots exchange visits are taking place between women's groups in Asia and Latin America, organized by Homeless International (UK), Fedevivienda (Colombia) and SPARC (India).

Information and action at the community level must also be brought to bear on action at policy level. The network can be used to channel the vioces of poor women to support NGOs and other powerful agencies. This is one function of having newsletter, which carries the stories of women's concerns and struggles in their own words.

Links to the United Nations system have also been a priority from the beginning, and are the focus of two items in the Plan of Action. Network members participated in the seminars on women and human settlements organized by the United Naions Centre for Human Settlements (Habitat) in all regions in 1988-89, as well as an interregional seminar in December 1989, which looked at women's role in the Global Strategy for Shelter to the Year 2000. This seminar recommended the establishment of a link between Habitat and the HIC Women and Shelter Group, so that the concerns of the network can permeate the international decision-making system. Such a link provides the potential for groups of women in poor neighbourhoods in different parts of the world to have their concerns heard by decision makers.

The same inter-regional seminar called for a full time post in the UN Centre for Human Settlements to address women's issues in the Global Shelter Strategy. This post has now been filled by a founder member of the group who acts as a formal liaison between the UN Centre and the HIC Women and Shelter Network.

Such preliminary steps leave women at the community level with very far to go before any real change can come about. Much will have to happen international agencies-including Habitat International Coalition itself-before anything more than lip service is given to the need to improve women's access to land and a safe, secure home. The HIC Women and Shelter Network provides the potential for change by setting up channels for the energies of women in poor communities so that in the long run they can have more impact.

Network membership forms and newsletters in English, French Spanish and Portuguese are available from the address below.

HIC women and Shelter Network Secretariat. Mazingira Institute Post Box 14564, Nairobi, Keneya

The Plan of Action for anglophone Africa is also available in English from this address.

NOTES AND REFERENCES

1. See paper by Maruja Barrig earlier in the issue of Environment & urbanization Vol 3 No. 2 1991 more details.
2. For more details, see NGO profile *Environment and Urbanization* Vol, 2, No. 1. April 1990.
3. For more details, write to the Asian Coalition for Housing Rights, P. O. Box 24-74. Klongchan, Bangkapi. Bangkok 10240, Thailand.

CHAPTER-9

Women, Environment and Urbanization : A Guide to the Literature

Judith Kjellberg Bell

I. INTRODUCTION

Women, Environemnt and urbanization as a distinct area of enquiry hardly appears as such in the literature, so the approach used in planning this Guide has been an indirect one, making use of two sets of different but nevertheless interlinked perspectives. One set of perspectives relates to the way in which women's in urban areas operate within their environment: this involves issues such as women's requirements for land and housing, the structure of households and families, women's responses to urbanization, their ways of earning income and their access to services. The other set relates to the impact on urban women of environmental degradation; women are in direct and daily contact with the environment through their use of resources (food, fuel and water) and through their efforts to maintain secure and healthy environments for their families.

The factor common to the way that all these elements impact on women across all geographical areas is poverty, which is very much a women's issue. Because of their economic and social status, women have access to fewer resources and fewer options in responding both to their own and their families needs, and to the demands that the environment places on them. Resource degradation and the feminisation of poverty are overlapping processes.

Much of the work included here, particularly the edited collections, is not limited to any one of these broad areas, but tends to consider them as inseparable elements in women's lives. This inseparability has resulted in considerable overlap between the sections of this Guide, which traces the women, environments and urbanization connection, then concentrates on women and shelter issues in human settlements, focusing on the household level to examine women's access to and use of resources. A brief review of some western work illustrates connections and differences in emphasis between First and

Third World issues. A section on international development has been included because of the significant role of agencies in generating and supporting policies and research projects.

The sections are as follow:

Environment and Urbanization: the Linkages for Women

International development Perspectives

Human Settlements and Housing

Household strategies

Collective Action

Law and Property

Some First World Work

Resources, Networks and Research

Substantial bodies of work exist in most of these areas. Only a very small number are Mentioned here, and these have been selected on the basis of their contribution to an understanding of the linkages. Much of the work included in the Guide is in the form of case studies, reflecting the lack of resources, both money and data, that have been available for major studies (a point referred to repeatedly in the literature). Only published work is included, with preference given to that which is recent and most accessible (some addresses are included at the end of the Guide). All the studies are in English which has contributed to the Guide's bias toward works by western researchers.(2) The participatory nature of much of the research has allowed women's voices to be heard.

II. WOMEN, ENVIRONMENT AND URBANIZATION

This section reviews work which has specifically addressed the built and natural environment linkage. A very new publication includes Caroline Moser, Frances Dennis and Dulce Castleton. "The Urban context: Women, Settlements and environment," Chapter 6 in sally Sontheimer, editor, Women and the Environment, A Reader: Crisis and Development in the third World (New York: Monthly Review Press, 1991, 192 pages, US $13, London: Earthscan Publications. Moser provides and introductory focus to the relationship between human settlements, or built environment, issues and the natural environment, approaching the linkage from the perspective of Vandana

Shiva's work[3] on the special relationship which women have with their natural environment by virtue of their daily tasks; and through these the extent to which they depend on natural systems, soil, water and trees, for survival in an urban context. Moser distinguishes between three roles for women: as managers, or maintainers, of the environment as it exists; as rehabilitators of the natural environment, in a sustainable development sense; and as innovators in the use of appropriate technology in the creation of new environments. The most critical issue in the urban context is land, because access to land is a prerequisite for access to shelter, and also because hazardous land conditions are so often the environment of Third World Urban women. Linked to land is housing; issues here revolve around housing design and settlement layout In addition, land zoning is a critical factor in women's income earning ability, separating places of work from residence. In their community managing role, women protect and care for the environment, working together, mobilizing, and challenging government for resources and access to services.

Two Latin Amrican case studies presented in the chapter address women's mobilization over environment issues. Moser draws on her Guayaquil, Ecuador work to show the critical role that women play in the formation, organization and success of Community protest groups to acquire land through invasion, or to pressure the state to allocate resources for basic infrastucture. The second study is of the Guarari Community Development project, an experiment in environmentally sensitive peri-urban low-cost housing in Costa Rica. Dennis and Castleton describe its origins in reaction to environmentally destructive squatter invasions and poor government response to infrastructure needs. Two community development organizations led the campaign for land for 3,000 houses. self-built in small groups to facilitate preservation of the natural habitat. The authors review the way this unique project works and the many measures of its success in community development, in strengthening the role of women, in skills training, and in environmental preservation.

"Women play a major role in managing natural resources soil, water, forests and energy. Their tasks in agriculture and animal husbandry as well as in the household make them daily managers of the living environment." Irene Dankelman and Joan Davidson. *Women and the Environment in the Third World: Alliance for the Future* (London: Earthscan, 1988, 210 pages) examine the relationships between women and their natural surroundings, and the way women deal with the kinds of environmental crises they face; they also look at the response of government agencies. Although the focus is on the natural habitat. Chapter six, "Human Settlements: Women's Environment of Poverty" provides a descriptive summary of the problems of environmental degradation faced by the poor, particularly by poor women: industrial pollution, poor services, human waste pollution, fumes from household fuel, and the consequences of soil erosion and flooding. Refugees, the majority of whom are women and children, live with especially severe environmental problems. The chapter concludes with a series of brief case studies, including those on squatter upgrading and urban agriculture in Lusaks, and the Baldia Soakpit project in Pakistan.

Forum 85 was organized as an NGO parallel event to the United Nations Conference of 1985 in Nairobi, which marked the end of the UN's Decade for Women. Two workshops are of particular interest. One was the Women and Habitat Workshop, described by Diana Lee Smith in "Nairobi 1985: Women and Habitat," *(Women & Environments,* Vol. 8 no. 1, 1986, pages 7-9). Strategies to address issues of food, water, energy, access to workplace, child and health care, and housing design are listed briefy; housing needs, especially those of female-headed households, and access to credit and materials are described along with recommendations made by the workshop. The Women. Environment and Development workshop series at Forum 85 were organized by the Environmental Liaison Centre (ELC) in Nairobi and published as a report on 'Women and the Environmental Crisis' (ELC's address is listed at the end of this review). For the most part they address natural environment issues, but a submission from UNCHS (the UN Centre for Human Settlements (Habitat)) stresses the linkage between environmental problems and their impact on the urban poor (particularly on women as the weakest component from economic, social and legal standpoints), and the rapid growth of cities.

III. INTERNATIONAL DEVELOPMENT PERSPECTIVES

The undecade for Women, 1975-85, played a crucial role in the legitimacy, focus and impetus it gave to research and discussion of women's social and economic issues, among them women and human settlements issues. H. Pictila and J. Vicker, Making Women Matter: the Role of the United nations (Zed Books, 1990), argue that the establishment of interrelationships between development processes and the position of women was one of the most important results of the decade.

The pivotal role of international development agencies in supporting both projects and research is examined by Eva M. Rathgeber, coordinator of the Gender and Development Unit of Canada's International Development Research Centre (IDRC). In "WID, WAD, GAD: Trends in Research and Practice" (Journal of Developing Areas, Vol. 24, July 1990, pages 489-502) Rathgeber shows the linkages between theories of development and women, and the different types of project that might flow from the application of each approach: Women in Development, Women and Development, and Gender and Development. WID came into use in the early 1970s after publication of Ester Boserup's ground breaking work on the differential impacts of development policies and projects on men and women.(4) WID was associated with the modernization paradigm, non-confrontational advocacy of legal and administrative changes to ensure women's better economic integration.The WAD perspective focuses primarily on the relationship between women and the processes of development, seeing women's condition primarily within the structure of international and class inequalities. Both WID and WAD are preoccupied with the productive at the expense of the reproductive part of women's lives. The GAD approach links these issues, taking into account all aspects of women's lives, and seeing women as agents of change rather than passive recipients of development assistance. As far as development agencies are concerned, the GAD approach is the most problematic because it is not easily integrated, but demands a commitment to structural change and power shifts that are unlikely to happen within agencies.

Caroline Moser also addresses the theme of different policy approaches in "Gender Planning in the Third World: Meeting Practical and Strategic Gender needs" (World Development, Vol. 17 No. 11. 1989, pages 1799-1825). Recognition of women's important role in Third World development has not necessarily been translated into the practice of socio-economic planning Moser describes the development of gender planning, which relates to the identification of women's triple roles - those of production and reproduction, with and additional one of community development - and the distinction between practical and strategic gender needs, concepts that she develops in her earlier work noted below. The article reviews gender needs in employment, in human settlements and housing (where housing design and facilitative zoning (practical needs) and tenure rights (strategic needs) are identified) and in delivery of basic services. Moser reviews defferent policy approaches to assisting poor Third World women: welfare, equity and anti-poverty, and the more recent approaches of efficiency and empowerment, discussing the kinds of programme and action that each produces, pointing out the necessity of a clear understanding of the practical and strategic needs that are addressed.

For a succinct and powerful view of the impact of development projects on women, see development, Crises, and Alternative Visions: Third World Women's Perspectives. The book was written by Gita sen and caren Grown for the project DAWN (Development Alternatives with Women for a new Era) and published by Earthscan in London and Monthly review Press in New York, 1987 (116 pages). Sen and Grown draw on evidence amassed during the UN Decade to point out that Third World Women's socio-economic status actually worsened over the period. They stress the importance of recognizing women's centrality to the production and distribution of food, and availability of water and fuel, and the distortions caused by development strategies. The book's notes and bibliography also provide useful information on organizations, issues and literature.

The importance of women's own voices is also a feature of Signe Arnfred, Agnete Weis Bentzon, editors. The language of development Studies (NewSocial Science Monographs, Copenhagen: Institute for Organization and industrial Sociology, 1990). The volume presents essays from a group of (mostly) Nordic teachers of development studies who share certain perspectives: the importance of "popular knowledge," of Third World people speaking for themselves: the complex ways in which people negotiate physical and cultural spaces resisting definitions and domination by forces beyond their control; and a perspective of "gender relations" rather than "women in development."Of particular interest from urbanization viewpoint is Suzanne Thorbek's comparative study of gender in slum cultures in Bangkok and Colombo (see the article in this issue of Environment and Urbanization); and Agnete Weis Bentzon's discussion of the role of law in the relationship between the post colonial, modernizing state and traditional lifestyles.

Irene Tinker's Persistent Inequalities; Women and World development (New york and Oxford: Oxford university Press, 1990,

320 pages) explores the expanding impact of women in development, from the point of view of scholars,practitioners and advocates. Policies supported by women have been able to influence the way development agencies design and implement programmes. An earlier attempt by development agencies to explore information about women's contributions to the economy of poor households, and the extent of women,s poverty, resulted in publication of mayra Buvinic, Margaret A. Lycette and William P. McGreevey,Women and Poverty in the Third World (Baltimore: Johns Hopkins, 1983).

IV. HUMAN SETTLEMENTS AND HOUSING

The literature in this area is extensive and diverse. The work described here has been selected for its own significance and also because it is representative of a range of issues and'approaches with an emphasis on the practical.

An excellent introduction to the issues of gender and urbanization is found in Lynne Brydon and Sylvia chant's Women in the Third World: Gender Issues in Rural and Urban Areas (New brunswick, NJ: Rutgers, 1989, 327 pages). This includes useful chapters on women and migration, urban health and services, urban planning, and household structure, reviewing for example work on how (or if) household structure is modified and transformed with urbanization and how this interrelates with the changing situation of women in cities. The introductory chapter provides an overview of women's roles and status in major Third World regions. The book includes a substantial bibliography.

Caroline O.N. Moser and Linda Peake, editors, Women Human Settlements and Housing (London and New York: Tavistock, 1987, 232 pages. US $14.95) makes a significant contribution to the literature on planning housing policy and settlements, both because of its theoretical approach in locating housing and gender issues within the broader political economy, and in its practical illustration of what interventions may or may not be successful in benefitting women. Caroline Moser presents a firm conceptual framework in chapter one; she distinguishes three interdependent roles of women: reproductive work (childbearing, family care), productive work as income earners, and a third, community managing - organizing the provision of items of community consumption. Of these roles, only production is recognized and given value in the dominant stereotypical conception of families, which means that women's lives are not understood nor are their needs properly addressed in policies and programmes. There is also a need to distinguish between different low-income household structures, uncovering the possibly one-third of the world's households which are female-headed (a figure which is much higher in latin America and parts of Africa). Sylvia Chant's chapter on the role of women in the housing process in Queretaro. Mexico, shows that women's participation is a critical determinant of dwelling standards, and that their participation and the resources allocated by the household to housing varies according to the household's composition, with those headed by women allocating the most. Leda Machado examines the extent to which a Brazilian site and service programme considers women's needs, and Paula Nimpuno-Parente approaches that question in a Nairobi project, where women's participation was impeded by selection criteria and an implementation process that discriminated against women. Marina Fernando examines the effects on women and on the community of an NGO community development project in Sri Lanka, which trained and empowered women in developing a housing project. Linda Peake assesses government housing policy in Guyana, and women's attempts to secure tenure rights. Irene Vance studies community participation in a self-help building Scheme examining the changes in gender roles that took place with "bottom-up" participation in a barrio project in managua, Nicaragua. In the final study, of Guayaquil, Ecuador, Caroline Moser focuses on the role of women in residential-level protest and struggle, suggesting that domestic based movements may be as important as workplace struggle in the development of urban social movements. In their concluding chapter. Moser and Peake express pessimism that the strategies and projects discussed in the book will be applied more widely because of the generally deteriorating shelter situation. The difficulties that women face in housing are likely to increase with the costs of structural adjustment, not only in terms of reduced governmental commitment to houseing, but also because of the tensions these costs impose on households. The chapter reviews the way that the case studies responded to women's gender needs, characterized as practical (services which assists women to fulfil their reproductive and productive roles, such as child care, clean water, and adequate housing), and strategic - those that stem from women's subordinate role and which can only be met through a different social organization. The volume includes a good bibliography.

Suzanne Thorbek's case study of women's daily lives in Khlong Toey' a slum area of Bangkok Voices from the City: Women of Bangkok (London and New York: Zed Books, 1987, 168 pages), examines the question of how women, as agents in the urbanization process, react to changes in their lives produced by their migration to urban slums. She makes liberal use of interview material in her examination of women's ways of earning money, their housework and family care, the structure of households, and social relations within families and between men and women. Thorbek documents the greater importance of family to women than to men, their reliance on helping and support networks and their involvement in organizing to improve conditions and to fight evictions - a starting point for her later work on women's role in social movements. She also raises the issue of prostitution as a response to women's dependent economic and sexual roles.

Two review documents from the UN Centre for Human Settlements make an important contribution: the first, Women and Human Settlements (UNCHS (Habitat), Nairobi, 1985, 92 pages, HS/OP/85/18) was presented as a contribution to the review of achievements of the UN Decade for Women, as well as a bridge to the 1987 International Year of Shelter for the Homeless (IYSH). While the report reviews evidence to support the need to treat women's housing issues as a distinct policy area, a literature review on housing as it affects low-income women uncovers the lack of a formal analytical framework, a lack of data and a "relative aimlessness" in research until that time. The report also cites the failure to view women as key participants in human settlements issues, and calls for recasting of women from a dependent to an independent actor in the process. Section two reviews policy approaches to the housing question for low-income women, and issues of education and training, access to services and credit, and to housing. The report is a useful general review of the area, and contains a good bibliographical list.

The context of the second report Women and Human Settlements Development (UNCHS (Habitat), Nairobi, 1989, 98, pages, HS/192/89) is an examination of progress made in light of housing strategies that emerged from the UN Decade. It reviews the literature on the roles of women in the development and management of human settlements, with an emphasis on shelter issues, examining the impact of housing policy on women, and discusses the effect of women's absence from settlements policy management. Section three is devoted to the access of women to land, with an overview of research in various countries; Section four reviews women's access to housing finance, the effect of macroeconomic policies, the employment of women in the financial sector, constraints on access to credit for women and some responses to these. Several case studies are given of credit programmes for women such as SEWA and the National Housing Trust of Jamaica. The construction sector and women's participation in construction and building materials production is the subject of Section five; the final section reviews women's involvement in grass roots efforts and low-income shelter projects. This is a really useful review of the research and issues, and is especially interesting in bringing together western experience of some of the questions with that of the situation of Third World women. The report has a lengthy bibliographical list.

The IYSH Women and Shelter Seminar, November-December 1987, Harare, Zimbabwe (Seminar Report 68 pages) was sponsored by the govts of Zimbabwe and Sweden to adress the inadequate shelter and unhealthy environments of a quarter of the world's population, the majority of the poorest being women. The report is a detailed resource document for governments. NGOs, donors and other agencies. It provides an overview and summary of women and shelter issues in Africa (for urban poor women, rural women and women on plantations and other work sites), health and services, shelter construction, land and legislation, organization and finance, research and information based on extensive secondary data from respondents in 13 countries who also participated in the meeting. It puts forward detailed recommendations and strategies for change within each of these areas, in the form of working group reports.

Women's role in housing production is examined by Anita Larsson, Modern Houses for Modern Life: the Transformation of Housing in Botswana (Report RI. Department of Building Functions Analysis, School of Architecture, University of Lund, Box 118, S-22100 Lund, Sweden, 1990). Larsson's slim volume, based on extensive interdisciplinary research, presents the challenging thesis that the modernization of housing in botswana has meant lower standards of use value; this is due to the erosion of women's traditional role in housing production, with utility becoming supplanted by status values.

Training project staff on the role of women in the execution of both sites and services and sqattter and slum upgrading projects is the subject of Caroline O.N. Moser and Sylvia Chant's course module. "The Role of Women in the Exectuon of Low-Income Housing Projects Training Module" (DPU Gender and Planning Working Paper No. 6, 1985). It indicates the reasons for the importance of women's participation in low-income housing projects. It also identifies different forms of women's participation in project execution, and the constraints that limit their participation, recommending ways to facilitate and improve their participation. The paper divides project execution into three stages: formulation (eligibility, recruitment, planning and financing), implementation (construction and services), and management (maintenance and cost recovery). Numerous examples or case studies from experience in different countries are used to illustrate approaches to each of these stages. The work formed the basis for the UNCHS publication: The role of Women in the Exection of Low-Income Housing Projects (1986).

V. HOUSEHOLD STRATEGIES

This section describes representative work which considers household survival and adaptive strategies, in both the "reproductive" area of family care and the "productive" area of income generation, notably informal work.

a. Housing and Households

Three reports have been published by the National Swedish Institute for Building Research, from a comparative project on five African capital cities designed to examine housing conditions of women-headed households, their housing strategies in various contexts, and governmental housing strategies, including upgrading and sites and services, in relation to women householders:

Ann Schlyter; Women Householders and Housing Strategies; the Case of George, Lusaka (Research report SB: 14, NSIBR, Gavle, 1988, 156 pages, SEK65); Ann Schlyter, Women Householders and Housing strategies: the Case of Harare (SB: 26, 1989, 203 pages); and Anita Larsson. Women Householders and housing Strategies: The Case of Gabarone, Botswana (SB: 25, 1988. 180 pages). Ann Schlyter has been engaged since 1968 on a longitudinal study of housing areas in southern Africa. Her data are drawn from official surveys and registers as well as from housing-household histories gathered through interviews. Women respond differently to upgrading than do men, being strongly committed to their housing, and having to overcome the constraints of being the sole income earner and adult for their families. Anita Larsson's parallel study reviews the factors governing the emergence of women householders and migration to urban areas, and their legal rights in relation to housing. She depicts housing "careers" open to women when they arrive in the city. All three reports review government housing policies in the respective countries (Zambia, Zimbabwe and Botswana), and the way these relate to women's housing strategies.

One area of importance to larsson is the situation of old and poor women. the ageing population in Third World cities is not an area which has been much addressed in the literature, but is bound to become of increasing concern with the rapid rise in the numbers of elderly people in urban areas.

Ann Schlyter's work also contributes to a recent collection produced in sweden, which focuses on the survival and adaptive strategies of the household/family as a way of approaching an understanding to Third World urbanization through an analysis of the interrelation between production and reproduction: Satya Datta, editor, Third World Urbanization: Reap praisals and New Perspective (Stockholm: Swedish Council for Research in the Humanities and Social sciences, 1990, 80 SEK plus postage). In Chapter 11, "Housing and Gender: Important Aspects of Urbanization," Schlyter draws on her empirical work in Lusaka and Harare, to argue that for poor and uneducated women on the margins of the urban labour market, house and neighbourhood are central to economic survival, a place of income generation as well as residence, and a means to have a secure investment, accommodate the family, and provide security against age and disability. She argues for a theoretical framework that is independent of the production/reproduction nexus, since "reproduction" cannot adequately explain some non-market activities within the household sphere; gender is a more significant concept in understanding household processes. Schlyter categorizes her work as a study of urbanization through the household perspective, since the women householders in adapting to urban life were changing conditions through their activities: "They were creators of an urban life form."

Further to these arguments, the work of cedric Pugh challenges the notion of housing as an arena of domestic consmption, arguing that it is a locus of human capital production which becomes dispersed in the form of social benefits and therefore interdependent with the wider economy. In "A New Approach to housing Theory: Sex, gender and the Domestic Economy" (Housing Studies, Vol. 5. No. 2, 1990, pages 112-129). Pugh suggests the need for a new economic theory of housing.

Ruth Mcleod's 1989 study of gender related differences in Household Shelter Behaviour among Low Income Households in Kingston, Jamaica (available from UNCHS in Nairobi) found that women household heads spend more than male heads on shelter because they tend to get caught in the rental market. They also give priority to income generation over shelter; are unlikely to take loans because of non-repayment fears; move more often; and are less likely to upgrade their dwellings. In light of the differences. Mcleod argues the need for housing policy makers to understand the feminization of poverty.

b. The Household and income: The Informal Sector

The informal sector is a major topic of discussion in much of the literature already included in this Guide, in addition to the range of perspectives mentioned below.

A classic collection of nine short articles by researchers from Britain, India, Argentina and Ghana presents an overview of the elements of the issue: "Women and the Informal Sector," a special issue of IDS Bulletin (Vol. 12, No. 3 1981, edited by kate Young and Caroline Moser). Informal work connected to the rapid growth of third World cities in the 1950s and 1960s gave rise to government support policies for male informal sector workers, although the data suggested that women rather than men were the majority of those involved. This collection reviews the interrelationship between informal work, women's domestic role, and the requirements of capital and labour and is an excellent introduction to this major area of research.

Sylvia chant, "Family Structure of Female labourers in Queretaro" (Chapter 12 in Janet H. Momsen and janet Townsend, Geography and Gender in the third World, London: Hutchinson. 1987) examines the role of household structure in influencing the access of women from the shanty towns of Queretaro in Mexico to income earning opportunities in both the formal and informal economy. She finds that nuclear families promote highly segregated male and female roles, while for women in extended families household support makes it more feasible for them to work, and women household heads have more freedom to determine their families earning strategies.

Ann Leonard, editor, SEEDS: Supporting Women's Work in the Third World (New York: Feminist Press, 1989,239 pages, US $12.95) presents a series of case studies originally published as pamphlets designed to provide information about the income generating programmes that provide women with cash, involve them in decision making and are economically sound. The studies include Ruth Mcleod's account of the Kingston Women's Construction Collective in Jamaica, which has provided basic training and skills upgrading, and resulted in a high rate of employment for its members. A second case study is on access to credit. Although women in Madras slums provide an average of 50 percent of their families' incomes from their work as small traders and vendors, they were denied credit. Marty Chen describes the creation of the Working Women's Forum, its community organization role around credit issues, and the further services that the organization now provides. Marianne Schmink describes the process of a community learning to manage the technical, economic and social aspects of a new, community based household waste management technology, SIRDO, in Merida, Mexico, the crucial role that women played in the process, and the strengthened position they gain within their families and communities as a result.

For a good and very detailed review of the urban (and rural) informal economy and credit programmes for women in latin America, see Marguerite Berger and Mayra Buvinic, Women'sVentures: Assistance to the Informal sector in Latin America (West Hartford, Conn: Kumarian Press, 1989, 266 pages).

The household provides the focus for an exploration of the gender dimension in the social impact of structural adjustment policies in third World countries: "Researching the Household: Methodological and Empirical Issues," edited by Naila Kabeer and Susan Joekes, IDS Bulletin, Vol. 22, No. 1, January 1991).

VI. COLLECTIVE ACTION

This section addresses the importance of women in popular

movements which in turn are important in urban change and in coping with environmental issues on a local scale.

Elizabeth Jelin, editor, (London: Zed Books, 1990, 226 pages) presents six studies by Latin American researchers on the role of women in social movements and organizations. Of the specifically urban case studies, one, by Cecilia Blondet, is an account of how a poor neighbourhood in Lima was established, and the central role played by women in setting up mutual aid networks, in organizations started outside the community, and in promoting change within community organizations. Teresa Caldeira analyzes the experience of women from six barrios in Sao Paolo when they became active in local popular movements, and the opportunity provided by these movements for encouranging politicization and growth of personal identity around issues beyond the initial family and community reasons for joining.

Suzanne Thorbek, "A Female Perspective on Urbanization in the third World" (Chapter 12 in Satya Datta, editor, see above), reflects on the importance of women in urban social movements as well as on men's and women's different interpretations of the problems they find in migrating to an urban environment. Like her article in this issue of Environment and urbanization, the paper is based on two field studies of slum cultures: one on the outskirts of colombo, and one in a central area of Bangkok. In Datta's book, Thorbek applies her analysis to various social movements, including the oppressive ones of nazism and the Moral Majority; and the popular one of Nicaragua, where women's issues and involvement were a crucial factor in the Sandinista revolution.

Among the best known organizing efforts for low-income living conditions is SPARC, the Society for Promotion of Area Resource centres. This community organization in bombay believes that by increasing the poor's participation and control of information and resources needed for the process of change, change can be made. Two articles illustrate the work of SPARC: "Women and Housing: A Training Program" (Open house International, Vol. 15, No. 4, 1990, pages 65-68) provides information on the collective action approach in searching for viable housing alternative, and how the women's groups, working with SPARC, developed a training programme which addresses preparation for resettlement, Skills in building and planning construction, and co-operative decision making. the other is a substantial profile of SPARC in Environment and Urbanization (Vol.

2, No. 1, 1990, pages 91-104), which provides a detailed review of SPARC's work over its first five years, its development and organization, and its commitment to process rather than projects.

Another well kmown organization in India is SEWA, the Self-employed Women's Organization in Ahmedabad, a trade union which has organised 40,000 workers. Ela Bhatt illustrates the situation of some of the Women in an account of SEWA's organising process (World Development, Vol. 17 no. 7 1989, pages 1059- 1065).

VII. LAW AND PROPERTY

The issues of access to land and tenure rights are addressed in most of the literature reviewed in the earlier sections on human settlements and housing. These few references are specifically on law and property.

A good anthropological introduction to property and its interaction with social forces and with the domestic/houschold locus in several countries, particularly in different parts of Africa, is provided by Renee Hirschorn, editor, Women and Property - Women as Property (London: Croom Helm, 1984).

For a review of women's issues in the administration of law in some African countries, see Alice Armstrong, Women and Law in Southern Africa (Harare: Zimbabwe Publishing House, 1987). To change the law we have to understand it: Mary Adhiambo Mbeo, Oki Ooko-Ombaka, editors, Women and Law in Kenya: Perspectives and Emerging Issues (1990) is an action-oriented study which contains a section on women's economic participation, including employment and property rights. Available from Public Law Institute, PO Box 52011, Nairobi, Kenya.

Land and property rights for women have been a frequent focus of Women's International news (WIN News), 187 Grant Street, Lexington, Mass. 02173, USA. The editor is fran Hosken: see also her article "Women and Property" in Women & Environments, Vol. 7 no. 3 fall 1985, pages. 10-13, and "Women, Urbanization and Shelter," in Development forum, may 1987.

VIII. SOME FIRST WORLD WORK

Western work on women and urban environments stems from a strongly spatial, built environment orientation. The body of work is considerable, so only a handful of publications are included here, to provide an idea of the approaches that have been taken.

An early work in the field edited by Gerda Wekerle, Rebecca Peterson and David Morley, New Space for Women (Boulder, Colorado: Westview Press, 1981, 332 pages), addresses issues for women in housing design, urbansuburban planning, and women's ability to influence the processes by which these are created. Environments designed, built and managed with male traditions and assumptions discriminate against women and contribute to their alienation, powerlessness and dependency.

The book was prepared following the 1976 UN Conference on Human Settlements in Vancouver, which provided a first international forum for these ideas. Another result of that conference was the founding (by the same editors) of Women & Environments magazine, which for 15 years has published work on women's built environments, and over the last several of those years has also addressed human settlements issues in the Third World. Through its articles and reviews the magazine provides a unique overview of the development of work in the area.

A central concept of western work, one which is problematic in a Third World context, is the separation of urban space between public (men's domain) and private (domestic, for women), or the production and reproduction functions, and the reciprocal effects of this on women and on urban change. Jo Little, Linda Peake and Pat Richardson's edited collection of papers by British geographers, (Women in Cities: Gender in the Urban Environment (London: Macmillan, 1988, 154 pages,) develops and critiques the concepts of gendered use of urban space; the papers link gender relations, the economy and urban spatial structure, and point to the need to analyze the relationship between production and reproduction in order to understand urban social, economic and environmental change.

Another British collection approaches the question of women's relationship to the urban environment from a design perspective. Making Space; Women and the man Made environment (London: Pluto, 1984, 148 pages) was written by Matrix, a collective of feminist designers, who argue that behaviour, travel and other activities of women in cities are mediated by urban layout and design, and that housing design and location based on the stereotypical nuclear family with car reinforces a gendered division of labour inside and outside the home.

Dolores Hayden, Redesigning the American Dream (New York: W.W. Norton, 1984, 270 pages, US $ 17.95), traces the emergence of suburban development in the US as an outcome of an emphasis on private ownership and domestic consumption. She puts forward ideas for restructuring urban space to eliminate the spatial separation of productive and reproductive functions.

A recent Canadian perspective on the issues of changing relationships between women's roles in paid labour and the household, the interconnection between public and private activities, and the ways in which our understanding of these is linked to changing urban environments is presented in Life Spaces: Gender, Household, Employment, edited by caroline Andrew and Beth Moore Milroy (Vancouver, University of British Columbia Press, 1988. 168 pages, $ 16.95). The volume includes and excellent bibliography of Canadian Work.

Women and Space: Ground Rules and Social Maps, edited by Shirley Ardener(London: Croom Helm, 1981 238 pages) helps to provide a bridge between First World work on Women's spatial relationship to the environment, and the cultural experiences of women in other countries, through cases studies centred on the Andes. Greece, Iran, Georgia, Nigeria and South Africa. Space reflects social organization, but once space has been bounded and shaped it exerts its own influence.

Another bridge between work on first and Third World human settlements issues is provided by "Women and Space in Human Settlements," a special issue of Ekistics, No, 310, Jan/Feb 1985, edited by Becky Dennison Sakellriou, which presents a cross-cultural perspective on how women in several first and Third World countries perceive their built environments, function within them, and change them. The articles examine the contexts for women of shelter, spatial patterning of house, neighbourhood and city, and activities within settlements, ranging from housework and community involvement to income generating labour and organized action. The collection provides a good and broad introduction to built environment issues and the work of some of the pioneers in the field.

IX. RESOURCES, NETWORKS AND RESEARCH

a. Resources

INSTRAW: The UN international Research and Training Institute for the advancement of women publishes INSTRAW News (in English, French and Spanish). An autonomous body of the UN, INSTRAW conducts research, training and information activities towards the integration of women in development. Recent issues of INSTRAW news have covered women and the informal sector (No. 12, Summer 1989); water supply and sanitation (No. 13, Winter 1989), focuses on women's present and potential roles in water and sanitation management and on efforts to integrate women into development projects in the water sector; No. 14 (Spring 1990) reviews the work of INSTRAW on statistics of women; No. 15 (Winter 1990) explores the nature of credit programmes for women, especially poor women, including those in the urban informal sector; types of credit available and uses made of it, and components of successful programmes. Cases studies are included. Available from INSTRAW, PO Box 21747, Santo Domingo, Dominican Republic.

The Tribune: A quarterly published by the International Women's Tribune Center addresses development issues for Third World women. Recent issues of the newsletter include No. 39, December 1987, on housing, which identifies the obstacles women face in housing, programmes: land, finance, access to infrastructure, location and transportation, design and participation. No. 40 is on women's participatory training issues and activities; No. 42 is on economics and women's lives; No. 44 is an organizing manual on women and new technologies. Each issue of The Tribune contains lists of resource materials and organizations.

Another IWTC publication is "The Tech and Tools Book" (1986), a highly practical guide to technologies that women are using. The Tribune and other IWTC materials are free to individuals and groups in the Third World. Order from IWTC, 777 UN Plaza, New York, NY 10017, USA.

The World's Women, 1970-1990: Trends and Statistics, United Nations, 1991, 135 pages, US $19.95. Available from UN Publications, Sales Section, DC2-853, New York, NY 10017, USA, or book shops. Several UN agencies, namely the Department of International Economic and Social Affairs, Centre for Social Affairs, Centre for Social Development and Humanitarian Affairs, UNICEF, UNFPA and UNIFEM, collaborated on this compilation of statistics presented in text, tables and charts, which portrays the situation of women's conditions and contributions. The project was an outcome of the UN Decade for Women. Sections are include on families and households, public life and leadership, education and training, health and childbearing, women's work and the economy. Country and area data are aggregated into regional and sub-regional averages; there are many gaps and blanks, but it is still the most complete statistical presentation yet published on women's situation worldwide. The section on work and the economy contains estimates of additions to various countries' GNP if women's unpaid housework were to be included.

International Center for Research on women has published Notes from the Seminar Series: The Determinants and Consequences of Female-Headed Households. These summaries are of four seminars on definitions, issues around the emergence and consequences of woman-headed households, lifecycle considerations, and family structure and poverty in developing countries. US $13 from ICRW, 1717 Massachusetts Avenue, NW, Suite 302, Washington DC 20036, USA.

b. Networks

Networking is one of the processes by which issues get onto the agenda - through making and using connections and pushing forward collectively. In the absence of more structured access to policy agendas, the building and use of networks is especially important to women. Here are some in the women, environment and urbanization area:

The International Housing and Gender Studies Network held a seminar in Lund, Sweden in October 1990. A report of the proceedings includes abstracts of the papers presented, as well as short summaries of discussions and questions raised. The network invites the interest of researchers on Third World housing and gender issues; to join or to request a copy of the report, contact the national Swedish Institute for Building Research, local Office in Lund, Finngatan 16, S-223 62 Lund, Sweden.

The HIC (Habitat International Coalition) Women and Shelter Network, mentioned elsewhere in this volume, publishes its own newsletter. The Co-ordinator, and focal point for anglophone Africa, is Diana Lee-Smith, PO Box 14564, Nairobi, Kenya.

SASH is official journal of the black Sash, a women's activist human rights organization in south Africa. Vol. 33, January 1991 of SASH is mostly on issues of the environment. A statement by the Black Sash says: General degradation of the environment is the price paid for not providing effective access to necessary resources such as clean water and fuel and waste removal services. In order to achieve a sustainable urban habitat...we need to work for Land (security of tenure), Affordable Housing, Safe Homes for All (free from eviction or extortionate rentals). Contact the Black Sash, 5 Long Street, 7700 Mowbray, South Africa.

The WEED (Women and Environments Education and Development) Foundation publishes the magazine Women & Environments, whose Fall 1991 issue will be produced as an environmental network; for information and/or inclusion in that issue, which will include information on international women's environmental groups, contact WEED at 736 Bathurst St.. Toronto M5S 2R4, Canada. A special issue of the magazine (Spring, 1991) carries the proceedings of WEED's major 1990 conference on Women and the Environment, WEED is also involved in Canada's NGO committee set up to participate in the preparation for UNCED, the UN Conference on Environment and Development, Brazil, 1992. Women and the environment will be the specific focus of the preliminary World Women's Congress for a healthy Planet, to be held in Miami in November, 1991.

c. Research

Women, Poverty and Environment in Latin America: The International Center for Research on Women (ICRW) in Washington DC is investigating the ways in which urban and rural latin American women's home and market roles can incorporate solutions to local environmental problems and, at the same time, lead to improvements in the economic and health conditions of themselves and their families. The questions the project is addressing concern the range of environmental problems confronting women: the strategies women use to conserve and protect the environment; the constraints on their ability to do this; the organizations which involve women in environmental efforts; and policy and programme changes which will increase their involvement. A report will be available in late summer, 1991. Contact

ICRW, 1717 Massachusetts Avenue NW, #302, Washington DC 20038, USA.

Urban Research in the Third World: The centre for Urban and community Studies at the University of Toronto is coordinating a major 18 month international consultative project directed towards the formulation of new urban policy approaches in developing countries. During the next year, urban research institutes in a dozen countries and sub-regions of latin America, Asia and Africa will be gathering information on research on urban questions that has already been carried out, is in progress or planned, including research on gender issues. The process will identify the areas that need to be researched, and will produce major review papers. The project is supported by the Ford foundation. For more information, contact Urban Research Project, centre for Urban and Community Studies, 455 Spadina Avenue, Toronto M5S 2G8, Canada.

X. SOME ADDRESSES FOR ORDERING PUBLICATIONS

DPU (Development Planning Unit), Bartlett School, London University, 9 Endsleigh Gardens, London WCIH OED, UK.

Earthscan Publications, 3 Endsleigh Street, London WCIH ODD, U.K.

Environmental Liaison centre, PO Box 72461, Nairobi, Kenya.

The IDS Bulletin is available from the Institute of Devlopment Studies, University of Sussex, Brighton BNI 9RE, UK.

Contact the Swedish Ministry of Housing and Physical planning, capakobsgatan 26, S-103 33 Stockholm, Sweden for the IYSH 1987 Seminar Report.

Kumarian Press, 630 Oakwood Avenue, Suite 119, West Hartford, Conn, 06110-1529, USA. The language of development studies is available from the Institute for Organization and Industrial sociology, Blagardsgade 23B, 2200 Copenhagen, Denmark.

Monthly Review Press, 122 West 27the Street New York NY 10001, USA

National Swedish Institute for Building Research reports are obtainable from Almqvist and Wiksell International, Box 45150, S-104 30 Stockholm Sweden.

Swedish Council for Research in the Humanities and social

Sciences: orders to Swedish Science Press, Box 118, 751 04 Uppsala, Sweden.

UNCHS (Habitat), PO Box 300030, Nairobi, Kenya.

Notes :

1. See, for example, Shiva, Vandana (1988). Staying Alive: Women, Ecology and Development, London: Zed Books: New Delhi: Kali for Women. "The poverty crisis touches women most severely, first because they are the poorest of the poor, and then because, with nature, they are the primary sustainers of society" page 5.
2. For an African view of the distortions imposed on Third World women by some western feminist work, see Ifi Amadiume's study of the ideology of gender in socio-cultural systems in Nigeria: Male Daughters, Female Husbands (1987, London: Zed Books).
3. Vandana Shiva, see note 1.
4. Boserup, Ester (1970), Women's Role in Economic Development, (London: Allen and Unwin). Among other issues, Boserup discusses the profound change in families; way of life and economy that has accompained a rural to urban slum move. This has been republished by Earthscan.

CHAPTER-10

Women and Solid Wastes in Poor Communities

Dr Christine Furedy

RESOURCE SCARCITY, WOMEN, AND SOLID WASTE MANAGEMENT

The subject of the use of waste materials by women to meet basic needs and generate income and work may seem to have no relevance to "infrastructure." The justification for addressing this topic is that solid waste management (SWM) is one of the essential services that any healthy community must have. To plan sustainable and equitable SWM in developing countries requires not only a knowledge of the nature of wastes generated by households, enterprises and businesses, but also an understanding of how wastes are used in communities, and what livelihoods are based on wastes. This is important because waste reduction and recycling are coming to be recognized as the basic premises of all waste management.

Equipment and procedures designed without any regard for waste recovery and recycling in resource-scarce societies rarely achieve their goals because those who depend upon wastes continue to try to gain access to them, thwarting, in the process, the plan of municipal managers. Despite this evidence of the needs of poor communities, municipal or corporate sector recycling schemes are sometimes suggested that would divert wastes from current users without assuring them access to substitute resources. These miscalculations occur partly because informal waste recovery is not seen to be relevant for the planning of basic services.

Because poor people extensively exploit wastes as resources, there are special relationship between waste management services, household management, and work which may not pertain to other dimensions of infrastructure. Since women in most societies tend to have initial control over the generation and reuse of wastes in the household, it is relevant to ask whether there are, within the "special relationships" of poor people to wastes, further distinctive aspects of women's work that warrant particular, even separate, attention. The practical issue for meeting basic needs is whether solid waste management (and environmental management in general) will be more successful if planners incorporate the findings of research on "women and wastes."

The work of urban women with waste materials is relevant for cities' economies and services in three principal areas: the use of wastes to meet household needs, informal work in waste recovery and recycling, and women's roles in municipal solid waste services (ref. 1).

WASTES AND HOUSEHOLD NEEDS

The use of wastes by poor households to meet basic needs is observed in all developing countries, although there is not even in a single case-study to provide a sense of how important wastes can be in household management. The use of wastes for fuel, particularly animal dung and agricultural residues, including urban vegetable wastes, such as coconut husks and shells, has been estimated in a number of areas (ref. 2). **Waste burning especially of cattle dung, is a routine matter for poor families of squatters and pavement dwellers in India.** Another use of dung is also common in the Indian sub-continent--the preparation of floors and sometimes walls with dung wash. Women, as the providers and organisers of daily household needs, are responsible for marshalling these waste products, although they may often relay on their children to gather dung or other wastes.

Prior to the building of a shelter, women may play the major part in assembling the materials for a squatter's shack. They **keep a look-out for items such as strong plastic, scrap iron, lumber, broken bricks, and rags that can be used to repair their shelters, repairs that they will make as routine housekeeping. One can hypothesize that the shorter a poor urban family is of ready cash, the more the women and children of the household must seek out wastes and resort to conservation and reuse as strategies** (ref. 3). This search for wastes frequently takes women and children beyond their immediate neighbourhood (for poor communities are not generators of large amounts of useful wastes) to the waste receptacles of rich districts, commercial areas, and, ultimately, to garbage dumps (ref. 4).

In these circumstances, the daily work of poor urban women becomes closely linked to the availability of various waste materials.

When these apparently trivial activities are multiplied by the millions of very poor households in cities and towns in developing countries, daily living can be seen as significantly waste-absorbing. At the same time, one can understand the importance that access to wastes assumes for low-income families.

INFORMAL WORK BASED ON WASTE RECOVERY AND RECYCLING

In most cities of developing countries, waste gathering extends beyond household needs as people find employment supplying the demand of small and large industries for wastes--paper, plastics, metals, rags, rubber, leather, glass and ceramics, bones--as substitutes for raw materials. Each large city manifests an intricate network of waste gathering, dealing and transportation--waste pickers and itinerant "announced" collectors, sorters and processors, buyers, dealers, and manufacturers. In South Asia some of these roles remain linked to traditional socioreligious statuses.

Although local systems usually have distinctive characteristics, the main status lines in waste recovery are uniform in developing countries: women and children predominate in the lowest levels of waste gathering, that is, those that depend on the least valuable wastes whose retrieval demands the greatest amount of simple labour for the lowest cash returns. Thus on dump sites that receive largely organic and inert rubbish in Asia one finds mainly women and children, except at times when men know that trucks will arrive from special areas such as the airport or certain commercial and residential neighbourhoods.

At Calcutta's Dhapa dump, for instance, most of the material retrieved consists of coconut shells, coal cinders, and pieces of wood. Besides pieces of glass, the manufactured wastes are very damaged and dirty fragments of paper, plastic, cloth, and leather. Unless they know that better materials are likely to be available, men resort to such a dump only if they can find no other kind of work at all. Casual observation suggests that cities where more valuable materials reach dumps in large quantities have larger numbers of male pickers. [It is possible that religious values máy influence male/female ratios among dump and street pickers; in Muslim societies women may not venture readily onto so public a place as a large garbage dump. In indonesia, more women are absorbed in sorting, packaging and simple processing of wastes than in collecting for industrial trading (ref. 5)].

The traders and managers of the waste recycling industries are, by all accounts, men. Women and children usually receive less for the wastes they sell and they find it harder to get advances or loans from buyers for equipment to reduce the burden of waste gathering. In South Asia women do not take the role of itinerant collectors who go from household to household, receiving, buying or bartering wastes. It must be extremely rare for a woman to "rise up" in a system of waste trading, unless she is part of a successful family business. I know of no instances of women acting as dealers or running independent waste trading enterprises.

How do these household strategies and informal work relate to the nature of solid waste services ?

The substitution of wastes for purchased materials, even if the wastes are not entirely free, represents important savings for poor households, and resource conservation for the society as a whole. This extensive waste recovery, incidentally reduces the amounts of wastes that cities have to collect, saves dump space, and allows the residues to break down into productive compost (ref. 6). Few municipal managers, however, see informal waste recycling in this light, and there has been very little discussion of ways to facilitate waste recovery by the needy (ref. 7). Most changes in equipment and techniques are explicitly designed to prevent or discourage scavenging of recyclables. The result of the introduction of large, lidded, containers (especially roll-on-roll off containers) is that recyclables are not retrieved in neighbourhoods, but are transported to dump sites (ref. 8). This means that less material is locally available for household needs; poor people are thus compelled to either purchase wastes from traders, or seek out waste transfer points and dump sites.

WOMEN MUNICIPAL WASTE WORKERS

The lowest jobs of the municipal cleaning system may be practically reserved for women in some countries, and they are rarely, if ever, promoted. In some countries of South America, women street cleaners are routinely subject to sexual abuse, but no explicit reference has been found to this in Asian cities. In some Indian cities, where municipal workers are given assisted housing, on the death of her husband, a widow immediately seeks work in the municipal corporation, and is usually regarded as having a right to the first cleaning job available, because, if she does families seek to place children and grandchildren in the municipal labour force. Thus the need for housing compels these children, who might have the chance of better work, to continue in the job of the father or mother. The working conditions for women sweepers are often very poor--they may have no footwear or gloves, no adequate implements for sweeping and waste collection. But fear of losing the valued municipal job, among other things, means few complaint about the situation, or request child care services and maternity leave. This menial work, however, gives these workers an insight into waste behaviours that could be valuable to municipal planners.

RESEARCH AND COMMUNITY ACTION

A number of ideas for research arise from this perspective on women and wastes, enquiries that can help community action and official policies for environmental improvement.

1. Household economy studies to estimate the importance of wastes in meeting basic needs, especially under conditions of increasing unemployment or scarcity of basic necessities. What are the waste reuse and waste disposal patterns in the household and how do they vary with income, education and the structure of the household, or other social characteristics ?

2. Surveys and interviews on attitudes of women to solid wastes. What is the level of knowledge about health hazards from uncollected solid wastes ? An important issue to probe is whether the use of wastes as reources affects the perception of wastes as hazards. What general concerns do women have about access to wastes, neighbourhood cleanliness, and municipal solid waste services ? These enquiries can move from individual perceptions to "collective diagnosis" (ref. 9, p. 240) that becomes a way of consciousness-building, laying the ground for community action.

3. Roles of women as waste pickers on streets and at dumps and in the sorting, processing, trading of wastes as feedstock for industry. It would be useful to know women's earnings, the conditions of their work, and the types of control exercised by men in the worlds of waste. Studies of the health risks of different kinds of waste work have yet to be undertaken.

4. Examination of the options for improving women's earnings and work, such as co-operatives [c,f. work of Self-Employed Women's

Association (SEWA) in organising some paper pickers' co-operatives (ref. 9, p. 236)]. Case studies of co-operatives or other forms of organization in this work would be useful. Community organisations can help identify productive but non-hazardous waste recycling work (for instance the makig of clothes and quilts from textile scraps) that could be supported to give women better opportunities for recycling work. Most of the general recommendations of the Government of India Commission of Self-Employed Women are relevant to waste work (ref. 9).

5. Knowledge and perceptions of women municipal waste workers of community needs and issues in solid waste services. Since most municipal workforces employ some women in city cleaning, their experience as both household managers and public cleaners could be drawn upon to provide insight into attitudes towards wastes and waste management behaviour in the community. Discussion groups of municipal workers could become a force for better adaptation of waste services to household needs. Showing respect for the knowledge and insight of women municipal workers is a first step in enhancing their self-esteem. Research must also identify the particular needs of women workers, with regard to child care, or possible risks for pregnant women, for instance.

Without waiting for research results, community development groups can explore the potential for integrating women's intimate knowledge of household wastes into a concern for "neighbourhood housekeeping"(ref. 10). By harnessing the knowledge that people have of their wastes, the activities of waste gathering and waste reuse, rather than being seen as largely problem-ridden, can be recognized as having environmentally positive elements. One hopes that this change in perception will lead to more constructive ways of accommodating informal practices to public management.

CONCLUSION

In striving for decent living and working conditions, communities need to look beyond the usual genralities of improving women's status, Supporting women's work and providing appropriate community facilities, to probing the specific needs and relationships that arise from the fact that wastes represent resources and create particular employment opportunities in low-income communities.

Ultimately, as research on waste management and waste work proceeds in developing countries, scholars and community leaders may decide that anything "special" about women's relationships to waste management and waste work is overridden by the social, economic, and environmental deprivations of all those associated with the lowest, most polluted, levels of waste work.

There is some basis for assuming, however, that, through their household roles and informal and municipal work, women acquire distinct insights into attitudes to wastes and waste behaviours that until now have not been used for environmental improvement. Whether or not it is worthwhile to pursue research on women alone, solid waste managers must eventually address the phenomenon of waste recovery by the poor and consider how conventional plans for SWM can be adapted to waste recovery and recycling.

REFERENCES

1. The needs of women in low-income communities for effective waste removal services are important and urgent, but are not of direct relevance to this paper.
2. Barnard G. and Kristonferson L.

   Agricultural Residues as Fuel in the Third World. London, Earthscan, 1985.
3. Giovanni A. Cornia notes the conserving aspect of "survival stategies" in the chapter "Adjustment at the household level: potentials and limitations of survival strategies," pp. 90-104, in **Adjustment with a Human Face**, edited by G. A. Cornia, R. Jolly, and F. Stewart. Oxford, Clarendon Press, 1987.
4. Generally it is only women living near dumps who can go there merely to get some fuel for the day. Dump picking becomes the preserve of those selling to buyers or making a business out of fuel-from-wastes.
5. Fatimah. N. "The Role of Women in the Scavenging System at Jati Dua, Bandung." Centre for Environmental Studies, Institute Teknologi Bandung, unpublished, 1982.
6. Furedy, C. "Appropriate Technology for Urban Wastes in Asia." **BioCycle,** July, 1989, pp. 56-59.
7. Cointreau suggested the design of transfer stations to allow for waste recovery in the late '70s but subsequently noted that no city has taken up this idea officially. COINTREAU S. **Environmental Management of Urban Solid Wastes in Developing Countries.** Washington, D.C., world Bank, 1982, and personal communication, 1989.
8. Furedy Social Aspects of Waste Recovery in Asian Cities. Environmental Sanitation Review, Environmental Sanitation Information Centre, Asian Institute of Technology, Bangkok,1990.
9. INDIA, GOVERNMENT OF. **Shramshakti. Report of National Commission on Self-employed Women and Women in the Informal Sector.** New Delhi, Govt. of India, 1988.
10. One can envisage modern version of the women's civic and sanitary groups in late 19th and early 20th century USA and Europe. See Hoy S. M. "Municipal housekeeping": the role of women in improving urban sanitation practices, 1880-1917. **Pollution and Reform in American Cities 1870-1930,** ed. M. V. Melosi, Austin, Univ. Texas Press, pp. 173-198.

CHAPTER-11

The Problems of Living with In-Laws

Shared accommodation entails living in close daily proximity with one's in-laws. In this respect, it is very similar to living in an extended households, and we may therefore look to studies of the extended households for insights into the problems of sharing a housing plot. To date, studies of the extended household in urban Mexico have tended to argue that it has positive implications for women, because of the opportunities for cooperation which it allows. But this is only half the story: there is also considerable potential for conflict.

Larissa Lomnitz[56] sought to counter the degrogatory aspects of some writings on urban marginality by analysing the mutual support networks enabling people to cope with extreme poverty. In her book, she wrote:

> One will find no stress on the more sensational aspects of poverty: the filth, the promiscuity, the arguments and fights between people who must live together in a tiny space.[57]

The social resources mobilisd by people in their efforts to survive included networks of reciprocal exchange and institutions such as *compadrazgo*.[58] Although networks could be based on friendship as well as kinship, "kinship is the most common social foundation for reciprocity networks",[59] and extended or 'joint' household structures played a key role in these networks.

Sylvia Chant[60] also emphasises cooperation in extended households. Women in extended households can "share and/or delegate gender-assigned duties"[61] more than women in nuclear households. They therefore face fewer restrictions on their ability to enter the labour market.[62] Decisions on household budgeting become more democratic, housework is shared, "the full-time mother-wife role tends to become redundant" and women seem to have "far greater personal liberty"[63] In short, extended households "reduce some of the excesses of patriarchy".[64]

Chant[65] examines different types of extension to the household in support of her arguments, particularly those involving the inclusion of women's sisters or mothers. The focus of this paper is narrower, since it is restricted to the incorporation of sons or daughters-in-law, but this is the most common pattern in household suggests that this type of extension and sharing. The literature on patrilocal extended households suggests that this type of extension is likely to lead to conflict between female relatives rather than cooperation:

> The authority structure of the patrilocal, patrilineal extended family, where father has authority over son and husband over wife, brings about conflict rather than cooperation between women in these groups.[66]

Since authority is in men's hands, women have to manipulate their relationships with men — their husbands, and later their adult sons — in order to gain influence. *As a result of the nature of gender relations in these societies,* mothers and daughters-in-law have conflicting interests. The stem family "introduces in the role of daughter-in-law a woman whose only hope of personal autonomy is division of her husband's natal family"[67] The consequences of this for dauther-in-law have been documented, for rural China, by Elisabeth Croll[68] and Margery Wolf,[69] and for rural India by Ursula Sharma,[70] although they stress that daughters-in-law are not without resources (including women friends) in dealing with their mother-in-law. The emphasis women place on strong relationships with their sons and the consequent strains between mother and daughter-in-law are summarised by Croll:[71]

> It was by forming and nurturing ties with her son which were personal and exclusive that women cultivated a source of power in a social structure dominated by menb. Any potential threat to this relationship by the daughter-in-law was felt deeply. Trapped all their lives, women, with the authority of being the mother-in-law, appeared to compensate for their own former suffering and impotence as outsiders by repeating the very same process of domination.[72]

This type of conflict has also been reported in rural mexico.[73] Krantz[74] describes the authority of the mother-in-law over her daughter (s)-in-law in such households as "overriding". Although the context of modern urban Mexico is a very different one, tension between in-law is still a significant problem, for which gender relations are ultimately responsible. The fundamental emotional significance of sharing was highlighted by one woman who answered my question as to why her married children (all daughters) didn't live with her by saying "Look, all my children hurt me *a lot*". She was referring, not to a family quarrel, but to the pain of childbirth. In a cultural context in which girls are seen as inherently less 'valuable' than boys,[75] a certain resentment of daughters, a feeling that they should stand on their own two feet just as their mothers had to do, can sometimes be detected, and probably helps to explain the gender bias in sharing. One woman in Mexico City particularly disapproved of married daughters bringing their husbands home, because, she said, they would expect her to cook for them.

Women's attitudes to their sons are different, reflecting the privileged nature of the moter-son relationship in Mexico.[76] In Puebla, a woman who blamed Mexican mothers for their men's machismo said that when a son marries, his mother will use all kinds of emotional blackmail (including pretending to be ill) to get him to stay with her. If she succeeds, however, she will have to face the presence of a younger woman in her household, a presence which will be interpreted as an intrucion. Given the limited opportucities for many women to wield power in other aspects of their lives, there is considerable potential for the home to become a battleground, and it seems almost inevitable that mothers will dislike their daughters-in-law, a feeling likely to be reciprocated. A resentment arising from the difficulties middle-aged women have faced in their own married lives, but which cannot perhaps be 'legitimately' expressed with their own daughters, can be given an outlet in criticisms of a daughters-in-law's habits particularly those concerning housekiiping or child care. The resulting tension, and the way in which it revolves around the son/husband, was summarised by a woman in Mexico City in these thems:

> Supposing your son comes home drunk one night, and you go out to tell him off about it. Then, his wife comes out and starts having a go at you for scolding her husband: she tells you to aly off and mind your own business.

Another put it more succintly: "I don't like having the daughters-in-law around!"

The misery that these problems can cause, for the older woman as well as the younger one, had become apparent during earlier work in Puebla. An old woman approached me in the street one day, and spontaneously started to tell me about the wickedness of her daughter-in-law. Another was locked out of her house by her daughter-in-law; and one 86-year-old woman without children of her own preferred ot live alone in a vecindad rather than living with her godson and his wife, because the two women didn't get on.[77]

For a woman sharing with her in-laws, the problem may be not only her husband's mother but also his sisters.[78] If, for example, a child is hurt in a fall, its mother may be blamed for being a 'bad mother' by her sisters-in-law as well as their mother; they react as though it is their child who has been hurt. Moreover, it may not be easy for women who are sharing to develop friendship networks to help them counteract such pressures, insofar as such networks depend on friends having access to each other's homes. Friends of whom the owner disapproves are unlikely to be welcome on the plot, and grounds for disapproval could readily be found by a hostile mother-in-law. Shopping or other work performed away from but spending too much time 'in the street' (which has strong sexual implications) can give a prying relative the chance to tell tales to a woman's husband.[79]

THE HOUSE OF TWO: RESPONSES TO THE PROBLEMS OF CO-RESIDENCE

The problems outlined above are widely recognised by people in low-income settlements in urban Mexico. What, then, can they do about them?

In the first place, sharing may be seen as a way of trying to reduce the potential for conflict associated with the extended household. Work in rural Mexico has shown the inportance of having separate cooking facilities "as a focus of identity".[80] The desirability of providing, ideally, separate accommodation and facilities or, at the least, as much autonomy as possible for the younger household was also withnessed both by people's comments and their practice in the areas studied in Mexico City, Guadalajara and puebla. Their ideas were summarised by a woman in Puebla, whose mother, she said, had taught her that *casados* ('married') meant *casa [de] dos* ('house of two'). In other words, married children must be given some independence. Although they might have little option but to live with their parents for a while, every effort should be made so small that they could push the door shut from the bed, the important thing was that they should have a door to shut behind them.

Thus, sharing can be seen as an attempt to avoid some of the problems associated with the patrilocal extended household. Tables 3-5 show that, overall, there are variations between the cities.

Secondly, conflict between women is not an *inevitable* outcome of co-residence. Instead of vying for men's affections, women *can* cooperate with each other to resist the exercise of patriarchal authority. As Chinas*81* notes in her study of the Isthmus Zapotecs:

> A surprising number of wives do adjust remarkably well to living with their mothers-in-law . . . and sometimes very strong bonds of affection form between them over the years. Frequently mothers-in-law side with the wife against their own son, especially when his behavious is obviously at the root of the trouble.

Nash[82] also talks of relationships between mother-and daughter-in-law which are "characterised by mutual cooperation". At the least, a conscious intention not to interfere was apparent on the part of many of the women I interviewed. Several women stressed that it was up to their sons and daughters-in-law to choose where they wanted to live, even if their own preference would be to have all their children close at hand. One widow with five married sons and daughters living elsewhere said she would happily evict her three tenants to make room for them, but accepted with philosophical resignation that "daughters-in-law don't want to live with you . . .". Once married, as another woman put it, sons "will live whereever their wives like - because they *don't* always like [to live with thier in-laws]". Thus many parents respect their children's need for autonomy, whatever their own feelings in the matter.

Thirdly: the fact that almost two-fifths of sharers are women indicates that parents also recognise their daughters' needs. In particular, they are concerned about the consequences of their daughters' marriages breadking down. The man who expressed more clearly than anyone else the idea that sharing is for sons nevertheless said that, in addition to the accommodation he was building for his two (as yet unmarried) sons, he was also trying to make room for his daughters as well. He would like to be able to help them if their marriages didn't work out well and they were left with nowhere to live. In the same street in Mexico City, a woman who had been living with her parents had just gone to live with her new boufriend. She wanted one of her married sisters to take her place, because "her in-laws are being right so-and-sos with her". And in Puebla, one woman, aged 22, was sharing with her parents. After getting married, she had spent a short time with her in-laws, but after problems with her mother-in-law she and her husband had moved to her parents' plot.

CONCLUSION

In research on gender and housing, the equation of 'traditional' and 'non-traditional' households with 'nuclear' households and 'women-headed' households, respectively, is problematic. The assumption that 'nuclear' means 'headed by a man' confuses structure and headship, and, ironically, reinforces the notion that where a male spouse is present, he should be regarded as head of household. By focussing predominantly on women-headed households, the literature on gender and housing runs the risk of rendering women in nuclear households, once agaijn, invisible. Therefore, it is important not to *restrict* discussion of gender and housing to the needs of women-headed households. Moreover, if there is a traditional norm in any society, it is not forced to be the nuclear household. This paper has examined a form of domestgic organisation, plot sharing, which may be regarded as non-traditional in the sense that it has been virtually overlooked in research on urban areas, but which probably constitutes a highly traditional living arrangement in rural areas, but which probably constitutes a highly traditional living arrangement in rural areas of Mexico and elsewhere. The nature of gender relations means that forms of domestic organisation involving patrilocal extended households or the sharing of accommodation may have negative consequences for women. These include women's dependence on their husband's relatives for a roof over their heads, and the potential for conflict between wives and members of their husband's family of origin. As Lamphere[83] concludes: "women quarrel with or dominate other women when it is in their interests as involving the manipulation of their relationship with their sons or husbands, rather than solidarity with other owmen in resisting male authority, then conflict rather than cooperation is likely to result. It is not, however, an *inevitable* outcome.

Thus, in order to understand the inplications of sharing as a housing strategy, we must take gender relations into account. Moreover, it is also important to remember that the home is *not* a separate sphere : state regulations permeate and circumscribe the supposedly private sphere. The next step in the exploration of sharing as a housing strategy should perhaps be to ask how the state intervenes in the interaction between gender relations, household structure and the housing process.

Finally, to return briefly to the question of 'traditional' and 'non-traditional' households: whilst married daughters as well as married sons were recorded sharing with their parents, single parents were, in all but one case, counted as part of their parents' extended household. It seems that it would be regarded as inappropriate for them to share their parents' plot as a separate, independent household. Sharing therefore reinforces the patriarchal norm of the nuclear family, insofar as it is a privilege accorded only to those who are 'married'. If, moreover, women without a partner are more likely to rent or to depentd on thier parents for accommodation, whilst sharing leads to home-ownership, then the patriarchal norm is also reinforced by material rewards for those who ascribe to it. In this sense, sharing is a highly 'traditional' housing strategy.

Acknowledgements—The research on which this paper was based was funded by grants from the University of London Central Research Fund and the Dean's Travel Fund (Faculty of Arts) and Department of Geography, University College London. I am grateful for this financial support and for the helpful comments of two anonymous referees.

Notes

1. This paper was was presented at a conference on *Shelter, Women and Development: First and Third World Perspectives,* held at the University of Michigan in Ann Arbor, 7-9 may, 1992. The reason for the discussion of 'traditional' and 'non-traditional' households is that the paper was presented in a session entitled "Non-traditional living arrangements: beyond the nuclear household".

2. A study evaluating research on low-income housing found that only 13 of 126 studies reviewed provided any information on the particular problems faced by women: W. van Vliet (ed.), *Women, Housing and Community,* (Avebury, Aldershot, 1988), pp. 1-5, see p. x.

3. S. Watson, *Accommodating Inequality*: Gender and Housing (Allen & Unwin, Sydney, 1988).

4. Although these introductory comments refer to English-language publications, a recent mexivan publication [A. Massolo, (ed.) *Mujeres y Ciudades: Participacion Social, Vivienda y Vida Cotidiana* (El Colegio de Mexico, Mexico D. F., 1992)] makes a similar argument concerning the latin American urban housing literature. In the literature in English, a number of specific issues have received more attention. Housing design has been addressed, in a British context, by the Matrix Collective, *making Space: Women and the Man-made Environment* (Pluto Press, London, 1984), and Marion Roberts, *Living in a Man-made World: Gender Assumptions in Modern Housing Design* (Routledge, London, 1991): for the U.S.A., see D. Hayden, *The Grand Domestic Revolution: a History of Feminist Designs for American Homes,*

Neighborhoods, and Cities (M.I.T. Press, Cambridge, 1981). Homelessness is a growth area in the literature as well as on the streets. It is examined, for Britain, by S. Watson with H. Austerberry, *Housing and Homelessness: a Feminist Perspective* (Routledge and Kegan Paul, London, 1986); M. Miller, *Bed and Breadfast: Women and Homelessness Today* (Women's Press, London, 1990); and J. Dibhlin, *Wherever I Lay My Hat: Young Women and Homelessness* (Shelter, London, 1991); for the United States, see M.R. Stoner, "The Plight of Homeless Women", in W. van Vliet (ed.), *Women, Housing and Community,* (Avebury, Aldershot, 1988), pp. 135-151, and S. Golden, *The Women Outside: Meaning and Myths of Homelessness* (University of California Press, Berkeley, 1992).

5. S.A. Radcliffe with J. Townsend, *Gender in the Third World: a Geographical Bibliography of Recent Work* (Institute of Development Studies, Brighton, 1988). J. Townsend, *Women in Developing Countries: a Select Annotated Bibliography for Development Organizations* (Institute of Development Studies, Brighton, 1988).

6. Housing is mentioned, but not analysed in any depth, in several recent studies of gender and the environment: A. Rodda, *Women and the Environment* (Zed Books, London, 1991); I. Dankelman and J. Davidson, *Women and Environment in the Third World: Alliance for the Future* (Earthscan, London, 1988); S. Sontheimer (ed.), *Women and Environment*: a Reader — *Crises and Development in the Third World* (Earthscan, London, 1991); C. Levy, "Gender and the Environment: the Challenge of Cross-cutting Issues in Development Policy and Planning", Environment and the Environment: the Challenge of Cross-cutting Issues in Development Policy and Planning", *Environment and Urbanization* **4**, 1 (1992), pp. 134-149.

7. C.O.N. Moser, "Gender Planning in the Third World: Meeting Practical and Strategic Needs", in R. Grant and K. newland (eds), *Gender and International Relations* (Open University Press, Buckingham, 1991), pp. 83-121; see p. 84.

8. L. Rodwin, (ed) *Shelter, Settlement and development* (Allen & Unwin, Boston, 1987).

9. Cited in A. Varley, "Review of L. Rodwin, (ed.), *Shelter, Settlement and Development,* 1987" *Transactions, Institute of British Geographers,* N.S. **14** (1989), pp. 115-117; see p. 116. An IYSH seminar on 'Women and Shelter' was held in Harare in December 1987.

[A. Schlyter, *Women Householders and Housing Strategies: the Case of Harare, Zimbabwe* (National Swedish Institute for Building Research, Gavle, 1989).]

10. Hayden, 1981 (see note 4). L. McDowell, "Towards and Understanding of the Gender Division of Urban Space", *Environment and Planning D: Society and Space* **10** (1983), pp. 59-72. O. Harris, "Households as Natural Units", in K. yound, c. Wolkwitz and R. McCullagh (eds), Of *Marriage and the Market: Women's Subordination Internationally and its Lessons,* 2nd edn (Routledge and Kegan Paul, London, 1984), pp. 136-155, E. Jelin, "Family and Household: OUtside World and Private Life", in E. Jelin (ed.), *Family Household and Gender Relations in Latin America* Kegan Paul Internation, London, 1991), pp. 12-39. Watson, 1988, see note 3.

12. Harris, 1984, *ibid.*, p. 151.

13. L. McDowell, "Space, Place and Difference: a Review of Ten Years of Feminist Geography", mimeo (1992).

14. *Ibid.*, p. 19.

15. J. Momsen, "Review of C.O.N. Moser and L. Peake, (eds), *Women Human Settlemants and housing", Transactions, Institute of British Geographers,* N.S. 14 (1989), pp. 119-120; see p. 119.

16. Despite the unsatisfactory implications, this paper follows the convention in the literature of describing households in which there is no resident male spouse as women-headed households. Such households may be either nuclear (a single woman with or without children) or extended (including, for example, grandchildren or other male or female relatives). The term 'community managers' is used byC.O.N. Moser, "Women, Human Settlements and Housing: a Conceptual Framework for Analysis and Policy-making", in C.O.N. Moser and l. Peake (eds) *Women Human Settlements and Housing* (Travistock,London, 1987), p. 12-32; Moser, 1991, see note 7.

17. A Larsson, "The housing Situation of Urban Female-headed Households in Botswana", Babitat International 12, 3 (1988), pp. 17-27. A. Larsson, *Women householders and Housing Strategies: the Case of Gaborone, Botswana* (National Swedish Institute for Building Research, Gavle, 1989). A. Schlyter, *Women Householders and Housing Strategies: the Case of George, Zambia* (National Swedish Institute for Building Research, Gavle, 1988); Schlyter, 1989 (see note 9).

18. A. Falu and M. Curutchet, "Rehousing the Urban Poor: Looking at Women First", *Environment and Urbanization* **3**, 2 (1991), pp. 23-38. The United States and United Kingdom literature also emphasizes single women women and women as single parents [Watson and Austerberry, 1986 (see note 4); G.R. Wekerle, "From Refuge to Service Center: Neighborhoods that Support Women", in W. van Vliet (ed.), *Women, Housing and Community* (Avebury, Aldershot, 1988), pp. 7-22; E.A. Mulroy, *Women as Single Parents: Confronting the Institutional Barriers in the Courts, the Workplace and the Housing Market* (Auburn House, Dover, MA, 1988); J.F. Sprague, *More than Housing: Lifeboats for Women and Children* (Butterworth Architercture, Boston 1991); Golden, 1992 (See note 4)].

19. See also S. Volbede, "Housing and Survival Strategies of Women in Metropolitan Slum Areas in Brazil", *Habitat International* **13**, 3 (1989), pp. 157-171. One little-explored line of inquiry concerns women's role in the construction industry. An exception to the general neglect of this topic is Olusola Adebola Labeodan's "Women in the informal House-building Industry in Nigeria", *Habitat Internation* **16**, 1 (1992), pp. 17-24.

20. L. Brydon and S. Chant, *Women in the Third World: Gender Issues in Rural and urban Areas* (Edward Elgar, Aldershot, 1989). Internationl Labour Ofice (ILO), *Women at Work*, No. 1 (1986).

21. J. G. Townsend and J.H. Momsen, "Towards a Geography of gender in Developing Market Economies", in J.H. Momsen and J.G. Townsend (eds), *Geography of Gender in the Third World*, (Hutchinson, New York, 1987), pp. 27-81.

22. M. Buvinic and **N.H**. Youssef with **B**. Van Elm, *Women-headed Households: the Ignored Factor in Development Planning* (International Center for Research on Women, Washington, DC, 1978). Moser, 1991 (see note 3).

23. Watson, 1988 (see note 3).

24. L.M.V. Machado, "The Problems for Woman-headed households in a Low-Income housing Programme in Brazil", in C.O.N. Mer and L. Peake (eds), *Women, Housing Settlements and Housing* (Tavistock, London, 1987), pp. 55-69. P. Nimpuno-Parente, "The Struggle for Shelter: Women in a Site and Service Project in Nairobi, Kenya", C.O.N. Moser and L. Peake (eds), *Women, Human Settlements and Housing* (Tavistock, London, 1987), pp. 70-87.

25. Moser, 1987, see note 16, p. 14. S. Chant and P. Ward, "Family Structure and Low-income Housing Policy", *Third World Planning Review* **9** (1987), pp. 5-19. D.L. Smith, "Women and Habitat: Nairobi 1985", in W. van Vliet (ed.), *Women, Housing and Community* (Avebury, Aldershot, 1988), pp. 185-189. M.S. Muller and D. Plantenga, *Women and habitat: Urban Management, Empowerment and Women's Strategies* (Royal Tropical Institute, Amsterdam, 1990). P.L. Sayne, "Food for Though: Making Women Visible", *Environment and Urbanization* **3**, 2 (1991), pp. 46-56. E. Wilson, *The Sphinx in the City: Urban Life, the Control of Disorder and Women* (Virage, London, 1991).

26. In two-thirds of the Latin American Countries analysed, women were described as de *jure* heads of between 10% and 20% of all households. The only figures over 30% were for Chile (32%) and Panama (40%) [Buvinic et al., 1978 (see note 22), pp. 87-88]. These figures were mostly for the 1970s, but in a paper presented to the *International Workshop on Insecurity in the 1990s: Gender and Social Policy* (5-6 April, 1993), Mayra Byviniv and Geetqa Rao Gupta report that "The prevalence of female headship in developing countries varies substantially across countries and situations, comprising anywhere from 10% to about 40% of all households". (I am indebted to an anonymous reviewer for this more recent informaion.)

27. N.H. Youssef and C.B. Hetler, "Establishing the Economic Condition of Woman-headed Households in the Third World: a New Approach", in M. Buvinic, M.A. Lycette and W.P. McGreevey (eds), *Women and Poverty in the Third World* (Johns Hopkins University Press, Baltimore, 1983), pp.216-243.

28. The temporary absence of men working illegally in the USA could account for under-reporting of *de facto* women-headed households; but in 10 Mexican cities, Selby *et* al. [1990 (see note 42), p. 201] found that only 11% of households had members working overseas.

29. Chant and Ward, 1987, see note 25. A.G. Gilbert and A. Varley, *landlord and Tenant: Housing the Poor in Urban Mexico* (Routledge, London, 1991). Volbeda, 1989 (see note 19).

30. The traditional concept of the household (usually defined as a residential unit sharing food and at least some budgetary resources) has been criticised as too static and too concerned with boundaries. Methodologically, it is argued that questionnaire surveys elicit

responses falsely depiciting a 'normal' conjugal family. [C. Fonseca, "Spouses, Siblings and Sex-linked Bonding: a Look at Kinship Organization on a Brazilian Slum", in E. Jelin (ed.), *Family, household and Gender Relations in Latin America,* (Kegan Paul International, London, 1991), pp. 133-160.] Such problems have led some authors to uncover *de facto* or 'hidden' women-headed households, doubling the overall proportion reported (Falu and Curutchet, 1991, see note 18), or to emphasise the importance of mother-child units in situations where "the overwhelming majority of households are normally nuclear" (Fonseca, 1991, p. 135). Unless the criteria used for defining *de facto* female-headed households are clear and consistently applied (following, perhaps, the categories proposed by Youssef and Hetler, 1983, see note 27), there is a danger of playing *cherchez la femme* in some of these approaches. [A. Varley, "Housing the Household, Holding the House ", in G. Jones and P.M. Ward (eds), *Methodology and Land and Housing Market Analysis* (UCL Press, london, in press).]

31. A.M. Goetz, "Feminism and the Claim to Know: Contradictions in Feminist Approaches to Women in Development", in R. Grant and K. Newland (eds), *Gender and International Relations* (Open University Press, Buckingham, 1991), pp. 133-57; see p. 140, my emphasis.

32. They were, in any case, never of great importance compared with the vast areas of 'spontaneous' housing in Latin America.

33. R. Burgess, "Helping Some to Help Themselves: Third World Housing Policies and Development Strategies", in K. Mathey (eds), *Beyond Self-Help Housing* (Mansell, London, 1992), pp. 75-91. J. Fiori and R. Ramirez, "Notes on the Self-help Housing Crituques: Towards a Conceptual Framework for the Analysis of Self-help housing policies in Developing Countries", in K. Mathey (ed.), *Beyond self-help Housing* (Mansell, London, 1992), pp. 23-31. C. Rakodi, "Cities and People: Towards a Gender-Aware Yrban Planning Process?", *Public Administration and Development* **11** (1991), pp. 541-559. The shift to a broader institutional level of intervention is unlikely to decrease discrimination against women unless specific safeguards are introduced. Brion and Tinker [M. Brion and A. Tinker, *Women in Housing: Access and Influence* (Housing Centre Trust, London, 1980)], and Watson (1988, see note 3) have shown how women in Britain and Australia are marginalised by housing allocation and finance systems, although Munro and Smith [M. Munro and S.J. Smith, "Gender and Housing: Broadening the Debate", *Housing Studies* **4** (1989), pp. 3-17] argue that

particular patriarchal outcomes cannot be assumed, because of the intervention of labour market variables.

34. For Mexico City see, for example, COPEVI (Centro Operacional de Vivienda y Poblamiento), *Investigacion sobre Vivienda 11: La produccion de vivienda en la Zona Metropolitana de la Ciudad de Mexico* (COPEVI, Mexico City, 1977). P. Connolly, "Uncontrolled Settlements and Self-Build: What Kind of Solution? The Mexico City Case", in P.M. Ward (ed)., *Self-Help Housing: a Critique* (Mansell, London, 1982), pp. 141-174. R. Coulombo and C. Sanchez Mejorada, *Todos Proprietarios? Viviends de alquiler y sectores populares en la ciudad de Mexico* (Centro de la Vivienda y Estudios Urbanos, Mexico City, 1991). A.G. Gilbert and P.M. Ward, *Housing, the State and the Poor: Policy and Practice in Three Latin American Cities* (Cambridge University Press, Cambridge, 1985). M.A. Michel, A. Azuela, P. Connolly, R. Coulomb, G. Garza, A. Iracheta, M. Maydon and M. Schteingart, *Procesos Habitacionales en la Ciudad de Mexico* (Universidad Autonoma Metropolitana-Iztapalapa and Secretaria de Desarrollo Urbano e Ecologia, Mexico City, 1988). M. Schteingart, *Los Productores del Espacio Habitable: Estado, Empresa y Sociedad en la Ciudad de Mexico* (El Colegio de Mexico, Mexico City, 1989). P.M. Ward, *Welfare Politics in Mexico: Papering Over the Cracks* (Allen & Unwin, London, 1986). P.M. Ward, *Mexico City: the Production and Reproduction of an Urban Environment* (Belhaven, London, 1990). For Guadalajara see Gilbert and Varley, 1991 (see note 29). R. Lopez Rangel, *Urbanizacion y Vivienda en Guadalajara* (Centro de Ecodesarrollo, Mexico City, 1987). D. Vazquez, *Guadalajara: Ensayos de Interpretacion* (El Colegio de Jalisco, Guadalajara, 1989). For Puebla see Gilbert and Varley, 1991 (see note 29). G.A. Jones, "The Impact of Government Intervention upon Land Prices in Latin American Cities: the case of Puebla, Mexico", unpublished Ph.D. thesis (University of Cambridge, Cambridge, 1991). P. Mele, *Los Procesos de Produccion del Espacio Urbano en la Ciudad de Puebla* Instituto de Ciencias, Universidad Autonoma de Puebla, Puebla, 1984). Universidad Autonoma de Puebla, Departamento de Investigaciones Arquitectonicas urbanisticas del Instituto de Ciencias (DIAU-ICUAP), *Memoria de la Primera Mesa de Trabajo sobre Investigaciones Universitarias de Urbanismo* (Universidad Autonoma de Puebla, Puebla, 1986).

35. CIDAC (Centro de Investigacion para el Descarrollo), *Vivenda y Estabilidad Politica: Alternativas para el Futuro* (Editorial

Diana, Mexico City, 1991). Ward, 1990 (see note 34).

36. R. Coulombm , "Viviends en renta Y dinamica habitacional en la Ciudad de Mexico", in M.A. Michel, A. Azuela, P. Connolly, R. Coulomb, G. Garza, A. Iracheta, M. Maydon and M. Schteingart (eds), *Procesos Habitacionales en la Ciudad de Mexico* (Unitersidad Autonoma Metropolitana-Iztapalapa and Secretaria de Desarrollo Urbano e Ecologia, Mexico City, 1988), pp. 141-182. Gilbert and Varley, 1991 (see note 29).

37. A Household is here defined as group of people 'eating from a common pot' and living on the same plot of land (see Varley,1993 see note 30). Where more than one household occupies a plot, the non-owner household (s) may either pay rent or share the plot, rent-free, with its owners. A nuclear household consists of a male or a female householder with or without a 'spouse' and with or without children; and extended household includes other relatives or non-relatives. A 'householder' is the person who originally bought or rented the house, either alone or with their 'spouse' (Gilbert and Varley, 1991, see note 29); this does not mean that householders have joint property rights.

38. Most sharers make some contribution to the costs of services consumed. Although the literature often fails to distinguish between extended households and sharing (see below), the question "*cocinan juntos o aparte*?" ("do you cook together or separately?") clearly makes sense ot people, and generally elicits a direct, clear response to questions seeking to establish the number of households present.

39. Fildwork in 1991 and 1992 included participant observation in a young self-help settlement on the eastern periphery of Puebla and a questionnaire survey in areas already studied in 1981-1982 (Mexico City) or 1985-1986 (Guadalajara and Puebla). *Loma de la Palma* developed in the 1970s on a hill in the north of Mexico City. Legalised in 1976, it received water and draninage in the 1980s and was being paved by the residents in summer 1991. *San Jose de los Leones* is a regularised and consolidated settlement in the west of Mexico City; it dates from the late 1960s. *El Salvador* is a 10-year old illegal settlement on the eastern periphery of Puebla. The streets are unpaved and many plots still unoccupied. *Veinte de Noviembre*, founded in the late 1940s as an illegal subdivision of private lands in northwest Puebla, now has a complex mixture of owner occupation, renting and sharing. *Buenos* Aires in Southern Guadalajafa dates from the beginning of the 1980s

and has experienced relatively lettle consolidation: the streets are unpaved and the area has still to be connected to the city's water and drainage networks. *Agustin Yanez*, in the east of Guadalajara, was founded by illegal subdivision in the early 1950s; as in Veinte de Noviembre, tenants now form an important part of the population.

40. The variation in the proportion of owners sharing their plot with other households is connected with the age of the settlement. The selection of settlements of widely differing ages was prompted by other research questions; it is unfortunate that in the Puebla and Guadalajara cases it means that there are relatively small numbers of sharers whose characheristics can be explored.

41. Although the workds 'married', 'wife' and 'husband' are used, no distinction is made between couples who are legally married and those living together in a consensual union. See also Gilbert and Varley, 1991 (note 29), Coulomb, 1990 (note 36); Gilbert and Ward, 1985 (note 34).

42. H.A. Selby, A.D. Murphy and S.A. Lorenzen, with I. Cabrera, A. Castaneda and I. Ruiz Love, *The Mexican Urban Household: Organizing for Self-Defense* (University fo Texas Press, Austin, 1990), p. 101. L.A. Lomnitz and M. Perez-Lizaur, "Dynastic Growth and Survival Strategies: the Solidarity of Mexican Grand-families", in E. Jelin (ed.), *Family, Household and Gender Relations in latin America* (Kegan Paul International, London, 1991), pp. 123-132; see p. 124. Arthur Wolf ["Family Life and the Life Cycle in Rural China", in R. McC. Netting, R.R. Wilk and E.J. Arnould (eds), *Households: Comparative and Historical Studies of the Domestic Group* (University of California Press, Berkeley, 1984), pp. 279-282] defines a [grand' family as having a minimum of *three* nuclear units — two married siblings and their parents. He difines a stem family as having only two nuclear units. If sharing is to be described as a variation on this theme, it is clear that there are both stem families and grand families involved.

43. L. Lamphere, "Strategies, Cooperation and Conflict among Women in Domestic Groups", in M.Z. Rosaldo, and L. Lamphere (eds), *Women, Culture and Society* (Standard University Press, Stanford, 1974), pp. 97-112; see p. 104.

44. *Ibid.*, see also E. Croll, "Rural China: Segregation to Solidarity", in P. Caplan and J.M. Bujra (eds), *Women United, Women Divided: Cross-cultural Perspectives on Female Solidarity* (Tavistock,

London, 1978), pp. 46-76. U. Sharma, "Segregation and its Consequences in India: Rural Women in Himachal Pradesh", in P. Caplan and J.M. Bujra (eds), *Women United, Women Divided: Cross-Cultural Perspectives on Female Solidarity* (Tavistock, London, 1978), pp. 259-282. M. Wolf, "Chinese Women: Old SKills in a New Context", in M.Z. Rosaldo and L. Lamphere (eds), *Woman, Culture, and Society* (Standard University Press, Stanford, 1974), pp. 157-172. Wolf, 1984 (see note 42).

45. G.M. Foster, *Tzintzuntzan: Mexican Peasants in a Changing World* (Little, Brown, Boston, 1967). B.L. Chinas, *The isthmus Aapotecs: Women's Roles in Cultural Context* (Holt, Rinehart & Winston, New York, 1973). J.W. Whitecotton, *The Zapotecs: Princes, Priests and Peasants* (University of Oklahoma Press, Norman, 1977). J.J. Gross, "Marriage and 'Family' among the Maya", in A.F. Marks and R.E. Romer (eds), *Family and Kinship in Middle America and the Caribbean* (University of the Netherlands Antilles and Royal Institute of Linguistics and Anthropology, Leiden, 1978), pp. 51-86.J.M. Ingham, *Mary, Michael and Lucifer: Folk Catholicism in Central Mexico* (University of Texas Press, Austin, 1986). L. Krantz, *Peasant Differentiation and Development: the Case of a Mexican Ejido* (University of Stockholm, 1991). L. Stephen, *Zapotec Women* (University of Texas Press, Austin, 1991). In an interesting exception to the rule, Nash [J.C. Nash, *Social Relations in Amatenango del Valle: An Activity Analysis,* Centro Intercultural de Documentacion (CIDOC), Cuernavaca, 1969] found that in Amatenango del Valle, Chiapas, where recently married couples used to live with the bride's parents, they were now equally likely to live with either set of parents.

46. 1990 (see note 42), p. 101.

47. 1991 (see note 42), p. 126.

48. L.A. lomnitz, *Networks and Marginality: Life in a Meixcan Shantytown* (Academic Press, New York, 1977), p. 119.

49. *Ibid.*, p. 120. The figures for 'initial residence' were 46% and 29%. The implication is that nuclear households were in the minority: 'the extended family previals in the great majority of households' (*ibid.*, p. 100). This finding is contrary to most studies of Mexican urban househods, although it is difficult to draw comparisons between Lomnitz' household classification shceme and those used by other authors. Many of the households she classifies as extended are more

easily enumerated as nuclear sub-groups (*ibid.*, p. 102). Sharers as defined in this study are found in Lomnitz' 'single-roof' and 'single-plot' extended household categories rather than what she classifies as 'jointed' households'.

50. More daughters and sons are recorded as living with their parents than with thier in-laws; this calls for comment. It may reflect under-reporting; but there is another explanation. Whereas almost all owners in the case-study settlements have enough space to accommodate another family, this is not necessarily true of their children's in-laws, who will come from a variety of housing types. Some, for example, will be tenants, who are more likely to lack the space to accommodate any other relatives (Gilbert and Varley, 1991, see note 29).

51. The custom by which a young man 'steals' his girlfriend from her parents, sometimes with the explicit support of his own relatives, has been widely documented in rural areas (Foster, 1967; Chinas, 1973; Whitecotton, 1977, see note 45) and is also, according to observations made during the fieldwork for this study, by no means uncommon in the cities.

52. Moser, 1991 (see note 7), p. 93

53. Volbeda, 1989 (see note 19).

54. Gilbert and Varley, 1991 (see note 29).

55. Gilbert and Varley [1991 (see note 29), p. 112] suggest that the deposit, rather than the regular montly payments on a plot of land, is one of the key elements dividing persistent tenents from prospective owners.

56.Lomnitz, 1977 (see note 48).

57. *Ibid.*, p. 31.

58. *Ibid.*, p. 3.

59. *Ibid.*, p. 156.

60. S. Chant, "Family Formation and Female Roles in Queretaro, Meixco", *Bulletin of latin American Research* **4**, (1985), pp. 17-32. S. Chant, *Women and Survival in Mexico Cities: Perspectives on Gender, Labour Markets and Low-Income Households* (Manchester University Press, manchester, 1991).

61. Chant, 1991 (see note 60), p. 156.

62. See also B. Garcia, H. Munoz and O. de Oliveira, *Hogares*

y Trabajadores en la Ciudad de Mexico (El Colegio de Mexico, Mexico City, 1982). M. Gonzalez de la Rocha, "Economic Crisis, Domestic Reorganisation and Women's Work in Guadalajara, Mexico", *Bulletin of Latin American Research* 7, (1988), pp. 207-223. Selby et al., 1990 (see note 42).

63. Chant, 1985 (see note 60). p. 22

64. *Ibid.*, p. 26.

65. Chant, 1991 (see note 60), pp. 144-153.

66. Lamphere, 1974 (see note 43), p. 105.

67. Wolf, 1984 (see note 42), p. 281.

68. Croll, 1978 (see note 44).

69. Wolf, 1974 (see note 44).

70. Sharma, 1978 (see note 44).

71. Croll, 1978 (see note 44), p. 50.

72. Interestingly, Croll [E. Croll, *Chinese Women Since Mao* (Third World Books, London, 1983), p. 83] notes that tension between mother-and daughter-in-law was the most common cause of divorce reported in 1980s Beijing.

73. Stephen, 1991, pp. 40-62; Chinas, 1973, p. 59; Ingham, 1986, p. 64 (see note 45). In her study of a village in Chiapas, where married children can live with *either* set of parents, Nash (1969, see note 45) found more harmonious relations between in-laws.

74. Krantz, 1991 (see note 45), p. 128.

75. R. Diaz-Guerrero, *Psicolgia del mexicano*, 5th edn (Editorial Trillas, Mexico City, 1990), p. 35. Stephen, 1991 (see note 45), p. 49.

76. L. Lenero Otero, "Valores familiares y dramaturgia social", in A. Hernandez medina and L. Narro Rodriguez (eds), *Como somos los mexicanos* [Centro de Estudios Educativos (CEE), Mexico City, 1987], pp. 253-299. Diaz-Guerrero, 1990 (see note 75), p. 75.

77. As Selby *et al.* [1990 (see note 42), p. 91] write "Living alone is almost unthinkable in urban Mexico", particularly for a woman in her eighties.

78. Krantz [1991 (see note 45), p. 136] notes the potential for confict between sisters-in-law discussing the problems of virilocal residence patterns in rural Central Mexico.

79. The phrase *subir y bajar* ('to go up and down') is used in two context: too-ing (as in visits to a government office in search of documentation, for example) and sleeping around. Women may be expected to take a child with them on 'legitimate' outings. Anzaldua [G Anzaldua, *Borderlands/La Frontera: the New Mestiza* (Aunt Lute, San Francisco, 1987), p. 16] records the prejudice against women who spend too much time 'in the street' from a *chicāna* viewpoint: "How many times have I heard mothers and mothers-in-law tell their sons to beat their wives for not obeying them, for being *hociconas* (big mouths), fcr being *callajeras* (going to visit and gossip with neighbors) . . . ?"

80. Whitecotton, 1977, see note 45, p. 254; Krantz, 1991 (see note 45). Writing about urban Greece, Hirschon [R. Hirschon, "Essential Objects and the Sacred: Interior and Exterior space in an UrbanGreek Locality", in S. Ardener (ed.), *Women and Space: Ground Rules and Social Maps* (Croom Helm, London, 1981), pp. 72-88]; indicates the importance of having separate kitchens as a "physical marker" of each household's autonomy when daughters marry and bring their husbands to live in their parents' home.

81. Chinas, 1973 (see note 45), p. 59.

82. Nash, 1969 (see note 45), p. 2/9.

83. Lamphere, 1974 (see note 43), p. 112.

CHAPTER-12

Women's Participation Strengthens NGO Projects : Sri Lanka

Vijita Fernando

Peoples' participation in community activities prevailed in Sri Lanka long before the term community participation became fashionable in modern development jargon. Self help groups, the forerunners of today's formalised Non Governmental Organisations (NGOs) existed in remote rural areas. In a country where 65 percent of the people live in rural areas, these were widespread as active, dynamic informal groups helping one another in activities directed to the common good.

Today community participation is acknowledge as an important tool in the country's mainstream development programmes such as the Integrated Rural Development Programme, the Million Houses Programme, the Janasaviya or Poverty Alleviation Programme of the government and in all development projects of the NGO sector.

Till a decade ago community participation meant men's participation with the women at the periphery - fetching and carrying and providing the men with hot meals and cups of tea. Several factors combined to make planners take a closer look at the enhanced roles, women could be called upon to play. Women's participation in development was already being highlighted through the UN International Women's Decade and the Year of the Child. This spilled over to the International Drinking Water Supply and Sanitation Decade (IDWSSD). Social Justice, equality and elimination of gender based discrimination in the development process were constantly being talked about. There was a particular emphasis on women's participation being crucial to achieving improvement in the health of the people through improved practices in water and sanitation. Women, half the world's human resource could, it was accepted, contribute positively to building sustainable systems both in their capacity as beneficiaries and as partners in development.

NGOs were also taking a closer look at the failure of water programmes. With their close links with the people and empathy with popular needs, it was not long before they faced the fact that without a supportive partnership with women, water/sanitation projects will always fail.

Involving women was not as easy as facing this realisation. Women's participation meant different things to different people, to different communities. Cultural and traditional practices and taboos had to be tackled just as strongly as men's and other elders' attitudes. Women's own conditioning to traditional attitudes, superstitious beliefs about water and waste disposal, which abound in Sri Lankan lore had to be overcome. The biggest stumbling blocks however, were not attitudes and beliefs but apathy and indiference born of poverty, constant ill health and malnutrition.

Innovative NGOs wooed women's participation by providing health clinics for their children. Women always respond to these and bring all their children to be measured, weighed and examined by a doctor/nurse team. The captive audience of mothers is treated to posters, flash cards, skits and illustrated talks on safe water and hygiene and the way is for a smoothed water sanitation programme.

WOMEN'S NGOS

Women's NGOs have the edge over others in winning women's participation. Talk of toilets and elimination of waste is easir between women and women, as the Girl Guide Association of Sri Lanka found in Heenatipone, a little village in the central hills. It was a women's story all the way, when a Buddhistnun, a former Guide, gifted land in the village to the Guides to set up a Centre. A resident Guide lives here as project officer and the Centre provides a meeting place for women. The women identified water and sanitation as basic needs. The men cooperated with them and the NGO as Guides are a respected community known islandwide in Sri Lanka.

The women admitted the need for toilets, for separate wells for drinking water and for bathing and washing clothes. They decided on the sites and took on the role of managers. Five years after the three wells and eighteen basic toilets were built, the women are still in charge. The toilet superstructures are now rather dilapidated but the insides are dry, clean and fly free. The men assist with occasional thatching of roofs and leave the credit of hygienic use to the women.

The wells are in mint condition, the aprons sparkling clean and divisions of washing, bathing and drinking are as strict as ever. There are informal caretakers - women of coursel - supervised by the Guide project officer. The caretakers keep the surroundings clean and flush the drains to prevent them being blocked with mud during the rainy season.

Women's participation in the water sanitation programme has given them new insights into their capabilities - several small income generating activities have been started and links have been forged with government agricultural and medical extension services to facilitate these, and set up a nutrition centre in the village. Four other villages have enrolled their women in these activities and in March when we visited the project there was one query - when are we getting wells and toilets for other villages? This is the very satisfying challenge that the Guide are now facing!

TECHNOLOGY

It is not easy for the sophisticated western mind to grasp the attitudes of simple rural people, especially women, to deep wells and hand pumps. A well to them is an open well where one can see the water sparkle when the sun plays on it. A certain kind of tree growing by it, its roots caressing the water means that the water in that well is pure and safe to drink. The branches overhanging the well keep the water tasty and cool. Certain kinds of fresh water fish in the water improves its quality. Resistance to using water that they do not see inside a tube well which comes to them through a pump can be grasped only if one appreciates these beliefs.

But where nature has not been so abundant with rain as in Heenatipone, deep wells and hand pumps are the only answer to women who have to walk miles to water holes ponds and drying streams for small quantities of water for drinking, in the dry north central and north eastern parts of the country. Winning womens participation for water projects here is a different story from areas where water is plentful. Sarvodaya, a large NGO with projects in 5000 villages islandwide has a success story.

Sarvodaya's development programmes had low participation from women in many of these villages. Water borne diseases, low productivity of the women, excessive time spent in water collection and storing were some facts that Sarvodaya identified. There was an overriding need to provide a simple low cost technology for safe drinking water conveniently at hand in there dry areas. The Sarvodaya plan was a costly one supplemented financially and technically by the International Development Research Centre, Canada and backed by research by Sarvodya workers. Padiyatalawa in the eastern province dry zone was selected and ten villages were identified for this innovative ambitious plan of involving women in manufacturing, repairing and maintaining hand pumps.

The first programme involved 20 girls. Ten girls were trained for two months in all aspects of technical details for constructing wells. The other ten were trained in planning fitting, welding lathework and smithy work required to manufacture handpumps, at the Sarvodaya's own engineering division close to Colombo. The final training was in assembling the handpumps in monitoring, maintenance and evaluation of performance.

A central workshop was built at Padiyatalawa and equipped with machinery to manufacture handpumps. Later ten subsidiary workshops were built in each of the selected villages to assemble, repair and maintain handpumps in use in the village.

UNFEMININE ?

It was not too difficult to select a suitable handpump which pleased the women. But Sarvodaya had many problems in selecting women to be trained. Technical work was not that fathers wanted for their daughters. Married women had other chores, so the selectees where unmarried girls between 18 and 25. Six dropped out of the first batch when they were repeatedly told by fellow villagers that their chances of finding a husband would be minimal if they continued to repair handpumps - an exclusively man's job and so unfeminine!

The programme, in spite of these drawbacks has been successfully carried out for six years. Sarvodaya achieved among many things women's participation in the technological aspects of water provision. After the initial hurdles if won men's approval when it was found that men did not have to run to the pump and repair it every time some little thing went wrong! The water problem was solved and later when Sarvodaya changed its thinking and recruited young married women who had greater leisure and did not face the prospects of leaving the village for employment, the project worked even better. It is steadily growing and spreading to other water starved areas today, and in every one of the projects sarvodaya has was hundred percent women's participation.

There is another aspects to this programme. The entry of rural girls into the field of water technology in the kind of exposed environment contrasts with women's scientific work behind closed doors in urban laboratories. This is a major breakthrough in changing traditionaly demarcated male and female work spheres and gender role perceptions that still prevail both among the women themselves and in society in general.

HEALTH WORKERS

In punchiwilaththawa's water/sanitation programme by the NGO Water Supply and Sanitation Decade Service (Decade Service) young women played a completely different role from the Sarvodaya programme. The village based NGO identified health education as a first priority when the Decade Service was able to get six open wells and sixty five basic toilets for its 250 families. Twenty five young school leavers, all under twenty five years of age were selected for training, first by the service and health extention staff is in the village and later at the town hospital eight miles away. The training was in all aspects of health education. The focus however, was on safe water and sanitation. Long before the wells were ready or the toilets were completed, each girl had in her purview ten households where mothers, grandmothers young women and children were given the message of safe water and sanitation by the girls. Keep the wells clean, buckets away from contamination and pass on these messages to the family's children, the girls exhorted, on their daily home visits.

Sometimes the girls were in tears! With the best of motives each girl was given the ten houses in her immediate neighbourhood whose inmates were people she had known all her life. The O. Level educated health volunteer had been the little girl the fimilies had watched grow, smiled at every time they passed her in the village, met at the temple and the market all her young life. Now she became an outsider, someone coming with an air of authority to tell them how to run their lives! It was tough.

But the girls won the women over and soon under the village spreading trees there were talks on safe water and hygiene illustrated with huge posters provided by the Decade Service, weighing babies, making notes and boiling water and storing them in large earthen containers covered with scraped coconut shells for safety. The girls also learnt to conduct simple surveys and within the next two years converted an unused school building and set up a nutrition centre. Weekly a nutritious meal of leaves and grains from the neighbourhood was cooked and distributed to pregnant and lactating mothers and children.

The Decade Service was able to leave the project sure of its sustainability in these capable young hands. The six wells and sixty five toilets were only the hardware for a spin off effect of better nutrition, clearner habits and more educated mothers - and of course, women's participation at every stage.

WOMEN MANAGERS

The Lanka Mahila Samiti (LMS) is one of the oldest women's NGOs in the country with a network of training women at community level in all 24 districts. When it launched on a water/sanitation programme in a dry zone village of 140 families where already a committee of trained volunteers worked at grassroots level, it went in with the philosophy that women should be involved in water and sanitation schemes not because it is they who go to the well and carry the pot of water, but because "women are a potential human resource and if they are actively integrated in water programmes at every stage there could be a definite impact on their own development".

Water and sanitation had only to be mentioned in this village and there was a ready response, from both men and women. This did not happen when other development activity was discussed - nutrition, family planning, even pre schools.

Building on this response the LMS got the women to do a house to house survey to get the actual water/sanitatioin picture, available water sources, toilets that were needed and then draw a map of the village. The women selected the sites, pinning flags on the map. To some women this was the first time they had seen a map, let alone drawn one! The LMS active involvement was only to assist them to get the funds. The women opened a Bank Account handled all the accounts, bought the bricks and selected the toilet sites with the advice of the health officials.

The women supervised the work and some were acutal bricklayers masons and combined these roles with those of monitor/evaluator.

Daily evaluations were conducted with the extension workers using IMS techniques of participatory evaluation.

Almost from the start of the project the women had gained a new status in the village. The specified the bathing hours at the wells and were ready to settle quarrels over the use of water... but they had a tough fight. First, they had to overcome their own inhibitions, then the attitude of their men and the men's interference. How much the men were convinced we will never know. But after some time the husbands, male officials in the village, the schools teacher and the monk in the temple agreed to let the women handle the project - they saw a new role for the women, other than cooking their meals and waiting on them.

The promise of the project could not be seen in full. No evaluation was possible. The pojeect had to be abandoned some tije later due to terrorist activity in this part of the country. But the LMS is determined to repicate the idea in another village to enable women to win greater participation in water/sanitation programmes as a stepping stone to being full partners in other areas of development, gaining a new status in their communities and fulfilling their potential.

A CONTRAST

The Kitulawa project - a small wet zone village subject to periodic flooding - is a study in contrasts. The provision of basic toilets to this rural community was a Guides project where a conscious effort was made to involve women in mainstream activities in sanitation and water. The Guides used the pre school related Mother Group as a focal point for dicussion on health and nutrition problems and their relationship to water and sanitation, thus motivating the women to participate actively in the programme, The 100 toilets were completed on schedule, sited where the women wanted and health education going on space long before they were completed. A visit this year - six years after they were completed - confirms their use and hygienic maintenance. The health officials report positively that diarrhoeal disease is much less. The health officials report positively that diarrhoeal disease is much less. The toilets still look good, their floors have no crac the roofs are in repair and the doors lock securely.

The six deep wells that were given to the village at the same time show less success. Women's participation was symbolised only by one of the wells being dug by the women.The participation ended there and six months after they were completed the handpumps were rejected by the community. The water from the tube wells was used only for washing as the women did not "trust" the water. Drawn through a handpumps was it safe enough for drinking ? There was a rusty colour and taste and the women did not use it for cooking. They did not even like to bath in the well water as the "hair turned brown". Today, six years later we find that the handpumps in three of the wells are not in working order.

The iron removal filters fitted at a later date for controlling excessive quantities of iron were broken and the pump in the well near the pre school which serves as a demonstration unit to the community is in a state of disrepair. The pre school kids have no source of water at hand.

The trained pump caretakers are all male and only one lives in the village. There has been no response to requests to have the pump repaired which is serious and needs expert help. Earlier there had been other development activity for the women, skills training in handicrafts batik printing and packeting condiments. Today there is no evidence of sustenance of women's involvement, though the pre school remains a potential focal point for such development.

SHARING EXPERIENCES

These are not great success stories of NGO efforts of winning and sustaining women's participation. But they are a good begining. Sri Lankan NGOs will always require special efforts to achieve women's participation and will need to address cultural constraints and barriers to women's participation in public.

Male attitudes must be overcome. More women in NGOs and more women's NGOs will have to be catalysts to involve women at every level. Women's role models are needed for rural women to be more confortable assuming new roles. The basic idea that water and sanitation is a masculine field will need to be revolutionised and the entire field feminized.

It has taken a decade for this process to get going. We have thanks to NGOs, reached a point where no longer is the concept to women's participation a source of amusement and resistance. At the highest levels they are realising the importance of full participation of women. But questions remain. The most important is 'how' in our little village, in my developing country, do we win the full participation of women ? The strategies may not be so different from your little village in your highly developed country. Let us share them.

CHAPTER-13

Women and Environmental Aspect of Human Settlement in the Third World

S.C. Sharma, R.L. Sehgal

Introduction:

Over the last fifty years, the relationship between women and the living systems which support their life has changed in response to ecological stress in many areas of urban & rural poor, developing economies. Rural women have inherited a situation where their rights and access to cultivable land have decreased and the fuelwood and water grown scarce. There is a belief that women are responsible for environmental destruction in rural areas. We can see the heavy loads of wood on thier heads and foraging for that last twig or bit of green in areas which have been stripped bare of vegitation. But laying the blame on women is to ignore the globally linked causes of environmental destruction which have created a situation of scarcity that often forces women into ecological destructive actions.

Throughout the under developed world, ecological equilibrium has been disturbed by a number of interacting factors, many of which are the direct result of development policies geared toward survival in that economy. For under-developed countries, economic survival has meant providing the raw material and agricultural products demanded by market in the developed countries, often at the cost of widespread natural resources depletion. Economic policies have supported the conversion of the felling of the forest for wood materials, bush and woodland for agricultural development, and the indiscriminate use of water resources for irrigation. At the same time growth of population continues to increase the number of men, women and children who depend on dwindling natural resources. The impact of scarcity of natural resources has been particularly very hard on rural women, who are mainly responsible for collecting water and wood, making those tasks increasingly arduous and time consuming in a day already burden by long hours of work on them. Because women's needs are always the last to be considered within the family and community, they are overlooked by development projects which might bring assistance and women always receive the least when scarce resources alloted to them.

Another phenomenon which has happend, is the growing number of women left behind in rural areas to carry the burden of their family survival alone because the men have gone in search of job facilities in urban areas. For the rural women who have also migrated to urban areas with their particular environmental crises and problems of poor sanitation, housing, pollution, and poverty brings another kind of hardship for them. This aritcle is an effort to indicate the too often untold story of silent sufferers, living in the face of ecological distress in the third world.

Environmental Aspects of Human Settlement in India

It is common to define women's environment as everything around her but excluding her. In terms of the natural system which supports all terrestrial life forms, a zone consisting of the earth's crust, waters and air space above these in which life can subsist, is known as the biosphere. A major concern of environmental management is to maintain the biosphere and its life support elements in a state in which they will continue to support life.

Women, as the only conscious life on earth, can induce change in many ways both in the physical environment and in other life forms. It will, therefore, be more appropriate to define nature as all that surrounds women, excluding women and what women herself has put therein, that is to say, all the elements of physical environment plus the biotic world except those elements of the physical environment which women has disturbed and those species of plants and animals which she has domesticated, eliminated or developed.

The biotic world bears an intimate relationship with the physical environment. The latter sustains the former. But this relationship is not unchanging. The physical world itself is changing, sometimes slowly and, at other times, dramatically. With every major change in the physical world, there takes place a corresponding change in the biotic world. In the past geologic periods several major changes in the physical world have literally wiped out large variety of animal and plant species from the surface of the earth. This is how the process of natural selection is functioning. Women, as the primate species of the biotic world, has herself come into being through this process of natural selection. In this perspective, nature would appear to be unyielding, limiting manoeuvrability within the rules framed by it.

However, the image of an unyielding nature softens as we review the history of achievement of mankind. Having arrived through the process of natural selection, she emerged as a unique species. She can observe, relate, assimilate and store and develop knowledge. Using these capabilities, she organized herself as a food-gatherer and, over a period of time, domesticated plants and animals. In a relatively shorter period in human history she organised herself first into small settlements and later into large cities. During the last 200 years she has acquired remarkable knowledge about the physical and living systems which has enabled her to realign some of the processes of nature for her own wellbeing. She superimposed on the process of natural selection, her own art of controlled selection. She domesticated species of plants and animals, developed new strains and is now even creating new life forms. She overcame the physical laws of nature in various ways. Nature, so it appears, yielded to her aspirations.

However at the same time, these historical developments have created situations of contradication. There are large variety of human actions which are apprehended as capable of causing upsets in nature, some of them of an irreversible character. Land which is for all purposes a non-renewable and inelastic resource has not been managed in a protective manner. The contact of water with land has created disadvantageous situation due to absence of scientific land and water management policies. The Ministry of Agriculture estimates that 175 million hectares (mh) out of the total land area of 304 mh suffers from environmental problems of one kind or another. Estimates show that we lose on an average 6000 million tonnes of top soil every year. Losses on account of floods aggregate Rs. 1000 crores a year. Even forest lands are not being fully protected. It is estimated that at least 20 million hectares of forest land is adversely affected by erosion. It is no longer tolerable that we treat forests as sources of timber only. Any endangering of forest land tends to disturb the total eco system. Alongwith this denudation of natural resource environmental pollution has emerged an another area which needs women concerted attention. Pollution has serious implications as it renders the resources (man made or natural) unfit for human use. The problem being created through water, land, air and noise pollution have undcarable dimensions.

All these environmental problems in Third World can be attributed to

a) those arising from conditions of poverty and under-development

b) those arising as negative effects of the very process of development.

The first category has to do with the impact on the health and integrity of our natural resources (land, soil, water, forests, wild-life, etc.) as a result of poverty and the inadequate availability, for a large section of our population, of the means so fulfil basic human needs (food, fuel, shelter, employment, etc.). The second category has to do with the unintended side-effects of efforts to achieve rapid economic growth and development. In this latter category would fall the distortions imposed on national resources from poorly planned development projects and programmes, as well as from lack of attention to long term concerns by commercial and vested interests. Thus it is clear that a concern for environment is essentially a desire to see that national development proceeds along rational sustainable lines. Environmental conservation is, in fact, the very basis of all development.

The environment policy in relation to human settlement has to be pursued in a manner that will satisfy all the human needs without any adverse affect on the environment. The lives of more than 75 per cent of our population living in rural areas is closely linked with nature and the natural environment. The environmental problems that manifest in rural areas are largely due to over-use or misuse of natural resources mostly because of sheer poverty and lack of alternatives. The denundation of vegetative cover due to indiscriminate removal for firewoods, and the over-grazing by cattle and other live-stock and consequent soil erosion are two common examples of the impoverishment of the environmental resources. Again, the non-availability of systems for disposal of community wastes in rural areas has led to the contamination of water courses and creation of insanitary living conditions. This, in turn, has had major impacts on the women's health of the population especially where unprotected sources of water have, of necessity to be used by the rural population. Despite all efforts so far about 2 lakh villages with a population of some 160 million are yet to be provided with potable water supply facilities while sewer age systems in the villages are non-existant. This has been a cause of water-borne diseases like jaundice, typhoid, cholera etc. The chronic unemployment and under-employment in these areas have led to the migration into towns and cities that have added to the already severe environmental problems in urban settlements.

At the same time, though the urban population is less than a quarter of the total population, its absolute size, over 12 crores, sheer numbers is collosal. The phenomenal increase in urban population both as a result of natural growth as well as immigration, has lead to the mushroom growth of slums and squatter settlements. The pressures on urban land have often resulted in an indiscriminate mixture of land uses resulting in a steady deterioration of already strained urban services and environmental quality. In order to provide additional land, ill-conceived reclamation has been carried out on water bodies and marsh lands which have curcial ecological roles to play in safe-guarding coastal towns and cities. Major instances of such coastal reclamation are to be found in Bombay, Cochin and Calcutta. Since Independence several new towns have been built and practically every city has been extended often at the expense of fertile agricultural land. When extensions of old cities have been made there have been inadequate assessments of the capacities of existing urban infrastructure to cater to the larger combined populations. Thus roads, water supply, drainage, sewerage services become over-loaded with the consequent frequent break-downs leading to unsatisfactory environmental conditions. These trends will only intensify in the future with the increase in population density and lower per capita availability of resources, both natural and man-made, thus aggravating problems of environmental health. So far attempts at environmental improvement in human settlements have come in a disjointed and piecemeal fashion with attention focussed on one particular function or the other (transportation, water supply, power generation, etc.) rather than treating settlements and their activities as a dynamic and organic whole. Vigorous and coordinated steps are now required for environmentally sound planning and development of human settlements.

The above delineation of the environmental problems into urban and rural should not be taken to imply that the rural and urban sectors are unrelated having their own special environmental problems which can be resolved independently of each other. The rural and urban sectors are part of a total system with intimate ecological relationships between each other. Thus, the problems of encroachments and slums in urban areas are a direct consequence of rural-urban migration resulting from lack of productive employment in the countryside. Any attempt to tackle the growth of urban slums without relating it to the economic stability of the rural country side has therefore, little hope of succeeding. Similarly, the increasing pressure on forests for industrial and urban needs, is dislocating the ecological relationship between the rural, particularly tribal, population and the forests. It is, thus, evident that the urban problems will have to be studied and tackled in their regional context. In other words, urban planning will have to define its objectives against the backdrop of regional planning. Town and country planning, called city and regional planning in the USA, will have to evolve as an integrated process.

Urbanization provides the stage for enacting development activities. It does not directly lead to economic growth and production but provides the spatial form for economic activities to take place. Viewed thus, it, by itself, is not a development sector like agriculture, industries and irrigation. This characteristic of urbanization has often lead to the erroneous inference that urbanization is the result of growth and development and not its cause. Operationally, this means that whenever economic activity, planned or unplanned, takes place, it creates the need for clustoring of activities making it necessary to provide basic urban facilities like roads, housing, water supply etc. Even international financing agencies have, as a rule, considered it appropriate to fund urban development only where the need for growth has been established by the market process and the investments are justified on grounds of financial viability. It is rarely that any effort is made to channelize and direct development by the provision of civic infrastructure at locations derived from regional optimization studies.

The pressure of urbanization has been significantly more in metropolitan and large cities than in smaller towns. This is largely influenced by the perception of enterpreneurs of the advantages to be derived by them through proximity to an existing already well developed infrastructure supported by investments by the State agencies to whom such investments offer immediate attractive returns. Actually, in most cases a stage has been reached where the economics of agglomeration have begun to be offset by the diseconomics that must inevitably follow the breakdown of the social and physical infrastructure. Unfortunately, governments do not take into account the cost of subsequently developing such infrastructure while encouraging economic growth in already congested urban centres. It should be obvious that corrective measures at a later stage may be prohibitively expensive or may just not be feasible.

Efforts have been made in the past to divert investment from the large urban centres for achieving balanced growth. The grant of capital subsidy and other incentives for industrial investments in backward areas is illustrative of such a policy. There is no doubt that this policy did succeed in attracting investments in the backward areas. However, in most cases, except developed land, water and electricity within the industrial areas, no supportive infrastructure development, namely, housing, shopping etc. in the associated town was planned or undertaken. Had this been done, the town would not only have been in a better position to absorb the growth but would also have given further impetus to it. The approach was totally sectoral, the sole objective being industrial development without consideration for related needs.

Recognizing the need for improving the absorptive capacity of small and medium towns for reducing pressure on the large cities and spreading development more evenly, a programme for development of small and medium towns was launched in the sixth plan. This was a major deviation from the policy being followed in earlier years during which, whatever allocations were available in the urban sector, were provided to only large cities, the lion's share being taken away by the metropolitan centres. The scheme, however, in most States, faced difficulties during implementation. One reason was the weakness in the organizational structure of the implementing authorities in the small and medium towns. The principal reason, however, was the inadequacy of the planning machinery to develop adequate town development schemes relating them to the regional dimensions of development. In reality, the schemes de-generated into area development schemes providing for housing plots and limited related infrastructure in specific locations without relating it to the total planning of the city or inducing a self-generating growth process. The biggest tragedy was that even the area development schemes, prepared in a hurry, were based on inadequate surveys and women's involvement and were, as such, sketchy and inadequate creating innumberable problems and delays during implementation.

The Indian experience in the development of industrial townships has also been far from happy. The coal mining areas are notorious for subhuman living conditions in the labour settlements with illplanned and unhygienic growth around them. Steel cities like jamshedpur, Rourkela and Bhilai, so also other industrial cities, particularly those associated with thermal power generation, present an ignominious combination of a well developed walled industrial township surrounded by shantly illplanned development for the supportive population. Korba in Madhya Pradesh is a classic case of lack of foresight, where a number of large industrial units have come up as separate walled entities and it is now impossible to tie up the urban infrastructure or provide common civic and urban facilities. In none of these cases, was any worthwhile planning study made prior to the setting up of the plants nor was any funding made available for planned growth. The unfortunate part is that even today, the planning of such centres is receiving callous attention which will inevitably lead to severe environmental degradation in the years to come.

This brings us to some difficult policy choice issues. If urban growth has to be given better direction, its financing will have to be improved which will evidently have to be at the cost of other sectors. What is even more important is that considerable strengthening of the planning mechanism will have to be done in order to enable it to meaningfully step in before growth takes place and not be over-taken by events. The planning authority evolving integrated investment plans will have to be clothed with adequate powers for coordinating and directing various activities in relation to both location and phasing of investment.

Developing countries are experiencing unprecedented urban growth on account of rural-urban migration due to lack of productive employment in the rural sector. Such large-scale dislocation of populations is costly and has innumberable sociological problems associated with it. An urbanisation policy will, therefore, have to be based on a sound population policy and a policy which improves economic stability in the rural sector. In other words, the urban-rural policy will have to be viewed in totality and a balanced investment plan evolved. Nonetheless there seems to be no way by which urban growth can be prevented. It will take place irrationally if we do not plan and provide for it, aggravating the existing environmental deficiencies in the urban centres.

While it is true that urbanization does not directly lead to economic growth, it provides the base for growth in the non-agricultural sectors. Even production of some of the agricultural inputs and marketing of the agricultural produce needs an urban base. It is now well recognised that for inducing industrial development, development of industrial infrastructure in the form of developed land, water and power, is essential. An adequate urban base is actually an infrastructure for development in the wider sense. In other words, if an industrial growth centre is being promoted, the infrastructure needed is not only in relation to the industrial area alone but for the supportive urban facilities in the form of housing, commercial centres, schools, etc. If urban development is viewed as infrastructure development, the conceptual error in treating it as consequence of economic growth, will disappear. In the development process, an infrastructure need has to precede or at least be fully comprehended and visualized in advance, if ill-planned growth has to be averted. This brings us back to the need for planning in totality rather than in sectoral compartments. It is significant to observe here that thinking in purely sectoral terms, industrial development agencies not only ignore the urban infrastructure needs but often consider intervention by the urban authorities as an intrusion. The need for coordinating planning authority can hardly be over-emphasised.

Funding for urban infrastructure has essentially to be in the form of seed capital for triggering off a process of self-generating growth. The seed capital needs have to be adequate in order to enable the urban authorities to initiate the growth process meaningfully. Land, the basic resource for urban growth, for the projected needs and development of the area required in the first phase, must be provided for at the outset. In the case of industry-related growth, a substantial diversion of resource takes place when the industries, projecting colourful pictures of employment generation and growth, succeed in securing land free or at a nominal cost. The States, competing with one another to attract central projects and private capital, go on increasing the concessions, depriving the urban authorities of their legitimate resources. It seems necessary to evolve a national consensus on this as well as treating and providing for the urban infrastructure needs as a part of total development.

Another policy issue pertains to limits to urban growth. It is true that it is only when an urban centre grows to a certain size, it becomes capable of supporting a range of economic and social activities interacting and assisting each other. It is also true that growth beyond a point becomes counter-productive not only in the provisioning of services but also in assuring reasonable environmental quality standards. Civic infrastructure including sanitation, watersupply, waste disposal and transportation tends to breakdown and problems of congestions, noise and traffic get aggravated. Transportation, needs grow exponentially with the growth of the city; as the city expands in population and activity not only do the number of trips to work multiply but the length of trips and the time spent on them increases substantially. In the developing countries, most cities were not planned for the growth they are experiencing and the road network, designed for casual slow traffic, is just not capable of taking the increased loads. With growth, the problems of waste disposal also become complex and prohibitively expensive. Medium cities crossing the million mark start, so to say, bursting in their seams. It, therefore, appears that policy should be directed to contain growth of cities beyond a point. However cities, unlike clubs, cannot restrict entry and attempts to do so lead to clandestine growth and jacking up of costs of urban properties. The only possible answer is to set up other urban centres as countermagnete bases on regional studies. Needless, to say, considerable initial investment will have to be made for developing the basic infrastructure in these countermanete. This will be a better investment from the long-range point of view, than allowing unbridled growth in the existing centres demanding heavy investments on strengthening the civic services at a later date without hope of satisfactory solution.

More important than the funding for urban development is adequate provisioning for planning studies. In most States, the urban planning organizations, due to insufficient allocation of funds, are grossly inadequate with the result that they are hardly able to handle the day-to-day work make less undertake long-range planning studies. Madhya Pradesh, whose planning office is recognized as better organised than most other States, has a skeletal organization consisting of a joint director assisted by a couple of assistant directors at the divisional level with, but for a few exceptions, no formation at the district level. The department has formulated development master plans for the major cities and a few tourist centres but is neither able to detail out these master plans by developing proper zoning regulations, nor has it the time to attend to the planning of smaller towns. Most of the master plans have now become outdated and need to be reviewed. The pressure of municipal sanctions and other day-today matters is so considerable that the various processes of planning are performed perfunctority or not at all. While the planning organizations are weak and inadequate, they are expected to perform miracles and, if they fail to attend to a planning job in time, they are hauled up or ignored. Traditional organisations like public works and police, find town planning an intrusion, and often proceed with projects without town planning or municipal clearance. Thus, town planning has still to get adequate recognition in India.

The processes of urban planning are complex and each planning job requires commitment of pertain professional time and costs, failure to provide which makes planning perfunctory and, what is more, it lags behind development thus rendering it largely ineffective. As has been stressed earlier, planning is basic to optimal utilization of available resources and must be adequately provided for without being made to compete with other sectors. Even the existing practice of preparing development master plans for a point of time in the future need to be replaced by the reiterative systems processes, which place substantially greater demands on the planning office. For a better understanding of this, a description of the recent developments in the perception and goals of urban planning will be useful.

For most of this century, town planning, even in the developed countries, saw its purpose in the preparation of unitary plans for a point of time in the future. In other words they were maps showing an ideal future spatial form projected on a spcified time horizon. An important characteristic of both the philosophy of the planning movement and the precepts of its practitioners has been to strive for comprehensiveness for many goals if not all of them, within the same plan. The aesthetic quality of the urban environment is one of the oldest goals of planning. It can be observed in the classical Greek towns, the renaissance towns of Italy, France, Spain and Northern Europe and in the elaborate stage-setting in Baroque planning, so also in the ancient and medieval towns of the east. The modern city planning movement, originating in Europe and North America at the beginning of the present century was strongly influenced by visual aesthetic goals established in the earlier periods. Next came the concern for healthy and sanitary living conditions, especially as these apply to residential areas. The early planning movement was given a particular impulse by the horror of the ugly and the degradation of human life that the industrial revolution promoted in the labour colonies. This provided one of the foundation stones of statutory planning in the West through the legislation of various laws relating to public health and hygiene. The industrial revolution also brought about economic prosperity and the growth of cities in size and population for the performance of the various economic activities. The economic prosperity generated impulses of an idealistic future. An element in the origin of planning was the scientific utopianism and a subsequent recurrent theme to embrace the future as an ideal worth striving for as part of man's perfectability. In this way, the planner has tended to be on the side of development as an expression of progress and human achievement.

In more recent times, the economic and social health of cities has come to the force as one of the principal aims of planning. This is based on the logic that economic activities occupy land areas and are sensitive to locational relationships, both of which are susceptible to the actions of physical planners. Planning has also become deeply concerned with social pathology based on health, education, standard of living, crime and delinquency, family structure and other elements. Finally, environmental quality based on ecosystem studies is now receiving increasing attention. These include not only environmental studies of forests, surface and subsurface water, features of unique visual quality, steep slopes, etc., but also the natural processes they support.

During recent times, largely from American sources, another meaning to planning has been provided. this is the idea of process, a sequence of events from objectives to results, to a reappraisal of the plan. Influenced by the developments in the study of systems natural as well as human activated, there has been a shift from planning as a spatial form projected into a specified time in the future, to planning as a reiterative process projecting possible courses of action, selecting an operational course based on cost-benefit and social values, studying the impact on the system of proposed changes and reviewing the plan to control deflections from the course charted or revalidating the course itself.

The development of systems theory has undoubtedly helped planners to see the inadequacy of relying on rigid plans of the old type but the transition from one style of planning to the other has not been easy and has caused great professional difficulties. In the United Kingdom, for instance, the traditional master plan approach evolved over years by the British planners, has been gradually replaced by less rigid structural planning which analysis and highlights the pattern and direction of growth but leaves detailed specification to action plans and zoning regulations which are subjected to periodic review and revision. Though this process may seem to reduce planning load in the preparation of the development plan, in actual fact, the studies behind the structural plan and the need for meticulously detailing the zonal plans so also their periodic review and updating, require substantial strengthening and upgrading of the planning machinery.

The developing countries, inadequate as they are in planning, have still to admit the new methodologies. Operating under severe resource constraints and faced with complex ecological problems, planning based on systems approach has special relevance to the developing countries and it is imperative that they inculcate it in their planning mechanism with the least possible delay.

Urban and regional planning is truly policy planning; it is an on-going, problem oriented activity, with no fixed end products, but with objectives set by perceived social goals, changing over time. complex systems require procedures of equal complexity to control them. So far, urban planning problems were handled by town planners as a rigid projection of the shape of things at a stipulated future point of time. What is now required, is for the urban systems (so also regional and rural systems) to become the focus of a new form of public management. In this process the disciplinary and professional skills will have to be re-grouped and strengthened under a new analytical and management oriented framework. Socio-economic systems and natural eco-systems are intimately interwined requiring similar professional skills and methodologies and the only logical place where all these activities can be appropriately performed is under the umbrella of the environment planners. While on the one hand, the systems approach to planning will enable holistic thinking on economic, social and environmental issues on a professional basis, on the other hand, the very processes of study of systems will bring about greater involvement of, and interaction with the women, local authorities and other agencies instead of the programmes being rigid prescriptions from above. Planning and a programme implementation will, thus, be a participative process, something which is sadly lacking today.

The above reorganisation of the planning processes may appear to idealistic. An urban planning machinery which can barely produce basic development plan for a few cities and which has no capacity to attend to the planning of most towns, or review, update and detail the plans already prepared, can hardly be expected to blossom into a pulsating organisation undertaking and reviewing integrated systems studies. Even if the required funds are provided, lack of professional staff and an inadequate data base will hold up the process for a long time.

Systems approach to planning is a way to look at human and natural systems in their totality, evolve solutions and admit corrections, involving the women for whom planning is being done. While technical expertise is an important ingredient of the process, the process itself and the experience in administering is, will develop and strengthen it. Once its relevance and benefits are understood and appreciated, it will be only a matter of time during which it will seep into the fabric of public management. Any delay in initiating women's involvement, this process will only mean loss of valuable time.

At the same time the planners have also to ensure that adverse environmental impact of development projects is made minimal if not eliminated altogether. In this respect we lack a well drawn out 'Environment Impact Assessment' system which is operated as part and parcel of project impact and evaluation mechanism. Poorly planned development activities are hazardous to the women and health of the people. Unplanned urbanisation, for example, has changed the ecological conditions in favour of the spread of filariasis Kala-bazar has also come back in a unprecedented manner. It was with this in view that in the Sixth Five Year Plan it was laid down that adequate pre-planning need to be undertaken, through use of techniques like environmental impact analysis for which the inter-disciplinary expertise will need to be built up., Environmental considrations must form an integral part of all planning for development and be supplemented by mechanisms to ensure that environmental safeguard proposals are implemented and that there is systematic monitoring to assess their effectiveness.

At the same time administriative and legislative arrangements for environment protection need strengthening. Though in the last few years many new legislative measures have been taken most others "remain outdated and are poorly implemented". In this context the Department of Environment at the centre and in the States and women involvement have a crucial role to play.

Since poverty is clearly the primary cause of ecological disruption, any environmental policy which may, wittingly or unwittingly, slow down the economic growth rate, would be self-defeating. Allowing a longer lead time for controlling poverty would virtually amount to giving further latitude to the process of environmental degradation directly resulting from poverty and irreversibly hurting the life support systems. Clearly, the most sound environmental policy would be one which speeds up the development process thus containing the environmental dislocation. For the same reason, a policy of speedy development withour consideration for environmental conservation leaving it for rectification later, would be dangerous. The ecological imbalance due to denudation of forests and degradation of land has already been so severe that any development policy which does not atempt to corrrect it would have very serious long-term negative effects irreversibly damaging the productivity of land and affecting the very survival of life. While enrichment of environmental quality standards and containing environmental degradation due to indiscriminate use of technology may be the prime concern in the developed world, the protection of the life support system being dislocated by presence of large women and poor populations, is a matter of immediate urgency in the developing nations. The policy choice is compulsive and immediate-there can be only one sound economic policy in the developing world and that is, speedy development with environmental protection measures fully integrated therein.

CHAPTER-14
Women, Shelter and UNCHS

Women and shelter

Although there have been three United Nations International Development Decades, the role of women in the process of development did not capture the attention of international planners until 1975, when the General Assembly of the United Nations declared 1976 to 1985 to be the united Nations Decade for Women: Equality, Development and Peace. It was not until the end of the Decade, however, that shelter issues of concern to women began to appear on the United Nations agenda.

Shelter issues were brought to the attention of women's movements and of Member States of the United Nations in 1985, when the World Conference to Review and Appraise the Achievements of the United Nations Decade for Women: Equality, Development, Peace adopted the Nairobi Forward-looking Strategies for the Advancement of Women; These called on governments to:

"integrate women in the formulation of policies, programmes and projects for the provision of basic shelter and infrastructure. To this end, the enrolment of women in architectural, engineering, and related fields should be encouraged, and qualified women graduates in these fields should be assigned to professional, policy-making and decision-making positions. The shelter and infrastructural needs of women should be assessed and specifically incorporated in housing, community development, and slum and squatter projects.

"Women and women's groups should be participants in and equal beneficiaries of housing and infrastructure construction projects. They should be consulted in the choice of design and technology of construction and should be involved in the management and maintenance of the facilities. To this end, women should be provided with construction, maintenance, and management skills and should be included in related training and educational programmes."[1]

The Global Strategy for Shelter to the Year 2000

The main objective of the Global Strategy is to facilitate adequate shelter for all by the Year 2000. "Shelter for all" means affordable shelter for all groups in all types of settlements, meeting basic requirements of tenurial security, structural stability, and infrastructure support, with convenient access to employment and community services and facilities.

Two important principles sustain the Strategy. The first is that governments must adopt an "enabling" approach-facilitating the activities of all the present and potential participants in the shelter production and improvement process. The second principle is that, while the main focus of the Strategy is on low-income population groups, it is not limited to any one group but, rather, is based on a comprehensive view of all demand actors.

The operational focus of the Global Strategy is on national strategies to be developed by all governments. International support is recognized as crucial for the success of the Global Strategy and must be directed towards enhancing national capabilities to formulate and implement national action components. The Global Strategy is a commitment by the world community and a mandate for the entire United nations system.

The answer to the question of encouraging the participation of women in the Global Strategy is to be found in the very processes of social and economic development sweeping the countries of Africa, Asia, the Caribbean, Latin America and Oceania. These processes have changed the roles and responsibilities of women. Women, as income-earners, home-makers, and heads of household, and women's organizations fulfil a crucial role as contributors to the solution of human settlements problems. This has to be fully recognized and reflected in the equal participation of women in the elaboration of housing policies, programmes and projects, and more specifically in the formulation and implementation of the Global Strategy for Shelter.

UNCHS (Habitat) activities related to women

Since the world Conference, the united Nations Centre for Human Settlements (Habitat), which has always placed housing policies and programmes in the context of national development plans, has been actively engaged in the promotion of women both as beneficiaries and as agents of change in the area of human settlements. One of the Centre's first follow-up activities after the World conference was an international seminar on women and shelter, organized jointly by the centre for Social Development and Humanitarian Affairs/Division for the Advancement of Women and the United Nations Centre for Human Settlements (Habitat). That Seminar, held in December 1985 in Vienna, brought together representatives of governmental and non-governmental organizations for women from many countries of the world.

The purpose of the Seminar was to familiarize women's organizations with key issues of settlements management. It was felt that, through familiarization with mainstream development issues, women's organizations could formulate proposals related to them for inclusion in national agenda for action. At the end of the Seminar, the participants had an increased appreciation of the broad scope of settlements but they felt that, in order to achieve the greatest impact, it was not enough for women's organizations alone to be made aware of the issues; policy-makers in the settlements sector also had to be familiar with women's perspectives on housing and residential environments. It was stressed that only through joint collaborative efforts could realistic and practical national plans of action evolve.

The Commission of Human Settlements, at its ninth session in May 1986, recommended that:

> "regional or subregional seminars be organized ... in order to exchange experiences on pilot projects and to define and evaluate the role of women and the organizations that represent then..."[2]

As a result, work intensified to promote the role of women in the management of settlements. In addition to the resources of the United Nations centre for Human Settlements (Habitat), funding required for regional seminars was received from the Governments of Netherlands and of Norway during and shortly after the tenth (Commemorative) session of the Commission which took place in April 1987.

The following regional and subregional seminars were organized by the centre and the respective host countries in 1988 and 1989.

(a) Asia and the Pacific: 24-29 February 1988 in Indonesia;

(b) French-speaking African countries: 28 March to 1 April 1988 in Tunisia;

(c) Caribbean countries: 6 to 10 June 1988 in Saint Vincent and Grenadines;

(d) English-speaking African countries: 31 October to 4 November 1988 in Zambia;

(e) Latin American Countries: 27 to 31 March 1989 in Argentina.

The participants, who were drawn from governmental and non-governmental organizations as well as from donor agencies, were all involved in human settlements activities, particularly those concerning women.

The objectives of the seminars were:

(a) To provide policy and procedural guidance to high-level policy-makers, in such ministries as housing, public works and industry, on the incorporation of women's concerns in their programmes;

(b) To provide technical information to representatives of governmental and non-governmental organizations on means of ensuring the effective participation of women in human settlements development and management, with particular emphasis on community participation;

(c) To facilitate the identification of special problems concerning the participation of women in settlements development and management;

(d) To enhance communication and co-operation between institutions dealing with issues concerning women and those dealing with mainstream sectoral development issues;

(e) To create a readiness in institutions to support policies, programmes and projects to mobilize the participation of women in the development and upgrading of settlements;

(f) To discuss the effectiveness of different communication and information technologies in promoting gender-awareness in the formulation, implementation and evaluation of policies, programmes and projects;

(g) To develop national advocacy strategies for the continuous promotion of the involvement of women in the development and management of settlements.

The following key issues were deliberated upon at each regional seminar:

(a) The role of women in the formulation and implementation of housing policies;

(b) Women and land;

(c) The participation of women in housing finance;

(d) The participation of women in the construction sector;

(e) The participation of women in shelter projects;

(f) Women, water, and sanitation;

(g) Community participation as a means of enhancing the role of women in the development and management of settlements;

(h) Communications and information as instruments to enhance the participation of women in the development and management of settlements.

Highlights of the findings and recommendations of the seminars are presented in Part One of this paper.

The interregional Seminar to promote the full Participation of Women in all phases of the Global Strategy for Shelter to the Year 2000 was convened to give further impetus to the process begun by the earlier series of seminars. The participants (governmental and non-governmental), observers, resource personnel and donors were drawn from each of the five earlier seminars. The Seminar built on regional experiences to develop a plan of action for the continuation of the process which the United Nations Centre for Human Settlements (Habitat) had initiated. Part Two of this paper provides an overview of the Seminar.

The process initiated by the United Nations centre for human Settlements (Habitat) is directed towards the achievement of the following long-term development objectives:

(a) Involving women at all levels of the planning and implementation of human settlements policies and programmes;

(b) Improving the residential/work environment of women, especially urban and rural low-income women, their families and communities.

The strategy developed during the Seminar was formulated in the total United nations context. In his introductory remarks at the regional meeting in Indonesia, the Executive Director of the United Nations Centre for Human Settlements (Habitat) had pointed out that the declaration of 1976-1985 as the United Nations Decade for Women had been a result of the recognition that the scales of world equality had been out of balance. Not only had women experienced negative effects of the shift from traditional to "moderinzed" societies through the development process, they had been, by and large, excluded from the development planning process itself.

During the Decade, efforts had been introduced to improve the status of women, and, despite difficulties confronted by all countries, those efforts had resulted in substantial achievements, although they had been unevenly distributed between developing and industrialized countries and among sectors of the economy. Noteworthy among the achievements had been the increase in visibility of women's issues throughout the world; the growth of worldwide women's networks; the expansion of research, writing, and scholarship on the status of women and world development; progress in legislation; the rapid expansion of the female labour force; the narrowing of educational gaps between men and women at the lowest levels of the education system; and a general acknowledgement of the need to include women in development policies and programmes not only for reasons of social equity, but in order to realize overall national development objectives.

The Fourth United Nations International Development Decade is about to be launched after a decade that has witnessed difficult and painful adjustments to the global economic crisis. As many studies have shown, the debt crisis has affected women and their dependent children especially.[2] The prospects for the 1990s, according to international analyses, indicate that the trends of the 1980s are likely to continue, given current policies. Macro-economic trends, particularly the continuing world economic crisis, have negatively affected the shelter conditions of women. Fewer employment and income-generation opportunities have resulted in more homeless women: reduced social expenditures on child care and education have pushed women into marginal, temporary and low-paid jobs. In addition, continuing social prejudices against women keep their needs secondary to those of men, and the process of including women in decision-making is agonizingly slow. The increased fragmentation of the family, because of migration, divorce, separation etc., has resulted in a greater number of households being headed by women, but the specific shelter needs of such households have been largely unrecognized.

For the majority of women in developing countries, the challenge is still one of survival and the satisfaction of the basic needs of their families. They still have to struggle for a bare minimum income, for food, for shelter and for employment. They still have to acquire literacy, an acceptable level of education and training, and health standards which will allow them to work productively and to enjoy the fruits of their work. However, there are signs that women and shelter issues have found a permanent place on the United Nations agenda-if not in the reality of daily life. The first such sign is the process initiated by the United Nations Centre for Human Settlements (Habitat) to ensure the full participation of women in the Global Strategy for Shelter to the Year 2000.

Human settlements are where organized human activity takes place. They function as a system at the global, regional, sub-regional, national and sub-national levels-down to the lowest unit of human habitation. Human settlements are not simply housing or the physical structure of a city, town or village but an integrated system of all human activities-residence, work education, health, culture, leisure-as well as the physical structures that support them.

Human Settlements form an important component of a country's fixed capital assets. Public investment in human settlements development-unlike investment in so-called "productive" sectors which, more often than not, suffer rapid obsolescence-are rarely wasted. Investment in human settlements invariably contributes to improvement of a society's ability to respond to basic development needs, such as shelter, education, health, mobility, and (generally) productive output, as well as to conservation of the natural environment.

It might be said, therefore, that while the United Nations centre for Human Settlements (Habitat) has a special interest in the provision of shelter (decent and affordable housing) for all, this is placed within a broad concept of human settlements which links the issue, as it should be, with almost every aspect of economic and social development. The strategy developed during the Seminar for the full participation of women, therefore, was squarely in this broad context-viewing women, the family and shelter as parts of integrated community development and the community into to as a contributor to national development plans and the Global Strategy for Shelter to the Year 2000.

It is becoming apparent that national development targets can only be achieved if women are approached as the main agents of change. The total sum of their available knowledge and talent is indispensable to progress and the development of humanity. Therefore, in the interest of national development as a whole, the contributions of women to development, which have remained unacknowledged for so long, must be seen by national planners as a valuable resource to supplement and balance those of the long-dominant male.

As development planners and activists look to the participation of local communities in the development process, they are finding that it is the women in communities who are the main providers of food, water and energy for their families, who build houses and who care for children and the sick. In addition to child-bearing and child-caring, women are often engaged in small-scale businesses in the informal sector. Reaching women at the community level is reaching the prime "agents for change": when only men are targeted for action and provided with resources, women, families and communities do not automatically benefit.

Human settlements activity requires a specific focus on women, because, in the majority of countries the shelter needs of women are still subsumed under those of the family, even though there is ample evidence that the specific needs of women and the contributions they can make are distinct from those of men. If it is accepted that human settlements are more than physical structures accommodating people- i.e., that they are "places to live and produce in, and a space within which the socialization process and social interaction occur, safeguarding the social fabric and social values of all its dwellers", as they were described by the Minister of Women's Affairs of Indonesia, H.E. Mrs. A. Sulaskin Murpratomo, at the seminar in Indonesia, it is essential to the social fabric of a country that the concerns and needs of women be taken into account in all policies, plans, programmes and projects related to human settlements. Women are, after all, the primary users and providers of the infrastructural facilities in a settlement, i.e., water supply and sanitary and health services, carrying out income-generating as well as household and child-caring tasks in extremely difficult conditions within the home and, also, contributing to the informal construction of shelter in poor rural and urban areas.

The earlier series of seminars had addressed the concerns and needs of women in general, but the focus of the meetings and the priority of the United Nations centre for Human Settlements (Habitat) were given to urban and rural poor and low-income women. Further delineations will not doubt result from future national and sub-national studies, as the process of involving women in the Global Strategy for Shelter progresses. For example, during the International Year of Shelter for the Homeless, two meetings on women and shelter (planned in consultation with the United Nations centre for Human Settlements (Habitat)), identified additional categories of low-income women. A seminar held in Harare, from 30 november to 5 December 1987, delineated the categories: urban poor women, women on peasant farms, and women on plantation and other worksites. The United States national congress Neighbourhood women conference on "Housing options for women." held at of Camden, New Jersey, in October 1987, focused on another growing category: the increasing number of homeless women in industrialized urban centres.

OVER VIEW OF REGIONAL SEMINARS

This Part of the report draws upon the work of the five seminars in the earlier series organized by the United Nations Centre for Human Settlements (Habitat) and on selected papers on the subject: women and shelter. It highlights only the main findings of the seminars; detailed regional and country reports are in the centre's archives for further reference. These highlights were also included in a background paper that provided a framework for the Interregional Seminar to Promote the Full Participation of Women in the Global Strategy for Shelter to the Year 2000. They are discussed below under housing policy, land, finance and construction, as they relate to women, and community participation and communications and information as means of enhancing the involvement of women in the development and management of settlements.

Women are central to the activities performed for the daily Subsistence of families and communities, yet are unrecognized and, hence, are marginal in the sweep of development planning and programmes. However, it has to be emphasized that each community and country should be analyzed in the context of its own history and culture, in order to design appropriate responses to women's issues in human settlements. Thus, when this overview states that women, generally, are experiencing certain problems, it should be kept in mind that there are many distinctions not developed within the scope of this document. These differences need to be studied before making specific plans for action at national and community levels.

Women and housing policy

1. Finding

In the formulation of shelter-development policies, the United Nations Centre for Human Settlements (Habitat) has identified two aspects of women's participation. The first is the direct participation of women themselves in the formulation of the policies; the second is the inclusion of considerations specific to women in the formulation of policy. Both are essential but, with few exceptions, both were found to be poorly developed in all regions.

One reason for the low levels of participation by women is the assumption that women are only potential recipients of the benefits generated in the human settlements sector, not contributors. This implies a purely welfare-oriented focus on women, even in those national economies that can afford welfare programmes. Another consideration is that shelter is often viewed merely as a physical structure accommodating a group of people-the family. The provision of shelter to the family is, thus, misinterpreted as being the same as the satisfaction of the shelter needs of women.

Changing social conditions, which tend to disrupt the traditional pattern of family and kinship, are increasing the number of households headed by women in low-income urban settlements. Rural-to-urban migration is also increasing the number of woman-headed rural households which must survive precariously on remittances from family members in urban areas, supplemented by income derived from subsistence-level agricultural production and/or paid agricultural work. The double burden of managing the household and generating income places women at a disadvantage in dealing with the complications of obtaining shelter through conventional housing programmes.

The gender-specific discrimination to which women heads-of-household are subjected costs society a great deal without benefiting any specific segment. Households headed by women are often excluded from programmes and projects simply because existing laws or statutes recognize only males as heads-of-household. In other cases, eligibility criteria for housing applications require a partner. Public announcements, application procedures, downpayment requirements and repayment procedures all discriminate against women-especially against women heads-of-household.

A particularly intractable difficulty identified at the seminars was the rapid rise in the number of people in need of housing at a time of a severe limitation on overall governmental resources, a situation exacerbated by adjustment policies being followed in many countries. It was pointed out that, in Latin America, economic stagnation and absolute poverty are spreading into the mushrooming spontaneous settlements (slums, shanty towns, ranchos and favelas) that girdle the urban centres of the region, casting doubt on the conventional belief that urban development and economic growth are positively linked. Rural poverty is being exported to the city, especially in the absence of positive urban-development programmes to raise the economic and social status of the poor, particularly women. This situation increases the need for national priorities and policies that will guide human settlements growth equitably.

The seminars addressed the question of why governments should single out women, in the face of the vast number of men and children who are also not benefiting from current housing programmes. The following points were made in this connection:

(a) Within the target universe of the disadvantaged population of a country (in many cases, as high as 80 per cent), the needs of the great majority of women are poorly addressed, even when policies generally correspond to the needs of the poor as a whole;

(b) Many women who are members of "conventional" households are at a disadvantage, because shelter programmes on the whole are not benefiting the poor, and, as a result women suffer disproportionately;

(c) Women who are not members of "conventional" households are at a disadvantage, because programmes actively discriminate in favour of "conventional" households;

The removal of the first type of disadvantage was considered to be relatively easy, because it does not necessarily result in a confrontation over the allocation of limited financial resources. Nevertheless, it does create a confrontation over attitudes and power-essential elements for lasting change-which it might be very difficult to avoid.

The consensus also recognized that shelter policies are a compromise between conflicting aspirations of different groups in a settlement and their respective stakes in the decision-making process. There appear to be two prevailing ways of viewing and treating urban growth. One approach views the city purely in terms of its market value and land purely as a commodity, the price of which must be maximized in order to sustain municipal finances through property taxes. This approach dismisses the urban poor, their informal economy and their residences as low-value occupiers of urban space. The second approach looks at the city in terms of its use-value as a place in which to live and produce, and tries to safeguard the traditional social fabric and the residential and economic activities of the informal sector. This people-oriented approach, however, is steadily losing ground to conventional economic analysis.

Planning instruments, such as building codes, redevelopment schemes, zoning ordinances and land-use regulations, tend to further the objectives of large-scale influential businesses rather than those of poor and disadvantaged households. Mixed-use restrictions (which contribute to the destruction of traditional crafts and small-scale workshops to the advantage of corporate manufacturers), banning of street vendors (who are often perceived as a threat to organized trade) and the introduction of various licensing and regulatory devices (which favour formal over informal businesses) all claim priority in urban space for the corporate economy. It is obvious that the losers from such trends are the informal sector and people who obtain their work and their housing from it, particularly women.

The demand for urban space created by market forces, narrowly defined, has an important impact on the traditional residential-cum-working neighbourhoods inhabited by the poor. It particularly affects women who earn a large portion of their income in the informal sector as well as in home-based crafts and manufacturing activities. Removed from their traditional locations, their employment opportunities disrupted and their transport costs increased, the urban poor in developing countries are often impoverished by the very policies which were ostensibly intended to benefit them.

The seminars acknowledged that progress has been made in all regions towards the achievement of equality for men and women in access to housing, land and credit, but reiterated that women are under-represented at decision-making levels and,therefore, make but a minimal contribution to the formulation of housing policies. In Latin America, the Costa Rican Government was cited as an exception, because its official programme gives priority to the housing problem and expresses the need for changing the role of women in society through improved conditions for the participation of women in the production process, as well as in social, political, and cultural life.

During the seminar for French-speaking countries in Africa it was reported that in Tunisia women have had the benefit of advanced legislation since independence. Wives are not under the guardianship of their husbands with regard to the management of their possessions, the acquisition of land or access to credit. Participants at the seminar stressed the need for ratification of the Convention on the Elimination of All Forms of Discrimination against Women, adopted by the United Nations in 1979, and for a popularization of women's legal rights-both of which require above all, a change of attitudes. A Moroccan woman stated that, in her country, laws currently in force were in women's favour and are not discriminatory, but that there was a difference between what the law said and the way things were actually done. Men were not ready to accept women in business, management or labour. Women's organizations still had a lot to do to sensitize women to the need to join together to assert their rights and their opinions. She cited a positive example which was beginning to bear fruit in Morocco-that of co-operatives. Women were creating women's co-operatives which gave their members negotiating power with financial institutions and local-government authorities. A woman from Niger also posed the problem this way: "Theoretically women are wanted; their place is reserved and recognized. But because of their inferior level of education they cannot participate." This clearly underscores the interrelatedness of all facets of development and the need to analyze and act on women and shelter issues withinthe scope of broad development policies and programmes.

It was also noted that, in recent years, efforts have been made by some governments in Asia and the Pacific to repeal laws and regulations which discriminate against women and to encourage the participation of women in the political process. None-theless, progress is slow, and obstacles persist.

In all regions, it was stressed that shortfalls in the formulation of human settlements policies and the gap between legal rights and enforcement had the greatest effect on the poorest urban social classes. In this situation, men as well as women are excluded from participatory processes. In the rural setting, too, there are distinct land and settlement configurations according to local customs and systems that must be factored into human settlements policies. Without exception, each region stressed the adverse impact of policies on women in all rural and urban economic and soicial categories.

2. Action needed to be taken

All the seminars confirmed the universally accepted dictum for bringing about policy change in favour of low-income women, their families and communities-there must be a political will to do so. In order to strengthen political will in this direction, they suggested the following:

(a) Help to establish housing and human settlement as a fundamental right, rather than a market decision;

(b) Develop plans at the national and local level to communicate this concept to policy-makers and to inform women, their families and communities of their rights and responsibilities as citizens-through public education;

(c) Campaign for the allotment of funds for research that can be applied to improve data on women and their shelter needs;

(d) Formulate appropriate policy recommendations on such issues as space distribution and design, acccss to basic public services and amcnitics, labour-saving technologies, construction-skill development, transport needs, employment options and the special needs of women heads-of-households;

(e) Analyse current policies and legislation in relation to the needs of low-income women, their families and communities in terms of sustainable human settlements, and determine changes that are needed;

(f) Work with women's bureaux to encourage other government agencies-particularly planning ministries and legislative bodies-to disaggregatc data by gender (and, where possible, by class and ethnicity, as well) and to apply gender analysis to all sectors at all levels of development planning and programming;

(g) Elicit the support of non-government organization (NGOs) - and community based organisation (CBOs)-for both men and women - to create an impact on national housing policy formulation, implementation and monitoring, in order to ensure inclusion of women's concerns in the process;

(h) Create regional, national and local committees, with equal participation of knowledge men and women from government, NGOs and CBOs, to plan, implement and evaluate the Global Strategy for Shelter.

Women and land

1. Findings

Each of the earlier seminars identified the access of women to land as a critical link that receives almost no attention in the human settlements chain. Monopolization of urban land by commercial interests, escalations in land prices and reluctance of governments to address land issues are obstacles to the acquisition and retention of land by the rural and urban poor in general. Poor women meet many added obstacles, such as low income, limited or no access to credit, and cultural biases reflected in restrictive policies on women's ownership of property.

The United Nations Centre for Human Settlements (Habitat) has observed that neither agricultural programmes with a land-reform component nor urban sites-and-services projects have addressed the issue of the right of women to own land. The rights of women, in general, and of women heads-of-households or of wives in polygamous marriages, in particular, have been neglected. With land providing one of the few recognized forms of collateral, the access of women to shelter and to investment finance in other sectors is constrained.

The Convention on the Elimination of All Forms of Discrimination against Women, which came into effect in 1981, deals with the property rights of women in three separate articles:

(a) With reference to rural women (article 14), the Convention calls for equal treatment in land and agrarian reform, as well as in land-resettlement schemes;

(b) With reference to the status of women before the law, article 15 calls for equal rights for women to coclude contracts and to administer property;

(c) With reference to marriage and family relations, article 16 calls for the same rights for both spouses in respect of the ownership, acquisition, management, administration, enjoyment and disposal of property.

Although the Convention does not make a general call for all categories of women - rural or urban, daughter, wife or mother - to have equal access to all forms of property, nevertheless, even those property rights agreed upon within the framework of the Convention are not recognized in a large number of countries which have signed and ratified the Convention.

The problem of the access of women to urban land presents additional complications, requiring understanding of the processes of urban land development and allocation. Access to legitimate and secure shelter in the vicinity of income-earning opportunities, with an acceptable level of essential services such as roads water supply and drainage, remains an impossible dream for millions in developing countries. Governmental strategies to increase the supply of land to the poor through public-sector interventions, such as squatter-settlement upgarding and sites-and-services schemes, have been insufficient to meet the need, and increasing numbers of low-income people are finding accommodation through informal channels. Non-commercial arrangements include unauthorized invasions of public or private land, encroachments on marginal lands or occupation of abandoned proper ties: unfortunately, the general tendency is for informal arrangements to be increasingly commercialized. Very often, residents are subjected to harassment and exploitation and are, therefore, reluctant to invest their savings. Commercial arrangements include the illegal sale of public land, substandard land subdivision land rental and land fragmentation. Such arrangements normally require a downpayment to the landholder and recurrent charges for services.

Public-sector intervention usually leaves out the lowest strata among low-income groups, since ability to repay is an eligibility criterion for public-sector schemes. These arrangements have a particularly adverse affect on women, because applying this criterion means that households headed by women are seldom deemed eligible for plots in sites-and services schemes (although actual repayment performance has not been shown to be related with certainty to apparent repayment ability). In the private sector, poverty, lack of information and social pressures place women in a particularly disadvantaged position with respect to both commercial and non-commercial land arrangements. The decreased availability of vacant land open to squatter invasion or encroachment, strict enforcement of legal measures by the authorities, the decreased supply of cheap rental accommodation in inner-city slums and rises in the number of evictions are factors that have changed the nature of the prevailing informal processes of land acquisition - again with particularly negative effects on women.

The participants in the earlier seminars stressed that much needs to be done by governments to increase the availability of land for shelter through legal and administrative means, so that the poor, the majority of whom are women, may gain access to land and shelter. Access to land for all has to be a component of human settlements development strategies, paying special attention to the needs and contributions of women and other marginalized groups in shelter and infrastructural development.

In Malaysia, the Federal Land Development Authority (FELDA) allocated land based on nuclear-family concept, the head of household was expected to be male, and the role of a woman was to assist in development. On the death of her husband, a woman could not claim title to the land; instead, the land was passed to the eldest son. If he was below the legal age, the widow might only hold the title deed until the son attained the age at which he could claim title.

In Papua New Guinea, land was described as falling into two categories - customary and alienated, i.e., where Western forms of land tenure obtain. Customary land is said to account for approximately 97 per cent of the land area and is viewed as being much more than a commodity. It plays a complex role in the economic, social, and cultural life of the people. Ownership rests with clans and tribal groups, and title is based on historic occupation. However, little or no attention is given to women's specific needs or concerns with respect to land and housing policies. The decision-making process is, by tradition, a male responsibility, and women have little or no control over land distribution, use, or demarcation.

In India, land is a very scarce resource, with 70 to 80 per cent of it owned by 20 to 30 per cent of the population. Land-reform legislation was enacted for redistribution of land, by placing a ceiling on holdings and providing for the takeover of "surplus lands" to be redistributed to the landless.

However, implementation of the land-reform law is not considered a success. Urban ceilings on land holdings have been a distinct failure. In any event, it was pointed out that if the law were to be successfully implemented, beneficiaries would be relatively few (less than 1 million) compared with the many millions in need. Guidelines with respect to land rights for women have been issued by the Government, instructing that whenever surplus lands or other governmental lands, house sites etc. are distributed, the title is to be held jointly by husband and wife. The rights of women heads-of-household are not mentioned. In the parts of India where a matriarchal system prevails, however, the access of women to land is reported to be good.

The Women's Charter of Singapore, passed in 1961, stipulated that married women had the possibility and capacity to acquire, hold and dispose of property in their own names. Creditors of the husband could have no claim against property given by the husband to the wife. Once again, there was no mention of the rights of unmarried women or women head-of-household in the Charter.

The participants in the seminars in Africa said that, in general, Africa has two systems of land tenure existing side-by-side. On the one hand, under the inheritance and customary systems dominant in rural areas, where the chief of a tribe is solely responsible for land allocation to different members of the community, women are not permitted to own land or participate in decision-making about land use and shelter policies, although they can have access to land through their fathers, husbands, brother or sons. On the other hand, there is the legal land-tenure system, introduced by colonial administrations, where land ownership changes according to an individual's capacity to pay; land is seen as a commodity which can be bought and sold. Land ownership has affected the production of housing for all income groups, in particular for low-income people. Land ownership also has implications for the extraction and production of building materials. Under the legal land system, anyone can own land, regardless of sex; however, as women are the poorest of the poor, access to land is, for them, an impossible dream. Evidence shows that, in most African countries, customary land tenure is quickly being transformed into legal land tenure, where titles of ownership are guaranted by governmental legislation. Modern systems discriminate against women more than traditional, even patrilinear, when women had right of use (as men did). Now "ownership" is vested in men only, even in previously matrilinear areas.

The population Division of the United Nations Secretariat has determined that the urban population of many large sub-Saharan cities - Nairobi, Dar-es-Salaam, Nouakchott, Lusaka, Lagos, and Kinshasa among them - grew more than sevenfold between 1950 and 1980. The demand for land for commercial and office, purposes and to build houses for profit is on the increase. This commercial pressure on urban land has given rise to land speculation. In recent decades, the urban poor, needing shelter close to their workplace and unable to participate in the land market, occupied vacant land on the outskirts of cities and made their own shelter arrangements. There is evidence that the amount of such vacant land for these informal arrangements is decreasing. Poor urban women in these areas, who cannot afford to buy food and would like to have a garden and livestock to feed their families, are often prevented by law from carrying on such activities in urban areas. There is a need for allotments in and around urban areas to allow low-income people, particularly women, to grow subsistence foods.

Governmental interventions in land issues to favour the poor were considered to be negligible, generally confining their role to planning controls and zoning. Even in recognized squatter settlements, governments have been reluctant to grant occupancy titles to residents. This is particularly stressful for women who need to own land for security purposes, e.g., old age and credit-worthiness.

In Zimbabwe, the Legal Age of Majority Act of 1982 secured for women the right to own land and property, but, in practice, women who wish to buy land have to have the husband as a referee, to secure the transaction. Women who live in rural or mining areas are at a particular disadvantage.

Land ownership is in the hands of large farm and mine employers (mines and farms occupy 40 per cent of the land and account for over 15 per cent of the population). Farmers and mine employers are responsible for providing housing and services for their employees, but occupancy rights for women are only possible through husbands who are employees. Should the husband cease to be an employees, become ill or die, the woman loses her right of occupancy.

In the United Republic of Tanzania, under modern law, every one over 18 years of age can acquire land. However, in practice, women are still restricted in land ownership because of complicated procedures, inheritance customs and the bureaucracy. In the Ujamaa village system, ownership of land is vested in the heads of households who, by governmental criteria, are men. Upon the husband's death or separation, a woman cannot claim a legal right to property which is in the husband's name.

In Zambia, women did not have customary rights to own land or buildings, but this has changed with legislation, since independence. Married women, however, must have their husbands consent to any transactions.

Current legislation in Swaziland was reported to forbid women's possessing land or property or engaging in contractual agreements. The position of women is aggravated by the existence of polygamy. Yet, the low position of women seems to contradict the realities of Swazi society. Historically, the country has a large number of women heads-of-household, as a result of male migration to South Africa (approximately 25,000 a year) and to urban areas. Women have been responsible for producing and maintaining their own shelter, but they have no access to land or property.

In Egypt, women have the right to own land and property, if they can afford it. A woman automatically shares half the husband's property on marriage.

The Caribbean seminar highlighted the Sou Sou land concept - the makings of a gender-aware policy on human settlements in Trinidad and Tobago. This concept allows for the development of an explicitly gender-aware approach to human settlements, so that the specific needs and aspirations of women for land and shelter can be understood and addressed. The Sou Sou land concept is a departure from the highly centralized, State-funded and bureaucratized system of settlement planning. If offers an opportunity for opening up dialogue on the variability of the social and economic situation of women who seek land and shelter as a fundamental human right. The non-zoning approach to land use and the organization of shelter, with respect to the provision and use of space, implicitly recognizes the triple role of women, in the home, at work and in the community - particularly in the informal sector of the economy. All three can be brought together under one roof, so to speak, thereby alleviating hardship for those women who must, of necessity, reconcile their triple involvements related to production, reproduction, and the management of both the domestic household and community action groups.

The Sou Sou land approach does not appear to assume that the household of the beneficiary needs to be male-headed. Financial viability is definitely not tied to the usual demand that there must be a strong collateral base linked to criteria, such as set income levels, proof of employment stability, and a credit record. While putting the burden of responsibility for financing settlement on the beneficiaries, this approach sustains the idea of State support by categorizing beneficiaries (e.g., squatters and non-squatters), by initiating the collection of "hands," or partial payments, from would-be beneficiaries and by making provision for a Government-arranged savings plan to be used for land purchase.

A gender-aware settlement policy requires sensitivity and responsiveness to the social and functional literacy levels of the large number of working women who need shelter. The communication network to make this happen must be "user-friendly." For example, in Trinidad and Tobago, community meetings are conducted to alert the citizenry to the need to participate in the determination and resolution of settlement problems.

Such meetings, which are held regularly in community centres or other suitable areas in the town or village, allow for face-to-face contact and understanding between settlement administrators and the people. Through such networking, the sensitivity of these "grass-roots" planners, many of whom have subsequently assumed public office in Trinidad and Tobago, can be easily attuned to the gender-aware dimension of development planning for settlements. The incumbent Minister of Settlements, for example, is a former Sou Sou land administrator, involved from the inception of the project. Her commitment to the institutionalization of the Sou Sou land concept, as an integral part of multisectoral State planning is highly regarded. So too, is her dedication to the task of uplifting the status of women in society. This augurs well for the movement to development a distinctly gender-aware policy on shelter needs.

Looking at the land issue from the perspective of development and the environment, the recent environmental report, *Our Common Future,* [3] points out that, in many countries where land is very unequally distributed, land reform is a basic requirement. Without it, institutional and policy changes, meant to protect the resource base, can actually promote inequalities by shutting the poor off from resources and by favouring those with large farms, who are best able to obtain the limited credit and services available. By leaving hundreds of millions without options, such changes can have the opposite of their intended effect, ensuring the continued violation of ecological imperatives.

2. Action needed to be taken

The primary focus of the recommendations from all the seminars, concerning women and land ownership, centred on legal aspects. There was a consensus that gender-awareness needed to be institutionalized in the formulation and execution of public policy. For that reason, they called for efforts to develop strategies for sensitizing policy-makers, technocrats, administrators, NGOs and other agencies to:

(a) Take account of the capability and needs of women in human settlements development and land tenure rights;

(b) Act on the principles stated in the Convention on the Elimination of Discrimination against Women, by establishing and implementing an equal-opportunity policy on land, by removing all customary and legal constraints which prevent access by women (including women heads-of-household) to land, by enforcing positive discrimination in favour of women, by setting up a publicity campaign aimed at informing women of their rights and, above all, by using planning power to make land available to the poorest group of the population;

(c) Ensure that planning standards and zoning regulations take into account the need for spatial arrangements allowing women to function as producers, reproducers and community members.

It was agreed that governments should use regulatory powers to intervene in the urban land market in order to release land for low-income housing which would otherwise remain vacant or be designated for other uses. Governments should also consider including land-sharing - the partitioning of a plot of land owned by one set of people and occupied by another - as a housing service. Such a mechanism has been applied successfully in Bangkok. Rural homesteads for women heads of families and single women could take the form of condominiums. Finally, governmental and non-governmental agencies should activate "grass-roots" efforts such as the Sou Sou land strategy described above.

Women and construction

1. Findings

In all regions, a large portion of the contribution of the labour of women to the construction sector is channelled through the family or the community and concentrated in the informal sector, particularly in rural and poor urban areas. Much of that labour is, therefore, unrecognized and unremunerated. In addition, the labour contributed by women is considered not to involve skills worthy of upgrading for improved human settlements development.

There is a great deal of cultural variation in the involvement of women in shelter and infrastructural development. Where cultural constraints control the social activities of women outside the home, their work contribution is often confined to the improvement of the family shelter unit. Where cultural norms do not prohibit the participation of women in "outside" activities, their contribution provides an important element in shelter and infrastructural development.

The participation of women in the formal construction sector is amazingly low - more so in developing than in industrialized countries. Reliance on high technology and imported materials in urban formal construction seems to have pushed women out of a sector in which they have traditionally played an active role. While women have achieved some penetration into the professional ranks of the sector, i.e., as engineers and architects, women constitute a minority among all ranks and levels of employment in the formal sector. Indeed, the female participation ratio in construction is far below the average for all industries.

According to International Labour Office statistics, female participation in construction in 1984 ranged between 0.18 and 18.84 per cent and averaged less than 5 per cent for countries for which data were available. The ratio tends to be highest in industrialized countries, because of the high ratio of clerical and related workers included in the count. In developing countries, however, women tend to be hired as production workers, Again, regional variations are significant. The participation of women in construction is particularly low in African countries, whereas, in several Asian countries, such as the Republic of Korea, Singapore, Sri Lanka and Thailand, the female ratio is relatively high.

Lack of training is one of the most limiting constraints to the participation of women in construction. Proper training of women could mobilize unemployed or underemployed labour, promote a balanced distribution of jobs in the construction industry, and help women to acquire shelter through self-help construction. However, existing conventional training institutions do not have the capacity to train the required numbers of skilled and professional workers and their training programmes are not comprehensive enough for the range of activities in the construction industry.

It was pointed out that training should not become an end in itself. The link between training and employment has to be made clear. Training, without job placement, credit, or technical assistance for resulting small businesses, is ineffective.

A training programme for Caribbean women in non-traditional skills was launched to provide an orientation for women in plumbing, refrigeration and electrical installation, that would allow them to assess whether they would wish to pursue long-term training in those areas. Eighteen young women between the ages of 18 and 25 participated - fourteen from Grenada and four from Dominica and Saint Vincent and the Grenadines. After the assessment, a special two-year accelerated programme was planned for the Grenada participants, most of whom did not have the initial academic qualifications to enter the regular programme at the Grenada Technical and Vocational Institute (GTVI). They did, however, have the potential to complete the entire technical training, and graduates will receive the normal GTVI diploma. Programmes for women in non-traditional fields are being strated in other Caribbean countries and are benefiting from direct contact with the Grenada programme. In Dominica, participants are being helped to undertake apprenticeship programmes that will qualify them to enter the technical college, if they wish.

An alternative to the technical colleges is exemplified by the Jamaican experience. The Women's Construction Collective initiated a programme for women, consisting of three month's basic training in carpentry and masonry. The women go directly on to work sites as paid apprentices and, as their skills develop, work their way up to fully-paid workers. At the beginning of the programme, 10 women were trained - with commitments from contractors to place them on-site on a trial "job audition" basis. Every woman who had auditioned had been hired, and the group then expanded (with national and international support) to 34 women from different communities. At the end of the course, more than 90 per cent of the women trained had been placed in employment that used their skills in plumbing, masonry, carpentry, electrical-installation, painting, and steel work.

Little by little, examples of women's construction training programmes are beginning to appear in all regions. As in Jamaica, training can lead to jobs and an income, and the construction industry acquires skilled labourers. In addition, employers are reporting the positive influence of women on building sites. In Jamaica, in addition to productivity increases, violence and pilfering decreased. It should be noted, however, that, if women are to be accepted in the use of these new skills, it is necessary to take measures to change the negative attitude of building-site supervisors.

Another important facet of the construction sector is the choice and use of building materials. The critical role of the informal sector, which accommodates a large proportion of women's work, and the importance of promoting small-scale indigenous building-materials production are largely unrecognized. As a result, the effective participation of women in the shelter sector, as beneficiaries and contributors, is hindered. The Importance of the informal sector in the construction of shelter is clear. In many urban areas of developing countries, up to 70 per cent of the population lives in buildings constructed by the informal sector, and rural housing is almost exclusively built by self-help and/or through the informal sector, which also produces a large proportion of the building materials used by the poor.

The choice of building materials is important for women, both as potential employees of the construction sector and as users of shelter and infrastructure. The use of imported building materials, produced with capital-intensive high technology, not only reduces employment in the national construction industry, but also diverts limited resources from employment-generating activities to other sectors. Traditionally, building materials have been readily available to both rural and urban people, because they have been obtained from the local surroundings. They took many forms - earth in the form of bricks, mud or adobe, fired by heat, sun-dried or solidified by stabilizing agents (lime, dung, ash, shell etc.); wood as timber - poles, beams, shingles, rods and branches; vegetable products, such as bamboo, reeds, palm leaves and grasses; skins and cloths; and stones, sands, gravel, lime, gypsum and cementitious mortars. New industrial products have recently taken over the market, supported by rules and regulations, standards and codes, and financing and credit facilities. Some of the new materials have become accessible for popular consumption - concrete wall blocks, flooring slabs and roof panels; asbestos-cement and steel sheets for roofing; steel rods and window frames; plywood panelling; Yet, these materials do not necessarily provide durable or comfortable shelter, are often more expensive than traditional materials and can have serious negative effevts on health.

The majority of developing countries have followed a policy of import substitution, establishing local industries which produce materials identical to those previously imported, e.g., machinery and equipment. What is needed, instead participants pointed out, is the adaptation of indigenous low-cost building materials that require minimal amounts of capital and foreign exchange and make use of locally available raw materials and skills in small-scale operations. The financial benefits of such a policy could be great. Construction prices could be lowered to a range affordable by low-income populations with the use of such inexpensive local materials; since, with proper design and treatment, they can last a long time. This would create significant savings in building and maintenance costs as well. Such a strategy would especially benefit women.

For women, the choice of appropriate building materials is very closely linked to their specific roles and associated needs as entrepreneurs, construction labourers, traders, or users of shelter and infrastructure. In construction work, small, light components could easily be handled by women who, with training, could play an important role in the installation of electrical, plumbing and sanitary systems and in the installation and maintenance of ceramic tiles and sanitaryware. As consumers of building materials, women have very specific needs. In Queretaro, Mexico, for instance, 27 per cent of families live in houses which are mixtures of brick and board, with earth floors. Women had been demanding floor materials which were easy to clean and maintain. The informal sector could easily produce soil-cement or lime-pozzolana blocks and clay tiles to meet such needs.

There is an enormous range of small-scale production units in developing countries, producing a variety of building materials. In the Philippines, for instance, cottage industries produce bamboo, bricks and roofing materials on a substantial scale. In Indonesia small-scale building-materials industries in both rural and urban areas (mostly unorganized, labour-intensive cottage industries run in traditional ways) produce clay bricks, tiles, cement products, lime, bamboo, timber elements, stone, gravel, sand and pozzolana-lime blocks. In Sri Lanka, small-scale and traditional production units produce bricks, country tiles, sand, and lime, supplying more than 35 per cent, by value, of the total building materials used in the country. In China, 80 per cent of the building materials, including bricks, tiles, fly ash, sand and stone, and 64 per cent of the cement is produced on a small scale by building brigades and communal enterprises.

In all these small-scale production units, women and, even, children play an important role in the production line, and there is scope for women to have an entrepreneurial role as well. Production in small units, located close to markets, creates local employment and lowers transport costs. It is not necessary to acquire large amounts of land through the formal market for installations. Finance, too, can often be of land through the formal market for installations. Finance, too, can often be informally acquired. Training of labour is done on the job through apprenticeship, with women and youths doing their share. Locally made machinery and tools are used, and, when foreign machines are brought in, innovative solutions are found to cope with any lack of spare parts.

While the question of infrastructure in connection with construction projects was not a specific topic of the regional seminars, it was woven throughout the discussions. In all countries in all regions, it was stressed that women tend to suffer most from inadequate water and sanitation services. An enormous amount of a women's energy is spent in procuring water from distant places. Where water supplies are contaminated, as is often the case, women have the task of nursing the sick or seeking health care to combat waterborne diseases. inadequate sanitation services also contribute to the high incidence of disease in slums and sqatter settlements and in rural areas. In all instances, children are an especially high-risk group.

Because of their traditional roles, women are the key target group for all water and sanitation projects in both rural and urban areas. Yet, in planning and development for shelter projects, authorities and, in households headed by men, husbands often prevent women from participating in various aspects of housing projects and infrastructural services. To look at housing construction without infrastructural supports bodes ill for the quality of life of a community. Women know this only too well. They are primary users who take care of their familie's needs and promote behavioural change. It makes good sense that they should be involved from the planning stage onward.

2. Action needed to be taken

Researchers, women's organizations and NGOs should collaborate in a plan of action concerning women and shelter construction, including: campaigns for changes in social attitudes and public policy; development of technical courses in building for women; promotion of self-help, low-income housing schemes that include infrastructural support; and recognition of the need for full participation of women.

Programmes should focus on women's interest in entering non-traditional fields and should initiate training programmes, keeping in mind lessons learned from other's experience. The following points are from the Caribbean experience in this area:

(a) Assess the market - the need or local demand for certain skills and potential job opportunities;

(b) Allow adequate time for pre-planning and preparation - clarify objectives and assess available human and material resources;

(c) Ensure thorough screening of participants, taking into account their level of education and seriousness of purpose, in particular paying attention to upgrading female trainees' competence in mathematics and basic science skills, so that they are not at a comparative disadvantage in relation to their male counterparts;

(d) Begin with an orientation programme for potential trainees to help them understand what will be expected of them during the training programme - this will also provide important guidelines for the training programmes;

(e) Sensitize tutors to the situation/needs and learning styles of women trainees, as well as the interrelatedness of the various skills being taught;

(f) In addition to basic theory, include appropriate tools for "hands-on" experience, as well as a personal development component to foster self-confidence and group cohesion and to cope with attitudes that trainees are likely to face in society;

(g) Pay particular attention to the needs of trainees who have children, so that their participation is not constrained by their domestic responsibilities;

(h) Ensure that the programme design includes exposure to role models of local tradeswomen, as well as audio-visual presentation by women working in different fields in the region;

(i) Contact governmental and private agencies to get their commitment for apprenticeship and job opportunities for trainees;

(j) Document the training experience, particularly the factors that promote or inhibit women's participation, and disseminate to authorities and other groups interested in promoting such programmes.

Governments should take measures to incorporate women in general adult education programmes - specific classes for women's groups in locations accessible to them, with child-care facilities as needed, would be appropriate. NGOs and community groups should pressure authorities to look at the needs of poor women, promote co-operatives or building groups based on existing communities, and promote building materials, products and industries based on local natural resources.

Women and housing finance

1. Findings

The world survey on the role of women in development, prepared by the United Nations for the World Conference to review and Appraise the Achievements of the United Nations Decade for Women: Equality, Development, Peace, suggested that the stabilization policies employed by many developing countries, in an attempt to cope with the world economic crisis, had affected women, particularly poor women, more negatively than they had men. While recent trends in the financing, insurance, real estate, and business service sectors had been found favourable to the employment of women, the occupational status of women in that sector had not improved significantly. Women tended to be clustered at the bottom of the ladder; their visible under-representation at the policy-making and decision-making levels contributed to the lack of consideration for women's concerns in the formulation of both macro policies and institutional rules and procedures.

The economic and financial policies, the priorities of financial institutions and the rules and procedures commonly employed for loans, mortgages and other forms of credit in both the formal and informal sectors have put women at a significant disadvantage in acquiring credit for housing, as well as for other types of investment in the housing sector. The constraints on women in obtaining housing finance are societal and operational, having to do with social prejudices and institutional practices. On the one hand, there is no social and economic recognition of the contribution made by women to the household; on the other, the income women earn outside the home, in the formal and informal labour markets, is viewed as "secondary", because it is dis-proportionately generated at the bottom of job hierarchies under unstable and temporary circumstances. Even when women are the sole or main supporters of their families, societal norms in general - and laws, regulations and institutional practices in particular - discriminate against them.

Loans taken to finance dwelling units are large, entailing long-term (10-25 years) repayment, require legal-tenure documentation and cover only a percentage (usually 60-80 per cent) of the price. Conventional lending institutions need to safeguard their capital, and applicants, thus, have to provide proof of an adequate and dependable (usually interpreted as formal employment) income as well as of ownership of the property. Applicants also have to provide a downpayment of 25-40 per cent of the cost of the dwelling unit. However, experience shows that many low-income applicants, especially women, have difficulty raising even 10 per cent.

The problems of downpayment requirements and savings are closely related. A woman's lack of formal savings precludes her from access to loans for house-building. Results of an International Centre for Research on Women survey of women heads-of-household who had applied for housing in the Solanda project at Quito, Ecuador, for example, showed that only 15 per cent of the women surveyed who were eligible in terms of income had sufficient savings to made a downpayment on a minimum-cost housing unit. Seventy per cent had savings that were not even half the minimum downpayment; and, even where the value of liquid assets, assuming stringent divestiture, had been calculated and added to savings, only 46 per cent of them could raise the minimal downpayment required. Unfortunately, reduced downpayment requirements would not necessarily improve the access of women to housing projects, because of the trade-off between low downpayments and high monthly payments.

Even where women do have savings, they might not be able to afford both the downpayment for the scheme and the costs of housing their families during the construction period. In sites-and-services schemes, people have to continue renting while they construct a habitable unit on the plot. That means having to find money not only for rent and materials but also for transport between the two sites.

Other factors are no less important in hindering the access of women to finance. For instance, women might be discouraged from obtaining an application form because of the payment required - money which they prefer to use to purchase stable food rather than to gamble on a "housing lottery"; or they might lack information on the availability of loan opportunities. Then again, women might simply lack the time or child-care support facilities to allow them to travel to commercial institutions, often inconveniently located vis-a-vis poor communities.

Participants of all regions noted that women have not been recognized as a special group of housing beneficiaries or contributors. Their view was that the removal of conventional barriers ot women's participation in socio-economic life and the ecnouragement of women to assume new responsibilities in the development effort in general are an important prelude to their full participation in all aspects of human settlements development. Accessibility to housing finance is a critical factor at both levels of involvement.

In Peru, the National Housing Programme proposes to establish the housing Mortgage Bank which is seen as a significant step towards the financing of public lending institutions with the provison that low-income groups be accorded priority.

The Government of Saint Christopher and Nevis encourages private-sector housing development to provide housing for low-income and middle-income earners. In implementing its housing policy, the Government will give due consideration to social infrastructure, recreational facilities and community development programmes. In its Low-income Housing Programme of 1987, 56 per cent of the houses went to women. In order to provide financial assistance to house-owners, the Government did not ask for a downpayment. The applicant paid $EC100 as one year's insurance and paid the cost of one month's rent. Today, the same system is followed. A building-and-repair loan programme was also put in place, so that sugar workers and employees of the Central Housing and Planning Authority could borrow up to $EC10,000 for house repairs or purchases. From 1983 to 1987,28 loans were granted, 50 per cent of them going to women.

Participants from Uganda reported that their Government had not taken action on counteracting the effects of inflation and its effects on prices of building materials. There have been some instances, in squatter-settlement upgarding schemes, where women have borrowed money for house construction but, because of increases in the cost of building materials, have been unable to complete the work.

To overcome a similar problem in the United Republic of Tanzania, loans are provided systematically according to the different stages of house construction. The lenders check each stage of construction before issuing the next instalment. This system also allows for changes in interest rates.

In Zambia, the Government provides loans at low interest rates for house construction and the provision of infrastructure, after every effort is made to mobilize individual and community financial resources and labour.

In Egypt, the Government subsidizes special banks which facilitate loans to low-income households at low interest rates. It was reported that, although this system is appropriate for supporting low-income households, it is often misused by clients who apply for a loan to build a second house with the intention of renting it. The Government has now introduced stringent criteria, and only first-time owners can apply for a low-interest loan.

In the Dandora sites-and-services project in Kenya, women were given financial support towards the cost of building materials, but, as the project developed, new contingency costs arose for which women were not prepared. The inclusion of a sewerage system increased the total cost of the units, and there was an increase in the price of building materials; but the women were unable to obtain extra loans from banks, because they did not fulfil credit requirements. Some women managed to raise the extra money from relatives and informal money lenders to finish their units: others, particularly women heads-of-household, were unable to continue with construction. Partial subletting of rooms was allowed to provide women with extra income for loan repayment. Again, women heads-of household were unable to take advantage of this measure, because their units had not been completed.

In Sri Lanka, women, through their own efforts, had formed co-operative societies. They placed their savings in rural banks managed by women, and, when interest had accrued, small loans were made to members at a 6-per cent interest rate. That facility was especially useful to women in the low-income bracket, who might also be heads-of-household.

The representative of the Philippines reported promising institutional reforms in that country. Lending policy had been altered to include private developers and a strong emphasis on low-income housing. The social housing package for low-income families provided funds for five to seven households which were then regarded as a mortgage unit. The self-employed in the informal sector were being recognized, and a mechanism for validating the informal income of low-income households had been introduced.

That development should be particularly benefical to women engaged in cottage industries. Another noteworthy development has been the promotion of livelihood projects at the community level. They were aimed at providing opportunities for women, who worked at essentially domestic chores and child-rearing, to engage in income-generating activities in their homes. That gave them an income which could be used for shelter and other human settlements improvements, while still allowing them to watch over the children. In general, housing finance in the Philippines was viewed as an integral component of the housing process. That meant that all financing packages were considered in connection with all other resources - land, building materials and labour.

In Indonesia, some efforts were afoot to increase the access of women to finance. The formal banking systems had instituted small credit programmes aimed especially at grass-roots people without collateral: women had equal access to such loans, However women had not taken full advantage, owing to low confidence and limited knowledge about the necessary procedures. A programme had been established to provide information and skills to women entrepreneurs, to enable them to understand and use the available facilities offering credit. Plans were also being made for an information and consulation centre on financial matters for women.

In India, housing is not regarded as an industry and, therefore, is not considered productive, Financial institutions give housing low priority, and about 70 per cent of the finance for housing comes from private sources. In high-income brackets, it comes mainly from such things as the sale of jewelry and other household assets. In rural areas capital is saved gradually in the form of building materials, and construction becomes a long, incremental process for low-income groups. Women suffer from restrictive credit facilities for housing. Because of their low incomes and the informal nature of their work, they fail to gain access to finance from banks and other formal institutions. It has been estimated that less than 1 per cent of the total loans made by banks went to women. The Government of India, therefore, decided to establish a National Housing Bank, so that women would have access to credit. Voluntary agencies have played an important role in implementing housing programmes. The India National Council of

Women, for instance, established a programme for grass-roots women to become familiar with finance procedures. One organization, SPARC, works with the pavement dwellers of Bomaby to improve their condition through education, advocacy and access to credit.

2. Action Needed to be taken

NGOs, CBOs and other relevant voluntary groups should advocate measures for the adaptation of terms and conditions of loans to meet the problems of affordability, credit-worthiness, downpayment, and repayment by low-income women. Governmental and non-governmental groups should institute income-generating projects for women prior to the start of shelter projects, perhaps in the production of construction materials, and allow reduced initial payments that might gradually be raised as in-comes increase. A revolving loan fund and a negative-amortization option might also be introduced.

Groups could be made responsible for repayment of loans (as a substitute for employment and income as collateral for low-income women), or the possibility of loan-insurance systems and guarantee funds set up by government could be pursued. Some programmes might even accept vendor operating licenses and the house itself as collateral.

Urban community groups could be encouraged to pool their savings to start their own credit systems - in much the same way as building societies when they were first begun. NGOs could be encouraged to disseminate the experience of successful women's credit systems (e.g., Grameen Bank in Bangladesh; Working Women's Forum, Madras, India; and Women's World Banking). This could encourage finances institutions to accept informal types of collateral, such as trusts or local leader's guarantees. NGOs can also document self-employed women's repayment-performance records in the various regions and develop methods of assessing informal sector activities and income and their impact on the lives of women and their families.

Community participation and communications and the implementation of programmes on women and human settlements

1. ***Community Participation***

The United Nations Centre for Human Settlements (Habitat) defines community participation as the voluntary involvement of people in making and implementing all decisions directly affecting their lives as well as the activities undertaken by low-income households, with or without outside assistance, to improve their living conditions. By this definition, community participation has always existed in the form of mutual aid in rural societies and was not invented by development agencies. However, with the rapid pace of urbanization in most countries, community participation has been given more attention and taken on new meanings and dimensions. It is sometimes viewed from outside the community as merely an "instrument" for causing change to happen, particularly in low-income settlements. This view has the limitation of organizing outside interventions by "mobilizing" the poor for achieving externally-conceived plans and programmes, rather than providing support for the empowerment of men and women themselves to determine the type, degree and direction of change they need and want - which is a basic tenet of democracy.

While some governments are still reluctant to encourage the latter type of community participation, an increasing number of governments, as well as national and international agencies, have become aware of the importance of full community participation in housing schemes. The disappointing experiences with conventional human settlements programmes in developing countries have helped to convince some governments that it is beyond their financial and administrative capacities to plan for and provide shelter and basic physical and social services for the expanding numbers of poor rural and urban households.Instead, governments are recognizing the necessity of fostering and complementing the efforts and investments that poor families themselves are making to meet their basic needs. They are seeing that community participation not only can improve the chances of project success but is a human right - an end in itself. People have the right and responsibility to participate in the planning, implementation and management of projects which affect their lives. Community participation in human settlements development can also stimulate people to seek participation in other spheres of life.

In an attempt to identify basic models for the application of community participation, the participants in the earlier series of seminars identified the following:

(a) The first model (usually found in situations where governmental policies explicitly encouraged independent community action) placed final planning and decision-making at the settlements level and assigned agency and technical personnel to advisory and regulatory roles.

(b) The second model saw the main planning initiatives in the hands or agencies, with community involvement limited to mere consultation on the plans. The pragmatic principle underlying that model was that, if the community agreed to the plans, it would not obstruct implementation and might prove co-operative in undertaking some role in the implementation and subsequent maintenance of development works.

(c) The third model, which was still the most prevalent, was the "sweet-equity" approach. This confines community participation to individual or group contributions of labour to the construction of houses, the installation of infrastructure or the carrying out of some services, such as garbage collection or drain-cleaning.

Participants identified several constraints that have been encountered when introducing community participation in human settlements programmes, including difficulties in altering established administrative procedures. National housing authorities and local governments did not enter into serious dialogue with communities but, instead, restricted community participation to the mobilizing of controlled self-help in housing construction and of labour contributions to infrastructure projects. Too often, government officials, whether professionals at the national planning level or technicians at the local project level, have been unwilling to change their established perspectives and procedures, to allow sharing of information and decision-making. As a result, the projects they initiate might be designed and implemented without any real consideration of the particular community's human and financial capacities.

Other dimensions of the attitudinal resistance of bureaucrats to community-participation approaches resulted from their genuine concern to maintain standards and procedures, as well as from a conservative mentality and a desire for predictable results within a preconceived time-span. Some of these attitudes can be changed over time, particularly if efforts are made to modify institutional links and internal reorganization and agencies (and recruitment of appropriately skilled personnel) is undertaken. Some of the obstacles to realizing the full potential of community participation derive from the fact that it is very new to agencies and to national administrative systems as a management strategy. It cannot be reduced to a tightly scheduled set of fixed procedures that can be replicated in every community. On the contrary, although the concept is transferable, its practical applications vary in accordance with the people, history, and conditions of each community.

The poor, particularly women, find the greatest difficulty in being informed about, participating in and benefiting from intended community-based projects. When families are struggling to survive and putting in long hours at low-income employment, they usually have little time or energy to attend project meetings and participate in various required activities at specified hours. The limited physical capacity to participate is often compounded socially and psychologically by vexed neighbourhood relationships by distrust and fear of officials accumulated from early negative encounters and by despair of any change going in their favour. In many cases people, who have experienced severe physical deprivation and have been downtrodden for too long react negatively to pressures to participate, and the whole process might only serve to deepen their isolation.

There are many other context-specific factors which hinder the participation of a community as a whole, including hetero geneity along economic, racial, ethnic, religious or political lines (and, as stressed earlier, there is also the culturally-biased gender factor). Often, the social and economic vulnerability of the poorest families forces them to seek the patronage or protection of others more affluent and better connected than they. Such patrons can deliver certain services and have contacts with prominent people and governmental officials which might prove of some benefit to their client families. The important point is that, whether they are genuine patrons or exploitative impostors, they have a vested interest in reinforcing attitudes of dependence among the people. Such attitudes and the social patterns crystallized by them are often difficult to change.

Participants pointed out that, where autonomous community organization was perceived by a government to constitute a threat to national stability, the degree of participation was usually very low. Established top-down patterns of decision-making were confined to activities of priority to government. Whatever has been achieved in social and physical terms through such participation could not be expected to be sustained, maintained or developed.

Even where governments were sincerely disposed towards fostering grass-roots participation in determining the directions of human settlements development, historical and contextual factors often constrained the capacity and willingness of communities to participate. High expectations about what newly established governments could deliver to their citizens sometimes resulted in communities being unwilling to participate in activities such as mutual-aid construction of settlements infrastructure, which they perceived to be the responsibility of their government. Frequent political changes damaged the potential for community participation, because programmes of a participatory nature did not have enough time to nurture the commitment and participation of hesitant staff and sceptical communities before they were scrapped and replaced by other programme approaches.

In most developing countries, the very centralized administrative systems that have been developed are not well-suited to the task of developing partnerships with communities at the local levels. Generally, local municipal authorities are not staffed with technicians who have been trained in participatory skills or who have been accorded the necessary discretionary or decision-making powers ot enable them to engage communities in effective participation.

It has also been observed that frequently the status accorded to community development departments and to community-development workers has been relatively low: that usually became a serious obstacle to the department's attracting able personnel to carry out crucial functions. All too often, community development work was seen as an optional activity rather than as the key to success of a project, and budget allocations reflected that attitude.

In the previous sections, where women and policy, land, construction and finance were discussed, many of the recommendations that were made have direct implications for community participation. Rural and urban communities are where poor and low-income women are already carrying out their daily subsistence tasks, including house-building. This is not always counted as community participation but it is indeed contributing to the welfare of the family and the community.

A quantum leap in strategic planning is required to provide women with options and channels to resources for the integral and sustainable development of human settlements at the community level. This will require a demonstration on the part of governments of a strong political will, supported by a sound systematic plan for sensitizing officials and technicians and for implementing national "enabling" strategies that bring together the governmental, for profit and voluntary sectors in new partnerships-with the full participation of women - in the creation of housing, essential water and sanitation services, transport and employment opportunities. NGOs can help "ready" communities to participate in these partnerships, by encouraging the start-up of CBOs. CBOs have begun to spring up all around the world, and a large percentage of them are women's organizations. The seminars identified many groups, too numerous to include in this document, whose experiences in organizing, motivating, and training community women and men in the participation process (i.e., planning, training, implementation and assessment) can be helpful to others. The participatory approach may be considered by many officials to be slow, but it stands the best chance of producing sustainable results in the long run.

2. *Communications*

While the fundamental causes of underdevelopment are essentially structural, it is increasingly recognized that deficiencies in information and communication processes are among the causes of policy, programme and project ineffectiveness and failure. Each of the seminars devoted time to the discussion of information and communication as an essential policy instrument in support of human settlements development. The impediments to and essential elements of communication methods were given detailed attention that is beyond the scope of this document to present. Each seminar discussed the steps that might be taken to develop a communication strategy for the implementation of specific national policies, programmes and projects.

It was pointed out, time and again, that women have been excluded from the information chain and that, because information is power, it is critical that links be established for their inclusion. If low-income communities, especially the women, do not have knowledge of the plans, programmes, and resources available to improve their communities and are not aware of their actual and potential roles, as well as of the constraints to participation in human settlements programmes, they are unlikely to exercise their rights and responsibilities in this area. If decision-makers and the general public are not provided with information and knowledge about the current contributions of women to human settlements, as well as the obstacles that must be removed in order for them to participate fully as contributors and beneficiaries, they are unlikely to respond appropriately to the needs, rights and responsibilities of women and their communities. Therefore in addition to the need for information, knowledge or data on human settlements, there is a need for communication - or means of transferring or relating this information to others. This calls for a range of social exchanges, i.e., transmitters and receivers on the personal and institutional levels.

At a recent Seminar on Women and Media in Asia, the status of women in the communications media, the skill-development needs of women in different communications media and the portrayal of women by communications media were examined. The seminar noted that issues tended to relate to educated and urban women, with very little attention given to rural women who constitute the majority in Asian countries. The Seminar also identified the need for training in order for women to increase their participation in communications professions and related activities.

The content of what is communicated should also be given high priority. Women's organizations, particularly community-based organizations, have an important role to play in collecting data on the views of women on housing and infrastructure and making them known to the relevant authorities and the local communications media. This cannot be overstressed as the voices of women have for too long gone unheard on matters that directly affect them and their families. It is known fact that many women and villages have been targets of research the results of which have not been shared with the women themselves or with decision-making authorities.

Participatory or action-oriented research is an approach that is being employed frequently. It involves women in a partnership with professionals (often students from local universities) in the collection of data on the community and analysis of the data from a woman's perspective. This not only provides baseline data for project design but is a tool for educating women and other community members on the history and current situation of their community. The information and analyses can also be communicated to authorities as a basis for advocating the type and direction of human settlements interventions needed and desired.

As communication implies dialogue, methods must be devised - with the collaboration of governmental and non-governmental agencies - to communicate policies, programmes and the availability of resources to women and their communities. Seminar participants cautioned that modern media, such as print and radio, often did not reach low-income women who have no time to listen to radio announcements, do not have radios or are illiterate. They found interpersonal communication to be an effective means not only of disseminating information but of effecting behavioural change. Demonstrations, verbal presentations, and displays had also been used to good effect.

Conclusion

It was apparent, from the discussion in all the seminars, that there was a universal concern about the lack of awareness of and attention to the question of women and human settlements. Participants underscored the urgency of working to place this question high on the agenda of national and international governmental agencies, as well as on the agendas of women's organizations. Another area of concern, highlighted across all regions, was the global trend of random urban growth that was having devastating effects on the urban poor everywhere, i.e., slum living conditions that were not only physically intolerable and psychologically impoverishing to the entire family but also particularly debilitating to the energy and status of women. The position of women heads-of-household and single women was another area of concern that regional participants insisted should be given special study and action, along with study of the informal sector and the importance it has in the lives of low-income urban/rural women and the general economy.

There was a heightened sensitivity to the need for women to find ways of working together with men at all levels and of establishing partnerships between poor-community women and professional women from other economic levels. In this regard, it is recognized that NGOs played an important role in joining their knowledge and skills to the knowledge and skills of low-income women and in helping to organize community-based women's organizations, skill-training programmes, advocacy for policy change, infrastructure and services, and participatory human settlements development. NGOs generally were flexible and adaptable, and could open up cost-effective ways for governments to invest in local communities.

Another concern of the seminars was the lack of accurate data on the contributions and needs of women. That constituted an obstacle to women's particularly poor women's, ever achieving the full benefit of development. Participants called upon national and international agencies to develop systematic disaggregated data-collectional methods and gender-sensitive analyses for all facets of human settlements plan and programmes. Some initiatives were under way and should be encouraged to develop indicators for measuring the impact on women and their families of action taken in the human settlements areas covered during the seminars, e.g., policy, land, construction, finance, community participation and communication.

THE FULL PARTICIPATION OF WOMEN IN ALL PHASES OF THE GLOBAL STRATEGY FOR SHELTER TO THE YEAR 2000

Introduction

In his opening address to participants at the Seminar to Promote the participation of Women in All Phases of the Global Strategy for Shelter to the Year 2000, Dr. Arcot Ramachandran, the Executive Director of the United Nations Centre for Human Settlements (Habitat) said;

> "if one conclusion has emerged from the regional seminars, it is the recognition that without the mobilization and participation of women - and the removal of obstacles to their full participation - the goal of the Global Strategy of providing adequate shelter for all cannot and will not be met."

The establishment of this basic premise by the Executive Director at the outset of the Seminar helped to allay some concerns of the participants that their work toward the design of a strategy might marginalize women from the mainstream implementation of the Global Strategy. Recommendations made by women about women too often have that kind of result. Because the Global Strategy has already been designed and is on its way to being elaborated and implemented by national governments, it is imperative that the strategy for the full participation of women also be elaborated immediately and be given priority in the formulation of national strategies for shelter.

Another basic premise of the Seminar was that the goal of improving shelter conditions for all must give priority to the poor and that, as the Executive Director said:

"in the world of the urban and rural poor, it is the women who are more often than not the poorest of the poor, and this is why one can speak with some justification of the 'feminization' of poverty in the third world, a condition that is most shockingly visible in the slums and squatter settlements which are such a prominent feature of the urban landscape in the developing countries."

This premise, the Seminar participants participants emphasized, makes it essential that formulation of the strategy for women's full participation be made not only at the global and national levels but at the community level as well, i.e., community strategies for shelter.

Objectives of the Seminar

The Seminar, which was held at the headquarters of the United Nations Centre for Human Settlements (Habitat) at Nairobi from 4 to 8 December 1989, was clearly a participatory event. Women (governmental and non-governmental) who had attended the five earlier seminars, observers, resource personnel and donor representatives (many of whom also had attended the earlier seminars) all participated in the discussions, and the active exchanges in the working groups laid the groundwork for eventual agreement on a strategy.

The Seminar's objectives were:

(a) To exchange information among regions on the experience each had since the earlier seminars;

(b) to develop a strategy for improving current practices and involving women in the implementation of the Global Strategy for Shelter to the Year 2000;

(c) To recommend the types of technical and financial resources needed by governmental and non-governmental agencies in the implementation of the strategy developed during the Seminar.

Update on regional activities

Following a brief review of the findings of the earlier seminars, as highlighted in Part One of the document, participants made informal presentations on some of the actions that had been taken under the auspices of the United Nations Centre for Human Settlement (Habitat). Because there had not been time nor had provision been made for a systematic assessment in each country represented at the earlier seminars, the report were more indicative than definitive. Nevertheless, they illustrated the types of actions taken in many of countries.

The participant from Zambia said that while no concessions were given to women, they were not discriminated against, either. After the earlier meeting held in her country, however, special attention was given to the issues of housing design and finance, and a new policy was being framed for implementation from 1990 onward. There was also some evidence that efforts were being made to treat women as a non-homogeneous group. The problems and needs of single women, women heads-of-household, and women in other situations, for example, were being considered for discrete treatment.

In Uganda, a Ministry of Women's Affairs, set up in 1988 under the President's Office, was conducting activities related to women and human settlements. Two projects had been launched to enable women to obtain loans without collateral.

Kenyan participants cited progress through the Ministry of Co-operative Development, which had broadened the possibilities for poor women to acquire land. A national housing policy has been drafted, and a Commission on Urbanization was recently established. The Land-Use Commission provided land along the coast to landless people, and slum improvement programmes were increasing. The need for revision of inheritance laws, that deprived a woman of access to her husband's property if she had only daughters, was also noted. It was also pointed out that town planning regulations should be modified to take into consideration the need for land for food production, even in urban areas.

Twenty-eight African governments and institution have established and were co-operating through the Company for Habitat and Housing in Africa (Shelter-Afrique) to help the poorest of the poor in Africa. Governments, by and large, seemed to have realized that the need for housing of the poor was a challenge which had to be faced. The emphasis was on establishing income-generating activities and improving the housing and sanitary conditions of the poor.

Indicative of the signs of advances being made in Asia were three developments in India since 1988:

(a) The National Commission on Urbanization had been creatd to address the issue of land titles, which had become more acute in the urban context than in rural areas;

(b) A National Housing Policy had been designed to cover the issues of access to land, housing finance, and the needs of the landless;

(c) Indira Awas Ujna, a rural projects, has initiated construction of houses in the joint names of housband and wife.

There had also been some success stories in slum-improvement projects, and the Government has decided to set up a national housing bank and has asked other banks to support housing as well.

Among significant developments in Pakistan were the creation of a People's Work's Programme and the emergence of trends towards decentralization of authority to local governments. A five-point grogramme had been established, to include the regularization of slums and the creation and the development of small plots of land in urban and rural areas. The policies and programmes are directed to helping the poor in general but, it was pointed out, no special attention had been given to the specific needs of women.

Some participants from the Latin American and Caribbean region reported having organized working seminars for town council officials and for professionals within ministries concerned with human settlements issues. However, because the economic and social situation in that region had become worse since the regional meeting at Buenos Aires in March 1989, the daily lives of poor women were becoming increasingly more difficult as a result of less employment, less investment, public and private, in housing, and deterioration in such public services as transport, health, water supply and education. Development of human settlements, therefore, had not received a high priority. Further, the number of women heads-of-household is increasing at a phenomenal rate as a result of war, natural disasters and the normal deterioration of the economic and social situation, while the gap of female unemployment was continuously widening compared with that for males.

The Sou Sou land concept, that had been discussed during the Caribbean seminar, focused on providing an opportunity for dialogue on the social and economic situation of women who sought land and shelter as a human right. Based on the concept and practice, the National Housing Authority of Trinidad and Tobago had defined its strategic goals as bringing affordable shelter solutions to low-income groups in society, particularly female heads-of-household who headed 30-40 per cent of all households, and fostering and encouraging self-help and self-reliance in the provision of shelter and community facilities and the creation of sustainable human settlements.

Participation underscored the need to reconcile the triple roles of women (production, reproduction and the managing of both the domestic household and community action groups) in shelter planning, to take into account the need for spatial arrangements allowing women to function adequately in those three areas. Research in Jamaica had found that, although 75 per cent of women who headed households were renters, housing policy did not address renters. Escalating speculation in urban land had eliminated "yards" and had commercialized open spaces. The aftermath of Hurricane Gilbert in 1988 had increased the housing crisis, particularly because relief had not reached renters.

Members of the Habitat International Coalition (HIC) Women and Shelter Group spoke of the Plan of Action on Women and Shelter launched by HIC in April 1988. The Plan of Action was a response to the Regional Seminar on Women and Shelter held at Harare in 1987 in connection with International Year of Shelter for the Homeless. It called for the setting-up of a global network on women and shelter. This is currently based at the Mazingira Institute, Nairobi, and operates as an outreach system, collecting and disseminating information from and to NGOs and CBOs in the different regions, through focal points. The HIC Women and Shelter Group acts as a policy group which will be constituted by the network of NGOs and CBOs, as it grows, and should represent poor women in rural and urban settlements. The first issue of the *HIC Women and Shelter Network Newsletter* has been produced in English, French, Portuguese and Spanish. It Contains news from slums and other low-income settlements in several regions.

The participant's statements indicated the following overall trends:

(a) There had been a gradual change in attitudes about the need to focus on women and human settlements;

(b) Policy-makers were beginning to view women as a force to be reckoned with, and women themselves were seeing the need to make their initiatives more visible;

(c) There had been an increase in popular and women's organizations and in international networking;

(d) The ease with which women worked in groups was a sign of hope as a "lead-in" to community level action.

At the same time, several participants pointed out that housing did not always appear on women's lists of priorities. Priority was given to the need for food, water, sanitation education, health, income-earning and transport, thus underscoring the wisdom of an integral approach to sustainable development of human settlements and addressing housing needs in that context.

Participants continually returned to the premise that, they stressed, must be repeated over and over again, even at the risk of annoying those in authority, namely, that global, national and community strategies for shelter must give priority to the poor and, especially, the poorest of the poor who are women. As the global economic crisis widened the gap between the rich and the poor, it was all too easy to lapse into general rhetoric or into plans and programmes for the development of human settlements without a focus on the poorest populations who constituted the majority in most developing countries. The dramatic structural changes required for bridging that gap would necessarily affect those at highest economic levels. (At a discussion meeting after a site visit, participants added that equally dramatic structural changes were needed in community structures as well, i.e., poverty alleviation and strategies that simply managed poverty were not good enough.)

The United Nations Global Strategy for Shelter to the Year 2000

The participants had before them General Assembly resolution 43/181, adopted on 23 December 1988, as a point of reference for the development of their strategy for the full participation of women in the Global Strategy for Shelter to the Year 2000.

The General Assembly had, among other things:

(a) Adopted the Global Strategy for Shelter to the Year 2000;

(b) Decided that the main objective of the Strategy was to facilitate adequate shelter for all by the year 2000, that the principal focus should therefore be on improving the situation of the disadvantaged and the poor, and that the following fundamental objectives and principles should form the basis of the Strategy:

(i) Enabling policies, whereby the full potential and resources of all governmental and non-governmental actors in the field of human settlements are utilized, must be at the heart of national and international efforts;

(ii) Women, as income-earners home makers and heads of households, and women's organizations fulfil a crucial role as contributors to the solution of human settlements problems which should be fully recognized and reflected in equal participation of women in the elaboration of housing policies, programmes and projects, and the specific interests and capabilities of women should be adequately represented in human settlements policy formumation and at all levels of government mechanisms for the implementation of housing policies, programmes and projects;

(iii) Shelter and development are mutually supportive and interdependent, and policies must be developed in full recognition of the important links between shelter and economic development;

(iv) The concept of sustainable development implies that shelter provision and urban development must be reconcilable with sustainable management of the environment.

(c) designated the commission on Human Settlements as the United Nations intergovernmental body responsible for co-ordinating, evaluating, and monitoring the Strategy, and the United Nations Centre for Human Settlements (Habitat) as the secretariat for the Strategy and the lead agency for co-ordinating and monitoring the relevant programmes and activities of other United Nations organizations and agencies concerned.

The general framework for the Global Strategy for Shelter was set up in the following plan of action:

1989-1991 : Establishment of national policies and strategies. Design of new institutional arrangements.

1992-1994 : Introduction of new institutional arrangement and strengthening of existing national programmes.

1995-2000 : Full-scale operation of national programmes. Progressive strengthening of institutions for activities beyond 2000.

The plan of action fixes the responsibilities of the various actors: the Member Staes of the United Nations, the General Assembly, the Economic and Social Council, the Commission on Human settlements, the United Nations Centre for Human Settlements (Habitat), United Nations agencies and organizations multilateral and bilateral agencies and non-governmental organizations.

It will be progressively updated and refined by the Commission on Human Settlements during its biennial sessions throughout the period up to the year 2000. A timetable, covering the period 1989-1991, is currently under implementation.

A strategy for the full participation of women in all phases of the Global Strategy for shelter

The intention of involving women as contributors to and beneficiaries of the Global Strategy for Shelter is eminently clear from the General Assembly resolution. The Interregional Seminar to Promote the Participation of Women in the Global Strategy for Shelter to the Year 2000 was organized by the United Nations Centre for Human Settlements (Habitat) to develop a strategy that would help transform that intention into a practical reality that could be acted upon.

The strategy (plan of action) outlined below envolved from the discussions and workshops which centred their attention on regional findings and methods for eliminating obstacles to the participation of women in human settlements activities. Participants addressed two basic questions:

(a) What is a gender-sensitive, enabling shelter strategy ?

(b) What is a gender-sensitive human settlement ?

In answer to the first question, the following links were emphasized between the enabling and the gender-sensitive shelter strategies:

Enabling (removing obstacles)	Gender-sensitive
Using public-sector resources to facilitate and encourage action taken by other sectors: private (formal and informal) and the community	Using public-sector resources to facilitate and encourage gender-specific action taken by other sectors (promoting women and women-in-development issues)
Stimulating the use of untapped capacities and resources in all sectors	Stimulating the use of untapped capacities of women (especially low-income women as individuals producers, home-makers and professionals); and effectively utilizing resources, including the managing and organizing skills of NGOs, CBOs and women's organization
Defining the complementary roles of the private and public sectors in the most efficient way possible	Recognizing and encouraging the role of women in the private and public sectors and defining the complementary roles of those sectors by promoting full participation by women's governmental and non-governmental organizations

Concentrating direct public-sector involvement on tasks not covered by the other sectors	Concentrating direct public-sector involvement on tasks specifically relating to women and not covered by other sectors; also directing public-sector support to the poor, taking into account that the majority of the poor are women

In answer to the second question, participants spoke in terms of the need for a "vision" (a term not uncommon to women and communities) of a gender-sensitive human settlement in order to work towards it. In familiar planning terms, there was a need to have a concept of what were the basic elements of a human settlement that took women, as well as men and children, into consideration.

First and foremost, the approach is integral and participatory. From the beginning, the planning includes women as well as men (particularly the poor of all ethnic groups). It responds to women's perspectives (as well as men's) on the use and function of private and communal living and working space. It ensures the co-ordination of the services of agencies that take into account practical family needs for water, sanitation, waste-recycling, health, child-care and education. There is no gender division of labour, and the burden of domestic chores is lessened. Of particular relevance to housing, insititutional forms of discrimination are eliminated by creating equal rights to land ownership and access to credit. There are opportunities for employment and/or income-generating enterprises for both men and women, with access to transport and markets. CBOs involving women are included in local-government planning and the implementation of programmes favourable to the sustainable development of the environment.

From discussions in working groups on community participation, training, communication and the roles of government, private and community sectors, several points arose that indicated the direction participants thought the strategy for women should take:

(a) As part of the Global Strategy for shelter, it should focus on poor women and not try to cover all levels.

(b) Within the Global strategy for Shelter it is analogous to the "life blood"(distinct from a limb) of the human system. There was no way to integrate the strategy for women in the Global Strategy; it is a vital part of it which had to become visible.

(c) It emphasis on progressively improving the conditions of women should ensure that the relations between male and female members of households and societies be structured in such a way that the advancements made by one generation of women were not lost to the next - and that new relationships were embodied in law.

(d) It implied a "paradigm shift" - from focusing on central government to decentralizing planning and implementation to local-government and community levels. It should stress that NGOs should function as a bridge between the official male-dominated policy-making mechanism, with its interdisciplinary and techinical language, and the practicality of local communities; that bridging should result in the emergence of a "shared language."

(e) It required a new system of training and communication within the human settlements and shelter sectors which provided for "bottom-up" activities. It recognized that women are, in great numbers, excluded from the existing formal education system while they were very much involved in non-formal learning-by-doing processes which should be developed and facilitated. Training as a learning and capacity-building process was currently being carried out for women by NGOs and CBOs and should be put on the agenda of governments and receive adequate support by international agencies. The new strategy called for a system of communication which was dependent not upon documents and papers only but also upon the deliberate creation of attractive information means, such as video and radio programmes, conducive to open exchange. Negotiating and leadership capacities were skills that women should acquire through specific training programmes.

(f) It should support the process of rethinking and reshaping the operational objectives and mechanisms and/or institutions of housing and human settlements, in order to be ready to function when governments wanted to "enable" NGOs and CBOs. Success full approaches needed to be documented, and their results disseminated for wide use.

(g) It should recognize and value the contributions of NGO and CBOs, both of which should increase their network activities - horizontally and vertically, in furthering the goals of the strategy. Enlisting the co-operation of NGOs and CBOs should be accompanied, when possible, by financial assistance, by, for example, making contracts related to human settlements activities open to bids from NGOs and CBOs.

(h) It should recognize that NGOs and CBOs had a vital role to play in closing the gap between government and the grass-roots, by being informed about governmental policies and programmes and by disseminating that knowledge for use by grassroots organizations. Conversely, they could make their knowledge about the conditions, needs and desires of grass-roots communities known to government and to society as a whole through the mass communication media. Institutional arrangements had to be worked out for NGOs to obtain local and national representaion, participation in decision-making processes and financial resources in recognition of the intermediary role they were ful filling.

(i) It should support the development of partnerships within the family and the community, and (in the context of the Global Strategy for Shelter) among the public, private and community sectors. It should look for further elaboration, in the Global Strategy for Shelter, of the role of the private sector, on which topic the participants in the Seminar limited their discussions to the need for employment and assistance in the starting up of informal small businesses. Further elaboration was also needed on ways of ensuring equality in the development of those partnerships.

(j) It should be set in the context of integral sustainable development of human settlements, as envisioned above. To that end, the strategy for women saw it as vital that there should be a further elaboration, in the Global Strategy for Shelter, of the infrastructural components needed in human settlements development, e.g., water, sanitation, roads and transport;

(k) It implied a heavy reliance on the ability of the United Nations Centre for Human Settlements (Habitat) to "enable" governments to make the strategy effective. One of the principle instruments would be the establishment of a focal point on women that would be provided with credentials and resources commensurate with the scope of the task assigned to it by the Commission on Human Settlements.

Plan of action

The Seminar participants developed a plan of action patterned after the Global Strategy for Shelter Plan of Action. The actions that need to be taken are identified specifically under :

A. Member States;

B. The General Assembly, the Economic and Social Council, the Commission on Human Settlements and the United Nations Centre for Human Settlements (Habitat)

C. United Nations agencies and organizations, multilateral and bilateral agencies and non-governmental organizations; and

D. Local governments and community-based organizations, an addition to the list of actors in the Global Strategy Plan of Action which the seminar participants saw as a necessary and logical progression from the insistence the particular attention be given to poor women at the local-government and community level.

The plan of action is set out in annex I. The material in bold type is taken verbatim from the Global Strategy for Shelter to the Year 2000: Plan of Action 1989-1991. These items are included to indicate how the Women's Plan of Action meshes with the Global Strategy for Shelter.

Monitoring and evaluation

The Global Strategy for Shelter has been characterized as a framework for a continuous process towards the goal of facilitating adequate shelter for all by the year 2000. The strategy for women developed at the Seminar could also be described as an evolving framework for the process, to include the full participation of women especially poor women, in the Global Strategy. As with the Global Strategy, the strategy for women would need to be monitored and evaluated continuously and modified accordingly.

To ensure that each national strategy and programme on human settlements, assisted by the United Nations Centre for Human Settlements (Habitat) and other agencies, included a woman's perspective in its formulation, implementation, monitoring, and evaluation, the participants asked that the most critical and practical indicators concerning women and human settlements be developed in consultation and partnership with the Commission on the Status of Women, the united Nations Children's Fund, the International Research and Training Institute for the Advancement of Women (INSTRAW) and International women's organizations in consultative status with the Economic and Social Council, and be tested as soon as possible.

With regard to evalutaion, participants proposed that :

(a) The Guidelines Manual of the United Nations Development Programme for technical co-operation project be reviewed from the perspective of gender, making use of the findings of the earlier series of seminars and the strategy for the full participation of women in the Global Strategy for Shelter;

(b) Technical co-operation projects and programmes incorporate indicators with gender differentiation (providing guidelines on, for example, disagregation by gender and income level among others) making use of the base-line data and impact-assessment system of the United Nation Development Fund for Women, the monitoring and evaluation recommendations and other studies related to human settlements development with a women's perspective.

Conclusion

In its resolution 9/9 of 16 May 1986 the Commission on Human Settlements recommended that :

> "... regional or subregional seminars be organized, within the framework of the preparations for the International Year of Shelter for the Homeless, in order to exchange experiences on pilot projects and to define and evaluate the role of women and the organizations that represent them, in the conception, financing and execution of such projects, such seminars to be funded from specific resources made available by Government and organizations in a position to do so;"

and in its resolution 10/17 of 16 April 1987 it urged :

> "... continuation of regional seminars initated during the International Year of shelter for the Homeless in order to exchange experiences on projects and to define and evaluate the role of women and the organizations that represent them, in the conception, financing and execution of such projects."

This report has presented the findings of those seminars and outlined actions needed to be taken concerning women and human settlements issus, i.e., policy, land, construction and housing finance. It has also presented the outcome of the Seminar to Promote the Participation of Women in the Global Strategy for Shelter to the Year 2000 which launched a strategy for the full participation of women in the Global Strategy for Shelter to the Year 2000. The participants in the Seminar expressed the hope that the report would be used to inform the Commission on Human Settlements of the Seminar's views on the essential contribution of women and of organizations for women to the development and management of human settlements.

The hope that the strategy for women would be taken as seriously as the drafters took the development of it stimulated the further hope that significant progress towards achieving the objective of involving women at all level of planning and implementation of human settlements policies and programmes, and of improving the residentail/ work environemnt of women, especially urban and rural poor women, their families and communities, would be seen by the year 2000.

Annex i

SUGGESTED REVISION OF THE PLAN OF ACTION OF THE GLOBAL STRATEGY FOR SHELTER TO THE YEAR 2000

Member States

Review progress in implementing a national shelter strategy (NSS) and adjust action programmes in light of experience.

Ensure that NSS is considered as an integral part of national economic-development strategies by:

- Designating a person to co-ordinate the strategy for women in the key economic ministry;
- Setting up a database system to support monitoring of NSS, with data collected as a normal procedure by gender, particularly those on households.

Take immediate action to improve living conditions of women in low-income settlements; projects for upgrading which include the participation of women should be given priority.

Strengthen the involvement of all participants in the shelter - delivery process.

Strengthen legal and institutional frameworks.

Expand the provision of training and information.

Develop an integrated approach to gender-awareness in NSS by:

- Forming or using existing interministerial committees (e.g., a national human settlements commission);
- Including women's representatives in the national machinery to formulate policy and establishing training programmes for those women;
- Ensuring that neighbourhood and women's groups are represented in local and national government;
- Developing ongoing communications between community based organizations (CBOs), non-governmental organizations (NGOs) and ministerial levels;
- Linking integrated sectoral committees with integrated ministerial committees;
- Conducting workshops on gender-awareness for public employees, both male and female.

Legislate to eliminate obstacles to women's equal access to housing, land, infrastructure, training, building materials and finance, with particular attention to the following points:

- Land titles should be granted on a family basis;
- Laws of inheritance and tenure rights should be non-discriminatory;
- Women need to be informed of their rights, and their rights should be facilitated.

Ensure that initiatives developed at the community level can be responded to at governmental level, by:

- Mobilizing and distributing financial resources;
- Ensuring financial support of NGOs that can provide the technical assistance needed for community groups to prepare proposals;
- Ensuring that the improvement of living conditions meets the basic needs of those concerned;
- Providing financial assistance, e.g., investments, grants and credit, needed by women to begin income-generating activities.

Continue holding national workshops and support sub-regional seminars.

Develop and integrated approach among government, the private sector and the community sector, and, especially, form or use joint co-ordination committees to ensure representation of women's agencies at all levels, e.g., women's bureaux, professional and business women's NGOs and CBOs.

Ensure that workshops and seminars are hold on women and shelter themes, to deal with:

- Communication/information/education needed for women;
- Training in participation, leadership, leadership, leadership skills, facilitation, concensus-building, caucusing, political organization and negotiation.

Prepare monographs and case studies on selected aspects of NSS

Create mechanisms for receiving proposals relevant to women's involvement in NSS;

Develop videos to inform government officials of the needs of women;

Prepare inserts in leading newspapers to highlight gender-sensitive shelter strategy;

Remove obstacles to land delivery, infrastructure installation, building-materials output and construction productivity;

Integrate approaches to planning settlements, through joint participation by agencies responsible for housing, services, health and transport and by women of the community;

Make planning standards and design of technology gender-sensitive, through:

- Legislation;
- Training of planners and executives;
- Consciousness-raising;
- Policy reformulation.

Relate water supply, sanitation, waste disposal and environmental management to gender-sensitive shelter strategies;

Emphasize training for the participation of women in all aspects of the construction sector, including planning and management.

Prepare a national report for submission to the Commission on Human Settlements at its thirteenth session and for worldwide dissemination.

Ensure that recommendations of the Seminar to Promote the Participation of Women in the Global Strategy for Shelter to the Year 2000 are taken into consideration in national reports.

Observe World HABITAT Day (WHD) by highlighting the achievements to date and plans for the future.

- Special attention should be given to the achievements of women whithin the chosen theme for WHD.

United Nations General Assembly, Economic and Social Council, Commission on Human Settlements and United Nations Centre for Human Settlements (Habitat).

Continue to provide Member State with substantive support for the formulation and implementation of shelter strategies and assistance in obtaining technical assistance

Ensure that gender issues are incorporated in an integrated manner across all sections of the Strategy from the very beginning, by:

- Appointing a woman to the staff of the United Nations Centre for Human Settlements (Habitat) to facilitate implementation of the strategy for the full participation of women in the Global Strategy for Shelter;
- Relating human settlements issues to other sectors of the economy and aspects of social life;
- Establising a link between the United Nations Centre for Human Settlements (Habitat) and the Habitat International Coalition Women and Shelter Group for outreach on human settlements issues at the national, sub-regional, regional and inter-regional levels;
- Involving other networks in these issues (e.g., Women and Law, Women and Environment;
- Consulting with the Commission on the Status of Women, the International Research and Training Institute for the Advancement of Women and international NGOs.

Plan an institutional framework to carry out the strategy for the full participation of women in the Global Strategy for Shelter, and establish a mechanism for maintaining dialogue between outhorities and women's organizations in regard to:

- Policy foumulation;
- Implementation;
- Monitoring;

Improve gender-sensitivity within all sections of the secretariat of the United Nations Centre for Human Settlements (Habitat) and the Commission itself through:

- Training programmes in all divisions;
- Placement of women at decision-making levels;
- Presentation of the strategy for the full participation of women in the Global Strategy for Shelter to United Nations Development Programme Resident Representatives and to other United Nations agencies;
- Giving of high priority in technical co-operation projects to the role of women and their participation in the conception, execution and maintenance of human settlements.

Continue to prepare and disseminate information on the Global Strategy for Shelter.

Increase public awareness dof the concern of the United Nations Centre for Human Settlements (Habitat) with women and shelter issues, by:

- Initiating mass media campaigns focusing on women and shelter within the Global Strategy for Shelter;
- Featuring "women and shelter" in *Habitat News.*

• Set up a database system to support monitoring of the Global for Shelter and ensure that data collected are disaggregated and analysed by gender for;

- Policy formulation;
- Implementation;
- Monitoring;

(breakdown of data by age and gender should be established as a normal procedure. It is particularly important to have data on households as beneficiaries/participants of programmes including women-headed households).

The Economic and Social council will receive a progress report on the Global Strategy for Shelter.

Carry out a follow-up evaluation on how recommendations have been carried out.

Prepare a monitoring report on national action on the Global Strategy for Shelter for submission to the Commission on Human Settlements at its thirteenth session.

Ensure that the recommendations of the Seminar to Promote the Participation of Women in the Global Strategy for Shelter to the Year 2000 are taken into consideration.

The Commission on the Human Settlements at its thirteenth session will:

(a) Review the monitoring report on implementation of the Global Strategy for Shelter;

(b) Review and recommend targets and timetables for the second phase of the Global Strategy for Shelter.

Place the final report of the Seminar to Promote the Participation of the Women in the Global Strategy for Shelter to the Year 2000 on the agenda of the Commission on Human Settlements at its thirteenth session.

The Economic and Social Council will receive a progress report on:

(a) Targets and timetables for the second phase of GSS;

(b) The 1992-1993 work programme of UNCHS (Habitat).

Ensure that the women's strategy on shelter is taken into consideration in progress report.

The General Assembly will receive a progress report on the Global Strategy for Shelter.

Ensure that women's strategies on shelter are taken into consid eration.

United Nations agencies and organizations, multilateral and bilateral agencies, and non-governmental agencies.

Circulate a summary of the report of the Seminar to Promote the Participation of Women in the Global Strategy for Shelter to the Year 2000 to United Nations agencies and organizations, multilateral and bilateral agencies, and non-governmental organizations (NGOs).

Regional commissions will review their activities in:

(a) Exchange of information on GSS;

(b) Policy research on GSS issues;

(c) Data collection for GSS.

Incorporate the women's strategy in the review of activities of the regional commissions and other organizations and agencies with reference to:

- Exchange of information on the Global Strategy for Shelter;
- Policy research on Strategy issues;
- Disaggregated data collection by gender;

Donor agencies should re-evaluate their assistance policies and channel more of their funding assistance to projects which directly benefit women in the human settlements sector;

Equal status should be given to NGOs and CBOs at international seminars;

Regional United Nations offices and other international organizations should make use of the Habitat International Coalition Women and Shelter Network's focal points as sources of information, so that the voice of poor women can be strong and also channelled to policy-makers;

Projects should be identified that can become demonstration projects;

Emergency support be given to poor, peasants and urban dwellers, of whom women are the poorest, and to those suffering from threats of eviction or dislocation due to natural disaster, drought, war or other disturbances;

Women's organizations hould be brought together with policy-makers to discusswomen's strategy issues in international fora;

Gender-sensitivity should be improved within the donor community, by:

- Demonstrating gender-based effects of specific loan conditionalities;
- Analysing connections between poverty, environment and women's subsistence roles;

The use of land by women for subsistence purposes (food, fuel, which is not planned for in land-use policies or economics, should be recognized and incorporated in the planning process.

Other United Nations organizations and agencies will prepare annual plans for Global Strategy for Shelter activities

Ensure that the recommendations of the Seminar to Promote the

Participation of Women in the Global Strategy for Shelter to the Year 2000 are taken into consideration.

Multilateral and bilateral agencies and NGOs will be invited to submit annual plans for Global Strategy for Shelter activities.

Ensure that rhe recommendations of the Seminar to Promote the Participation of women in the Global Strategy for Shelter to the Year 2000 are taken into account;

Submit status reports to the Commission on Human Settlements at its thirteenth session.

All agencies and organizations will be invited to participate in WHD celebrations to mark the end of the first phase of GSS to distribute information material focussed on this themse.

Local governments and community-based organizations

Circulate a summary of the report of the Seminar to Promote the Participation of Women in the Global Strategy for Shelter to the Year 2000 to CBOs;

Local governments should become involved in NSS both in planning and implementation. Local governments should then channel information from and into the community to local decision-makers and poor women through:

Local meetings;

- Traditional fairs;
- Local social gatherings;
- Posters;
- Radio announcements;

Strengthen the capacity and voice of activists within government and NGOs by:

- Allocation financial resources for training programmes for interface personnel in NGOs and government agencies;
- Ensuring the participation of these interface personnel on inter-ministerial and intersectoral committees;
- Supporting direct donor contributions to NGOs and CBOs active in women's shelter strategies,

- Including the representations of women's organizations in decision-making positions in bodies responsible for shelter programmes;
- Developing vertical communication channel using existing women's organizations as facilitators at all levels:
- Forming an umbrella organization for lobbying, networking and outreaching CBOs, and ensuring that there is local representation on its board;

Publicize work implemented at the community level by:

- Inviting decision-makers to specific functions so that they can see at first-hand what is happening and be informed of needs "on the spot";

Neighbourhood women's groups should:

- Identify their needs and priorities;
- Establish their autonomy;
- Develop an informal grassroots network;

Training seminars for local groups should provide:

- Information sessions;
- Assertiveness training;
- Videos on women's needs and women's issues;

At the local level, there is need to:

- Review and, if necessary, change zoning regulations to enable women to work for remuneration at home;
- Use extension workers for outreach systems. (It is important to have independent extension workers employed by local NGOs, in addition to local government employees.)

Women should be encouraged to become both small-scale and large-scale entrepreneurs through:

- Practical training apprenticeships for unskilled women;
- Skill-training programmes;
- Credit facilitation;
- Consciousness-raising.

REFERENCES

Joint United Nations Information Committee/NGO Programme on *Women and Shelter,* Kit No. 4 (1988). English, French and Spanish versions.

United Nations, *Official Records of the Forty-third Session of the General Assembly Supplement No. 8* (A/43/8), The Addendum, Report of the Commission on Human Settlements on the work of its eleventh session; Global Strategy for Shelter to the Year 1990.

United Nations Centre for Human Settlements (Habitat), *Building-related Income Generation for Women - Lessions from Experience* (Nairobi, 1990) (HS/197/90E).

— *Case Study of Women Block Makers in Kenya* (Nairobi, 1988) (HS/08/86-20E).

— *La Mujer y los Asentamientos Humanos en America Latina.* Bibliografia anotada (Nairobi, 1989).

— *La Participacion de la Mujer en la Gestion y el Desarrollo de los Asentamientos Humanos* Manual de formacion (Nairobi, 1989) (HS/155/89S).

— *La Participation des femmes a la gestion et au development des etablissements humans,* Maual de formation (Nairobi, 1990) (HS/155/89F).

— The Role of Women in the Execution of Low-income Housing Projects, Training module (Nairobi, 1986) (HS/75/85). Avialable in English, French and Spanish.

— *Women and Human Settlements* (Nairobi, 1985) (HS/DP/85/18).

— *Women and Human Settlements: The Experience.* Bibliographic Notes No. 15 (Nairobi, 1989).

— Women and Shelter. Bibiligraphic Notes No. 7 (Nairobi, 1985).

— *Women in Human Settlements Development and Management* (Radstock, Tilden Communications Ltd., 1990).

CHAPTER-15

Women in Human Settlement Development and Management

D. Subramaniam

Introduction

This essay focusses on the role women can play in the Human Settlement Development and Management in the back drop of Habitat Day-1993's theme WOMEN AND SHELTER DEVELOPMENT. As part of the overall strategy it is envisaged that the human settlement development and management can be achieved on sustainable basis by involving women in shelter development activities. In other words, "shelter" and "women" are made king-pins of human settlement development.

Section - I

1.0 Status of Human Development of Women in Human Settlement Planning

Both the Equity and efficiency criteria of development have been compromised in India because of the left handed treatment women are meted out in national life. One reason for neglecting development of women in human settlement planning in India is due to the lack of emphasis which successive development plans have placed on women development vis-a-vis physical development. While physical plant and equipment were accorded primacy in resource allocations and organizational inputs, human development aspects of women such as health and education were put on the back burner. A point in evidence is the meagerness of resources ear-marked for human development of women in human settlement planning.

In India, from the First Plan (1951-1956) to the Seventh Plan (1985-90) the public sector plan outlay on different human substantially decreased. For example, on social services the percentage decreased from 21 percent in 1951-61 to 17.5 percent in 1985-90. On education it decreased from 7.5 percent in 1951-56 to 3.5 percent in 1985-90.

On healfh it decreased from 3.5 percent in 1951-56 to 1.9 percent in 1985-90. And on social welfare and related fields it decreased from 6.7 percent in 1951-56 to 5.0 percent in 1985-90.

Women's development suffered not only because of the comparative neglect of human development in Indian Plans, but also because of deep-rooted politico-economic and socio-cultural prejudices which militated against women's interest. Politically, women's preferences do not got adequately reflected in decision-making. Women are required and are made to conform to the political preferences of their husbands or sons. Woman do not exercise their vote prerogative on their own volition either for lack of relevant knowledge or lack of courage to act on their own. Their courage was eroded and their personalities stunted by the weight of the oppression and suppression they suffered over centuries.

1.2 Economic development of women

Economically, women have few opportunities for remunerative work. They do work in agriculture, but for most part, as unpaid workers on own-farms, where they are hired for work, their wages are often a pittance. While women's remunerative work is underpaid, and spread over unevenly over the year and is characterized by irregular hours, the work load carried by them is so heavy as to border on the inhuman. In addition to work in agriculture either paid or unpaid, they put in long hours as wives and mothers. A normal day's work for woman spans twelve to fourteen hours of routine toil, including approximately four hours fetching fuel wood and drinking water. Women have precious few opportunities for work in non-agricultural activities, where they manage to get work in urban areas, they end up doing menial jobs mostly in the service sector. They are not only poorly paid, but the nature of their work is stultifying and demanding.

1.3 Social Development of Women

Socially, women are discriminated against in a myriad ways. This discrimination takes place in the household, in the work place and in the folk-place. In the household, they are either daughters or wives or mothers. As daughters, they demand a liability; their nutrition, health and education receive a residual preference. Either in the matter of financial resource allocation or food allocation theirs is often a negligible share because they get only the balance remaining after needs of boy-children are all met. Their marriages are arranged not by their choice or considerations of future happiness but by their social convenience and anxiety of their parents to get rid of them some how before their marriageable age passes which is in some cases pretty early in life. As wives, more correctly as daughters-in-law, they become work horses, ill-fed and over worked. A good percentage of them become mothers over and over again, often against their will, either because the husbands are considerate or because the mother-in-law goad them to bear more children than their health permits. Every successive child born becomes a greater draft on their health and well-being. Quite often, they become old women at the end of their child-bearing years:

The participation of women in social life is minimal. Custom, lack of optional time, physical weariness which envelopes them as a miasma preclude which envelopes them from participation in recreational activities. Vicissitudes of life hit them most severely off all; a crop failure means they become the ones most vulnerable to scarcity, infections and epidemics affect them first; and they are the last ones to be reached by programs of social development because they happen to have the least access to the benefits of these programs with due to ignorance or prejudice or just lack of will.

Social restrictions and inhibitions arising from the rigidity of household structures militate against their cultural growth. Lack of education, submission to age-old social customs and sanctions, local optional time, and personal fear of offending their husbands or family elders preclude them from any attempts of cultural resumption. Add to it the fact that cultural events meant exclusively for women are rare to the point of non-existence. And there develops a social milieu which keeps women chained to the basic spots as workers, mothers, baby sitters, and generally untrained human beings bereft of development. Essentially, they become wasted human beings, their household and social rigidities and obligations, and their potentialities unrealized.

1.4 Gender inequality - A Constraint of Women Development in Human Settlement Planning

This unrelieved and gloomy existence of women and the wretchedness of their lives get reflected in a number of ways in the decreasing sex ratio (the ratio of the number of women per 1000 men), in their higher mortality pattern (at least up to the age of 35 years), and their relative illiteracy (compared with men). These are only a few indicators, but they suffice to show to what extent the almost half the country's population of women lack human development both in the absolute sense, and relatively to men.

1.4.1 Sex Ratio

The sex ratio in India was 972 to 1000 men in 1901. It fell down to 929 in 1991. True, a part of the decrease may be attributable to under enumeration of women in successive censuses. But the monotonic decrease in the ratio over 90 years with almost no exception shows that some fundamental factors have been at work in swelling the ranks of "missing women".

1.4.2 Mortality

The mortality of women, up to the age of 35 years is greater than that of the males. As of 1986 in the age group of 0-4 years it is 11 per cent greater; in the age group of 5-14 years it is 22 per cent greater; and in the age group of 15-34 years, it is 31 per cent greater. It is only after the age of 35 years for women their relative mortality rate in comparison with men declines. These mortality differentials only mean that the natural biological advantage of life-expectancy which women as a gender group enjoy is more than counter balanced by the socio-economic disadvantages from which they suffer up to the age of 35 years.

1.4.3 Literacy

The above argument, supported by facts, which are accepted all around, goes to show that human development in India leaves very much wanting, and that even in the potency of human development which took place, such as it has been, women fare distinctly worse.These two deficiencies do not augur well for future development. Of the two, the gender inequality is more important as a factor in overall development because it is a compelling negative power. It detracts from the development achievements which otherwise, can become an engine of socio-economic progress all around. This is even apart from the purely equity considerations which demand justice between the genders, as a matter of "failures" (Rawls).

The women movement in India, as elsewhere, failed to grasp the nature of women's problems. It concentrated on women's rights and privilege rather than develop of framework of action which, when implemented could lead to an amelioration of the women's condition. Moreover, the women's movement tilted towards women in urban areas; the movement itself was high-jacked by socialite women who did not adequately appreciate the nature of the women's problems in the rural areas.

SECTION - II

2.0 What is Human Settlement Development and Why it is Important?

HUMAN SETTLEMENT DEVELOPMENT is a study of mankind in acquiring the basic requisites of well being for human development, and effectively using them to achieve equity and efficiency at settlement level. It is not only concerned with optimizing development, but equally important, it is also concerned with the augmentation of physical, human, (skill), and natural resources for development and an in-built provision for their renewal, replacement, conservation, and growth where applicable on a sustainable basis.

In other words, human settlement development is about meeting the needs of the people without compromising the basic objectives of development, equity and efficiency and in the process without making any discrimination on the grounds of sex, caste, creed etc. However, a pre-condition for this to happen is the promotion of inter-human-group equity. Unless systematic attempts are made to promote equity within groups of individuals, it will not be possible to organize and motivate them to participate in the process of human settlement development.

The human settlement development is a lead factor in a country's over all socio-economic progress. As such, if the nature and tempo of human settlement development becomes a characteristic of national development, the necessary formulations are laid for the country's take-off on its journey towards progress.

2.1 Human Settlement Development becomes sustainable when

- — Its income and output are produced at constant or even increasing returns to scale;
- — When its method of production can augment employment of labour without an undue diminution of its marginal product.

— When minimum levels of living are ensured to its inhabitants especially the special groups such as women, children, poor etc.

— When institutions undergo a continual renewal to maintain their relevance to the needs of the human settlements management.

— When people's attitude becomes cooperative, positive and development oriented; and finally,

— When the planning policy becomes responsive to the needs of the prople and responsible for their welfare.

Human Settlement Development is important because they contribute to the gross domestic product; they sustain exports and provide a market for imports; and they house country's agricultural and non-agricultural stock (capital). They are centers of health and education; arts and science; technology and innovation; and transport and communications. As such, a country's chances for political development hinge around variable and feasible human settlements growth.

2.2 Unfortunately however, the human settlements development is hampered by several factors :

a) gender inequality, displaced and rootless human groups and social unrest.

b) inadequacy of the capital stock to provide for their growing needs, especially housing;

c) congestion and pollution;

d) crime and corruption;

e) unemployment and low productivity of labour; and

This pathology of human settlement settlements development can be completed in two ways; one, by providing for an affective maintenance and renewal of capital stock and the other, by facilitating the augmentation of captial stock. It is argued below that housing (shelter) and other shelter related programs could provide a large part of the answer to the problems faced by human settlements, and by making women responsible for implementation and management of these programs can significantly facilitate human settlement development on sustainable basis.

2.3 Women in Human Settlement Development : Some Issues

Majority of the Indian women do not have adequate knowledge about the developmental aspects of human settlements such as the importance of environment, resource conservation etc. Lack knowledge on environment of their missusing the environment led to the problems such as ecological inequilibrium, pollution etc. Their social, economic and cultural constraints discussed earlier influence their behavioural patterns and they are reflected not only how the environment around is influencing them but what is important is how they are influencing the environment, which is vital to the sustenance of human settlement development. The resultant problems (mentioned below) are not only inter-linked but also cyclical.

2.3.1 Environment

An understanding of environmental problems is vital to planning for survival of the earth's rapidly expanding human population. Survival not only depends on how much fresh water and food.

2.3.2 Ecological Inequilibrium

Any human settlement can ecologically sustain only a minimum number of people beyond which sustaining it becomes virtually impossible. The uncontrolled population growth without concern for matching increase in resource base creates burden on their environmental capital and further on the economic development. This situation led to the problems of environmental inequilibrium and unfavourable economic conditions in which the human wants cannot be satisfied. If the importance of population control and subsequent problems of environmental inequilibrium are to be achieved, it is the women who have to be taken in to confidence not only on the issues of resource conservation and ecological inequilibrium but also about the population control measures.

2.3.3 Inefficient Resource Management

While it is not claimed that the strategy adopted by Government of India had militated against the prospects for human settlement development, it is a fair comment to say that a consideration of the cost of development and an appreciation of the relative importance of resource management and resource husbandry did not receive adequate attention. In point of fact, the Indian economy has recently come close to a collapse in her balance of payments because of the sad neglect of some elementary precautions such as limiting the size of government expenditures, and even the size of the development plan to available resources, and avoiding inflationary finances. The point arising out over here is what is reflected at national level is nothing but what was happening at household level in the resource husbandry and management.

2.3.4 Exhaustion of Non-Renewable resources

Non-renewable raw materials from forests, fossil fuels, denuded hulls, clay from fertile river banks etc. are increasingly exhausted in various activities of human settlement development. These have been extensively put to use by women due to innocence or out of the compounding necessity, thereby destroying scarce natural resources. Educating women on the importance of non-renewable energy resources and informing them the alternative sources such as solar energy would curtail the exhaustion of these resources.

2.3.5 Pollution

Instead of socio-economic development leading to balanced human settlement development, unbalanced economic development led to environmental deterioration. Such situation led to the generation of solid and liquid wastes generated by the low income groups. Further inadequacy of waste disposal capabilities and pollution cleaning/ control mechanisms led to the disposal of untreated wastes in to the ecosystem thereby causing major environmental problems like water pollution, air pollution, noise pollution etc. At a neighbourhood level these problems of pollution can be controlled by building the pressure groups preferably managed by women activists because they are the ones who have to face the brunt of the disasters caused by the pollution.

These factors led, and rightly so, to the cry of women involvement in human settlement planning. But how to promote it is the question elaborated in the remaining sections be\

SECTION - III

3.0 Shelter as a LINK between Women Development and Human Settlement Development

Shelter (housing and other building of industry and commerce) accounts for a quarter of the capital stock in the urban areas. It also accounts for over 30 per cent of national investment. That is to say, the proportion of shelter investment in the total is becoming larger over time in response to (a) population growth, and (b) the lack of shelter short fall over the years in the past. The currently achieved increases in the proportion of shelter investment in the total are grossly inadequate. They can not even provide for the growth in population, and as a result the backlog of housing shortage cannot but grow. The situation call for a substantial increase in shelter investment - the returns from which could be handsome, if only the choice of projects for such investment is judiciously made with an eye on promoting equity and meeting a socially feltneed.

Capital is the link between the present and the future, and adequate capital stock *can cetris paribus* ensure sustainability of development. Among all kinds of capital, buildings (shelter) seem important because they serve a dual purpose. At once, they meet a consumption need for shelter and an investment need for accelerated development. The employment multiplier of buildings is more often than not, the highest of all types of captial as also the re-investment quotient. A judicious development of housing (shelter) including other buildings of an industrial and commercial value could become the main plank.

Shelter is not only an economic asset, but it is a "piece of development" in itself.

The economic value of housing (shelter) is high Now and is likely to be higher as time passes:

1. A house is not merely an abode but quite often it is an income earning capital asset. Properly built houses can house not only the owner but also one or two tenants.
2. The capital value of houses appreciates, often substantially so that considerable capital gains can be derived by the owners.
3. Ownership of houses is a matter of pride for those who become new owners, and almost invariably such ownership enthuses them into a self and family improvement programme; their marginal propensity to consume is likely to shift upwards.

4. Increase and improvements of the housing stock make it possible to utilize the personal skills of the potential owners such as masonry, carpentry and planning for building houses not only for individual use but also as a professional input of the building programme on general.
5. Housing starts which are made on a planned systematic basis can release people's creative energies in a larger measure than other community activities because housing provides a concrete, usable, and socially edifying physical asset.

Shelter development helps promote human settlement development in several ways.

a) Ameliorating harsh conditions of living accommodation goes a substantial part of the way in redressing environmental and ecological problems.
b) Shelter is usually a backage and include more effective health services. As a result, there will be a decline not only of general morbidity but also in childhood diseases like diphtheria, tetanus and whooping cough.
c) Drop-outs from schools will show a declining trend, with female education becoming more popular, because of the improvement of the living conditions in human settlements and an increase in the level of their consciousness.
d) The rate of population growth in human settlements will decline not only because of an increase in individual and household income which often accompanies improved the living conditions but also because of a more ready acceptance of family practices through female education.
e) Income generation activities will grow, especially own-businesses.
f) There will be a more interested and more intensive cooperation in the delivery of public services.
g) There will be a more enthusiastic participation of the community in building community assets like roads, meeting halls and schools.

3.1 How Women and Shelter can Facilitate Human settlement Development

Equally important is providing equal opportunities to women in every walk of life. To enable that to happen, women may be involved in shelter development activites. Educating women in shelter related human settlement developmental activities, to put it briefly, is the hen that lays the golden eggs. Inter-temporal and cross-sectional studies go to show in-controvertibly and categorically that women's involvement in shelter development reduces infant mortality, reduces the total fertility rate, gives employment to women, make them into independent human beings in the sense that they attain social adulthood, in spite of the several family-and group-based constraints they suffer from. It is because shelter embodies factors in sustainable human settlement development like water supply, proper sanitation and drainage, and access to transport networks. The other variables of human development, such as health education, employment, basic infrastructure etc. are built around bousing as a pivot. The *primus inter parus* status of shelter may be explained in terms of its advantages for human development and opportunities for parallel development of institutions and organizations for human settlement development and management.

3.2 How Women can help human settlement development indirectly

An elaboration of the short statement made above on human settlement development comprises aspects of inter-personal

3.2.1 Inter-personal Equity

Human settlement development becomes sustainable when it promotes inter-personal equity by creating an environment where equal opportunities are made available for both the genders for developing themselves and also the settlements they live in. Unless systematic attempts are made to promote equity within groups of individuals in a country it will not be possible to organize and persuade them to participate in the process of human development planning. Hence inter personal equity especially the gender equity should be treated as a foundational requirement of human settlement development.

3.2.2 Steady Growth

The functioning of an economy on an even keel without major fluctuations in the pattern of sectoral outputs and their rates of growth is essential for bringing human settlement development about on a sustainable basis. A steady growth also implies that cyclical fluctations are smoothed by short term policy measures as well as long term structural changes, for which the economic at human settlement level should be strong. The economic base at human Settlement levels becomes strong only if the gender equity is ensured.

3.2.3 Balanced Regional Development

Balanced regional development is a sine-qua-non of balanced human settlement development. equity does not only relate to personal income distribution (among genders) and per capita income growth rate of different groups but also to the regional growth rates, and their congruence to the volume of inter-regional transactions. unbalanced human settlement development can lead to spatial and functional distortions in the socio-economic profile of the country such that the interests of future development are given a go-by in trying to cope with the economic pathology thrown up by unbalanced regional development. It need no elaboration to say that the same thing applies to balanced human development among gender's.

3.2.4 Self-Reliance

Self-reliance is not a point which is based on the relationship between exports and imports. it is more a schedule related to the success of the country in promoting human settlement development. As a country becomes more successful in promoting continuous growth without prejudice to its resource base, the nature of self-reliance will undergo a change. So much so, a dependence on external resources which might currently imply a negation of self-reliance will, with the onset and advance of human sustainable settlement development, become consistent with self-reliance due the very momentum of growth and its congruence to the needs of the people. no matter how the factor of self-reliance is viewed, either as a point in time or a schedule over time, adherence to it as a national policy promotes habits of thrift and economy in resource use which, among others, guarantees sustainable human settlement development.

3.2.5 Raising Productivity of Women

Employment, nutrition, health, education and economic information are the best guarantors of raising the productivity of the women. Studies made in regard to the productivity of labour which has underfed, as well as studies relating to the elimination of food deficiency in the developing countries go to show that the fulfillment of the basic needs can significantly raise the productivity of the women. A ten per cent increase in the productivity of the women can contribute a 3 to 5 per cent rise in the national income (provided adequate productive employment opportunities are created), while at the same time laying the base for sustainable development. The women work mostly with their labour and rather simple technology neither of which makes exhaustive demands on the resource base. On the contrary, raising the productivity of the women can, more often than not, raise resource productivity also.

SECTION - IV

4.0 Enabling Strategies for Women in Human Settlement Development in general and Human Development of Women in Particular

A coherent and well-coordinated strategy of sustainable development has not yet been enunciated, but its contours seems to be emerging, and a consensus is slowly developing around the major elements of the strategy.

4.1.1 Population Planning

Population planning is vital to human settlement development. An addition of hundred million people every year to the world's population poses problems of food, resource management, employment, health, and education which the country is not geared to cope with. For instance, India adds to its population every year a Malaysia. It is ideal to expect under such a population growth milieu that the country would be able to feed, clothe, preserve, and employ its labour productiviely and gainfully. The additional income growth rate is eaten up by the additional population. It is a situation aptly described by the saying that "what is gained in the swings, is lost in the round abouts." The result has been a persistence of poverty in growing numbers.

4.1.2 Family Planning

There is no denying that countries everywhere are aware of the population problem, but their approach to its solution is neither wise nor realistic. Targets are fixed for contraceptive coverage of couples; but such targets come into force only after the first two or three children are born to a couple. The result has been that by the time woman accepts the contraceptive at the age of thirty or so, the damage has already been done. Preoccupation with the arbitrarily set targets of contraceptive coverage has been the bane of population policy everywhere. Because of such a pre-occupation, the socio-economic and the humanitarian considerations in population planning given a go-by. Family planning has become a bother for the individual, if not a matter of resentment. The shift in policy, in order for it to succeed, should be such that family planning becomes a pleasant exercise rather than a social or government compulsion.

4.1.3 Resouce Management

Development of human settlement cannot be sustained with the resources candle being burned at both ends as under a regime of profligate consumption and irresponsible investment whereby projects are played by time and cost-overruns. While most definitively resources such as building materials (cement, steel, stone etc.) have to be used as an input of development, the use of resources will have to be efficient in terms of costs and also effective in terms of attaining the ojectives of the sustainable human settlement development programme. The demand for resources either by the government or individuals should be tempered by considerations of resource management with a view to providing for the future.

4.1.4 Energy Planning

Of equal importance with population planning is energy planning as an aspect of the strategy for human settlement development. It is well known that the finite stocks of petroleum would swiftly decline in the 21 st century, the rate of their decline being a function of the proven reserves and the acceleration in the demand for their use. every one knows that the Sun is the father of energy. But solar energy is harnessed only on an experimental basis. Though to a very small extent, encouraging women in using solar cooker and smoke less chullahs as a part of conservation practice go long way in human settlement development. Using solar energy for developmental purposes would be a powerful booster of sustainable settlement development in the long run.

4.1.5 Recycling, Renewal, Rebuilding and Redeployment of Resources

The older values of thrift and husbandry, both at the level of the family and the government, should be encouraged in order to provide a lasting foundation for sustainable human settlement development. As a part of promoting such attitudes and values, recycling, renewal, rebuilding and redeployment should be given a high priority in economic decision-making, both among the private individuals and the government. The art and practice of recycling has got to be spread far and wide as a first step in the conservation of resources. Recycling not only cuts costs but also greatly aids in removing debris and thus acts as an anti-pollution agent. An example of wide visibility in India is the women rag-pickers. A national rag picking mentality is not to be laughed at in the context and interests of sustainable human development.

4.1.6 Maintenance and Replacement of Assets

Almost as a part of the recycling ethic a practice of providing for maintenance and replacement of assets on a nation-wide basis is a key element of the strategy of sustainable human settlement development. In this area, the developing countries are the worst offenders. They build but do not preserve; they erect but do not sustain; they create but do not maintain. Probably this is one important where women can play a vital role. The attendant disabilities of the low forest cover are many and varied. Droughts become more extensive and more frequent; flooding increase progressively; soil erosion takes place at a phenomenal rate; desertification envelops wider and still wider area and pollution rises and becomes more insidious without the influence of chlorophyll. In fact, development Policy should be concerned not only with the need for physical capital formation but with the maintenance and augmentation of the inputs for physical capital which, by and large, happen to be the natural resources. Though the order of their importance might decrease with the spread of technology, no one can gainsay the need for improving the quality, and where possible, the quantity of natural resources.

4.1.7 Gender ineauality and Development

Fighting gender inequality is an aspect of the strategy of human settlement development. It has a global significance. Equally importantly, women's development in general can made a tremendous contribution to human settlement development. Human settlement development is predicated on the well-being of the women. Subsidies aimed at alleviating sufferings of the women are not generally defensible. A large part of the amount of subsidy ends up in the wrong hands, and even where a part of the subsidy goes to the intended beneficiaries, they might become addicted to it with the result that their motivation and initiative to develop are stifled. The important thing to ensure in the women development programs is an upward movement of the productivity of the women. The women need capital; they need technology; and they need markets; and they need organization. Most of women development programs do not adopt a comprehensive attitude towards these four elemental requirements. Even more important than fulfilling the basic needs of the women is the provision of these essentials. If the women are enabled to earn increased income through an Important of their productive capacity, they themselves can pay for food, health, education, and other necessities. Hence a programme of organizing the women for higher productivity can not only provide a sustained flow of income to these people but through their increased productivity can guarantee sustainable national development in the future. Promoting social adulthood of women can also produce a substantial and lasting national asset. For instance, if the rural women are freed four hours a day-the time which they now spend on fetching water and fuel-there would be scope for creative investment of the same length of time in optional activities which are after all the pith and substance of development.

The need for subsidies cannot be denied entirely. In dealing with the destitute and other starkly poor groups direct subsidies are the only means (a kind of negative income tax) which stand between them and extinction. But such subsidies need not always be only at the expense of the state. The regional or local community can handle a part of them. Where ultimately the need for the state to intervene arises, subsidies can be directly administered by the government.

4.1.8 Community Support

Sustainable human settlement development also contains a strong commitment to the widest possible public participation. Effective and comprehensive human settlement management requires the mobilization and involvement of all those who can contribute to solutions, all those whose interests are affected, and all those whose cooperation is necessary for a successful implementation of the related policy and projects. This is not a task which can be accomplished by 'government' alone. Instead, the public sector, the private sector and the community and non-governmental organizations should be involved. The objective of such cooperative participation would help to achieve "economic efficiency in the use of devlopment resources; social equity in the distribution of development benefits and costs; and avoidance of unnecessary foreclosure of future development options".

4.2 Strategy to promote Human Development of Women as part of Human Settlement planning

Women's education should receive a far greater emphasis. Not only does their education help from human captial of a greater efficiency and higher quality that would powerfully contribute to family welfare through a more humane regulation of human birth rate than the existing population control programs do. There is ample evidence that women's education is conducive to a lower fertility rate and a reduced infant mortality rate.

Women's health should receive far more attention than it does at present. Maternity and child health should be cardinal element of primary health care. Vastly more resources than at present should be earmarked for primary health care and within it to women's health.

A sustained effort should be made to increase women's optional time. The immediate need is to emancipate women from the drudgery of fetching fuel and water. Firewood plantations in villages, bio-gas development, and facilitating drinking water supply, should be undertaken on a warfooting. Such initiatives, if sincerely undertaken, will have vast indirect effect on human development as well as national development in general.

As a matter of social action for the upliftment of women, girls in the age group of 15 through 19 should be given specialized and specific training in matters related to sex and child-bearing, and the need for spacing children at long enough intervals so as to keep the birth rate in check and protect the health of young mothers. A separate training programme should be undertaken for the mother-in-law with a view to changing their attitude to the newly acquired daughters-in-law. At the same time the women's movements should focus on promoting nuclear families in the place of joint families.

Women in India, as elsewhere, should attain their 'adult-hood' by which is meant they should be economically and socially independent in order to play an equal role with men in national affairs. This is one of the surest recipes for an accelerated development of the country, informed at once by gender equity in play.

In government service, at different cadres, the same reservation formula should apply. Even in the existing reservation provision, women should occupy 30 per cent of the positions.

CHAPTER-16

Women and Human Habitat

Susmita Bhatt

Introduction

Food, clothings and shelter have been three basic needs of human existence upon which depends any measurement of quality of material life. Ever since the dawn of human civilization these three have been taken to be the parameters of material advancement of any society. No doubt human needs and aspirations are not confined to material wellbeing alone, but they do constitute the very foundation upon which the intellectual and spiritual enhancement is grounded.

In any human settlement planning it is necessary to take a comprehensive and integrated view of different dimensions of human existence and attempts should be made to ensure fulfilment of minimum basic needs in a balanced way. In this context the notion of human habitat becomes highly pertinent and significant. Here again it should be remembered that the notion of human habitat should not be viewed separately or in isolation from over-all natural habitat, housing animals, plants and other inanimate phenomena with all of which human existence is inseparably and intricately related and on which alone human existence is inevitably dependent.

Though in India the history of human habitat planning goes back to the vedic times and Indus valley civilization and we have evidences of developed sciences live vastu shashtra, shilpa shashtra, Nagar Rachna Shashtra, Manasara etc., the need and requirement of such a planning has become a matter of alarming necessity in the modern times. It is not that we are not aware of this necessity, or that there is lack of knowledge, skill, expertise or even availability of resources but what is miserably missing is a will and a preparedness on our part. There is a passing on of the buck in a vicious circle from the government agencies to the NGOs and conversely from the NGOs and conversely from the NGOs to the government agencies resulting in increasing degradation of the eco-systems under the impact of haphazard and reckless human settlements involving damaging land, water, air, sound and space pollutions This is more so in the urban sprawl where there are limited and depleting resources and increasing demands.

Unprecedented population growth, unplanned industrialisation, unregulated urbanisation, misdirected technology coupled with human selfishness have caused environmental hazards jeopardising physical, social, moral, cultural, aesthetic and spiritual well-being of human kind, demeaning the very existence of human beings, what to say of quality of life.

It is not that many of us are not conscious or even painfully aware of all this, but all of us seem to be passive and helpless spectators witnessing the spectacle in bewilderment. But human kind lives by hopes alone and let us hope that our wish for a normal or ideal human habitat may not remain a more utopean dream and a blue-print on the paper. Let us hope that the wings of will may get attached to our wish and stimulate human endeavour to realise this dream even though in a faltering way, as something is better than nothing.

The notion of habitat, as we have pointed out earlier, is highly complex and multidimensional involving human beings, animals, plants and inanimate objects, all of which are inter-dependent. Within human habitat, again, there are multiple facets, involving a complex and integrated network of housing, health and sanitation, community services and civil suppliers, communication and transport, educational and recreational facilities, places of worship and spiritual discourses etc. catering both to the individual and social life of the human being. In the modern context human habitat is linked with every thing which is necessary to ensure a good standard of living.

Role of Women

In human society women play central and foundational roles of multiple types. To ignore their contribution or to belittle it is to lose a vital human resource in the development process. The advancement of women therefore, is a necessary pre-condition for the development of society as a whole. No society can be considered as developed if half of its population is not able to contribute to and benefit fully and equally from the achievements of its objectives. This is the reason why development projects which tend to ignore women's needs and contributions have often failed, as wastage or misuse of half of human resources have detrimental effects on human enterprises. These projects not only point out the inequality meted out to women, they also under scrore the need for women to have the same opportunities as men. Incapacitating or preventing women from improving their existential situation, Living Conditions, and from participating fully in social and national development programmes have always resulted in backwardness, retrogation and pathology,

It is happy augury that in recent times there is a growing awareness of the significance and need of the role of women and there is an increasing assignment to the women's participation.

Since the beginning in 1976 of the United Nations Decade for women considerable amount of work has been done in the developing and developed countries on how to bring women in the mainstream of economic and social development. This work which is extra-ordinary in both quantity and quality has led to creating an environment where in the developing countries have begun to realise, admit and recognise that the status of these women - folk is extremely low and subordinate and that it is a major source of their underdevelopment.

As the programmes for the International decade progressed, the role of women has received increasing focus and recognition. At the 'World Conference to Review and Appraise the United Nations Decade for Women: Equality, Development and peace' held at Nairobi in July, 1985 a 'Joint statement on women and settlements' was adopted. This statement drew attention to the poor condition of women in slums and squatter settlements, to problems faced by single, divorced, widowed and abandoned women and mothers and to the need for governmental and other agencies to take appropriate measures through legislation and other means to ensure equal opportunities for women with respect to access to housing, land and security of tenure as well as access to credits and loans for shelter improvement.

Women and Housing

Housing has always been a focul point of human settlement. Acquisition of adequate shelter is a life - time ambition of people throughout the world. Some achieve this objective early in life, some during their life time but some fail to do so. Possession of a home provides, above all, dignity and roots for a family. For the poor it can also be a location for Income - generating activities or a base entering into the world of entrepreneurship. House-owning serves the physical, psychological, aesthetic, social and vocational needs of human being and provides a sense of settlement to his or her existence.

In a house landlady is the central figure. It is she who turns the shelter in a home and is responsible for setting-up all the family's survival system, food, water, health and education. Even though employed outside, most of the times she has to stay indoors and on her lies the responsibility of house-upkeeping.

Even though women plays pivotal role in house-keeping, she is rarely consulted in the planning of the house, particularly the kitchen, which needs to be constructed as per her comforts, convenience and requirements. A well-ventilated house with proper sanitation, clean surroundings and adequate facilities for waste disposal are the basic considerations which meet with the housing requirements of women as they have to suffer the most from their absence. Not only they have to spend most of the time within the home, it is they who must nurse the house - inmates, both grown up and children when fall sick because of the non-sanitary conditions within and around the house, it is unfortunate that millions of women are forced to live in slums and squatter settlements and raise their families is sordid misery. They bear most of the brunt of all the problems which arise from the lack of adequate shelter and supporting services. This apart in many of such poor households women have to be the main bread-earner as their men-folk are either vagabound or extravagant or drunkards who spend most or all of their earnings on themselves. As a consequence their women are forced to use their houses for income-generating activities leading to inconvenience.

For a women to own a house is a matter of necessity. It provides not only a psychological satisfaction or a sense of settlement and permanence, it also gives a social security to a woman. If she owns a house in her name she can partly be independent in monetary terms. Since she is not to pay rent for not staying in a rented accommodation, house-owning is an asset as well.

Except in a few cases of employed women and in cases of families having huge properties, there is no practice of having a house in the name of a women. There is a need for a change in our psychology and social custom. Patriarchical form of our society is responsible for this situation as the ownership passes on to sons only and daughters are generally denied share in parental properties.

There are some other advantages also in women's ownership of house. In those families where male is a drunkard he may have the tempation of to sell movable properties but it may not be easy to sell a house. Likewise, in situations of emergency like loss of husband a woman can find support if she owns a house. The same thing holds good in old age also. Thus house-owning is a part - substitude of the disintegrating joint-family system as it provides a sort of social security.

Importance of Women's Participation

There are three main reasons for advocating the incorporation of women's participation in the execution of housing projects:—

(a) Women's participation is an end in itself:

Women, as much as men, have the right and duty to participate in the execution of projects which profoundly affect their lives. Since women, as wives and mothers, discharge primary responsibility for child bearing and rearing, they are most affected by housing and settlement projects. They should, therefore, be involved in the planning and decision-making as well as in the implementaion and management of projects which relate particularly to their lives.

(b) Women's participation is a means to improve project results:

Since women have a particular responsibility for the welfare of the household, they are the primary users of housing. They, therefore, are better aware than men of the most urgent, needs for infrastructure and services and are also more committed to the success of a project-which improves living conditions in settlement. Their active involvement in the project can often improve the outcome, a project will respond to the perceived needs and priorities of women in housing and settlement planning.

(c) Participation in housing activities stimulate women's participation in other spheres of life:

Through active involvement in housing projects, women may be encouraged to participate fully in the community, help them to overcome apathy and lack of confidence, and it can make women visible in the community. It can enable women to come out of their houses and show them the potential of self-help solutions. In so doing, it may raise awareness that women can play an important role in solving problems in the community.

In the formulation of shelter policies two aspects of women's participation are essential. First is the direct participation of women in formulating such policies so that their needs and requirements get reflected in them. The second is the inclusion of gender-specific considerations in the policy formulation. For example, women's participation in housing and town planning may get incorporation of five types of housing for different categories as follows:—

(a) Housing for single woman

(b) Housing for distressed woman

(c) Housing for aged woman

(d) Housing for disabled woman

(e) Housing for working woman

Global strategy for shelter

The Global strategy for shelter upto the year 2000 (GSS) was adopted by the United Nations General Assembly in its resolution 43/181 of 23, December 1988. Its principal objectives are:—

— To facilitate shelter for all by the year 2000;

— To focus on improving the situation of the disadvantaged and the poor.

The following fundamental principles form the basis of the strategy:—

(a) Enabling policies, in which the full potential and resources of all governmental and non governmental actors in the field of human settlements are utilized, must be at the heart of national and international efforts:

(b) Shelter and development are mutually supportive and interdependent, and policies must be developed in full recognition of the important links between shelter and economic development:

(c) The concept of sustainable development implies that shelter provision and urban development must be reconcilable with sustainable management or resources and within national economic institutional capacities;

(d) Women and women's organisations - fill a crucial role as contributors to the solution of human settlements problems which should be fully recognized and reflected in equal participation of women in the elaboration of housing policies, programmes and projects, and the specific interests and capabilities of women should be adequately represented at all levels of planning, implementing, monitoring and evaluating of housing policies, programmes and projects.

For the first time in history, the forward looking strategies, adopted at the 1985 World Conference to Review and Appraise the United Nations Decade for Women, made specific calls to governments to integrate women's concerns in the formulation of policies and programmes for the provision of basic shelter and infrastructure. Since then, UNCHS (Habitat) has actively promoted women as agents of change and beneficiaries in the area of human settlements. The process initiated by UNCHS (Habitat) is directed at :—

(a) Involving women at all levels of formulation and implementation of human settlements policies and programmes;

(b) Improving women's access to credit for both property ownership and business development;

(c) Protecting and improving women's shelter tenure;

(d) Opening up employment opportunities for women at all levels of the human settlements sector;

(e) Improving the residential environment of women, especially low-income women, their families and their communities.

Women, health and family welfare

Health is the real foundation upon which human happiness and development rest. Women's health status is basic to their advance in all fields of endeavour. Any serious attempt to improve the health of women must deal firstly with biased social customs and cultural traditions that have an impact on their health status. The cultural norms that specially affect women's health are the attitudes to marriage, age of marriage, the value attached to fertility and sex of the child, the pattern of family organisation and the ideal role demanded of women by social conventions. They determine her place within the family, the degree of her access to medical care, education, nutrition, and other accessories of health.

Women face high risk of malnutrition, retardation in growth and development, disease, disability and even death at three critical stages in their lives, viz, infancy, early childhood and adolescence and the reproductive phase. In old age, they face threats of cancer-breast cancer and uterus cancer-and-menopause related problems.

The Indian women on an average has 8-9 pregnancies, resulting in a little over six live births, of which 4-5 survive. She is estimated to spend 80 percent of her reproductive years in pregnancy and lactation.

Dietary surveys have shown that the intake of women is low income groups is deficient by 500 to 600 calories. The corresponding findings for pregnant and lactating women reveal daily deficiency of 1100 calories and 1000 calories respectively. Over 50 percent of pregnant women have a haemoglobin level of less than 10 grams. Anaemia in pregnancy accounts directly for 15-20 percent of all maternal deaths in India and indirectly for a much larger population.

Women and Poverty

The role of women in the urban areas, particularly their role in poverty alleviation which is one of the most formidable problem currently facing the urban areas of the developing countries, has received comparatively minor attention. In the context of the urban areas, some work has been done to highlight the discrimination that women are subjected to particularly in respect of their access to the labour market, but questions such as whether women help in the reduction of poverty in the urban areas; in what ways do women help in reducing poverty; what exactly do women do in the urban poor households; what is the impact of women's work on the levels of literacy, health, nutrition etc; are women able to take advantage of the development programmes to the benefit of families they belong to; and in what way are the families where women work different from those where women do not work, have not been directly and systematically adressed in the work done during the women's Decade.

It is in the context of increasing urban poverty that the developing countries have begun to ask whether 'women' who constitute 50 percent of the total number of the poor have any role in the reduction of poverty, and if so in what way can they be enabled to play that role more effectively and efficiently.

A very large number of programmes and initiatives have been taken both to reduce the incidence of poverty and to involve the women into the mainstream of socio-economic development and to enhance their contribution of national welfare. There are two streams of initiatives - first related to poverty alleviation, and the second to women's development,

In the first stream all programmes like the Urban Basic Programmes, Self Employment Programme for the urban poor, Housing for the economically weaker sections and Environmental Improvement of urban slums. All these programmes are neutral to gender except the Urban Basic Services Programme which is particularly designed to reach more women and children who are more disadvantaged among the urban poor households.

The second stream consists of a large variety of programmes like Training and skill upgradation, access of poor women to basic services. Training and skill upgradation constitute a major plank of the development initiatives that have been taken so far to reach and benefit the urban poor women. Evidently, this plank assumes that training is necessary to bring urban poor women into the mainstream of socio-economic development. Improving access of poor women to basic services (water supply, sanitation, primary health and education) is also a major development initiative that takes note of the needs of particularly the urban poor women.

But most of these programmes are not reaching to majority of them are in case they one reaching them it is not so in an effective and efficient manner. There is an urgent need to take some initiative by good NGOs, government agencies, planners and policy makers to develop strategies or policies to involve women's participation in decision-making and other important activities.

Women and Employment

According to the census of India 1981 only 8.3 percent of the total females in the urban areas are economically active, the balance, by implication, do not "work" and make no contributions to the national economy.

Another feature of female's work which is no less disturbing lies in the casual nature of their jobs and employment. According to the National Sample survey, an estimated 28 percent of the total female workers are "casually" employed, and another 45 percent are in the category of "self-employed:.

In Situations where families cannot survive on the wages of the male head of the household, women have to contribute whatever they can to the family budget. Women who are heads of households have to earn an income for the entire family. If they have no employment openings within the settlement or if land-use regulations do not allow income-earning activities in residential areas, these women are forced to look outside the neighbourhood for work. This often causes severe hardship for the children who are left on their own. Therefore in comparison, the incidence of casualisation is low among male workers, as compared to females, as given in Table below :—

Percentage Distribution of Workers According to usual status of employment categories,

Employment Categeries	urban					
	Male			Female		
	1972-73	1977-78	1983-84	1972-73	1977-78	1983-84
Wage employment	50.69	46.41	44.58	27.89	24.94	26.23
Non wage-Employment:						
(a) Self Employment	39.25	40.38	40.67	48.40	49.47	46.50
(b) Casual Employment	10.06	13.21	14.75	23.71	25.51	27.27

Women's earnings as a share of family incomes are extremely significant, and, if these are excluded from the family earnings at least 23 percent of the low income households would plunge deep into the state of poverty. Nearly 30 percent of the working women contribute as much as 26-50 percent of the family incomes, indicating a very high degree of dependence of these families on women's earnings and work. For11 percent of the households, women's earnings are the only source of survival, these households being the female headed households. Seven percent of working women have no independent income as they work together with the other members of the households. The surveys also revealed that where women participate in a joint endeavour with men of the household, there is a greater likelihood that the income is controlled by the men which is often not spent on the essentials. Thus the need to reach women with opportunities to earn independent income is important.

Contribution of Female (+15 years) to the monthly Household Incomes

Contribution of females to Household Incomes	percentage of Households
1-25	43.20
26-50	32.04
51-75	5.80
76-90	0.84
91-100	11.06
No Independent Income	7.06

Women do mainly unskilled work and are not organised; they are domestic servants or are invloved in petty commercial activities because of illiteracy and their responsibility for domestic work, child bearing and rearing. They are usually paid less than men for the same kind of work. In order to make a living, they,therefore, have to work more hours per day than men and are generally not protected by social security.

Usually women are also involved in the construction process, but in a supportive manner. They tend to carry out 'secondary' chores; fetching and carrying wetting bricks, mixing mortar, passing tools, cleaning up the tools and providing male partners with food merely as an intensification of their routine domestic duties. Women frequently deny that they have any role to play in the construction sector.

There is an urgent need to design and inplement strategies which could permit women for economic activities in their houses; such as shop-keeping and renting of rooms. This would (a) allow women to combine economic activities with their domestic roles, (b) allow families to increase their total income, (c) provide women with a source of independent in-come, and (d) lead to a housing solution for female-headed households which cannot afford to buy land or property, (e) create confidence and give full exposure to women as to how to deal with the outside world.

Women and Access to Credit

Women have had no traditional access to capital assets or to institutional finance and credit for housing. If they do not have a savings account, they will often also have problems obtaining a loan from a bank for their composite credit needs (shelter construction, repairs, consumption, emergency, social purposes, income-generation, asset creation, working capital etc.). They have to resort to borrowing from traditional credit sources at exorbitant rates of interest.

In addition, they have to face such problems as lack of information about credit programmes, low and irregular incomes, lack of collateral, complicated loan application procedures, discrimination on the part of male bureaucrats, high interest rates and lack of legal-standing in certain areas. Formal banking and financial institutions are increasingly reluctant to advance credit to women because of the fear of non-repayment. But the fact is that willingness to pay is a vital ingredient for successful cost-recovery, and women appear to be more reliable than from experience it has come to be established that women are more responsive and more willing to repay their loan. Men as compared to women treat the repayment issue more casually and are less strong. Therefore, there is a need of the change of psychology on the part of bankers and money lending institutions. In recent times various agencies have come out to play an intermediary role in creating access for women to institutional credit but their reach has been limited. It may however be hoped that soon there will be an improvement in the situation.

Women and low-income settlements

In many low-income settlements women, constitute almost half of the adult population. Because they are responsible for child bearing and rearing, they have to spend the entire day in their houses and in the neighbourhood. Moreover, because they have their domestic duties they are the primary users of the infrastructunal facilities in the settlement.

The crucial role women can play in the development of the settlement is rarely recognized by the planning authorities and by male sections of the community due to a gender blindness. Gender blindness is a failure by the authorities to recognize that men and women may have different needs and priorities. Consequently, despite their importance as users, women often participate much less than men in the execution of low-income housing projects. When they do participate, their contribution is often not sufficiently acknowledged.

Sites-and-services projects aim to provide shelter for those people who are too poor to afford 'conventional' housing but not so poor that they will be unable to make regular repayments for land, housing and services. Usually, eligible families need to have an income greater than that of the poorest 10 percent of the population. As a result, women are frequently excluded from the target group of sites-and-services projects.

Women and Infra-Structure

Without adequate infrastructure like clean water, sanitation facilities etc. domestic labour is very heavy and can cause severe physical and emotional strain for the women.

Access to clean water and fuel is yet another need. In villages in west Bengal it was observed that women spent over half the day (15 hours) in household chores of which nearly 2 hours were spent in fetching water and fuel. Household chores were so time consuming that they denied access to community life. Massive deforestation in many regions is making this worse as women have to walk greater distances.

The provision of sanitation has an extremely low priority because the burden of work related to hygiene falls on women and because men, unlike women, do not require the same privacy in order to perform ablutions. Women who do not have adequate private toilets are relieving themselves before sunrise and after sunset, which can cause severe medical problems. In the slums, low-income women are equally in need of private toilets, otherwise they have to perform their ablutions in isolated spots in which they are particularly vulnerable to rape and molestation.

The same kind of problem they are facing in case of storage of garbage. Women usually find ways to cope with deficiencies in absence of infrastructure and services, but these solutions are often time-consuming and tire-some. Women take their laundry outside the settlement to wash it in rivers or storage tanks; they dump and/or burn their garbage at great distances from their houses. This work and the lack of time prevent them from attending to all other necessary household chores and from participating in community activities.

Women and Communication

Communications are systems, methods or means of transferring, transmitting, transporting or disseminating information; as such they are infrastructure consisting of roads, telephone network etc.

Information consists of knowledge or data. Communication is the transfer of information. It is, at the same time, a social process by which information is transferred from a sender to a receiver in order to influence the knowledge, opinion, attitudes and/or behaviour of the latter. This influence can aim to change attitudes, behaviour etc. or to reinforce existing ones. Senders and receivers can be individuals, groups, organisations or other collectivities.

Ensuring equality between women and men, and increasing the effiectiveness of the participation of women in society, requires basic structural and attitudinal changes. It also requires the attainment of a balance in social, economic and political power between the two sexes. Traditional perceptions and attitudes are often major constraints in the process of such a change. To eliminate these perceptions and attitudes, women and women's groups have strengthened their communication activities.

Despite the realization of the importance of communications in shaping the image of women in society, efforts to use communication as an input to policy, as a device to bring women's voices into development planning, and as a means to facilitate the contributions of women to development activities have thus far received secondary importance.

On the whole, the reach of mass media in India is rather limited especially in rural areas, among women and slum dwellers. This is mainly due to four mutually reinforcing factors. These are:—

— Low literacy

— Low purchasing power (about 40 percent of the population lives below poverty line).

— Poor means of transportation for timely delivery of news papers, or maintenance of radio T.V. sets; and

— Lack of relevant information.

Women are particularly deprived of such information; they neither have information of settlement's conditions, nor on opportunities that might be available to them to improve their living conditions. Also lacking information on alternative actions that they can take, women often fail to voice their problems and formulate their demands. This deficiency in the settlements field is partialty being remedied by recent activities of women's organisations; but, their current efforts are rather marginal and are confined to the Compilation and dissemination of information on women's legal entitlements, credit opportunities and organisational matters.

When settlements development efforts aim at enhancing the participation of women in settlements management; the accompanying development support communication may assume the following objectives :—

(a) create awareness of the multiple roles women play in the development and management of settlements; raise consciousness of the need to ensure full participation of women in settlements management as beneficiaries and contributors;

(b) Develop and re-inforce positive and favourable images of women in settlements management;

(c) Change unfavourable, stereotypical images of women which hinder an adequate policy response to their needs and which prevent the participation of women in the sector as planners, decision-makers, professionals, and skilled and semi-skilled workers;

(d) Create or increase a willingness among policy-makers, private employers, local leaders, communities, development specialists, and among women and men, for positive and sustained action, including education and training, to ensure equitable participation of women in settlements policies as beneficiaries and contributors;

(e) Stimulate action and co-operation between central and local governments, non-governmental organisations, communities and individuals to facilitate the participation of women in settlements management.

Women and Education

Women's level of education is considerably lower than that of men. Consequently, rates of female illiteracy is rather high. Inspite of concerted efforts to improve the enrolment of girls by complusory primary education and to provide adult education for women, their educational status is still far from satisfactory. Female enrolment in educational institutions is low as compared with males and drop-out rates are high. As per the 1981 census, 75 percent of women are illiterate. This is compounded by the high dropout rate for girls which is estimated at 55.5 percent at the primary stage and 77.7 percent at the middle school stage. Enrolment of girls in higher education has been almost static from1975 to 1985. There are also substantial disparities in the enrolment of girls and boys at the university stage, and in technical and professional colleges.

The Programme of Action of the National Policy on Education (1986) lays stress on women's equality and has identified for the first time three areas for special attention viz ;—

(i) review of school text books to remove sexist bias and developing approaches to promotion of the value of equality through school curricula;

(ii) re-orientation of teachers to promote gender equality through their teaching and

(iii) Increasing the coverage of women and women's issues in the research and teaching activities of higher education.

Issues in women's education are not issues only of educational sector, but they extend to issues of environment, employment, production processes. Indeed, the entire gamut of social and economic policy has a bearing on women's education. In urban areas, by and large, there is a greater acceptance of its need than in rural areas. Some other factors responsible for low enrolment are:—

(i) The requirement for older girls to stay at home to take care of siblings when mothers are away at work;

(ii) Need for girls to work in order to help in augmenting the family income;

(iii) Early marriage of girls;

(iv) Social customs that hinder female mobility after puberty;

(v) Lack of relevance of school curriculum, and

(vi) Lack of facilities in the form of school buildings, hostels and women teachers etc.

Women & Legislation

The struggle for legal equality has been one of the major concerns of the women's movement all over the world. A central theme of the women's movement has been violence against women, both in their homes and outside, and directly linking it to their unequal positions in a patriarchal society, and cutting across both class and community.

Since the establishment of the United Nations, legislation to eliminate discrimination against women has been an important area of progress. Starting with the charter of the United Nations, many international instruments have aimed at improving the status of women. These improvements, while not dealing systematically with the status of women within the settlements sector, dealt, neverthless, with settlements issues through their focus on such matters as women's employment, access to credit, social issues (dowery, rape etc.), and property ownership. Through a large number of international instruments, working conditions were regulated to reduce discrimination against women.

Women and women's orgainsations have networked and communicated within and across national boundaries to ensure equal legal status. Greater efforts have to be made to inform women of their rights and there is a need to make some changes in the legislation to have it more effective. For this purpose what is required is that :—

(a) It must be known by women who are to benefit from it;

(b) It has to be understood and accepted by both women and men;

(c) Mechanism must exist for its enforcement. These mechanisms includes institutional and organisational provisions, the willingness of law enforcement personnel and the ability of women to demand remedy if deprived of opportunities provided by such legislations.

Suggestions

Having discussed the concept of Human Habitat in relation to women a few suggestions may be put forth for improving the lot of women is this respect:

— From time to time govt. designed and implemented different programmes, plans and strategies but most of them have failed because of some drawbacks in designing and lack of devotion, enthusiasm and dedication on the part of the implmenting officers. There is an urgent need that good NGOs should come forward to help the women.

—There is a strong need for a strategy that focuses on and enlists the full participation of women because no one is more committed to changing the wretched conditions of poor families than women themselves.

— Studies have been done and from experiences it has come to be established that women are more hard worker, sincere and responsible, but they are not aware of their rights and capabilities. More and more non-governmental organisations should come forward and help them is forming Community Based Organisations (CBOs) which in turn should collectively solve some of their problems and help each other in solving community related problems like water, sanitation, housing etc.

— In India at least 80% of females are illiterate. They can neither read nor write. They are not aware of their rights and are not exposed to outside world. It is necessary to change the present education policy both formal and non-formal and design some more liberal policies which will generate confidence among females towards education.

—Appropriate training is always necessary to give innovative ideas and skills to people to perform any task. The training of women is also very important for two reasons:-

(i) Most of the females who are engaged in employment market are working in informal sector as domestic servants, construction workers etc. because they lack skills. Training should be given to them to increase their skills and employment opportunities.

(ii) Skills training can build up spirit of self-reliance and solidarity among women. It can also raise awareness and generate confidence.

—Information is lacking at both national and local levels about the acute problems women face in access to education, health care, nutrition, water, sanitation, employment, finance, shelter, contribution of women in settlement, difficulties which are faced by them in negotiating with powerful landlords, their contribution in uplifting the family and national development. Therefore, information and communication system should be so geared to give priority to their needs and potentials.

— Houses should be so constructed as to enable women to have house based earnings through self-employment or cottage industry. The geographical location of the house should also be conducive to the maximum use of their earning potential.

— Deptt. of women's affairs, ministry of urban affairs, ministry of rural affairs, etc. Should work as nodel agencies to wordinate efforts of urban-rural housing boards (HUDCO, NABARD, NHB, etc.), national and international agencies.

— While constructing houses and providing infrastructure facilities, needs and priorities of females are neglected and due attention is not given. More and more females should be given professional training as architect, so that they can design and help in constructing houses according to their needs and requirements.

Without the full mobilization and participation of women and the removal of obstacles to their full participation, the goal of improving the status of women cannot and will not be met.

While concluding it can be said that let us help nature to help us so that it can serve our needs adequately. Nature has made both males and females without any distinction. There fore, male people do not have any right to stop realisation of the rights of women. Let us help them to come up, grow and help in nation's development. Let every flower enjoy the cur it breathes.

Bibliography

1. Community Participation in health and family welfare: innovative experiences in India - Dr. Ashok Sahni & Dr. Sudha Xirasagar
2. Focus on women - United Nations Centre for Human Settlement (Habitat), Nairobi
3. Communication Development and women's participation in human settlements management - Mine Subuncuoglu, United Nations Centre for Human Settlements, Nairobi
4. Shelter: From projects to National Strategies, International year of shelter for the homeless-United Nations Centre for Human Settlements, Nairobi
5. Global Strategy for shelter to the year 2000: Sub-regional seminars to support national action —United Nations Centre for Human Settlement, Nairobi
6. The Role of women in the execution of low-income housing projects—United Nations Centre for Human Settlement, Nairobi
7. National Perspective Plan for women - 1988-2000 A.D. —Deptt. of women & child development, Ministry of Human Resource Development, Govt. of India.
8. World Population situation 1993-UNFPA Publication.
9. Women, Urban Poverty and Economic development—National Institute of Urban Affairs
10. Slum Habitat : Hyderabad slum improvement project Edited by H.V. Bijlani & Prodipto Roy.
11. Women and development : R.K. Sapru
12. Women's Rights —M.J. Antony

CHAPTER-17

Indian Women and The House

Anjali Krishan

The women; a house maker is a revelation and elevation of the lives of women, who performed the tasks that Indian have considered central to the survival of its culture. In the early times gender roles were defined by tradition, if not by written code. Most Indian were farmers and women performed a mediating central role in the family. Women were empowered with the responsibility & authority to transform the raw materials of the field and forest into useable goods. Thus they preserved and worked food stuffs grains and other produce into food to be eaten. So too they transformed sheep's wool, cotton into line thread and textile. Also most of the responsibility of child rearing fell on them.

Women operated in the intermediate spaces of the house while performing these functions; with built structure as their framework. The boundries between authority and responsibility were clearly defined and understood; women possessed little of the dormer and much of the latter, or at best they found themselves in a situation where their responsibility was for greater than their authority. Indians have done little to alter this imbalance. There was still the responsibility to cook, clean launder and rear the children. Technology made it possible for women to jettison some activities, usually only to take on others.

The urban metropolis with consumers oriented society emerged middle class household The economic pressure compelled these women to take to work. Working class women, whether they worked outside the home or not had to worry, since many a day-laborer, on his return at evening from his hard toil, is repelled by the night of a disorderly house and a comfortless supper.

THE INDIAN WOMEN :

Traditionally the Indian women held a very dignified status in the family: her word is heard but authority still lied with the head of the family ie normally a man. As per the Hindu mythology the women is viewed as a mother young/old has definite recognition in religious context. Her image is thus a complex network of culture; religion & social responsibilities. The connotations are imbibed with in a women in Indian society are an inherent part of upbringing. She lives with it and even dies with it. This image has existed for years & centuries and continues to exist. But in today's revised role her interpretations of all these may vary but conceptually the continuity is still very evident. This transformed image is not a regular feature with all women but with a certain section of society, basically concentrated in an urban context as it has severe economic pressure. Conventionally her decision on socio, cultural, religion related issues are valued, recognised and implemented too. This explains why the Indian cultural ties are so strong.

Before we starts with Indian women's contemporary image: needs & her requirements etc. It is important to understand and be aware of her backdrop as most of the factors still affect her; their respective weightage may vary in the urban context/rural context etc or for a women from MIG/HIG/LIG or EWS section etc. Even if the educational backdrop has enabled her to develop certain logic &rational to analyse and accept and reject the continuity of certain rituals and practices. This is also pastly attributed to the fact of shortage of time due to working hours etc.

Therefore unless one understand the Indian women's in correct perspective, to draw any kind of conclusions regarding her needs etc may not work. The backdrop study shall enable one to start with a correct footing. Thus if one were to analyse the responsibilities/duties of an Indian Women, can be summerised as follows:—

1) To transform four walls and a roof into a home with certain identity.

2) To ensure sustainance of religious/cultural practices.

3) To bind the family with the joint family/relatives.

4) She and her kitchen/

5) To bring up children in a specific social fabric/ethnic group

6) To be a conservationist by approach

7) To be a bread earner - an added responsibility

8) To build houses;

FOUR WALLS & THE ROOF : A HOME

The four walls and the roof defines only a physical space of certain proportion & size when a women walks in after her marriage its she who is the decision maker for that space. She has a total freedom the express herself in terms of assigning of functions like seating (draming area); sleeping area; priya corner (religious riche to workship) etc.

The allocation of these functions with in the space is never done randomly as the culture as religious codes refer about them For example: the workship zone for a Hindu has to face east and for a muslim west (for India); entrance perch to the main living area to face east etc etc.

Conventionally the life styles guides about the furniture that is to be housed. With in the dwelling unit exists hierarchy of spaces ie covered, semi-covered open to sky (room; verandahs/porches & the coustyand respectively) The climatie conditions prevailent in India encourages most of the living in verandah's; coustyand or terraces and even sleeping in hot summer months.

With reference to the hindu mythology on architecture, the manual "Vastushilpa" refers to the act of building buildings. The space allocation for each individual with respect to the social stratification, the layout of the house; disporition of spaces with in and extent of coverage for all four groups.[1] The built structure then sits on a piece of land with landscape well integrated with in as per the geographical location; then it is referred as a complete dwelling unit. Normally more than single entrances to the house exist, the secondry for semicos etc.

This traditional built form has been deviated from as the social stratification is based on economic status & not on the baris of birth in a particular family. But can ceptually the combination of spaces continues to be same with similar utilities as their life styles: eating habits; living habits etc etc haven't changed much.

Though the uncoded conduct of the society empowers the lady of the house to take all decisions but the soical/religious aspects make her to consult her husband on final decisions. Thus it is more or less a co-ordinated effort; preference is given to her decision as eventually its her who has to maintain and decorate it: the scale/height of the layout to be essentially manageable by her.

SHE AND HER KITCHEN

Kitchen is not viewed as a mere cooking area in the house but much more than that ie. a typical Indian women often decides to have her Puja corner there. Every day cooking to occassional/festival cooking varies & so does the act of eating[2] it. Its then when the family gets together with women cooking hot and Serving her husband and kids and then eats later. Though this conventional image is deviated from in an urban context when she is a bread earner and thereby shortage of time. None the less even today, majority of the women still follow the conventional image.

The kitchen is considered an auspicious space therefore cleaned/ washed every day thus hygenic and clean. For a joint family ie. a set of parents with married children & grand children etc. A single kitchen shall mean their togetherness while seperate kitchen indicates a seperate family. This interpretation has even been accepted legally and documented as such. In some parts of India cooking is also a social get-together, For example "Sanjza Chulha"[3] which means the ladies of the neighborhood get together sing & dance and cook together, basically "rotis"[4]. Thus cooking even encourages social get-together & folk music/group singing etc.

WOMEN — THE BINDING FACTOR:

Its normally her that takes up intiative to be socially abrest with latest in the family sharing the responsibility of new born; fixing up bride/bride groom-match making; coring for older members of the family during their sickness etc etc. The older women of the family also share the responsibility of the women, if living together as in case of a joint family. The harmony and co-ordination always exist as the hierarchy is honoured and accepted ie older women's (mother-in-law's) decision over rules daughter-in-law's decision etc etc. Though one heans of the nuclear families in majority in urban metropolis but when they get together they also abide by this code of conduct.

Various cultural/religious practices are tools for the lady of the house to ensure of the Social dependence and thereby a binder for the family. For varying occasions certain duties are to be performed by specific persons in the family - also binds the family together.

LIFE STYLE & BRINGING UP CHILDREN:

It's her who is responsible to attend to children's requirements physical & pshycological both. It's her who gradually introduces the young ones to various rituals and customs. This gradual process is integrated well with in the life styles of the people. India with its various geographical zones nutuses a wide range of life styles catering; to its climate; landform etc; so much so that the eating habits; living habits other than socio/cultural connotations also blends with the geographical location too: environmentally conscious approach. For example: 1) people living in hills never cut trees for domestic use unless the tree is old/borken etc and uses dry twigs for cooking 2) people living along the coastal region: use the coconut trees virtually for most of the things like eating; making utensils; building houses roofs etc and a multiple use of it has cultural expressions too.

Arrival of the new born is considered an occassion by itself various stages of the development of child is recognised as a landmark in one's life and of the family too. Thus the child grows up with specific exposure to a certain life style and since it is ingrained in a child's mind the ties are strong and thereby stranger roots and continuity of culture/ social etc. For the above process a women is the constant factor as a guide; a friend; a reference; a mentor etc above all as a mother in all respects.

TO BE CONSERVATIONIST BY APPROACH:

Economic pressure is a typical characteristic of Indian society (third world developing country). Earlier it was prevalent in the large section of the society but today with the MIG class emerging as a major part of the society also has financial constraints. The lady of the house being conscious of this pressure always tries to be careful about her resources and the supplies. Most of the things are either recycled or had multiple use. Thus the management is basically her outlook and the means resorted to may vary from one to another depending upon their priorities. But conceptually every women indulges in the conservationist approach. For example: 1) Water is scarce in hills thus the limited water so say used for bathing is latter used to flush the water closet which drains on to the fields: thereby recycling the water and waste too. The crop sown is also chosen carefully which further uses up waste & water thus the environment remains balanced and pollution free. 2) Multiple use of clothes ie. eldest child weans it and gets passed on to the younger brothers or sisters and so on and latter the same piece of cloth is used for dusting & moping the floor/furniture etc.

All these examples depict a conscious approach of an Indian women; this is further strengthened by social intereaction which forms a platform for exchange of such ideas/approaches etc. This attitude is directly related to the buying capacity for the lady of the house but the affluent class forms only a fraction of the society

TO BE A BREAD EARNER:

With the economic pressure surrounding and reaching enormous proportions has compelled women to take to work. Besides this the educational awareness among women has made them carrier conscious. Issues like Identity; self expression; to achieve something; ambition and success etc etc are gradually becoming important. It's fairly well expressed with in the urban middle class and partly in higher income while the lower class following the suit. The educational backdrop for a women has reviewed her rationale and now she takes decisions for more objectively.

Studies have shown that the women are for more sensitive professionals (with respect to certain issues) than men. This gives a healthy competition with in the society and thereby better development. Since most of the women are not very educated they end up with jobs of low wages or if self employed the income is fairly low. Its only those who attain higher education manage good wages. Even as of today there are only few disciplines that women have made their mark, while some of the fields are still untouched. For example: medicine; engineering; sports etc for former and latter one's example are defence; astronomy; space study etc.

None the less the whole process has triggered off a bend towards education, which is gradually picking up pace. The urban fabric clearly shows the working women as a large number. This has direct repurcussions on to the family life and life styles of it. The former as the schedule of the day is revised as per working hours; with work and family as primary and the other responsibilities as secondry. The life styles have improved as the income is two fold. Refering to the secondry responsibilities ie. socio-cultural; binder of family etc suffers as that doesn't come through due to lack of time for the women. This phenomenon who takes over as a general phenomenon may damage to the continuity; and homes for aged etc may become a regular feature etc; Inspite of these implications the women can't be debarred of their educational rights.

Thus the working women have tried to draw a balance so as to cope with added responsibility ie by taking to home based jobs so that the twenty four hours can be utilised efficiently. Keeping home as the base the multiple functions can be done and as and when occassions & festivals come the priorities shift towards the social commitments etc.

The home based work has had direct implications on the designs of the dwelling unit ie. earlier the kitchen was located in such a way that the cooking; keeping an eye on the young ones; social intereaction with in the neighborhood all occured as kitchens were located such but with work taking over some covered space be allocated with spill over in same open area. The work place to be strategically located such that if it is a group work women of the same cluster could share the county and mutually for the same or different jobs.

Thus the conclusion is that a space be allocated for the lady of the house to work. The space requirement is definiately related to the nature of job handled; Further each section/ethinic group has certain kinds of job associated with them. This broad based conclusion is valid for each part of India respectively.

TO BUILD HOMES:

In India except for the urban metropolis which are consumer's the rest of the country both men and women have to work for every small to big things including building their own houses. Each geographical zone has some construction technology available which utilises the local materials to its maximum efficiency and have the vernacular technology to execute the structures. The women folk share the responsibility equally with in their physical capacity. Thus once the construction activity is shared equally the built structure after completion becomes a women's domain.

They highlight the entrance with a threshold and a "rangoli" laid out first in front of the entrance door. Niches or seating platform are left on either side of the entrance door (the niches are used to light up the entrance by placing lamps etc while the seating platform encourages social intereaction with in the neighborhood/adjacent neighbour etc). Each house has a contyard around which various functions are laid out. This typical layout is the conceptual plan and varies a bit for a wealthy person to a poor one. This Layout is also climatically very effective and thus the enclosed coustyand becomes the usuable open to sky space, usually the focus of the house. Every courtyard is characterised by some plantation/landscape depending on the size of the countyard For example: either a "tulsi" (scered plant to hindu religion and worshipped daily); pipal etc.

In an urban metropolis the building activity in slums/outskirts etc is basically a self help effort using cheap materials; industrial waste etc. to build their dwelling units, for which women are also a part of it. Other than the self help women actively participate in construction field as source of income.

WOMEN IN AND URBAN CONTEXT

Her changing role in the society : The broad classification of the society into ie rural &urban: the women in the rural sector has for less constraints thereby less problems as compared to the women in the urban sector. The former one has fairly less exposure to happening and activities but that goes for the men of sector too also oming to our poor communication links. The statistics indicate half the world's population shall be living in urban area by the turn of the century which implies they are almost half the world's population.

Refering to the constraints if one were to list down it shall probably be closer to, as follows:— a) Shortage of space b) economic pressure-a part of consumers society c) rearing children d) to earn a living e) to build their own homes f) to educate the children g) to take care of old parents h) to share the responsibilites of old parents as the family may have 6-8 children: getting the sisters married; settling the younger brothers etc. i) social intereaction with the neighbourhood inhabitants/relatives etc. j) cultural & religious practices & customs etc etc. to name some. Though not all factors are applicable to all women as the higher class is usually spared beacuse of better financial status, relatively less spared are middle class women and worst hit are the lower class women and so on.

The middle class women are normally better educated because of their better awareness towards education and exposure etc. Thus they end up taking jobs which takes them away from home ie. dividing the time between office and home and travelling up down which is considerable amount of time in an urban metraplois. In the process the home duties get a back slot and do the base minimum ie bring up children and some social gathering on fesitvals/occassions etc. Thus the courstsey visits to old parents are ignored/ neglected and live seperately resulting in nuclear families. Also place of work takes a nuclear family away from the joint family to form a nuclear family. Since the transition is on these days that one comes across joint and nuclear families both. Gradually the nuclear families are out numering the joint families. With better education facilities & women taking to higher education three major implicaions have come about a) system of marriages b) weightage to work hours & c) Number of kids.

Conventionally the marriages are arranged by the parents by match making of "Janampatri". With growing awarness and education the blind faith in such a system which decides who is the life partners because questionable. The younger generation wanted to take thier own decisions. This encouraged mixing with people from other community/ ethnic groups. This whole system thus effect the girl's pshysic condition while majority of the girls still have to endure the conventional system.

Once settled may she be MIG/LIG settles down with her house hold chores. The MIG with her educational backdrop is conscious of her family size; health; hygenic etc. While the women from the LIG lands up with normally large family sizes; smell dwelling units etc. Thus the economic pressure and the shortage of space put together had major repurcussions on to her along with the balance list of responsibilities. It's her who is the worst hit in the urban sector and they form a sizable number of them therefore to focus on them. [some of the studies conducted clearly shows that women in the LIG/EWS sector have stronger socio-cultural ties continuity while in MIG/HIG is relatively less.].

Working initially started to cope up with the growing financial crisis but now women look upon the hours of working in a different perspective. They wish to make a mark in it, an ambition to achieve success in their work & recognition too. The attitude is currently a typical characteristic of MIG and some HIG. Women in urban metrapolis while LIG etc are gradually following it up. Thus for a dedicated professional/worker to give in working hours alot of concentration etc leaves the individual with little enthusisom; energy; time and consident attitude towards home front. Every women has her own set of measurement to decide which is important work or home and by how much. None the less the conflict exists and is a constant debate on her mind. With the growing consciousness towards the quality of time for her work she has a similar approach towards her home & kids: More the kids the equal distribution of such time with all never happens as other responsibilities come through.

Studies conducted for women in urban poor have indicated that they interspect the weightage to work & home in a different way ie. house is the first priority. Their family ties are stronger with old parents; married brother and sisters; relatives etc. As an offshot of their strong family ties that they share the responsibility mutually or as per their capabilities. Its very ironic considering they are the worst hit in all respect & they manage to keep up with the continuity of traditional rituals & customs. But now the yield point has come streched beyond this point they may not be able to sustain there-fore they need immediate attention.

WOMEN FROM LIG/EWS IN URBAN CONTEXT & HER NEEDS:

Once the need is highlighted and the focus established it can be summerised as follows:—

a) Women a determinant for the design of dwelling unit: active participation of women for developing the brief & programmes for designing of the dwelling units or accounting of their work designing of the dwelling units or accounting of their work space; spill over etc.

b) Avilability of space usually minimum with in the dwelling unit with poor infrastructure facilities & its related implication on the life & life styles of the inhabitants.

c) Translation of her needs in terms of physical space requirements and psychological frame of mind to be in a healthy state mentally & physically.

Since the women largely contribute for building of homes their participation shall not only affect the utilisation of the space but shall relocate the wasteful space into better use: As the dwelling units are being worked out with minimum areas as 25 sqm, to as low as 9.5 sqm. In a typical urban metrapolis these areas are a typical feature arrived at by the planners with certain determinant in mind which normally fails to meet the requirements. As such no reference or standards exist for work space and dwelling unit. Other than the need to develop one, very rarely that the designes analyse the women's needs therefore the translation never comes about. Thus the layouts and programmes do not attain maximum efficiency. An intereaction with women as main users shall enable one to understand their needs & also give cues to arrive at solutions which are essentially their own interpretation of a problem. It's critical when one talks of housing a family in a small area of 25 sqm or 9.5 sqm with common toilets facilities. These base minimum standards are more of experiments or an offshot of an architects migenuity. Most of the time they fail to give the right frame of mind for the women to work. These are essentially single room dwelling unit with/without kitchen facility with shared toilets. These kind of dwelling units restricts the expression of women & eventually she has to sacrifice/compromise to a larger extent.

THE ISSUES:

Having previewed the context & needs of the women from LIG/ EWS urban metrapolis the next step shall mean outlining the specific issues involved to understand them so that direct inforness could be drawn and incorporated to enable women to live in a friendly environment.

The first and the most important issue is to have women's participation in developing a housing brief. This reflects in inappropriate house designs ie kitchen & working area are too small; neighbourhoods are designed in a way that does not allow women to work in & around the home; food growing is either prohibited or unplanned for; women's personal safety is not taken into account. While locating recreation facilities; public lighting & other amenties etc. While the zoning regulations also prohibit the commerical activity with in the neighbourhood; ownership & rental housing procedure by emphasis on male headed. Thus the women has to be legally sound so that authorative she can ascertain her right to work, permissible by regulations etc. To work the legal aspects & zoning regulations regarding commerical activity women should be involved for framing all ot it as then it shall ensure a complete women's perspective.

The second issue ideally should focus on the socio-cultural profile of the community to be housed. The weightage of this parameter gets decided upon by the fact that which ethnic group they belong to their customs & rituals; their life style & way of living; their source of income; the social fabric for that group and community intereaction a factor of the place they come from ie. specific geographical location; its climate etc. The last factor gets reflected in various ways their nature; their lifestyle; sense of dressing up etc etc. All above mentioned parameters are important but their weightage may vary from one ethinic group to another. The inter-relationship amongst these factors may also vary but by & large it is a major deciding factor for their life style.. While the source of income may be common for two different ethinic groups but their system of working and quality of product/end results shall have a strong relation with the group they belong. Thus the socio-cultural aspect is directly proportional to the woman and has direct bearing.

The next issue on the list is the design of dwelling units & of residential neighbourhoods. There is need to emphasize better shelter for women: the family member who spends maximum time has least to do with the designing of it. Ideally there should be community participation of the users or some consences which talks of the ethnic group they belong to? Do they share the some kind of jobs etc. Once that is decided upon then residential clusters could be grouped, the tentative number arrived at after intereaction with the users. The second issue shall clearly convey information regarding their life styles etc & thus one arrives at the kind of spaces required semi-open; open; covered in what ratio? Their life style shall give a cue to the infrastructure facilities either shared or individually along with each dwelling unit. The layout of spaces within the common open space of the residential neighbourhood with circulation within. The circulation area kind of subdivide the open space & effects the flexibility of the open space which needs to be viewed with women's work in mind. The size & proportion of the space and its linkage with the adjacent neighbourhoods and access to them. All there are basically design determinants resolved while designing so if done with women's prospective shall respond to the women's needs better. Once the residential cluster is tentatively frozen the design of the dwelling units features again the socio-cultural issue helps one to evaluate the efficiency of the dwelling units thus designed and adequate changes be incorporated for maximum efficiency. Some space be allocated with in the house design for work area of women.

Since women play a major role in maintaining the built environ; the significance of the various concepts related to conservation, recycling; utilisation of solar energy etc etc are necessary. Though these concepts are integrated in the rural sector but the urban context lacks this attitude as a consequence of it a lot of energy is wated and thereby effects the environment also. This can be counter-to some extent by involving women into some Co-operatives and then made aware of such concepts and measures to be taken. An active participation on their account shall result in an environment friendly & harmonious.

The next issue is the changing role of the women and its relationship with the house. The Changing process is on and its only transition phase therefore a similar kind of flexibility should be there in the design of the dwelling unit & neighbourhood too.

The last is to develop common references for the planners to fall back on a data with women's backdrop for which women professionals or participation shall enable one to achieve better results. Once these are formulated it should be mandatory to account for the women determinant in the rehabilitation Schemes.

This exercise shall not only safe guard women's interest's needs and thus achieve an environment congenial & harmonious to live in.

NOTES :

1) Four groups refer to traditional social split of society as per hierarchy ie Brahmin; Kshatriya; Vaishya & shudara. This division relates to the kind of profession/jobs they do.

2) Act of eating refers to the elaborate decoration that goes along with each plate served ie each plate/banana leaf (used as a plate in the southern parts of India) has a design/flowers placed in some aesthetic way all around the plate and then the food served. For example in case of wedding the bride and the bridegroom shall have the most elaborate design/decoration. The design are made out "rangoli" - a white powder used dry or mixed with water usually made of rice ground to powder. Traditionally the whole act occurs after sitting on the ground/fields, never on a higher level ie dinning table etc.

3) "Sanjza" means together & "Chulha" means cooking area. Normally Sanjza chulha occus in northern parts of India.

4) "Roti is similar to bread: basic food in northern India unlike rice in Southern India.

REFERENCES :

Ali, Syed Ameer, *The Legal Position of Women in Islam*. London 1912.

All-India Women's Conference Report, Fifth Session. 1931

Bader, Clarissa, *Women in Ancient india*. London 1925.

Bhattacharya, P., *Ideals of Indian Womanhood*. Calcutta 1921.

Butler, C., *Pandita Ramabai Saraswati*. New York 1923.

Cousins, Margaret C., *The Awakening of Asian Womanhood*. Madras 1922.

Dutt, G.S., *A Woman of India*. London 1929.

Field, harry H., *After Mother India*, London 1929.

Frazer, R.W., *Indian Thought, Past and Present*. London 1915.

Garratt, G.T., *An Indian Commentary*. London 1928.

The Indian Year Book. Bombay 1930-31.

Kelman, J.H., *Labour in India*. London 1923.

Macnicol, Nicol, *Pandita Ramabai*. Calcutta 1926.

Mayo, Katherine, *Child Marriage in India, Volume Two*. London 1931.

Mulla, D.F., *Principles of Mohammedan Law*. Bombay 1912.

Murdoch, J., *The Women of India*. Madras 1895.

Natarajan, K., *Miss Mayo's Mother India*. Madras 1928.

Progress of Education in India, Quinquennial Reports. Calcutta 1930.

Radhakrishnan, S., *The Hindu View of Life*. London 1927.

Rai, Lajpat, *Unhappy India*. London 1914.

Shajahan Begum, *Why Purdah is Necessary*. Calcutta 1922.

Urquhart, M., *Women of Bengal*. London 1925.

Wingfield-Stratford, B., *India and the English*. London 1922.

Winslow and Elvin, jack, C., and Verrier, *The Dawn of Indian Freedom*. London 1931.

CHAPTER-18

Women and Water in Rural Maharashtra

Brinda Rao

I. INTRODUCTION

THE PAPER CONSIDERS what water scarcity means for poor rural women and how responses to such a scarcity can address other aspects of women's struggle. It illustrates this theme through a description of the inadequacies in government response to water scarcity in the Pune district of the state of Maharashtra in India, especially in understanding and addressing the needs of those who were responsible for water collection (a task undertaken by women). It also describes the community based `water councils' set up in many villages which improved poorer groups access to water but also gave no special consideration to women's water needs and rights. The final section discusses how a scarcity of water other ecological resources have the potential for both encouraging and hindering women's movements fighting for access to production conditions (since women have little or no control over land and water for crop production) as well as for new self-definitions which break existing oppressive moulds.

In 1972, a male member of India's Planning Commission admitted in a public lecture that if men had to fetch water, all the country's 230,000 villages would have had drinking water after 25 years of planned economic development. (1) These last years of the International Drinking Water Supply and Sanitation Decade (1981-1991) is a good time to make known to those who take Indian rural women for granted the facts about their condition of life and their struggles a subject which is inextricably connected with that of water.

Access to water has always been an important symbol in Indian society. Water signifies many things-a poor woman's forgotten dream, a politician's promise, the government's benevolent intentions and its not-so benevolent planning, the essence and expression of a Brahmin's caste purity, and a rich farmer's wealth and power. Yet water has not been given the attention it deserves. State policies gloss over the issue and the Planning Commission has pushed ;the date for providing water to all the villages further into the future. Even ecologists and feminist critics of development do not dwell much on water, save for brief references in discussions of general issues such as drought and deforestaion or the invisibility of women's work. This is significant because drinking and household water is a "women's issue" wherever water is collected with difficulty and effort-be it queuing at 2.00 am at the lift pump in an urban slum or walking five miles a day over difficult terrain in the countryside.

This paper is a study of water scarcity and what this scarcity means for poor, rural women in the Pune district of Maharashtra. The fundamental premise is that neither the situation of rural women nor the problem of drinking water (and ecological conditions generally) can be understood without reference to one another, How women relate to water and water scarcity, and how the social construction of water scarcity is itself based on images of women, are different aspects of the same general process. "Drought" is a social construct that can be used to understand (or conceal) a varied set of phenomena that have natural or social origins or both. For example, women can not "experience the drought" but they can and do experience acute scarcity of drinking water. Similarly, the women of the Chipko movement did not "experience development" but rather the shortage of cooking fuel, and recurring floods during the monsoon rains.[(2)] It is thus through a focus on specific, local issues, as experienced by women themselves, that their non-local origins and implications can be better understood.[(3)]

Water scarcity is one of the most important of these issues. Water is a condition of production whether used for irrigation or for household purposes. Yet the division of sexual labour, the low status associated with women's work, and government apathy about the conditions under which human life is produced, mean that the production of crops is regarded as more important than the production and sustenance of life.[(4)] Therefore, a focus on women's role in the production and maintenance of life, is a way of questioning and subverting misplaced priorities and raising the question of how women's access to and control over water and other production conditions can be achieved.

II. WOMEN, ECOLOGY AND DEVELOPMENT

TWO BODIES OF literature contain information about rural women in India-those on women and development and those on ecology and ecological movements. The former has made progress in understanding the nature and implications of the division of sexual labour as well as the impact of economic development on women's lives. Feminist studies in India (and the Third World generally) have successfully redefined the concept of work to include women's work.(5)

Besides agricultural work, women are solely responsible for collecting fuel, fodder and water for their households. These tasks consume between four and six hours a day, depending on the region. In recent years, depletion and destruction of resources have made these tasks extremely difficult, often costing women their health and sometimes their lives. One woman suffered a prolapsed uterus because she had to carry too much water too far during the drought in Madras in 1983. Since there was no one to help her, she continued to carry water after her operation.(6) The drinking water situation is generally grim. Walking several miles a day to get water, then returning home with two or three large full pots takes from three to five hours, depending on the terrain and the proximity of the water source. the water available to poor women is of poor quality. In Kutasa village in Vidarbha region of Maharashtra, for example polluted water has led to an increase in infant mortality in recent years. Furthermore, it is harder to get firewood suitable for cooking and women have had to use biomass products such as cowdung cakes, waste crops, and weeds for fuel. These sources of energy are not only inefficient but also unhealthy. The toxic fumes emitted during cooking were identified in Gujarat as the main cause of respiratory disease, a leading health problem for women and girls in India.(7)

The general finding of the literature on women and development is that the backbreaking work of women and the division of sexual labour are the primary causes of women's subordination in the family. the community, and society. These studies have established the connection not only between the invisibility of rural women and their work, but also their marginalization in the planning process.

One drawback of this literature is that it tends to divide women's lives into two different spheres, production and reproduction, or "work" and "family life". Because the focus of development studies is "women's work", what women do becomes mixed with who they are and what they want and desire. This kind of descriptive research, which concentrates on women's "roles" in the labour force and household, has little room to take up issues such as domestic, state, religious and social violence, or issues of caste and class, except where these issues impinge directly on women's work or family life, Hardly any material on women's world views, aspirations, and goals, and how these have changed historically, can be found in women and development studies. Another drawback is that such studies are centred on a search for causal, even unilinear, relationship between two entities "women" and "development".

The second body of literature, that on ecology and ecology movements in India, also provides valuable accounts of the destruction of natural resources and its connections with women's lives.(8) This research first appeared during the Chipko movement, and grew thereafter, which is probably the reason why it attempts to transcend a "victim" approach by describing women and the poor as potential harbingers of a new era of an ecologically conscious existence.

These and other works on ecological degradation in India acknowledge that women are the worst affected by the destruction of natural resources. But they do not provide specific information about water scarcity, other than to point out that it is widespread, and that it is more difficult for women to collect water. There is a tendency to consider household water scarcity as an effect of drought.

The main recurrent theme of these writings is that the social costs of ecological scarcity in India are borne by the poor, the lowly and the marginalized, The main beneficiaries of "development schemes" are the state, the multinational corporations, and urban and rural entrepreneurs.

Writings on India'a ecology and ecological movements depict a conflict that is centred on the use of nature for profit versus the reclamation of nature for survival. Contrasts between the forces of capitalism and the needs of the people are sharply drawn: the destruction of humans and nature versus sustenance and survival. Such conflicts are also represented as struggles between two world views, one based on hegemonic, western science, the other on indigenous knowledge and ecological consciousness.

Precisely at this point, there is some ambiguity. No one explains how "ecological consciousness" is acquired, whether naturally by rural people simply because of their precarious existence, and/or because of the severe and direct threats arising from ecological disasters, or in other ways. And once acquired, can this consciousness be regarded as permanent and unchanging? The point has actually been made that when survival is threatened, poor people, including women, may also become ecologically destructive, either indirectly, by seeking employment in the cash economy responsible for ecological destruction, or directly, for example, by being forced to uproot plants to stave off hunger. There is also the practical question of where women and the poor in general, working 16 hours a day, find time and energy to mobilize, organize, and engage in sustained struggle against ecologically destructive forces.

It is fair to conclude that while the literature on women and development is distinctly pessimistic, the emergent writings on ecological movements are often characterized by a kind of romantic idealism. This article tries to steer clear of both tendencies, and to focus instead on giving a more accurate picture of the complex relation between women, development, and natural resources.

III. DECONSTRUCTING WATER SCARCITY, RECONSTRUCTING RURAL WOMEN

MAHARASHTRA IS A highly populated and politically important state in western India. The birthplace of the Indian renaissance during the 18th century, as well as of key political revoulutionaries during India's freedom struggle, Maharashtra has a political and historical legacy which is evident in the frequency of peasant riots and the abundance of leftist and women's organizations. These protests have been closely linked with ecological disasters. Between 1970 and 1973, years of severe drought and famine, rural men and women were very active in organizing themselves, and the strength of sheer numbers was soon evident. Over five million people were involved in the rural workers' strike at that time, which compelled the government to create employment and to pass a law granting equal wages for equal work of men and women. Since then, dispite the steady growth of mass-based organizations such as the *Shramik Sanghatana* (Toilers Association) and the *Shetkari Sanghatana* (Peasants' Association). and autonomus women's organizations and environmental groups, ecological struggles in Maharashtra have been sporadic and issue based. Likewise, the struggles of poor women for water have been confined within their immediate locality. The scarcity of drinking water remains acute in more than one third of the state of Maharashtra, but still the issue has not been able to command the attention deserves.

The main resons relates to the way that water scarcity is perceived by the state. Government documents and state policies explain water scarcity (and drought) as arising from "natural causes". Attributing water scarcity to "natural causes" is an effective way for the government to absolve itself of any serious responsibility other than the provision of short term relief measures. The implication is that, if water scarcity is "naturally" caused, it will be resolved "naturally" as well. In general, the attitude of the government is apathetic and fatalistic. A government official, who did not wish to be named, told me that the solution to scarcity of ecological resources was ultimately in the hands of God.

The government's approach to the issue of water scarcity is extremely fragmented. Maharashtra's Department's of Rural Development, Irrigation and Water Supply are not only situated in different locations but are funded differently and have different priorities. This lack of an integrated approach to planning makes it possible for the state to ignore connections between the increase in tubewells of rich peasants and the drying up of common wells: increases in sugar cane cultivation and shortages of household water; and encouragement to "cooperative" sugar mills and the formation of a powerful social and political elite.

The issue of drinking and household water receives low priority not only by the state government but also by the central government. In the water supply schemes both at the central and state levels, water scarcity is not regarded as seriously as crop failure. Household water scarcity is categorically subsumed under concerns about drought; and, by a backward chain of logic, policies formulated to tackle drought are assumed to also address drinking water scarcity.

In their elaborate plans for the provision of water supply, neither the central nor the state governments mention women at all. The census does not include time spent by women to get fodder or water as "work". As the boundaries of state jurisdiction are currently drawn, neither rural women nor drinking water scarcity are subjects of concern in their own right. As mere appendages of larger categorical entities, household water shortage is conflacted with drought, while concerns about women (both rural and urban) are often coupled with those about children and the disabled.

In effect, the state does not acknowledge the existence of women, especially rural women, in any other light than as child-producing objects or machines. The same patriarchal values which lead individual men to ignore the contributions of women in their households (at the same being aware themselves of their own dependence on these contributions) form the cultural and ideological background for state policies that are anti-woman.

IV. GRASSROOTS ALTERNATIVES: FROM FACT TO FICTION

THE WATER ISSUE has been raised periodically by environmental activists and women's groups. This section discusses one of these efforts, that of the *Pani Panchayat* (Water Council), and of some women's organizations in Pune district.

The *Pani Panchayat* was the idea of V.B. Salunke, a Pune based engineer who was deeply moved by the plight of the rural poor. The drought of 1972 killed a number of villagers in the district, and adversely affected crops and trees for the next several years. Salunke moved to a village called Naigaon, starting his water council experiment there. Since then, it has been adopted by 50 other villages. The naigaon experiment consisted of lifting water from the nearest water site with the help of electric pumps, and then transporting it to the village by means of canals and pipes so that it could be shared by the villagers. Salunke attempted to achieve not only a technological transformation, but also a social one, based on egalitarian principles for the equitable distribution of water.

The water Council was composed of one member from each family (nearly always male) and was based on the following principles:

1. The project was financed partly by a percentage of the villagers money, payable at once or through fixed instalments.

2. Sugarcane and other high water use cash crops were not to be grown.

3. All members of the Council had water rights, even if they were landless.

4. These rights were not transferable, and unused water rights, as in the case of family moving away from the village, would revert to the Council.

5. Regardless of the number of acres owned by each member, s/he was alloted water just sufficient to feed her/himself and the family. This worked out to one-half of an acre of irrigated land person

(equivalent to one fifth of hectare). A family of five would be entitled to two and one-half acres (one hectare) of irrigated land.

These principles have done much to ensure that water is shared equally. Women benefit from the scheme as they do not have to walk miles to get water. It would appear that a movement like *Pani Panchayat* would have potential of helping women gain access to production conditions and in recognizing them as producers. How ever, the ideology of the Water Council does not acknowledge rural women in their own right. Women appear as "family" of the male members of the Council. Traditionally, only men can own land; and,under the Water Council scheme, only men can hold water rights. Although landless men can have water rights, women, who are traditionally landless, cannot. Moreover, the workload of women that have adopted the Council plan has not lessened, In Shinewadi, for example, women reported to me that their workload has not decreased at all because the men had delegated some of their own tasks to women, arguing that since women did not have to spend time fetching water, they had a lot of "free time" at their disposal.

Women's organizations such as the *Stree Aadhar Kendra* (Women's Foundation Centre) and the *Samajwadi Mahila Sabha* (Socialist Women's Organization) are doing extensive work in rural areas. Women activists have a profound knowledge of water scarcity in their own regions, the manner in which it affects rural women, and of grassroots efforts to overcome drought. The critical question is whether to focus on general issues or on specific issues which reinforce women's subordinate status in society. Women's organizations currently tend to focus on the latter. They do not deny the interconnectedness between women and ecology, but assume that women's awareness of themselves and their oppression as women is a prerequisite to empowering them to struggle for access to water.

By contrast, a more dailectical approach to women and water scarcity is portrayed in *Pani* (Water) a film made by Sumitra Bhave. *Pani* depicts the unified struggle of women to get a well dug in their village. The village is typically drought- ridden while irresponsible development policies have decreased ground water levels. The village well has dried up, and the women have to walk far over hilly areas to obtain water. A woman is battered by her husband for attempting to ration his use of water, and is forced by him to get more water after sundown. The woman sets off with her pots and her six-year-old daughter, but in the dark the child slips, falls into the dry well, and is badly injured. Following this incident, Kushakaki, a sensible village elder, mobilized other women, and the struggle for drinking water begins. The contours of the struggle are finely drawn, beginning with the strong, silent stare of a heavily pregnant woman when admonished by her husband for sending his old mother to fetch water, to the sarcastic exchanges between women and the men ("if men had to get water, a well would have been dug her long ago"), and culminating in the victory of both Kushakaki's knowledge of her terrain ("I know that there is water right here. This is where we have to dig.") and the unified struggle that the women are able to offer. In a brief 30 minutes, this amazing film manages to depict a number of struggles- between men and women, between women and village authorities, between women and the state, between activists and the state-and slao to highlight the interconnectedness of the themes.

V. IDENTITIES AND IDEOLOGIES: EXPLORING WOMEN-WATER CONNECTIONS

THE CONNECTION BETWEEN people's identity and natural resources can be traced back to nature worship in Ancient India during the Vedic Age. Some gods like fire and air were invariably male, while others, like water, were female, The easy interchange between the properties of humans and nature suggests a recognition of a symbiotic existence with nature, and people's awareness of themselves as another natural form.

The water element in nature has been associated with female qualities. *Ganga* (ganges), the primal source of water, was regarded as the eternal purifier, and the provider of salvation, a form of bridge between this world and the next. The water element was also associated with great power, being the source of both creation and destruction. Fetching water for household use as an activity closely linked with women's daily lives is deeply embedded in Indian folklore, mythology and literature. Numerous references can be found in popular, regional folk songs and dances, and religious stories, in which bringing water is depicted as a wonderful and liberating task. In contemporary times, the growing alienation between people and nature is clearly manifest in the adverse conditions under which women have to obtain water, and also in the lack of an integrated approach to the question of water scarcity. Fetching water is neither a liberating task, nor does it ensure power to women within or outside their homes.

How then do women relate to water under present conditions, which are far from liberating? What kind of links can be make between the transformation of ecological conditions and changes in women's choices and strategies?

Since the water element has been associated with purity and porification, water has served to make the class and caste distinctions more rigid in rural areas. In rural Maharashtra, as in most other parts of India, class and caste positions often go together. In times of drought, the awareness of caste and class privileges, and the associated discrimination, are intensified. In drought-ridden villages which are supplied with water by trucks once every three days or so, it is not uncommon for the trucks to go the house of the sarpanch (head-man) first, then to other prominent characters of the village, before it reaches the Dalit vasti (settlement of the downtrodden). Water scarcity is created (or intensified) primarily by the use of caste and class power by richer farmers. Thus, although women normally have the responsibility of collecting water for their households, when drinking water is scarce, it comes under the control of men of higher castes and/or classes. Gender distinctions, like those of caste or class, are intensified, along with women's awareness of their gender.

Another way in which water scarcity transforms gender relations is through male out migration and desertion. Patriarchal relations and the low position of women in the caste and class hierarchies deny them these options. Instead, the social structure of the village gets transformed, since women often have to plough the land, and manage a large, extended family.

Women's relations with other women are also altered by ecological scarcity. Longer hours spent collecting water can mean less time for women, and the water site as a common meetting place gradually disappears. Furthermore, changes in ecological conditions are linked to changes in the relationship of women to their communities. The Kashtakari Sanghatana in Dahanu, a tribal grassroots organization, has recently connected the revival of the horrible anti-women practice of witch-hunting to deforestation in the area. Excessive deforestation has resulted in the disappearance of several medicinal herbs, plants and roots, which has increased disease and infant mortality. Deaths and disease are being attributed to the practice of "witchcraft" by women, especially widows and deserted wives. Compaigns to hunt and kill such women are currently underway.

As in the case of migration. access to water for women can imply both a liberation and a form of upward mobility. In Shinewadi, a village under the Pani Panchayat scheme, it appeared that the Shinewadi women's presentations of self were less deferential and more confident than those of women in other areas experiencing water scarcity. Another activist helping with the acquisition and instalment of borewells in villages near Karjat noticed a similar change in the poor women of that area. She told me that access to water had made women more confident and outgoing. The other change which occurred in this village was the feeling of cleanliness and superiority experienced by some after they had access to water.

VI. CONCLUSION

Struggles of women to gain access to ecological resources, or to escape the trauma of ecological disasters, have the potential to enhance women's awareness of their oppression as women. The acquistion of gender consciousness is strongly realted to the struggle for ecological resources; often women have to confront and defy the men within their own families and communities when they participate in these struggles. The film *Panillustrates* this clearly: once the women mobilize to have a well dug in their village, the wrath of the menfolk descends of them. Daily, in the course of their work, they are harassed. digging a well is ridiculed as a whimsical and illogical notion. Another constraint on women's participation in struggle is the perception of women's defiance as a moral violation of "true woman hood". Activism on the part of women, especially without the involvement of men, threatens to divest them of their identity as women.

Yet, despite their oppression, rural women still maintain real and potential sources of power which they can use against men. the sources of women's power, and the forms in which they are manifested, change with ecological conditions. And these conditions in turn, change depending on the level and forms of women's power. Ecological crises provide not only pretext and context for struggles by women redefining their identities but also much of the content of these struggles. Scarcity of water and other ecological resources have the potential for both encouraging and hindering movements of women fighting for access to production conditions, as well as for new self-definitions which break oppressive capitalist and patriarchal moulds.

REFERENCES

1. Agarwal, A. and S. Narain (1985), "Women and natural resources", *Social Action* Vol. 35.

2. Editors note see Bhatt, Chandi Prasad (1990), "The Chipko Andolan forest conservation based on people's power" in *Environment and Urbanization* Vol. 2, No 1. April, pp 7-18 for more details of the Chipko movement.

3. "Although grass roots struggles are seemingly local episodes their reverberations are global in import, if only because survival on the local plane is impinged upon by forces which are non-local in origin . . . . .local struggles are part of the process of global transformation currently underway". Shiva, V. (1986). "Ecology movement in India", *Alternatives* Vol. 10, pp. 256-257.

4. This term (rather than the more common "sexual dividson of labour") is used because the "sexual division of labour" has come to be understood in a somewhat static way. By switching the terms around, the author hopes to address the fluid, changing and culture specific tasks which men and women perform in any given society.

5. Leacock E. and H. Safa (editors) (1986), *Women Work: the Division of Labour by Gender,* Bergin and Garvey, New York Sen, G (editor) (1987), *Development, Crises and Alternative Visions,* Monthly Review Press, New York, Beneria, L. (1982), *Women and Development,* Preager, New York; mazumdar, V. (1982), "Another development with women; a view from Asia", Development Dialogue, No 2, Tinker 1. (editor) (1990). *Persistent Inequalities.* Oxford University Press Dube, L.E. Leacock and S. Ardener (editors) (1986) *Visability and power,* Oxford University Press, Bombay.

6. See note

7. Batliwala S (1983), "Women and cooking energy", unpublished manuscirpt.

8. Shiva (1986), see note 3; Omvedt, G. (1987), "India's green movements", *Race and Class,* Vol 28, No 4. pages 29-38; Parajuli, P. (1989), "When subalterns speak; the politics and pedagogy of ecological movements in Jharkhand, India", manuscript; Agarwal and Narain (1985) see note 1.

CHAPTER-19

Women's Roles in Creating the Urban Habitat[1]

Lillian Van Wesemael-Smit

"Men are cowards, they do not want to take risks and only think about their own well-being. We women are different, we defend our property with tooth and nail, Why? Because we think of our children, it has always been the women who have defended our houses, if necessary only with sticks. The men were not there, not did they concern themselves with community affairs. It was the women who went ahead leaving men behing. Just imagine it, those bandits. After wards they said that we are weak, that men protect and always watch over women.

Women of a barrio[2]

In the above quotation the woman takes a high tone to make it clear that in daily life men have not recognised the role of women in the struggle to defend their dwellings. The signal is clear: the specific role of women in defending the urban habitat is a subject that has not received much attention. This lack of attention can also be noticed in case-studies and theories[3] on the participation of slum-dwellers in community affairs. In order to correct this lack of information on the activities of women, I will refer largely to women's activities in the creation of the urban habitat.

During my fieldwork in Peru it became clear that women have been very active in creating the urban habitat. And nowadays women's organisations in the barrios of Lima and other cities, like Cuzco for example, strive for the provision of social services for the community. Not all barrios have an active and successful women's organisation

[1] Parts of this paper have been published in van Wesemael-Smit, 1988a.

[2] In this paper urban living districts which arose in an informal way are indicated by the Spanish word barrio. This preferred to the English word slum which has certain negative connotations. The quotation is taken from Huaman (1985a, p. 98). translation L.v.W.

[3] In the writings of, for example, Gilbert and Ward (1984a, b), Mangin (1967), Portes (1972, 1976), Saloma (1984), de Soto (1986), Turner (1963, 1965), no gender specific data are included concerning the participation of *barrio*-habitants in community affairs.

Part of the explanation for this may lie in the role that women have played during the formation of the barrio, which seems to vary considerably according the specific form that this process of barrio-formation has taken.

This article attempts to identify women's role in creating the urban habitat. It appears that women's activities in this process are different according to the specific stage in the process of creating the urban habitat. To specify women's role it is useful to distinguish three stages:

stage 1- the struggle for a terrian and a dwelling;

stage 2- the struggle for basic services (like water, electricity, sewerage etc.);

stage 3- the struggle for social services (like health service, infant schools etc.)

Huaman (1985a) makes a similar distinction in what she calls the urban consolidation process. In my opinion it is more appropriate to speak of *creation* of the urban habitat. The dwellers actually have formed their own living environment, sometimes out of nothing. This effort is much more far reaching than just consolidation.

The three stages distinguished should not be seen as a necessary historical sequence in stages which have taken place in certain clean-cut periods. In some recently formed barrios where the struggel for a terrain and a dwelling may not have been solved, the barrio-dwellers may also be involved in the struggle for basic services and for social services. In some of the more ancient barrios the different stages seem to succeed each other. Whereas stages 1 and 2 cannot be placed in a certain time-period, stage three finds its major impact in the eighties. partly due to the economic crisis at that time, women started the struggel to retain their living conditions and try to create social services.[4]

The Peruvian cities Lima and Cuzco are taken as cases to illustrate the differences in the process of barrio-formation. While in Lima most of the barrios find their origin in the invasion of terrains, the situation in Cuzco is different. There the illegal purchase of terrains lies at the basis of barrio-formation. In the description of the process

[4] For a more detailed discussion of the different factors that have influenced the rise of women's organisations see van Wesemael-Smit (1988b).

of barrio-formation, special attention will be paid to the activities of women's organisations in order arrive at an insight into the characteristics of these organisation which, in part, the specific process of barrio-formation may have brought about. In conclusion, some therories on the participation of barrio-dwellers in community affairs will be looked at in order to see if these theories also apply to the participation of women.

This article is based on the results of fieldwork and the study of literature on urban development. During the period 1983-1988 several short and medium length visits were made to Cuzco and to a lesser degree to Lima. Points of investigation were urban development and the changes which women's organisations have been able to bring about.

CREATION OF THE URBAN HABITAT IN LIMA

The writings of Turner (1963, 1965) on the development of the barrios in Lima are well known. He describes vividly the inventive and ingenious way in which urban dwellers creaet their dwellings and their environment. He, however, never makes an explicit differentiation between the activities that men and women undertake in order to create their habitat. This is an omission which is reflected in many writings on this subject (see for example Mangin, 1967, and de Soto, 1986), although is should be said that this is merely a lack in international studies. Nowadays in Peru a fair amount of attention is given to the role of women in urban development (see Tocon de Armas *et al*; Huaman, 1985a; Haak and Diaz Albertini, 1987). The investigation of Huaman (1985a), for example, has made visible the role of women in the various stages of urban development in Lima.

The first stage

In the last four decades the city of Lima has grown by 1,200%. In 1981 the city of Lima had, according to the National Census of Peru (Instituto Nacional de Estadistica, 1981), 4,993,032 inhabitants. This growth has mainly taken place through the informal estalishment of new neighbourhoods on the margin of earlier city-districts. As de Soto states (1986, p. 18), in 1984 these informally created districts housed 47% of the population and contained 42.6% of the buildings, which had an estimated value of 8,319.8 million US$. Most of these districts started with the invasion of open ground and to a lesser degree from illegal purchase of terrains (de Soto, 1986, p. 19) Nowadsys invasions continue to be the order of the day. The struggel for land is thus not only an historical event, but also a contemporary issue.

It is generally acknowledged that the preparations for invasions were largely taken by men who formed invasion committees and made their demands public. Women, however, played a more hidden role by giving rise to these demands. As Huaman (1985, p. 100) points out, women played an important role in the decision to move away from earlier dwellings and to participate in urban invasions. Since women have to confront a variety of daily problems which arise from living in inadequate housing conditions and which have consequences for all members of their family, women seem to be more aware than man of the needs of their family with respect to the dwelling (Huaman, 1985, p. 101). Huaman describes that women, even at the cost of the opposition of their husbands, have left their earlier, often rented, dwellings in order to participate in an invasion.

But women's activities have also taken a more overt form. In the battle to defend their houses against police and bulldozers it was the women who led the way and made the firmest stand (see Tocon de Armas et al., 1982, pp. 76-77 and Spessart, 1980, p. 44). Several reasons for this have been proposed.

Some argue that women have to defend their dwellings by necessity, since most confrontations take place during day-time, when men have left their dwellings in order to work and women have stayed behind in order to carry out their household related activities. Although it should be noted that not all men go out to work and neither do all women stay at home, I think that these parctical circumstances form a plausible argument, be it only a partial one. Apart from these practical circumstances, more strategic considerations deserve attention in order to explain women's important role in the defence of their dwellings. De Soto (1986, p. 22) asserts that, by allowing women and sometimes also children to bear the brunt of the attack, the authorities could be sensitised and made to realise that their attack is vicious. Huaman (1985, p. 98) takes another standpoint. She states that women have more courage than men, and that women watch over their families better than men. Huaman says that the participation of women in the struggle has even led to the emergence of informal female leaders, who have played a significant role in defending the barrios. These women become aware of their possibilities and their strength.

In my opinion all three arguments should be taken into account in explaining women's role. Huaman's point of view in this is most far-reaching, since she indicates that in this struggle female leadership may emerage.

Apart from these struggles, amounting occasionally to outright battles, other attempts to safeguard the dwellings and the terrains should be mentioned. In Peru there is a large tradition of forming barrio-committees in order to protect and to legitimise the barrio. These committees also function as a planning and regulation unit and as a mobilisation front. Men are the main leaders of these committees, and it is primarily men who participate actively in the meetings convocated by these committees.

So far the discussion of men and women's activities has centred on the public sphere. In the private sphere, men's efforts to construct and to improve their dwellings have been discussed intensively since the writings of Turner on this subject. Less known are the activities of women; the role they play in the daily struggle to survive in an environment devoid of all amenities. As even the most elementary amenities like water, electricity, food-stores and transport are lacking, it is an enormous burden to fulfil daily household task. Providing water, washing clothes, preparing food and taking care of sanitation become very time consuming and difficult tasks. It is largely women who are responsible for arranging these daily life activities in order to keep their family functioning.

The second stage

In the second stage, the struggel for basic services like water and electricity is central. As the government do not normally provide basic services, subcommittees are formed in order to reach out for these amenities. As in the central barrio-committee, men are the main leaders. But here again, women too play an important role. Women, for example, arranged special marches to claim the right to have water connections. Women not only put forward requests to the government, but also denounced the fact that many of the barrio organisations - which consist of men- became co-opted by the government and had stopped fighting on behalf of their barrio (see for example Huaman, 1985, pp. 103-104). In the so- called women's committee they tried to form their own organisation. Figueroa and Anderson (1979, p. 13) give the following picture, which may serve as an illustration:

"Sometimes stimulated by government mobilisers, sometimes out of frustration with the inoperability [. ..] of female community participation, the idea of forming women's committees took hold in more and more pueblos jovenes [barrios, L.v.W.]. From the start they were positioned on a very traditional patriarchal notion of the division of men's and women's spheres. The women's committee was to occupy itself with health, education, food programmes and young children while the men took care of the big problems: getting potable water pipelines installed, electricity, and deciding the community's political affiliation. There was a surprise for the men in this neatest of all arrangements, however. The men's possibilities for action were almost nil, whereas the women with less global problems assigned to their sphere, were in a good position to achieve results."

Not much is known about the scale and the dispersion of these women's committees. It is possible that during the seventies these committees were located mainly in Lima.

Although women's committees seem to have been an important phenomenon, they existed for only a short stretch of time. In my opinion this may be caused by the fact that women only have a direct interest in these committees in order to obtain basic services and that when these goals are reached, they lose their significance. On the other hand the creation of so-called `clubes de madres' (mothers clubs) may have elbowed these committees aside.

In the seventies, ecclesiastic organisations organised these, in origin mostly very traditional and paternalistic, mothers' clubs in order to distribute food-donations. Figueroa states (Figueroa et al., 1983, p. 139) that there is a great difference between the women's committees and the mothers' clubs. Whereas the women's committees tended to organise activities around necessities felft by the barrio-dwellers, the mothers' clubs were based on general outlines made by the ecclesiastic organisations. Co-operation with the central barrio-committee was in some cases prohibited. Although these mothers' clubs received much criticism in Peru,[5] it is generally acknowledged that through their formation the biggest mobilisation of women up to that moment was achieved. Exact data with respect to the number and the dispersion of the mothers' clubs are not available. It is clear, however, that in such cities as Cuzco. Arequipa, Chimbote and Trujillo, mothers' clubs were formed.

The third stage

The third stage consists of the struggle for social services. Contrary to the previous stage, the activities of men are seldom mentioned. Portes (1976, p. 102), when reflecting on experiences of invasions in Peru, Chile and Brazil, even states that:

"[. . .] onces the most acute developmental problems are resolved, rates of participation in community associational activity and all forms of political action tend to decline sharply."

He suggests that participation in community activities and all forms of political actions decline, a conclusion which others, like Gilbert and Ward, also draw (Gilbert and Ward, 1984b, p. 917).

Portes does not make clear what he considers to be the most acute developmental problems. His statement is so general that it is difficult to affirm or to reject. I think, however, that the general tendency which he seems to indicate does not apply to the situation in Lima. There the participation of women in community affairs has grown during the various stages of formation of the direct urban habitat. An important role is played by women's organisationswhich try to retain or to improve that daily living conditions by creating social services like infant schools, provisional primary health-care posts, communal kitchens, etc. Some of these women's organisations have arisen through the experience in the mother's clubs. the influence of transformatory ideas of assessors, be it from ecclesiastic or from feminist origin, on these former mothers' clubs has been significant. It is not possible to give an exact picture of the number of these women's organisations. With respect to communal kitchens in Lima, Diaz-Albertini (1986, p. 8) speaks of a number of 700 in which 14,000 women participate and which serve 70,000 beneficiaries. So 3% of the people living in the barrios benefit from communal kitchens.[6] An important number of female leaders have emerged out of the organisation of these communal kitchens, a phenomenon which also took place in other women's organisations, like for example the glass of milk' campaign.

Several observations should be made at this point. In the first place it should be noticed that men do not seem willing to put energy in the creation of social services. This may spring from the existing sexual division of labour. Women tend to be responsible for securing the well-being of their family, and creating services that may ensure the families' well-being might be thought to be relevant to women and less to men. Another observation is that it may look as if better living conditions will be created through the activities of the various women's organisations. But taking into account the lowering of the living standard in the eighties it should be seen as an effort to combat the negative effects of the economic crisis.

THE CREATION OF THE URBAN HABITAT IN CUZCO

In Cuzco the formation of barrios started in 1950. A tremendous earthquake had demolished 80-90% of the dwelling[7] and solution had to be sought in order to shelter people. At the same time, migration from the surrounding rural areas to the city increased tremendously. The city grew from 52,000 habitants in 1950 to 220,000 in 1982 (Saloma et al., 1984, p. 1). Almost 50% of these inhabitants live in barrios (Instituto de Investigaciones UNSAAC-NUFFIC, 1984, p. 14; Fernandez Baca, 1987, p. 244).

While in Lima the growing need for dwellings has been largely satisfied by the invasion of terrains, this need was met differently in Cuzco. Here, the majority of barrios were formed by small groups of people who contacted landlords, the municipality or the church in order to buy a piece of land and to create a dwelling area. In Cuzco only 10% of the 127 barrios have come into existence through invasion.

The first stage

Whereas in Lima the main struggle in this stage consisted of the invasion of terrains and afterwards the sometimes outright battles in order to defend the dwellings, in Cuzco the situation was different. Here the struggle consisted of long and time-consuming attempts to get official recognition and to secure title-deeds. Although women probably played an important role in the decision-making process, men led the negotiations for obtaining land and acquiring the official entitlement. The purchase of the terrains has often caused long-lasting conflicts, either because of the large amount of money involved, or because of the uncertainty of the title-deeds. In some cases land was sold by someone who was not entitled to do so and even years afterwards the property was claimed by others (Saloma *et al.*, 1984, p. 2). Until now many barrios have not received entitlement for their dwelling area (cf. Fernandez Baca, 1987, p. 240 *ff.*). It was largely the task of the central barrio-committee, which consisted of men, to settle the entitlement.

Whereas in Lima women have been active in the overt struggle to defend their houses, in Cuzco the situation was different. Women's activities seemed to be more hidden in the private sphere. An exception forms in a barrio where an invasion took place. In this case women played a significant role and one woman achieved a sort of informal leadership, which is still in force.[8]

The second stage

Just as in Lima, the government did not provide the basic services. The barrio-dwellers themselves had to arrange water installations, electricity and sewerage. This was done with the money and the labour-power of the barrio-dwellers. Every family provided labour, in most cases a man's, and the work was done collectively on Sundays. Women provided food and drinks during the working days. Some barrios received financial support from development organisations or ecclesiastic organisations.[9] and during the military regime (1968-1980) those barros that acquired official recognition received the support of government instituions. By 1984, 60% of the barrios had obtained electricity, 40% sewerage and 40% had access to water, although not always drinking-water (Saloma et al., 1984, p. 4).

There is no information concerning the specific role of women in this stage. But, in general, women did not participate in the central committee nor in the subcommittees. Neither could the formation of women's committees be observed, as in the case of Lima. The presence of mothers' clubs with a very traditional character, however, was very strong in Cuzco. It is estimated that 50 clubs were functioning in 1984 (van Wesemael- Smit, 1985). In these clubs about 1,500 women were involved. Whereas in Lima various marches in order to get water or electricity were organised by women, I have no information that similar marches were organised in Cuzco during this stage. In a barrio that was formed by invasion in which women took an important part, it is known that a women's organisation has recently played a significant role in obtaining considerable financial support from external development organisations for the installation of water connections.[10]

The third stage

In the third stage, the struggle for social services, men hardly have played a role. As in Lima, women have formed communal kitchens, health committees and have taken other initiatives in order to retain or to improve the living conditions. It should be noticed, however, that the scale of these organisations is more limited than in Lima, In Cuzco the formation of these organisations has not been stimulated by the assessors of the mothers' clubs as in Lima. The number of communal kitchens may serve as an illustration. Whereas in 1986 in Lima the communal kitchens covered 3% of the barrio habitants, in Cuzco only 2% was reached.[11]

Although the scale of these organisations is rather limited, the intensity with which women struggle is in some cases very striking. The following may serve as an illustration. In 1986 the municipality planned to close a primary school in a barrio. The barrio-committee did not mobilise the populatiom, neither did it take other steps to prevent the closing down of the school. The local women's organisation, however, organised meetings in the barrio in order to mobilise the population. They organized several protest marches in which it again was women who formed the majority of the participants. Finally the cases was evern taken to court. The judge considered that the school should keep functioning. But not in every aspect could the event be seen as a success for the women's organisation. The municipality took complete control over the functioning of the school and declared the womem's organisation was no longer allowed to hold meetings in the school as they had done before.

There is an interesting feature in the urban development of Cuzco. It appears that women's participation in public affairs at barrio level was observed to be significantly higher in a barrio where women played an active role in the invasion than in other barrios which were formed through purchase of terrains. In a barrio that was formed by invasion in which women took an important part, the women's organisation has recently played a significant role in obtaining considerable financial support from external development organisations. This may indicate that through the active participation in the struggle during the first stage, women's participation in later stages will be higher.

My argument thus far is that the urbanisation process in Lima has profound differences from the urbanisation process in Cuzco. Whereas in Lima the overt struggle in order to defend the dwelling is a major characteristic, in Cuzco this type of struggle is largely absent. Very striking is that women's participation in invasions led to the emergence of informal leadership, which is largely absent in Cuzco. I have also pointed out that women's organisation in order to create social services in Cuzco lagged behind in comparison with the situation in Lima. This can be explained in part by the difference in the role that women have played from the start in creating the urban habitat. Another factor mentioned is the stimulus on the part of the assessors of ecclesiastic and feminist orgnisations for forming these types of organisations in Lima, but which was largely absent in Cuzco.

LINKING UP WITH SOME DEBATES ON URBAN ISSUES

In this paper attention has been paid to the participation of women in creating the urban habitat. Several points which have been raised deserve to be placed in a broader context. In the literature on the praticipation of barrio-dwellers in communal activities and political participation, some general remarks are made, which seem to be achieving acceptance as a kind of model of participation. The issues that will receive attention here relate to:

(1) the level of political participation during the different stages;

(2) the probability of radicalisation of barrio-dwellers;

(3) the importance of the barrio as a territorial basis for collectie action. I will first draw a picture of the different issues at stake and then give a commentary with respect to the role of women.

Political participation

In the first place it is stated that barrio-dwellers who have participated in invasions participate to a higher degree in community affairs than barrio-dwellers who have not.[12] As Portes concludes;

"In all cases, invaders exhibit higher levels of political militancy and activism than non-invaders." (Portes, 1976, p. 103)

Furthermore it is suggested that there are different stages in the participation of barrio-dwellers. Mangin (1967), for example, argues that in the barrios of Lima the organisations of dwellers reach the peak of their importance at the time of the land invasion and tend to decline after the settlements have become established. Portes has studied several investigations on this subject and concludes:

"The extent of political participation by the urban poor in Latin

America is equal to the extent of political provision for basic collective needs. That these needs are seen as limited to housing and urban services and not to other aspects of poverty is a reflection of the individually centered ethic of these groups." (Portes, 1976, p. 102)

His point of view is that over time all political participation and participation in community affairs tend to decline sharply. Janssen (1978b) has a somewhat different standpoint. He point out that the urban space is under a constant pressure to adapt itself to the changing demends. And he concludes:

"So the struggles of the barrio for their land or for public services are not a temporary matter, something that is over when these goals are achieved." (janssen, 1978b, p. 158).

Janssen (1978a, b) asserts that the continuity of the struggle, however, depends on the articulation of the barrio-organisations and the proletariat.

Probability of radicalisation

There have been many speculations with respect to the probability of radicalisation or in other words to the extent to which barrio-dwellers could be expected to undertake collective actions. As Portes summarises (1972, pp. 268-270), towards the end of the fifties and during the sixties, ideas and theories were being developed in which barrio-dwellers became portrayed as radical, irrational and aggressive individuals by nature. In these studies barrio-dwellers and other marginal groups were considered to see the fury and to radicalise. The agruments for this were derived from non-Marxist political sociology.

Another important trend has been the theory around the Culture of Poverty, brought up by Lewis (1963). According to these ideas, an active role of barrio-dwellers in improving their situation was not to be expected. The explanation for this is found in the disappointment that barrio-dwellers encounter in their efforts to fulfil their aspirations because of structural barriers, which consequently leads to apathy and fatalism. Here, the argument is that barrio-dwellers are apathetic because of their personal characteristics and will not bring about any change.

The numerous investigations on barrio- dwellers demonstrate, however, that barrio-dwellers have formed various kinds of organisations. It has been proved that barrio dwellers cannot be seen as merely apathetic and fatalistic. And it has been made clear that structural limitations, because of unequal social relations, account for the difficult situation which barrio-dwellers encounter, rather than individual characteristics that are ascribed to barrio-dwellers (see also Portes, 1972; Perlman, 1976; Janssen 1978a, b, for a more detailed criticism).

The territorial basis for collective action

The empirical findings are reflected in the attention given to the importance of the barrio as a territorial basis of collective action as expressed by Pansters (1986, 1987). In his view barrio-dwellers seem to have taken over the role of the poor working class, the proletariat, as revolutionary vanguards. Now it is not poor because of the individual characteristics of barrio-dwellers, but because of the structural situation, as expressed in the reproduction relations and in the relations to the State, that they are seen as revolutionaries. Because of these relations, barrio-dwellers have a common problem to face with respect to consumption, and this should form the basis for further organisation, according to Pansters.

There is much to be said on this subject. Portes (1972, pp. 268-286; 1976, 70 *ff.*) offers an explanation, which dismisses the more `apathetic and fatalistic' view and the more revolutionary view of barrio-dwellers. He takes the view that barrio-dwellers act and also organise themselves according to the evaluation of two aspects:

(1) the structural conditions and the possibilities and viability of revolutionary initiatives in concreate instances;

(2) The interpretation of this situation by the people themselves.

These form the two ingredients that, according to Portes, lead barrio-dwellers to action as rational people and to evaluate whether, in certain instances, collective action can be possible and advantageous for them. this also accounts for the fact that organisations of barrio-dwellers tend to increase and decline according to the necessities felt by the participants. The organisations as such, Portes declares, have no intrinsic value. The organisations do, however, remain as potential instruments which can be employed if necessary.

The question should now be asked if these theories also hold true for women, and if they explain the participation of women in community affairs and political affairs.

The first point that has been brought up is that invaders tend to participate more actively than non-invaders. In Lima the main way of obtaining land has been by invasion, while in Cuzco the purchase of plots has been the most common feature. If the activities of women in the barrios in Lima and the barrios in Cuzco are compared, then an interesting feature becomes apparent. In the first and the second stage, women seem to have been more active in Lima than in Cuzco. And the formation of women's organisations directed to retain or improve the daily living conditions has taken a higher rate in Lima. In Cuzco in one of the few invasion-settlements a woman acquired some kind of informal leadership. Although other background factors may have been at work, this can be an indication that women acquire a higher participation rate in invasion-settlements and that from this some kind of self-esteem and informal leadership may arise. Further investigation on this subject would be very valuable and interesting.

The second point raised is the fact that participation rates and political activity tend to decline after having fulfilled the most pressing living needs. Here, a differentiation concerning gender seems to be indispensable. As has become clear from the case in lima, in the second and third stage women tend to become more active in community affairs. Many authors seem to have overlooked the activities that women undertake in order to safeguard the necessities of their family with respect to basic services and social services. And the remark made by Portes with respect to the "individually centered ethic of these groups" does not account for women's organisations. Elsewhere I have paid attention to what moves women to be active.[13] The main motivation of women to participate in communal kitchens is to confront the economic problems which beset lower class families. Of course this has certain benefits for the women, but they bring forward that the well-being of their children and their husband is of supreme importance.

The ongoing struggle of women cannot be attributed to the articulation with the proletariat, as janssen has brought forward. It seems to have another logic.

And now the question is raised why it is that women continue their struggle for social services to a greater extent than men? Some explanations for this difference may be found in the sexual division of labour. As I have explained elsewhere in more depth, women, more than men, are responsible for their families' well-being.[14] They have to provide basic services. And in reality they appear to feel this is their responsibility.

But why is it that men seem to have been more active in the first stage of settlement formation? On the one hand this may be due to the incomplete picture of men and women's activities; whereas the role of male barrio-dwellers has been largely recognised, the role of women has been underestimated, as has been made clear before. On the other hand this may be due to one of the characteristics of the first stage of barrio-formation. At that time the formation of committees is an important activity. This is an affair in the public sphere, which is mainly a male domain. But there may be another argument involved as well, which is related to the property rights of the dwellings. Men are the owners and not women, so maybe that is why men are more involved with the construction of the dwelling and its legalisation. I dismiss the argument that men are physically more capable than women of constructing houses and doing `heavy' jobs. In practice nowadays in Peru, women have proved more than once to be capable of constructing their own houses, and in big construction and infrastructure programmes women participate in large numbers.

Thus, it is not because of the nature of the work that men are more involved, but rather because of the property rights, which is of high interest of men, and because of the male domination in negotiations in the public sphere.

Probability of radicalisation

Another issue which is frequently raised concerns the interpretation of the extent to which barrio-dwellers will radicalise. In general the ideas developed in non-Marxist political sociology and the culture of provery theory do not seem to fit the reality. I will not go into these arguments as they have been sufficiently criticised and rejected elsewhere (see also Portes, 1972; Perlman, 1976; Janssen, 1978a,b). Neither for men nor women can it be stated that barrio-dwellers are apathetic or, to the contrary, revolutionary vanguards.

The territorial basis for collective action

More interesting are the opinions of Pansters and Portes. In my opinion, Pansters tends to put too much emphasis on the structural aspects of participation. It is a great advance that he, just as other theoreticians of the new social movements, no longer sees the production relations as the major force behind social action. But in my opinion, the emphasis that Pansters puts on the reproduction relations in the barrios and the specificity of relations with the State is not sufficiently problematisised. From what he writes, the suggestion arises that on these bases there is unity between the barrio-dwellers with a socio-cultural and a political-ideological content. But he overlooks the differences between the barrio-dwellers, and this seems to me an oversimplification. Is there really such a kind of unity which prevails over other differences, as, for example those based on man-woman or ethnic relations?

Some of the consequences of his arguments are that he does not differentiate between the different interests that barrio-dwellers may have. I think that this is untenable if we look at the man-woman relationship. Women have, in part, the same interests as men, but also have quite conflicting interests.[15] The disputes which women's groups in Cuzco had with the (male) barrio-committees because of the use of communal dwellings, the control of public watertaps, the necessity of social services, the provision of food-products and the like, confirm the idea of conflicting interests between men and women. These conflicting interests occur not only at an organisational level, but also at the private level. In cases of divorce, there are, for example, conflicts concering the property of the house and the responsibility for the children. And in daily life, there are different interests with respect to the way money is spent and tasks are to be performed.

Pansters also overlooks the difference in the role that people have played in the process of the creation of the barrio. If it is correct that invaders tend to be more active that non-invaders, what will be the consequences with respect to their attitude to the state? And will they react in the same way as non-invaders when facing problems at the level of individual consumption?

My major point of criticism of Pansters" viewpoint is the fact that he leaves out the personal aspects. It looks as if people react to certain structures in a necessary way. But are we not taking a step backwards in the theoretical analysis, and are we not transferring the primacy of the proletariat to that of the barrio-dweller? Does a mechanical approach help us to grasp reality? I think that in all circumstances personal aspect should be taken into consideration.

My plea for taking into account the personal aspects as well as the structural aspects is in line with thinking of urban sociologist as in the later work of castells (1983), Leeds and Leeds, Van der Linden,

Portes. But I want to add that a differentiation on basis of sex and of race is needed in order to detect the different ways in which structures influence men and women. The same argument goes for the personal interpretation of the situation.

In this paper I have tried to highlight the role that women have played in creating the urban habitat. It turns out that women play a far more active role than is generally acknowledged. Although in all stages distinguished women's participation in community affairs is present, in the third stage their participation is most striking. At that moment men frequently refrain from participation in the struggle for social services. In Lima many womn's organisations have arisen around issues like food, health and work. In Cuzco, however, the organisation of women is at a lower level. Apart from the role of assisting organisations, this may be due to the specific history of barrio-formation. Unlike in Lima, in Cuzco barrios formed by invasion tend to be a minority. I think that the specific history of barrio-formation plays an important role in the formation of women's organisation and of female leadership. General theories on urban development and participation of barrio-dwellers do not give us many clues to discover this relation. Further investigation in this area could be valuable. Issues seen in this light which deserve special attention are:

—do invasion settlements have a more active women's organisation than other settlements?

—does the composition of women's organisations show a major participation of women who have been active during invasions or other struggles?

—do leaders of women's organisations tend to have been active in invasions or other struggles?

Acknowledgement—I am grateful to Peter Kloos, Roelie Lenten and Jan van der Linden for their valuable comments on earlier versions of this text.

REFERENCES

Castells, M., *The City and the Grassroots. A Cross Cultural Theory of Social Change.* Arnold, London, 1983. de Soto, H., *El Otro Sendero.* Instituto Libertad y Democracia, Lima, 1986.

Diaz Albertini, J., La Alimentacion Popular Urbana y las Estrategias de Supervivencia. DESCO, Lima, unpublished paper, 1986.

Fernandez Baca, I., Estrategias Frente a la Vivienda y Titulacion de los Pobladores Barriales de la Ciudad del Cusco: su Historia y Situacion Actual. *In Estrategias de Vida en el Sector Urbano Popular,* Haak, R, and Diaz Albertini. J. (Editors). DESCO and FOVIDA. Lima, 1987.

Figueroa, B, and Anderson, J., Women in Peru. In *Change, International Reports: Women and Society,* No. 5, 1979.

Gilbert, A. and Ward, P., communal Action by the Urban Poor—Democratic Involvement, Community Self Help or a Means of Social Control? *Wld Devl.* 12, 769-782, 1984a.

Gilbert, A. and Ward P., Community Participation in Upgrading Irregular Settlements: the Community Response. *Wld Devl.* 12, 913-922, 1984b.

Haak, R. and Diax-Albertini, J. (Editors), *Estrategias de Vida en el Sector Urbano Popular.* DESCO and FOVIDA, Lima, 1987.

Huaman, M.J., La Mujer y el Desarrollo Urbano. In *Mujery Desarrollo,* Tristan, F. (Editor, pp. 93-114, 1985a.

Huaman, M.J., Comedors Populares y Estrategias de Sobrevivencia. In *TAREA Revista de Cultura,* No. 1, pp. 16-21, 1985b.

Instituto de Investigaciones UNSAAC-NUFFIC,*Problematica General de los Asentamientos Urbano-Popular de la Ciudad de Cusco.* UNSAAC-NUFFIC, Cuzco, 1984.

Janssen, R., *Wij Hebben Zelfs Geen Recht op de Stad. Vogelvrij wonen in Bogota.* Ekologische uitgeverij, Amsterdam, 1978a.

Janssen, R., Class Practices of Dwellers in Barrios Populares. *Int. J. Urban Region. Res.* 2, 147-159, 1978b. Lewis, O., *Five Families: Mexican Case Studies in the Culture of Poverty.* University of Illinois Press, Urbana, 1963.

Mangin, W., Latin American Squatter Settlements: a Problem and a Solution. *Latin Am. Res. Rev.* 2, 65-98, 1967.

Pansters, W., Urban Social Movements and Political Strategy in Latin America. *Bol. Estudios Latinoameri-canos Caribe* **41,** 13-28, 1986.

Pansters, W., De Politieke Theorie van Stedelijke Strijd—het Voorbeeld van Mexico. *Derde Wereld* **87-1**, 55-71, 1987.

Perlman, J.E., *The Myth of Marginality. Urban Poverty and Politics in Rio de Janeiro.* University of California Press, Berkeley, 1976.

Portes, A., Rationality in the Slum: an Essay on Interpretive Sociology. *Comp. Stud. Society Hist.* **14-3,** 268-286, 1972.

Portes. A., The Politics of *Urban Poverty. In Urban Latin America; the Political Condition from Above and Below,* Portes, A. and Walton, J. (Editors), University of taxas Press, Austin, 1976.

Riofrio, G., barrig, M., Montes, O., jaruillo, T. and Jurado, R., *Los Programas de Promocion Dirigidos a la Mujer en los Barrios de la Legua y el Augustino.* CENCA, Lima, 1982.

Saloma, A., Cual es la Problematica o en que Consiste la Problematica Urbana de la Ciudad del Cusco. Paper presented at the First Forum with respect to the Construction and Titulation of Popular Urban Settlements, Cuzco 1984.

Saloma, A., Castillo, M. and Cespedes, J., Problematica de Asentamientos Populares. Paper presented at the First Forum with Respect to the Construction and Titulation of Popular Urban Settlements, Cuzco, 1984.

Tocon de Armas, C., Rodriguez Atilano, M. and Urbina Herrerra, C., *La situacion de la Mujer en Chimbote. Ensayo* I.P.E.P., Chimbote. No. 7, 1982.

Turner, J.F.C., Minimal Government-Aided Settlements. *architect. Des.*, 379-380, 1963.

Turner, J.F.C., Lima's Barriadas and Corralones: Suburbs versus slums. *Ekistics* **19**, 152-155, 1965.

van der Linden. J., *The Sites and Services Reviewed; Solution or Stopgap to the Third World Housing shortage?* Gower, Hants, 1986.

van Wesemael-Smit, J.L, *Vrouwengroepen: Naaikransjes of Vrouwenfronten? Een Analyse van Vrouwen-groepen in Volksbuurten van Peru.* Gografische en Planologische Notitie, Amsterdam, No. 50, 1985.

van Wesemael-Smit, J.L., Communal Kitchens in Peru; Women's Groups Striving for their Interests in the Face of Outside Interference. Urban Research Working Papers, Amsterdam, No. 16, 1988a.

van Wesemael-Smit, J.L., Autonomy and Women's Groups; the Newkey to Theory and Policy on Women and Development? In *Development and Religion,* quarles van Ufford, Ph. and Schoffeleers, M. (Editors), 1988b.

BIBLIOGRAPHY

Diaz Albertini, J. and Haak. R., Las experiencias de promocion y desarrollo en las estrategias de vida. In *estrategias de Vida en el Sector Urbano Popular,* Haak, R. and Diaz Albertini, J. (Editors), pp. 13-29, 1987.

Estudios y Promocion del Desarrollo, *Mujer y Desarrollo.* Serie Experiencias de Desarrollo popular, No. 4. Tarea, Lima, 1985.

Huaman, M. J., Comedores populares y estrategias de sobrevivencia. *TAREA Revista de Cultura* 1, 16-21, 1985.

Hupperts, P. and de Wit, H. (red.) *De "Revolutie" van de Generaals. 12 Jaar. Reformisme in Peru,* Latijns Amerika Publicaties, Utrecht, 1981.

Instituto nacional de Estadistica, *Censos Nacionales, VIII de Poblacion, III de Vivienda. Tomo,* Lima, 1981.

Montes, E., El Comedor Popular: de la Gestion Individual a la Participacion Collectiva. In *Estrategias de Vida en el Sector Urbano Popular,* Haak, R. and Diaz Albertini, J. (Editors), DESCO and (FOVIDA, Lima, pp. 75- 95. 1987.

Spessart, S., *Garant oder Gegner? Militarregierung und Stadtische Marginalitat in Lima, Peru, 1968-1975: Vier Fallstudien.* Saarbrucken, 1980.

CHAPTER-20

Women and Urban Housing Crisis: Impact of Public Policies and Practices in Uganda

Hilda Ntege

I Introduction

As recently as 1982, the government admitted that while housing is the most central human need without which Uganda's public service cannot survive, it was long since anyone did a scientifically detailed study of the country's housing and settlement problem [Public Service Review Commission (PSRC) 1982]. The commission also admitted that even its own review and policy recommendations lacked the basis of such research and it urged government to quantify the problem through a housing planning unit in the department of housing. So although there is a general acknowledgement of the housing and settlement crisis, it would be difficult to imagine a sensible national housing plan by governments that could not even establish the number of existing habitable houses, their class, their state of repair their residual life expectancy, location and future demands. As the commission noted, without such a study the conventional solutions to housing and settlement crises have been indiscriminately applied only to be disarmed and overtaken by socio-economic events such as political unrest, population explosion and economic depressions. The implication is that while the current housing and settlement crisis cannot be disconnected from the national housing, settlement and land utilisation policies, there is a need for viable and sustainable policies which must be founded on a critical and detailed analysis of the problem. Judging from the recent (though scanty) data of the 1989-90 Public Service Review and ReorganisationCommission, it seems the National Resistance Movement (NRM) government has already done some general quantification of the problem. Secondly, enough housing commissions have been set up in the past (and probably more will be set up) and they have dwelled enough on the subject of recommending policies that would increase the general housing stock, although they all believed that at no foreseeable time will the problem be totally solved by government. My contribution to the debate is the gender perspective, and area that has so far been under-researched. This shortage of a detailed analysis of subject is reflected in the 1982 PSRC's half-hearted admission that the public housing and settlement policies are *apparently* sexist and classist especially in terms of married women officers and the low income officers (my emphasis) [PSRRC 1989-90, 153].

Apart from this background, this paper cannot be uprooted from my personal experiences (as a women) of the marginalisation and discrimination by the sexist housing and settlement practices, which are clearly, but not totally, illustrated in the following incident: In 1991, I got involved in a desperate hunt for a job and a house, a hunt which led me into applying for the office of a field researcher (on issues of birth control), in one of the city-based companies which is closely affiliated to the famous United States Agency for International Development (USAID). As an academician neither I nor my two male interviewers doubted my ability to do the work, but before I even sat the interview, I was told that the company wanted a male employee. During the interview, I was asked whether I was married, and to my 'No' reply, I was asked if and when I hoped to do so (question which were totally out of tune with the job requirements) adding that the company did not want to employ women who had the potential of getting pregnant. Not to my surprise, after months of constant checking on the results, I had not been offered the job because in the words of one of the interviewers, "We want a man and while I would have loved to give you the job on the basis of your academic merit, my colleague is very reluctant". But as I later learnt from another staff member, "the job has the fringe benefits of a car and a bungalow and no one can bear the sight of a young single woman with benefits which are meant for a family man. These people are so obsessed by this fact that over the years the job has been done by an unqualified family man who made a daily tourist ride around the city, and slept in the bungalow, but could not produce any meaningful research data."

Certainly, I had not been offered the job because of a sexist housing practice, a case which I could have filed in a legal court under tha NRM bill of Sectarianism. But it looked as if I had no legal evidence, and even if I did, I had neither the time nor the financial means, nor the words to compose my case. And so, like many other women do/would do, I explained away my ordeal in terms of the fact that in Uganda, failure to be offered a job without any reason is normal. Months later, I was struck and provoked by Akwi Ojogo's one-page article 'Public Service Housing is Sexist' (1991). Suddenly I realised that these were the words I needed to explain my case and that of many other unhoused or ill-housed urban women. These were the words. And this paper is my partial attempt to pursue them.

The gender perspective of Uganda's housing and settlement policies and practices is biased against women, an issue that has escaped the minds of policy-makers architects and designers who perceive themselves as planning for people and not for engendered men and women [Moser and Peake on women, Human Settlement and Housing 1987]. This error which is manifested in the present sexist housing and settlement policies and practices is rooted in the recommendations of the past public service review commissions, particularly the 1954 Lidbury Commission, whose critical review will feature prominently in this paper. Following from this statement, the main argument is that regardless of Uganda's general urban housing crisis, the public housing and settlement network is sexist in favour of men. Therefore women deserve special attention in any scheme that aims at alleviating the housing crisis.

The article specifically focuses on urban housing in Kampala city mainly because much of the scramble for land, housing and settlement is in the urban world where it is warranted by the scarcity of resources against an ever increasing population. The choice of Kampala in particular is dictated by the relative availability of secondary data which can be supplemented by primary and my 10 years experience in this city. Secondly being the capital city, the policies which are made in its context almost automatically filter out into other urban area of the country. The primary data used are those-gathered during my research and interviews in Katanga, one of Kampala's slums in 1991. This article draws a lot of information from the income women in Kampala's slum settlements.

II Women in Housing Policy and Programmes

The general housing shortage in Uganda is attributed to high population growth against low housing construction rate since independence, the destruction of some units during the civil wars shortage of capital, lack of construction skills, high construction costs particularly in terms of buying imported materials and technology, the collapse of the local raw material industries such as cement, asbestos and iron sheets, the low priority which housing has so far occupied in government planning uneconomic rents for government units which has prevented the housing industry form self-sustenance corruption and swindling of housing funds. wastage of housing funds into 'dollar houses'. poor maintenance of the existing housing stock, the narrow capital base of the Housing Finance Company and the National Housing and Construction Corporation, lack of adequate salaries for the private sector to boost the housing market, and the high costs of urban plots.

Like many African cities of colonial times, Kampala was planned and developed for white colonial masters, Asian business men and African male immigrants, in that order Sometimes, the segregation was not only sexist but also classist and tribalistic especially in the case of Africans. If there at least existed the compoundless, tiny and poorly ventilated quarters for African male immigrants nothing was planned for independent African women. Compelled by the desire to preserve the African culture and moral fabric, both the colonial masters and African society were determined to keep its supposed guardians, the women, within the Class family and trible authority where the social codes of behaviour, discipline and customs were founded [Obbo 1981]. Against this attitude, unmarried women who challenged this position were ridiculed and stigmatised as prostitutes deviants, unruly argumentative and unmarriageable-people with low moral fibre who must be rejected persuaded or forced out of the city. According to Obbo, by the 1950s, the *1981 Adultery and Fornication Law and the 1914 Law to Prevent Prostitution* which required the repatriation of single women who were found 'loitering' in Kampala were still enforced [Obbe 1981, 26]. Parents constantly warned their daughters against "the lazy city-prostitutes, who move virtually naked in miniwears, painting their nails and faces with artificial colours, and making themselves barren in order to snatch away other's men".

These images have not changed much for even as recently as the 1970s. Amin's government was convinced that all unmarried urban women were prostitutes. Thus with the support of his officers, he wasted no time in mounting a verbal and physical war against them. Making them the target of his 1975 'city-cleaning and purification campaign' in preparation for the 1975 OAU summit in Kampala, Amin passed a decree to round up 'these prostitutes' into a camp. But because he never specified the camp, those who were rounded up were simply beaten, raped or killed by his blood-thirsty soldiers [Akello 1979. 14]. On the other hand, the 'good' married women were suddenly rewarded in apresidential decree which encouraged them to work in the informal and public sectors and granted three months' maternity leave instead of the former one month. Amin constantly reminded women that their goodness is in motherhood and wifehood and his general batred for the urban elites was extended to school girls who were often rounded up and abused by his soldiers.

It is possible to explain away Amin's sexist behaviour in terms of his general 'madness' with everybody but this position is greatly challenged by the prevalence of sexist practices within many public policies and practices of Uganda's 'sane' regimes. A critical evaluation of the existing policies suggests that whether consciously or unconsciously, society still believes that urban women are 'a thorn in the flesh' of urban planning and development. They are among those who must leave the city and the general labour market so that the little available housing and other resources can be distributed to the 'more useful' population.[1] This is evidenced in a series of the following discriminatory policies which date as far back as the pre-independence times and which have been faithfully preserved.

Class Divisions

Originally, the racist nature of colonial policies classified and confined the urban African population into the rent-free African quarters. But faced with an increasing rate of rural-urban migration, the colonial government was advised by the 1948 Holmes Commission that in order to avoid future housing problems, it should arrange to divest itself of the unlimited responsibility to house public servants and the urban population in general. The proposal was taken up by the 1954 Lidbury commission which went further in classifying the housing problem by introducing the criteria of 'Entitled'. 'eligible' and 'Others' which still operate in form of the Standing Orders. The 1962 Prosser Commission concurred with this position and it went further to suggest that in order to effect this position without fail, "government should not build any more houses for civil servants" [PSRC 1980-82, 156]. a position which was also taken up by the 1963 Ani Salaries Commission.[2] In all their attempts to solve the growing housing crisis, the pre-and post-independence governments and housing commissions made it clear that Uganda could no longer afford to maintain public housing as a service sector. For this reason, all of them suggested or implied the introduction of an economic rent for public housing. Time and again, it wassuggested that a percentage of each housed worker's salary should be charged to cover the rents; but as the wages were progressively devalued by inflation, the suggestion was not feasible and it was constantly shelved. Nevertheless, the mere fact that the suggestion appeared, and continues to reappear, suggests and explains the domination of the private housing market by the high income bracket who can afford to rent or build own house, and of whom women are a minority.

Secondly, looking back at the standing orders, government restricted itself to housing only special categories of workers. First are those who hold 'status posts'- the expatriates, the ministers, the permanent secretaries, the judges and those who belong to the super salary scales A and B. These are entitled to housing; that is, they must be accommodatd at any cost. In 1982 government passed a bill to the effect that this class would only be limited to expatriates but as often happens, the amendment remained on paper. What worsens the situation is the constant expansion of this category by an increasing number of returned exiles who had left the country in search of greener political and/or economic pastures. Next are the 'permanent and pensionable workers who are eligible for housing; that is they are accommodated if and when possible. Otherwise they can be billeted with other officers or pesons. Alternatively, they can be given a housing allowance in lieu of housing and this allowance is supposedly 20 per cent of the individual worker's salary. Other public workers, the others, are neither entitled nor eligible for housing save in exceptional circumstances and on temporary basis [PSRC 1980-82, 159]. Suffice it to note that of the total 2,39,528 public workers, only 1,36,269 fall under the Entitled and the Eligible categories (even then, many of the latter are not housed) and this leaves the 1,02,898 Others knocked off the list including the informal sector-workers. For female workers of both sectors most of whom are others, this legislation serves to exclude them from public housing.

It is also important to note that according to Baingana compared to about 599 men in the super salary scale A and B, there are about 68 women only, 14 in the former and 54 in the latter. This further shows how women are disproportionately represented in Uganda's public service and salary scale. Baingana observes that the entry for professionals into the public services is at U5A-3 and although the total number of women professionals in and above USA-3 is high in absolute terms, it is surprising that so few of these women have so far been promoted to the U1, U2, and U3 super salary scales. For instance, by the start of 1992, Uganda's so-called broad-based cabinet had only two women cabinet ministers out of a total of 21. And out of a total of 10 ministers of state there was only one woman. Similarly, out of 10 deputy ministers, only one was a woman. Out of 40 permanent secretaries only six were women, and out of 26 judges of the high court, only four were women [Baingana 1992].

As already noted, the colonial masters pursued a racist housing policy where by Europeans and Asians monopolised the high and middle class pool houses respectively while the Africans occupied the poor 'African Quarters'. While this caused a lot of resentment and hatred for the former, the post-independence governements have never seen any contradiction in replacing the recist system with a sexist and classist one. For instance, while they concurred with the sexist and classist Standing Orders, the 1980-82 PSRC was outraged by the Ani Commission's racist suggestion that government housing provision should be limited to the expatriates. In a moving statement on the subject the former said that such a suggestion had to be shelved because they could not imagine ''swarthy businessmen heaving and gallivanting around golfcourse-skirted dwellings of our former colonial masters, now preserved for the high echelons of the administration in the country'' (PSRC 1980-82, 156)[3].

Commenting on the practice of classifying housing needs in Bogota, Glaser (1986) said that certain terminologies such as 'the undeserving and the deserving' (which are the equivalents of Uganda's 'entitled, eligible and others') sound too crude for modern use. Thus he cited Schaeffer's alternatives of the working class and the lowers class or 'the poor and the poorest of the poor' or 'the formal and the informal workers'. But as he also admits, changing the classification terminologies makes no difference and, to put it loosely, if one looks at the classification from a gender perspective, much of it is tantamount ot sexism where by the number of advantaged men far exceeds that of women. Secondly, even when terminologies are changed and amendment bills passed in favour of women, the gap between policies and practices remains so unchallenged that many policies remain on paper. In Uganda, the situation is worsened by the frequent and violent changes of regimes and the subsequent discontinuity between the past and the present policies This is evidenced by the number of recommendations which various PSRCs have passed but which have since then remained on paper. So even as the present government provides much room for women's participation in many spheres of life, the continuity of this relative freedom is subject to the next government's attitude towards women.

'Points System' and Women's Marital Status

The few women who are eligible and entitled for government housing are often discriminated against on the grounds of their marital status. Among the educated middle and upper-class population, women's share of the natinal housing is comparatively low. It is assumed that those who are married are housed by their husband and that the unmarried do not need any formal housing because they are assumed to live with their parents, relatives or friends. Therefore most unmarried women seek to rent rooms in private units. But even here they are considered undesirable for fear that they will destabilise the landlords's marriages. This reflects the gender ideology that a women's true and complete identity is in the man/marriage and that any adult single women is either abnormal or a prostitute unless she proves otherwise. All this results in the concentration of single mothers, widows and divorcees in the free world' of the shanty towns.

According to the sexist Standing Orders, "a married woman is only housed by government if her husband is not housed (by the same). A woman public officer thus forfeits her housing rights by getting married" (PSRC 1980-82, 161). There is no official provision for her once she is divorced or widowed because then she becomes a pitiable second class citizen who needs special qualification if she must be housed in her own right. By losing her husband, she loses the most automatic way through which she has access to public housing, that is, her being affiliated to a family man, for according to the Points System, special favour is given to "the more senior family man" and not the more senior family women, and this clause was considered justifiable by the 1980-1982 PSRC. In fact the commission's complaint was that at the time, the clause was not being strictly adhered to. So since the list of the more senior family men' will never end, women will never be a priority category unless they rise up and protest now.

Although it is claimed that an unmarried woman can apply for her own housing, the way she must raise the points makes the exercise unrealistic, especially amid the severe competition for the few housing units. First, if she is divorced, she must prove it which is problematic because formal divorces are rare; this is due to the complicated and expensive nature of court divorce procedures. Secondly-albe it indirectly- she must have many children because each child carries four points. This too is problematic because it contradicts family planning, and discriminates against the childless and those whose children are under the fathers' custody. Thirdly, she must have worked in the public service for at least four years. which automatically wins her 15 points. The longer she has worked, the more able she is to compete with other. But by the end of the first four years, most women are married and are thus knocked off the competitors' list. Others might be single parents, but since priority is given to the more senior family man, it will be long before they win houses, even if they have families. This reflects a clear misrepresentation of what constitutes a family/ household in an African setting. Consciously and/ or unconsciously, government planners assume a Victorian nuclear family or husband, wife, and two or three children within which there is a clear sexual division of labour in which the man works outside as a breadwinner and the woman is a house wife [Moser on *Women, Human Settlement and Housing* 1987]. So the idea of a single family woman and her housing needs seems to be alien and unaccommodated in public policies and practices which are set and implemented by westernised authorities.

Against this background, unceremonious eviction of widows from public houses goes on unabated. Even when the widow and the deceased husband, or any other of their household members, were public servants, it does not automatically follow that the woman retains the house. In this case the injustice to the woman is institutionalised by a regulation which registers the couples houses in the names of the husbands so that when they die, the fate of the wives and children is a foregone conclusion. Sometimes, the justification behind such evictions is that depending on the widow's status in public service, she may not qualify for the deceased's class of housing. But given the general housing shortage, a woman who is thus evicted may not necessarily get resettled in her supposed class of housing. Eviction of women applies with greater force in case of non-public servant females who are housed by public servants, either as wives or as 'squatters', for in this case, the former's non-eligibility is undebatable. In recent times, the situation has worsened if the husband happens to be an AIDS victim (whose eventual death is sure) because people begin to apply and to lobby for the house long before he dies.

The presence of a very high percentage off ill-housed or unhoused women is not surprising given the fact that in Uganda, women form the majority of the poor, illiterate and semi-literate population who have no access to good jobs and good housing. By 1985, the women who had completed primary school formed only 38 per cent of the total population of these, only 5 per cent had completed secondary school level which means that the remaining 33 per cent were semi-literate. The basis for women's low level of education is the constant reproduction of the gender ideology which stresses the breadwinning man and the dependant mother and housewife. When school girls get pregnant they tend to be humiliated, harassed and expelled or with drawn from school, and that ends their academic career. At the earliest opportunity, they are sold off into marriage at a reasonabale bride price or else they escape into the city which seems to be 'the land of beginning again'. But because such women lack the skills to compete for good jobs and good houses, and the standards to compete for the rich and well-housed men, their hopes are shattered and they retreat into the shanty towns.

Given the host of cultural and economic factors which militate against women's education, the idea that men and women have equal education, employment and housing opportunities can no longer be entertained. First many parents are still reluctant to educate their daughters who according to tradition, are primarily bred for marriage. Secondly, compared to boys, girls get so preoccupied with domestic chores that they tend to have less time to concentrate on their education. Moreover even those who make it through the system tend to be groomed for non-professional careers which "can be easily combined with motherhood and wife hood" [Baingana 1992,12]. Still, those who manage to get good careers tend to be bypassed when it comes to higher training and refresher course opportunities. Sometimes, they might be too preoccupied with house hold cares that they have no time to take up such opportunities. In the end, as long as their education levels remain lower than those of their male counterparts, their chances of being promoted to senior offices, to which housing is attached, are also very limited.

During the second half of the 1960s, government declared its intentions to enable civil servants to champion the housing programme through the clolonial practice of direct purchase and/or direct construction of own housing. Accordingly, 1968 saw the founding of the National Finance Company and the verbal determination to strengthen the 1964 National Housing Corporation (the present NH and CC) in order to increase the housing stock for sale. But due to lack of funding which intensified from he mid 1970s. the projects were not fruitful. The only units which were sold (in 1975) were the 216 up-country units and the 244 unfinished ones at Ntinda and Nsambya. Even then, instead fo recycling the funds into construction, they were diverted and this sealed the bankruptey of the schemes. In the vacuum that followed, all banks opened up housing credit schemes but their role in increasing the housing stock has been negligible, cautious and highly inflexible particularly in case of the poor of whom women are a large proportion.

Although women are ready to throw off the gender yoke which prevents them form owning houses and other property, their poverty and lack of access to credit facilities is a great obstacle. The credit schemes are not only inefficient but also sexist in favour of men-albeit indirectly. Reporting as early as 1957, Gutkind and southall noted that because common sense is often vaquished by commercial needs and greed, a major contradiction in Uganda's housing credit schemes is that the poorer the applicant is, the less likely (s) he is to secure the credit [Southall and Gutkind 1957, 47]. As often happens, lending decisions are made on the basis of one's prior earnings or savings and credit history; this makes it difficult for the low income people and the potential beginners to penetrate the credit system. For women, an additional problem is the lenders' tendency to demand that the credit forms must be countersigned by one's husband. Behind this is the false assumption that men are the heads of households and that as "the" income earners, they are more reliable in paying the loans. So it is not surprising that with their low initial capital, women, particularly the single, are the last to be considered because they are thought to be risky clients.

Because of the women's low and fluctuating earnings, their distrust for banks, plus their overspending on the household budget, they tend not to keep savings account. As such, their bargaining power is greatly jeopardised; the moneylenders stereotype them as potential loan-defaulters on the ground that they cannot present a substantial amount of inital working capital or maintain fixed monthly payments on the mortgages. The problem is aggravated by the moneylender's tendency to estimate every applicant's income on the basis of his/her regualr earnings rather than his/her total incomes from other sources such as friends, relatives and petty trading. Whenever this income requirement is applied to loan applicants, the results are biased in favour of men whose incomes are higher and more regular [Moser 1985]. In some cases, not only do the schemes demand loan security (in form of fixed assets) which most women lack, but they also tend to insist on urban-based security which is easier and more profitable to develop. Yet if there are any women who have security it is in form of rural land; by rejecting it the financiers do not only wound the women by they also contradict government's efforts to develop the rural world.

Another problem which excludes women from credit schemes are the intimidating and complicated bureaucratic procedures through which credit institutions allocate loans. The application forms tend to be complex, with suspicious questions about one's personal details which must be substantiated with official documents such as identity cards, tax tickets, bank statements, and employer's reference; the self-employed may be required to prodcue business registration certificates, balance sheets and growth projections of their businesses. For credit schemes, the aim is to minimise risks of loan-defaulting; but as most women are self-employed (in the informal sector) without regular and/ or documented incomes, these demands are exclusive. Many informal business operators, particularly the female petty traders rarely keep such records, party because their incomes are irregular and/ or insignificant, and partly because they are not trained in the economics of running their enterprises.

Most of them, ''rely on either their instinct or the experience of a friend or relatives... they keep no formal records and they engage in duplication of efforts. If one of them is engaged in a venture that seems profitable, there is a mad rush (by other) to establish a similar business...only to soon find the market saturated and their hopes shattered. (Suddenly, they start another venture) [World Council of Churches 1985, 41-42].

Secondly, given their low mobility, their general marginalisation in the formal sector, and/or their low literacy levels, many women have not full information about formal credit procedures, but they may feel insecure and afraid to show their ignorance. This, plus their preoccupation with domestic chores, survival activities and child care deny them access to credit. The problem is compounded by the common practice that even when one meets all the necessary criteria and has undergone all the necessary procedures, (s)he might wait indefinitely before the transaction is effected, a process that is often punctuated by a series of bribes in the attempt to lubricate the officials so they can effect and/or hasten the transaction. The tendency is that in addition to the official criteria, one must have a wide range of differentiated contacts which (s)he can activate to help her/him. As Jacobson said, In the urban area, almost any service or item...can be made more readily accessible by the strategic manipulation of such contacts and connections. Whether one...is applying for a position as a bank clerk, or obtaining a licence to operate a stall on the market, makes no difference, all transaction are carried out more efficiently if there is a social connection between the participants. Where aid is given, a return is expected either an equivalent service or the provision of another contact, or sometimes participation in the formation of a clientele. These alternatives failing, the service must be bought... There are various ways in which (all this) can be accomplished, and the higher one stands in the social hierarchy, the greater the range of possible contacts... The school and university are ideal for they provide a setting in which people make the right kind of friends (Helga Jacobson (on Ceba city, Philippines), quoted in Elliot, 1975, 270).

In all these problems men, particularly those in the high income bracket, are favoured because of their high lobbying power. Given their low mobility and their marginalisation in the education system, women are less likely to make useful contacts and this seals their fate. So it is not surprising that rather than the poor, established business men and government bureaucrats are the major beneficiaries of the credit schemes.

Thirdly, the interest which is levied on the mortgages is often beyond the means of most women. For instance, according to the 1980-82 PSRC, for a Shs 4-5 million houses, the Housing Finance's mortgage could be as little as Shs 3,00,000; and for that relatively small loan, it would make unimaginable profits by laying a total claim on the building. "In a different setting, this would be tantamount to usury (and) it is certainly discouraging to would-be house owners" [PSRC 1980-82, 158]. Moreover , in view of the high inflation rates, the mortages progressively lose their value and the creditor must face the problem of covering the gap. This might involve longer working hours, subletting, multiple borrowing or a total abandoning of the housing project. Government's failure to save women, and the poor in general from the strains of funding their own housing schemes does not only contradict its 'women's liberation theology' but it is also out of tune with its intentions to let the private sector champion the housing cause.

Women and Land Tenure System

Land is an indispensable part of any houseing scheme, but in Uganda, its special importance lies in the absence of a single national tenure system. Generally, Uganda's land tenure system(s) is a catalogue of confusion, but it is even more so in and around the urban areas where the high population pressure and capitalist interests have put government policies and customary practices at antagonistic ends. Ever since the colonical government whittled away the Baganda's customary system (in the 1900 Buganda Agreement) by nationalising some of their land and by privatising the rest into the hands of political monarchs, it is impossible to talk about land issues without generating high emotions. The tension is particularly high whenever mention is made of the total nationalisation and bureaucratisation of land administration and the suppression of kinship inheritance and individualisation systems which enhances the individual landholder's rights. The tension is not only responisble for the marginalisation of women's land rights but it also explains the haphazard nature in which Kampala city has developed in terms of housing. For women, the ways in which the universalist state laws and policies exist within the context of the conservative and particularistic customary systems pose a serious threat to their land ownership and optimum utilisation. One one hand there are cases where the customary system gave women land ownership but in an urban setting, the system is weak and irrelevant, for it can be overridden by the state power. On the other hands, there are cases where state laws and land policies which would give women more land rights (compared to customary systems) fail to break through the front that is set by the latter so that women become victims of the tension between the two.

State intervention in Buganda's customary land law[4] datea as far back as colonial times and it has been faithfull followed and reinforced by successive post-colonial government sometimes with a few but unsuccessful attempts towards some modification. Before colonialism, land was owned communally, administered and distributed by clan and lineage heads on behalf of the king. As divorcees, widows or spinsters women were also entitled to land use for the Baganda believed in their proveb that "an abandoned property (in this case the abandoned woman) must return to its own people and must be given refuge". With Buganda's territorial expansion however, the king replaced the clan heads' land authority with that of a political elite who distributed land among clans without necessarily altering its communal and non-capitalist use value. The only power which a landowing individual gained was political and social prestige. But with the coming of colonialism, the introduction of the cash crop economy led to the commoditisation of land which included the right of individuals to purchase, sell and inherit land in their independent right. About 8,700 square miles of land were given to top political figures[3] who later sold away some of it. Thus at the start of 1900, there were 4,000 mailo landowners most of them Baganda males, plus a few chiefs from Bunyoro, Busoga, Toro and Ankole. With the eventual divisions and subdivisions however, the number rose to about 50,0000 in 1953 (Southall 1989), Another 6,800 square miles were set apart as Crown/ Public land and of this, 104 square miles were particularly reserved for foreigners who had no contact with the landowning elites. However, with the rapid expansion of the city, the latter miles were encroached on as well and consequently, the 1962 government as compelled to re-emphasise the 1903 Ordinance stressing that,

...no citizen or person in private enterprise should entertain the idea that the Government of Uganda cannot, whenever it is desirable in the interests of the people, nationalise any or all privately owned interests, mailo (mile) and freehold land and all productive assets or property, at any time, for the benefit or the people. The Party, therefore, directs the government to work along these lines [Article 36, Uganda Constitution 1962 in Mafeja A 1973, 22-23].

Whatever other shortcomings it had, the main problem of this policy is that in practice, it ignord the fundamental issue of nationalising all the land, particularly the unutilised mailo land, and instead, it concentrated on the nationalisation of only that land which government needed/needs at a particular point in time. With hindsight, the opportunity to effect this change was lost at a time when the newly independent nation was capable of absorbing such major traumatic changes. Today the undertaking is more complex and the reconciliation of the customary land rights with the state policies is so politically sensitive that despite the constant suggestion to carry out a land reform in public interest, successive regimes have been reluctant to effect the paper measures. Thus, right in the city-centre, are chunks of land which are covered by slum settlements because the successive governments and the private landowners have failed to agree on the issue of nationalising them. A good example of this cold conflict is manifested in the traditionalists' stronghold on Kibuli hill and the surrounding areas, a conflict which has provided a conducive atmosphere for the survival of an extensive slum settlement which extends as far as Namuwongo and Wabigalo. The question at issue is how to compensate the present occupants, and how to nationalise the land without opening the 'land grabbing' conflicts between the traditionalists and the state. The problem is that some of the male political-bureaucratic elites who would enforce the land-reform measures are an economically weak class who live more by consuming than by investing in land. Their control over land is therefore minimal and they are in constant fear of causing a rebellion among the land elites who are their main political-economic supporters [Mafeje 1973]. Other elites are powerful landlords themselves, and for fear of signing their own death warrant, they are resistant to land reform.

For women, the major effect of the 1962 Uganda constitutional land policy was/is that all factors remaining constant, they can buy land in their own right. But by the same token, the land reform decree created strong class differentiations on economic grounds, for it was clear that outside kinship inheritance, which is rarely extended to women, land ownership was/is for the rich. But since the majority of women have less access to good income-generating activities the land decree marginalised most of them, particularly those in the urban areas where the communal tenure system has been totally eroded. In order to compensate for this anomaly, government left room for the poor people to acquire land through a tenancy system, "ekibanja". Under this arrangement, one could buy land at a very subsidised price, settle on it and use it as long as (s) he continued to pay a little annual tax to the landlord.

According to this provision, the tenant's land rights were so strong that (s) he could even pledge the land as security for a loan. This was confirmed even by 1969 Public Land Act which went further to add that a person could lawfully occupy, by customary tenure, any land which was not alienated in leasehold or freehold. Acoording to this Act, without the consent of the customary tenant at issue, neither government nor any private person could give or lease out his/her land. The trend was to expand the individual's rights of land and to make state intervention in land issues a matter of last resort [Kisamba-Mugerwa 1989, But in Practice, the law did not work and more than men, women have had to pay a greater and more painful price for their tenancy since they were a large proportion of the tenants. The problem was that as land became more commoditised in the urban world, landlords prrferred to terminate their tenants' contracts and to divide the land into smaller plots (for building purposes) which sell very expensively and whose money is paid in a lump sum, thus making it more investible). Because of the constant fear of eviction, tenants lack the security to put permanent housing, or perennial cropping,. on the land. Although the law stipulates that the landlord has no legal sanction to evict a tenant who has not failed to pay her annual tax, illegal and violent eviction of tenants continues unabated. The tenants may not be in good financial position to endure the costs and delays which are associated with court appeals. In their disussion of this issue in Kisenyi slum, southall and Gutkind (1957) confirmed that these disadvantages tend to apply with greater force to women who are a large proportion of the tenants.

As if to sanction the eviction of tenants, Amin's 1975 Land Reform Decree (LRD) which, though intended to abolish the mailo land system, ended up strengthening it while it at the same time left everybody confused. Hoping to free the tenants from the land tax which made them 'debt peons', the decree repealed the tenants' annual land tax. But by the same token, the move left no obligation for the mailo landowners to ensure the security of their tenants. All tenancies were converted to customary tenure and their holders had no legal title to the land which they, to this day, hold at sufferance. At the ruling of the Land Office, they can, at a notice of six months be evicted, either by government, leaseholders, or private companies. Thus without any security of tenure, the tenants were reduced to the status of squatters who can be evicted once the former claims his intentions to develop the land, whatever this may mean. Although the LRD stipulates that the landlord must compensate the tenant for her/his investment on the land, the money thus paid tends to be too small to afford the tenant another plot on the open market.

Althought this LRD has never been systematically implemented the fact that it has neither been repealed suggests that it is condoned and it can be manipulated or invoked by whoever wants to use it to hi/her advantage. Indeed government and a few private landlords and companies have often used it. According to Kisamba-Mugerwa, in an increasing number of cases, land has been leased out even without the knowledge of the tenants, who are simply bulldozed by powerful lords, particularly commercial companies who are not bound by socio cultural ties and who easily use lawyers to effect the eviction [Kisamba-Mugerwa 1989]. As long as they have lawyers to shrewdly interpret the law, they can find refuge in the law and the state. This is particularly possible since the tenants are too poor to hire lawyers, and sometimes they are not even fully aware of the land law itself. For instance, until now, without the knowledge of most customary tenants the land office operates only two registers-the mailo land and the lease hold land files, and this suggests that government does not recognise the customary tenants' rights of ownership to land.

Apart from the mailo system and the customary tenancies which are held at suffernace, the present government operates on the leasehold system, at least in principle. Southall and Kisamba-Mugerwa have contradicting information on the duration of the leases although it is apparent that the present leasehold rules were basically rooted in those of the 1975 LRD. According to the latter, as per 1975 LRD, all freeholds and mailo land had to be leased for 99 years, while land which belonged to institutions and charitable organisations was to be leased for 199 years [Kisamba-Mugerwa 1989]. But according to Southall, the 1989 Land Commission adjusted the 1975 LRD, ruling that all mailo land was supposed to be leased for 99 years, and the rest for 49 years [Southall 1989]. Consequently, all mailo tenants, together with the mailo owners were to be granted leasehold titles. This however, is total confusion, for then both parties would become legal owners of the land and unless the tenant leaseholder is very self-assertive and powerful, the mailo leaseholder is very self assertive and powerful, the mailo leaseholder is likely to use his social-financial position to evict him/her.

If it is not that government simply fears to provoke a social-political conflict with the landowning elite, then the aims behind its desire to protect mailo landowners at the expense of the mailo tenants are unclear. One argument would be that government wanted to discourage land fragmentation and encourage large-scale investment on land. But clearly, given the poor financial positon of the mailo-landowners, the realisation of this dream might require more than a whole centruy. Almost 100 years since the landed aristocrats acquired their estates form the colonial masters, they have not put any large-scale investment on the land, Instead, the best they do is to trade in land plots, selling them to very peasants from whom the very land was grabbed away in 1900 Agreement and the 1903 Crown Land Ordinance. While countries like Kenya and some central African republics struggled against the colonial large-scale landalienators, in Uganda, it was the Baganda sub-imperialists who stole a march against the peasants. As Southall says, the Ugandan mailo tenants/settlers received no consideration whatsoever in the 1900 and the 1903 arrangements.'' They were sold by the British like nameless chattels in return for the allegiance of their owners'' [Southall 1989, 23]. To this day, they resent their fate and it is no wonder that in some cases they are a threat to the life and property of any land-owners who evict tenants without adequate compensation or notice [Kisamba-Mugerwa 1989]. In fact, apart from the financial handicap of the mailo landowners, this cold war between them and the peasants has played a significant role in preventing them from utilising their parcels of land, or even selling it away anyhow. Surprisingly in some cases, if a group of peasants take their stand against an eviction, even government, unable to defend and implement its own policies, tends to act in their favour by stopping the eviction.

All these problems and confusions aside, there are cases where women's land ownership is complicated by the gender ideology that women should not own property, particularly land and housing. Women who own property tend to be stereotyped as self-assertive and unruly, and therefore unmarriageable. This tactic is used to discourage women from buying land and/or from pursuing their inheritance rights (where they might exist) as much as it discourages them from its optimum utilisation. Society's fears about self-sustaining women are not unfounded for among other factors, it is the economic power of men which has always given them control over women. To let this power shift into the hands of women is to sign the men's death warrant. And this is the basic reason why young women are often threatened that if they go 'too far' in education, own property, or too much money, their chances of getting married and/or maintaining a stable marriage are greatly jeopardised. It is constantly claimed that as far as women are concerned, house-ownership is for the hopeless those who will never marry-the widows, the prostitutes, the senior spinsters, the frustrated, and the divorcees. Some women themselves have absorbed this ideology so much that even if they are lucky to have inherited land they abadon it, or sell it off before marriage. Other might be in position to buy land out of personal savings yet, buying land is the last thing they can think of.

For most people however, the major obstacle to owning a house is the expensiveness of urban plots including those that are sold by government. Apart form this problem, the official prices.ground rent for government leasehold plots are unknown to the public and they are easily inflated by the land officers. For instance depending on what ground rent each or them paid, about five oral informants gave me different prices, ranging from Shs 2,00,000 to 2,000,000 of what they believe the ground rent is. It is interesting to note that the informant who suggested Shs 2,00,000 was a top government offical confirming the common knowledge that the higher one is in the social-political confirming the common knowledge that the highter one is in the social-political hierarchy, the less likely s(he) is to be cheated. There are also cases on record where the land office has, whether out of administrative error of corruption sold a plot of land to more than one client. The only way the two buyers discover themselves is when they meet at the constructionsite, each of them trying to lay a claim on the plot. In such cases, if the first client had bought but left the land unutilised for more than five years, the land office might take cover under the 1989 Land commission which gives the land office powers to terminate, without reimbursing the ground rent, the lease of anyone who, after five years fails to effectively develop the leasehold.[6] But if this is not the case, the two clients and probably the land officers must resort to the law of the jungle, unless the land office acts quickly.

Multiple-selling is not only limited to the land office, it is widely practised even by private landowners, and any potential land buyers does well to carry out detailed research on the plot (s) he may want to buy. The best way to do this is to ascertain from the City Coun cil registry the land-seller's legal claim on the land and whether (s)he has not sold it to someone else before. To establish this even further, the buyer must, through a wide range of contacts (such as the landlord's neighbours, relatives, friends and even enemies) do a lot of research on the subject. Thus is addition to the actual land price, one must be ready to spend a substantial amount of money on the 'research contacts' other middlepersons. (S)he must also tip or bribe the official land surveyors who, though they should be simply doing their duty, expect the 'tip', more as an obligation than as a favour. All these costs, togother with the 'official' ground rent and the complicated bureaucratic procedures make it difficult for low income women to acquire urban land. With their low rate of mobility, their little knowledge of the 'city games' and their low incomes, women are less likely than men to get urban land.

Prices become more inflated as one moves into the city-centre and this explains people's withdrawal into the city suburbs which were once unpopular. The trend has the effect of circling the poor into slum settlements which survive well on disputed acreage. The rich house-owners, both private and public figures, have devised a series of tactful regulations in form of inflated land-price, complicated bureaucratic procedures, expensive building regulations and practices, through which they protect their colonies from the poor who are stereotyped as uncultured. An important effect of this informal zoning is the concentration of basic infrastructural services in the rich zones at the expense of the poor zones. For the poor women, problems such as constant water and power cuts, the broken sanitation infrastructures and the poor road maintenance mean the prolonging of their working day on both the domestic and the market levels. As already mentioned, poor women and children are constantly roaming the city in search of water sometimes, they line for long hours, baked by the sun, hit by the dust, and exposing their children to unhealthy conditions. Sometimes, the struggle for water can be explosive particularly when the male water vendors push into the line with several containers and kick aside the women and children's containers. If the water is fetched from open wells, it is certainly polluted with sewage and rain run off, and sometimes, it is drunk unboiled in a bid to save time and fuel. But when the family falls sick, the consequences fall back on the women who must nurse the sick and/or meet the medical bills.

Compared to the poor infrastructure in the poor zones, the rich ones tend to be much better, with street/security lights, good sewerage systems, better roads, and a more regular supply of water and power. Whenever the system breaks down there tends to be a mad rush to fixit it, on the contrary, it may take months before a similar breakdown in poor zones is fixed. Even then, the residents may have to bribe the technician (who may not even be qualified) in order to effect the repair. In fact in many poor areas, the power system is more or less entirely manned by 'self-trained'/illegal technicians who constantly disrupt the system so they are constantly bribed into fixing it. Similarly in cases of water shortage, richer zones are more readily supplied with tank trucks. This alternative failing, the rich can drive long distances and stock their houses with water, or they can hire labour. In a nutshell, the inflated prices of urban plots and the subsequent informal zoning which separates the rich and the poor have caused a great infrastructuaral imbalance between the rich and the poor zones. And since women are the major users of the housing infrastructure, this marginalisation increases the weight of their household work.

III Women's Survival Strategies

Despite enormous odds, the number of women in Kampala and other urban areas has continued to grow by the year, rising from 42.5 per cent in 1967 to 51 per cent in 1991. This is due to the relatively higher education and Job opportunities offered to girls/women in towns, the instability in the rural areas and the increasing unattractiveness of village life in terms of agricultural producer income and public infrastructure. Despite its economic constraints, most women are convinced that given the extreme forms of poverty and/or insecurity in Uganda's rural areas, town migration is inevitable. Urban life is relatively soft. It gives them access to a wide range of social services, such as education and medical services, it provides some access to money so they can purchase basic commodities (such as clothing, salt, sugar and fuel), it frees them from monotonous and backbreaking domestic chores (such as digging, cooking on firewood, and fetching water over long distances) which are done without any labour-saving technology, and relatively, it sets them free from some oppressive traditional practices such as early pregnancies and forced marriages.

Town migration is no longer a male phenomenon, nor do women migrants have to accompany, or be accompanied by their parents, spouses or other male reltives. Secondly migration is no longer limited to married adults and educated elites. On the contrary, the age and status profile of Kampala's female population reveals a characteristically youthful and mid-age composition. Many of them are unmarried, illiterate or semi-literate, they are concentrated in the informal sector, and compared to men, their incomes are reltively low and unstable. Because of their low education status, their chances of getting into the formal labour force are very slim and so is the possibility of getting housed by government. At the same time, their low and unsteady incoems make it hard for them to rent, buy or build their own housing.

Some women, particularly those in the low and the high income brackets, tend to take advantage of the urban multi-cultural setting to resist gender norms which forbid them from owning houses and other property. As one shack-owner interviewee, Tendo, put it.

Every woman must own a house, no matter what it looks like, the nature of the dwelling does not matter as much as the fact *it is mine* (her emphasis). I can close it and open it any time. And I can use it anyhow without the policing figure of a husband, parent , or land-lord.

On the other hand, some women, particularly those in the mid-income and some low-income groups tend to survive by manipulating various gender norms in order to be housed. Among them are those who look out for housed male relatives or spouses, those who use lovers to generate money for own housing or for rent and those who lobby informally in government housing committees to allocate them government units. A third category includes those whom I call 'squatters' or 'nomads' and the sub-renters. The latter refers to those who rent independent rooms of the same housing unit from single houseowner, but it can also mean relatives and/or friends who pool resources to rent a single housing unit or room. The 'housing nomads' are those who are housed by the day without necessarily sleeping the streets.[7] Among these are the pentecosta Christians who spend nights in trans-night prayer gatherings; and those who live by visiting relatives and friends one short period after another. The ''squatters'' are more difficult to ground; the major difference between them and the nomads is that the residence within any single household tend to be more permanent, at least in principle However, suffice to note that although various survival strategies are present here in clear-cut categories, on the ground women tend to use more than one strategy.

Insights from Katanga Slum

The total number or Kampala's female houseowner/occupiers is unknown but there is no doubt that it is on the increase particularly among the urban poor. There is an increasing number of women who toil day and night to construct their own rooms and/ or houses in order to free themselves from the yoke of rent and constant eviction. As one Katangee[8] argued, the basis of their actions is that every woman who constructs her own house must believe that owning a house is normal. She must break the outdated gender shackles which bind her to men's houses and other property. She must be deaf to those who wish to tarnish her brave image by stigmatising her as a prostitute. If need be, she must construct her own dwelling; she must not listen to the conservative moralists who claim that construction work makes women lose their sexual decency. She must bravely challenge traditional authorities and the so-called moral fabric of African traditional society which sentences women to life house-arrest. As Mama Juma put it :

After all, in the context of Katanga's mulitcultural composition, what are the norms, and from which tribe are they ? In some tribes women are the hosue-builders while in others they are simply housed. But when all of use meet here, we form our own culture which is highly flexible. There are no norms here, every one creates his/her norms; in the slums, everythings is normal. You just have to introduce an idea, stick to it self-assertively, and you will be surprised how you get followers. We cannot afford to rent these tiny mud rooms when other women build theirs and save their money.

No doubt there are many self-liberating women who take advantage of the multicultural nature of the city setting and, in my view more should be encouraged to do so. In fact, available evidence suggests that in comparison to their rural and upper class counterparts, lower class urban women are more desirous of and more successful in breaking gender norms. For instance, circumstances have forced them to be less mindful about breaking the silence of marital tensions and it is common for them to divorce, abuse and fight their men. Their being ridiculed as marriage failures or social misfits is just a passing chapter. They chase their money freely and they are eager to achieve material independence at any cost. Yet certain tribal norms which marginalise women persist. Even in the 'free world' of slums where acquisition of land and housing takes place illegally, women's self-liberation should not be grossly exaggerated. Many are still marginalised by the desire to maintain their feminine identity and decency at the cost of their survival, a syndrome which is even stronger among the middle class women.

Self-funding women and the nature of their houses vary according to their incomes. The few rich ones do not constitute a big problem. They might easily get access loans. They also lend to hire technical labour, use good quality materials, and their houses are certainly upper or middle-class in quality. However, for many poor women, self-funding and direct involvement in construction work is not an option. Many of them learn their construction skills not from a professional source. Sometimes they might seek the helping hand of their female friends and at times they might hire men to lift some heavy weights such as poles and cement and to do the roofing, but on the whole, they construct their own houses. Their units may not be very impressive but as the local proverb goes, ''the little one owns is better than the plenty that is borrowed''. Many house owners rarely know the pains of the manual labour which construction work involves for, in most cases, their task is to search for money and to hire labour. With out government support and/or a viable source of income, the women at issue reject traditions, and get physically involved sweating in the tropical sun with water, poles, bricks, roofing material, mud or cement. Mirembe was one such woman who demonstrated that despite their low earnings women can build their own houses without necessarily resorting to 'city games' or the help of lovers and that once they have asserted their position, they turn out to be respected and admired.

Born to mid-income Christian parents Mirembe was the first born in a family of 10. Influenced by their own literacy, her parents ensured the education of all their children regardless of their sex, for they believed that education was the only lasting inheritance which cannot be take away from a person. After repeating many classes. Mirembe concluded that she did not have the brains to pursue this treasure. Convinced that her parents had failed to appreciate her handicap she escaped at 15 to live with an illiterate family whose interpretation of the bible was so warped that they believed that poverty is a Christian virtue. Education and the search for wealth were seen as worldly pursuits which divert people from the kingdom of god. Using the second Corinthians as their justification, they constantly reminded her that true success lies in contentment, for the grace of god is sufficient.

They were so absorbed in their belief that they left no room for Mirembe to doubt or regret her decision.

They promised her a better life among the brethren suggesting that she should never even return to her own family because they were too blind in sin to bring her up in the knowledge of god. Since then, Mirembe and many other girls/women of her type moved and stayed among several brethren and learned to treasure them as their only wealth. Wherever they stayed, they performed a variety of domestic chores without being paid, for a members of the household and as 'sister' in the Lord, they were simple doing their duty. At 23, Mirembe revisited her family for the first time and she was shocked by how far her brothers and sisters had gone in education. Even the youngest sister had a job and a well-furnished room of her own. "I felt so envious and I spent the next years evaluating my life and regretting how I had wasted my years. You see, early in my life I had decided never to marry. The very fact that I have no children to bother me should have enabled me to make enough money and even to own a house of my own. But there I was a woman of 30 loitering among brethren and eating the crumbs that fell from their tables. Jesus did not tell people not to work; he was a carpenter himself". she said.

At 30, Mirembe had made up her mind to leave the circle of these unprogressive Christians and joined a more 'awakened' group. Through her sister she got a job as a cleaner in the hospital where she was so devout that within a short time she was promoted to the office of head cleaner. As she put it.

I worked hard because I was happy. I was working for my personal well-being. My Christian commitment also helped me to be very faithful so I was quickly trusted with the hospital property. I got many friends both rich and poor, doctors, administrators, medical students, nurses and fellow cleaners. My salary is not so high but since I was used to using very little money. I had no problem saving even from the meagre earnings. More over, sometimes my friends would tip me for my faithful services and this has always helped me to balance my budget.

Mirembe spent the first one year renting a small room in Mulago slum at Shs 4,500 per month. But conscious of her meagre salary her brothers and sisters often paid the rent particularly for the first eight months. In the meantime, Mirembe saved much of her salary and she began looking for land where to put up at least one room of her own. Finally one of her friends, a doctor, put her in touch with a relative who was a landlord in a Katanga slum and who gave her a smal plot free of charge. After that she spent her evenings making mud bricks at the site until she had accumulated enough for a room. She had no major problem with brick-laying because she had done it all while she lived among the brethren. Fortunately, she laid her bricks in the dry season so she escaped the problem of having her bricks washed away. She used her savings to buy a door, a window and eight iron sheets for the roofing. When all was set, her brother came and put up the room in a matter of three days while Mirembe fetched water and did other minor on-site jobs. Two weeks's later, Mirembe entered the room with two stools, a mattress, a blanket two saucepans, one cup 'and other rubbish', as she put it. "Until now that is my basic wealth. But one great thing is that I don't pay rent. This is my house."

Asked what others thought of her, she adamantly said that her possession of a house gave her such a high sense of self-worth that in reality, what others thought was immaterial. "Anyway, they admire and respect me particularly because my room is out of my own labour. People can only gossip about you if you owe your wealth to theft or to lovers. But I am an elderly woman, an auntie to all my neighbours, and to the best of my ability, I live an honest life."

One admirable thing about Mirembe is her sympathy towards her homeless friends and her desire to squeeze them in her room whenever she can.

> Sometimes, [she said], it is not easy to house people whose characters are strange, but on the other hand, it feels nice to help rather than to be helped. I love it when they ask me to help them with accommodation for some days. In fact I cannot imagine life without someone sleeping with me in this room. I am even planning to add another room so I can have a living room and a bed room. I will even furnish my house; you cannot believe my determination.

Manipulating Gender Norms

The ways in which women raise money is interesting too; apart from the usual petty trading and casual employment about which Obbo and Southall and Gutkind have written extensively, there is a women-sanctioned norm of using men as "income-generating project". Over the years, some feminists have suspected that men's praise of women, for example in marital relationships, is partly motivated by a desire to keep them in restricted places [Flax 1989]. But in Kampala, there is also evidence that some women praise men in order to reap financial benefits from them, even if for a moment. Available studies in Katanga. Namuwongo, Wabigalo, Mulago and Kisenyi suburbs suggest that, bound by their gender felters, some men toil all day long to prove themselves the bread-winners, the ideal men who forbid their women to work because it is shameful on their part. Taking advantage of the situation, some women decide to look out for such men and save money form the occasional 'gift' and the allocations for the daily domestic expenditures. As though they are proud of their subordination, they avoid confrontation and resort of manipulation for a while. They accept domestication while working towards a long-terms target. The flattering tones with which they voice their love for their men and the willingness with which they cook for them wins them the admirations of other richer men who flock to their homes every other night. Even when the woman in question has a side source of income there is a tendency not to disclose it to the lover especially if the latter is a higher income man who is likely to grossly under-estimate her earnings.

For instance aware of the temporary nature of Katanga's marital unions. Mama Nandawula, one of the interviewees commented that "a woman who is ignorant enough to violate this principle is as stupid as an eagle which dismantles its nest before it soars in the sky in the false hope that it will forever stay in the sky. We can stay with out men as long as love lasts, but we must acquire our own property in preparation for the rainy season." She recalled an incident when she used this method, saved money and bought a plot of land without the knowledge of her lover Joh.

When he learnt about it, he quarrelled and heaved like a bull. He insisted that my workmate Bob was my lover and that he was the one who bought the land for me. I tried to deny but he started beating me. The fight quickly gained momentum. I wasted no time in hitting his head with a chair in order to quickly weaken him. Men are like rats for even when they grow up into your own house, as Joh did, they will steal your foodstuff, Well, after this fight we broke out relationship but at least I have my land title.

In her research in Wabigalgo and Namuwong, Christine Obbo (1981) found the prevalence of a similar phenomenon, suggesting that women used traditional virtues of submission and service and their roles of motherhood and wifehood to strategise for their survival. She said that some women who bore children out of casual sexual relationships tended to use their men to court in order to get financial support from them in the name of financing the children's education, food and clothing. Thus, a rich man might be required to pay Shs 400 a month while a middle class man might pay shs. 100 Some women might not be able to afford the corruption and the costs which are associated with court procedures, but by threatening to leak the information to the men's wives, they might induce their lovers to give them financial support. Others even flatter men into fathering children and thus demand financial support from them. "Some smart women [can] even get the men to find them jobs or build them houses for the sake of the secret" [Obbo 1981, 103]. In this way, some women have risen from humble beginnings to mid-in-come levels.

The justification behind this strategy is that some women are so overwhelmed by the gender bias around them that they can never hope to survive if they attempt to challenge men head-on. Other women see it as a 'tit-fo-tat' affair whereby they strike a balance with men's exploitation of their sexuality and domestic labour. According to one elderly woman in Katanga, what is more upsetting about men is that if a women gives them sexual services without any financial demands, they stigmatise her as a 'communal baisn', meaning that she is loose and available for any man. She suggested that to be an outright prostitute is better and less oppressive than to be called a 'communal basin' by the very men whom she seeks to please with her generosity. So, in order to strike a balance, one should either resort to prostitution or to manipulation. She even stated that if she was younger she would actually have resorted to prostitution because prostitutes are at least assured of money and sex without being bound to the militant men. Moreover, "we Katangees have no name to protect, because to outsiders all of us are prostitutes anyway". The impression was that while prostitutes and manipulators are publicly despised, They are privately envied for their wealth and their courage to ply their trade despite enormous odds.

Contrary to common thought manipulation of gender virtues and roles is not limited to 'low class' women. It is also common among the educated and 'respectable' middle class women although sometimes it may take quite different forms. Although this category rarely invests in own housing (partly) becuase they set their housing dreams so high that they never seem to accumulate enough money to start off), nevertheless, some also manipulate gender virutes in order to balance their housing budgets. Most of them, as office workers, tend to concentrate on renting decent houses or rooms, eating well and dressing up in order to maintain a public appearance especially within their social groups. Others seek well-housed spouses, and if they are lucky to be the wives, they have struck a good bargain, at least for a time. Apart from this some women who are eligible for public housing might develop love affairs with male officials who might help them to lobby for government housing. As one case illustrates :

X had been a graduate public servant for two years. Because of her short period in public service and the fact that she had no dependents, she was not on the priority list for public housing. Her boss happened to be a member of the Housing Allocation Committee (HAC). Having realised the interest of her boss, X manipulated him into lobbying for a house for her, in exchange for a love affair. Thus after the following HAC meeting to the surprise of many long-time applicants, X got a house. Unfortunately once she entered the house, she pulled out of agreement with the boss. Imbued with the desire to protect his big name, the boss was too handicapped to threaten her in any way, lest she leak the secret. Instead he resignedly commented thus, 'You see, only smart people can survive these city games'.

However, such deals are not always broken. Sometimes, they might be the beginning of a lasting relationship which the woman can exploit to secure housing for some of her friends and relatives. True, the relationship might end some day, but still the woman retains the house unless the big man goes all the way to cause a malicious termination of her public services. Then she might lose the job and the house.

Indeed, as the case of Linda illustrates, manipulation of gender norms and personal charms is a fragile venture which, if it backfires, can cause very disastrous effects. In 1973 Linda had just returned from abroad, a 'been-to[9] as such returnces are admiringly tagged. With her newly acquired western looks and high-income airs, she was determined to hook a rich married man into a relationship that might eventually secure her one of his dollar houses in Lungujja. Against warnings from various friends, Linda conceived on purpose, married the man and got him to separate form his wife Felicity. Linda thought that as long as she had the man's son she could, in the event of a separation or death, inherit a house through her son. In 1987, the man died but when Linda tried to claim her share of the household property, she discovered that the great houses had been registered in the names of the deceased and Felicity. All that her son inherited was plot of land from which he quickly evicted his mother swearing to kill her should she lay any claim on it. In the words of Linda.

I suddenly fell from a high-class respectable woman to a nothing. Felicity's children had grown up and for all the crimes that I had committed against them and their mother they violently drove me out of her house. They almost killed me during the funeral. They did not allow me to take even a plate, and perhaps the were right, because throughout our marriage, I was just a housewife. Since I had left my job, I was entirely dependent on the man. I never contributed anythings to the home, not even domestice labour for the man surrounded me with house-girls and house-boys.

At the time of the interview Linda, then aged 44 had joined a nearby Pentecostal Christian Church and she had worked for three years as a voluntary councillor and this gave her the benefit of the use of the back room for sleeping in. She also did a variety of casual work including the sweeping of a nearby motor-repair workshop. Occasionally she would visit her only sister who lived at Nsambya but since the sister had a large family, she never attempted to stay for long. Asked why she could not return to her premarriage nursing profession, she said that no one would employ her because she had been out of practice for so long. She was so resigned to her fate that she had no housing plan for the future. "As long as this church lives. I will stay and die here". she said.

The Landladies

As the housing crisis intensifies, a few women have taken to the business of being landladies either as sub-renters of their own units[10], or as owners of separate rooms/houses for renting. A lucky few, particularly those in the peri-urban areas, have owned their land and houses through inheritance or direct purchase long before the city expanded into their areas. Some can still use their land to grow some food for household purposes and the rest can be sold off. Those who have built houses specifically for renting are admired particularly if they are rented for shop-keeping or to rich tenants who can pay a four-six months rent at once. The beauty of the houses vary and the better they are, the higher the profits. On the whole, however, any house owner is almost certain of his/her daily bread. Among the poor, houses tend to be designed for double purpose, that is, they tend to have a family room at the back and a double doored front room which, if some opportunity arises, can be turned into a shop. Secondly, the houses, particularly the semi-permanent mud and wattle ones, are often constructed in such a way that they can be easily extended to suit one's changing household needs.

For most women the initiation of a successful housing trade takes long years of hard work and self-denial. Even then, due to constant theft of materials, lack of funds and time to supervise the builders, and lack of authority in relation to contractors, most women build their houses very slowly [Larsson 1991, 163]. Thus it is understandable that successful traders tend to be women above 30 years. Another possible explanation for this age group's extraordinary involvement in own housing is that compared to the younger women whose hopes in the husbands' houses are still high, the older women have, from years of experience, learnt that marriage is a whirlwind. Once death and divorce strike, for the woman, homelessness and poverty are imminent. Therefore as Larsson says, a woman's own house offers a fixed place of abode, particularly outside marriage. It enables her to run her own social and economic activities; it eliminates the costs of renting; it enables her to live with her children; and through letting, it is a lasting investment. Besides, if she dies or returns to the villages, the house can be handed over to her children as a permanent inheritance.

In view of all this, many women are determined to work for their own houses. Some are upper class interstate traders while others have excelled in the despised small scale services such as selling cooked foodstuffs in open markets, selling local brews, second-hand clothes, vegetables, etc.[11] Unfortunately in evaluating their success, society tends to ignore their hard work and concentrates on stigmatising them as senior prostitutes, suggesting that they owe their wealth to long years of prostitution and adultery. One cannot deny that some of them have lovers who help them out on bad days, but this does not qualify them as prostitutes for frequently, they return the help. Secondly, society knows that most of them are financially independent; what they want is not money but sex without marriage ties for many of them believe that apart from sexual services, men are a nuisance in general [Obbo

1981]. In fact, because of the women's financial independences their lovers are despised as opportunists or manipulators ('abalebeesi') whose position is similar to that of the female manipulators.

These women and their movement towards own housing are not a recent phenomenon. As early as 1957, Southal and Gutkind wrote about them. According to them, for instance, by that time out of 199 house owners in Mulago slum, as many as 75 were women. Among others they cited one woman who resided in Mulago slum whose wealth was attributed to her independent hard work as a beer and banana seller.

She felt that independent work is the key to future riches...She thought that men did not like women do this sort of thing as it interfered with the 'power' which they have over women. This woman is known in the village for being extremely fastidious in her choice of lovers. She had saved a considerable amount of money and had managed to put up a number of houses for rent. Once when a man called her a prostitute, she beat him almost senseless, explaining that women without husbands are much better than those with husbands, because the latter are dishonest with their husbands in any case [Southall and Gutkind 1957, 178].

In more recent research, Obbo found similar women in Namuwongo and Wabigalo suggesting that "shop-keeping and house owning were regarded...as a sign of arrival at the top of the economic ladder" [Obbo 1981, 139]. Among others, she cites one Eseza, who had been in Kampala since 1952 and owned three brick houses each with three rooms. She lived in one of the houses while she rented out the others at a substantial profit. In addition, she was a successful seller of local brews who could afford to hire some labour for her business. She maintained a wide network of contacts particularly with the local authorities-the policemen, local chiefs and tax collectors. Another similar, but lower income woman could not attain Eseza'a standards but she was quite content with four mud and wattle grass-roofed houses brick house with a corrugated iron roof.

Tatu, who lived a few metres outside katanga is another interesting case. Aged 45, Tatu came to the city in 1978 after her husband had divorced her for being barren. She stayed with her brother, a widower, who had suffered from a long illness, which, in retrospect seems to have been AIDS. His illness had alienated him from all his relatives, leaving him desperate and lonely. Because Tatu patiently saw him through his painful last months, he left her his plot of land and his mud-and-wattle house. He asked her to bring up his children, Mandy and Suzie, then six and eight years old. At his death, Tatu, desperate to protect her land from money-hungry relatives and to ensure the children's survival, forced herself and the children into a slow and painful bricklaying project. Each day, each child had to lay between five to 10 mud bricks. They had to fetch their own water and to prepare the.

CHAPTER-21

Gender in Two Slum Cultures : Sri Laka and Thailand

Susanne Thorbek

I. INTRODUCTION

This Paper Considers the lives of women through comparing and contrasting two Asian slum areas in Bangkok (Thailand) and Colombo (Sri Lanka). It examines their lives through focusing on gender struggle, and the conflicts between men and women, and considers the reasons for the women's different experiences in each of the two areas. It also describes the ways in which urban life exacerbates the problems which women have to cope with and the differences in the ways in which they coped in the two slums. It also considers how these coping strategies were shaped by gender relations.

People in the Third World have been migrating to cities in large numbers in recent decades. When they move, they have to find new ways of living. They find new ways of understanding their world and their own role within it and they develop new practices. In studying slum areas, my intention is to focus attention on such new practices to better understand and analyze what poor urban people create.

Of course, the urbanization and daily life in the slum areas are influenced by structural factors such as the dominance of waged work. the separation of workplace and family, and the policies of the state, all of which are beyond the control of people themselves. However, it is usefull to focus attention on what people create and how they do so and how they interact with social institutions as well as their own past. Such a focus on people's practices in everyday life has been relatively strong in the social sciences in the last decade and this may help us to understand how social structures are created and how they may change." (1)

These kind of studies are of political significance because urbanization trends have been so strong and because social revolutions in the last two decades or more have, by and large, been based in cities. Such social movements will probably continue to be urban based.

Social movements must necessarily build on the concepts and ideas, the needs and interest of poor urban people. In this context, I believe that the question of gender, and the understandings and concepts which have developed around gender will become of utmost importance for the direction of social movements as well as their forms of organization.

The two field studies. one in a slum area of Bangkok and the other in a slum area of Colombo, have focused on women and the relationship between the genders as women see it. These two studies were intensive in depth, examinations of the daily life of slum dwellers. I lived (as for as possible) in the slum areas and tried to follow the daily activities of people there. I spoke some Thai but no Sinhalese and in both areas I worked with the help of translators.[(2)]

II. GENDER STRUGGLE

THE CONCEPT OF gender struggle is chosen because it focuses on the dynamic aspect of gender relations and on the public or semipublic activities which men and women undertake in order to keep a balance between the genders. It refers to direct conflicts between men and women, between spouses or between fathers and daughters. But it also includes possible conflicts between women (or men), and among friends and kin where these have an essential impact on gender relations.

In the Bangkok area, it was very obvious that both men and women took an active part in gender struggles. It mostly took the form of verbal conflicts-for example, a husband and wife might discuss the use of money, a wife might argue against her husband's gambling and drinking or women in a family might oppose a daughter (or sister) in law moving. Physical violence did occur but was not common. The women's concept of their relationship with their husbands showed a kind of equality as exemplified in the following statements:

"We are like friends, we discuss everything."

"If he can do it. I can do it too."

"There ought to be democracy in the family too. In these times." Women had friends and appreciated them greatly. In the daytime, women and, occasionally, a few men could be seen chatting in small groups, whereas in the evening the groups were mostly dominated by men with perhaps a few middle-aged women. Women fought in the gender struggle and told many stories about what they had done to get what they wanted, with varying degrees of success. Marriages were by and large stable, including second marriages. In regard to the division of income within families, in most instances, women were given a fixed amount of fimily income for household expenditure. Men generally administered most of the income although in a few cases this was done by women. The men usually allocated any surplus income but sometimes it was discussed and joint decisions made.

However, success was only relative. Accroding to the women, men squandered large amounts of money on gambling, especially when drunk. Men often had a minor wife (mistress) but, at the same time, were very possessive of their wives or daughters and allowed them no freedom.

By contrast, in the slum area in Colombo, I never came upon the concept of gender struggle, but rather talked about wife-battering. The women did not talk about conflicts with their husbands or fathers although the men were very offensive and often used physical violence, occasionally resulting in hospitalization. Conflicts were often within kin groups where discussions of a dowry or lack of a dowry, or of a son's responsibility towards either the new family or his family of origin played a major part. Such conflicts could continue for years and develop on many minor points. Help from other women was less evident, or rather it came very late in the conflict, mostly when a woman's life or health were at risk (for instance, when a wife fled from her husband and was naked at a neighbour's door). Women's groups (ie. women's contact with other women outside the family) were unusual. There was talk about friendships but also much talk about gossip and envy between the women, and the men certainly opposed gossiping among their wives. Women mostly fought for their needs in private and were generally not inclined to talk about such conflicts (for fairly good reasons as discussed below).

Compared to the area in Bangkok, the outcome of the gender struggle in the slum in Colombo was worse for women. Marriages were unstable and nearly half the women were no longer in their first marriage. Later marriages were even more unstable and often not considered as real marriages. The distribution of income within families was generally more skewed. Many women did not know how much their husband earned not even how much they would be given so insecurity was very high. The women did not complain much about other women and their husbands relationships with other women but rather about drinking and drugs, especially when combined with beating and scolding.

III. URBANIZATION

URBANIZATION IS NOT just a question of the movement of people from villages and the countryside to towns or big cities. It is also a question of changes in social processes: the introduction and eventual domination of wage labour as the way of earning a living and related to this, the destruction of the family as an economic unit active in production.

As I have argued elsewhere, urbanization tends to strengthen gender struggle, leading to a relative deterioration in the women's sphere of action and material conditions when compared to men's.[(3)] Perhaps this is most clearly seen in the division of labour between the sexes. In all big modern cities men are seen as the providers, as the main labourers who are paid for their work producing "things", while women are seen as housewives, whose work and main responsibility is the production of life, a job which is unpaid. These concepts do not correspond to the actual facts of men's and women's activities but they function as important ideas with serious material consequences.

In Thailand, rapid urbanization is relatively recent and most women in the study area came from the provinces with the greatest agricultural problems.[(4)] Most had parents who owned some land or at least a house, and most had kept up contact with the family of origin. In Sri Lanka, most of the women failed to keep up contacts with their region of origin and they all had (or had once had) parents who worked for money and did not own land, Likewise, they were drawn he political system before migration although many had moved from one village or smaller urban centre to another, mostly as domestic servants, before they reached the slum area. In a sense, they were urbanized before they reached the slum area on the outskirts of Colombo.

The long drawn out and disruptive process of urbanization which the Sri Lankan women had experienced may be major cause of their relatively worse material conditions as well as contributing to their relative passivity in the public or semi-public gender struggle. they had lost much of their influence in the home because the home was no longer an economically important unit engaged in social and economic activity. But they were expected to be confined to the home and to work producing and maintaining life there.

Gender struggle is stronger in the towns because women (but not men) are materially dependent upon the division of income within the family. The form that urbanization took in Sri Lanka contributed to an erosion of the women's basis for fighting within this struggle and to an erosion of their identity as women. In Thailand, on the other hand, women came directly from villages to Bangkok, and often from subsistence agriculture. There they experienced a stronger gender struggle and growing contradictions in the family, but their basis for active and public struggle was much stronger because of their experiences in the village, where they had contributed to family production in many ways.

The stronger, and for women more detrimental, impact of urbnization in Sri Lanka becomes even more evident when examining the special forms that urbanization takes for women in the two areas. In Thailand, roughly as many men as women migrated (now there is a slight majority of women) and they mostly moved to the city when they were young (15-25 Years old) and unmarried, Nearly all the women in my area came with friends or family. Nearly all had a place to stay where they could get help in the initial difficult period, whilst finding work and a place to live. Their reasons for migrating were mainly to help their family by earning money either simply to support themselves or to send something home. When they met a boyfriend, they returned home to their mothers, paid the brideprice and were properly married (a ceremony involving family and kin). The women have the support of (mostly female) kin or friends in the new area but retain links with home.

In the slum area in Colombo, among the migrants, men vastly outnumber women. Women of all ages came to the area. Young women mostly came to join their husbands-to-be or their husband's family while older women came with family or alone. Only one third (22 out of 64) knew someone in the area besides their own family, and for the young that meant their husband (to-be) and his family and friends. Their reasons for coming to the area were mostly family reasons, either their marriage of family conflicts in their former home. Only four (out of 64) came to get work in the nearby industrial zone and one of these had a further reason: she was going to take care of her brother's children whilst his wife was a domestic servant in the Middle East. Most women knew no-one except their husband and his family.

The women in Bangkok were very divided in their evaluations of city and village, whereas the women in Colombo agreed that life was better in the countryside, As one said:

" . . . .. it is much better in the countryside, more peaceful. It is true that there is more money have the men like it better here because they have more amusements. But as a woman I like life in the village better."

Thus, it seems that the form of urbanization experienced was especially disruptive for the women in Colombo, even if they had come from families who owned nothing in the countryside. From the moment that they arrived in the slum area, they were much more dependent upon their husband and his family than they had been before.

It appears that the relatively worse situation for women in the Colombo area is partly the result of a long drawn out and disruptive process of urbanization which places them in a difficult position within the gender struggle and which further contributes to their difficulties. The welfare system does not compensate for this in any substantive way.

IV. GENDER IDENTITY

The Concept of gender identity refers to people's understanding of the tasks and proper ways of behaving for men and women as such thoughts are formulated and discussed. It is thus a sociological category which refers to public or semi-public concepts. Men and women may share the same ideas but often their ideas vary. especially when formulated in semi-public areas where only one gender is present or one gender is dominant.

I think that such gender concepts show variations and probably contradictions in most cultures. Nevertheless, there seem to be some ideas which everyone supports, or at least is influenced by even if not totally accepted. For instance, in the slum area in Bangkok, nearly all the women told me that they loved their mother or did this or that for their mother's sake. This might be correct or they might have other motives, but the important thing is that all seemed to agree that a woman loves her mother.

In the area in Colombo, despite great differences in the stories told by women, everyone seemed to agree that proper marriage (ie. one which was registered at the public office) was very important. This may be unsurprising when one woman talked about a long life with her husband, her own family of origin and seven pregnancies. But it was more surprising when a former prostitute tolde me about abduction and rape, and then when her man married her shortly before the birth of the third child she commented: "That was how the knot was bound. If it had not been for that, I and my four children would still have been nothing."

Such ideas concerning the genders and their relationship, expressed in everday language, can be termed gender identity. They do not go into the individual women's feelings in any great depthsome of the women in the Bangkok area may have had more dubious relationships with their mothers and not all women in the Colombo area put such a high social value on marriage. But they do denote what is considered proper, and to a degree I think they match people's actions.

Some of these ideas are considered in more detail below, in particular: the perceptions about husband and wife which partly overlap with perceptions about men and women; the perceptions around women's paid work; and the perceptions around family form.

In both slum areas, men were thought to be physically stronger than women but it was also thought that they were the ones who should make the decisions. Taking care of children and the household were seen as women's work; and men's proper work was the kind done in workplaces, for which they were paid. But there were great differences which could be detected in the words used for husband and wife and the relationship between them.

In Bangkok they used a slang word *faan* which denoted each person in a couple, irrespective of whether they were properly married or not and irrespective of the speaker's gender. Such words hardly exist in English (but do in Danish), and mean something like common law husband or wife. In the area they actually laughed at me when I used the word I had learned at the university that was not how they talked.

In the Colombo area, no such word existed. A marriage in the slum area was called "to live under a husband" (a woman talking) or "to obey a husband" and as noted already, strong social values were attached to marriage. A woman might explain what a good wife she was by saying that she never discussed anything with her husband when he was drunk but waited and talked nicely to him later on: "Did he beat you when he was drunk? No. Another woman would try to fight in such circumstances, but I waited and talked nicely to him. I talked with him later. I was golden and that is why people say I reformed him with my mouth." My translator did not believe her and asked: "Did he stop drinking then?" And the answer was no. But the concept of a woman who loves a man being able to reform him through her kind love was widespread: this woman could be a wife but might also be a daughter or even a child.

In the Bangkok area, women often discussed shatters with their husbands. One proudly told of how she threatened to leave him once so that now: "No, he doesn't have minor wives. There is nothing doing there." In general, the women felt they could if necessary, leave a husband and find a way to support themselves (although as mentioned earlier marriages were more stable than in the Colombo area). Indeed it was thought quite fitting for a woman to work and earn money to help her family especially when she was young.

In the Colombo area too, women might say to a husband that he could leave but I only heard about it once and it was not the woman herself who told me she was not proud of it, rather it was a mild criticism form her mother.

By and large women talked about men as people from whom you could expect help and support: husband, father, brother, uncle were relied upon. When Charlet, a woman with three adult daughters, was asked if they could help her if she ill. she answered: "No, there are no special advantages (in living close to the daughters). If they need help, we will give it. Or if they have something . . .But they don't have anything to give. This one she might give us something if they had anything because she has a husband living with her. So it is not because there are any advantages that we have them here, it is because of the difficulties.

We asked three more questions about the advantages of mother and daughters living close to each other and whether any help was exchanged. Then she said: "Well, yes. If I became ill, they might make some food and bring it to me or wash my clothes. I have not been seriously ill so far. What I could do, what I hope to do, since my daughters cannot help either. I had a brother. He used to help me . . But since he is no longer here, and I don't think my daughters have the means to help me . . . ." Thus, in this area, the idea among women that they were dependent upon men was strong. This is in spite of the fact that close to half of the men in the area (16 of the 36) did not support anyone, some of them not even themselves.

The concept of women's work for income was surprising. Women's work was badly paid compared to men's work in both areas (particularly in the Colombo area) but it was socially accepted and valued in the Bangkok area whereas it was often stigmatized in the Colombo area. Yet most women (more so in the Colombo area) did something in order to earn money. Some of these activities were so badly paid that comparable work in the Bangkok area was not counted as work at all. In the Colombo area, women work was, in principle, accepted. But nearly everything women could do was looked down upon by the society around them. Going to the Middle East as a domestic servant was a dream of many and a reality for a few women in the slum area. But this was considered a disgrace because the children were left at home and the husband would find himself another woman. Besides the woman's chastity might be endangered, as was considered to be the case in factory work. These occupations were valued in the slum area, but domestic work in the nearby area (especially on a part-time basis) was considered close to begging. Selling fruit or similar activities was also calling attention to the woman and begging which a few women did, was despised. Thus, the occupations that women were able to undertake were stigmatized in society as a whole and often also in the slum area. Men here were hardly able to cook a meal (which was very time consuming and required skill) and thus often complained if the wives were not home to prepare the food. Women in the Colombo area were, however, often satisfied or proud that they could earn something but they rarely talked about it in public and some even refused to say what kind of work they did.

Female centred families were quite common in both areas: young couples lived close to their parents or the wife's mother slightly more often than to the husband's and the relationship and the help exchanged was much greater with the woman's mother than with her parents-in-laws.

In the Bangkok area, women talked about the reciprocal help and, even if they did not live close to their mothers, they would visit them, often daily. They were conscious of the value of their mothers living close by in terms of help and in terms of the gender struggle. One of them put it this way: "When the husband lifts the foot in order to kick (his wife), he will think of his mother-in-law."

In the Colombo area, this pattern of living was more surprising both beacuse it received very little recognition and because of the reasons the women gave for migrating (going to live with their husbands or their husbands' families). Part of the reason may be found in the fact that nearly all women in the area aged over fifty lived without a husbands. This type of family form, centering around the mother, was very much seen in terms of terms of loss and lack of males: "We have nobody, Madam."

Women's identities seemed quite different in the two areas. In the Bangkok area, women built up their self-esteem in a variety of ways and they appreciated a pleasant easy life with some fun. In the Colombo area, women's self-esteem seemed much more closely connected to their different roles in the family: virgins when young, chaste and obedient housewives and responsible mothers who would feed their family well in older age.

There are clear connections between the gender identity of the women in the two areas and the ways in which the gender struggle was fought. In the Colombo area, it was difficult for women to fight openly for their needs. For example, since a good wife could reform her husband of bad habits, it was difficult for a woman to discuss her problems at home with other women. They would usually only learn about such conflicts when they were acute and the wife had more or less given up. Even then the first question asked would most often be "What did she do?" Or "What did she say to him?"

Women's friendships were also hampered by the great importance placed on chastity and (sexual) morality for women. Since very few could in fact live as expected and condemnation was often harsh. friendships easily broke up when dealing with such questions. It appeared that the contradictions in ideas about women's proper behaviour created problems for the women. These ideas were more like ideals for a good life, peaceful and with love and harmony, but the facts were very different and so most women had something to hide. The ideas were often self-contradictory as, for example, the idea that women should feed a family well yet the condemnation of any money earning activities. Or the need for chastity, and the need to find some work or even simply the pleasure in talking with others. Obviously, such ideas made it more difficult for the women to participate in mixed groups.

It is quite tempting to look to history to find explanations for the differences in the two areas. In a sense, an historical expalnation of the notion of gender begs the question. It is still not understood why the most partiarchal trends of thought are picked up and integrated into the Sri Lankan culture and it is still hard to understand why women actively share and support them.

Women's own self-identification with their role in the family may, however, be seen in another light. If able to shoulder their heavy responsibilities, they developed great strength, and a few women managed to keep their families together, took care of children and adults and created a good atmosphere in their homes and surroundings. The high value placed on the family may possibly be understood both as a dream of a better life and as a protest against modern life with all its hardships.

V. SLUM CULTURE AND GENDER

THE CONCEPT OF slum culture is used here to mean the common understandings and interpretations of everyday life, of individuls, the community and the society at large among the urban poor. My contention is that a slum culture is more achievable in slums and squatter settlements where people have the opportunity to talk and discuss things together, But their culture need not differ markedly from other poor urban cultures.

The two slum areas were both Therevada Buddhist cultures and they also shared a degree fo opposition to their surrounding societies. But there were important differences in the way in which each area was integrated into these societies. In the Bangkok area, people clearly expressed that they were Buddhist and felt that they belonged to a community which centred around their beliefs. They sometimes interpreted Buddhism somewhat differently from the middle-classes but they were actually integrated into the institutions of Buddhism: a monk was seen every now and then in the area, boys were sent as novices to temples, people went to temples in Bangkok on different occasions and the active attachment to the Buddhist institutions was clearly seen in the trips which slum dwellers organized to temples in the country and from which they both got merit and blessings, and much fun and pleasure. The temples were open to these people and they in turn brought their own (usually repressed) culture to the temples.

The slum dwellers in the Bangkok area were firmly integrated into the very tolerant Buddhist culture of their society but they were much less integrated into other social institutions, including the state. They were often directly suspicious of or hostile to such institutions. The schools were sometimes criticized or ridiculed (although also much valued for their support during evictions). The free hospital was called a slaughter house, and people clearly expressed feelings about the port authorities, the police and sometimes the rich, which were ambivalent if not outrightly hostile.

In the Colombo area, people also clearly expressed that they were Buddhists but their links with the institutions of Buddhism were different and seemed much weaker. During the six months I worked there, I did not see one monk in the area and people did not usually go to the temples. In the few cases where they did, it was elderly women who went for meditation while they were fasting. The only other instance was a mother who needed a monk to help get a proper school start for her two girls, but that was, she explained, because she knew no other respected person. People did not seek the pleasure the Bangkok women found, but rather their participation in the activities was connected to control of mind and body, and their active involvement was weak.

This fits Kapfere's[5] analysis of an area close to Galle (in his study around devil exorcism) where he showed that the Buddhist temples and the monks mostly gave services for the middle classes whereas the poor people or proletarians created their own culture. The Buddhist Sangha in Sri Lanka reorganized itself at the beginning of this century into a more efficient form and it seems that the monks have been much more active in politics than the Thai Sangha, first in education and today in development projects.

The slum dwellers in the Colombo area were, however, much more integrated into the instituions of the state. They were active in their relationship with the local school (as parents) and to trade unions and political parties. They went to hospitals as well as to the police on several occasoins and they went to different government offices for papers. They did not always achieve their goals but they knew where to go and how to act. Indeed, those who translated the interviews were, in some cases, very impressed by the women's ability to take care of such things and by their independence in relation to the authorities.

The differences between the two slum areas relationships with the wider society were thus quite marked. Although they shared certain attitudes of distance and sometimes hostility or suspicion towards society, the Bangkok slum dwellers were much more integrated into the tolerant Therevada Buddhist institutions whereas the Colombo slum dwellers, although also feeling Buddhist, did not participate actively.

There were also differences in the degree of participation by women in the day to day group talks in the two slum areas. In the Bangkok area, they participated quite actively and sometimes as leaders of the groups although not as often during the evenings. In the Colombo area, women participated less and were more confined to the small groups of family and close neighbours.

Both of the slum areas had organizations but they were very different. None included all the inhabitants and people were involved in them to varying degrees. In the Bangkok area (as in similar areas in the city), there was a welfare organization, originally created by a woman born in the area, which was quite well developed. It was democratically organized with the election of leaders in the different parts of the area, but also with a council of well-meaning middle class supporters. It worked with welfare issues such as schools, creches, asylums and the distribution of (poor quality) free rice to the poorest and it fought against eviction and organized rehousing. Women as well as man played an active part, although the men tended to dominate decision making. This slum organization dealt with the problems of women's everyday lives including water and sewage, housing schooling and feeding the family. but nobody seemed to think of these as solely women's problems; they were rightly considered to be common problems for both men and women, for all who lived there, and everybody participated in trying to address these problems.

In the Colombo area, the organization which existed was very different. It was organized by a man who had surrounded himself by "tough guys". Some years earlier he had nearly been killed by a rival gang and was now partly disabled, but he had won the fight and some of the others were now dead. He had built up a large business and owned the shop which served the area, the local bus, fishing boats and nets (from which men in the area got work), a coconut plantation and a distillery. He also provided small interest bearing loans against security. He had built up a political position and was secretary of the local UNP branch and aspired to the position of Justice of the Peace. He had asked two government ministers to come to the opening of a lantern show that he had organized at Vesak. He did not want the police in the area (and they did not come during the six months I was there) but he thought that he and his gang of about 40 young men should maintain order. Thieves were roughly treated: so too were possible heroin users.

He claimed in an interview that most of his time was spent in negotiations and help to couples and their families when they disagreed or fought. His advice was similar to that of the police. To the woman he would say: "Go home and please your husband, don't give him occasion for jealousy or anger." And to the husband "Don't you ever beat your wife again or I shall beat you up." Another individual had tried to rule the area before him but he had lacked sufficient economic and political power to do so.

This organization did not concern itself with the problems and the tasks of women's everyday lives. It barely considered women at all, except in terms of the services they provided. When asked about women's role in the organization, he replied that four young girls served food and tea to male members. When women were considered at all it was as problems, in the course of the negotiations he conducted.

Although this seems a somewhat special case of organization in a slum area, it might be quite common practice that if women's problems in everyday life are not taken up and treated as common problems women themselves may be seen as the problem. This is what usually happens when women ask for money for the household or complain of problems with water or sick children.

VI. CONCLUSIONS

ONE OF THE reasons for the strategic importance of gender in the slum cultures of big cities may be that the main problems are those of creating life and maintaining it. These are seen as women's tasks in large cities all over the world. Since these are serious problems among the urban poor, they may be viewed as problems which concern everybody. The direction of slum cultures and any organiztions which develop on this basis would thus be concerned with questions of people's welfare and with the possibilities for creating a good or better life.

But if the questions surrounding women's daily tasks are not taken seriously, men may not be made aware of the miserable conditions under which women produce life but may only concentrate on any problems the women identify through their talk and complaints of daily life. Then women themselves may be seen as the problem and pushed out of the public sphere, or their problems over shadowed and seemingly forgotten. Thus it seems that the conditions in slum areas make the production and maintenance of human life a real and great problem for all, and the daily tasks in this connection are the tasks of women. Women therefore become central to slum cultures.

But urbanization also turns women into a strategic force in the struggle for better conditions. They have experienced the most radical changes in connection with urbanization. They share with men the new importance of wage-paying work and the changes this brings about (although they are treated as a secondary labour force). But family changes impact hardest on them. Not only do they themselves lose the opportunities for production within the family context but the whole family changes its meaning. It is no longer a base for creating wealth or power. It becomes a social unit which has as its main purpose the creation of life, something not given much value in society. So women become economically and materially dependent upon others, mostly men.

These changes create a need among women for co-operation with other women in the slum settlement. If the local culture allows, they might create a degree of power around family, kin and neighbours. In many contexts, it may be of great importance to organize around these networks of women. which may have a strong influence in the slum settlement.

Life in the slum puts the question of gender and the relationships between men and women on the agenda. In some contexts, urbanization upsets the normal rhythms of everyday life, especially women's daily life, and the slum gives them a need to co-operete with other women who may be important asscsts in the struggle for a better life.

In the two slum areas which I studied, the connections between the slum cultures' understanding of gender relationships and the possibility for creating organizations are evident. In Bangkok, where the women were visible and where they participated in daily discussions, they could make their influence felt; both men and women were aware that problems such as those connected with housing and water were important and that it was worth struggling to find a solution to them.

But in Colombo, women were much more closely identified with the family and their role in it, and the great contradictions between what was said and what was done made discussion of their problems much more difficult. Thus, a (relatively) wealthy man ran the community organization in his own interests and in a very authoritarian fashion, and women were seen as a problem. The women certainly did not develop this kind of organization themselves but they and their men (who also did not always like this situation) had less opportunity for taking part in other kinds of organization, In addition, women's problems were much less visible as common problems.

REFERENCES

1. Ortner, S. (1984), "Theory in anthropology since the Sixties". Comparative Studies in Society and History, Cambridge.

2. The article is based on two field studies which I conducted in slum areas, one in a slum area in Bangkok (1981), the other in a slum area at the penphery of Colombo (1987). In Bangkok, I lived in the area for six months, spoke some. That although I worked with a translator and visited the area both before and after the main study. I chose 24 houses close to the one in which I lived and the study covered 132 persons, 45 women, 41 men and 46 children.

   In Colombo, I could not live in the area for more than a month (for health reasons) but I came to the area every day and talked with the women although I could only work through translators. The study from Colombo covered 31 houses in depth, that is 131 persons, 36 men, 38 women and 57 children and is supplemented by a small survey of 107 houses. I used "soft" sociological methods daily talk, participation in work or festicities. After a while I had longer talks with the women and finally I conducted taped interviews with 8-10 of them.

   The study from Bangkok is published in Thorbek, S. (1987), Voices from the City. Women of Bangkok. Zed Press, London. The other is forthcoming.

3. Thorbek, S. (1988), "Women and urbanization". Acta Sociologica, Oslo.

4. Phipatseritham, K. (1979), Trends in land Tenure and Security in Thailand, Bangkok.

5. Kapferer. B. (1983), A Celebration of Demons, New York.

Additional reading :

Jayawardena, K, and S. Jayaweera (1986), A profile on Sri Lanka. Women's Education Centre, Clombo

Leach, E.R, (1960), Pul Eliya, Cambridge.

Morrison, M.B etal (editors) (1979), The Disintegrating Village, Lake House, Colombo.

Myrdal, G. (1968), An Asian Dream, New York.

Obeysekere, G. (1963), "Pregnancy cravings (Bola-Duka)...", American Anthropologist.

Obeysekere, G. (1984), The Cult of the Goddess Pattina, Chicago.

Potter, J.M. (1977), Thai Peasant Social Structure, New York.

Potter, S.H. (1977). Family Life in Northem Thai Village, New york.

Schrijvers, J. (1985), Mothers for Life, Delft.

Sharma, U. (1980), Women Work and Property in North West India, London.

Tambiah, H.W. (1961), Sinhalese Laws and Customs, London.

Yalman (1967), Under the Bo Tree, California.

CHAPTER-22

Gender and Housing

The Provision of Accommodation for Young Adults in Three Mexican Cities

Ann Varley

INTRODUCTION: 'TRADITIONAL' AND 'NON-TRADITIONAL' HOUSEHOLDS IN RESEARCH ON GENDER AND HOUSING[1]

Women's housing needs do not seem to attract much attention. They do not figure prominently in the housing literature, as can be seen, for example, from the contents of journals such as Habitat International or Housing Studies.[2] Similarly, housing has received little attention in the gender studies literature. There are relatively few books on the subject. Notable exceptions, in recent years, include Sophie Wastson's book on Britain and Australia, *Accommodating Inequality: Gender and Housing*,[3] and the collections on *Women, Housing and Community and Women, Human Settlements and Housing*, edited by Willem van Vliet and by Caroline Moser and Linda Peake, respectively.[4] In comparison with other subjects, there are few entries on housing in Sarah Radcliffe and Janet Townsend's[5] bibliographies on women in developing countries, and the authors surveyed tend to take 'squatter settlements' as a context for their study rather than focussing on housing *per se*.[6]

How can we explain this? In part, it may result from unwillingness to accept the relevance of gender: "most authorities responsible for development planning have only very reluctantly recognised gender as an inportant planning issue".[7] In their introduction to Lloyd Rodwin's edited collection on Shelter, Settlement and Development, published to mark the International Year of Shelter for the Homeless (IYSH) in 1987,[8] Rodwin and Bishwapriya Sanyal call for special attention to be paid to the shelter needs of women and especially of women-headed households. But there is no chapter on this subject. The United Nations/ IYSH leadership decided that it "should be dealt with in other ways".[9]

But what of feminist scholars? Could their apparent reluctance to work on housing stem from the fear that they will be criticised for suggesting that 'a woman's place is in the home'? Such fears would not be groundless. In his foreword to Women, Housing and Community, Willem van Vliet deprecates "the limited scope of feminist critiques that have juxtaposed the private home and the public community as a dichotomy of female and male spheres".[10] This criticism is misdirected: feminist writers have played a central role in exposing the ideological nature of the supposed dichotomy between public/male and private/female spheres, work and home, production and reproduction.[11] Nevertheless, given "the empirical foundation to this dualism",[12] it is all too easy to reinforce the notion of home and work as separate female and male spheres rather than recognising their interdependence.[13] Rather than trying to "reconceptualise the links between home and work",[14] it may (deceptively) seem safer simply to steer clear of the domestic sphere. As Janet Momsen[15] has written, "recent work on women in Third World countries has, in most cases, concentrated on moving the research focus from women's reproductive roles to their productive contributions", emphasising paid employment outside the home.

Unconscious anxiety about upholding an unacceptable ideology may also explain why research on gender and housing in developing countries has largely portrayed women outside the confines of the nuclear household. The literature emphasises, firstly, 'women-headed households', and, secondly, women as 'community managers' mobilising around housing construction or the introduction of services to their settlement.[16] Most chapters in the Moser and Peake collection, for example, focus on women-headed households, and a series of parallel projects on women householders in Africa have led to several publications.[17] The theme has also been taken up in a Latin American context.[18] Regarding women as community managers, all but two of the case studies in Women, Human Settlements and Housing are concerned with housing/upgrading projects, and Moser's chapter on Ecuador documents women's struggle for services. An emphasis on specific housing projects is also apparent in the other studies cited.[19]

There is a clear rationale for work on women-headed households. Firstly, as they tend to be more common in cities (at least in Latin America), continuing migration and urbanisation increase their numbers.[20]

Secondly, women-headed households are likely to be among to poorest members of society, although this is by no means universally or inevitably the case.[21] Thirdly, they have been neglected by planners.[22] In particular, they have been marginalised by the eay, in which "housing policy and provision...assumes, and is structured around, the patriarchal family form".[23] Thus, an emphasis on women-headed households is intended to redress a general imbalance, and specifically to expose discrimination against women.[24]

However, the emphasis on women-headed households may have some rather unfortunate consequences. There is a danger of exaggerating the quantitative importance of women-headed households—surely not a good way to convince the planning community of their importance. And there is a danger of rendering many women (the majority?) once again 'invisible'.

It has become almost commonplace to argue that "one third of the world's households are now headed by women" and that "in urban areas, especially in Latin America and parts of Africa, the figure exceeds 50 per cent".[25] The original source of such figures about female headship is often cited as Buvinic *et al.* (see note 22), but the authors of that study regarded a figure of one-sixth of all households in developing countries as nearer the mark.[26] Given the difficulties of working with National Census data on household structure,[27] information on the subject is often based on small-scale surveys of particular locations. Taking Mexico as a case study, Table 1 presents the results from Various micro-surveys and one larger study of Mexican cities in the last decade. In only two cases does the figures for women-headed households reach one-third of all households.[28] The findings for tenants are particularly significant. Women-headed households face particular difficulties in building their own home. They may therefore be

Table 1. Percentage of of women-headed households in Mexican cities, 1981-1992

	Single women/ mothers only*	All female heads**	*N*
Various 1980s!			
Low-Income settlements	7	12	9464
Mexivo City 1988			
Young settlement (owners)	na	6	78
Young settlement (owners)	na	18	80
Older settlement (mixed)++	na	15	216
Older settlement (mixed)++	na	11	210
Inner city rental area (tenants)	na	29	73

		Single women/ mothers only*	All female heads**	N
Mexico City 1981-1982				
Young settlement (owners)	A	16	16	25
Older settlement (owners)		0	4	25
Young settlement (owners)	B	16	16	25
Older settlement (owners)		0	4	25
Mexico City 1991				
Older settlement (owners)	B	8	15	78
Older settlement (owners)	A	6	11	72
Puebla 1986				
Young settlement (owners)	C	2	5	100
Older settlement (owners)	D	6	14	76
Older settlement (tenants)		11	15	80
Inner city rental area (tenats)		9	12	115
Puebla 1991				
Young settlement (owners)	C	0	5	55
Older settlement (owners)	D	12	33	33
Guadalajara 1985-1986				
Young settlement (owners)	E	5	12	102
Older settlement (owners)	F	9	13	64
Older settlement (tenants)		10	16	96
Inner city rental area (tenants)		15	19	120
Guadalajara 1992				
Young settlement (owners)	E	5	8	77
Older settlement (owners)	F	5	11	56
Puerto Vallarta 1986				
Yound settlement (owners)	13	17	23	
Older settlement (owners)		9	20	69
Leon 1986				
Young settlement (owners)		4	9	23
Older settlement (72% owners)		6	11	54
Queretaro 1982-1983				
Young settlement (owners)		9	14	92
Young settlement (owners)		8	10	52
Young settlement (owners)		10	15	100
Monterrey 1990				
Older settlement (owners)#		10	11	402
Oaxca settlement (66% owners)		18	42	50

Sources - Various, 1980s: Selby *et al.*, 1990 (see note 42); Mexico City, 1988: A.G. Gilberit, O. Camacho, R. Coulomb and A. Necochea, *In Search of Home* (University College London Press, London, in press); mexico City 1981-1982: A. Varley, "*Ya Somos Duenos: Ejido* Land Development and Regularisation in Mexico City", unpublished Ph. D. thesis (University College London, 1985); Mexico City and Puebla, 1991: questionnaire survey, summer 1991 (author); Guadalajara, 1992: questionnaire survey, summer 1992 (author); Guadalajara and Puebla, 1985-1986: Gilbert and Varley, 1991 (see note 29); Puerto Vallarta, Leon, Queretaro: S Chant, 1991 (see note 60) Monterrey, 1990: D. Villareal, *La Politica de Vivienda Del Gobierno del Estado de Nuevo Leon 1970-1990* (Universidad Autonoma de Nuevo Leon and Universidad Autonoma Metropolitana-Xochimilco, Monterrey, 1992); Oaxaca, 1990: K. Wills, "Women's Work and Social Network Use in Oaxaca City, Mexico", *Bulletin of Latin American Research* 12. 1(1992) pp. 65-82

Notes

* Excludes extended households headed by women.

** Includes extended households headed by women.

\+ Mexico City, Mexicali, Merida, San Luis Potosi, Queretaro, Tampico, Villahermosa, Mazatlan, Reynosa, Oaxaco.

++ A mixture of tenants, owners and sharers were interviewed, tenants being the most numerous group

\# Although these settlements are officially local government subdivisions belonging to the Monterrey Metropolitan Trust, FOMERREY, several of them originated in invasions and the government did not select the residents (Villarreal, 1992,p. 68)

na Not available.

Definition of women-headed households : see note 16. Percentages for different cities are not stricitly comparable. Some of the studies cited exclude, for example, single-person households or households composed of unmarried siblings, although the majority include such households.

'Young' settlements : self-help housing areas over 15 yaears old. In some cases, these were about 20 years old, but the one in Guadalajara was about 35 years old, and the Puebla one bout 40 years old in 1985-1986.

A, B, C, D, E, F - letters identify the same settlement surveyed in different years.

Table 2. Percentage of women-headed households in various Latin American cities 1968-1990

Country and town/city	Type of area	Percent, female headed of area	Year	Source
Argentina, Buenos aires	Not specified	18	1982	I.L.O., 1986
Argentina, Cordoba	Housing project	16+	1988-1990	Falu and Schmink, 1991
Brazil, Belo Horizonte	Various, all income groups	17	1983	Merick and Schmink,1983
Brazil*	Various	18	1984	Goldeni, 1990
Brazil, Sao Bernardo do Campo	Housing project	13	1980s	Volbeds, 1989
Chile, Santiago	Various, low-income owners	20-38	1988	Girbert et al., forthcoming
Chile, Santiago	Various, low-income tenants	9-20	1988	Gilbert et at., forthcoming
Colombia, Bogota	Not specified	19	1982	I.L.O., 1986
Colombia, Pereia	Various, self-help	20	1987	Gough 1992
Costa Rica, San Jose	Not specified	17	1982	I.L.O., 1986
Costa Rica, various	Low-income	14-15	1989	Chant, 1991a
Ecuador, Manta	Low-income	13	1970s	Middleton, 1991
Honduras, various	Various	33	1970s	Cited in Chant, 1991b
Mexico, Oaxaca	Low-income	22	1977	Hackenberg, Murphy and Selby, 1984
Mexico, Mexivo City	Various	17	1969-1970	Garcia, Munoz and de Oliveria, 1982
Nicaragua++	Various	48	1975	Vance, 1987
Panama, Panama City	Not specified	23	1982	I.L.O., 1986
Peru, Lima-callao	Not specified	18	1982	I.L.O., 1986
Venezuela, Caracas	Not specifed	21	1982	I.L.O., 1986
Venezuela, Caracas	Various, low-income owners	15-29	1988	Gilbert et at., forthcoming
Venezuela, Caracas	Various, low-income tenants	14-22	1988	Gilbert et al.,forthcoming
Venzuela, Various	Not specified	20-25	Various	Cited in Chant, 1991b

Source — I.L.O. (International Labour Office), *Women at Work, No. 1* (I.L.O. Geneva, 1986); Falu and Curutchet, 1991 (see note 18); T.W. Merrick and M. Schmink, "Houscholds headed by Women and Urban Poverty in Brazil", in M. Buvinic, M.A. Lycette and W.P. Mc.Greevey (eds), *Women and Poverty in the Third World* (Johns Hopkins University Press, Baltimore, 1983), pp. 244-271; A.M. Goldani, "Changing Brazilian Families (in press) (see Table1); K. Gough, "From Bamboo to bricks: Self-help Housing and the Building Materials Industry in Urban Colombia", unpublished Ph. D. thesis (University College London, 1992); S. Chant. "Gender, Households and seasonal Migration in Guanacaste, Costa Rica" *European Review of Latin American and Caribbean studies* **50** (1991a), pp. 51-85. D.R. Middleton, "Development, Household Clusters, and Work-Wealth in Manta", *Pobre de Oaxaca* (Instituto Nacional Indigenista, Mexico City, 1974); R. Hackenberg, A.D. Murphy and H.A. Selby, "The Urban Household in Dependent Development", in R.McC. Netting, R.R. Wilk and E.J. Arnould (eds), *Households: Comparative and Historical Studies of the Domestic Group* (University of California Press, Berkeley, 1984), pp. 187-216; Garcia *et al.*, 1982 (see note 62); I. Vance, "More than Bricks and Mortar: Women's Participation in Self-help Housing in Managua, Nicaragua", in C.O.N. Moser and L. Peake (eds), *Women, Human Settlement and Housing* (Tavistock, London 1987), pp.139-165.

*Figure from 1984 National Household Survey, which includes some rural areas but is more representative of the urban areas (Goldani, 1990, p. 536).

+See note 11. It should be remembered that some housing projects may discriminate against women-headed household (Machado, 1987).

+One-half of the Nicaraguan population lives in Managua.

under-represented in self-help settlements, but not in rental accommodation.[29] If, therefore, between 10% and 30% of tenant households are headed by women, it is unlikely that women-headed households constitute 50% of urban households.

Earlier Mexican work and other Latin American studies also suggest that the proportion of women-headed households is lower than has been suggested. Figures below 20% are often reported (see Table 2).[30]

The significance of women-headed households is, as I have indicated, not merely a question of statistics. But a legitimate concern for the housing needs of single woman should not lead us to neglect the housing problems facing women who live with a male partner. Otherwise, there is a danger that many women will once more be rendered 'invisible' — this time, ironically, by feminist scholars. Discussion of the housing strategies of female -and male-headed households, for example, easily slips into a comparison of 'women' and 'men', as if there were no women in the (so-called) male-headed households.

It is tempting to see the gender and housing literature's emphasis on single woman as an example of the irony identified by Anne-Marie Goetz:

> the liberal feminist language of *integration* has been based upon a *separating* out from the context of development of the category 'women' as a self-contained identity . . . The effect has been to ignore the importance of relations between men and women . . with the result that women, seen as separate rather than central, have been added into the process of development *at the margin*.[31]

If the archetypal gender-and-housing study concerns women-headed households in a housing project the danger of marginalisation is increased by the change of emphasis in World Bank thinking, with ramifications for national housing policies. Individual projects such as sites-and-service schemes are no longer in favour.[32] Instead, city-level attempts to unblock housing markets characterise the new emphasis on shelter delivery/urban management systems or *programmes* rather than *projects*.[33] This change should be acknowledged in research on gender and housing. A land tenure legalisation programme, for example, is likely to influence far more women's lives, for better or for worse, than all the sites-and-services projects in the country. We need to understand the housing problems facing low-income women from all types of households, 'traditional' and 'non-traditional', and not only those headed by women. The next section tries to put this principle into practice.

THE PROVISION OF ACCOMMODATION FOR YOUNG ADULTS IN URBAN MEXICO

The housing problems of Mexico City (1990 population almost 15 million), Guadalajara, the country's second largest city (1990 population approaching 3 million) and Puebla, Mexico's fourth largest city (1990 population over 1 million), are well documented.[34] The economic crisis of the 1980s aggravated a situation in which two-thirds of the population was already denied access to ownership via the conventional private or public housing markets.[35] Extensive areas of self-built housing had grown up since the 1940s, but the pressures on incomes, land prices and building material costs in the 1980s created further difficulties for people seeking to house themselves in such areas. The three cities already had an unusually high proportion of tenants and the recession of the 1980s seems likely to have increased the number of families unable to gain access to ownership.[36]

One response to such difficulties is to share accommodation with kin.[37] As here defined, 'sharing' refers to two or more separate households occupying the same plot: one household owns the plot, and the other/s live/s there rent-free as a result of kinship or friendship links with the owners.[38]

Table 3 provides basic information on sharing in six self-help settlements of different ages and degrees of consolidation: two in each city.[39] Overall, one in five owners were currently sharing their plots with at least one sharer household, but in the areas about 20 years old in Mexico City, the figure was two in five.[40] Most sharers are the sons or daughters of the owners. They are married and approaching 30 years of age, with an average of two children.[41] Table 3 also reveals that plot owners tend to let their sons share more often than their daughters. Overall, less than two-fifths of sharers are women.

If instead of living as separate households the members of these families all lived together, they would form extended households. As the literature on extended households is highly relevant to the following discussion, Table 4 provides some information on extended households in the case-study settlements to complement Table 3. The finding which I wish to underline concerns the proportion of those still living with their parents who are women. Overall, women with a husband or child are as likely to form part of their parents' extended household as their male counterparts; but if single parents are excluded, the proportion falls to about two-fifths—the same as for sharers.

These findings suggest that providing accommodation for young adults in this way is characteristic of what anthropologists have described as the patrilocal 'stem' or 'grand' family.[42] These multi-

Table 3. Basic information on sharing in case-study settlements

	Mexico city		Puebla		Guadalajara		All
	Loma de la Palma	San Jose	El Salvador	Veite de Nov.	Buenos Aires	Agustin Yanez	
Percentage of owners who share their plot with other households (s)	37	38	7	27	10	9	22
Mean no. of sharer households*	1.6	1.6	1.0	1.8	1.0	1.0	1.5
N	78	72	55	33	77	56	371
Of sharers:							
Percentage who are daughters/sons of owners	85	77	75	100	88	60	83
N	47	44	4	16	8	5	124
For sharers who are daughter/sons of owners:							
Mean age (to nearest year)	29	29	25	30	26	23	28
Percentage who are women	33	44	67	38	0	67	37
Percentage with spouse and children	95	85	100	94	86	100	90
Percentage with spouse but no children	5	12	0	6	14	0	8
Percentage with children but no spouse	0	3	0	0	0	0	1
Mean no. of children	2.3	2.1	1.7	2.3	1.7	1.3	2.1
N	40	34	3	16	8	5	103

Source: Questionnaire survey, 1991 and 1992.

Notes: In El Salvador and Buenos Aires, there are as yet few sons/daughters of plot owners forming their own families; hence the very small number of sharers.

'Sharer': within the sharing household, the person with the closest blood relationship (or friendship) with the owners of the plot.

* Only for plots with at least one sharer household.

Table 4. Yound adults living as part of their parents' extended household in case-study settlements

	Mexico city		Puebla		Guadalajara		All
	Loma de la Palma	San Jose	El Salvador	Veite de Nov.	Buenos Aires	Agustin Yanez	
Percentage of owners with an extended household including daughters/sons with spouse/child	9	18	15	15	17	21	16
Mean no of dauthers/ sons with spouse/child in these households*	1.1	1.2	1.1	1.0	1.3	1.0	1.2
N	78	72	55	33	77	56	371
For daughters/sons with spouse/child living in their parent's household:							
Mean age (to nearest year)	24	24	28	26	22	26	25
Percentage who are women:							
—overall	25	67	33	60	56	75	54
—excluding single parents	14	50	25	60	45	71	43
Percentage with spouse + children	38	47	67	80	56	50	54
Percentage with spouse but no children	50	7	22	20	13	38	21
Percentage with children but no spouse	13	47	11	0	31	13	25
Mean no. Of children	1.0	1.3	1.9	1.6	1.3	1.3	1.4
N	8	15	9	5	16	8	61

Source: Questionnaire survey, 1991 and 1992.
Notes: The table refers to extended households including one or daughters/sons with spouse/child.
* only for households extended in this way.

generation households are formed when, rather than moving to a new house on marriage, sons bring their wives to live with their parents. Later, older siblings and their families may move to independent accommodation. Such households have been found in "peasant communities in state societies",[43] including Latin America, China and India.[44] They have often been mentioned in studies of rural mexico.[45]

Some authors have argued that patrilocality is no longer significant in urban Mexico. Selby *et al.*[46] argue that the tendency to live with the man's parents ''has disappeared from urban households'' and Lomnitz and Perez-Lizaur[47] find that ''instances of patrilocality are not substantially greater than those of matrilocality''. However, in the case study on which this statement is based, Lomnitz[48] argued that "partilocality is predominant in the shantytown", although it declined over time as married children moved away from their parents' home. Some 35% of households were classified as patrilocal at the time of study, compared with 25% which were matrilocal (giving a ratio almost identical to the one noted above).[49]

In the surveys in Mexico City, Guadalajara and Puebla, information was sought about the housing status of *all* living children of the people interviewed. If there is a tendency to patrilocality, those living with their in-laws should display the opposite pattern from the one described above: more women than men should live with their in-laws. Table 5 shows that this is indeed the case. Again, the patrilocal bias is not dramatic, but it is noticeable: whereas the ratio of men to women is about 3:2 for those living with their parents, the ratio is reversed for those housed by in-laws.[50]

Further evidence comes from people's accounts of how they decide which of their children should share their plot. In one house in La Palma, one son was sharing with his parents. Another son, who now

Table 5 : Young adults relying on their in-laws for accommodation

	Mexico city		Puebla		Guadalajara		All
	Loma de la Palma	San Jose	El Salvador	Veite de Nov.	Buenos Aires	Agustin Yanez	
Percentage of those sharing with their in-laws who are women:	50	89	100	0	60	0	64
N	10	9	2	1	5	1	28
Percentage of those living in their in-laws' extended households who are women:	71	57	60	—	75	100	67
	71	57	60	—	75	100	67
N	7	7	5	0	4	1	24

Source: Questionnaire survey, 1991 and 1992.

Notes: The table includes the daughters/sons of interviewees who share with their in-laws or live as members of their in-laws' extended households.

In all, 558 sons/daughters of interviewes who were over 15 and had a spouse/child were recorded, 216 (39%) of them shared/lived with their own parents/their in-laws, and women constituted 49% of this latter group.

owned his own home, also used to share; but their two married sisters were both tenants and had not shared with their parents since marrying.

The explanation for this was that "*se las llevaron*", the daughters' husbands had "taken them off" to live elsewhere. This phrase was echoed by other people interviewed. It is a husband's responsibility to house his wife, particularly when, as this phrase hints, the couple had eloped.[51] Other people were quite clear that sharing is a privilege to be granted to *sons*. Parents may build additional accommodation in anticipation of their sons getting married, or a man may build a room on his parents' plot in order to set up home with his girlfriend.

THE IMPLICATIONS OF SHARING AND EXTENDED HOUSEHOLDS FOR WOMEN'S HOUSING OPTIONS

The effect of the patterns observed is to increase women's dependence on others in their efforts to accommodate themselves and their children. Tenure has been identified as a key concern in women's access to housing: "For women, tenure rights are a strategic gender need which ensures protection for themselves and their children".[52] The problem of tenure becomes particularly acute for a women whose right to her home depends on her relationshop with someone who does not himself own the property, and whose family may view her with hostility (see below). If the relationship breaks down, she will probably have to leave, as the owners are likely to support their son, and continued co-residence is likely to be distasteful to all concerned.

The difficulties facing women-headed households wishing to build their own home have already been noted. On separation from her husband, a women who has been living with her in-laws would seem to have few options but to return to her own parents' home, or to move into rental accommodation. Regular rent payments pose particular problems for families with only one earner, especially when the children are still young.[53]

On the other hand, women who live with their husband's family may find themselves upwardly mobile in the housing market, since sharing probably helps people to become owners.[54] It enables them to save money that would otherwise have gone on rent payment, until they have enough for the deposit needed for their own plot.[55] Later, they can dedicate a larger share of their income to purchasing building materials than tenants would be able to do.

The Problems of Living with in-laws

Shared accommodation entails living in close daily proximity with one's in-laws. In this respect, it is very similar to living in an extended household, and we may therefore look to studies of the extended households for insights into the problems of sharing a housing plot. To date, studies of the extended household in urban Mexico have tended to argue that it has positive implications for women, because of the opportunities for cooperation which it allows. But this is only half the story: there is also considerable potential for conflict.

Larissa Lomnitz[56] sought to counter the derogatory aspects of some writings on urban marginality by analysing the mutual support networks enabling people to cope with extreme poverty. In her book, she wrote:

> one will find no stress on the more sensational aspects of poverty: the filth, the promiscuity, the arguments and fights between people who must live together in a tiny space.[57]

The social resources mobilised by people in their efforts to survive included networks of reciprocal exchange and institutions such as *compadrazgo*.[58] Although networks could be based on friendship as well as kinship, "kinship is the most common social foundation for reciprocity network".[59] and extended or 'joint' household structures played a key role in these networks.

Sylvia Chant[60] also emphasises cooperation in extended households. Women in extended household can "share and/or delegate gender-assigned duties"[61] more than women in nuclear households. They therefore face fewer restrictions on their ability to enter the labour market.[62] Decisions on household budgeting become more democratic, housework is shared, "the full-time mother-wife role tends to become redundant" and women seem to have "far greater personal liberty".[63] In short, extended households "reduce some of the excesses of patriarchy".[64]

Chant[65] examines different types of extension to the household in support of her arguments, particularly those involving the inclusion of women's sisters or mothers. The focus of this paper is narrower, since it is restricted to the incorporation of sons or daughters-in-law, but this is the most common pattern in household extention and sharing. The literature on patri local extended households suggests that this type of extension is likely to lead to conflict between female relatives rather than cooperation:

> The authority structure of the patrilocal, patrilineal extended family, where father has authority over son and husband over wife, brings about conflict rather than cooperation between women in these groups.[66]

Since authority is in men's hands, women have to manipulate their relationships with men — their husbands, and later their adult son — in order to gain influence. *As a result of the nature of gender relations in these societies,* mothers and daughter-in-law have conflicting interests. The stem family "introduces in the role of daughter-in-law a women whose only hope of personal autonomy is division of her husband's natal family".[67] The consequences of this for daughter-in-law have been documented, for rural China, by Elisabeth Croll[68] and Margery Wolf,[69] and for rural India by Ursula sharma,[70] although they stress that daughters-in-law are not without resources (including women friends) in dealing with their mothers-in-law. The emphasis women place on strong relationship with their sons and the consequent strains between mother and daughter-in-law are summarised by Croll:[71]

> It was by forming and nurturing ties with her son which were personal and exclusive that women cultivated a source of power in a social structure dominated by men. Any potential threat to this relationship by the daughter-in-law was felt deeply. Trapped all their lives, women, with the authority of being the moter-in-law, appeared to compensate for their own former suffering and impotence as outsiders by repeating the very same process of domination.[72]

This type of conflict has also been reported in rural Mexico.[73] Krantz[74] describes the authority of the mother-in-law over her daughter(s)-in-law in such households as "overriding". Although the context of modern urban Mexico is a very different one, tension between in-laws is still a significant problem, for which gender relations are ultimately responsible.

The fundamental emotional significance of sharing was highlighted by one women who answered by question as to why her married children (all daughters) didn't live with her by saying "Look, all my children hurt me *a lot*". She was referring, not to a family quarrel, but to the pain of childbirth. In a cultural context in which girls are seen as inherently less 'valuable' than boys,[75] a certain resentment of daughters, a feeling that they should stand on their own two feet just as their mothers had to do, can sometimes be detected, and probably helps to explain the gender bias in sharing. One women in Mexico City particularly disapproved of married daughters bringing their husbands home, because, she said, they would expect her to cook for them.

Women's attitudes to their sons are different, reflecting the privileged nature of the mother-son relationship in Mexico.[76] In Puebla, a woman who blamed Mexican mothers for their men's *machismo* said that when a son marries, his mother will use all kinds of emotional blackmail (including pretending to be ill) to get him to stay with her. If she succeeds, however, she will have to face the presence of a younger women in her household, a presence which will be interpreted as an intrusion. Given the limited opportunities for many women to wield power in other aspects of their lives, there is considerable potential for the home to become a battleground and it seems almost inevitable that mothers will dislike their daughter-in-law, a feeling likely to be reciprocated. A resentment arising from the difficulties middle-aged women have faced in their own married lives, but which cannot perhaps be 'legitimately' expressed with their own daughters, can be given an outlet in criticisms of a daughter-in-law's habits, particularly those concerning housekeeping or child care. The resulting tension, and the way in which it revolves around the son/husband, was summarised by a women in Mexico City in these terms:

> supposing your son comes home drunk one night, and you go out to tell him off about it. Then, his wife comes out and starts having a go at you for scolding her husband; she tells you to lay off and mind your own business.

Another put it more succintly: "I don't like having the daughter-in-law around!" The misery that these problems can cause, for the older women as well as they younger one, had become apparent during earlier work in Pueble. An old women approached me in the street one day, and spontaneously started to tell me about the wickedness of her daughter-in-law. Another was locked out of her house by her daughter-in-law; and one 86-year-old women without children of her own preferred to live alone in a *vecindad* rather than living with her godson and his wife, because the two women didn't get on.[77]

For a women sharing with her in-laws, the problems may be not only her husband's mother but also his sisters.[78] If, for example, a child is hurt in a fall, its mother may be blamed for being a 'bad mother' by her sisters-in-law as well as their mother; they react as thought it is *their* child who has been hurt. Moreover, it may not be easy for women who are sharing to develop friendship networks to help them counteract such pressures, insofar as such networks depend on friends having access to each other's homes. Friends of whom the owner disapproves are unlikely to be welcome on the plot, and grounds for disapproval could readily be found by a hostile mother-in-law. Shopping or other work performed away from the home may provide some opportunity for women to resist such restrictions; but spending too much time 'in the street' (which has strong sexual implications) can give a prying relative the chance to tell tales to a women's husband.[79]

The House of two : Responses to the Problems of Co-residence

The problems outlined above are widely recognised by people in low-income settlement in urban Mexico. What, then, can they do about them ?

In the first place, sharing may be seen as a way of trying to reduce the potential for conflict associated with the extended household. Work in rural Mexico has shown the importance of having separate cooking facilities "as a focus of identity".[80] The desirability of providing, ideally, separate accommodation and facilities or, at the least, as much autonomy as possible for the younger household was also witnessed both the people's comments and their practice in the areas studied in Mexico City, Guadalajara and Puebla. Their ideas were summarised by a women in Pueble, whose mother, she said, had taught her that *casados* ('married') meant *casa [de] dos* ('house of two'). In other words, married children must be given some independence. Although they might have little option but to live with their parents for a while, every effort should be made to provide somewhere for them to be together, in private. Even if the room was so small that they could push the door shut from the bed, the important thing was that they should have a door to shut behind them.

Thus, sharing can be seen as an attempt to avoid some of the problems associated with the patrilocal extended household. Table 3-5 show that, overall, sharing is more common than living as part of the parental household, although there are variations between the cities.

Secondly, conflict between women is not an *inevitable* outcome of co-residence. Instead of vying for men's affections, women *can* cooperate with each other to resists the exercise of patriarchal authority. As Chinas[81] notes in her study of the Isthums Zapotecs:

> A surprising number of wives do adjust remarkably well to living with their mother-in-law ... and sometimes very strong bonds of affection form between them over the years. Frequently mother-in-law side with the wife against their own son, especially when his behaviour is obviously at the root of the trouble.

Nash[82] also talks of relationship between mother-and daughter-in-law which are "characterised by mutual cooperation". As the least a conscious intention *not* to interfere was apparent on the part of many of the women I interviewed. Several women stressed that is was up to their sons and daughter-in-law to choose where they wanted to live, even if their own preference would be to have all their children close at hand. One widow with five married sons and daughters living elsewhere said she would happily evict her three tenants to make room for them, but accepted with philosophical resignation that "daughters-in-law don't want to live with you...". Once married, as another woman put it, sons "will live wherever their wives like - because they *don't* always like [to live with their in-laws]". Thus, many parents respect their children's need for autonomy, whatever their own feelings in the matter.

Thirdly: the fact that almost two-fifths of sharers are women indicates that parents also recognise their daughters' needs. In particular, they are concerned about the consequences of their daughters' marriages breaking down. The man who expressed more clearly than anyone else the idea that sharing is for sons nevertheless said that, in addition to the accommodation he was building for his two (as yet unmarried) sons, he was also trying to make room for his daughters as well. He would like to be able to help them if their marriages didn't work out well and they were left with nowhere to live. In the same street in Mexico City, a women who have been living with her parents had just gone to live with her new boyfriend. She wanted one of her married sisters to take her place, because "her in-laws are being right so-and-sos with her". And in Puebla, one woman, aged 22, was sharing with her parents. After getting married, she had spent a short time with her in-laws, but after problems with her mother-in-law she and her husband had moved to her parents' plot.

Conclusion

In research on gender and housing, the equation of 'traditional' and 'nontraditional' households with 'nuclear' households and 'women-headed' households, respectively, is problematic. The assumption that 'nuclear' means 'headed by a man' confuses structure and headship, and, ironically, reinforces the notion that where a male spouse is present, he should be regarded as head of household. By focussing predominantly on women-headed households, the literature on gender and housing runs the risk of rendering women in nucler households, once again, invisible. Therefore, it is important not to *restrict* discussion of gender and housing to the needs of women-headed households.

Moreover, if there is a traditional norm in any society, it is not forced to be the nuclear household. This paper has examined a form of domestic organisation, plot sharing which may be regarded as non-traditional in the sense that it has been virtually overlooked in research on urban areas, but which probably constitutes a highly traditional living arrangement in rural areas of Mexico and elsewhere. The nature of gender relations means that forms of domestic organisation involving patrilocal extended households or the sharing of accommodation may have negative consequences for women. These include women's dependence on their husband's relatives for a roof over their heads, and the potential for conflict between wives and members of their husband's family of origin. As Lamphere[83] concludes: "women quarrel with or dominate other women when it is in their interest to do so; they share and exchange with other women when it suits their own goals". When women see their interests as involving the manipulation of their relationship with their sons or husbands, rather than solidarity with other women in resisting male authority, then conflict rather than cooperation is likely to result. it is not, however, an *inevitable* outcome.

Thus, in order to understand the implications of sharing as a housing strategy, we must take gender relations into account. Moreover, it is also important to remember that the home is *not* a separate sphere: state regulations permeat and circumscribe the supposedly private sphere. The next step in the exploration of sharing as a housing strategy should perhaps be to ask how the state intervenes in the interaction between gender relations, household structure and the housing process.

Finally, to return briefly to the question of 'traditional' and 'non-traditional' households: whilst married daughters as well as married sons were recorded sharing with their parents, single parents were, in all but one case, counted as part of their parents' extended household It seems that it would be regarded as inappropriate for them to *share* their parents' plot as a separate, independent household. Sharing therefore reinforces the patriarchal norms of the nuclear family, insofar as it is a privilege accorded only to those who are 'married'. If, morevoer, women without a partner are more likely to rent or to depend on their parents for accommodation, whilst sharing leads to home-ownership, then the patriarchal norm is also reinforced by material rewards for those who ascribe to it. In this sense, sharing is a highly 'traditional' housing strategy.

Acknowledgements—The research on which this paper was based was funded by grants from the University of London Central Research Fund the Dean's Travel Fund (Faculty of Arts) and Department of Geography, University College London. I am grateful for this financial support and for the helpful comments of two anonymous referees.

NOTES

1. This paper was presented at a conference on *Shelterm Women and Development: First and Third World Perspectives,* held at the University of Michigan in Ann Arbor, 7-9 May, 1992. The reason for the discussion of 'traditional' and 'non-traditional' household is that the paper was presented in a session entitled "Non-traditional living arrangements: beyond the nuclear household".

2. A study evaluating research on low-income housing found that only 13 of 126 studies reviewed provided any information on the particular problems faced by women: W. van Vliet, "Communities and Built Environments Supporting Women's Changing Roles", in W. van Vliet (ed.), *Women Housing and Community,* (Avebury, Aldershot, 1988), pp. 1-5, see p. x.

3. S. Wastson, *Accommodating Inequality: Gender and Housing* (Allen & Unwin, Sydney, 1988)

4. Although these introductory comments refer to English-language publications, a recent Mexican publication [A. Massolo, (ed.) *Mujeres y ciudades: Participacion social, Viviends y Vida Cotidiana* (El Colegio de Mexico, Mexico D.F., 1992)] makes a similar argument concerning the Latin American urban housing literature. In the literature in English a number of specific issueshave received more attention. Housing design has been addressed, in a British context, by the Matrix Collective, *Making Space: Women and the Man-made Environment* (Pluto Press, London, 1984), and Marion Roberts, *Living in a Man-made World: gender Assumptions in Modern Housing Design* (Routledge, London, 1991): for the U.S.A., see D. Hayden, *The Grand Domestic revolution: a History of Feminist Designs for American Homes, Neighborhoods, and Cities* (M.I.T. Press, Cambridge, 1981). Homelessness is a growth area in the literature as well as on the streets. It is examined for Britain, by S. Watson with H. Austerberry, *Housing and Homelessness: a Feminist Perspective* (Routledge and Kegan Paul, London, 1990), and J. Dibblin, *Wherever I Lay Hat: Young Women and Homelessness* (Shelter, London, 1991); for the United States, see M.R. Stoner, "The Plight of Homeless Women", in W. van Vliet (ed.), *Women, Housing and Community,* (Avebury, Aldershot, 1988), pp. 135-151, and S. Golden, *The women Outside: Meanings and Myths of Homelessness* (University of California Press, Berkeley, 1992).

5. S.A. Radcliffe with J. Townsend, *Gender in the Third World: a Geographical Bibliography of Recent Work* (Institute of Development Studies, Brighton,

1988), J. Townsend, *Women in Developing Countries: a Select Annotated Bibliography for Development Organizations* (Institute of Development Studies, Brighton, 1988).

6. Housing is mentiond, but not analysed in any depth, in several recent studies of gender and the environment: A Rodda, *Women and the Environment* (Zed Books, London, 1991): I. Dankelman and J. Davidson, *Women and Environment in the Third World: Alliance for the Future* (Earthscan. London. 1988); S. Sontheimer (ed.). *Women and the Environment: a Reader—Crisis and Development in the Third World* (Earthscan, London, 1991); C. Levy, "Gender and the Environment: the Challenge of Cross-cutting Issues in Development Policy and Planning", *Environment and Urbanization* **4**, 1 (1992), pp. 134-149.

7. C.O.N. Moser, "Gender Planning in the Third World: Meeting Practical and Strategic Needs", in R. Grant and K. Newland (eds). *Gender and International Relations* (Open University Press, Buckingham, 1991), pp, 83-121: see p. 84.

8. L. Rodwin, (ed) *Shelter, Settlement and Development* (Allen & Unwin, Boston, 1987)

9. Cited in A. Varley, "Review of L. Rodwin, (ed), *Shelter, Settlement and Development*, 1987", *Transactions, Institute of British Geographers*, N.S. **14** (1989), pp. 115-117; see p. 116. An IYSH seminar on 'Women and Shelter' was held in Harare in December 1987. [A Schlyter, *Women Householder and Housing Strategies: the Case of Harare, Zimbabwe* (National Swedish Institute for Building Research, Gavle, 1989).]

10. Van Vliet, 1988 (see not 2)

11. Hayden, 1981 (see not 4), L. McDowell, "Towards an Understanding of the Gender Division of Urban Space", *Environment and Planning D: Society and Space* **10** (1983), pp. 59-72. O. Harris, "Households an Natural Units", in K. Young, C. Wolkowitz and R. mcCullagh (eds), *of Marriage and the Market: Women's Subordination Internationally and its Lessons*, 2nd edn (Routledge and Kegan Paul, London, 1984, pp, 136-155, E. Jelin, "Family and Household: Outside World and Private Life", in E. Jelin (ed.), *family, Household and Gender Relations in Latin America* Kegan Paul International, London, 1991), pp. 12-39 Watson, 1988, see not 3.

12. Harris, 1984, *ibid.*, p. 151

13. L. McDowell, "Space, Place and Difference: a Review of Ten Years of Feminist Geography", mimeo (1992).

14. *Ibid.*, p. 19.

15. J. Momsen, "Review of C.O.N. Moser and L. Peake, (eds), *Women, Human Settlements and Housing*", *Transactions, Institute of British Geographers*, N.S. **14** (1989), pp. 119-120; see p. 119.

16. Despite the unsatisfactory implications, this paper follows the convention in the literature of describing households in which there is no resident male spouse as women-headed households. Such households may be either nuclear (a single women with or without children) or extended (including, for example, grandchildren or other male or female relatives). The term 'community

managers' is used by C.O.N. Moser, "Women, Human Settlements and Housing: a Conceptual Framework for Analysis and Policy-making", in C.O.N. Moser and L. Peake (eds), *Women, Human Settlements and Housing* (Tavistock, Londown, 1987), pp. 12-32; Moser, 1991, see note 7.

17. A. Larsson, "The Housing Situation of Urban Female-headed Households in Botswana", *Habitat International,* **12,** 3 (1988), pp. 17-27, A. Larsson, *Women Householders and Housing Strategies; the Case of Gaborone, Botswana* (National Swedish Institute for Building Research, Gavle, 1989). A. Schlyter, *Women Householders and Housing Strategies: the Case of George, Zambia* (National Swedish Institute for Building Research, Gavle, 1988); Schlyter, 1989 (see not 9)

18. A. Falu and M. Curutchet, "Rehousing the Urban Poor: Looking at Women First", *Environment and Urbanization* **3,** 2 (1991), pp 23-38. The Uniter States and United Kingdom literature also emphasizes single women and women as single parents [Watson and Austerberry, 1986 (see not 4); G.R. Wekerle, "From Refuge to Service Center: Neighborhoods that Support Women", in W. van Vliet (ed.), *Women Housing and Community* (Avebury, Aldershot, 1988), pp. 7-22; E.A. Mulroy, *Women as Single parents: Confronting the Institutional Barriers in the Courts, the Workplace and the Housing Market* (Auburn House, Dover MA, 1988); J.F. Sprague, *More thatn Housing: Lifeboats for Women and Children* (Butterworth Architecture, Boston 1991); Golden, 1992 (see note 4) .

19. See also S. Volbeda, "Housing and survival Strategies of women in Metropolitan Slum Area in Brazil", *Habital International* **13,** 3 (1989), pp. 157-171. One little-explored line of inquiry concerns women's role in the construction industry. An exception to the general neglect of this topic is Olusola Adebola Labeodan's recent article on women in the informal house building industry in Nigeria: O.A. Labeodan, "Women in the Informal House-building Industry in Nigeria", *Habitat International* **16** (1992), pp. 17-24.

20. L. Brydon and S. Chant, *Women in the Third World: Gender Issues in Rural and Urban Areas* (Edward Elgar, Aldershot, 1989). International Labour Office (ILO), *Women at Work,* No. 1 (1986).

21. J.G. Townsend and J.H. Momsen, "Towards a Geography of Gender in Developing Market Economies", in J.H. Momsen and J.G. Townsend (eds), *Geography of Gender in the Third World,* (Hutchinson, New York, 1987), pp. 27-81.

22. M. Buvinic and N.H. Youssef with B. Van Elm, *Women-headed Households: the Ignored Factor in Development Planning* (International Center for Research on Women, Washington, DC, 1978). Moser, 1991 (see note 7).

23. Wastson, 1988 (see not 3).

24. L.M.V. Machado, "The Problems for Women-headed Households in a Low-income Housing Programme in Brazil", in C.O.N. Moser and L. Peake (eds), *Women, Human Settlements and Housing* (Tavistock, London , 1987), pp. 55-69. P. Nimpuno-Parente, "The Struggle for Shelter: Women in a Site and Service Project in Nairobi, Kenya", in C.O.N. Moser and L. Peake (eds), *Women, Human Settlements and Housing* (Travistock, London, 1987), pp. 70-87.

25. Moser, 1987, see note 16, p. 14 S. Chant and P. Ward, "Family Structure and Low-income Housing Policy", *Third World Planning Review* 9 (1987), pp. 5-19, D.L. Smith, "Women and Habitat: Nairobi 1985", in W. van Vliet (ed,). *Women, Housing and Community* (Avebury, Aldershot, 1988), pp. 185-189, M.S. Muller and D. Plantenga, *Women and Habitat: Urban Management, Empowerment and Women's Strategies* (Royal Tropical Institute, Amsterdam, 1990). P.L. Sayne, "Food for Thought: Making Women Visible", *Environment and Urbanization* 3, 2 (1991), pp. 46-56. E. Wilson, *The Sphinx in the City: Urban Life, the Control of Disorder and Women* (Virago, London, 1991).

26. In two-thirds of the Latin American countries analysed, women were described as *de jure* heads of between 10% and 20% of all households. The only figures over 30% were for Chile (32%) and Panama (40%) [Buvinic *et al.*, 1978 (see note 22), pp. 87-88]. These figures were mostly for the 1970s, but in a paper presented to the *International Workshop on Insecurity in the 1990s: Gender and Social Policy* (5-6 April, 1993), Mayra Buvinic and Geeta Rao Gupta report that "The prevalence of female headship in developing countries varies substantially across countries and situations, comprising anywhere from 10% to about 40% of all households". (I am indebted to an anonymous reviewer for this more recent information.)

27. N.H. Youssef and C.B. Hetler, "Establishing the Economic Condition of Women-headed Households in the Third World: a New Approach", in M. Buvinic, M.A. Lycette and W.P. McGreevey (eds), *Women and Poverty in the Third World* (Johns Hopkins University Press, Baltimore 1983), pp. 216-243

28. The temporary absence of men working illegally in the USA could account for under-reporting of *defactor* women-headed households; but in surveys in 10 Mexican cities, Selby *et al* [1990 (see note 42), p. 201] found that only 11% of households had members working overseas.

29. Chant and Ward, 1987, see not 25. A.G. Gilbert and A. Varley, *Landlord and Tenant: Housing the Poor in Urban Mexico* (Routledge, London, 1991). Volbeda, 1989 (see not 19).

30. The traditional concept of the household (usually defined as a residential unit sharing food and at least some budgetary resources) has been criticised as too static and too concerned with boundaries. Methodologically, it is argued that questionnaire surveys elicit responses falsely depicting a 'normal' conjugal family. [C. Fonseca, "Spouses, Siblings and Sex-linked Bonding: a Look at Kinship Organization in a Brazilian Slum", in E. Jelin (ed.), *Family, Household and Gender Relations in Latin America,* (Kegan Paul International, London, 1991), pp 133-160.] Such problems have led some authors to uncover *de facto* or 'hidden' women-headed households, doubling the overall proportion reported (Falu and Curutcher, 1991, see note 18), or to emphasise the importance of mother-child units in situations where "the overwhelming majority of households are normally nuclear" (Fonseca, 1991, p. 135). Unless the criteria used for defining *de facto* female headed households are clear and consistently applied (following, perhaps, the categories proposed by Youssef and Hetler, 1983, see note 27), there is a danger of playing *cherchez la femme* in some of these approaches. [A. Varley, "Housing the Household, Holding the House", in G. Jones and P.M. Ward (eds), *Methodology and Land and Housing Market Analysis* (UCL Press, London, in press).]

31. A.M. Goetz "Feminism and the Claim to Know: Contradictions in Feminist Approaches to Women in Development", in R. Grant and K. Newland (eds), *Gender and International Relations* (Open University Press, Buckingham, 1991), pp. 135-57, see p. 140, my emphasis.

32. They were, any any case, never of great importance compared with the vast areas of 'spontaneous' housing in Latin America.

33. R. Burgess, "Helping Some to Help Themselves: Third World Housing Policies and Development Strategies", in K. mathey (eds), *Beyond Self-Help Housing* (Mansell, London, 1992), pp. 75-91. J. Fiori and R. Ramirez, "Notes on the Self-help Housing Critique: Towards a Conceptual Framework for the Analysis of Self-help Housing Policies in Developing Countries", in K. Mathey (ed), *Beyond Self-help Housing* (Mansell, London, 1992) pp. 23-31. C. Rakodi, "Cities and People: Towards a Gender-Aware Urban Planning Process?", *Public Administration and Development* **11** (1991), pp. 541-559. The shift to a broader institutional level of intervention in unlikely to decrease discrimination against women unless specific safeguards are introduced. Brion and Tinker [M. Brion and A. Tinker, *Women in Housing: Access and Influence* (Housing Centre Trust, London, 1980)], and Watson (1988, see not 3) have shown how women in Britain and Australia are marginalised by housing allocation and finance systems, although Munro and Smith [M. Munro and S.J. Smith, "Gender and Housing: Broadening the Debate", *Housing Studies* **4** (1989), pp. 3-17] argue that particular patriarchal outcomes cannot be assumed, because of the intervention of labour market variables.

34. For Mexico City see, for example, COPEVI (Centro Operacional de Vivienda y Poblamiento), *Intestigacion sobre Vivienda II: La produccion de vivienda en la Zona Metropolitana de la Ciudad de Mexico* (COPEVI, Mexico City, 1977), P. Connolly, "Uncontrolled Settlements and Self-build: What Kind of Solution? The Mexico City Case", in P.M. Ward (ed.), *Self-Help Housing: a Critique* (Mansell, London, 1982), pp. 141-174, R. Coulomb and C. Sanchez Mejorada, *Todos Proprietarios? Vivienda de alquiler y sectores populares en la ciudad de Mexico* (Centro de la Vivienda y Estudios Urbanos, Mexico City, 1991). A.G. Gilbert and P.M. Ward, *Housing, the State and the Poor: Policy and Practice in Three Latin American Cities* (Cambridge University Press, Cambridge, 1985), M.A. Michel, A. Azuela, P. Connolly, R. Coulomb, g. Garza, A. Iracheta, M. Maydon and M. Schteingart, *Process habitacionales en la Ciudad de Mexico* (Universidad Autonoma Metropolitana-Iztapalapa and Secretaria de Desarrollo Urbano e Ecologia, Mexico City, 1988). M. Schteingart, *Los Productores del Espacio Habitable: Estado, Empresa y Sociedad en la Ciudad de Mexico* (El Colegio de Mexico, Mexico City, 1989), P.M. Ward, *Welfare Politics in Mexico: Papering Over the Cracks* (Allen & Unwin, London, 1986), P.M. Ward, *Mexico City: the Production and Reproduction of an Urban Environment* (Belhaven, London, 1990). For Guadalajara see Gilbert and Varley, 1991 (see note 29). R. Lopez Rangel, *Urbanizacion y Vivienda en Guadalajara* (Centro de Ecodesarrollo, Mexico City, 1987). D. Vazquez, *Guadalajara: Ensayos de Interpretacion* (El Colegio de Jalisco, Guadalajara, 1989). For Puebla see Gilbert and Varley, 1991 (see note 29). G.A. Jones, "The Impact of Government Intervention upon Land Price in Latin American Cities: the Case of Puebla, Mexico", unpublished Ph.D. thesis (University of

Cambridge, Cambridge, 1991), P. Mele, *Los Procesos de Produccion del Espacio Urbano en la Ciudad de Puebla* (Institute de Ciencian, Universidad Autonoma de Puebla, Puebla, 1984). Universidad Autonoma de Puebla, Departamento de Investigaciones Arquitectonicas y Urbanisticas del Instituto de Ciencias (DIAU-ICUAP), *Memoria de la Primera Mesa de Trabaja sobre Investigaciones Universitarias de Urbanismo* (Universidad Autonoma de Puebla, Puebla, 1986).

35. CIDAC (Centro de Investigacion para el Desarrollo), *Vivienda y Estabilidad Politica: Alternativas para el Futuro* (Editorial Diana, Mexico City, 1991). Ward, 1990 (see note 34).

36. R. Coulomb, "Vivienda en renta y dinamica habitacional en la Ciudad de Mexico", in M.A. Michel A. Azuela, P. Connolly, R. Coulomb, G. Garza, A. Iracheta, M. Maydon and M. Schteingart (eds), *Procesos Habitacionales en la Ciudad de Mexico* (Universidad Autonoma Metropolitana0Iztapalapa and Secretaria de Desarrollo Urbano e Ecologia, Mexico City, 1988), pp. 141-182. Gilbert and Varley, 1991 (see note 29)

37. A household is here defined as a group of people 'eating from a common pot' and living on the same plot of land (see Varley, 1993 see note 30). Where more than one household occupies a plot, the non-owner household(s) may either pay rent or share the plot, rent-free, with its owners. A nuclear household consists of a male or a female householder with or without a 'spouse' and with or without children; an extended household includes other relatives or non-relatives. A 'householder' is the person who originally bought or rented the house, either alone or with their 'spouse' (Gilbert and Varley, 1991. see note 29); this does not mean that householders have joint property rights.

38. Most sharers make some contribution to the costs of services consumed. Althought the literature often fails to distinguish between extended households and sharing (see below), the question "*cocinan juntos o aparte?*" ("do you cook together or separately?") clearly makes sense to people, and generally elicits a direct, clear response to questions seeking to establish the number of households present.

39. Fieldwork in 1991 and 1992 included participant observation in a young self-help settlement on the eastern periphery of Puebla and a questionnaire survey in areas already studies in 1981-1982 (Mexico City) or 1985-1986 (Guadalajara and Puebla). *Loma de la Palma* developed in the 1970s on a hill in the north of Mexico City. Legalised in 1976, it received water and drainage in the 1980s and was being paved by the residents in summer 1991. *San Jose de los Leones* is a regularised and consolidated settlement in the west of Mexico City; it dates from the late 1960s, *El Salvador* is a 10-year old illegal settlement on the eastern periphery of Puebla. The streets are unpaved and many plots still unoccupied. *Veinte de Noviembre,* founded in the late 1940s as an illegal subdivision of private lands in northwest Puebla, now has a complex mixture of owner occupation, renting and sharing. *Buenos Aires* in southern Guadalajara dates from the beginning of the 1980s and has experienced relatively little consolidation: the streets are unpaved and the area has still to be connected to the city's water and drainage networks. *Agustin Yanez,* in the east of Guadalajara, was founded by illegal subdivision in the early 1950s; as in Veinte de Novimbre, tenants now form an important part of the population.

40. The variation in the proportion of owners sharing their plot with other household is connected with the age of the settlement. The selection of settlement of widely differing ages was prompted by other research question; it is unfortunate that in the Puebla and Guadalajara cases it means that there are relatively small numbers of sharers whose characteristics can be explored.

41. Althought the words 'married', 'wife' and 'husband' are used, no distinction is made between couples who are legally married and those living together in a consensual union. See also Gilbert and Varley, 1991 (note 29), Coulomb, 1990 (note 36); Gilbert and Ward, 1985 (note 34).

42. H.A. Selby, A.D. Murphy and S.A. Lorenzen, with I. Cabrera, A. Castarieda and I. Ruiz Love. *The Mexican Urban Household: Organizing for Self-Defense* (University of Texas Press, Austin, 1990), p.101, L.A. Lomnitz and M. Perez-Lizaur, "Dynastic Growth and Survival Strategies: the Solidarity of Mexican Grand-families", in e. Jelin (ed.), *Family, Household and Gender Relations in Latin America* (kegan Paul International, London, 1991), pp. 123-132; see p. 124. Arthur Wolf ["Family Life and the Life Cycle in Rural China", in R. McC. Netting, R.R. Wilk and E.J. Arnould (eds), *Households: Comparative and Historical Studies of the Domestic Group* (University of California Press, Berkeley, 1984), pp. 279-282] defines a 'grand' family as having a minimum of *three* nuclear units— two married siblings and their parents. he defines a stem family as having only two nuclear units. If sharing is to be described as a variation on this theme, it is clear that there are both stem families and grand families involved.

43. L. Lamphere, "Strategies, Coperation and Conflict among Women in Domestic Groups", in M.Z. Rosaldo, and L. Lamphere (eds), *Women Culture and Society* (Stanford University Press, Stanford, 1974), pp. 97-112; see p. 104.

44. *Ibid.*, see also E. Croll, "Rural China: Segregation to Solidarity", in P. Caplan and J.M. Bujra (eds), *Women United, Women Divided: Cross-cultural Perspectives on Female Solidarity* (Tavistock, London, 1978), pp. 46-76. U. Sharma, "Segregation and its Consequences in India: Rural Women in Himachal Pradesh", in P. Caplan and J.M. Bujra (eds), *Women United, Women Divided: Cross-Cultural Perspectives on Female Solidarity* (Tavistock, London, 1978), pp. 259-282. M. Wolf, "Chinese Women: Old Skills in a New Context", in M.Z. Rosaldo and L. Lamphere (eds), *Women, Culture, and Society* (Stanford University Press, Stanford, 1974), pp. 157-172. Wolf, 1984 (see note 42).

45. G.M. Foster, *Tzintzuntzan: Mexican Peasants in a Changing World* (Little, Brown, Boston, 1967). B.L. Chinas. *The Isthmus Zapotecs: Women's Roles in Cultural* (Holt, Rinehart & Winston, New York, 1973). J.W. Whitecotton, *The Zapotecs: Princes, Priests and Peasants* (university of Oklahoma Press, Norman, 1977). J.J. Gross, "Marriage and 'Family' among and Maya", in A.F. Marks and R.E. Romer (eds). *Family and Kinship in Middle American and the Caribbean* (University of the Netherlands Antilles and Royal Institute of Linguistics and Anthropology, Leiden, 1978), pp. 51-86. J.M. Ingham, *Mary, Michael and Lucifer: Folk Catholicism in Central Mexico* (University of Texas Press, Austin, 1986). L. Krantz, *Peasant Differentiation and Development: the Case of a Mexican Ejido* (University of Stockholm, Stockholm, 1991). L. Stephen, *Zapotec Women* (University of Texas Press, Austin, 1991). In an interesting exception to the rule, Nash [J.C. Nash, *Social Relations in*

Amatenango del Valle: An Activity Analysis, Centro Intercultural de Documentacion (CIDOC), Cuernavaca, 1969] found that in Amatenango del Valle, Chiapas, where recently married couples used to live with the bride's parents, they were now equally likely to live with either set of parents.

46. 1990 (see note 42), p. 101.

47. 1991 (see note 42), p. 126

48. L.A. Lomnitz, *Networks and marginality: Life in a Mexican Shantytown* (Academic Press, New York, 1977), p. 119

49. *Ibid.*, p. 120. The figures for 'initial residence' were 46% and 29%. The implication is that nuclear households were in the minority: 'the extended family prevails in the great majority of households' (*ibid.*, p. 100). This finding is contrary to most studies of Mexican urban households, although it is difficult to draw comparisons between Lomnitz household calssification scheme and those used by other authors. Many of the households she classifies as extended are more easily enumerated as nuclear sub-group (*ibid.*, p. 102). Sharers as defined in this study are found in Lomnitz 'single-roof' and 'single-plot' extended household categories rather than what she classifies as 'jointed' household'.

50. More daughters and sons are recorded as living with their parents than with their in-laws; this calls for comment. It may reflect under-reporting; but there is another explanation. Whereas almost all owners in the case-study settlement have enought space to accommodate another family, this is not necessarily true of their children's in-laws, who will come from a variety of housing types. Some, for example, will be tenants who are more likely to lack the space to accommodate any other relatives (Gilbert and Varley, 1991, see not 29).

51. The custom by which a young man 'steals' his girl friend from her parents, sometimes with the explicit support of his own relatives, has been widely documented in rural areas (Foster, 1967; Chinas, 1973; Whitecotton, 1977, see note 45) and is also, according to observations made during the fieldwork for this study, by no means uncommon in the cities.

52. Moser, 1991 (see note 7), p. 93.

53. Volbeda, 1989 (see note 19)

54. Gilbert and Varley, 1991 (see note 29)

55. Gilbert and Varley [1991 (see note 29), p. 112] suggest that the deposit, rather than the regular monthly payments on a plot of land, is one of the key elements dividing persistent tenants from prospective owners.

56. Lomnitz, 1977 (see nte 48)

57. *Ibid.*, p. 31.

58. *Ibid.*, p. 3.

59. *Ibid.*, p. 156.

60. S. Chant, "Family Formation and Female Roles in Queretaro, Mexico", *Bulletin of Latin American Research* 4. (1985), pp. 17-32. S. Chant, *Women and Survical in Mexico Cities: Perspectives on Gender, Labour Markets and Low-Income Households* (Manchester University Press, Manchester, 1991).

61. Chant, 1991 (see note 60), p. 156.

62. See also B. Garcia. H. Munoz and O. de Oliveira *Hogares y Trabajadores en la Ciudad de Mexico* (El Colegio de Mexico City, 1982) M. Gonzalez de la Rocha, "Economic Crisis, Domestic Reorganisation and Women's Work in Guadalajara, Mexico", *Bulletin of Latin American Research* 7, (1988), pp. 207-223. Selby *et al.*, 1990 (see note 42).

63. Chant, 1985 (see note 60), p. 22.

64. *Ibid.*, p. 26.

65. Chant, 1991 (see note 60), pp. 144-153.

66. Lamphere, 1974 (see note 43), p. 105.

67. Wolf, 1984 (see note 42), p. 281.

68. Croll, 1978 (see note 44).

69. Wolf, 1974 (see note 44).

70. Sharma, 1978 (see note 44).

71. Croll, 1978 (see note 44), p. 50.

72. Interestingly, Croll [E. Croll, *Chinese Women Since Mao* (Third World Books, London, 1983), p. 83] notes that tension between mother-and daughter-in-law was the most common cause of divorce reported in 1980s Beijing.

73. Stephen, 1991, pp. 40-62; Chinas, 1973, p. 59; Ingham, 1986, p. 64 (see note 45). In her study of a village in Chiapas, where married children can live with *either* set of parents, nash (1969, see not 45) found more harmonious relations between in-laws.

74. Krantz, 1991 (see not 45), p. 128

75. R. Diaz-Guerrero, *Psicologia del mexicano,* 5th edn (Editorial Trillas, Mexico City, 1990), p. 35. Stephen, 1991 (see note 45), p. 49.

76. L. Lenero Otero, "Valores familiares y dramaturgia social", in A. Hernadez Medina and L. Narro Rodriguex (eds), *Como somos los mexicanos* [Centro de Estudios Educativos (CEE), Mexico City, 1987], pp. 253-299. Diaz-Guerrero, 1990 (see note 75), p. 75.

77. As Selby *et al.* [1990 (see note 42), p. 91] write "Living alone is almost unthinkable in urban Mexico" particularly for a women in her eighties.

78. Krantz [1991 (see note 45), p. 136] notes the potential for conflict between sister-in-law in discussing the problems of virilocal residence patterns in rural Central Mexico.

79. The phrase *subir y bajar* ('to go up and down') is used in two context: tooing and fro-ing (as in visits to a government office in search of documentation, for example} and sleeping around. Women may be expexted to take a child with them on 'legitimate' outings. Anzaldua [G. Anzaldua, *Borderlands/La Frontera: the New Mestiza* (Aunt Lute, San Francisco, 1987), p. 16] records the prejudice against women who spend too much time 'in the street' from a *chicana* viewpoint: "How many times have I heard mothers and mother-in-law tell their sons to beat their wives for not obeying them, for being *hociconas* (big mouths), for being *callajeras* (going to visit and gossip with neighbors)...?"

80. Whitecotton, 1977, see note 45, p. 254; Krantz, 1991 (see note 45), Writing about urban Greece, Hirschon [R. Hirschon, ''Essential Objects and the Sacred: Interior and Exterior space in an Urban Greek Locality'', in S. Ardener (ed.) *Women and Space: Ground Rules and Social Maps* (Croom Helm, London, 1981), pp. 72-88]; indicates the importance of having separate kitchens as a ''physical marker'' of each household's autonomy when daughters marry and bring their husbands to live in their parents' home.

81. China, 1973 (see note 45), p. 59

82. Nash, 1969 (see note 45), p. 2/9

83. Lamphere, 1974 (see note 43), p. 112.

CHAPTER-23

Rehousing the Urban Poor : Looking at Women First : Argentina

Ana Falu and Mirina Curutchet

1. INTRODUCTION

1. **THIS PAPER CONSIDERS** the suitability for poor women headed households of a housing project in Cordoba, Argentine both in the planning and in implementation. The project was designed to rehouse squatters who occupied land needed for public works. The paper examines the extent to which women headed house holds participated in the project and documents a considerable number of "hidden" women headed households. It also analyzes the deficiencies in the housing project which include: plans for the relocation which did not consult women headed households as to their needs and priorities; housing designs and layouts ill-suited to their family size, needs and incomes; and, unrealistic assumptions about the "free time" that women could contribute to self-help. For many women headed households, this meant unrealistic demands for self-help contributions in view of their other responsibilities for earning the family income, managing the house and raising and caring for the children. The paper ends with recommendations as to how housing and human settlements policies can and should become gender aware.

The programme to relcoate squatters was carried out by the municipal government of the city of Cordoba after the return to democratic rule in Argentina in 1983. Cordoba is the second largest. (1) The study focused on the Quintas de san Jorge project which was designed by the new local government to relocate people who were illegally settled on land needed for public works.

The context for the project in Argentina (and in the rest of Latin America); The increasing inadequacy of government housing and basic services provided for the urban poor and the significant and growing number of households under the *defacto* responsibility of women, especially in the poorest social sectors, who were confronted with particularly difficult economic circumstances.

Both of these were further aggravated by the structural adjustment policies implemented in the region.

The objective of the study, focusing on one example of a social housing policy implemented by a local authority, was to make women and their need "visible," particularly women with primary responsibility for their households. Another objective was to contribute towards developing a greater understanding of how women are affected by social housing policies directed at the poor urban sectors. The study began during the project's final stages of implementation in 1988 and continued for the first two years of the new dwellers occupation.

The first stage of the study was an analysis of the project's objectives, the technical data/information and the implementation process. This was followed by a number of interviews with women heads of households and key informants. Finally, a study was made of the new settlement and its facilities and dwellings of including any enlargements and improvements undertaken by the dwellers. The research finding essentially confirm the thesis of Caroline Moser that planning for housing is base in inaccurate stereotypes and incorect paradigms as to the nature of "the household", including a failure to recognise the triple role of poor urban women a condition further aggravated in the case of women headed household (see Box 1)

Box 1: Inaccurate Stereotypes of Households and Women's Work

". . . there are two severs problems with the abstract stereotype model of Third World urban society. Firstly, it fails to recognize the triple role of women. In most low-income households "women's work" includes no only reproductive work required to guarantee the maintenance and reproduction of the labour force, but also productive work, often as secondary income earners located either in the home or at the neighbourhood level in informal sector enterprises. In addition in many urban areas it includes managing work, the organizational work undertaken by women not only in the household but also, and more importantly, at the community level. Secondly, the abstract stereotype model of Third World urban society fails to recognize that low income households are not homogeneous in

terms of family structure, and that, although nuclear families may be the dominant type, a diversity of other structures may also occur. The most important of these are de facto women headed households, in which the male partner is absent, either temporarily or permanently. It is estimated that today one-third of the world's households are headed by women, while in urban areas, especially in Latin America and part of Africa, the figure reaches 50 percent or more.

Source : Moser, Caroline (1985), "Housing policy and women: towards a gender aware approach". draft document commissioned by UNCHS-DPU, University College London, Working Paper No. 7.

II. Structural Adjustment and New Urban Poverty

THE IMPLEMENTATION OF social policies in Argentina already faced serious problems during the democratic beginning in 1984. But since then, the situation has deteriorated still further, due to the growing economic crisis and the structural adjustment policies affecting the whole Latin American region. Particularly in Argentina, this has meant a destruction of the stock of societal capital accumulate over generations as a result of a process of privatization that benefits a few local and external groups. Reductions in state expenditure, a rationalization of the productive sector, increasing concentration of industry with the closure of small and medium enterprises and, more recently, and massive privatization of state owned companies and their re-structuring, have brought alarming social and economic changes. This phenomenon, begun in the mid 1970s, has resulted in the "new urban poor." intitiated in the 1970s. a relatively young population unable to find employment in the formal productive sector in the last 10-15 years. The growing numbers of new urban poor have increased the number of people living in illegal settlement (the *villeros*) in Cordoba.

Cordoba experienced a strong industrial and economic expansion from the 1950s, followed by rapid population and urban growth but unlike the late 1970s and the 1980s, this did not produce a significant growth in the *villero* population. An example of the impact of the present structural adjustment in the housing and urban sector in given by graffiti that reads "*Se acepta clase media!*" ("We honour the middle-class!"). This subtle irony has an undeniable sociological content; the depth and persistence of the crisis pushes ever wider sectors of society into poverty.

a. Poor Women, The Adults Most Affected by the Economic Crisis

The various different economic policies implemented since 1983 have increased the level of poverty in large sectors of the population.[(3)] This is the result of a combination of factors including falling incomes, increased prices, rising unemployment and government cuts in social expenditure. There are important differences in the impact of these factors on men and women as a result of the social role assigned to women and because of the variety of activities they perform within the family and the community, especially in the poorest groups.[(4)] While men are responsible exclusively for productive work, women's responsibilities include the reproduction, care and raising of children, administration of households budgets, and working as a second income earner, often in low-paid jobs. In addition, women take care of the elderly and sick within the family and undertake a variety of community tasks. As a result of the economic crisis, their workload has increased in all these areas without any reduction in their domestic obligations. Women must compensate for the rising costs of food and shelter, the lack of day care centres and school support, and cuts in public services. They are also taking on an increasing number of community tasks that have to be done because of the crisis and cuts in government social expenditure such as the creation of communal kitchens, family gardens, community stores and improvement of facilities all of which are urban activities.

III. The Quintas Desan Jorge Housing Project

The Local Government of Cordoba, elected in 1983 and re-elected in 1987, has undertaken a range of social policies, including the construction of dwellings and site and service schemes for the population living in squatter settlement (villas miserias[(5)]. They have also constructed schools, health care centres and children's day-care facilities on the periphery of the city and they run a food programme for poor children under 12 years of age.

Their social housing policy planned to relocate the inhabitants of the *villas miserias* to free up the public or private land on which they has developed their homes, because this land was needed for the ambitious public works plan of the new democratic government. According to a census carried out by the municipality in 1984, 8,000 families were found to be living in more than 70 *villas miserias*. The majority of these had an urban background and can be classified as "new poor". About 30 percent of these families were categorized as women headed households. The quintas San Jorge project was the first stage of the *villas* relocation process. It involved approximately 600 families, a total of about 3,000 persons.

The project was initially directed at resettling 365 families from two squatter settlement located on land reserved for a city ring road: villa 3 de Mayo (with 343 families) and Villa la Canada (with 22). The project was later enlarged to about 6000 dwelling because of the need to accommodate those moved from other squatter settlements, most of them small and scattered around Cordoba. The project wás located on the outskirts of the city. The dwellings were built and allocated to squatter households in various stages over a two and a half year period. The allocation of housing to the former squatters was tied to the land that had to be cleared for public works, although this was never openly acknowledged by the local authorities who declared that the objective of the project was to provide decent shelter for the *villeros.*

The only data available on the population prior to relocation was from a study of 50 families undertaken by the municipality in Villa 3 de Mayo.[6] According to this, 23 percent of the population was between 19 and 30 years old, 46 per cent under the age of 12, and only 8 percent between 12 and 19 years old. Thus, 77 percent of the whole population was under 31 years old 70% had previously lived in other neighbor hoods of Cordoba which suggests a down-ward trend in social mobility: 20 percent came from rural areas while 10 percent had been living in other slums. Sixty percent of the people had lived in the *villa* one or two years. In this group of 50 households, 58 percent were married couples, 28 percent common law unions and 6 percent separated or divorced, the rest being widows or single people. Only 25 percent of the economically active population had a permanent job.

a. The Women Heads of Household become Visible

Owing to a shortage of reliable data at the beginning of the study-aggravated by the difficulties in obtaining municipal figures a survey was carried out involving 397 households resettled in Quintas de San Jorge. The data show that 55 percent of families had four to six members, 22 percent eight or more, and 22 percent one to three members. Sixty percent of the population were between two and 40 years old and 57 percent were born in the city of Cordoba. An analysis of the survey returns confirmed that a significant proportion of the households were under the responsibility of single women. There was also a considerable variety of complex kinship relations within many households which differed from the "typical" nuclear family. The first classification led to the definition of the following categories (see Table 1).

i. Nuclear households

A father, mother and their children; this type of household fits the stereotype generally accepted by planners where the father is the main income earner and the mother takes primary responsibility for reproduction and management tasks within the family.

ii. Households under the Responsibility of Women (Women Headed Households)

Women living alone with their children. Different children often have different fathers. The women usually assume the triple role of production (earning income), reproduction and management of the household simultaneously. Households with two or more generations of women and their children are also included.

iii. Household of Varying Composition

Men and women co-habit in "common law" unions, with their children and/or the children of either the women's or the man's former unions. These households often included relatives or *allegados* (friends) and more than two generations.

iv. Special Households

Households in which one person lives on his/her own, or two or more adults live with or without a kinship relationship. An example of this type of situation is sisters or a single man Single men with children under their responsibility are included in this category since they are not the object of this study.

Table 1 : type of Household

Types of Household	Number	Percent
Nuclear Households	220	56
Households under the Responsibility of Women (WHH)	63	16
Households of Varying Composition	81	21
Special Households	26	7
Total Surveyed Cases	390	100

N.B. From the total survey, seven were not considered because of lack of verification.

The data suggests that 16 percent of households are women headed households compared to the figure or 20 percent registered by the municipal census of 1985. The reasons for this decrease emerged from the interviews, especially those conducted with young mothers.

Some of the women headed households who had been surveyed in the squatter settlements did not obtain a house in the Quintas de San Jorge programme.

Some of the women headed households did not continue with the process of housing construction within the project because of the difficulties which are described below.

Analyzing the women headed households, 54 percent were separated, 25 percent were single and 21 percent widows. Most of the separated women were between the ages of 25 and 45 years old, that is to say young women. Fifty six percent worked outside their home, 9 percent were unemployed, 9 percent were retired or pensioners and only 23 percent were home workers (the remaining 3 percent did not respond).

After the first classification, an exploratory semiopen survey was undertaken on a sample of women heads of household and on the dwellers of households of varying composition. On closer analysis, we found that the percentage of women headed households increased if some of the other classifications were broken down. In the ''households of varying compositions ''there were several cases of women in charge of multiple responsibilities vis-a vis-their children. It was necessary to denominate and classify the different situations encountered, which was done under the general classification of "hidden women headed household" as shown in Table 2.

Table 2 : Hidden Women Headed Households within Households of varying Composition

Type of Household		Number	%
a.	Women with their own children without children in common with their partner	16	4
b.	Women with children from their and their partner's previous relationships but not children in common	7	2
c.	Women with own children and only one child in common with partner	10	3
d.	Women with own children and two children in common with partner	14	4
	Total	47	12

These cases corresponded to the households with higher numbers of children, the majority with children of more than one father. In most cases, the youngest child under the age of three, was the son or daughter of the women. This seemed to indicate the temporary nature of the "father"/man at the time of the census. Even when the man was not a temporary relationship, in the first two cases in Table 2 the children were the responsibility of the woman.

Furthermore, it was observed that in case (b), although the fathers assumed productive responsibility for their own children, it is the women who assumed the reproductive and management responsibilities for the whole dwelling for their and the men's children-and also generated income to satisfy their own children's needs. In cases where the women had a child/children with her actual *companero* (man-friend), he assumed a differential responsibility with regard to the women's children.

These women are close to being women heads of households because they assume full responsibility for productive and reproductive roles, as well as management of their scarce resources and time.

Therefore, we consider them as "hidden women heads of households". Data from both households of varying compositions and women headed households revealed the existence of single women with children living with their parents, mothers or grandmothers. These cases usually corresponded to very young mothers with children "without a father" living with close relatives. These women, who have to assume responsibility for taking care of and raising their children, as well as guaranteeing economic support, are labelled "women mothers alone". We found 17 such cases, which is 4 percent of the sample.

If all the survey evidence reaffirmed by the interviews is taken into account, the real perçentage of women haeded households in Quintas de San Jorge is 33 percent. These women headed households can be disaggregated into three categories (see Table 3).

Table 3 : A Disaggregation of Women Headed Households Showing the Proportion that are Hidden

Types of Household	Number	Percent
Women headed households evident in settlement	63	16
Women headed households within households of varying composition	47	12
Hidden women headed households women mothers alone	17	4
Total number of cases	127	33

This analysis suggests that during the design, implementation and evaluation of social housing policies, more attention should be paid to the *invisibility* of different household cases which are under the sole responsibility of women and also to the *magnitude* of the verified data.

b. Different Types of Houses

The Quintas San Jorge project was developed in defferent phases, with a different type of housing constructed at each stage. The study analyzed five different types of housing. Even thought the whole urban lay-out and the multiplicity of housing solutions were the responsibility of the municipal technicians and professionals, there was a notable diversity in the design alternatives and in building types.

With reference of design criteria, the analysis centred on the number of rooms, the relative functionality between them, the relationship between constructed and utilized areas, the positioning in the lay-out of the wet cell (bath-kitchen), and the size and use of the kitchen and its relationship to other functional areas. The potential for expansion of the dwelling was also incorporated into the research. Two different production methods were adopted. The first was private contractors who produced finished houses. The second was self-help construction programmes carried out by mutual aid groups where the group built a number of houses and when all units were completed, they were assigned to different group members.

An indicator called "functional performance" was used to evaluate the house designs. This compares "total of dwelling. This analysis showed significant differences between the different lay-outs. An indicator relating to the efficiency of the built area is essential in the assessment of social housing programmes; the rooms are generally small and of insufficient size and therefore a design appropriate to the needs of the inhabitants is very important. In cases such as Quintas de San Jorge, which gave people a "core house", maximization in the use of the resource and optimization of the living areas should be basic design criteria. Table 4 illustrates this.

Table 4 : Functional Performance* Analysis According to House Type

HOUSE TYPE AREA	LAYOUT AREA	TOTAL LAUNDRY	KITCHEN	BATH ROOM IZED	HALLS UTIL PERFORMANCE	FUNCTIONALMM FOR EACH HOUSE TYPE	
A	27,13	4,00	3,42	4,59	15,12	55,7	47,6
B	28,31	incorp.	2,94	4,97	20,40	72,0	4,9
C	38,08	incorp.	6,8	4,70	27,3	71,7	14,4
D	37,68	5,80	7,44	5,24	19,20	50,9	3,4
E	29,32	4,00	3,4	4,52	17,40	59,03	8,3
F	19,05	3,00	2,8	2,61	10,64	55,8	21,4

* The ratio between total built and effectively used area.

From information summarized in Table 4, we wanted to analyze the two type of dwelling which optimize the functional performance of the built areas: these are labelled type B and C to be compared to types A and F, the types of dwelling to which most women headed households were assigned, and the dwellings with lower functional efficiency scores and smaller total built areas. Type D, with the lowest functional performance of all the analyzed houses, was not considered in this study because of the low proportion of women headed households allocated this type of house. Type E was not included because the houses were built for civil servants working in local government and not for the relocated squatters.

Table 4 shows that only 5 percent of women headed households are in dwelling type B with 14 percent in type C, 48 percent in type A and 21 percent in type F. Type A is one of the housing models which was built by the dwellers (ie self-help construction models) whilst the others, types B, C, and F, were built by private contractors.

Two lay-outs optimize the functional efficiency of the built area, namely types B and C. In both cases, the kitchen is not conceived as separate room but is integrated into the "living room" of the dwelling, a euphemism referring in type B to the only space in the house and in type C to the other room of the unit. While type B and C give higher percentages of useful area related to total built area (72 percent and 78 percent), the opposite is true of types A and F.

Type A, the self-built houses, perform worst: one example of a type A house is given in Box 2. Yet women headed households were assigned the worst dwellings and they had to work to build them. Twenty-two percent of women headed households obtained type F dwellings: one example of this type is given in Box 3. Type F dwellings are the ones with the least built-up area and also among the worst in terms of functional performance. In both cases, the room for the kitchen represented nearly one-third of the total built area. This is related to the house design, particularly regarding the kitchen and how it functions, the intended furniture and kitchen equpment: it does not respond to the needs and/or perferences of the women, who only have access to very old-fashioned and large kitchen equipment which does not fit into the allocated spaces. Where the kitchen was planned and designed as a separate room, it has rarely been used as a kitchen except for washing dishes (because of the water pipe) or to store belongings. In general, cooking activities take place on the patio, the open space at the back of the house, in mud ovens or on open fire places, using firewood or charcoal as fuel. Firewood and charcoal are much cheaper than gas or kerosene (which the interviewed women heads of households indicated they could not afford).

From observations and the opinions of the interviewed women, it appears that dwelling types B and C are more efficient, although they do not fulfil even the minimum needs of the relocated families who mostly live in overcroweded conditions, especially those living in type B. Although this analysis is valid for the whole population of Quintas de San Jorge, Whether nuclear households or not, when one takes into account the indicators of functional performance related to potential for expansion (analyzed in the next section), the housing policy as if affected women heads of households indicates a lack of awareness of the reality of these women's lives.

c. House Enlargement : From Plan to Reality

All the houses, even those offering the best functional efficiency and the ones with two rooms, were thought of as "core houses" to which the occupants could add additional rooms. It was for this reason that a "materials bank" was planned. The "materials bank' created by the local government, functioned over a very short period of time and benefited only a small number of residents. Analyzing the present situation in the settlement, the number and volume of modification and enlargement that have taken place in the short time (three years) since the houses were assigned is surprising. However, only a few of the enlarged dwellings belong to women headed household.

Of the women heads of households interviewed, 50 percent could not afford any king of building improvement. The other half have made only small modifications most of them consisting of fences to delimit their plot and to protect their family and belongings, in direct response to the lack of security in the neighbourhood. Of this 50 percent, only for women hired labour to enlarge their houses, and each of these four women manage their own small, stores. In only one case has a woman household head taken on the responsibility of enlarging the house herself. On the other hand, 50 percent of all households in the neighbourhood have expanded their dwellings in the three years reaching, in several cases, the maximum size of three bedrooms, a large kitchen and a living room plus gallery.

d. Self-help Construction : Between Self-confidence and Exhaustion

Opinions differ among the residents of Quintas de San Jorge with regard to the benefits of the self-help scheme. On the one hand, their statements on the method of housing production are very positive. On the other hand, there are complaints, especially from women, about the strenuous efforts they have had to make. A comment by one interviewed woman illustrates her feelings."... self-help construction is not adequate: men get drunk while women do not leave the spade." To have participated in this experiment has meant gaining self-confidence, particularly for women, who faced the challenge of coping with "male work", as construction work is defined. This is the women's general conclusion in spite of the heavy and exhausting work they have had to do.

All but two of the women interviewed admitted that they had obtained help during the process, but this help was never free and something was always demanded in exchange. The help came mainly from family members or relatives such as adult children and brothers; only in a few cases was labour hired. In the case of relatives, the women paid with food, clothes and other kinds of services. They also stated unanimously that without help, it would have been impossible to fulfil the requirements for unpaid work expected by the programme. The women believe that their participation in the programme, apart from the physical and psychological impact, caused many other problems. These include all health, a significant reduction in child care and a curtailment of income generating activities even though these incomes are essential for the subsistence of the family. These problems are not surprising considering the many responsibilities these women face : they work over 30 hours a week in low-paid jobs, they spend between one and two hours a day travelling to their place of work and they have sole responsibility for caring for the children at home.

One of the interviewed women, only 35 years old and suffering from Chagas disease-an illness that causes serious heart problems which can lead to death[(7)] gave the following commentary :

"No body at home wanted to help. My husband had no confidence in the programme and never went to work. My grown-up boys only helped when our house was nearly finished. But my husband-from whom I was actually separated, but my husband-from whom I was actually separated, but not formally - was the first and most active in organizing the move to the new dwelling. For more than a year, every day, I went to the building site after my job in the hospital. I worked as long as it was required by the programme with the sole help of my eldest daughter, who was 16, and I did all the tasks. I know it hurt me very much to work in such a way and I know my heart is serously damaged but I wanted to have a house of my own. What is terribly sad now is that I still have problems with my husband and he does not want to leave the home. He wants me to leave! Do you understand? From the house I built but which the municipality allocated to both to us because we were married..."

All of these women affirm that the construction work was heavy but neither difficult nor unpleasant. According to the technicians and social workers involved in the project, women managed the whole construction process efficiently. Dona Delia, aged 50, said"...watching with the eyes, you learn," This statement reflects the motivation of these women who did not mind the construction work even when they generally had to do the most physical, least specialized, tasks such as loading and unloading lorries, mixing the mortar and concrete and digging foundations.

Another significant commentary was given by Sandra :

"I worked harder than men although I was pregnant. In the beginning I was ashamed of being a women involved in construction work but later I liked it and worked happily among men."

Beyond the effort, women enjoyed the challenge of being able to accomplish tasks traditionally regarded as "men's". According to the women, the problems that arose during the construction processing were of an organizational and management kind, including a lack of Co-ordination among the municipal government's agents, delays in the provision of building materials and a shortage of water and transport. One of the major organizational problems was the amount of work that had to be done by beneficiaries, which had to be reduced from 20 to eight hours per week. All of the problems arising during the long process of construction reduced the beneficiaries interest. In addition, they did not know which house they would be allocated in the end.

The lack of precise control over the work done by beneficiaries led considerable conflict and even of some of them abandoning the programme. For the women headed households involved in this programme there was no choice; they either participated or became homeless. The possibility of obtaining a shelter of their own was enough to mobilize these women and to push them into accomplishing tasks for which they were neither physically nor culturally prepared - despite some (inadequate) training. Participation in the programme was highly positive, since women gained self-confidence and social prestige.

Nevertheless, analyzing the costs that these efforts imply, as in the case of the woman suffering from Chagas, the balance is not so positive. It is made less so when, depending on the level of involvement of each villa and their inhabitants, some households have to make enormous efforts to obtain and build a shelter, whilst others receive finished houses built by the private contractors. This illustrates the lack of equity in the programme's design.

e. The Variety of Criteria in the Development of the Programme

The analysis of dwelling types using the indicators of functional efficiency, capacity to enlarge the house and production methods showed that the programme had different consequences for the different types of household, especially in the case of women headed households. It does not appear that these consequences were foreseen by the municipal government since they did not examine the social and cultural realities of the target population. The design and implementation of their programme responded to other criteria and interests. What were the criteria underlying the selection of the production methods, the variety in the lay-outs and the decisions about dwelling allocation?

A first explanation might be found in the various stages of implementation and in the intervention by differnt municpal departments and agents at each stage. The first stage was optimistic and enthusiastic. It coincided with a return to democracy and was expressed in the comments of the Human Development Department of the municipality which was responsible for the self-help and mutual aid project. As one leading municipal official commented: ''Our intention is to move from the squatter (villero) to the neighbour, with all the rights and responsibilities this move implies...'' This stage was characterized by the intention to set up within the municipality a sector for formulating policies and projects for social housing and community development where social promotion through mutual aid would overcome poverty.

Later stages of the programme came under the responsibility of the ''efficiency-first'' sector, who were mainly concerned with the implementation of public works and who demanded the villeros relocation. The various stages and different characteristics of the housing solutions have been affected by the intervention of different municipal agents and departments which worked with little co-ordination or agreement. Moreover, budget decisions have been influenced by the underlying electrol pressure which demanded the completion of the plan of public works.

IV. FINAL COMMENTS

THE LOCAL ADMINISTRATION of Cordoba has shown that, not only does it have resources and management capacity to implements its plans but it also has the freedom and independence of ideas to design its own social policies. The major commitments to free urban land and to undertake important and much-needed public works are linked to the responsibility for rehousing those who had to be evicted. In spite of the serious problems highlighted in the preceding analysis, there is a significant difference between the concerns of the democratic government of Corodoba and the practices under the military dictatorship the fell in 1983. In Buenos Aires, the military government had simply bulldozed the squatters off the land it needed for public works with no compensation and no provision for rehousing.

Looking at Quintas de San Jorge from a gender perspective, focusing mainly on the self-help and mutual aid scheme we conclude that it is typical "assistance and efficient housing project" like many others implemented by government organizations and NGOs, often with external help. These rely on women to guarantee their success but ignore women's real situation and their needs. Quintas de San Jorge, without doubts, was an answer, however partial, to practical gender needs. However it is important to draw attention to the problems found in this settlement, which are similar to those analyzed in other fieldwork studies and which give evidence of the lack of any policies which take into account the specificity of women's needs, and particularly those of women headed households.(8)

Some of the most significant critical observations are :

Self-help housing production methods were promoted among those who were least table to manage the requirements of this type of housing construction: this is evident in the incoherence in the policy of assigning the different types of dwellings to different types of household.

-There was a lack of essential services for women in charge of children.

-The location of the settlements was on the urban periphery, far from places of work and basic urban services, and this increases time and costs incurred in travelling.(9)

-The form and design of the dwellings were based on ideological assumptions alien to the beneficiary group.

Based on the research, we would say that, in spite of the census conducted by the municipality prior to the implementation of the Quintas de San Jorge programme which showed that women headed households accounted for 30 percent of the total, this was not taken into account in the formulation of the programme. This social group, which probably makes up 36 percent of the households involved in the projects, was not specifically considered in the development and implementation of housing policy.

Evidence from the study shows that women headed households share similar aspirations to other beneficiaries of the programme but, due to their particular situation, they are among the least able to develop their homes. In our opinion, gender awareness in designing housing policies in the case of Quintas de San Jorge should have implied a different housing allocation policy, and should have **positive discrimination** towards women, including giving them special consideration in designing the layout and functioning of the dwellings. This would mean that :

-Dwellings allocated to women headed households should be among the largest, because this group has evident difficulties in undertaking enlargements.

-Dwellings, particularly if they are "core houses", should incorporate a kitchen area into the multi-functional area. This allows women headed households to achieve a greater efficiency in the use of the built-up area and allows a better performance from the limited area in which these women have to perform the multiplicity of domestic tasks. Because of their low incomes, the women cannot afford gas or kerosene, and continue to cook in the open air with charcoal or firewood, which means a more limited use for the kitchen area.

-To allocate finished dwellings to women headed households would not involve them in the personal and social costs incurred through self-help which, in this project, put an excessive burden on them.

It is critically important to make women visible and, as a consequence, to consider them in planning theory and the process by which houses, neighbourhoods and settlements are produced.

This is for several reasons. First significant numbers of poor urban women have sole responsibility for their children, having to play a triple role but also being the main group most affected by the present economic crisis. Secondly, the increasing inadequacy of the state's social polity towards the poor is all too evident. The third is the lack of effort to identify women headed households as specific subjects for social housing policies with specific needs. This means developing gender awareness in planning theory and the processes of habitat production.

On the other hand, the reflections arising from the findings of this research, highlighting self-help and mutual aid, suggest the need to continue the debate initiated by Beatriz Cuenya. Does the participation of women in processes of habitat production such as Quintas de San Jorge constitute a progressive and emancipatory action in relation to the subordinate position of women or does it reinforce the situation of social discrimination.[10] In our opinion, this research reveals similar contradictions to those evident in the majority of projects - the women are overexploited but, through the experience, they gain an increased awareness of their social situation, which means a step forward in the field of strategic gender interests.

REFERENCES

1. According to preliminary data from the 1991 national census; city of Cordoba, 1,179.067 inhabitants: a growth rate of 18.7 percent for the decade; 555,744 men, 613,293 women and 330.093 dwelling units.

2. Moser, Caroline (1986), "Women needs in the urban system: training strategies in gender aware planning" in Schmink, M., J.Bruce and M.Kohn (editors). "Learning about women and urban services in Latin America and the canbbean". Population Council, New York, mimeo.

3. Editors note for a discussion of the "new urban poor" in Buenos Aires and their involvement in community organizations, see "Land invasions and grassroots organization: the Quilmes settlements in Greater Buenos Aires, Argentina" by Cuenya, Beatriz, Diego Armus, Maria di Loreto and Susana Penalva (1990), Environmental and Urbanization Vol. 2, No. 1, April.

4. Sanchis, Norma and Blanca Ibarlucia (1991), published in Pagina 12, a short but consistent article based on research work on "Structural adjustment: the differential impact on men and women".

5. The name given to squatter settlements in Argentine cities the literal translations is misery villages or misery settlements.

6. Nardini, B. and M.Y. Peralta (1984), survey undertaken at the request of the municipality of Cordoba, Argentina on a sample of 50 families from the squatter settlement 3 de Mayo due to be eradicate.

7. Chagas disease (American trypanosomiasis) is a debilitating parasitic disease usually transmitted by the triatomine insect it is found only in the Americas 24 million people are already infected and 65 million live in conditions which put them at risk of infection.

8. Studies carried out in Latin America and Africa by several research Schlyter (1988-89) Nimpuno Parente (1986), Buvinic Lycette and Berger (1986), Vance (1985) Bohman (1984) Chant (1985), Larsson (1985-89), among others (see Guide to the Literature for more details)

9. Other studies on the specific topic of urban services and poor women such as the work of Barrig, Maruja and Amelia Fort (1987), "De vecinas a cludadanas, la mjuer en el desarrollo urbano", SUMBI, Lima and Aguirre, Rosaria (1990), "Descentralizacion iniciativas locales de servicios de cuidado infantil en Montevideo", presentation to the second woeking group meeting of the regional group "Mujer y Politicas Socials a Nivel Local", Chile, mimeo.

10. Cuenya, Beatriz (1989), "Participacion de de la mujer en la gestion barrial, significados y orientaciones para la planificacion delos servicios habitacionales", contribution to the seminal "Mujer y Habitat", CLACSO-IIED, held in Buenos Aires, October 1989, mimeo.

CHAPTER-24

Gender and State Bias in Jamaican Housing Programs

*Thomash. Klak and Jeanne K. Hey**

Introduction

This paper assesses the Jamaican state's responsiveness to women's housing needs. The National Housing Trust (NHT) is Jamaica's largest housing financier, public or private. NHT was created in 1976 as part of Michael Manley's broad social welfare package (Girvan, Bernal and Hughes. 1980. pp. 117-118) to finance large number of working-class housing units, and to distribute them according to "housing needs" (*The Gleaner,* 1976a, 1976b; NHT, nd). Given that female-headed households are concentrated in the low-income groups that endure the most dire housing needs (Statin, 1987a, p. 20; Massiah, 1983), it is important to analyze the degree to which NHT provides loans to women, especially those of low income.

Female-headed households comprise half of the total in many cities of Latin America and the Caribbean (Moser, 1987b, p. 14). The Jamaican census reported that women headed 46.8% of households in Kingston in 1984 (Statin, 1987a, p. 15). Despite the urgent need for research on women's housing needs and access, most studies of state housing programs pay scant attention to women. The literature on housing and poor in Third World cities is predominantly oriented to men's experience. This bias may reflect the fact that in other regions (e.g., Africa and Asia, Dwyer, 1979, pp. 65 206). men 20-35 years old are the most prominent recent urban immigrants, and thus find themselves without housing in a shelter-scarce metropolis. This trend in no way relieves housing studies of their obligation to pay particular attention to the housing crisis of women, particularly in Latin America where women comprise much of the urban migrant population. Across the Third World, the relationship among women, shelter, and the state has not been investigated rigorously. Most of the empirical work has concerned Central and South America (Moser, 1987a, p. 5) In the Caribbean, despite extensive female poverty, gender-sensitive housing studies are clearly in short supply.

Research on Jamaican women's housing conditions, needs and opportunities is particularly lacking. Blackwood (1983) has performed the only quantitative study. It addressed the relation between gender and the repayment of state housing loans. Unfortunately, Blackwood was only able to access government data aggregated into tables, rather than at the individual level. Blackwood's data analysis nonetheless revealed that women are more likely than men to repay housing loans (similarly see *The Tribune,* 1987, p. 24). Besides Blackwood's study, women's housing issues have received remarkable little publicity or research attention that could lead to better housing policy.[1] For example, a historical review of Jamaica's natonal newspaper, *The Gleaner,* which has documented and discussed Jamaica's housing crisis in general (*The Gleaner,* 1975; 1976a; 1976b; 1976c; 1982; 1983; 1984; 1985), found a virtual silence regarding women, hosing, and the state. This silence in discussion and analysis of women's access to state housing resources is particularly notable considering their acute housing problems.

The following analysis contributes to rectifying this negligence. We are specifically concerned with how gender shapes Jamaicans' access to NHT housing loans. In Section2, we review the obstacles separating women from decent housing, both Latin America and the Caribbean in general and in Jamaica specifically. Women's numerous family and employment responsibilities make their housing needs great but often work against their ability to secure state housing loans. Societal prejudices against women also hinder them from obtaining housing assistance, as state agencies tend to assume that men remain principally responsible for home finances.

Section 3 systematically examines Jamaican women's access to state housing loans and their loan repayment performance. Drawing primarily on quantitative records from NHT, we explore four dimensions of the housing loan process: (a) eligibility and application, (b) allocation of mortgages, (c) state employment and mostgage allocation, and (d) repayment and (nu) arrears. We appraise women's performance and rates of exclusion or inclusion at each stage of the loan process, from application to allocation repayment. We identify two levels of gender bias that operate in different directions. First, there are biases against women in the work force which exclude many of them from the beginning stages of the selection process during which a person's eligibility for state loans is determined. Women receive a very small share of the loans relative to their participation in the work force. Second, there is a bias in favor of women once they have entered the state mortgage system through stable formal employment. Women of marginal income have a better chance of receiving a loan than men in the same income group. NHT also awards loans to a slightly higher percentage of eligible women than of eligible men. This bias in favor of women within the NHT system, however, does not overcome the effects of bias against them in the work force. Far more women are excluded from the system than are favored by it. In absolute terms, men obtain most of the loans, and a disproportionate share of the loans compared to their participation in the official work force, which itself undercounts informal workers who are mostly women. Including all informal employees in the work force would make the male bias in loan allocation even greater.

Through our exploration of gender biases in Section 2 it becomes clear that NHT maintains a heavy bias in favor pf state employ, most of whom are women. NHT loan allocation to state employees, however, exhibits a bias against women. State-employed men receive the greatest share of all NHT loans. Our examination of women's loan repayment records addresses whether women's relatively low likelihood of obtaining loans can be explained by an inability to repay their mortgages. Despite their economic hardships, women in fact have better loan repayment records than men.

In the concluding section, we place our findings in the context of a feminist perspective on housing problems. Women have primary responsibility for the home, yet housing policy has not addressed their needs. Although NHT favors those women who are able to access the system. NHT's rules of inclusion reflect societal prejudices against women. The overall effect is that most women are excluded. A feminist perspective is crucial to understanding the greater societal biases against women that must be addressed before any institution can properly meet their needs.

2. Women's Housing Needs

Women's housing needs are particularly great for two reasons. First, women perform a triple role in society, acting as reproducers, community managers and wage earners (Moser. 1987b). Each role generates particular housing needs. Second, women represent a disproportionately large segment of the poor populaton, who suffer the most dire housing crisis (UN Habitat, 1987 Jones, Webber and Turner, 1987; Statin, 1987a p. 20). This section reviews these two issues that create women's particular housing needs.

Moser (1987b) observes that women, particularly those living in poverty, maintain a triple role of reproducers, community managers and producers. As reproducers, women are responsible for childcare, home maintenance and ensuring a protected and stable environment within which their families can grow and prosper (Blumberg, 1989). Women are the "primary users of space both in their homes and in the local community, utilizing their homes throughoutt the entire day more than men do (Moser, 1987b, p. 17).

In their role as community managers, women organize themselves to provide services for their communities that the economy and state fail to produce. Because women spend a large proportion of their time in the home and local community, they have a particular interest in maintaining community services such as housing, childcare facilities, and the utilities required of a well functioning neighborhood. Poor areas are usually in dire need of services and it is women who suffer from inadequate services the most because their work is so often centered in the community Despite their unique understanding of community needs, women are ususlly excluded from official decision making on the provision of community services. Their collective work performs some of the tasks that public and private housing and neighborhood service organizations have failed to perform for the poor. This work also takes women's time and energy away from their other duties (Harris, 1989; Moser, 1987b).

Examples of community management projects in Jamaica include the St. Peter Claver Free Trade Zone Women's Group which organizes female heads of household to upgrade their housing conditions. With the aid of this non-governmental organization, women in the group pool financial resources to improve their community's housing facilities (Hinds, 1989, p. 24). The "partner" system is another means by which Jamaicans, particularly women, have organized themselves to better their household and community conditions. Partners are savings institutions usually operating in the informal sector and almost always headed by women. Members of the community bank contribute financial resources and are able to draw on it for, among other things, upgrading shelter conditions (McLeod, 1987, pp. 133-136). These documented examples of community management projects in Jamaica represent a fraction of women's community efforts that are too often neglected by academic study and the Jamaican state.

Their roles as reproducers and community managers place a far greater burden on poor women than on most men and wealthy women. This means that poor women have less time for the wage earning work necessary to qualify for housing loans. It is to this producer role that we now turn.

Working conditions in Jamaica, particularly for women, are characterized by low pay, a shortage of formal employment, and widespread informality (Boyd, 1988). Jamaica's per capita GNP was US$940 in 1985, which was low for Latin america and the Caribbean (World Bank, 1987, pp. 202, 268-271). GNP undoubtedly excludes much informal production, but the lack of data on informal enterprise prohibits knowing its contribution to income or comparing Jamaica to its neighbors.[2]

Almost all formal workers earn the official minimum wage or more, and have better access to state resources (Lawson and Klak, 1990). The formal sector employs many more men than women. Women represent only 36.1% of all NHT's contributors. who are almost exclusively formal sector workers.

To compensate for limited job opportunities in the private formal sector, some women are drawn to employment within the state. Women are well over half of all Jamaican state employees (55.7%).[3] The state nonetheless remains a limited resource for improving women's income for two reasons. First, state salaries are lower than those in the private sector for comparable jobs (Wines, 1987). Fewer men will accept the relatively low wages the state offers, and thus the state positions are relegated to women, Second, the state cannot absorb many more women into its work force. To the contrary, state employment shrank dramatically for both sexes during the 1980s, falling 20% in one 2.5 year period (April 1984-October 1986). While the greater proportion of state employees are women, less than 11% of the total female work force is state employed (Statin, 1987b, p. 24).

Finding few decent jobs in the formal sector, many Jamaicans turn to informal work, Perhaps half of the Jamaican work force is employed in informal enterprise. Women must resort to informal wage-earning activities more than men. The fact that workers often choose informal occupations over formal jobs should not imply that informal work is well paid or stable. The choice of infomal work is more a reflection of the miserable conditions in the available minimum wage formal employment (Bromley and Birkbeck, 1988; Portes, 1989).

Official statistics do not fully document informal activities such as street vending and piece rate homework, and therefore understate women's participation in the work force and obscure the full extent of their poverty (Blumberg, 1989; Bromely and Birkbeck, 1988). The Jamaican census does not distinguish formal from informal employment. Rather, some of the more regular informal employment is apparently lumped with petty bourgeoisie in the "self-employed" category (Statin, 1987b, p. 25; PIJ, 1989). A large portion of informals are officially considered "not in the work force" or "unemployed" (Gross and Bingham, 1985, pp. 115-116). For example, the official work force contains only 79% of working age men, and 63% of working age women. Within the official work force, 13% of men and 33% of women were considered unemployed (Statin, 1987b, p. 22). Of working-age men under 25, 25.9% were categorized unemloyed, while the comparable figure for young women is a remarkable 50.8% (PIJ, 1989). With little public welfare to fall back on, however, few Jamaicans can afford the luxury of not working. Thus most of the 18.9% of the work force that was officially unemployed in 1988 worked informally. Women were concentrated in the undocumented occupations. The state's lack of recognition of informal work also means exclusion of informal workers from state housing assistance.

Informal work typically provides irregular wages and little job security (Moser, 1987b, p. 26; Massiah, 1983). There is considerable diversity of wage levels among both formal and informal employees (Portes, Castells and Benton, 1989). On average, however, informal workers earn much less. In Bogota in 1984, for example, more than half of informal workers earned less than the official minimum wages, while only 3% of formal workers did (Portes, 1989, p. 25). Further, the recession that besieged Latin America and the Caribbean during the 1980s put at least as much downward pressure on informal wages as formal ones. Layoffs and real wage cuts in the formal sector made earning a living through informal work far more difficult (Gilbert, 1986; Portes, 1989; Moser, 1989).

Both informal employment and poverty are concentrated among women. Whereas one survey found that women individually head 41% of poor Kingston households in which informal work predominates (McLeod, 1987, p. 27, the official census found them to be the sole heads of only 24% of households in which the head is employed formally (Statin, 1987b, p. 32). Much of women's informal sector work is performed at home (Machado, 1987, p. 67; Moser, 1987b, p. 21). The households is thus for many women a center not only of reproduction and community service, but of wage-earning production as well. Decent housing conditions and community services are therefore crucial to women's ability to earn a living in the informal sector.

The argument that maintains that women usually provide a second income to their house-holds would appear to make these figures on women's proverty less severe. The assumption that women are primarily second-income earners is, however, flawed. In many cases, women are the only or primary income source for their households. A 1984 Jamaican census reported that 41.2% of all Jamaican households were headed by women and 58.8% were headed by men (Statin, 1987a, pp. 14-15). An independent sample of poor Kingston households found that 41% were female headed, 42% male headed, and 17% joint headed (McLeod, 1987, p. 27). Thus for poor Jamaicans, female-headed households appear to be as common as any type of living arrangement. Even when residing with men, women generally are responsible for shelter, childcare, household finances, and other domestic necessities (Massiah, 1983, p. 34; Moser, 1987b).

The main points of this discussion of women's triple role and housing needs are: (a) women require better housing conditions to perform their multiple household reponsibilities; (b) women are concentrated in informal work characterized by low pay, insecurity, and a lack of state recognition; and (c) women represent a larger share of household head and primary wage earners than is generally acknowledged. These conditions make women's housing needs particularly acute. As will be discussed in Section 3, however, women's triple role also obstructs their access to state housing loans and impedes their ability to improve their housing conditions.

3. Assessment of Gender Bias in NHT's Housing Programs

NHT is Jamaica's principal housing finance agency, drawing

mandatory payroll deductions from employees and their emplyers equal to 5% of wages to provide housing mortgages. NHT has survived two regime changes and has grown to be the third largest financial institution in Jamaica in terms of assets (private banks hold the first and second positions). While NHT is by far the largest housing agency, it is not expected to contend with all of Jamaica's housing problems. Its is one of seven state and parastatal agencies attempting to expand and upgrade Jamaica's housing stock (Jones, Webber and Turner, 1987, p. 42). Private financial institutions, of which the most well endowed are building societies, trusts, and life insurance companies, also offer mortgages. But these are too few in number and too expensive to supply housing to those most in need (Grose, 1979; Golding,

An assessment of gender bias in government housing data requires methodological choices and interpretative caution. Because official data reflect culturally-based attitudes that favor men and thus are biased toward men (Moser and Peake, 1987), we must devote a substantial portion of our discussion to methodological issues. Housing agents assume that the man is the primary breadwinner and household head, even though the woman may take on primary responsibility for assuring loan repayment (Moser, 1987b). If there is a male applicant present, his name generally appears first on the mostgage even in a household in which the women has similar or greater income and job security. The man's name may appeae alone on the mortgage if his income is enough to qualify, even if in practice the women assures that monthly payments are made. The woman's name appears first on the mortgage only when she applies individually or brings in a second mortgagor to pool enough wages to qualify. For gender analysis, these males biases in data recording methods obscure the extent to which women have shelter responsibility. Male biases in the data also mask variations in repayment depending on whether men or women are responsible for it.

Keeping these data problems in mind, we use the first mortgagor to define gender. In fact, the vast majority of NHT loans (81.7%) are written to a single mortgagor. Of these strngle mortgagor loans, 63.7% have been allocated to men, suggesting their relative stength in wages, saving, and credit histories. Whereas only 9.8% of male morgagors, have taken 9 women as a second Mortgator 20.2% of female mortgagors list a man secondly the opposit sex for female first MortgagtorsThe higher rate of shared legal repayment responsibility with a member of suggests theirgreater reliance on men, owing to both financial and cultural constraints (Black wood, 1983, p.43; Moser, 1987b). Although we distinguish analytical between male and female NHT mortgagors, we recognize that their homes are generally not sexually segregated (Statin, 1987b, p. 32). For many single mortgagors of either sex there are persons of the opposite sex who benefit from the improved liring arrangements. No matter how many loans are allocated to men from which females in the household benefit, they do not improve houring Conditions for the many household heads who are women.

(b) Gender differences within NHT's contributor and applicant populations

Contribution to the NHT fund is a prerequisite for obtaining a loan. It is therefore essential to examine NHT's rules and its contributor population to find who is excluded from applicant eligibility screening, selection and application process toward obtaining an NHT housing loan at the broadest level by comparing the population most in need of housing to that which participates in NHT. In proposing NHT, Prime Minister Manley and his allies promised that loans would be distributed to Jamaicans according to "housing need" (The Gleaner, 1976a; The Gleaner, 1976b; NHT, nd). Our earlier discussion of women's poverty and triple role revealed that femaleheaded households have greater housing needs than those that are male headed. Poor women, however, are largely excluded from participating in NHT, and thus most of the bias against women in the work force occurs at this selection stage. We will next delineate how this bias is achieved.

NHT's contributors are almost exclusively formal sector employees, who are legally required to lend 2% of their wages for seven years to NHT The employee escrow with NHT earn 3% interest, far less than the inflation rate and what can be earned in private banks. Their employers contribute another nonrefundble 3% of the employee's wages. Despite the requirement to contribute to NHT, employees and employers from many formal sector firms, especially the more tenuous, smaller, and less vzisible ones, avoid paying NHT. In particular, many firms escape contributing to NHT because they have folded by the time (typically a number of years) NHT investigates their account status (Green, 1988).

For self-employed and informal workers, who have grown as a

proportion of the wokforce since at least the 1970s (Boyd, 1988, p. 101), contributing to NHT is voluntary and in practice rare. Voluntary participation is ecconomically irrational for poor people for three interrelated reasons. First, contributing 3% of earnings to NHT is unaffordable when basic and immediate needs (including shelter) are not being met. Contributing to NHT by no means guarantees housing assistance. Less than 10% of all contributors have received loans since NHT's inception (NHT, 1988a; NHT, 1988c). A voluntary contributor thus makes an extreme gamble. Second, NHT's token interest payments to contributors do not encourage participation. Funds deposited with NHT lose real value over time. Third, the probability that a low income contributor will obtain a loan is disproportionately low. The probability of obtaining a loan is seven times higher for a contributor in the ninth income decile than for one in the bottom third of contributors (NHT, 1988a; 1988b). Excluding the nonformal workers reduces the number of contributors to one-half of the work force. When employees in noncompliant formal sector firms are removed, NHT manages to tap at most about one-third of the work force has recently numbered just over one million, the total number of NHT contributors has fluctuated since its inception with economic trends and state employment policy within the 200-350,000 range (Statin, 1987b; NHT, 1988c Boyd, 1988, p. 101-102). Women more often Poor and informal workers, are more frequently excluded by NHT's participation structure than men. Nearly 64% of NHT contributors are men (Table 1), whereas the official work force statistics report only 53.7% men (Statin, 1987b, p. 24).

To summarize, NHT contributors are concentrated in the more secure or stable portions of the formal sector, and so represent the relatively privileged one-third of Jamaican workers. Those employees who have even a small chance for a NHT housing loan generally represent the relatively affluent and protected elements of Jamaica's work force. The vast majority of Jamaicans with the greatest housing needs fall in the lower two-thirds of the work force with respect to income, and do not participate in NHT, NHT's funding Source of a compulsory savings tax on the formal sector creates a gender disparity toward formal sector men, particularly those with more secure positions. A large share of female workers are excluded at the outset from NHT's housing program. NHT's emphasis on more secure formal workers neglects female.

Table 1. NHT contributors by gender and income 1981

Row % Column % Total %	Females	Males	Row total
Wage category			
J $-12.000*	37.7	62.3	90.4
	94.5	88.1	
	34.1	56.3	
Over J$12.000	20.7	79.3	9.0
	5.5	11.9	
	2.0	7.6	
Column total	36.1	63.9	100.0

Source : NHT (1988 a)

*In 1981, J$1 = US$ 1.78 (wiffer 1983)

household heads, many of whom have a dire need for housing. Keeping in mind that over 40% of jamaica's households are female headed and that many women perform the duties of their triple role in the home. NHT's exclusion of poor and informal female workers assumes particular severity (Blackwood, 1983; McLeod, 1987).

Thus far we have been concerned with gender biases that inhibit women in the work force from NHT eligibility. It is necessary also to consider the gender aspects of NHT's contributor and applicant populations. Within NHT's contributor population, women earn less than men. For example, in 1981, women were 37.7% of contributors below J$12,000 while they were only 20.7% above it (J$1 = US$1.78) Witter, 1983). (See Table1.) In other words, among the more privileged workers of the formal sector that contribute to NHT, women are concentrated at the lower end of the pay scale. A woman's wages earning capacity is directly related to her ability to obtain a housing loan because NHT is interested mostly in the ability to repay loans when assessing an applicant's eligibility for a mortgage (*The Gleaner*, 1982). Women's roles as reproducer- and community managers, which should be important to a program allocating assistance based on "housing needs, " are generally ignored when they apply for loans (Moser, 1987b; CHFC, (1989).

Unlike the data sets for NHT contributors and beneficiaries under examination in this analysis (NHT, 1988a; 1988b), there are no reasonably error-free computerized records representing the contributors who have applied for loans.[5] We are therefore forced to rely more on qualitative evidence for applicants, gathered through discussions with key decision makers at Jamaica's state housing agencies. Our evidence is drawn from NHT and from another Jamaican state housing agency, the Caribbean Housing Finance Corporation (CHFC).[6]

Arguably, fewer people are excluded through the application process than during other selection stages. Owing to the extreme shortage of private formal sector housing, there is a virtually insatiable demand for NHT housing in all socioeconomic groups. This shortage assures that there will be far more male and female applicants from all income groups than there will be loan recipients (Jones, Webber and Turner, 1987). It is common to hear of NHT contributors who have expended much time applying for loans over the years and have given up trying to receive one. This is true even for applicants for small home improvement loans for which they would easily qualify. If the applicant pool underrepresents any Socioeconomic groups, these probably include poor female household heads. Their triple role allows little discretionary time to apply for laons when the likelihood of success is very low7. The poor are also less likely to have access to the newspapers in which NHT programs are advertised. Those with less formal education also find completing the application forms more difficult (Batley, 1983). Thus whatever socio-economic biases exist at the application stage are likely to be contrary to NHT's objective of allocating assistance based on "housing needs."

Despite the possible exclusion of some of the most disadvantaged contributors, including women, at the application stage, the impression inside Jamaica's state housing agencies is that women as a group demonstrate much more interest in housing loans than do men. This impression has both statistical and qualitative support. According to Blackwood (1983, p. 35), while women are 36.1% of NHT contributors, they were 39.9% of applicants through 1982. It is worth exploring why women convey a *presence* in the state agencies, as this is key to understanding women's circumscribed successes in obtaining and repaying state housing loans. At CHFC, it is reported that women are more accepting of a "match box start"- i.e., women are more interested in the modest housing options made available in government programs (CHFC, 1989). Similarly, Massiah (1983, pp, 36-37) report that Jamaican women surveyed by Jamaica's public research institute

(ISER) seemed remarkably capable of adapting to life's situations, including occupations, that are less suitable than what they had earlier aspired to. Mortgagor files document that women more often than men visit Jamaica's housing agencies to deal with arrears problems (CHFC, 1989; similarly see Blackwood, 1983). At NHT one can observe queues of women submitting loan applications, checking on their application status, coming for interview, paying the household's mortgage, and dealing with loan repayment problems, even if they are not the primary mortgagor. This observation may have led NHT's Acting Managing Director to her mistaken belief that "all of [NHT's] mortgagors are women" (Francis, 1989). While the next section documents that this statement is untrue, NHT has responded to women's greater reponsibility for housing by offering loans to women with marginal incomes and savings when men with the same economic attributes are rejected.

(c) *Gender differences in the allocation of mortgages*

From over 400.000 household heads in Jamaica, the vast majority of whom are in need of housing, about 25,000 have obtained NHT loans from 1976 to the present (The Gleaner, 1984; Statin, 1987b, p. 32; Jones, Webber and Turner, 1987; Kelly, 1989). In this section we are concerned with the gender profile of those mortgage recipients.

Contrary to NHT's mandate that need would be the principle criterion for allocating housing assistance, its lending Policies privilege those with more regular employment and credit histories, and therefore discriminate against poor women. The likelihood of receiving a loan increases with an applicant's ability to demonstrate regular employment and income. Informal worker can rarely document enough regular income to satisfy NHT's lending criteria. Further, because of historical differences between men and women regarding records such as bank accounts, access to family finances, job experience and status, and unemployment, women possess less information about state programs, and are able to bring fewer of the critical documents to housing laon applications than men (Blackwood, 1983, p. 9; Moser, 1987). A large portion of the women in the Jamaican informal sector are street vendors, called higglers, They sell goods that are more attractive around holidays and although many are quite successful, their income has a marked seasonality. In contrast, NHT requires monthly payments, and provides no special payment programs that would adjust to seasonal income fluctuations. Higglers are thus handicapped in obtaining NHT loans both by their lack of documentation and by their irregular income.

Nearly 60% of all NHT loans were granted to men and just over 40% were granted to women, indicating a substantial bias in favor of men. This bias reflects NHT's overall orientation toward higher income and more stable formal sector workers, who are predominantly men (Table 1). In absolute terms, NHT allocates more loans to men than to women.

Relative to their proportion of NHT contributors, however, men do less well. While they are 63.9% of the contributors, they have received 59.5% of loans. In other words, female Contributors have a slightly higher probability of obtaining a loan than men. This trend represents a gender-progressive pattern of loan allocation and can be attributed to NHT's cognizance of women's conscientious attitudes toward loan repayment and women's high representation in the public sector to which NHT is most responsive.

A second gender-progressive element of NHT's mortgage allocation record is the income level it requires of men and women to qualify for loans. There is virtually no difference between men and women in the size of their loans (NHT, 1988a; 1988b). The median income for male mortgagors, however, was J$7,301 in 1981, whereas the median for female mortgagors was only J$5,456 (NHT, 1988a; 1988b). That is, women on average have been able to obtain the same sized loans as men with only 75% of men's income (Table 2).

Gender-sensitive analysis should also consider the distribution of loans among income groups within the contributor population. The median income in 1981 of NHT contributors who had not received loans was J$3,428. It was J$6,193 in that year for those receiving NHT loans during 1976-88. A person in the ninth income decile of the contributor population has the highest probability of obtaining a loan (NHT, 1988a; 1988b). Thus loan recipients are on average drawn from high-income contributors (Peterson and Klak, 1990).

Additionally, there are gender differences in the income levels of NHT mortgagors relative to contributors (Table 2). At lower income levels (below J$8,000), female contributors have a higher probability of obtaining an NHT loan than male contributors. Above J$8,000, the probability of receiving a loan is much higher for male than female contributors. Further, where as the probability of receiving a loan for male contributors generally increases with income, for females it peaks at the sixth to eighth income deciles of the contributor population.

Compared to men, female contributors are slightly more likely to receive loans and female mortgagors have substantially lower income levels. From this evidence one might be tempted to conclude that NHT is contributing to the equalization of housing opportunities between the sexes. For both men and women, however, income groups above the median income of the contributor population have the highest probability of receiving a loan. Earlier discussion judged that the contributor population approximates the most privileged third of Jamaican workers. Thus even the gender-progressive features of NHT's loan allocation concentrate loans in the wealthier portion of the upper third of Jamaican worker. NHT's bias in favor of female contributors does not overcome the effects of the biases that prevent women, particularly poor women from entering the contributor population. The loan award procedure should not be separated from the multistage process of selection and screening of which it is only a part. Prior to the selection of loan applicants, NHT's attachment to the more secure portion of the formal sector has excluded

Table 2. NHT contributors, mortgagors, and arrears by gender and income

Wage category (J$ 1981)	%of Contributors	Number of Mortgagors Number of Contributors	Mean months in arrears
Entire population	100.0	0.041	10.6
No income reported	0.1	0.000	na
Female	0.1	0.000	na
Male	0.01	0.000	na
J$1-2,000	34.8	0.010	14.7
Female	11.4	0.012	12.6
Male	23.4	0.009	16.2
J$2,000.01-4,000	18.1	0.029	12.2
Female	7.3	0.035	9.4
Male	10.8	0.026	14.8
J$4,000.01-6,000	16.6	0.066	11.4
Female	6.8	0.083	9.8
Male	9.8	0.054	13.0
J$6,000.01-8,000	9.6	0.075	9.8

Female	4.2	0.083	7.7
Male	5.4	0.069	11.7
J$8,000.01-10,000	6.6	0.073	9.4
Female	2.7	0.064	7.9
Male	3.9	0.079	10.2
J$10,000.01-12,000	4.5	0.073	9.1
Female	1.7	0.050	7.2
Male	2.8	0.087	9.8
J$12,000.01-14,000	3.0	0.072	9.4
Female	0.9	0.034	9.9
Male	2.1	0.089	9.3
J$14,000.01-16,000	2.0	0.073	7.6
Female	0.4	0.025	9.9
Male	1.6	0.087	7.4
J$16,000.01-18,000	1.5	0.068	8.0
Female	0.3	0.007	7.5
Male	1.2	0.080	8.1
J$18,000.01-20,000	1.0	0.054	8.4
Female	0.1	0.006	1.0
Male	0.9	0.062	8.5
Over J$20,000	2.0	0.040	7.4
Female	0.2	0.007	3.0
Male	1.8	0.044	7.5

Source: Calculated from NHT (1988a, 1988b).

*Note that the critical information in this column is the relative ratios of the number of mortgagors to the number of contributors per income group. The absolute values of the ratios are less meaningful because the data sets for both mortgagors and contributors, while representative of their respective total populations, are not 100% samples (see Section 3a).

most poor women. The structure of housing policy by which workers participate in or are excluded from NHT is not socially neutral, but rather is a product of decisions by NHT and other state agents (similarly, see Maia Gomes, 1986). Female participants in NHT are fewer than their proportion of the work force as defined by the official census, and much fewer than their proportion of households in need of housing. Female contributors on average are also more affluent than women in the work force and in need of housing. Relative to Jamaican society, NHT's female contributors are already relatively privileged, owing to their stable formal sector jobs. Any emphasis on female contributors within the NHT system cannot overcome NHT's exclusion of the most needy women.

(d) Mortgages, gender, and state employment

The bias in lending toward state employees is so heavy that is requires us to consider the interaction between state employment and gender in loan allocation. Although state employees comprise less than 10% of the official work force, they obtain 58.3% of all NHT loans (Table 3). The overwhelming bias toward state employees applies to both sexes. This massive state-funded loan allocation to state employees documents one way that the state serves itself (Block, 1980; Bunker, 1985).

State employment is a major avenue toward state housing loans. More women work for the state than men (55.4% of state employees are female compared to 44.6% male). A key reason for women's greater participation in the public sector is that the state pays substantially less than the private sector for comparable jobs (Wines. 1987). Becuase the private sector offers women fewer opportunities and lower pay, they are more willing than men to take state jobs. Men prefer and take higher paying private sector jobs, relegating more of the state jobs to women.

The question arises as to whether women, disadvantaged in the private sector, use state employment as a means to obtain better housing conditions, The evidence shows that many women do. Calculating from Table 3,63.5% of all female mortgagors are state employees, while only 54.8% of all male mortgagors work for the state. These female beneficiaries are concentrated in roles customarily open to women: office workers such as clerks and secretaries, teachers, and nurses (NHT, 1988a; Statin, 1987b, p. 60-61).[8] Women must use state employment as a means to obtain NHT loans more than men do. In other words, privately employed men have better access to state housing loans than do women in the private sector. Private sector men represent 49.6% of the total official work force and receive 26.9% of NHT's loans. Privately employed women are over 40% of the official work force but obtain only 14.8% of the loans (Table 3).

Table 3. Work force and NHT mortgagors by gender and public or private sector employment

	Females			Males			Totals both sexes		
	% Workers	% Mortgagors	M/W Ratio*	% Workers	% Mortgagors	M/W Ratio*	% Workers	% Mortgagors	M/W Ratio*
Work in the private Sector	41.2	14.8	0.36	49.6	26.9	0.54	90.8	41.7	0.46
Work in government	5.1	25.7	5.04	4.1	32.6	7.95	9.2	58.3	6.34
Totals public & private	46.3	40.5	0.87	53.7	59.5	1.11	100.0	100.0	1.00

Sources: Statin (1987b, p. 24), data are for October 1986; NHT (1988b), data are through May 1988. *M/W ratio is (%Mortgagors/% Workers), a measure of proportionality. A value of 1.00 means that the group has received a share of NHT mortgaes equal to its share of the official work force; the value of 6.34 for government workers means that they have received over six times their proportional share of mortgares.

Do the biases hindering privately employed women's ability to obtain NHT loans also work against women employed by the state? This is overwhelmingly the case. Looking at the labor force as a whole, we find that while state employed men comprise the smallest portion of the offical work force (4.1%), they haye capatured the largest share of NHT laons (36.2%, Table 3). In contrast, state employed women comprise 5.1% of the official work force but have received only 25.7% of the loans. In sum, the relatively few men working in government have had more success in obtaining NHT Loans than female state employees. These figures reflect the same biases found in loan allocation to the private sector work force.

Together these trends indicate that (i) state employees have a much better chance of obtaining an NHT loan than private sector workers, (ii) women in the private sector are less likely to obtain NHT loans than privately employed men, and hence women use state employment as a means to obtain housing loans more often than men. and (iii) most important, male bias in the state sector exceeds that in the private sector. The relatively few men working for the state have captured a larger share of loans than female state employees. Although women use state employment to improve their housing conditions, male state workers reap the most housing benefits. Bais against women occurs in both the private and the public sectors.

(e) *Gender differences in loan repayment and arrears*

Jamaican state housing programs are plagued with the problem of housing loan default. The average NHT loan slips more than two months into arrears per year (Peterson and Klak, 1990). Besides financial hardship, which should not be underemphasized, these arrears are also related to an "attitude of noncommitment" in jamaica regarding state assistance. Resources allocated by the state are considered "free" or "a gift". While the "state gift" attitude is widespread therre are significant gender differences in the degree to which attitude is embraced. Men are much more likely to hold to this attitude toward the state than women (Blackwood. 1993, pp. 71-79; CHFC, 1989). This gender difference in attitude is directly related to women's responsibilities as household reproducers.

One might think that the burden of women's triple role would make them incapable of paying back their loans. In particular, the budgetary demands of immediate expenses such as food, clothing, and education would seem to leave little for loan repayment. Women's greater responsibility for household reproduction, however overcomes their poorer financial conditions so that female mortgagors are less in arrears than males. The average mortgage allocated to a woman is 10.4 months behind in payments. whereas the average for men is 12.2 months (the difference is statistically significant at 0.001) Blackwood (1983.p 48) also found in a study of NHT through 1982 that female mortgagors were on average fewer months in arrears. The two sets of findings add confidence to an assessment that women's better repayment record is consistent over time. Women are poorer than men but nontheless present NHT with fewer economic risks. Women's repayment records are better than men's at virtually every income level (Table 2). Women in both the public and private sectors have lower rates of arrears than men (Table 4). In fact female mortgagors working in the private sector have received disproportionately few loans (Table 3) but have the lowest arrears rate *and* the lowest income level (Table 4) Further evidence from other countries suggests that when women are able to break through the gender biases in the housing ;programs, they are more reliable mortgagors than men."[9]

Women's triple role increases their sense of responsibility. Because so many tasks of their triple role are performed in the home. women can little afford to maintain a noncommittal attitude toward housing finance that might put their home in jeopardy. Blackwook (1983, pp. 68 69) found that women were more likely than men to visit

NHT to apply for loans, check on the progress of the loans, and to repay their loans on time. NHT employees communicated that women's failure to pay back loans on time was usually a function of economic difficulties while men's failure to repay stemmed more from a lack of commitment to repayment (Blackwood, 1983)

Table 4. Arrears and income levels by gender and public or private employment

	Mean months in arrears	Mean income J$ 1981
Femal government	10.5 (5.256)	6.051 (969)
Male government	11.2 (6.674)	7.713 (1.282)
Female private	10.2 (3.022)	5.538 (935)
Male private	13.4 (5.498)	8.884 (1.678)

Source : Calculated from NHT (1988a : 1988b).

* The difference between the rows is statistically significant at 0.001.

* The number of cases is listed in parentheses. See Section 3a for a description of the data.

NHT grants only a limited number of loans to low-income household heads of either sex because of the widespread belief that low-income households are greater credit risks, In fact, lower income mortgagors as a whole are not substantially more in arrears than high-income mortgagors. Correlating mortgagor income with the number of months he or she is in arrears yields a correlation coefficient of -0.10 (from data in Table2). If one measures arrears in monetary costs to the state rather than by the number of payments, the relationship between arrears and income disappears (Peterson and Klak, 1990). Becuase female mortgagors, despite lower income levels, have lower arrears, a policy of granting them more loans would be economically rational. In fact, based on these arrears records, NHT would reduce its overall arrears rate by granting more laons to lower income women and fewer loans to even higher income men (Table 4). Finally, we can find no justification for the present lending policy that is biased against the poor if one judges it relative to social need, which is concentrated among the poor, especially women.

5. SUMMARY AND CONCLUSIONS

Women perform the roles of reproduction, production, and community management but receive payment for only their role as producers. In this capacity they are underpaid in the formal sector and disproportionately employed in the informal sector. As informal workers, they earn low and irregular incomes in often insecure jobs. They are thereby overburdened with the amount of work they are required to do. Women in Jamaica are obligated to maintain the upkeep and integrity of the household and represent over 40% of all households heads. These conditions make it clear that state housing policies should address women's needs as a Priority As women maintain primary responsibility for household management, a focus on women's housing needs would also address family housing needs in general.

It is therefore fitting to ask to what degree the state has addressed and met the housing needs of women. This is a particularly appropriate question for Jamaica's National Housing Trust. It was designed by a self-proclaimed Democratic Socialist government that claimed as its responsibility the allocation of housing resources to those most in need. According to its own objectives, NHT is supposed to provide housing to the poor on a priority basis. Women are most in need of housing loans in Jamaica. NHT nonetheless maintains no office devoted to women in housing and its operational rules are biased against lower income women in their quest for housing assistance.

The greatest bias against women is in their exclusion from NHT's contributor population, Women are structurally excluded from NHT first because of their disproportionate participation in the informal sector, NHT is also biased toward those portions of the formal sector that have more stable incomes and are thus less likely to include women. That 63.9% of NHT contributors are men indicates this bias against women's work.

If we assess NHT according to its own criteria that housing loan recipients must also be contributors to the Trust (excluding informal sector and less privileged formal sector workers), we find two dimensions of bias in favor of women within this relatively privileged group. First female contributors have a slightly higher probability of obtaining a loan than male contributors. Second, women are able to obtain loans with lower incomes than men. Women have achieved this access to state housing through greater persistence in pursuing state housing assistance, greater reponsibility in loan repayment, and, most significantly, state employment. NHT nonetheless awards more loans to men than women. The bias in favor of women within the NHT system does not compensate for the bias against women in the work force.

A much stronger bias than toward female contributors is toward state employees of either sex, as they capture 58% of all NHT loans while comprising only 10% of the work force. Some women have used state employment as a means of obtaining better housing than is available to women in the private sector. State employment, particularly for women, however, provides lower salaries for comparable jobs in the private formal sector. Most importantly, despite women's use of the state to obtain housing, men in both public and private sectors capture a much larger share of state housing loans than women in the same sector.

This analysis has demonstrated that despite some of NHT's gender-progressive tendencies. the institution's rules of eligibility are biased against women. NHT has thus largely failed to meet women's housing needs. A feminist perspective on housing contributes to understanding how this might be rectified. Moser (1987b) identifes a feminist approach to housing as one that addresses itself to both practical and strategic needs of women. Practical neeeds are those specific to women as a function of their place in the division of labor. Women's practical needs therefore include such things as housing, acess to child care and other services that facilitate their work. Strategic needs are those that arise form women's subordination. The fulfillment of strategic needs empowers and emancipates women. They require changes in societal organization and attitudes to allow women not only to gain equal access to social opportunities but to raise their consciousness as well.

As we have been concerned with the degree to which NHT fulfills its own stated objectives, we have necessarily confined our study to women's practical needs. Our evidence show that the Jamaican state has allocated a relatively small portion of housing to women. Housing is arguably the primary practical need of women performing triple roles. It is worthwhile to consider at this point whether a policy aimed at meeting practical needs can ever achieve its objectives within a society in which women's strategic needs are not met.

As long as Jamaican housing programs operate within the constraints of a society that fails to recognize and value women's work, state institutions such as NHT will continue to reflect cultural biases against women. These policies will thus repeatedly fail to meet women's practical needs. In other words, Jamaican society's failure to meet women's strategic needs leads to its failure in meeting their practical needs. A sole focus on practical needs addresses problems superficially and does not address the greater societal questions regarding women's emancipation and empowerment within the state and society. When women's strategic needs are met, their practical needs will be addressed by institutions that no longer reflect biases against women. Perhaps only through policies aimed at women's strategic needs will their seemingly more immediate practical needs be met.

NOTES

1. Global recognition of women's issues has infiltrated some institutions devoted to housing policy in the Caribbean. The caribbean Mininsters of Settlements and Shelter recommended recently that the gender dimension of shelter issues be investigated (Ministry of Settlements and Public Utilities, 1988 Annex XI, p. 2). The Jamaican government in 1987 released a national policy statement "recognizing the deficiencies of housing supply . . . .and the extraordinary number of household heads who are women." The document calls for "special efforts" to aid women in obtaining shelter (*National Policy Statement,* 1987, p. 4). Similarly the US Agency for International Development (1989) has identified women in development as a theme of their lending programs. These institutional commitments, however, have not been met with programs, that directly attack the women's housing crisis in Jamaica. While the leadership of a housing agency may call for sensitivity to women's issues, that sensitivity has not yet emerged in policy, let alone investment.

2. Despite the prominence of informal work in Jamaica, there has not been 'a serious and sustained attempt to collect and order the available data" (Thomas, 1988, p. 370). We must therefore rely on incomplete and sometimes impressionistic characterizations of women in informal employment.

3. Virtually all state employees are contributors to NHT. The entire contributor populataion on which much of our study is based consists of both private and public sector empolyees. Therefore, the 55.7% of state employees who are women are included in the proportion of women represented in the entire NHT contributor population (36.1%).

4. Building societies hold the next largest share of mortgage assets, 20%. Compared to NHT, this group represents disproportionately fewer individual mortgages because of the much higher value per unit (Peterson and Klak, 1990, p. 2).

5. NHT's data tapes that are supposed to contain this information are particularly

suspect. For example, the population sizes are far smaller than they should be. The relatively poor quality of data for applicants compared to contributors and beneficiaries may be attributable to the financial stakes attached to the latter two populations. Whereas NHT's financial solvency relies on decent records for contributors and mortgagors, thorough record keeping for applicants has no economic justification for NHT. In fact, applicant data could be incriminating if they reveal that low income people are excluded.

6. This section in particular draws heavily from field work experiences in Kingston, Jamica that included extensive interaction with housing decision makers. During 1988 the first author obtined office space at NHT and ÇHFC as an independent researcher. In 1989 the first author was a consultant to USAID and the Jamaican Government on a project assessing the performance of the housing programs and suggesting improvements. In addition, both authors researched gender biases in housing policy in Jamaica during the summer of 1989.

7. Recall that less than 10% of contributors have received loans, and that the likelihood for poor contributors is much worse. Women's triple role leaves them responsible for shelter, but this responsibility does not negate the economic irrationality of applying for a loan if income is very low or unstable. Similar to the Jamaican case, Batley (1983) argues that bureaucratic red tape was used as a screening device to reduce the number of applicants for loans from Brazil's National Housing Bank.

8. Both female and male state employees with housing loans work in offices in the government bureaucracy and teach. Additionally, male state workers with NHT mortgages are police officers, soldiers, and technicians (NHT, 1988a).

9. For example, see Peake (1987) for Guyana and Nimpuno-Parente (1987, p. 84) for Kenya.

REFERENCE

Batley, Richard, *Power Through Bureaucracy: Urban Political Analysis in Brazil* (New York: St. Mrtin's Press, 1983).

Blackwood, Florette, "The performance of men and women in repayment of mortgage loans in Jamaica," Mimeo (New York: Population Council of New York (1983).

Block, Fred, "Beyond relative autonomy: State managers as historical subjects, "*Socialist Register* (1980), pp. 227-242.

Blumberg, Rae, "Making the case for the gender variable: Women and the wealth and well-being of nations" (Washington, DC; USAID, Office of Women in Development, 1989.

Boyd, Derick, *Economic Management, Income Distribution, and Poverty in Jamaica* (New York: Praeger, 1988).

Bromley, Ray, and Chris Birkbeck, "Urban economy and employment," in Michael Pacione (Ed.), *The Geography of the Third World: Progress and Prospects* (London: Routledge, 1988).

Bunker, Stephen *Underdeveloping the Amazon: Extraction, Unequal exchange, and the Failure of the Modern State* (Urbana, IL: University of Illinois Press, 1985).

CHFC (Caribbean Housing Finance Corporation), Personal communication with several managers (Kingston, Jamaica: 1989).

Dwyer, D. J., *People and Housing in Third World Cities: Perspectives on the Problem of Spontaneous Settlements* (New York: Longman, 1979).

Francis, Yvette (Acting Managing Director of NHT), Personal communication (Kingston, Jamaica: 1989.

Gilbert, Alan, "Latin America, the world recession and the new international division of labor," *Tijdschrift Voor Economische y Geografie,* Vol. 77, No. 2 (1986), pp. 368-377.

Girvan, N., R. Bernal, and W. Hughes, "The IMF and the Third World: The case of Jamaica, 1974-80," *Development Dialogue,* Vol. 2 (1980), pp. 113-155.

The Gleaner, "Prices of NHT housing units increased" (March 4, 1983).

The Gleaner, "NHT: Now it's points system" (December 29, 1982).

The Gleaner, "Builders have some hope in Housing Trust" (May 5, 1986a), p. C-10.

The Gleaner, "House approves National Housing Trust" (March 18, 1976b), pp. 12, 16.

The Gleaner, "Proposed National Housing Trust operations outlined" (February 17, 1976c), p. 5.

The Gleaner, "Text of Prime Minister's statement" (October 9, 1975). p. 1 Acf.

Golding, Bruce, *A National Housing Policy for Jamaica* (Kingston: Ministry of Construction (Housing, 1982).

Green, Dennis (NHT Compliance Department manager), Personal communication (Kingston: 1988).

Grose, Robert N., *Squatting and the Geography of Class Conflict: Limits to Housing Autonomy in Jamaica* (Ithaca, NY: Cornell University Program on International Studies in Planning, 1979).

Gross, S., and M. Bingham, *Women in Latin America-Volume II* (St. Louis Part, MN: Glenhurst Publications Inc., 1985).

Harris, Sonia (officer in the Canadian International Development Agency in Kingston), Personal communication (Kingston: 1989).

Hinds, Suzanne Francis, "Low income housing," unpublished paper (Kingston: Women's Housing Group, 1989).

Jones, Eleanor, Maureen Webber, and Margery Austin Turner, *Jamaica Shelter Sector Strategy, Phase 1- Final Report* (Washington, DC: USAID Sponsored Urban Institute Project 3666-02, February 1987).

Kelly, Sylvester (NHT Mortgage Accounts Manager), Personal communication (Kingston: 1989).

Lawson, Victoria, and Thomas Klak, "Conceptual linkages in the study of production and reproduction in Latin American cities," *Economics Geography,* Vol. 66, No. 4 (1990).

Machado, Leda M. V., "The problems for woman-headed households in a low-income housing programme in Brazil," in C. Moser and L. Peake (Eds.), *Women, Human Settlements, and Housing* (London: Tavistock, 1987), pp. 55-69.

Maia Gomes, G., *The Roots of State Intervention in the Brazilian Economy* (New York: Greenwood Press, 1986).

Massiah, Joycelin, *Women as Heads of Households in the Caribbean* (New York: UNESCO, 1993).

McLeod, Ruth, "Low income shelter strategies in Kingston: Solutions of the informal sector," Report for RHUDO (Regional Housing & Urban Develpment Office) (Kingston: USAID, 1987).

Ministry of Settlements and Public Utilities, Trinidad and Tobago, *Report of the First Meeting of Caribbean Ministers of Settlements/Shelter* (Port-of-Spain, Trinidad and Tobago: September 27-28, 1988).

Moser, Caroline, "The impact of recession and structural adjustment policies at the micro-level: Low income women and their households in Guayaquil, Ecuador," Mimeo (London: Department of Social Administration, London School of Economics and Political Science, 1989).

Moser, Caroline, "Introduction," in C. Moser and L. Peake (Eds.), *Women, Human Settlements, and Housing* (London: Tavistock, 1987a), pp. 1-11.

Moser, Caroline, "Women, human settlements, and housing: A conceptual framework for analysis and policy-making," in C. Moser and L. Peake (Eds.), *Women, Human Settlements, and Housing* (London: Tavistock, 1978b), pp. 12-32.

Moser, Caroline, and L.Peake (Eds.), *Women, Human Settlements, and Housing* (London: Tavistock, 1987).

NHT, contributor file, computer data file containing records for NHT contributors and 1981 contributions (Kingston: 1988a)

NHT, Mortgage master file, computer data file containing records for NHT beneficiaries (data current to May 1988) (Kingston: 1988b).

NHT, "National Housing Trust, Contributor Accounts System," Report No. RCP400 (Kingston: Compliance Department, 1988c).

NHT "Objectives of the NHT," Internal document (Kingston: NHT, n.d.).

National Policy Statement on women (Kingston: Government of Jamaica, July, 1987).

Nimpuno-Parente, Paula, "The struggle for shelter women in a site and service project in Nairobi, Kenya," in C. Moser and L. Peake (Eds.), *Women, Human Settlements, and Housing* (London: Tavistock, 1987), pp. 70-87.

Peake, Linda, "Government housing policy and its implications for women in Guyana," in C. Moser and L. Peake (Eds.), *Women, Human Settlements and Housing* (London: Tavistock, 1987, pp. 113-138.

Peterson, George and Thomas Klak, "Shelter sector mortgage credit and subsidy policy; The National Housing Trust and Caribbean Housing Finance Corporation," Executive Report (Kingston: USAID and the Jamaican Ministries of Construction (Housing and Development, Planning and Production, Contract #PDC 0000-I-00-6168-00, 1990).

PIJ (Planning Institute of Jamaica), *Economic and Social Survey* (Kingston: PIJ, 1989).

Portes, Alejandro, "Latin American urbanization in the years of the crisis," *Latin American Research Review,* Vol. 24, No. 3 (1989), pp. 7-44.

Portes, Alejandro, Manuel Castells, and Lauren Benton (Eds.), *The Informal Economy* (Baltimore, MO: Johns Hopkins University Press, 1989)

Statin (Statistical Institute of Jamaica), *Household Expenditure Survey 1984 Volume II* (Kingston: Statin, 1987a)

Statin (Statistical Institute of Jamaica), *Statistical Abstract 1986* (Kingston: Statin, 1987b).

Thomas, Clive, *The Poor and Powerless : Economic Policy and Change in the Caribbean* (New York: Monthly Review Press, 1988)

The Tribune, "Women and Housing," *International Women's Tribune Centre* (New York: United Nations, 1987).

United Nations Habitat, *Global Report on Human Settlements* (Nairobi, Kenya: UN Habitat, 1987).

US Agency for International Development, *A.I.D. Program for Women in Development ; A User's Guide to the Office of Women in Development* (Washington DC: USAID Office of Women in Development, 1989).

Wines, Sarah, "Staff salaries and incentives in Jamaica's Town Planning Department," Working paper of the USAID Assisted Town Planning Review Project (Washington, DC: The Urban Institute, 1987).

Witter, Michael, "Exchange rate policy in Jamaica; a critical assessment, "*Social and Economic Studies,* Vol. 32, No. 4 (1983), pp. 1-50.

Woolcock, Joseph. *The Contribution of the Building Societies to the Development of the Jamaican Society* (Kingston: Institute for Social and Economic Research, University of the West Indies, 1987).

World Bank, *World Development Report* (New York: Oxford University Press, 1987).

CHAPTER-25

Equality for Women—What we Need Doing

T.K. Sarojini

NO FORMAL NETWORK SYSTEM OF INFORMATION exclusively for women, exists today. Whatever information is available is merely constituent in the total information network system in the country. The major sources of information on demographic and socio-economic aspects of women are the Office of the Registrar-General and Census Commissioner, the National Sample Survey Organisation (NSSO) and the Central Statistical Organisation (CSO) and Planning Commission. In addition to these, the related Central Ministries/ Departments like Health, Education, Rural Development, Labour etc., generate information on women. A brief description of these networks is given below:

Registrar General, India

The Registrar-General and Census Commissioner is responsible for conducting population census in the country. The census operations are undertaken once in ten years. The data available from the census include changes in the age-sex structure of the population, expectation of life at birth, their socio-economic characteristics, level of literacy etc. The economic tables classify all persons by their main activity and subsidiary activity and categorise them broadly as workers and non-workers. Data also provide information on the distribution of currently married women, births and deaths during the previous year, age at marriage by religion and education, present age and duration of marriage etc. This information is available separately for urban and rural areas. Information is also available on the classification of occupations, e.g. professional, technical and related workers, administrative, executive and managerial workers, clerical workers etc. Besides the decennial census, specific studies viz. Sample Registration Surveys (SRS) on different socio-economic aspects of the people, including studies on infant and childhood mortality and fertility and mortality differentials are carried out by the Census Organisation.

National Sample Survey Organisation (NSSO)

Originally constituted for conducting large scale surveys to provide data for National Income Estimations and for Planning and Policy formulation, the NSSO has embarked upon a variety of fields, particularly in conducting socio-economic surveys. It has a wide network Zonal, Regional and sub-regional offices located across the States, districts and sub-divisions in the country. The socio-economic rounds are planned to be conducted in the cycle of ten years, periodically in cases like population, including maternity and child care and family planning, debt and investment and capital formation and land holdings and live-stock enterprises, and five years in the case of employment, rural labour, consumer expenditure etc.

Central Statistical organization (CSO)

The CSO, which is a part of the Department of Statistics, is responsible for coordination of statistical activities in the country, maintenance of statistical standards, conducting economic census and surveys, plan work relating to development of statistics, dissemination of statistical information etc. The Social statistics, Population and Manpower Research Division of the CSO is engaged in the coordinated development of social statistics, including population, manpower and employment, education health and social welfare and maintenance of standards.

Planning Commission

The Planning Commission is a supra-level agency responsible for formulation of policies and plans at national level. The main functions of the Planning Commission are carried out in a number of technical Divisions, e.g. Perspective Planning Division, Monitoring and Information Division, Social Welfare and Nutrition Division. The Divisions scrutinise and analyse various schemes and projects to be incorporated in the plan, conduct technical studies and research on plan projects and programmes, prepare study materials and reports on the plan and follow up the progress of the Plan Programmes. The Plan evaluation work is carried out by the Programme Evaluation Organisation (PEO), an independent agency working under the general guidance and direction of the Planning Commission.

Ministry of Labour

The Ministry of Labour plays an important role in generating and providing data and statistics on women, on a continuing basis. There is a Women's cell in the Ministry which addresses itself to the various problems relating to employment of women workers.

Directorate General of Employment & Training (DGE&T)

The DGE&T in the Ministry of Labour, which is responsible for development and coordination of programmes relating to Employment Service and Vocational Training, Scheme, including women's vocational training collects data under the Employment Market Information (EMI) Programme. The data is complied and brought out in the form of a Quarterly Employment Review. The Review provides information on women employment in the organised sector, employment of women by industry and State-wise.

Labour Bureau

The Labour Bureau, another organisation under the Ministry, of Labour collects and publishes Statistics on employment, wages, absenteeism, labour turnover, working conditions, etc. of labour force. The Bureaw also conducts research studies/surveys and brings out reports and pamphlets on women labour force, their earnings, working conditions etc. To monitor the progress in the sphere of equality of men and women in respect of human rights, the Labour Bureau brings out a publication entitled 'Women in Employment' presenting a picture of the trends of women employment in India, the laws and regulations governing their employment, wages and earnings etc.

Ministry of Health & Family Welfare

The Directorate General of Health Services (DGHS) of the Ministry of Health and Family Welfare collects statistics on the performance of various health programmes from the States and consolidates them at the national level. The Ministry undertakes and also sponsors ad-hoc studies on specific problems through various agencies viz. The Indian Council of Medical Research (ICMR), National Institute of Nutrition (NIN), Hyderabad etc.

Department of Education

The States are primarily responsible for collection and compilation of basic data on education. The State Education Directorates collect data on educational institutions, enrolment, manpower, etc. The Department of Education collects the compiled statistics from the States on an annual basis, which are brought out in annual publications such as 'Education in India'.

Surveys are also conducted by the Department of Education, National Council of Educational Research and Training (NCERT) and other organisations to collect detailed information on the educational facilities for Planning the spread and improvement of education at various levels.

Department of Rural Development

The Department of Rural Development is responsible for alleviation of rural poverty and creating infrastructure which has supportive role for income generation, self and wage employment. A Comprehensive monitoring system exists for monitoring various programmes of this Department. The District Rural Development Agencies (DRDA) provide a strong structural base for collection and compilation of data. The same base is proposed to be utilised for the purpose of developing an information network system for women also.

Ministry of Programme Implementation

The Ministry of Programme Implementation was created in September, 1985 for effective monitoring of the implementation of certain projects and programmes. The Division for Programme Monitoring in the Ministry is responsible for monitoring the Progress of implementation of the 20-Point Programme. Point No. 12 of the 20-Point Programme refers to 'Equality for Women'-a strategy adopted for advancement of women in the country. Progress reports are brought out on monthly/quarterly basis and action is initiated to correct any deviation or deficiency in the achievement of targets.

Department of Personnel and Training

The Department of Personnel and Training collects and publishes data on women employees's representation in various services in Government. They also bring out brouchures on special concessions/privileges granted to women in Government services.

Ministry of Welfare

The Ministry of Welfare safeguards the interests of socially, physically and mentally deprived classes of society through various welfare and legislative measures. The State Directorates of Social Welfare and the Tribal Research Institutes form the network for collection of data relating to these categories and to feed the National Machinery-for formulating necessary policies and programmes for betterment of these special groups.

Networking through NIC

The National Informatics Centre (NIC), a plan project of Government of India Under the Department of Electronics has been given the responsibility of creating appropriate information system to facilitate the planning and decision making process in the Ministries/ Departments of the Government in the country.

In the Phase-I, of their projects, NIC has developed an intracity computer network in Delhi with interactive terminals in various Ministries/Departments including the Department of Women Child Development-the national machinery for women's development. All these terminals are connected to a large computer system-CYBER 170/ 130. In the Phase II, NIC in introducing a similar network to cover the country by connecting all state capitals with super micro systems. The PC/AT compatible systems installed in the district head-quarters will form the third level of NICNET. The District Computer Centres (DCCs) will have information relating to administrative data, monitoring data and socio-economic data which includes information on women. The national centre will be able to query the data base created at the State levels. The State centres in turn can query the district centres for any information. The NICNET has been so designed that querying in the reverse direction would also be possible.

In the Phase-III, all the villages in the country will be linked up to the DCCs to facilitate flow of information right from the field level to national level through the linkages at district and state headquarters. Once the entire network system comes into operation, the national machinery for women is going to take the full advantage of the system developed under NIC so that the information required for the formulation of policies and programmes for the advancement of women could be made easily available to the planning bodies for effective and timely decision making.

Linkages with regional and international agencies

Apart from the linkages with in the country, the national machinery is maintaining close liaison with regional and International Agencies including UN Systems working for the development and advancement of women. This ensures regular flow of information on women's development from these agencies.

Obstacles encountered

As already pointed out, there are several deficiencies and gaps in the information available for formulation of policies and programmes for the advancement of women. Some of these, as could be listed, include: lack of up-to-date and complete data on various demographic and socio-economic parameters, non-availability of processed data for operational use, lack of information on emerging social problems and women's contribution to labour market, non-availability of programme statistics, etc. Besides, the absence of a separate information network for women has resulted in dependency even for basic information on other sources. Related to this are the problems. Like lack of trained personnel for collection and interpretation of data and adequate machinery for timely processing as well as publication of the data collected. All these constitute some of the obstacles which are causing hindrances to the national machinery in its effective functioning.

However, with the initiative now being taken for building up an information network system through the National Informatics Centre and also the cooperation and support expected to be received from the regional and international organisations, especially ESCAP and SAARC, it is hoped that the national machinery will be able to overcome the present problems and become self-sufficient in meeting its information needs.

Information aided decision-making

In the history of Indian planning for women, there are many instances to quote regarding effective utilisation of information aided decision-making. The first and foremost among such instances is the setting up of a separate administrative machinery to take care of the interests and welfare of women. As stated earlier, a Committee on the Status of Women in India was set up in 1971 to make a detailed study of the situation of women in the country. This Committee brought forth many revealing facts about women in India and suggested a number of measures for the development of women which *inter-alia* included setting up a separate machinery at the central and State levels to liik after the interests and well-being of women. Accordingly, a separate Bureau for women's welfare was set up in 1976 as part of the then Department of Social Welfare.

Followed by the IWY in 1975 was the declaration of the International Women's Decade 1976-85. The information explosion that took place during the women's decade exposed the bare facts about the situation of women in India in comparison with that of other developing countries and demanded an immediate intervention of the government. The first effective step that took place in this direction was strengthening of the existing national machinery into a full-fledged Department of Women and Child Development to meet the emerging needs of women effectively.

A review of the progress made by the country in general and women in particular since its independence in 1947 forced the Indian planners to believe the old saying that 'no country can advance while a segment of its population lags behind'. The women who represented 50 per cent of country's total population were lagging much behind men in every sphere of life as revealed by the socio-economic indicators of development. It was therefore, for the first time in the history of Indian planning that 'Women's Development' was given due recognition as one of the major areas/sectors of development and also a separate place in the Plan Document of Sixth Five Year Plan 1980-85.

The socio-economic situation of women in mid 70's had prompted Indian planners to have an immediate shift in their policies and programmes for the development of women as the earlier approach of providing curative and ameliorative services proved ineffective as women in India still continued to be socially backwrd and economically dependent Accordingly, policies and programmes relating to women were given a shift in approach from 'curative' to 'preventive' and 'welfare' to 'development'. Economic development through income generating activities was given the highest priority so that women could become economically independent and self-reliant to take part in the socio-economic development of the country. In line with these policies, the Seventh Plan 1985-90) has launched many new programmes with a special thrust on 'Employment and Training' for women throughout the country.

Introduction of the scheme of Integrated Child Development Services (ICDS) for children and mothers is yet another example of how decision-making is aided by the information base. The past experience of two development decades in implementing programme of health, nutrition and immunisation for mothers and children through separate departments proved to be ineffective in bringing about the desired impact on the over-all development of children and mothers. Therefore, the basic services essential for the over-all development of children and mothers were brought under one single roof with an 'integrated approach'—in the name of ICDS under the Development of Women and Child Development.

Information collected through research and evaluation studies has proved not only effective for introduction of new policies and programmes but also in bringing about modifications in the on-going programmes for welfare and development of women. For instance, the findings of various evaluation studies on the scheme of 'Hostels for Working Women' have pointed out a glaring deficiency in the services under the programme as no facilities were provided for the dependent children of the working women residing in these hostels. As a result of this, immediate measures were taken to expand the scope of the scheme by adding day care facilities to these hostels. This has made the scheme much more popular than before with more demand and increased budgetary support.

Lack of information, a problem

About the instances where lack of information has become a problem for decision-making, we may refer back to Part-I of this paper where information gaps have been listed. Besides those, there are a few specific instances where lack of information has become a stumbling block in decision-making. These include-contribution of a house-wife to GNP; changes in women employment trends; socio-cultural and attitudinal barriers; access to social legislation etc. These are explained below:

According to 1981 census, only 14 per cent of the total female population in the country fall in the category of 'workers'. The unpaid economic activities of women and their contribution through work in the domestic sectors remain unreported in the census. An ILO study has estimated that the value of unpaid household work contitutes 25-39 per cent of the total gross national product in developing countries.

But until and unless some supportive data on this particular aspect is made available the value of women's contribution to GNP can neither be estimated nor compensated.

There has been a reported decline in the employment of women in sector like Jute, textiles, plantations and also in some areas in the public sector. But, lack of data on this problem has become the major drawback to arrest the decline in these primary sectors where women can contribute and represent themselves as partakers of the development. Investigative studies need to be undertaken with a view to finding remendies in case of any proven decline in women's employment in any of the sectors. Simultaneously, new areas which have potential for promoting women's employment need to identified.

Socio-cultural and attitudinal barriers, like feudal ideologies, elitist conception of women's role and negative aspects of ethnic, cultural and religious revivalism have kept women away from developing their full potential and actively contribution to and benefitting duly from socio-cultural and economic progress. Socio-economic barriers are operating in almost every sector. Until and unless these barriers are identified, programmes to counteract them can never be planned.

The household conceals several differences within it. Just as only women perform most of the household chores, such as fetching water and fuel, cooking and cleaning and most of the child care, women are also uniquely employed in paddy transplantation, tea leaf picking and hand spinning etc. In most processes of production, this task differentiation takes place and it is universally found that women cluster in the most monotonous, least skilled and least paid jobs. Under-remuneration of women workers adds to the invisibility of women, not only in their capability to receive benefits, such as bank loans, but also in the awareness of policy makers and programme implementors of the occupations that women are in fact engaged in.

There has been minimal involvement of women in planning, execution and evaluation of local and national programmes. From the women's point of view, the statistical measures that were customarily used in economic and social analysis, are inadequate and sometimes even inappropriate. Therefore, there is an urgent need to develop gender-wise data wherever necessary for effective decision-making.

Suggestions

To sum up, the present system of collection of information on women in India is still in the process of evolution and as such it is one of the weakest links in the total information system. Information on women in India suffers from a number of shortcomings which are common to several other sectors also. Although a mass of data is collected through censuses, surveys and administration of public services, yet only a fraction of these are subsequently analysed and published due to various constraints—such as shortage of trained manpower, equipment, printing facilities etc. Sometimes, even the published data are not fully utlised for purposes of planning and decision-making due to the defective systems through which it was collected.

In order to overcome the existing lacunae and deficiencies in the information on women and in the system of its collection, the following suggestions are worth considering:

— One of the main reasons for the poor statistical reportage in the field of women, is the lack of proper infrastructure at various levels. Firstly, there is no proper machinery to collect data on regular basis. Secondly whatever little is done it is only throught the administration staff at lower levels who are not oriented towards this type of work. It is therefore, necessary to build up appropriate machinery with trained personnel right from the grass-root levels. These schemes should become part of the plan budget proper financial backing and push.

— The nodal Department of Women and Child Development should issue specific instructions to all the concerned both at national and state levels to publish relevant statistics—not only of the routing official statistics, out also those collected through special surveys sponsored from time to time by (i) Sex (ii) age group (iii) rural/urban (iv) education (v) training status (vi) employment position wherever relevant (vii) classification by groups like socially/physically/mentally handicapped (viii) by levels of more income/expenditure groups.

— In the case of sponsored studies, some uniformity in the concepts and definitions, methodology and tabulation should be ensured by the sponsoring organisations for each type of studies undertaken by them. It should include a core format of enquiries and tabulation programme, so that all India picture is rendered possible. In this connection, preparation of some standard manuals for the various types of studies in the different fields may be sponsored by the CSO on the pattern of UN manuals.

— At the State level, the concerned Departments should be encouraged to bring out statistical publications with similar formats as those brought out by the different central Ministries. Similarly at the District/Block levels, also, such information Should be collected and supplied to the State Level Focal Points and through them to the National Focal Point. The frequency should be quarterly, half-yearly and annual.

— In the case of beneficiary-oriented programmes implemented by various Ministries/Departments, autonomous and voluntary organisations, the sex-wise and age-group wise, wherever relevant, and area-wise break-up of the beneficiaries, should be published to throw light on the extent of benefit/participation by these segments of population. State/National level seminars/workshops should be encouraged to create a common forum for exchange of views and experiences amongst the personnel involved in the task.

— Pre-service and in-service training for the personnel involved should be encouraged so that a uniform pattern, structure and techniques in collection, compilation and collation of data could be developed. A regular system to disseminate the data relating to women should be developed for the use of planners and administrators.

A model information network

In a developing country like India where financial resources are a major constraint, it is difficult to develop a parallel network system exclusively for women. Instead, it would be more pragmatic and economical to strengthen the existing system by adding a few 'Focal Points for Women', wherever necessary, so that the present day requirements of information on women could be met. Later, the same could be developed into an independent system depending upon the availability of resources and trained manpower etc.

The information network system for women as visualised in the Chart envisages flow of information/data both vertical and horizontal. The existing Focal Points for women at national level/state level are expected to maintain a close liaison with the office of the Registrar General and Census Commissioner, National Sample Survey Organisation,

Central Statistical Organisation on the one hand and with Planning Commission, concerned governmental and non-governmental organisations and research organisations on the other. Information thus collected will be processed and stored as 'ready to use' in the mini computer installed by the NIC in the Department of Women and Child Development. Similarly, the State level focal Points will also maintain a very close contact with the State Bureau of Economics and Statistics which are the major sources of data, besides the concerned Departments. For this, the State Focal Points are being strengthened with NICNET system. The District, Block and village level Focal Points (yet to be installed) are expected to function as intermediary links ensuring smooth flow of information. The main 'nerve centre' for both horizontal and vertical flow of information will be the District Headquarters under the overall Control of the Distric Collector. The District level data-base on women will be developed and maintained in the District Computer Centres (DCCs) where the disaggregated information could be transmitted to the concerned quarters. The Planning Commission has already made provision for building up village level data base through DCCs of the National Informatics Centre. The Focal Point for women at District level (preferably a Statistical Officer to be appointed) will be part and parcel of the District Computer centre and working in close collaboration with the NIC set-up.

As far as collection and compilation of data from grass root levels is concerned; services of Extension Officers available at the Block level will be made use of. All the data thus collected from the grass-root levels will be computerised under the guidance of the National Informatics Centre and published at regular intervals to make it easily available for decision-making, formulation of policies and programme implementation for the advancement of women in India.

It is encouraging to note that the Women's Section in the Social Development Division of ESCAP has already initiated action in developing Women's Information Network for Asia and the Pacific (WINAP) in collaboration with the national networks on women available with its member countries.

The SAARC Technical Committee on Women in Development is another regional agency which is coming up with a similar plan of action to develop information network on women in the South Asian region. Their efforts to bring out-i) Bibliography on women in development; (ii) Directory on Audiovisual Aids. (iii) Directory of existing instituions and expertise available in the field of women's development; and (iv) updating of national reports on the status of women, are under way as a first step in sharing the existing information amongst the SAARC countries.

Viewed from the Indian context, however, there is considerable scope for initiatives in collection and exchange fo information and research findings and for building up of a network of information system for women with the cooperation of various regional and UN/ international agencies. Some of the areas where substantive work could be started and where the UN and other international agencies like UNICEF, ILO, WHO, UNESCO, UNDP, Statistical Office of U.N., ESCAP, SAARC etc. could contribute are :

— setting of a data base at the national level, with appropriate software and hardware systems;

—Institutionalisation of exchange of information and experiences on the status of women between various countries particularly in the region on a regular basis;

—transfer of expertise within the region and between regions;

— Dissemination of innovative experiments through various media;

— training of personnel for development of skills in collection and processing of data as 'ready to use' information, monitoring and evaluation and other allied area.

Regional and international co-operation

The Mexico Conference on International Women's year emphasised the need for data collection, exchange of information and research findings, promotion of a network of institutions, both national and international, including the UN agencies to facilitate regular exchange of information and linkages. The Nairobi Conference on UN Decade for Women in 1986 also reiterated the above line of action. For this, the Conference visualised a well-knit network system at the national, regional and international levels for monitoring the improvement in the status of women. These are indeed laudable ideals set forth and implementation of the same would go a long way in evolving meaningful policies and programmes for the advancement of women.

CHAPTER-26

Shelter, Women and Development : Beating a Path Towards Women's Participation

Meera Bapat, Sheela Patel

This paper is based on the experience of community organisation work that the Society for Promotion of Area Resource Centres (SPARC) has been involved with since its formation in 1984.

SPARC is a non-government organisation (NGO) based in Bombay, India. SPARC's founders are professionals who have worked in areas of social work, social activism, social sciences and related research. In order to work towards establishing equity and social justice they felt a need to set up an organisation which aligned as a partner rather than as a patron of marginalised communities and organisations of the poor. To fulfil its endeavours SPARC has set up resource centres in areas geographically accessible to the groups that need them. In such centres people find information, interact with their neighbours and others in similar situations as themselves, develop skills and learn to make their own representations. In these resource centres management is gradually passed on to the communities that use them.

SPARC has two partner organisations : Mahila Milan (MM) and National Slum Dwellers Federation (NSDF). MM was formed in 1987 initially as an organisation of women who live on pavements and who trained themselves with the help of SPARC to lobby for their rights among which is access to secure shelter. The organisation has developed strategies to ensure that the women are supported by the entire community of which they are a part. Women are encouraged to work not only within their own community but also with women from other communities to help them to take on similar initiatives. In the process they gather strength as the membership of their collective grows.

NSDF had been in existence for several years prior to becoming a partner of SPARC and had worked sporadically on issues concerning slum dwellers. After SPARC conducted in 1985 an enumeration of pavement dwellers living in a central ward of Bombay, NSDF was drawn to the methodology of using the creation of an information base for mobilising people and began to interact with SPARC, NSDF has member federations in Bombay and in other cities in India.[1]

SPARC began its work with women from families living in hovels on pavements in Bombay. The reason for choosing this group with which to start its work was that it saw pavement dwellers as the most deprived and isolated among the urban poor and those who have least organisational and political skill. Women among them, as compared to women from poor households, are greater sufferers in the struggle for survival because of their added vulnerability arising from the ever present threat of demolition of their dwellings. By starting with the most vulnerable, SPARC believes it addresses the challenge of developing an alternative that is relevant in the context of the worst-off; if it proves relevant to the most marginalised it can be adapted for the less deprived because of its built in flexibility.

When SPARC began its work, the organisation had a philosophy of work but did not have a set course of action or a methodology. As its involvement in its work grew, it formulated its approach almost intuitively. The outcome so far of this work has perhaps little to show in terms of concrete results or gains, but the process it has set in motion, we believe, attempts to contribute towards changing the marginalised position of disadvantaged groups and in particular of women.

I

Reviewing Approaches of Women's Development

The experience of SPARC's work needs to be viewed against the background of approaches used for achieving women's development and strategies adopted for countering their subordination, especially since 1975 when the United Nations decade for women began.[2]

The almost uniform conclusion of the International Women's Decade research is that with a few exceptions, relative access to economic resources, incomes, and employment has worsened, their burdens of work have increased , and their relative and even absolute health, nutritional and educational status has declined.[3]

What is significant is that this decline in women's situation has occurred in spite of all the information, publicity and pressures surrounding women in the last two decades or so.

Policy approaches that have been successively adopted in an attempt to change women's status have been described[4] as welfare, equity, anti-poverty, efficiency and empowerment. Each approach was born out of an understanding at that time of women's role in development. These approaches have been operationalised not singly but in combination. Most of these approaches, however, have failed of address the fundamental problems that women suffer from.

In order to analyse why women's status has altered little a distinction needs to be made between the 'condition' and 'position' of women5. A women's condition means the material state that she finds herself in (eg, poverty, lack of education, burden of work, lack of access to credit or technology, etc). Her 'position' means her social and economic standing relative to men.

The condition of women is the subject of much of development literature on women and a major part of development concerns centres on finding ways of improving women's condition by targeting ameliorative resources to them rather than by radically changing underlying structures. The emphasis on women's condition has two consequences. Firstly, there has been a tendency to emphasise women's practical and day-to-day needs-giving greater access to credit, special training schemes, etc. Secondly, the approach makes it difficult for structural issues concerning women's position to be raised. It in hibits posing the question of whether women's condition is related to their structural position, and/or whether any serious and sustainable improvement in their condition is possible without structural changes. As a result while women's needs as mothers, producers, etc, are highlighted, their interests as women are not.[6]

When discussing women's needs it is essential to differentiate between "the needs of women as occupiers of particular social roles and interests of women as a social category with unequal access to socially valued resources (both economic and social) and political power".[7] This differentiation has been further developed as practical needs and strategic interests.[8]

> Examples of practical gender needs to derive from the necessity of fulfilling particular roles allocated to them by the division of labour : e.g, care of children, maintenance of the house, care of the elderly, servicing of family and community. Strategic gender interests arise from women's growing recognition that the

age-old structures of male dominance and privileges are not sacrosanct, but social impositions and as such amenable to change.[9]

The approach to the development of women that is concerned centrally with the position of women and her Strategic interests is the 'empowerment' approach. Strategic interests are defined on the basis of an analysis of gender subordination and a formulation of a vision of alternative gender relations.

It is clear that if women are to attain justice in society it is necessary that the structure of subordination are transformed-i e, changes in laws, civil codes, property rights, labour codes, social and legal institutions that underwrite male control and privileges. The empowerment approach, however, recognises the limitations of top-down government efforts to meet strategic gender interests. Even when these strategies are adopted, in order to implement them, sustained efforts in the form of political mobilisation, consciousness raising and popular education are required. The empowerment approach sees the importance of using practical gender needs as the basis on which to build a secure support base and a means through which more strategic interests may be reached.

Popular education is regarded by adherents of the empowerment approach as an important component of a strategy that challenges gender subordination. Popular education "is concerned with developing critical consciousness amongst the marginalised groups, with strengthening behaviours and attitudes which lead to more confident and assertive practices and to formulating strategies to contribute to the changing of their marginalised position".[10]

The approach develops from the needs and aspirations of the marginalised groups and leads to the self-discovery among the people of their own capacities to analyse, challenge and transform their own reality.

II
Why Focus on Women Pavement Dwellers

In the work done by SPARC, as now seen with hindsight, the element of popular education which attempts to address the situation of women's subordination, evolved as a critical component. The group arrived at its methodology of work not from studying any manuals or handbooks on the subject, but from their commitment to take as the starting point needs and aspirations of marginalised groups as defined by the groups themselves; the workers in SPARC have been acutely conscious of not imposing their own values, attitudes and ideas on the people and communities with whom they work.

The focus on women pavement dwellers'' arose form the experience of some of the individual members of SPARC of earlier work with such communities. It had shown them clearly that these women, on the one hand, have to face an extremely hostile and difficult situation, but on the other, are a key to the survival of their families and communities. They not only nurture and create the physical and psychological space for fulfilling family needs but also create the community's survival system based on mutual support which is so essential for getting by in a highly competitive and alienating environment of the city. They manage resources in such a way as to ensure their conservation and equitable distribution. And yet, their contribution to the building, consolidation and development of their settlements remains unacknowledged. Women do not give any credit to themselves for their own contribution either. They are never consulted in formulating interventions (by NGOs or government agencies). In order to address the needs and aspirations of marginalised groups, however, those who face crises and devise survival strategies (i e, women) must play a central role in decision-making, in designing strategies and implementing them. Hence SPARC focuses on women. This is a means of acknowledging existing proceses and building upon them.

Right form the start in SPARC's work, therefore, central participation of women is a critical component of a gendersensitive community organisation. It attempts to achieve this by facilitating the renegotiating by men and women of relationship within their families, communities, federations in an effort to achieve the goal of equity.

III
Reorganisation of Communities and Gender Sensitivity

Changing Self-Image of Women

The reorganisation of groups in order to be gender sensitive must occur in large enough numbers of communities to provide the environment in which new relationships can not only sustain themselves but also get reproduced. Popular education becomes a critical tool to create the new environment. By starting popular education with women, it is ensured that both women themselves and communities constantly acknowledge women's central role in the process of change.

In the popular education programme, as the first step towards self-discovery by women, SPARC initiates individual introspection by women into their past. Starting from childhood, women are encouraged to share their experiences. This narration includes events, views, feelings, opinions and much reflection. The listenner (catalyst) is not a passive audience, but demands accountability from the speaker to ensure that self-promoted myths do not creep in.

It is not that the women do not talk about their lives or know about each other's histories. What is different in this new narration is the value that is ascribed to that experience. It not longer remains an isolated, individual experience; instead it is linked to critical milestones in the history of the settlement. This ensures that in future women's role and contribution to making decisions on issues that affect the settlement/community can no longer be marginalised. This introspection enables women to see themselves as agents of change. It reveals to them that this experience is a process of their own creation and worthy of becoming a reference point in subsequent discussions.

The next step in the process of selfdiscovery is to move from individual stories to group histories. Small groups of women are assisted to discuss collectively their experiences and issues related to themselves. When women know about each other's life histories, it is easier to refer to individual incidents in group meetings and discussions. In such discussions, the role of the catalyst is to help women form a collective experience and then build on it.

In subsequent discussions women as well as men participate. At this point the catalyst supports men a narrate the perception of their life history and then integrate it with women's experience in order to build the history of the settlement. From this point onwards any discussion on the past experience refers to what women and men have contributed to the settlement/community history. This is one of the most difficult stages and marks a watershed in the process.

In this process of reorganising the community's history there is an ongoing debate which discusses who in the community will spearhead the process of change. There is an agreement that it should be those who build and consolidate the settlement, face crises and solve problems. Invariably on these criteria women are endorsed to work as agents of change. The process is difficult and long drawn because it challenges existing leadership patterns and upsets existing power equations within the community. Women generally avoid confrontation over this matter. They cajole, connive and even manoeuvre situations to gradually develop a working relationship with men in the community. The catalyst helps by providing the women space to use their new-found knowledge to facilitate changes in their community equations in a manner and at a pace that they can cope with and make use of. In such an environment, the women that SPARC has worked with have clearly displayed that they have a desire to play crucial roles in decision making. They have demonstrated that it is possible to develop strategies to set in motion a process leading to the transformation of their situation of subordination within their families and communities.

This experience is significant in itself and especially when viewed against the recognition by the international women's movement that there has been little success in finding ways of effectively challenging gender subordination. An important reason identified[12] for this is the perceived lack of acceptable alternatives which do not entail intolerably high costs. The experience of oppression and subordination that women may suffer is mediated by experiences which may lead many women to conclude that their situation cannot be changed or that attempting to change it will worsen their existing situation which they have learnt to cope with. This belief may not only deter women from taking action to change their situation but may even lead certain categories of women to support the structures and institutions of male domination. In SPARC's work, the transformation of women's situation of subordination is linked to improved life for the entire community and therefore it is accepted by men and the community as a whole.

The scope provided in the approach devised by SPARC to transcend women's anxiety about the cost of challenging their existing situation has proved to be a crucial feature. After the alliance with MM was initiated, men and women whose roles were reorganised through this process began to participate as partners with SPARC. NSDF are more effective in this process since they demonstrate to the communities the benefits of this rearrangement; and when men discuss this transformation it is even more effective. This is the point after which SPARC no longer plays the role of a catalyst, but hands it over to members of MM and NSDF. They reproduce the process that they have been through with other communities that join the federation.

Establishing Collective Leadership

A critical part of the popular education strategy devised by SPARC is the upgrading of information levels of all members of communities. This is essential for facilitating their participation in the process of mobilisation and for establishing collective decision-making. It is also crucial for enabling the communities to demand accountability from the collective leadership. Building people's capabilities to introspect, systematise their knowledge and use it to advance their collective cause is central to community organisation initiated by SPARC. This is contrary to the traditional pattern of community structures, especially in poorer settlements, in which leaders are often brokers of (political) patronage. They prop up their own position as leaders by exploiting their access to information or knowledge (of the working of government agencies, banks, welfare schemes, etc). They thrive in a situation where people in the community do not have the exposure to the working of such institutions and therefore lack the confidence to seek information themselves. The community leaders use this situation for abtaining gains for themselves. They are, therefore, not interested in changing this situation by building people's capabilities to take on such tasks. In the popular education and community organisation strategy devised by SPARC, these traditional leaders usually get sidelined and replaced by a responsive collective leadership.

IV
Popular Education Using Question of Shelter

Women living on pavement express as their first priority the need for secure shelter, mainly for the sake of their children. Owing to this consideration SPARC evolved its popular education programme around the question of shelter.

Shelter is the most critical question for pavement dwellers. Their lives are fraught with an acute sense of insecurity arising from repeated demolition by authorities of their shelter and consequent loss of belongings. Demolitions rarely achieve the objective of clearing pavements as their residents almost always manage to return to the same location and erect their shelter all over again. Demolitions, however, not only deplete the meagre asset base of these families but also torment and terrorise them. They are made to feel powerless and begin to regard their situation as hopeless. Apathy sets in as a result. The trauma, anguish and rage felt on account of demolitions gives way to passive acceptance of the situation. The psychological damage caused by demolitions is severe and difficult to remedy. The feeling of apathy and powerlessness incapacitate people and make them incapable of participating in efforts aimed at changing their situation. This is even more true for women in such groups. This poses a big challenge for devising strategies that will change this situation of inaction. In this environment, identifying shelter as a focal point of intervention and women as agents of change is a strategic choice made by SPARC.

In mid-1985 SPARC conducted an enumeration of pavement dwellers (a people's census)[13]. It revealed that nearly 6,000 families (27,000 people) lived on pavements in just one district (ward) and four arterial roads in Bombay. The enumeration was conducted as much as a strategy to mobilise the people as to generate information about them (which was scanty) in order to create public opinion against mass demolitions and to deter the local authority from taking such a drastic action. [14] The objective was to bring into focus the reality that a problem of such a magnitude and complexity could not be solved by demolishing huts and evicting the people.

Tension and anxiety mounted as the day after which demolitions were expected to begin drew closer. To pavement dwellers' and their supporters' relief, however, mass demolitions did not occur. (This was as much due to intensive work of mobilising of pavement dwellers done by various organisations as of a play of diverse forces in the local politics.) But the event brought home to pavement dwellers the stark reality of the extent of their vulnerability. Women began to ask how long they would go on accepting such a precarious existence and whether their children's children too would be born on pavements. Not only was their situation desperate- the poverty, hand-to-mouth existence, isolation and hopelessness- but difficulties seemed insurmountable and no solution was in sight.

The imminent threat of demolitions provided the critical historical moment for building an alliance between SPARC and pavement dwellers. SPARC felt that the apathy of pavement dwellers could be turned into a positive force galvanising the people into action provided they :

(1) Developed a vision of an alternative : The people needed to develop an alternative, working towards which would provide the motivation to shed apathy and take action.

(2) Conducted organised action : A large enough number of people needed to believe that a change was possible.

(3) Built stamina and capacity for sustained action : They needed to develop stamina and capacity for a long drawnout process of negotiations and lobbying to legitimise and institutionalise the change they desired and demanded.

The impending threat of mass demolitions and acute anxiety caused by it provided the impetus to focus on the question of shelter. The enumeration of pavement dwellers and subsequent discussions with the people on its findings had created the background for conducting a training programme[15] which explored possible ways of changing the prevailing situation.

Essential features of this training can be described as :

1 (A) To organise, along with the community concerned and its leadership, existing knowledge, information and practice that the people have used in working out their present shelter strategies.

(B) To examine them in order to understand the circumstances in which the strategies have evolved and to analyse their advantages and drawbacks.

2 (A) To identify areas where changes are needed and to articulate why these changes are essential.

(B) To identify various actors involved other than the community itself, in bringing about the change in order to identify the required skills and resources, and who can contribute them.

(C) To develop the required skills within the community to undertake the process that aims at achieving the desired change.

3. Having developed this understanding, the next phase is to develop skills to articulate the alternative to people within the community, to other communities who are in a similar situation and to outsiders (professional, citizenry and government officials).

Integral to this training is sustained community mobilisation that is essential for carrying on the action through a long drawn process before the alternative can be achieved. Therefore, this training process ensures an outcome (i) a clear-cut understanding of aspirations, (ii) a statement on how the community proposes to achieve them, and (iii) developing of insights into internal and external factors that will lead to achieving the alternative. (iv) recognition of the fact that most critical problems of the poor cannot be resolved without structural changes. The outcome of this training programme becomes the foundation for community action.

The decision to treat this training process as an educational component of community mobilisation was somewhat intuitive. On hindsight, its rationale can be described thus. In order to enable poor communities, especially women among them, to work with SPARC as partners in building an alternative, a reorganisation of the communities' way of functioning must form an essential feature of this process. A sustainable change in not possible without such a reorganisation. Developing specific skills through training cannot ensure their use leading to equity and justice even within these communities if their traditional structures are not reorganised.

A critical part of the training is to upgrade information level of the entire community, for without this all its members are not in a position to participate in the mobilisation process. Community members (and not SPARC) then develop criteria for selecting leaders. This ensures that the leaders are accountable to the community. Members of SPARC discuss, argue and negotiate with the people each other's ideas regarding leadership and the final concept emerges out of a consensus. Creating processes which allow for negotiations to occur in order to arrive at a consensus is as much part of the training methodology as building actual skills.[16]

Group discussion is the mechanism used for arriving at a consensus. The entire community (i e, men and women) participates in these discussions.

In the process of transformation, the twin factors of women's central participation and collective decision-making once endorsed by the community become the most important aspect of the organisation process. Some groups and individuals in the community (e.g, the traditional male leaders) may continue to deride these features. Rather than exclude the traditional leaders for their derogatory behaviour, the process of debate and discussion challenges their views until and internal consensus is reached. Once women's participation in creating alternative shelter emerges this in itself creates the basis for a collective leadership.

V
Shelter Training Programme

In order to understand the shelter training programme in practice, it is useful to describe the first cycle of this training that SPARC and women pavement dwellers developed in 1986-87. In the specific case of pavement dwellers, public meetings were arranged in order to discuss impending demolitions and work out strategies to avert them/deal with them. Women's participation, in case such an eventuality occurred, was linked to the 'need' rather than to a 'right', by emphasising that the question of shelter concerned women the most since it was they who made a pavement dwelling (or any dwelling) a home. Further, as crisis such as a demolition was faced generally by women since men are at work when it occurred. After a series of meetings it was accepted (by men) that women would spearhead the training programme. This position was publicly ratified. The key role given to women put women in a position of responsibility which they were willing to shoulder. Any fears, anxieties and doubts that this responsibility created among women were openly discussed so that they did not act as deterrents to their participation. The group took the responsibility of coping with the work collectively.

The first training programme was conducted for 600 women participants. Besides, men also participated sporadically. It way undertaken in an atmosphere that was conducive and congenial to participation by women and the community. Days, timings and agenda of meetings were flexible and organised by the women participants.

Members of SPARC made sure that all critical issues were discussed, however, difficult some of them were. They were dealt with by the community in a manner and at a pace that they could handle. The informal atmosphere in which the training took place made women feel at ease. The training used language, from and manner that made sure that the participants were not intimidated. They were in fact, put in a position of advantage because the discussion began from a narration of their experience.

A number of questions were discussed in the training programme. For example, since the demolition of dwellings was a major concern for pavement dwellers, a detailed discussion on this problem was included in the training. During these discussion women made analytical observations on a number of issues related to demolitions (i e. which settlements had to face demolition squads more frequently than others, why it was necessary to build huts using materials that could be dismantled quickly and costs involved in maintaining such structures, the loss of belongings, including food and stored grains, confiscated during demolitions and consequent hardships suffered by them, violence during demolitions. etc). Attention of the participants was then drawn to the distinction between demolition (i.e, destruction of dwellings) and eviction (i.e. preventing people form occupying the pavement). This distinctions helped them to differentiate between their inability to save their homes and their strength in resisting from being evicted altogether from the pavement. The group then listed all the actors involved in the drama. This led to an exploration of possible alternative responses to impending demolitions.

It became clear in these discussions that these families did not wish to reside on pavements. To attain secure shelter they were willing to move to alternative sites in the city which met certain minimum requirements. Until this alternative became a reality, which the participants recognised would be a very long process, it was essential to devise ways of minimising the psychological and economic damage caused by demolition of shelter. Several steps were planned to deal with such an eventuality (and subsequently executed).

Some of them were :

Women delegates visited the municipal ward office and the local police station, and demanded and obtained clear information on the stipulated procedure to be followed during demolitions. It became clear to them, for example, that the presence of the police was as much to protect the people as to effect violence-free demolitions. This information was passed on to all members of the community to be made used of when required.

A 'battle plan' was drawn up to face demolitions collectively with residence of neighbouring settlements coming to assist (e.g, in dismantling huts in order to save the ignominy and indignity of the hacking of dwellings by the demolition squad, providing food to the affected families on the day their homes are demolished). This plan is now routinely practised when facing demolitions. This has helped break the feeling of isolation and create a feeling of solidarity among pavement dwellers.

The next stage was to develop an alternative for the question of shelter. The crucial issue here related to the question of availability of land. Pavement and slum dwellers have repeatedly been told by the local and housing authorities that there is no land available in Bombay where they can be accommodated. This myth had to be broken and in order to do that vacant stretches of land were located (on the Development Plan of the city, from information received from slum dwellers living in other areas, from professionals in the relevant departments of the state government). Visits were arranged to inspect these sites. The training programme included the gathering of information, checking out its validity and arranging visits so that each member of the community saw the vacant land. For many, especially women, this was their first visit to another area of the city, using public transport. The site visits provided an opportunity for the people to interact with other communities and this strengthened the basis of net working.

Having established that vacant land exists in Bombay, the next complex question that needed to be thrashed out was why it was not officially available to the poor. This discussion illustrates how people began to grasp that their deprivation was a result of a number of external forces. It made them aware of the magnitude of change that is required to fulfil their aspiration of secure shelter.

By now people felt comfortable being part of large groups. However, it became unwieldy and unrealistic for everyone to participate in everything. Not everyone had the time or the capability for doing various concrete tasks that needed to be done. By this time a stage had been reached when some of the participants had shown qualities of prime movers and leaders.

The group in turn was, by now, seeking representative for doing future work and a process of identifying collective leadership began. Essentially leaders were to be those who could share, nurture, support and assist, those who sought to do the work rather than wield power, those who wished to contribute their efforts and found time to do what needed to be done.

From every 15 houses one woman was chosen to assume the responsibility of carrying our concrete tasks. Such representatives together formed area committees. They had to conduct regular meetings with members of the 15 houses and be a link for communication between them and between this group and the rest of the community. This is a mechanism that is used even today by which every person in the community is kept informed and which ensures that the communication chain in maintained.

The women chosen to be members of area committees had to acquire various skills and play specific roles. They were required to learn to involve everyone and also facilitate collective decision-making. They received support and feedback on their work from SPARC and members of the community. These women representatives, because of their communication skills, subsequently became trainers in other communities.

In order to collect basic information which was necessary for planning their alternative settlement each cluster had to do a simple exercise of counting the exact number of families that lived there. Since they had never been involved in such a task before, the exercise was important for undertaking the gathering of statistical information about themselves and using it with confidence in discussion to support their arguments. Besides, SPARC's experience had showed that an enumeration can be used as a powerful tool for mobilising people. For these reasons, it was decided that area committee members would perform this task for their individual groups of 15 houses (although information about each cluster existed in the census of pavement dwellers conducted earlier by SPARC).

This exercise was watershed in the training programme. An anomaly surfaced in that the number of structures (huts) did not match the number of families that lived in the cluster (because of renting out of part of huts, huts, being used for conducting income earning activities, vested interests attempting to claim more space, stronger families trying to outdo weaker ones and so on).

TABLE 1 : MAHILA MILAN HOUSING UNIT— BANK SAVINGS

Areas	Number of Account Holders	Amount in Bank (Started 1986) (Rs.)	Amount in HDFC* (Started 1991) (Rs.)
Apna	99	71,542	6,450
Water Street	85	75,249	16,100
Tank Pakadi	23	7,101	500
Dimdimkar Road	53	49,516	11,800
Peer Khan	33	36,575	9,560
Sophia Zubair	41	8,158	41,860
Shanti Nagar	41	12,118	57,560
Jula Maidan	45	27,519	18,690
Dockyard Road	19	1,570	38,150
P D Mello Road	117	12,864	47,500
Total	556	3,02,212	2,48,170

Total amount : Rs. 5,03,383

Statement covered period till March 3, 1992.

* Housing Development Finance Corporation— a private financing agency.

TABLE 2 : MAHILA MILAN— HDCF DEPOSITS

Date	Amount (Rs.)
15.09.1990	5,150
3.04.1991	200
5.04.1991	200
10.04.1991	160

23.05.1991	150
3.07.1991	12,990
31.07.1991	110
21.08.1991	8,920
9.09.1991	30
16.10.1991	13,640
23.10.1991	560
6.11.1991	12,320
14.11.1991	14,700
27.11.1991	12,410
Total	92,540

Number of account holders : 534.

There was tension that had to be resolved. Enumeration was conducted in each cluster several times until the findings satisfied a majority and a consensus was reached. The whole process contributed significantly to group-building.

For women the enumeration exercise was the first major concrete task that they did collectively. This gave them a sense of accomplishment and boosted their confidence. They got insights into the community dynamics and began to understand processes by which area committee members could be co-opted by outsiders or community members. The process made them aware of the need to set carefully norms for space allocation so that needs of every member of the community could be fulfilled. They developed a team spirit which formed a basis for a collective leadership in place of traditional leaders.

The next step in the training was to design the dwelling and settlement. While women dreamt of the kind of houses they would want to live in, they were realistic about their means and resources, and needs of the community. They analysed the existing allocation of space for various functions in their dwellings. This helped to identify family space against collective/community space. The importance of sharing space and amenities was discussed.

On the basis of this analysis requirements of individual dwellings were worked out. They were discussed with professionals. Women defended their choices/decision.[17] Architects/engineers explained the importance of natural light and proper ventilation, and space management. They discussed the importance of developing a prototype. The presence of SPARC at these meetings ensured that the professionals were informed and sympathetic, they were neither overbearing nor romantic about people's participation, and that there was frank dialogue. After a series of meetings designs of dwellings and settlement evolved.

The training programme included a discussion on existing public housing schemes for the poor. Officials from the housing authority were invited to make presentations before groups of women. Visits to public housing projects by a core group of women were arranged in Bombay and other cities. Pamphlets giving information about various housing schemes were obtained and translated by SPARC staff members into appropriate languages.

Women compared their dwelling and settlement designs with those in official schemes and assessed public housing designs for suitability for their own needs. During visits to housing projects they asked their residents those questions that they had asked themselves when they planned their dwellings. They explained their design choices to these residence. In this process a critique of public housing projects emerged.

The whole exercise involved :

(1) An analysis of their own life styles, and their means and resources in order to arrive at relevant dwelling/settlement designs.

(2) Articulating their design choices to professionals and defending their decisions.

(3) Developing prototypes with the help of professionals.

(4) Collecting information of public housing schemes and assessing them for suitability.

Subsequently, full scale dwelling models were built by women (using timber, cloth, paper in the first training programme; in subsequent programmes other materials such as brick and concrete were also used). An exhibition was organised which was visited by slum dwellers, professionals and government officials. Women showed and discussed the dwelling models with the visitors who had diverse interests in the exhibition. To slum dwellers it demonstrated ways of upgrading their houses and settlements; to government officials and professionals it was not only a clear expression of people's ability to plan shelter meticulously but it also broke stereotyped images of the poor being incapable of working out suitable alternatives.

Starting from an analysis of their existing situation to working out a concrete structure for shelter took a period of nearly 18 months. Having conceptualised dwelling and settlement designs, the next phase in the training programme was to discuss the 'hardware' of housing i e, the three major components of building materials, finance and land.

(i) Building materials : Women visited building material depots to determine which material were appropriate for their use and enquired about their prices. They also learnt actual construction, estimating cost of construction, delivery systems and later supervising construction work.

(ii) Finance : Pavement dwellers are fully aware that alternative shelter would not be given free of charge. They started putting aside small amounts of money regularly in a bank for paying for shelter. In addition, they made inquiries about loan facilities for housing from established credit sources.

Each household has an account in a bank in the name of the woman. Community leaders assist each family to open a bank account. Periodic assessment of total savings is done against the target set on the basis of estimates of dwelling cost. Women who once regarded entering a bank intimidating and operating bank accounts formidable, now do this work with ease and confidence. Regular saving of money has inculcated discipline among the people and awareness regarding planning for the future-both values alien to those leading a hand-to-mouth existence.

Discussions with housing finance institutions have now been initiated and are going on. Considerable amounts of money put aside as housing saving so far by pavement dwellers as a group show the level of preparedness of the people to participate in housing projects. This is contrary to a normally held view by government authorities that pavement dwellers are neither willing to pay towards housing nor are they capable of saving money regularly.

(iii) Land : In the case of pavement dwellers the acquiring of land is the most difficult proposition. They have had to start with a struggle for recognition of their legitimacy. Even this has been achieved only marginally. Establishing a right to land to live on is a distant goal.

TABLE 3 : DHARAVI MAHILA MILAN— SAVINGS AND LOANS

Area (Society Name)	No of Ac. Holders	Savings (Rs.)	No of Loans Disbursed	Amt. Disbursed (Rs.)	Amt. Repaid (Rs.)
Ashirwad Society	17	468			
Bharatiyar Society	169	5,022	3	700	
Chambra Bazar	169	26,791	15	27,672	1,430
Maharashtra Seva	30	1839			
Rohidas Society	26	2442			
Rosa Vilas	---	56			
Sakinabai Chawl	30	980			
Tagore Society	---	453			
Vijay Nagar	5	106			
Vir Savarkar Society	24	363			

Statement covers period till March 31. 1992.

Negotiating with government authorities for land has been initiated but constitutes a long drawn and painful process.[16]

Urban land is a highly valuable resource. To tilt its allocation in favour of the urban poor (i e, those who are incapable of competing in the land or housing markets) is a major political battle.[19] The complexity of and enormous difficulties in the task of obtaining secure shelter have not so far deterred pavement dwellers from refining their training programme or assisting other groups of urban poor in developing their shelter alternatives. It is a continuing evidence of solidarity among marginalised groups that pavement dwellers have assisted in designing constructing houses those groups of slum dwellers who have been allotted land, although their own quest for land remains unfulfilled. Because the struggle for shelter is a part of the larger struggle for social change, every small step forward in either the specific shelter situation or in the context of urban poverty and deprivation feeds into the other and strengthens it.

VI
Illustrating Outcome of Popular Education

In conclusion, this section illustrates various elements described in the paper. There are :

(a) The challenge of ensuring women's participation in the process of change and specifically in the shelter situation.

(b) strategies of popular education which not only create means for people to participate in formulating these strategies but in reproducing them in a manner which ensures women's central participation and community control over the adaptation and reproduction of these processes.

Most existing shelter training material for women[20] is a case of a top-down approach. It embodies an approach which refers to the 'condition' of women and not to their 'position'. Such an approach has severe limitations for improving the status of women. In the shelter training programme devised by SPARC, the focus is on empowering women. It has, firstly, created a positive self-image of women and, secondly, has created mechanisms to sustain it. This has transformed their perception of themselves from individuals who are not worthy of associating with the better-off and professionals and who are incapable of making any contribution to individuals who can act as catalysts in the process of change. Their increased self-esteem has changed their role within their families and the community. Thirdly, by locating the process of reproduction of this training within women's collectives, it has ensured that women's participation is sustained in all decision-making both in their communities and in federations of which these communities are members. For example.

A. This empowerment process acknowledges women's need to integrate their own empowerment with the fulfilment of needs of their families and communities. This has always remained a challenge to educators working with poor women. In SPARC's approach, women's self-esteem is enhanced by taking up issues in those priority areas which have helped resolve crises faced by such communities. For example :

(1) Obtaining of ration cards which have entitled the families to buy foodgrains, cooking oil and fuel at subsidised rates.

(2) Dealing with harassment by the police—changing humiliat-

ing treatment given previously by officials to due respect to women's opinion.

(3) Transforming the feeling or intimidation by and a lack of access to institutions like banks into a situation where bank staff welcome poor women to open bank accounts and invite women's collectives to advise on loan applications by members of their communities.

(4) Dealing with municipal officials at the local ward level—transforming the fear and the feeling of helplessness caused by repeated demolitions into ensuring accountability form public servants.

Women's judicious decision-making has established their credibility among not only their community members, but also with larger federations and public authorities. This has created an effective spiral where women's capacity to undertake tasks related to community well-being is supported by the community and this, in turn, creates the space for collective introspection into women's strategic interests.

B. The empowerment approach devised by SPARC uses shelter as a focus because this is regarded as the most pressing and critical problem by pavement dwellers with whom SPARC has chosen to begin its work. However, the question of shelter is only a means to achieving the alternative vision that women have built collectively. The devising of a strategy for action is a complex process for it must be harnessed both to resolve immediate problems and address long-terms goals. In the case of pavement dwellers efforts to gain access to secure shelter addresses their immediate predicament, at the same time it lays the foundation for contributing to the fulfilment of their alternative vision.

This approach acknowledges that having explored possible alternatives, isolated efforts at achieving them cannot bring much result; the larger context of mobilisation of increasing numbers of communities is an essential factor. Creating educational strategies to give impetus to larger and larger numbers of people to take action contributes to this end.

A number of federations of slum and pavement dwellers now have educational tools to assist communities.

(1) To undertake enumeration—a process by which they create a data base which is required for designing strategies and negotiating with the state.[21]

(2) To design mechanisms of savings and credit to fulfil community members' needs for tiding over family crises, needs for loans for small business and saving for shelter. (See Tables 1, 2 and 3.)

(3) To design dwellings and execute house construction, and manage basic amenities.

(4) To link communities which are doing any of the above with those who aspire to take action, through a horizontal exchange between communities.

While the scope of the work that SPARC, MM and NSDF have embarked on together has expanded, it has so far primarily involved internal reorganisation of poor and deprived groups. The challenge of securing adequate shelter has now moved to a larger arena, for it is a struggle for a greater share of resources. This is related to the political economy of urban development. The struggle for secure shelter is even harder in the present context of globalisation and liberalisation of the Indian economy and proposed privatisation of various services, for access to even basic necessities of decent living for the poor cannot be achieved without the intervention by the state in their favour.

REFERENCES

1. Member federations are the Pavement Dwellers Federations, the Railway Slum Dwellers Federation, Dharavi Vikas Samiti, Dharavi Vyavasay Ekta Samiti, the Federation of the Airport Authority Land Dwellers. Taken together these federations have a membership of nearly 3,15,000 families.
2. The following review draws extensively on an overview presented by Walters, shirley in 'Her Words on this Lip : Gender and Popular Education in South Africa', *ASPBAE Courier,* No 52, 1991.
3. Sen, Gita and Caren Crown : *Development, Crises and Alternative Visions,* Third World Women's Perspective, Monthly Review Press, 1987.
4. Moser, Caroline : 'Gender Planning in the Third World : Meeting Practical and Strategic Gender Needs', *World Development,* 1989.
5. This 'tool' for analysis has been develop by Kate Young, cited in Shirley, Walters, opcit.
6. Shirley, Walters, ibid.
7. The differentiation identified by Maxine Molyneux, referred to in shirley, Walters, ibid.
8. Developed by Kate Young referred to in Shirley, Walters, ibid.
9. Shirley, Walters, Ibid.

10. Shirley, Walters ibid.

11. It is estimated that 35,000 families lived on pavements in Bombay in 1985.

12. By Kate Young, *referred* to in Shirley, Walters, ibid.

13. SPARC, *We, the Invisible,* Bombay, 1985.

14. The demolishing of pavement dwellings in Bombay was expected to begin any time after October 31 (the end of the monsoon) that year. In a judgment given by the Supreme Court, the Bombay Municipal Corporation (BMC) was directed not to remove dwellings on pavements during the monsoon in order to save the residents' hardships caused by being rendered homeless in the rain. In 1981 after the BMC attempted to evict pavement dwellers after demolishing their huts, a write petition was filed in the Supreme Court challenging this action. The Supreme Court in its judgment given in 1985 ruled out that the BMC was empowered by the Bombay Municipal Corporation Act to remove encroachments, including huts, from pavements.

15. What is undertaken under this training programme is, no doubt, an exercise in community organisation/mobilisation. We call it 'training' because it is a process which once developed can be used by other marginalised and poor groups in their struggle to achieve their goals. It is essentially a systematisation of knowledge and information and designing of strategies to develop requisite skills.

16. By negotiations we mean a debate between people holding different points of view to arrive at a consensus/agreement. Deprived groups generally do not have any experience of negotiating with authorities who allocate resources. The poor are regarded as beneficiaries for whom decisions are made. The training process provided opportunities for them to build skills to negotiate.

17. For instance, women, opted for shared toilets— one toilet to be shared by four families. This was contrary to professionals' view that each dwelling should have its independent toilet facility. Women argued that placing a toilet in the confined space of their small dwellings is not hygienic. Further community toilets would be constructed by the authorities at their cost while internal toilets would increase considerably the dwelling cost to be borne by the occupier. Further, shared toilets would

serve as a deterrent to higher income groups buying out the poor households and dispossessing them of the dwelling.

18. Even today, there is not public housing scheme that mentions pavement dwellers. However, the Planning Commission, Government of India, has allocated Rs. 7,50,000 in 1988 for each of the four metropolitan cities in India, towards setting up rehabilitation projects for pavement dwellers. This money to this day remains unutilised in Bombay because the local authority still refuses to acknowledge the presence of slum dwellers in the city, let alone allocate land for rehabilitating them.

19. Bapat, Meera: 'Allocation of Urban Space; Rhetoric and Reality—Evidence from Recent Jurisprudence', *Economic and Political Weekly*, July 14. 1990.

20. For example Moser, Caroline and Sylvia Chant : *The Role of Women in the Execution of Low-Income Housing Projects Training Module*, DPU gender and Planning Working Paper No 6, Development Planning Unit, London 1985.

21. See SPARC : *'Beyond the Beaten' Track: Resettlement Initiatives of People who Live along the Railway Tracks in Bombay, 1988*. Nearly 18,00 families (97,000 people) who live along railways tracks in Bombay were enumerated in conjunction with government officials.

An enumeration of pavement dwellers in Madras in the state of Tamil Nadu in south India was conducted in 1989-90 in order to design rehabilitation scheme for pavement dwellers. This work was officially assigned by the Madras Metropolitan Development Authority to SPARC, MM and NSDF.